The Philosophy of Philosophy

The Philosophy of Philosophy

Timothy Williamson

Second Edition

WILEY Blackwell

To my children Alice, Conrad, and Arno

Contents

Preface to the Second Edition

It was Marissa Koors, Philosophy editor at Wiley-Blackwell, who in 2018 proposed renewing *The Philosophy of Philosophy* in a second edition, with extra material on developments since 2007, when the book was first published. I liked the idea, without feeling tempted to rewrite the first edition. Since its publication, I have continued to stand behind all its main ideas and most of the details. In subsequent writings, I have further clarified and developed its lines of thought, responded to critics, and filled in omissions. However, those later pieces were scattered about, hard to survey and in some cases hard to find even for me, let alone anyone else. It may be helpful for readers to have all this material collected together into one volume, constituting a more comprehensive philosophy of philosophy, with replies to the sorts of questions and objections it tends to provoke.

My other projects delayed work on the second edition for over two years. This preface, written in the Oxford of 2020, under partial lockdown as a result of Covid-19, is an opportunity to look back, and forward, in briefly introducing the new material.

The most constructive additions are Sections 9.1–9.4, four essays that substantially extend the first edition's picture of philosophy, both its methods and its recent history. Each was written not so much as a contribution to an ongoing conversation as an attempt to start a new one. Those attempts already seem to be succeeding. Section 1, "Widening the picture," explains the topics of the new conversations, and how I came to be interested in them.

The other new sections, most of them quite short, and some of them quite polemical, were all written in something more like response-mode. Thus the distribution of topics in them is some evidence of what was happening in the philosophy of philosophy in the years after the publication of the first edition. The two response-mode sections of full article length, Sections 10.2 and 10.4, are defenses of armchair philosophy against attacks from "experimental philosophers." Of the shorter sections, twenty were my invited replies to book symposia on the first edition, in *Analysis*, *Philosophical Studies*, *Philosophy and Phenomenological Research*, *Analisi* (the bulletin of SIFA, the Italian Society of Analytic Philosophy), and the *Croatian Journal of Philosophy*, and to a symposium in *Epistemology and Philosophy of Science* (Moscow) on a paper in which I briefly summarized my updated view of philosophical methods (2019c).[1] Another five short sections originated as book reviews invited for *The Times Literary Supplement*, *Philosophy*, the *European Journal of Philosophy*, and *The Journal of Philosophy*. One commentary (14.5) originated in an invitation to review a large group of works of popular philosophy collectively for *The Times Literary Supplement*, another (14.6) in an invitation to contribute to the blog *Daily Nous*. Section 11.5 developed out of an invited reply for the *New York Times*' philosophy blog "The Stone" to a defense of naturalism by Alex Rosenberg against my original post, out of which developed Section 11.4, itself provoked by "naturalist" responses to the first edition. I usually accept invitations to contribute to symposia on my books and articles, and to review books on topics on which I am currently working, though for many years my policy has been not write unsolicited replies to reviews or criticisms of my work; life is too short. Thus the balance of topics discussed in the additional response-mode sections is not an artefact of my selection.

All the sections have been written to be readable by themselves, which occasionally involves some local repetition. The response-mode material is overtly one-sided, since it includes only my half of each exchange – altogether, with nearly thirty philosophers, based in Australia, Canada, Croatia, Italy, Russia, the United Kingdom, and the United States. Of course, to judge properly whether I have been *fair* to my interlocutors, readers will have to read their side too. In any case, I am deeply grateful to all those who have spent so much time and effort carefully reading my work and articulating their responses.

In contrast to the first edition, the additional material is designed to be read selectively, according to the reader's interests. It also varies in how wide a readership it was written for, depending on its original

---

[1] For citations in this form, "Williamson" is understood.

place of publication, another dimension on which readers may wish to choose. But the underlying view of philosophy is the same throughout.

Sections 2 to 5 of this Preface briefly introduce the new response-mode material. Section 1 concerns the more spontaneous sections.

1. Widening the picture

My deepest instincts about the nature of philosophy have changed little over my career. For instance, I recall thinking as an undergraduate that transposing philosophical questions from the material to the formal mode, Carnap's way of unmasking them as inviting linguistic decisions, really just disguised quite intelligible non-linguistic questions behind linguistic masks. Taken all the way, the "Linguistic Turn" struck me as in practice not clarifying but obscuring. Such critical instincts are manifest in *The Philosophy of Philosophy*.

However, soon after the book was published, I started to regret not having said more in it about aspects of philosophy which had long mattered greatly to me, but had been occluded by my more urgent preoccupations in writing the book. One such occluded topic was the *abductive* nature of theory choice, in philosophy as it should be, and to some extent in philosophy as it is. Just like theories in natural science, philosophical theories can be compared for fit with the evidence – both their consistency with it and their ability to bring it under illuminating and powerful generalizations – but also for strength, in the sense of informativeness, and for simplicity, elegance, and avoidance of the *ad hoc*. The method is sometimes called *inference to the best explanation*, though philosophical explanations are constitutive rather than causal. The first edition is quite consistent with the abductive aspect of philosophy, which is implicit in the chapter on evidence in philosophy, but somehow it remained in the background.[2] The omission was brought home to me when I gave a week-long colloquium based on the book at the University of Göttingen in 2009, invited by the students: I found myself answering question after question with reference to the role of abduction in philosophy, and wondering why I had not said more about it in the book itself. For the abductive aspect

---

[2] Abductive arguments in philosophy are mentioned in the first edition (184, 210, this volume). Unless specified otherwise, page references in this preface are to the first edition of this book, as reprinted here.

xiv   Preface to the Second Edition

of philosophy was nothing new to me. During my doctoral studies at Oxford in 1976–1980, my closest friend amongst my fellow graduate students in philosophy was Peter Lipton, whose DPhil thesis later turned into his classic treatment *Inference to the Best Explanation*.[3] The relevance of the topic to assessing philosophical theories was salient to me even then. In my book *Vagueness*, the overall case for classical logic was fundamentally abductive (e.g. 1994a: 186). In this second edition, the additional Section 9.2, "Abductive Philosophy," fills this gap in the first edition; Section 9.5 briefly responds to some criticisms of the approach.[4]

Another omission was the methodology of *model-building*. I had started thinking seriously about it thanks to having the economist Hyun Song Shin as a colleague at University College Oxford in 1990–1994, trained in philosophy too, with a degree in PPE (Philosophy, Politics, and Economics) from Oxford. We shared an interest in epistemic logic, on which we published two joint papers (Shin and Williamson 1994, 1996). Our collaboration gave me fascinating experience of the differences in research culture between two disciplines when dealing with the same phenomena, in this case knowledge and ignorance of one's own or another's knowledge and ignorance. As an economist, he was used to a model-building approach, on which models are assumed from the outset to involve drastic simplifications of the reality under study, so that a mere discrepancy between model and reality is not news, and just pointing it out is not considered a significant intellectual contribution. Rather, what displaces a model is *a better model*. He once remarked to me, of Gettier's seminal paper (1963) refuting the analysis of knowledge as justified true belief by counterexamples, that in economics it would have been considered unpublishable. As a philosopher, used to treating counterexamples as the gold standard, I was shocked. Did these economists not care about *truth*? On second thoughts, however, I realized that the model-building methodology was just as oriented towards truth as the potentially naïve

---

[3]   Peter died far too young, in 2007. His work reminds me of Beethoven's view of Handel: a master of achieving great effects by simple means.

[4]   My work in continued defense of an abductive methodology for choosing between rival candidates for the first principles of logic and mathematics (2013a: 423–9, 2017b, 2018b) is too specialized to be appropriately included in the present volume. For a more "popular" account of abduction in philosophy see 2018a: 66–81.

falsificationism of conjectures and refutations by counterexamples (thought experiments), though in a subtler and less direct way. One of our joint papers used an explicitly model-building methodology, and it was employed in an increasingly prominent role in some of my own publications from that period on.[5] "Must Do Better," the Afterword to the first edition, recommends the use of mathematical models to test philosophical ideas (293, this volume), though without discussing such methods in detail. Later reflection on the nature of progress in philosophy convinced me that, like progress in natural science, much of it takes the form of building better and better models of the phenomena under study, rather than discovering exceptionless universal laws, and that failure to recognize the model-building methodology is one of the reasons for widespread overestimation of the difference between philosophy and natural science. In that respect, the additional Section 9.3, "Model-Building in Philosophy," goes far beyond the first edition, while Section 9.6 briefly considers a proposed alternative.[6]

A recent side interest, which played no role in the first edition, has been the surprisingly effective dialectical role of moral and political considerations in philosophical debates which seem to have nothing specifically to do with the moral or political – for example, over general relativism, general skepticism, and general internalism in epistemology. The story of how I first came to notice this phenomenon tempts me into a digression.

As a graduate student at Oxford, I used to attend meetings of the Radical Philosophy group, associated with the journal *Radical Philosophy*. In practice, what was philosophically radical about it was its rejection (and often ignorance) of analytic philosophy, in favor of just about anything which then counted as "continental" – they discussed Nietzsche, Saussure, Althusser, Derrida, the more arid parts of Foucault's corpus, and so on, with varying degrees of reverence. The "analytic"-"continental" distinction cut at an obvious joint in the sociology of philosophy, however artificial it may have been in other respects. I experimented with those alternative traditions because I felt oppressed by the style and assumptions of the kind of analytic

---

[5] For uses of model-building in my work see Shin and Williamson 1996, various passages in 2000a, and 2013c, 2014b, 2015a, 2019b, 2020b.

[6] For a more "popular" account of model-building in philosophy see 2018a: 127–40.

philosophy then most fashionable in Oxford, and hoped that I might find different ideas for use in my own work. I didn't get much out of the experiments, though I enjoyed reading Nietzsche and Saussure. I came to realize that those who led the discussion often understood the obscure texts they talked about no more clearly than I did, although they certainly had a far more extensive acquaintance with them than mine, and were willing to "go on in the same way" as their authors. On the rare occasions when I asked a question or made an objection, they never seemed in danger of getting the point. There were one or two exceptions, fully open to rational discussion of ideas from both sides of the divide – one was Michael Rosen, now at Harvard. After I had left Oxford for my first proper teaching job, at Trinity College Dublin, I felt liberated to discover that what had really oppressed me about the then-predominant style of Oxford philosophy was not that it was too analytic but that it was not analytic *enough*. However, one of the things I did learn from my Oxford experience of Radical Philosophy was this: within such an intellectual world, much of the resistance to the relativist-sounding extremes of Post-Modernism came from Marxists and others on the far Left, who feared relativism as a threat to their political hopes. How far will those who view the case for revolution from a relativist stance commit to the revolutionary cause? In that world, objections to relativism from common sense, natural science, or logic had much less credibility. Later, while in Dublin (1980–1988), I was intrigued to hear from a talk by Richard Kearney (now at Boston College) of Richard Rorty describing absolutism about justice as much harder to give up than absolutism about truth. I was never tempted to give up either, but I could imagine how someone more concerned with morality and politics than with logic might feel that way.

I did nothing with those thoughts at the time, but they stayed with me. Much more recently, in responding to Paul Boghossian's epistemological internalism, I found myself objecting that it counts as justified (though false) a consistent neo-Nazi's belief that he ought to kill members of a target group, and wondering whether such a view would also count as justified (though wrong) his acting on that belief (Boghossian and Williamson 2020). That got me thinking more carefully about why emotive cases are dialectically effective, and whether invoking them is some kind of cheat. That is an obvious danger, especially in the current philosophical climate, where morally or politically wrong-footing one's opponent is all too often used as a convenient excuse for not engaging properly with their arguments or objections. Nevertheless, I came to the conclusion that it *is* legitimate to use such examples in order to make vivid the practical consequences of a philosophical theory, especially one which had seemed to have none. The justification of belief and the justification of action should not be treated as orthogonal issues: the considerations for and against internalism are similar in the two cases, and after all the distinguishing mark of a belief is the agent's willingness to act on it. The additional Section 9.4, "Morally Loaded Cases in Philosophy," encapsulates my reflections on these issues.

The Preface to the first edition starts by expressing my long-held view that the self-images then salient for contemporary philosophy failed to fit its actual development over the preceding decades. The book aimed to help put that right. I had also long been aware of a related strangely growing gap in the historiography of analytic philosophy. When I started as an undergraduate at Oxford in 1973, historical narratives of analytic philosophy tended to stop the story around 1960. Naturally, I expected that, as time went on, the lag between the time of writing and the end of the period written about in narratives of analytic philosophy would remain roughly constant. It did not happen. Thirty years later, historical narratives of analytic philosophy *still* tended to stop the story around 1960. Although that generalization is not exceptionless, there really was very little serious historical work on post-1960 developments in analytic philosophy. The time lag was far longer than needed to gain some historical perspective on the past – it was far shorter for serious historical work on post-1960 (and indeed post-1989) developments in politics, society, and culture. Many younger philosophers felt that Saul Kripke, David Lewis, and others had effected a revolution in philosophy after 1960. I found it frustrating that no one seemed interested in achieving a proper historical understanding of so significant a change.

It was as though such a revolution was not *supposed* to happen. Whether historians of analytic philosophy preferred its logical positivist or its ordinary language strand, its predicted further development would not be in the direction of pre-Kantian metaphysics. From an older perspective, philosophers such as Kripke and Lewis looked like anomalies, anachronisms, to be swept away by the *zeitgeist*, unworthy of serious historical treatment. Instead, the opposite happened.

Their ways of doing philosophy gradually prevailed, to an extent increasingly hard to marginalize historically, whether one approved of them or not. The first edition of this book was obviously a product of that turn in philosophy, but did not say very much about its history.

Some years later, the historian of philosophy Miroslava Trajkovski encouraged me to give a talk at the University of Belgrade, to help bring later developments in analytic philosophy alive for her students by drawing on my personal acquaintance with many of the protagonists. I used the opportunity to reflect historically on the transition from linguistic philosophy to contemporary metaphysics, and describe how it felt to one person at the time. The result was my article "How did we get here from there? The transformation of analytic philosophy", now included as the additional Section 9.1. It is not meant as a work of serious historical scholarship, but rather as a provocation to others to produce such works on post-1960 developments in analytic philosophy. Indeed, things had already begun to improve in that respect. Such historiography is now flourishing. For example, the massive influence of David Lewis has become well-recognized, and his key role in the history of post-1960 analytic philosophy is being analyzed in detail. After all, the period from 1960 to 2020 is just as long as that from 1900 to 1960, and just as deserving of historical study.[7,8]

The reception of the first edition and of "How did we get here from there?" was in many ways gratifying. However, I will not resist one grumble. The experience brought home to me that not all historians of philosophy read a contemporary philosophical text with the professional accuracy or empathy one might expect. I give samples without naming names. Where I wrote "looked," it was irritating to be read as if I had written "is"; I used the past (not present) tense and the verb "to look" (not "to be") for a reason. It was irritating too to be read as if I must be using the word "analytic" in Kant's sense, not in the clearly broader sense standard in analytic philosophy for the last half-century. It was also irritating when my deliber-

---

[7]   Incidentally, one of those now engaged in this much-needed work is Paolo Tripodi, with an earlier incarnation of whom I take issue in Chapter 13.5.

[8]   For a more general and "popular" discussion of the relation between philosophy and its history see 2018a: 98–110.

ately casual introduction of the phrase "armchair knowledge" for an overtly heterogeneous range of cases was read as aiming to replace the term "*a priori*" by a more precise substitute better suited to epistemological theorizing (171, this volume). Alas, no philosophical text is proof against determined attempts to interpret it to suit the interpreter's purposes.

2. *Experimental philosophy*

The first edition treated another topic only briefly: the "negative program" of some "experimental philosophers" against "armchair philosophy." It explained why their talk of "philosophical intuitions" failed to pick out a psychologically distinctive kind, and why thought experiments are not cognitively exceptional, as they assumed, but I did not engage with their texts in much detail.

However, the fashion for experimental philosophy was growing, and I often encountered (and still encounter) surprisingly crude misunderstandings of my objections to the negative program. Do the rejected obsolescent armchair methods include reading a philosophical text carefully and grasping its dialectical structure? In particular, many people took for granted that the book "defended philosophical intuitions," when in fact it argued that thinking in terms of philosophical "intuitions" leads one hopelessly astray. I was also persistently classified as an "enemy of experimental philosophy," despite having engaged in it myself (Bonini, Osherson, Viale, and Williamson 1999). Indeed, given the book's keynote anti-exceptionalism about philosophy, it would have been absurd for me to argue that experimental results are *in principle* irrelevant to assessing the reliability of a philosophical method. But to assess it properly, you must first understand both what the method is and how it is being applied in particular cases. In practice, proponents of the negative program often – though not always – violated these conditions, either by seeing the methodological issues through the distorting lens of the category "philosophical intuitions," or by making sundry naïve or impatient errors in handling the first-order philosophical issues themselves.

The negative program worried me because it had the potential to do serious damage to intellectual standards in philosophy – though its proponents' intention was undoubtedly the opposite. Of course, no particular thought experiment is above criticism, just as no particular experiment in natural science is above criticism. But the negative program aimed at a much less banal conclusion: roughly, that no thought experiment in philosophy should carry significant weight until its result has been independently endorsed by a large and varied sample of non-philosophers. That is one step towards doing philosophy by opinion poll.

If the negative program were to triumph, its effect would be to drastically impede the use of ordinary *examples* in philosophy, since each example would require a large and expensive research program over several years to test whether folk worldwide agree that it exemplifies what the philosopher takes it to exemplify (the "philosophical intuition"). That would constitute a strong disincentive to introducing new examples in the first place, since they could always be neutralized, at least for several years, by the generic demand for such experimental testing. Yet, from Socrates on, in both Western and non-Western philosophy, apt and ingenious ordinary examples have been one of the most effective ways of keeping philosophers honest. Without them, high-sounding abstract generalities are liable to go unchecked. Examples bring us back down to earth.

But why should not experiments themselves provide an alternative reality-check on philosophical theorizing? The trouble is that experimental philosophers' experiments do not test most philosophical hypotheses. They test psychological hypotheses as to whether people's judgments accord with philosophical hypotheses. For example, they do not test the moral hypothesis that it is a wrong to torture a child for fun; they test the psychological hypothesis that most people *think* that it is wrong to torture a child for fun. Of course, one can derive a moral hypothesis from the psychological hypothesis that most people accept it, given the auxiliary hypothesis that a moral hypothesis is true if most people accept it, but how is the auxiliary hypothesis itself to be tested? One can experimentally test the psychological hypothesis that most people accept the auxiliary hypothesis, but that is just to embark on an infinite regress of auxiliary hypotheses. I have never seen a plausible account of how philosophy would in practice work better (or at least not worse) once reformed in line with the negative program.

Fortunately, within experimental philosophy, the negative program has receded in recent years. Perhaps the main reason has been that many of the original results suggesting variation with ethnicity and gender in verdicts on thought experiments have failed to replicate, when the experiments were repeated to higher standards. In other cases, the experiments were irrelevant because the questions asked of ordinary subjects involved terms (like "refer") which philosophers use in technical senses. Indeed, to a surprising extent, philosophers' thought experiments may be tapping into a universal human cognitive system. As one small branch of cognitive psychology, experimental philosophy is well-suited to investigating nuances of the human cognitive system, including how far they are products of nature, how far of culture. For that fruitful inquiry, an animus against thought experiments is merely a source of bias, conscious or otherwise. The five additional sections, 10.1–10.5, on experimental philosophy in this edition are mainly directed against the negative program, to combat the danger it posed to standards of argument in philosophy, although they also consider problems for the category of "philosophical intuitions" irrespective of the negative program. However, none of this implies any hostility on my part to the general idea that experimentation sometimes plays a legitimate part in philosophical activity.

Reflection on the negative program did help persuade me that, by itself, the method of cases is insufficiently robust. In principle, there is nothing wrong with using thought experiments to learn about possibilities, some of which are counterexamples to philosophical generalizations. Our verdicts on thought experiments are not peculiarly liable to error. But, on the same anti-exceptionalist grounds, they are also not peculiarly *immune* to error. The general fallibility of human cognitive faculties applies as much to our verdicts on thought experiments as to our judgments in any other sphere. Of course, when a philosopher makes an idiosyncratic mistake, it will probably be picked up by other philosophers. But suppose that some glitch in our cognitive system disposes humans in general to misjudge a specific thought experiment, perhaps because we are unconsciously relying on a usually reliable heuristic which goes wrong in this special case. How will we notice our collective mistake? By hypothesis, in this case there is no significant variation in ethnicity or gender for experimental philosophy to identify. We may thus treat our false judgment as giving us a datum or Moorean fact, which we use as a counterexample to philosophical theories. If the rest of our data come from verdicts on *other* thought experiments, what is to alert us to our error about *this* thought experiment? The danger is that we treat the thought experiment as refuting what is in fact the *true* philosophical theory in the vicinity, sweep it off the table, and never return to it. That is naïve falsificationism at its worst.

A good strategy to deal with this problem is to hedge one's bets, by using more than one method. Each method acts as a potential corrective to the others. Where different methods converge on the same answer, our acceptance of it is correspondingly more robust. In particular, we can sometimes use both the case method and the method of model-building, neither having priority over the other. For example, I have used formal models of epistemic logic to argue that knowledge is not equivalent to justified true belief (as epistemologists traditionally use the word "justified"), the same conclusion normally reached in epistemology by Gettier-style thought experiments. Thus the two methods converge on the same answer.[9] Although each method by itself may provide knowledge under normal conditions, in the long run we can expect more reliable results from using two or more methods to explore overlapping aspects of an issue and keep a check on each other.

One kind of normal human judgment about hypothetical cases which may sometimes go systematically wrong concerns *conditionals*. In *Suppose and Tell: The Semantics and Heuristics of Conditionals* (2020a), I explore what is arguably the primary human heuristic for cognitively assessing conditionals, a procedure which works well under most conditions, allowing us to extract and communicate valuable information stored in our dispositions to judgment about hypothetical cases, which are miniature thought experiments. This procedure is what we use to make judgments for or against the sample "if" sentences which provide most of the data for semantic and logical theories of conditionals in natural language. However, the heuristic *cannot* be fully reliable, for it is internally inconsistent. That explains why philosophers and linguists have had so much trouble agreeing on how "if" works. But the usual methods of experimental philosophy would not bring the limitations of the heuristic to light, if it is indeed a human universal, since all those who apply it are liable to the *same* errors. Rather, the heuristic's inconsistency is demonstrated by logical and

---

[9]   See 2013c, 2015a. These papers are not included in the present volume because they are mainly occupied with epistemological and technical issues, exemplifying rather than discussing philosophical methodology.

mathematical argument. The role of psychological experimentation lies elsewhere: in testing how far humans do indeed rely on that heuristic. That is a task for cognitive psychology, though not specifically for experimental philosophy.

In general, philosophy and cognitive psychology have much to learn from each other about the nature of human thought and its characteristic vices and virtues. Collaborations between philosophers and cognitive psychologists are likely to become increasingly fruitful, and trying to separate philosophy from psychology in the results may often be fruitless. Whether any of that should be described as "experimental philosophy" is another matter. Anti-exceptionalism about philosophy suggests that the psychology of human philosophical thinking is best understood as just a special case of the psychology of human thinking in general. Schematically: philosophers will have most to bring to their collaboration with psychologists by cultivating their distinctively philosophical skills, not by aping the psychologists, just as psychologists will have most to bring to the collaboration by cultivating their distinctively psychological skills, not by aping the philosophers – though, in a successful collaboration, the philosophers will surely learn lots of psychology and the psychologists lots of philosophy. One reason for the qualifier "schematically" is that there is already a continuum between "pure philosophy" and "pure psychology," with different people at home on different points of the continuum. That is as it should be, and as it is on the continua between "pure philosophy" and "pure mathematics," "pure physics," "pure biology," "pure computer science," "pure linguistics," "pure economics," "pure history," and so on. Philosophy has deep natural connections with many other disciplines; to give exclusive privileges to any one of them is to misunderstand the nature of philosophy.[10]

3. Naturalism

Of philosophers who self-identify as "naturalists," the more extreme tend to dismiss *The Philosophy of Philosophy* as an anti-naturalist tract, while the more moderate tend to wonder why it does not make its implicit naturalism explicit. The first edition defends armchair

---

[10] See 2018a: 111–26 for brief "popular" discussions of some close links between philosophy and various other disciplines.

philosophy against extreme naturalistic attacks, while also defending anti-exceptionalism about philosophy as much less different from other sciences in nature and methods than many philosophers like to think. It presents philosophy as an investigation of the same world which other sciences investigate too, and philosophical knowledge as the product of ordinary human cognitive capacities.

As best I can tell, there is an asymmetry between those who regard the book as implicitly naturalist and those who regard it as anti-naturalist: the former are more likely than the latter to have read it. After all, reading a book is an armchair method of learning what it says.

For the front cover of the first edition, I chose Picasso's "Portrait of Olga in an Armchair," because the sitter is a young woman, not the stereotypical philosopher in an armchair – an old man with a long beard and a pipe. The subliminal message was that armchair philosophy is not what you might think it is.

In a very loose sense of the term "naturalist," I probably count as one. The trouble is that the term is also often used much more narrowly, for one who takes the *natural* sciences (physics, chemistry, biology, ...) to provide the model which all other attempts at systematic inquiry should emulate in method. By that standard, even mathematics falls short, since it does not use observation or experiment in the intended sense, even though all the natural sciences rely on mathematics. It is the most obvious example of a science which is not a natural science in any distinctive sense. Another example, I suggest, is philosophy. The reliance on armchair methods is one of the most salient features of both mathematics and philosophy. That is not to deny the relevance of natural science to philosophy, or even to mathematics. It is just to insist that armchair methods have a central role to play in philosophy, and even more obviously in mathematics.

The second edition contains six short additional sections on naturalism, 11.1–11.6. Their main concerns are to separate extremist versions of naturalism from moderate ones, to emphasize the implausibility of the extremist versions, and to show that the moderate versions are fully compatible with armchair methods.

4. Concepts, understanding, analyticity

Some reactions to the book made me wish that I had been more explicit about my terminology. For example, I often used the words "concept" and "conceptual," but did little to define or clarify them.

The reason was that I borrowed those words from my *opponents*, primarily to articulate their views and arguments – to the effect that philosophy is in some distinctive sense a "conceptual" activity. I wanted to be fair to my opponents by not defining or clarifying the terms in ways which they might reject. Moreover, such views of philosophy come in numerous sub-varieties, which gloss the words in different ways, as I acknowledged (17, this volume). Since the same forms of argument often worked against different sub-varieties, I used the words "concept" and "conceptual" in a somewhat schematic way, to avoid unnecessary repetition.

The upshot of Chapter 4 is that there are no "conceptual" truths or connections in any sense helpful to my opponents. If one likes, one can define a "concept" to be the actual or potential meaning of a linguistic expression, which it shares with all synonymous expressions, appealing to whatever standard of sameness in meaning is made available by a well-developed semantic theory. However, I argued that such a standard will be too coarse-grained to serve my opponents' purposes. For example, it will not make even the most elementary logical truths "conceptual" in any distinctive sense. Such conclusions should have made it clear that "concept" and "conceptual" were not load-bearing terms in my statements of my own positive views.

A little unwisely, I sometimes also wrote of applying "concepts" and of "conceptual" practices in stating my own views, not only in going along with my opponents' ways of talking for the sake of argument. I could just as well have written instead of applying *words* and of *linguistic practices*. In those cases, the step of abstraction from linguistic expressions to concepts was idle. For instance, all the work can be done by the word "vixen" and the property of being a vixen, cutting out the useless middle man, the concept *vixen*.[11] In retrospect, I wish I had stuck to the more perspicuous metalinguistic formulations in stating my own views, and not muddied the waters by sentimentally continuing to employ the term "concept."

For similar reasons, it would be more open to replace currently fashionable talk of "conceptual engineering" by talk of "linguistic engineering." After all, our direct conscious and social control is of

---

[11]   A more accurate statement replaces "the property of being a vixen" with a second-order analogue, as explained in 2013a.

linguistic practices rather than ways of thinking, and our indirect influence on the latter is typically through the former.[12]

For some readers, my use of the word "analytic" was also misleading, since they adhered to its older, historically and etymologically justified sense in which analytic truths are corollaries of conceptual analyses. On that view, "Vixens are female foxes" is both analytic and a conceptual truth, whereas "Red shades are not green" is not analytic but may still be a conceptual truth. I followed much current philosophical usage, which treats "analytic truth" and "conceptual truth" as interchangeable.

With these health warnings, I have left the terminology of the chapters from the first edition unchanged, since readers may wish to see how I originally put things, for purposes of comparison.

The six short additional sections, 12.1–12.6, are all replies to philosophers who took issue with the book on these topics.

5. *Other topics*

As a student at Oxford in the 1970s, my exposure to Wittgenstein's influence helped me build up enough antibodies to resist it for a lifetime (see Section 9.1). Although his influence had greatly declined by the time I wrote the first edition (and has since declined further), he was still too salient a landmark to be ignored in a discussion of philosophical methodology, especially since in some respects my viewpoint stood directly opposite his. Responses to the first edition showed that his ideas were still widespread in the international community of philosophers. The six short additional sections, 13.1–13.6, all reply to philosophers whose approach to the philosophy of philosophy is strongly marked by Wittgenstein's influence.

In the book, I did not intend to cast Wittgenstein, or anyone else, as the villain of the piece. Obviously, I am no Wittgenstein scholar; I am happy to leave detailed engagement with his texts to those with more interest in them. My primary interest has been in combating mistaken assumptions about philosophy widely held by living philosophers, without worrying too much about their historical origins. But philosophers with Wittgensteinian sympathies were strongly represented amongst the authors whom I was invited to respond to or review, perhaps because editors hoped for a lively debate.

---

[12]   Both negative and positive associations of the word "control" are intended.

The final group of additional sections, 14.1–14.6, contains six short pieces which did not fit neatly into any of the previous sections. Two discuss popular philosophy; two reply to critical responses to the first edition; two review books about the nature and value of philosophy.

6. Work published elsewhere

It may be useful to sketch other work in which I have developed themes from the first edition, which has not been included here because it took a more general approach, in either epistemology or the philosophy of language.

Chapter 6 of the first edition analyzed the arguments underlying thought experiments in terms of counterfactual conditionals. The latter were parsed in the traditional way, as the result of applying a two-place sentential operator to a pair of input sentences, the antecedent and the consequent. The envisaged semantics was of the kind proposed by David Lewis in his classic treatment. This approach involved some awkwardness in formalizing the natural language arguments, specifically in handling the anaphoric dependence of pronouns in the consequent (the judgment about the scenario) on quantified terms in the antecedent (the original description of the scenario). A technical appendix is devoted to that issue (307–10, this volume). Another technical appendix concerns the derivation of the logic of metaphysical modality within the complex logic of the counterfactual conditional, given definitions of the former in terms of the latter (295–306, this volume). That appendix furthers the book's anti-exceptionalism: as argued in Chapter 5 of the first edition, philosophers' metaphysical modality is just a limiting case of counterfactual constructions integral to ordinary, practical thought.

Much more recently, I have come to a quite different view of the semantics of the counterfactual conditional. It is best understood as a contextually restricted strict conditional, the result of composing the contextually restricted local necessity operator "would" with the ordinary "if," read as a material conditional (2020a: 103–58, 166–88). In place of $A\,\square\!\!\rightarrow B$ one has $\square(A \supset B)$, but with $\square$ restricted to contextually relevant possible worlds. As a welcome side-effect, this drastically simplifies the treatment of anaphoric relations between antecedent and consequent, since they are no longer separated by a modal operator. It also provides greater flexibility in selecting the contextually relevant worlds to verify the scenario to suit the needs of the thought experiment. Metaphysical necessity becomes a straightforward limiting case of "would." The overall effect is to preserve the anti-exceptionalist spirit of the original, but in a streamlined and more flexible framework (2020a: 229–41).[13]

The epistemology of counterfactual conditionals is correspondingly central to the epistemology of philosophers' thought experiments and modal judgments, in the first edition. It emphasizes the key cognitive role of the imagination in determining what *would* hold on a counterfactual supposition. On my account of conditionals, our primary heuristic for cognitively assessing conditionals involves suppositional thinking, in a reinterpreted Ramsey test (2020a: 15–88). We apply a derivative form of the heuristic to assess counterfactual conditionals (2020a: 189–213). I have also explored the general cognitive function of the imagination more extensively (2016c, 2020c). This work on the cognitive role of supposing and imagining has not been at all specific to philosophical thinking, but subsumes allegedly puzzling aspects of it under much more general forms of human cognition, vindicating the anti-exceptionalist approach.

The first edition uses the role of the imagination in ordinary counterfactual and modal thinking to cast doubt on the idea that the distinction between *a priori* and *a posteriori* knowledge cuts at the cognitive or epistemological joints (167–171, this volume). In later work, I have sharpened and deepened that critique of the distinction, and replied to objections to it (2013b, 2021b, 2021c; Boghossian and Williamson 2020). Again, those arguments are not at all specific to philosophical cognition, but also tend to vindicate anti-exceptionalism about its nature, insofar as it is taken to be *a priori*.

Chapter 4 of the first edition, on epistemological conceptions of analyticity, originated in a symposium with Paul Boghossian at the 2003 Joint Session of the Aristotelian Society and Mind Association, chaired by Crispin Wright – Paul and I talked at such length that no time was left for Crispin to present his comments; I still feel bad about that. Since then, Paul and I have had a series of further exchanges on understanding, the *a priori*, and intuition, culminating in our book (Boghossian and Williamson 2020). Section 12.2 is my

---

[13]   2017e, 2018c, and 2021d defend the counterfactual approach to modal epistemology but were written before my change of view on the semantics of counterfactual conditionals.

half of one of those exchanges, in a book symposium on the first edition. The later rounds are also relevant to the epistemological arguments of this book, although they are not specific to the epistemology of philosophy.

Chapter 7 of the first edition, on evidence in philosophy, in effect applies the general account of evidence defended in *Knowledge and its Limits* to the special case of philosophy. I have continued to uphold that account of evidence, though usually without special reference to philosophy (2021e).

I have also written for a much wider readership on what philosophy does and how (2018a, 2018d).[14]

The Preface to the first edition ends with an expression of my enjoyment in doing philosophy. I am happy to report that, fourteen years later, it continues to provide just as much pleasure.

---

[14] The present text of the first edition corrects mistakes which escaped my proofreading, on pages 166, 180, and 306: thanks to Andrew Melnyk, Chi-Yen Liu, and David Etlin respectively. I have silently corrected a few similar mistakes in the added sections. I have also made various verbal adjustments in the added sections for the sake of smooth reading in the new context of the second edition.

Preface to the First Edition

This book grew out of a sense that contemporary philosophy lacks a self-image that does it justice. Of the self-images that philosophy inherited from the twentieth century, the most prominent – naturalism, the linguistic turn, post-modern irony, and so on – seemed obviously inadequate to most of the most interesting work in contemporary philosophy: as descriptions, false when bold, uninformative when cautious. Less prominent alternatives too seemed implausible or ill-developed. Although an adequate self-image is not a precondition of all virtue, it helps. If philosophy misconceives what it is doing, it is likely to do it worse. In any case, an adequate self-image is worth having for its own sake; we are not supposed to be leading the unexamined life. This is my attempt to do better.

I considered using the phrase "philosophical method" in the title, but decided against on the grounds that it seemed to promise something more like a recipe for doing philosophy than I believe possible. When asked for advice on some occasion, the Duke of Wellington is said to have replied "Sir, you are in a devilish awkward predicament, and must get out of it as best you can." My advice would be scarcely more useful. At the crucial point, I can only say "Use your judgment." The primary task of the philosophy of science is to understand science, not to give scientists advice. Likewise, the primary task of the philosophy of philosophy is to understand philosophy, not to give philosophers advice – although I have not rigorously abstained from the latter.

I also rejected the word "metaphilosophy." The philosophy of philosophy is automatically part of philosophy, just as the philosophy of anything else is, whereas metaphilosophy sounds as though it might try to look down on philosophy from above, or beyond. One reason for the survival of implausible self-images of philosophy is that they have been insufficiently scrutinized as pieces of philosophy. Passed down as though they were platitudes, they often embody epistemologically or logically naïve presuppositions. The philosophy of philosophy is no easier than the philosophy of science. And like the philosophy of science, it can only be done well by those with some respect for what they are studying.

The book makes no claim to comprehensiveness. For example, it does not engage in detail with critics of analytic philosophy who do not engage with it in detail. I preferred to follow a few lines of thought that I found more rewarding. I hope that philosophy as I have presented it seems worth doing and not impossibly difficult. At any rate, I enjoy it.

Acknowledgments

First come the acknowledgments from the first edition. My three Blackwell/Brown lectures, given at Brown University in September 2005, constituted the occasion for the book, although the material had evolved considerably since then. I thank both Blackwell Publishing and Brown University for the invitation and their generous hospitality. Jeff Dean at Blackwell was a helpful and supportive editor.

My further debts of gratitude are huge. An earlier version of some of the material was presented as the Jack Smart Lecture at the Australian National University in July 2005. Various later versions were presented as four Anders Wedberg Lectures at the University of Stockholm in April 2006, where the commentators were Kathrin Glüer-Pagin, Sören Häggqvist, Anna-Sara Malmgren, and Åsa Wikforss, as eight José Gaos Lectures at the Instituto de Investigaciones Filosóficas of the Universidad Nacional Autónoma de Mexico in September–October 2006, and as three Carl G. Hempel Lectures at Princeton University in December 2006. Other occasions on which the material in one form or another came under scrutiny included a week-long graduate course at the University of Bologna in May–June 2005, a week-long Kompaktseminar at the University of Heidelberg in February 2006, three lectures I gave as the Townsend Visitor in Philosophy at the University of California, Berkeley, in September 2006, a lecture and workshop at the University of Munich in June 2005, two lectures I gave as Tang Chun-I Visiting Professor at the Chinese University of Hong Kong in March 2007, and lectures at a graduate conference on epistemology at the University of Rochester in September 2004, where Richard Feldman was the commentator, the University of Arizona, Tucson, and the University of California, Los Angeles, and a meeting of the Aristotelian Society (my Presidential Address) in October 2004, a workshop on the epistemology of philosophy at the University of Bristol in May 2005, a conference on philosophical methodology at the Research School of Social Sciences at the Australian National University in July 2005, a conference on philosophical knowledge in Erfurt, and at Rutgers University in September 2005, the University of Warwick in November 2005, an Arché workshop on modality at the University of St. Andrews in December 2005, a workshop on metaphysics at the University of Nottingham in January 2006, the first conference of the Dutch-Flemish Society for Analytic Philosophy at the University of Amsterdam and the University of Leeds in March 2006, the Universities of Turin and Milan, the "Is there anything wrong with Wittgenstein?" conference in Reggio Emilia and the third conference of the Portuguese Society for Analytic Philosophy at the University of Lisbon in June 2006, the Joint Session of the Aristotelian Society and the Mind Association at the University of Southampton in July 2006 (my address as President of the Mind Association), the GAP.6 conference of the German Society for Analytic Philosophy and the subsequent workshop on Implicit Definitions and A Priori Knowledge, where Frank Hofmann was the commentator, at the Free University of Berlin in September 2006, the University of Santiago de Compostela in November 2006, the Massachusetts Institute of Technology and the Eastern Division meeting of the American Philosophical Association, for which Gillian Russell was the commentator, in December 2006, the Royal Institute of Philosophy and the University of Calgary in February 2007, and the University of Cambridge in June 2007. I presented still earlier versions of the ideas at a workshop on intuition and epistemology at the University of Fribourg, where Manuel García Carpintero was the commentator, a conference on modalism and mentalism in contemporary epistemology hosted by Aarhus University at the Carlsberg Academy in Copenhagen, a conference in the Centre for Advanced Studies at the Norwegian Academy of Science and Letters in Oslo, which also hosted me for a term of leave in the summer of 2004, a workshop at the University of Amiens on John Cook Wilson and Oxford realism, a conference on externalism, phenomenology, and understanding in memory of Greg McCulloch at the Institute of Philosophy in the University of London's School of Advanced Study, a summer school on epistemology at the Sorbonne, and a conference on meaning and truth at St. Andrews, and talks at the universities of Bilkent, Edinburgh, Michigan, Minnesota, Padua, Rijeka, and Stirling. Most of the material had also been presented in classes and discussion groups at Oxford. Much of the development of themes in this book was provoked by reflection on the questions and objections raised on those occasions. It would be hopeless to try to enumerate the questioners and objectors, but they may be able to trace their influence.

Those who had helped with discussion or written comments outside the occasions above include Alexander Bird, Stephan Blatti, Davor Bodrožić, Berit Brogaard, Earl Conee, Keith DeRose, Dorothy Edgington, Pascal Engel, Tamar Szabó Gendler, Olav Gjelsvik, John Hawthorne, Thomas Kroedel, Brian Leftow, Brian Leiter, Peter Lipton, Ofra Magidor, Mike Martin, Nenad Miščević, Michael Pendlebury, Oliver Pooley, Gonzalo Rodriguez-Pereyra, Helge Rückert, Joe Salerno, Laura Schroeter, Nico Silins, Jason Stanley, Scott Sturgeon, Hamid Vahid, Alberto Voltolini, and Ralph Wedgwood. John Hawthorne, Joshua Schechter, and two referees read the book in manuscript and provided comments on which I drew extensively during the final revisions.

That list of acknowledgments is undoubtedly incomplete: special thanks to those who have been undeservedly omitted.

The book was based on a series of articles in which earlier versions of the ideas were formulated, although hardly any pages have survived completely unchanged. Chapters 1 and 2 derive from "Past the Linguistic Turn?," in *The Future for Philosophy*, edited by Brian Leiter (Oxford: Oxford University Press, 2004), pp. 106–28. Most of Chapter 3 was new. The first section of Chapter 3 and much of Chapter 4 constitute an expanded version of "Conceptual Truth," *Aristotelian Society*, supplementary volume 80 (2006), pp. 1–41, with much subsequent material (for example, on tacit knowledge and on normative conceptions of analyticity); the germ is to be found in "Understanding and Inference," *Aristotelian Society*, supplementary volume 77 (2003), pp. 249–93. Chapters 5 and 6 derive from an initial sketch in my Presidential Address to the Aristotelian Society, "Armchair Philosophy, Metaphysical Modality and Counterfactual Thinking," *Proceedings of the Aristotelian Society*, volume 105 (2005): 1–23. An intermediate step on the way to Chapter 5 was "Philosophical Knowledge and Knowledge of Counterfactuals," *Grazer Philosophische Studien*, volume 74 (2007): 89–123, also appearing as *Philosophical Knowledge – Its Possibility and Scope*, edited by Christian Beyer and Alex Burri (Amsterdam: Rodopi, 2007), the proceedings of the Erfurt conference on philosophical knowledge. Chapters 7 and 8 derive from "Philosophical 'Intuitions' and Scepticism about Judgement," *Dialectica* 58 (2004), pp. 109–53; the volume constitutes the proceedings of the workshop on intuition and epistemology at the University of Fribourg, Switzerland, in November 2002 (the talk I gave there is not recognizable in this book; I gave it to make myself think seriously about the topic). Chapter 7 in particular was greatly expanded; sections 1 and 7 were new; the probabilistic material in section 4 was expanded from pp. 683–5 of "Knowledge and Scepticism," *The Oxford Handbook of Contemporary Philosophy*, edited by Frank Jackson and Michael Smith, (Oxford: Oxford University Press, 2005), pp. 681–700. The Afterword is a slightly modified version of "Must Do Better," in *Truth and Realism*, edited by Patrick Greenough and Michael Lynch (Oxford: Oxford University Press: 2006), pp. 177–87; that volume constitutes the proceedings of the St. Andrews conference on meaning and truth.

The enlarged edition reprints the following previously published pieces, sometimes rearranged; for each, I was the sole author and all required permissions have been obtained, which I hereby acknowledge: "Replies to Kornblith, Jackson and Moore," *Analysis Reviews*, 69 (2009): 125–35; "Replies to Ichikawa, Martin and Weinberg," *Philosophical Studies*, 145 (2009): 465–76; "Plato Goes Pop," *Times Literary Supplement*, 5529 (2009): 15; review of Robert Brandom, *Reason in Philosophy*, *Times Literary Supplement*, 5579 (2010): 22–3; "Philosophical Expertise and the Burden of Proof," *Metaphilosophy*, 42 (2011): 215–29; "Reply to Peacocke," "Reply to Boghossian," "Reply to Stalnaker," and "Reply to Horwich," *Philosophy and Phenomenological Research*, 82 (2011): 481–7, 498–506, 515–23, and 534–42 respectively; "Three Wittgensteinians and a Naturalist on *The Philosophy of Philosophy*," in Richard Davies (ed.), *Analisi: Annuario e Bollettino della Società Italiana di Filosofia Analitica (SIFA) 2011*, Milan: Mimesis (2011), 127–37; "What is Naturalism?" and "The Unclarity of Naturalism" in Matthew Haug (ed.), *Philosophical Methodology: The Armchair or the Laboratory?*, London: Routledge (2013): 29–31 and 36–8 respectively; review of Joshua Alexander, *Experimental Philosophy: An Introduction*, *Philosophy*, 88 (2013): 467–74; "Replies to Trobok, Smokrović, and Miščević on the Philosophy of Philosophy," *Croatian Journal of Philosophy*, 13 (2013): 49–64; review of Paul Horwich, *Wittgenstein's Metaphilosophy*,

European Journal of Philosophy, 21 (2013): e7–e10; "How Did We Get Here From There? The Transformation of Analytic Philosophy," *Belgrade Philosophical Annual*, 27 (2014): 7–37; review of Peter Unger, *Empty Ideas: A Critique of Analytic Philosophy*, *Times Literary Supplement*, 5833 (2015): 22–3; "Abductive Philosophy," *Philosophical Forum*, 47 (2016): 263–80; "Philosophical Criticisms of Experimental Philosophy," in Justin Sytsma and Wesley Buckwalter (eds.), *A Companion to Experimental Philosophy*, Oxford: Wiley Blackwell (2016): 22–36; "Model-building in Philosophy," in Russell Blackford and Damien Broderick (eds.), *Philosophy's Future: The Problem of Philosophical Progress*, Oxford: Wiley-Blackwell (2017): 159–73; review of Penelope Maddy, *What Do Philosophers Do? Skepticism and the Practice of Philosophy*, *Journal of Philosophy*, 114 (2017): 492–7; "Morally Loaded Cases in Philosophy," *Proceedings and Addresses of the American Philosophical Association*, 93 (2019): 159–72; "Reply to Dennett, Knobe, Kuznetsov, and Stoljar on Philosophical Methodology," *Epistemology and Philosophy of Science*, 56 (2019): 46–52; "Popular Philosophy and Populist Philosophy," *Daily Nous* (2020), http://dailynous.com/2020/06/08/popular-philosophy-populist-philosophy-guest-post-timothy-williamson. Many of those pieces were indebted to various philosophers for their feedback. They are acknowledged at the relevant places in the text, since that is more informative.

I thank Marissa Koors, the acquisitions editor at Wiley-Blackwell, for first suggesting an expanded edition of the book to me, and for her patience, flexibility, and enthusiasm in facilitating its implementation, and Charlie Hamlyn, also at Wiley-Blackwell, for his detailed help in the later stages of the project.

Finally, as in the first edition, thanks above all to my wife Ana, who still does not let me forget what matters.

Part I

Introduction

Introduction

What can be pursued in an armchair?

Every armchair pursuit raises the question whether its methods are adequate to its aims. The traditional methods of philosophy are armchair ones: they consist of thinking, without any special interaction with the world beyond the chair, such as measurement, observation or experiment would typically involve. To do justice to the social and not solely individual nature of philosophy, as a dialectic between several parties, we should add speaking and listening to thinking, and allow several armchairs, within earshot of each other, but methodologically that brings philosophy little closer to the natural sciences. For good or ill, few philosophers show much appetite for the risky business of making predictions and testing them against observation, whether or not their theories in fact have consequences that could be so tested. Without attempting to define the terms precisely, we may put the difference to a first approximation thus: the current methodology of the natural sciences is *a posteriori*; the current methodology of philosophy is *a priori*. What should we make of this difference?

Opposite reactions are possible. *Crude rationalists* regard philosophy's *a priori* methodology as a virtue. According to them, it makes philosophical results especially reliable, because immune from perceptual error. *Crude empiricists* regard philosophy's *a priori* methodology as a vice. According to them, it makes philosophical results especially unreliable, because immune from perceptual correction.

Few contemporary philosophers have the nerve to be crude rationalists. Given the apparent absence of a substantial body of agreed results in philosophy, crude rationalism is not easy to maintain. Many contemporary philosophers have some sympathy for crude empiricism, particularly when it goes under the more acceptable name of "naturalism." However, that sympathy sometimes has little effect on their philosophical practice: they still philosophize in the grand old manner, merely adding naturalism to their list of *a priori* commitments.

A subtler response to naturalism, or empiricism, is to scale down the ambitions of philosophy. Holding fixed its a *priori* methodology, one asks what it could be good for. Not for answering ordinary factual questions, it is claimed: that is best left to the natural sciences with their *a posteriori* methodology. Nevertheless, what we already have in the armchair is the intellectual equipment we bring to *a posteriori* inquiry, our conceptual or linguistic competence. Perhaps philosophy can find some sort of legitimate employment by investigating, from within, what we bring to inquiry. Rather than trying to answer ordinary factual questions, it seeks to understand the very possibility of asking them – in some way, yet to be properly specified, that does not involve asking ordinary factual questions about the possibility of asking ordinary factual questions. The "linguistic turn" in twentieth-century philosophy comprises a variety of attempts in that general spirit. Since confinement to an armchair does not deprive one of one's linguistic competence, whatever can be achieved through exercise of that competence and reflection thereon will be a feasible goal for philosophy. If one regards thought as constituting a more fundamental level of analysis than language, one may generalize the linguistic turn to the "conceptual turn," and consider what can be achieved through exercise of our conceptual competence and reflection thereon, but the outcome will be broadly similar: philosophical questions turn out to be in some sense conceptual questions.

Crude rationalists, crude empiricists, and linguistic or conceptual philosophers (those who take the linguistic or conceptual turn) share a common assumption: that the *a priori* methodology of philosophy is profoundly unlike the *a posteriori* methodology of the natural sciences; it is no mere difference between distinct applications of the same underlying methodology. One apparently distinctive feature of current methodology in the broad tradition known as "analytic philosophy" is the appeal to *intuition*. Crude rationalists postulate a special knowledge-generating faculty of rational intuition. Crude empiricists regard "intuition" as an obscurantist term for folk prejudice, a psychological or social phenomenon that cannot legitimately constrain truth-directed inquiry. Linguistic or conceptual philosophers treat intuitions more sympathetically, as the deliverances of linguistic or conceptual competence. Of course, the appeal to intuitions also plays a crucial role in the overt methodology of other disciplines too, such as linguistics.

One main theme of this book is that the common assumption of philosophical exceptionalism is false. Even the distinction between the *a priori* and the *a posteriori* turns out to obscure underlying similarities. Although there are real methodological differences between philosophy and the other sciences, as actually practiced, they are less deep than is often supposed. In particular, so-called intuitions are simply judgments (or dispositions to judgment); neither their content nor the cognitive basis on which they are made need be distinctively philosophical. In general, the methodology of much past and present philosophy consists in just the unusually systematic and unrelenting application of ways of thinking required over a vast range of non-philosophical inquiry. The philosophical applications inherit a moderate degree of reliability from the more general cognitive patterns they instantiate. Although we cannot prove, from a starting-point a sufficiently radical skeptic would accept, that those ways of thinking are truth-conducive, the same holds of *all* ways of thinking, including the methods of natural science. That is the skeptic's problem, not ours. By more discriminating standards, the methodology of philosophy is not in principle problematic.

Some may wonder whether philosophy *has* a method to be studied, especially if it is as methodologically undistinctive as just suggested. Forget the idea of a single method, employed in all and only philosophical thinking. Still, philosophers use methods of various kinds: they philosophize in various ways. A philosophical community's methodology is its repertoire of such methods. The word "method" here carries no implication of a mechanically applicable algorithm, guaranteed to yield a result within a finite time. On this loose understanding of what a methodology is, it is disingenuous for a philosopher to claim to have none.

Another main theme of this book is that the differences in subject matter between philosophy and the other sciences are also less deep than is often supposed. In particular, few philosophical questions are conceptual questions in any distinctive sense, except when philosophers choose to ask questions about concepts, as they may but need not do. Philosophical questions are those philosophers are disposed to ask, which in turn tend, unsurprisingly, to be those more amenable to philosophical than to other ways of thinking; since the philosophical ways of thinking are not different in kind from the other ways, it is equally unsurprising that philosophical questions are not different in kind from other questions. Of course, philosophers are especially fond of abstract, general, necessary truths, but that is only an extreme case of a set of intellectual drives present to some degree in all disciplines.

In most particular cases, philosophers experience little difficulty in recognizing the difference between philosophy and non-philosophy. Being philosophers, they care about the difference, and have a professional temptation to represent it as a deep philosophical one. But just about every institutionally distinct discipline acquires a professional identity, and its practitioners experience little difficulty in recognizing the difference between what "we" do and what "they" do in most particular cases. They care about the difference, and have a professional temptation to represent it in the terms of their own discipline. But such temptations can be resisted. The distinction between the Department of Philosophy and the Department of Linguistics or the Department of Biology is clearer than the distinction between philosophy and linguistics or biology; the philosophy of language overlaps the semantics of natural languages and the philosophy of biology overlaps evolutionary theory.

The unexceptional nature of philosophy is easier to discern if we avoid the philistine emphasis on a few natural sciences, often imagined in crudely stereotyped ways that marginalize the role of armchair methods in those sciences. Not all science is natural science. Whatever crude empiricists may say, mathematics is a science if anything is; it is done in an armchair if anything is. In no useful sense are mathematical questions conceptual questions. If mathematics is an armchair science, why not philosophy too?

Most philosophers are neither crude rationalists nor crude empiricists nor, these days, linguistic or conceptual philosophers. Many would accept the theses just enunciated about the methodology and subject matter of philosophy. But a third theme of this book is that the current philosophical mainstream has failed to articulate an adequate philosophical methodology, in part because it has fallen into the classic epistemological error of psychologizing the data. For example, our evidence is sometimes presented as consisting of our intuitions: not their content, since it is allowed that some of our intuitions may be false, but rather our psychological states of having those intuitions. We are then supposed to infer to the philosophical theory that best explains the evidence. But since it is allowed that philosophical questions are typically not psychological questions, the link between the philosophical theory of a non-psychological subject matter and the psychological evidence that it is supposed to explain becomes problematic: the description of the methodology makes the methodology hard to sustain. Again, philosophy is often presented as systematizing and stabilizing our beliefs, bringing them into reflective equilibrium: the picture is that in doing philosophy what we have to go on is what our beliefs currently are, as though our epistemic access were only to those belief states and not to the states of the world that they are about. The picture is wrong; we frequently have better epistemic access to our immediate physical environment than to our own psychology. A popular remark is that we have no choice but to start from where we are, with our current beliefs. But where we are is not only having various beliefs about the world; it is also having significant knowledge of the world. Starting from where we are involves starting from what we already know, and the goal is to know more (of course, how much more we come to know cannot be measured just by the number of propositions learnt). To characterize our method as one of achieving reflective equilibrium is to fail to engage with epistemologically crucial features of our situation. Our understanding of philosophical methodology must be rid of internalist preconceptions.

Philosophical errors distort our conception of philosophy in other ways too. Confused and obscure ideas of conceptual truth create the illusion of a special domain for philosophical investigation. Similarly, although perception clearly involves causal interaction between perceiver and perceived, crudely causal accounts of perceptual knowledge that occlude the contribution of background theory create the illusion of a contrast between world-dependent empirical beliefs and world-independent philosophical theory.

Clearly, the investigation of philosophical methodology cannot and should not be philosophically neutral. It is just more philosophy, turned on philosophy itself. We have the philosophy of mathematics, the philosophy of physics, the philosophy of biology, the philosophy of economics, the philosophy of history; we also need the philosophy of philosophy.

The rethinking of philosophical methodology in this book involves understanding, at an appropriate level of abstraction, how philosophy is actually done. Philosophers of science know the dangers of moralizing from first principles on how a discipline should ideally be pursued without respecting how it currently is pursued; the same lesson applies to the philosophy of philosophy. The present opposition to philosophical exceptionalism is far from involving the idea that philosophers should model themselves on physicists or biologists. The denial that philosophical questions are conceptual questions is quite compatible with a heavy emphasis on issues of semantic structure in philosophical discussion, for the validity or otherwise of philosophical reasoning is often highly sensitive to delicate aspects of the semantic structure of premises and conclusion: to make our reasoning instruments more reliable, we must investigate those instruments themselves, even when they are not the ultimate objects of our concern.

That philosophy *can* be done in an armchair does not entail that it *must* be done in an armchair.[1] This book raises no objection to the idea that the results of scientific experiments are sometimes directly relevant to philosophical questions: for example, concerning the philosophy of time. But it is a fallacy to infer that philosophy can nowhere usefully proceed until the experiments are done. In this respect, philosophy is similar to mathematics. Scientific experiments can be relevant to mathematical questions. For instance, a physical theory may entail that there are physically instantiated counter-examples to a mathematical theory. A toy example: one can specify in physical terms what it takes to be an inscription (intended or unintended) in a given font of a proof of "0 = 1" in a given formal system of Peano Arithmetic; a physical theory could predict that an event of a specified physically possible type would cause there to be

---

[1]   In this respect Hilary Kornblith seems to misunderstand the claim that philosophy can be done in an armchair (2006: 19). I have even dabbled in experimental philosophy myself (Bonini, Osherson, Viale and Williamson 1999).

such an inscription. Less directly, psychological experiments might in principle reveal levels of human unreliability in proof-checking that would undermine current mathematical practice. To conclude on that basis alone that mathematics should become an experimental discipline would be hopelessly naïve. In practice, most of mathematics will and should remain an armchair discipline, even though it is not in principle insulated from experimental findings, because armchair methods, specifically proof, remain by far the most reliable and efficient available. Although the matter is less clear-cut, something similar may well apply to many areas of philosophy, for instance, philosophical logic. In particular, on the account in this book, the method of conducting opinion polls among non-philosophers is not very much more likely to be the best way of answering philosophical questions than the method of conducting opinion polls among non-physicists is to be the best way of answering physical questions.

Although this book is a defense of armchair philosophy, it is not written in a purely conservative spirit. Our ideas about philosophical methodology, however inchoate, are liable to influence the methodology we actually employ; bad ideas about it are liable to tilt it in bad directions. A reasonable hypothesis is that our current methodology is good enough to generate progress in philosophy, but not by much: ten steps forward, nine steps back. Nevertheless, we can improve our performance even without radically new methods. We need to apply the methods we already have with more patience and better judgment. A small increase in accuracy of measurement may enable scientists to tackle problems previously beyond reach, because their data lacked sufficient resolution. Similarly, small improvements in accepted standards of reasoning may enable the philosophical community to reach knowledgeable agreement on the status of many more arguments. Such incremental progress in philosophical methodology is a realistic prospect, for current standards in the profession exhibit large variations significantly correlated with differences between graduate schools. Philosophical methodology can be taught – mainly by example, but fine-tuning by explicit precept and discussion also makes a difference. For instance, the level of rigor in philosophical statement and argument which Frege achieved only by genius (with a little help from his mathematical training) is now available to hundreds of graduate students every year: and we know how to do even better. That is not to imply, of course, that we must strive for maximum rigor at all times, otherwise this impressionistic introduction would be self-defeating. At any rate, if the philosophical community has the will, it can gradually bring up a much higher proportion of practice to the standard of current best practice, and beyond. Such progress in methodology cannot be relied on to happen automatically; not all of us love the highest at first sight. Although the envisaged incremental progress lacks the drama after which some philosophers still hanker, that hankering is itself a symptom of the intellectual immaturity that helps hold philosophy back. No revelation is at hand; any improvement in accepted standards of philosophical discussion will result from collective hard work and self-discipline. One hope with which this book is written is that by contributing to the current tendency towards increasing methodological self-consciousness in philosophy it will play some role, however indirect, in raising those standards. Philosophizing is not like riding a bicycle, best done without thinking about it – or rather: the best cyclists surely *do* think about what they are doing.

This book is an essay. It makes no claim to comprehensiveness. It does not attempt to compile a list of philosophical methods, or of theories about philosophical methods. It touches on historical matters only glancingly. Instead, it explores some interrelated issues that strike me as interesting and not well understood. It starts by inquiring into the nature of philosophical questions. It proceeds in part by detailed case studies of particular examples. Since all examples have their own special characteristics, generalizations from them must be tentative. But many long-standing misconceptions in philosophy are helped to survive by an unwillingness to look carefully and undogmatically at examples, sometimes protected by a self-righteous image of oneself and one's friends as the only people who do look carefully and undogmatically at examples (some disciples of the later Wittgenstein come to mind).

It is difficult to displace one philosophical picture except by another. Although discussion of philosophical methodology is itself part of philosophy, it is less often conducted with a clear view of the theoretical alternatives than is usual in philosophy. David Lewis once wrote that "what we accomplish in philosophical argument" is to "measure the price" of maintaining a philosophical claim; when his remark is cited as an obvious truth, it tends not to be noticed that it too is subject to philosophical argument, and has its price – not least the danger of infinite regress, since claims about the price of maintaining a philosophical claim are themselves subject to philosophical argument.[2] Another hope for this book is that it will clarify an alternative to widespread assumptions about the nature of philosophy.

---

[2]   See his 1983a: x. Lewis himself gives a brief philosophical argument for his claim about measuring the price, based on the premise that "[o]ur 'intuitions' are simply opinions," against a foundationalist alternative. He also qualifies the claim, allowing that Gödel and Gettier may have conclusively refuted philosophical theories, and that perhaps the price of a philosophical claim "is something we can settle more or less conclusively."

1

The Linguistic Turn and the Conceptual Turn

The Linguistic Turn is the title of an influential anthology edited by Richard Rorty, published in 1967. He credited the phrase to Gustav Bergmann (Bergmann 1964: 3; Rorty 1967: 9). In his introduction, Rorty (1967: 3) explained:

> The purpose of the present volume is to provide materials for reflection on the most recent philosophical revolution, that of linguistic philosophy. I shall mean by "linguistic philosophy" the view that philosophical problems are problems which may be solved (or dissolved) either by reforming language, or by understanding more about the language we presently use.

"The linguistic turn" has subsequently become the standard vague phrase for a diffuse event – some regard it as *the* event – in twentieth-century philosophy, one not confined to signed-up linguistic philosophers in Rorty's sense. For those who took the turn, language was somehow the central theme of philosophy.

The word "theme" is used with deliberate vagueness. It does not mean "subject matter," for the linguistic turn was not the attempted reduction of philosophy to linguistics. The theme of a piece of music is not its subject matter. Those who viewed philosophy as an activity of dispelling confusions of linguistic origin did not see it as having a subject matter in the sense in which a science has a subject matter. But merely to regard linguistic analysis as one philosophical method among many is not yet to have taken the linguistic turn, for it is not yet to regard language as central. We will be more precise below.

There is an increasingly widespread sense that the linguistic turn is past. We will ask how far the turn has been, or should be, reversed.

Language has been regarded as central to philosophy in many different ways, which cannot all be treated together. A history of the many different forms that the linguistic turn took would be a history of much of twentieth-century philosophy. That is a task for another book, by another author. Self-indulgently, I will use a thin slice through history to introduce the contemporary issues by briefly considering some of my predecessors in the Wykeham Chair of Logic at Oxford.

A. J. Ayer was the first holder of the Chair to take the linguistic turn.[1] In 1936, back from Vienna and its Circle but not yet in the Chair, he announced an uncompromisingly formal version of linguistic philosophy:

> [T]he philosopher, as an analyst, is not directly concerned with the physical properties of things. He is concerned only with the way in which we speak about them. In other words, the propositions of philosophy are not factual, but linguistic in character – that is, they do not describe the behaviour of physical, or even mental, objects; they express definitions, or the formal consequences of definitions. (Ayer 1936: 61–2)

Ayer traced his views back ultimately to the empiricism of Berkeley and Hume (Ayer 1936: 11). His contrast between definitions of words and descriptions of objects is, roughly, the linguistic analogue of Hume's contrast between relations of ideas and matters of fact. For an empiricist, the *a priori* methods of philosophy cannot provide us with knowledge of synthetic truths about matters of fact ("the behaviour of physical, or even mental, objects"); they yield only analytic truths concerning relations of ideas ("definitions, or the formal consequences of definitions"). A rather traditional empiricism later overshadowed the linguistic theme in Ayer's work.

Ayer was the predecessor of Sir Michael Dummett in the Wykeham Chair. Dummett gave a much-cited articulation of the linguistic turn, attributing it to Frege:

> Only with Frege was the proper object of philosophy finally established: namely, first, that the goal of philosophy is the analysis of the

---

[1]   Ayer's three immediate predecessors were John Cook Wilson, H. H. Joachim and H. H. Price.

structure of *thought*; secondly, that the study of *thought* is to be sharply distinguished from the study of the psychological process of *thinking*; and, finally, that the only proper method for analysing thought consists in the analysis of *language*. . . . [T]he acceptance of these three tenets is common to the entire analytical school. (Dummett 1978: 458)

On this view, thought is essentially expressible (whether or not actually expressed) in a public language, which filters out the subjective noise, the merely psychological aspects of thinking, from the intersubjective message, that which one thinks. Dummett's own corpus constitutes one of the most imposing monuments of analytic philosophy as so defined. Unlike Ayer, he does not describe philosophical claims as definitions. Unlike Rorty, he characterizes the linguistic turn as involving distinctive claims about the subject matter of philosophy, not only about its method. On Dummett's view, Frege's insight replaced epistemology by philosophy of language as first philosophy. But this methodological innovation is supposed to be grounded in the account of the proper object of philosophy.

Elsewhere, Dummett makes clear that he takes this concern with language to be what distinguishes "analytical philosophy" from other schools (1993: 4). His account of its inception varies slightly. At one points (1993: 5), he says: "[A]nalytical philosophy was born when the 'linguistic turn' was taken. This was not, of course, taken uniformly by any group of philosophers at any one time: but the first clear example known to me occurs in Frege's *Die Grundlagen der Arithmetik* of 1884." Later (1993: 27), we read: "If we identify the linguistic turn as the starting-point of analytical philosophy proper, there can be no doubt that, to however great an extent Frege, Moore and Russell prepared the ground, the crucial step was taken by Wittgenstein in the *Tractatus Logico-Philosophicus* of 1922." Presumably, in Frege the linguistic turn was a fitful insight, in Wittgenstein, a systematic conception.

That "analytical philosophers" in Dummett's sense coincide with those usually classified as such is not obvious. Some kind of linguistic turn occurred in much of what is usually called "continental [supposedly non-analytic] philosophy." That Jacques Derrida did not subscribe in his own way to Dummett's three tenets is unclear: if some stretching of terms is required, it is for the later Wittgenstein too. Conversely, Bertrand Russell did not subscribe to the three tenets, although often cited as a paradigm "analytical philosopher." Over the past 20 years, fewer and fewer of those who would accept the label "analytic philosophy" for their work would also claim to take the linguistic turn (I am not one of those few). Even philosophers strongly influenced by Dummett, such as Gareth Evans, Christopher Peacocke, and John Campbell, no longer give language the central role he describes. For Dummett, they belong to a tradition that has grown out of "analytical philosophy" without themselves being "analytical philosophers" (1993: 4–5). In effect, they aimed to analyze thought directly, without taking a diversion through the analysis of language. In the 1980s it became commonplace in some circles to suggest that the philosophy of mind had displaced the philosophy of language in the driving seat of philosophy.

For philosophers of mind who accepted Jerry Fodor's (1975) influential hypothesis of a language of thought, the priority of thought to public language did not imply the priority of thought to all language, since thought itself was in a language, the brain's computational code. In principle, someone might combine that view with Dummett's three tenets of analytic philosophy, contrary to Dummett's intention; he did not mean a private language. Moreover, the first-personal inaccessibility of the language of thought makes such a version of the linguistic turn methodologically very different from the traditional ones.

For those who deny the methodological priority of language to thought, the minimal fallback from Dummett's three tenets is to reject the third but maintain the first two. They assert that the goal of philosophy is the analysis of the structure of thought, and that the study of thought is to be sharply distinguished from the study of the psychological process of thinking, but deny that the only proper method for analysing thought consists in the analysis of language. If thought has constituents, we may call them "concepts." On this view, concepts take the place of words in Dummett's analytical philosophy.

In practice, linguistic philosophers were often happy enough to speak of concepts rather than words, for they regarded a concept as what synonymous expressions had in common; their primary interest was in the features common to synonyms, not in the differences between them. It is therefore not too misleading to describe as *conceptual philosophers* those who accept Dummett's first two tenets –

that the goal of philosophy is the analysis of the structure of thought, and that the study of thought is to be sharply distinguished from the study of the psychological process of thinking – whether or not they accept the third. We may also describe them as doing *conceptual philosophy*, and as having taken the *conceptual turn*.

The conceptual turn constitutes a much broader movement than the linguistic turn. It is neutral over the relative priority of language and thought. We think and talk about things – truly or falsely depending on whether they are or are not as we think or say they are. The aboutness of thought and talk is their *intentionality*; the conceptual turn puts intentionality at the centre of philosophy. This terminology indicates how little the conceptual turn is confined to what would ordinarily be called "analytic philosophy." The phenomenological tradition may constitute another form of the conceptual turn. In the hermeneutic study of interpretation and various shades of postmodernist discourse about discourse the conceptual turn takes a more specifically linguistic form.

Have we stretched our terms so far that all philosophy is conceptual philosophy? No. On a natural view, concepts constitute only a small fraction of a largely mind-independent reality. That the goal of philosophy is in some sense to analyze that small fraction is no platitude. To put it very schematically, let *absolute idealism about the subject matter of philosophy* be the view that philosophy studies only concepts, in contrast to *ontological absolute idealism*, the wilder view that only concepts exist.[2] Although absolute idealism about the subject matter of philosophy does not entail ontological absolute idealism, why should we accept absolute idealism about the subject matter of philosophy if we reject ontological absolute idealism? Of course, we might reject absolute idealism about the subject matter of philosophy while nevertheless holding that the correct method for philosophy is to study its not purely conceptual subject matter by studying concepts of that subject matter. This methodological claim will be considered later; for present purposes, we merely note how much weaker it is than those formulated by Ayer and Dummett.

The claim that concepts constitute only a small fraction of reality might be opposed on various grounds. Recall that concepts were

---

[2]   The "absolute" is to distinguish these forms of idealism from the corresponding "subjective" forms, in which concepts are replaced by psychological processes.

defined as the constituents of thought. If thought consists of Russellian propositions, complexes of the objects, properties, relations, and other elements of reality the proposition is about, then those objects, properties, relations, and other elements of reality are by definition concepts. In that case, ontological absolute idealism may be a triviality, because whatever exists is a constituent of various Russellian propositions, and thereby counts as a concept. However, even conceptual philosophers who accept the Russellian view of propositions will distinguish *conceptual structure*, the structure characteristic of propositions, from other sorts of structure. For example, they will analyze the atomic proposition that this crystal is translucent as the object-property complex ⟨this crystal, translucency⟩, but they will not regard it as any of their business to analyze the structure of the crystal itself: that is chemical structure, not conceptual structure in the relevant sense, otherwise the proposition would not be atomic. Their goal for philosophy – to analyze the structure of thought – is still only to analyze one sort of structure among many. Thus one might accept the Russellian view of propositions and still oppose the conceptual turn, on the grounds that philosophy can appropriately investigate general features of nonconceptual structure too, such as the general mereological structure of physical objects.

Alternatively, take a more standard view of concepts, as something like modes of presentation, ways of thinking or speaking, or intellectual capacities. Still, the claim that concepts constitute only a small fraction of reality might be accused of violating Dummett's second tenet by confusing thought with the process of thinking. Almost everyone agrees that psychological events constitute only a small fraction of reality, but that is not yet to concede that thought in a non-psychologistic sense is similarly confined. John McDowell (1994: 27), for instance, argues:[3]

> [T]here is no ontological gap between the sort of thing one can mean, or generally the sort of thing one can think, and the sort of thing that can be the case. When one thinks truly, what one thinks *is* what is the

---

[3] Although McDowell is sometimes classified as a "post-analytic" philosopher, he finds his own way to accept Dummett's "fundamental tenet of analytical philosophy," that "philosophical questions about thought are to be approached through language" (1994: 125).

case. So since the world is everything that is the case . . . there is no
gap between thought, as such, and the world. Of course thought can
be distanced from the world by being false, but there is no distance
from the world implicit in the very idea of thought.

For McDowell, the sort of thing one can think is a conceptual
content: the conceptual has no outer boundary beyond which lies
unconceptualized reality. He denies the accusation of idealism on the
grounds that he is not committed to any contentious thesis of
mind-dependence.

The sort of thing that can be the case is that a certain object has
a certain property. McDowell's claim is not that the object and the
property *are* concepts, but merely that we can in principle form concepts *of* them, with which to think that the object has the property.
Indeed, we can in principle form many different concepts of them:
we can think of the same object as Hesperus or as Phosphorus. In
Fregean terms congenial to McDowell, different senses determine the
same reference. He admits "an alignment of minds with the realm of
sense, not with the realm of reference . . . thought and reality meet in
the realm of sense" (1994: 179–80). For objects, his claim that the
conceptual is unbounded amounts to the claim that any object can
be thought of. Likewise for the sort of thing that can be the case: the
claim is, for example, that whenever an object has a property, it can
be thought, of the object and the property, that the former has the
latter. But, on a coherent and natural reading of "the sort of thing
that can be the case," such things are individuated coarsely, by the
objects, properties, and relations that they involve. Thus, since Hesperus *is* Phosphorus, what is the case if Hesperus is bright *is* what is
the case if Phosphorus is bright: the objects are the same, as are the
properties. On this reading, McDowell's claim "When one thinks
truly, what one thinks *is* what is the case" is false, because what one
thinks is individuated at the level of sense while what is the case is
individuated at the level of reference. Although McDowell's claim is
true on weaker readings, they will not bear the weight his argument
puts on them.

McDowell's argument in any case seems to require the premise
that everything (object, property, relation, state of affairs, . . .) is
thinkable. That premise is highly contentious. What reason have we
to assume that reality does not contain *elusive objects*, incapable in

principle of being individually thought of? Although we can think of them collectively – for example, as elusive objects – that is not to single out any one of them in thought. Can we be sure that ordinary material objects do not consist of clouds of elusive sub-sub-atomic particles? We might know them by their collective effects while unable to think of any single one of them. The general question whether there can be elusive objects looks like a good candidate for philosophical consideration. Of course, McDowell does not intend the conceptual to be limited by the merely medical limitations of human beings, but the elusiveness may run deeper than that: the nature of the objects may preclude the kind of separable causal inter-action with complex beings that isolating them in thought would require. In Fregean terminology again, a sense is a mode of presenta-tion of a referent; a mode of presentation of something is a way of presenting it to a possible thinker, if not an actual one; for all McDowell has shown, there may be necessary limitations on think-ing.[4] Although elusive objects belong to the same very general onto-logical category of objects as those we can single out, their possibility still undermines McDowell's claim that we cannot make "interesting sense" of the idea of something outside the conceptual realm (1994: 105–6). We do not know whether there actually are elusive objects. What would motivate the claim that there are none, if not some form of idealism very far from McDowell's intentions? We should adopt no conception of philosophy that on methodological grounds excludes elusive objects.[5]

Suppose, just for the sake of argument, that there are no elusive objects. That by itself would still not vindicate a restriction of philosophy to the conceptual, the realm of sense or thought. The practitioners of any discipline have thoughts and communicate them,

[4]   McDowell's invocation of humility (1994: 40) addresses contingent limitations, not necessary ones.
[5]   Mark Johnston (1993: 96–7) discusses "the Enigmas, entities essentially unde-tectable by us." He stipulates that they are collectively as well as individually undetectable; thus our elusive objects need not be his Enigmas. If we cannot have good evidence that there are no Enigmas, it may well be a waste of time to worry whether there are Enigmas. But it would not follow that it is a waste of time to worry whether there *can be* Enigmas. Their definition does not rule out knowledge of the possibility of such things; such knowledge may itself be philosophically useful (indeed, Johnston uses it for his philosophical purposes).

but they are rarely studying those very thoughts: rather, they are studying what their thoughts are about. Most thoughts are not about thoughts. To make philosophy the study of thought is to insist that philosophers' thoughts should be about thoughts. It is not obvious why philosophers should accept that restriction.

Even within what is usually considered analytic philosophy of mind, much work violates the two tenets of conceptual philosophy. Naturalists hold that everything is part of the natural world, and should be studied as such; many of them study thought as part of the natural world by not sharply distinguishing it from the psychological process of thinking. Those who study sensations or qualia without treating them as intentional phenomena are not usually attempting to analyze the structure of thought; their interest is primarily in the nature of the sensations or qualia themselves, not in our concepts of them. Even when the question of veridicality arises, it is not always conceded that there are structured thoughts: some philosophers claim that perception has a conceptually unstructured content that represents the environment as being a certain way. Their interest is in the nature of the nonconceptual content itself, not just in our concept of it.

Despite early hopes or fears, philosophy of mind has not come to play the organizing role in philosophy that philosophy of language once did. No single branch of philosophy does: philosophy is no more immune than other disciplines to increasing specialization. Nor is any one philosophical method currently treated as a panacea for philosophical ills, with consequent privileges for its home branch. Once we consider other branches of philosophy, we notice much more philosophizing whose primary subject matter is not conceptual.

Biology and physics are not studies of thought. In their most theoretical reaches, they merge into the philosophy of biology and the philosophy of physics. Why then should philosophers of biology and philosophers of physics study only thought? Although they sometimes study what biologists' and physicists' concepts are or should be, sometimes they study what those concepts are concepts of, in an abstract and general manner. If the conceptual turn is incompatible with regarding such activities as legitimately philosophical, why take the conceptual turn?

There is a more central example. Much contemporary metaphysics is not primarily concerned with thought or language at all. Its goal is to discover what fundamental kinds of things there are and what properties and relations they have, not to study the structure of our thought about them – perhaps we have no thought about them until it is initiated by metaphysicians. Contemporary metaphysics studies substances and essences, universals and particulars, space and time, possibility and necessity. Although nominalist or conceptualist reductions of all these matters have been attempted, such theories have no methodological priority and generally turn out to do scant justice to what they attempt to reduce.

The usual stories about the history of twentieth-century philosophy fail to fit much of the liveliest, exactest, and most creative achievements of the final third of that century: the revival of metaphysical theorizing, realist in spirit, often speculative, sometimes commonsensical, associated with Saul Kripke, David Lewis, Kit Fine, Peter van Inwagen, David Armstrong and many others: work that has, to cite just one example, made it anachronistic to dismiss essentialism as anachronistic.[6] On the traditional grand narrative schemes in the history of philosophy, this activity must be a throwback to pre-Kantian metaphysics: it ought not to be happening – but it is. Many of those who practice it happily acknowledge its continuity with traditional metaphysics; appeals to the authority of Kant, or Wittgenstein, or history, ring hollow, for they are unbacked by any argument that has withstood the test of recent time.

One might try to see in contemporary metaphysics a Quinean breakdown of divisions between philosophy and the natural sciences. But if it is metaphysics naturalized, then so is the metaphysics of Aristotle, Descartes, and Leibniz. Armchair argument retains a central role, as do the modal notions of metaphysical possibility and necessity. Although empirical knowledge constrains the attribution of essential properties, results are more often reached through a subtle interplay of logic and the imagination. The crucial experiments are thought experiments.

Might the contrast between the new-old metaphysics and the conceptual turn be less stark than it appears to be? Contemporary metaphysicians firmly resist attempts to reconstrue their enterprise as

[6]   On essentialism see, for example, Kripke (1980), French, Uehling, and Wettstein (1986), Fine (1994, 1995) and Wiggins (2001). For a good statement of the outlook of contemporary metaphysics see Zimmerman (2004).

the analysis of thought – unlike Sir Peter Strawson, who defined his "descriptive metaphysics" as "content to describe the actual structure of our thought about the world" (1959: 9). But can one reflect on concepts without reflecting on reality itself? For the aboutness of thought and talk is their very point. This idea has been emphasized by David Wiggins, Dummett's successor and my predecessor in the Wykeham Chair, and author of some of the most distinguished essentialist metaphysics, in which considerations of logic and biology harmoniously combine. Wiggins (2001: 12) writes: "Let us forget once and for all the very idea of some knowledge of language or meaning that is not knowledge of the world itself."

Wiggins is not just stating the obvious, that language and meaning are part of the world because everything is part of the world. Rather, his point is that in defining words – natural kind terms, for instance – we must point at real specimens. What there is determines what there is for us to mean. In knowing what we mean, we know something about what there is. That prompts the question how far the analysis of thought or language can be pursued autonomously with any kind of methodological priority.

Dummett claimed not that the traditional questions of metaphysics cannot be answered but that the way to answer them is by the analysis of thought and language. For example, in order to determine whether there are numbers, one must determine whether number words such as "7" function semantically like proper names in the context of sentences uttered in mathematical discourse. But what is it so to function? Although devil words such as "Satan" appear to function semantically like proper names in the context of sentences uttered in devil-worshipping discourse, one should not jump to the conclusion that there are devils. However enthusiastically devil-worshippers use "Satan" as though it referred to something, that does not make it refer to something. Although empty names *appear* to function semantically like referring names in the context of sentences uttered by those who believe the names to refer, the appearances are deceptive. "Satan" refers to something if and only if some sentence with "Satan" in subject position (such as "Satan is self-identical") expresses a truth, but the analysis of thought and language is not the best way to discover whether any such sentence does indeed express a truth. Of course, what goes for "Satan" may not go for "7." According to some neo-logicists, "7 exists" is an analytic truth (what

Ayer might have called a formal consequence of definitions), which "Satan exists" does not even purport to be. Such a claim needs the backing of an appropriate theory of analyticity.

After this preliminary sketch, it is time to get down to detailed work. The next three chapters examine different forms of the linguistic or conceptual turn. Chapter 2 uses a case study to consider in a microcosm the idea that philosophers' questions are implicitly about language or thought when they are not explicitly so. Chapters 3 and 4 assess a wide range of versions of the idea that the armchair methodology of philosophy is grounded in the analytic or conceptual status of a core of philosophical truths, which need not be *about* language or thought, even implicitly. In each case the upshot is negative. Although philosophers have more reason than physicists to consider matters of language or thought, philosophy is in no deep sense a linguistic or conceptual inquiry, any more than physics is. But it does not follow that experiment is an appropriate primary method for philosophy. Similar arguments suggest that mathematics is in no deep sense a linguistic or conceptual inquiry, yet experiment is not an appropriate primary method for mathematics. The second half of the book develops an alternative conception of philosophy, on which a largely armchair methodology remains defensible, as it does for mathematics.

From this perspective and that of many contemporary philosophers, the conceptual turn and *a fortiori* the linguistic turn look like wrong turnings. It is pointless to deny that such philosophers are "analytic," for that term is customarily applied to a broad, loose tradition held together by an intricate network of causal ties of influence and communication, not by shared essential properties of doctrine or method: what do Frege, Russell, Moore, Wittgenstein, Carnap, Ayer, Quine, Austin, Strawson, Davidson, Rawls, Williams, Anscombe, Geach, Armstrong, Smart, Fodor, Dummett, Wiggins, Marcus, Hintikka, Kaplan, Lewis, Kripke, Fine, van Inwagen and Stalnaker all have in common to distinguish them from all the non-analytic philosophers? Many who regard the linguistic and conceptual turns as serious mistakes have ties of influence and communication that put them squarely within that tradition. "Analytic philosophy" is a phrase in a living language; the attempt to stipulate a sense for it that excludes many of the philosophers just listed will achieve nothing but brief terminological confusion.

Historians of philosophy on the grand scale may be too Whiggish or Hegelian to regard the linguistic or conceptual turn as merely a false turning from which philosophy is withdrawing now that it recognizes its mistake. We are supposed to go forward from it, not back. At the very least, we should learn from our mistakes, if only not to repeat them. But if the conceptual turn was a mistake, it was not a simple blunder; it went too deep for that. A new narrative structure is needed for the history of philosophy since 1960; it is clear only in the roughest outline what it should be.

2
Taking Philosophical Questions at Face Value

How often are philosophical questions implicitly about thought or language when they are not explicitly so? As a case study, I will take a question closely related to the problem of vagueness, because it looks like a paradigm of a philosophical question that is implicitly but not explicitly about thought and language. For vagueness is generally conceived as a feature of our thought and talk about the world, not of the world itself. Admittedly, some philosophers find tempting the idea of mind-independently vague objects, such as Mount Everest, vague in their spatiotemporal boundaries and mereological composition, if not in their identity. That kind of vagueness is not my concern here. I will consider an example of a quite standard type, involving a vague predicate.[1] Yet the reconstrual of the question as implicitly about thought or language turns out to be a mistake. If it is a mistake here, in such favorable conditions, it is a mistake far more widely.

1

Suppose that there was once plenty of water on the planet Mars; it was clearly not dry. Ages passed, and very gradually the water evaporated. Now Mars is clearly dry. No moment was clearly the first on which it was dry or the last on which it was not. For a long intermediate period it was neither clearly dry nor clearly not dry. Counting the water molecules would not have enabled us to determine whether

---

[1] On vagueness in general see, for a start, Graff and Williamson (2002), Keefe (2000), Keefe and Smith (1997), and Williamson (1994a). On vague objects see Williamson (2003b) and references therein.

it was dry; other measures would have been equally inconclusive. We have no idea of any investigative procedure that would have resolved the issue. It was a borderline case. No urgent practical purpose compels us to ask whether Mars was dry then, but only a limited proportion of thought and talk in any human society is driven by urgent practical purposes. We should like to know the history of Mars. When necessary, we can always use words other than "dry." Nevertheless, we reflect on the difficulty of classifying Mars as dry or as not dry at those intermediate times, even given exact measurements. We may wonder whether it was either. We ask ourselves:

Was Mars always either dry or not dry?

Henceforth I will refer to that as *the original question*. More precisely, I will use that phrase to designate that interrogative sentence, as used in that context (the word "question" can also be applied to what interrogative sentences express rather than the sentences themselves).

The original question is at least proto-philosophical in character. It is prompted by a difficulty both hard to identify and hard to avoid that we encounter in applying the distinctions in our repertoire. It hints at a serious threat to the validity of our most fundamental forms of deductive reasoning. Philosophers disagree about its answer, on philosophical grounds explored below. A philosophical account of vagueness that does not tell us how to answer the original question is thereby incomplete. Without an agreed definition of "philosophy," we can hardly expect to *prove* that the original question or any other is a philosophical question; but when we discuss its answer, we find ourselves invoking recognizably philosophical considerations. More simply, I'm a philosopher, I find the original question interesting, although I think I know the answer, and I have no idea where one should go for an answer to it, if not to philosophy (which includes logic). But before we worry about the answer, let us examine the original question itself.

The question queries just the supposition that Mars was always either dry or not dry, which we can formalize as a theorem of classical logic, $\forall t \, (\text{Dry}(m, t) \vee \neg \text{Dry}(m, t))$.[2] In words: for every time t,

---

[2] Classical logic is the standard logic of expressions such as "every," "either . . . or . . ." and "not" on the assumption that there is a mutually exclusive, jointly exhaustive dichotomy of sentences into the true and the false.

either Mars was dry at t or Mars was not dry at t. The question is composed of expressions that are not distinctively philosophical in character: "Mars," "always," "either . . . or . . . ," "not," "was," and "dry." All of them occur in a recognizably unphilosophical question such as "Was Mars always either uninhabited or not dry?," which someone might ask on judging that Mars is both uninhabited and dry and wondering whether there is a connection. Although philosophical issues can be raised *about* the words in both questions, it does not follow that merely in using those words one is in any way engaging in philosophy. One difference between the two questions is that it is not obviously futile to try to argue from the armchair that Mars was always either dry or not dry, whereas it is obviously futile to try to argue from the armchair that Mars was always either uninhabited or not dry.

The original question does not itself *ask* whether it is metaphysically necessary, or knowable *a priori*, or analytic, or logically true that Mars was always either dry or not dry. It simply asks whether Mars always *was* either dry or not dry. Expressions such as "metaphysically necessary," "knowable *a priori*," "analytic," and "logically true" do not occur in the original question; one can understand it without understanding any such philosophical terms of art. This is of course neither to deny nor to assert that it *is* metaphysically necessary, or knowable *a priori*, or analytic, or logically true that Mars was always either dry or not dry. For all that has been said, the proposition may be any combination of those things. But that is not what the original question asks.

In other circumstances, we could have answered the original question on philosophically uninteresting grounds. For instance, if there had never been liquid on Mars, then it would always have been dry, and therefore either dry or not dry. In order to pose a question which could not possibly be answered in that boring way, someone who already grasped one of those philosophically distinctive concepts might ask whether it is metaphysically necessary, or knowable *a priori*, or analytic, or logically true that Mars was always either dry or not dry. The meaningfulness of the philosophical jargon might then fall under various kinds of suspicion, which would extend to the question in which it occurred. But the original question itself cannot be correctly answered in the boring way with respect to the originally envisaged circumstances. Its philosophical interest, however contingent, is actual.

We could generalize the original question in various ways. We might ask whether *everything* is always either dry or not dry. Then we might notice that discussing that question is quite similar to discussing whether everything is either old or not old, and so on. We might, therefore, ask whether for every property everything either has it or lacks it. The coherence of such generalizing over properties might itself fall under various kinds of suspicion, which would extend to the question in which it occurred. Someone might even doubt whether there is such a property as dryness. But the original question itself does not attempt such generality. That it has the same kind of philosophical interest as many other questions does not imply that it has itself no philosophical interest. If that interest is obscured by problematic features of the apparatus with which we try to generalize it, we can refrain from generalizing it, and stick with the original question. In order not to be distracted by extraneous issues that arise from the apparatus of generalization, not from the original question, we do best to stick with the original question in its concrete form.[3] We can still help ourselves not to be distracted by unimportant features of the question, if we remember that there are many other questions of a similar form.

What is the original question about? "About" is not a precise term. On the most straightforward interpretation, a sentence in a context is about whatever its constituents refer to in that context. Thus, taken at face value, the original question is about the planet Mars, the referent of "Mars" in this context; perhaps it is also about dryness, the referent of "dry," and the referents of other constituents too. Since the original question contains no metalinguistic expressions, it is not about the name "Mars" or the adjective "dry." Evidently, the original question is not explicitly about words.

Is the original question implicitly about language? Someone might claim so on the grounds that it is equivalent to questions that are explicitly about language, such as these:

Is the sentence "Mars was always either dry or not dry" true? (Does it express a truth as used in this context?)

Did Mars always belong either to the extension of the word "dry" or to the anti-extension of "dry" (as the word "dry" is used in this context)?

[3]   See also Quine (1970: 11).

But parallel reasoning would lead to the conclusion that the unphilosophical question "Was Mars always either uninhabited or not dry?" is also implicitly about language, since it is equivalent to these questions:

> Is the sentence "Mars was always either uninhabited or not dry" true? (Does it express a truth as used in this context?)
>
> Did Mars always belong either to the extension of the word "uninhabited" or to the anti-extension of "dry" (as the word "dry" is used in this context)?

Indeed, we could make parallel arguments for all everyday and scientific questions. Since they are not all about language in any distinctive sense, the reasoning does not show that the original question was about language in any distinctive sense. Even if the equivalences did show that the original question was in some sense implicitly about language, they could be read in both directions: they would also show that the explicitly metalinguistic questions were in an equally good sense implicitly not about language.

The equivalences between the questions are in any case uncontroversial only if the corresponding disquotational biconditionals are:

(T1) "Mars was always either dry or not dry" is true if and only if Mars was always either dry or not dry.

(T2a) For any time t, Mars belongs to the extension of "dry" at t if and only if Mars is dry at t.

(T2b) For any time t, Mars belongs to the anti-extension of "dry" at t if and only if Mars is not dry at t.

On the face of it, these biconditionals express at best contingent truths. For perhaps the word "dry" could have meant *wet*, in which case Mars would have belonged to the extension of "dry" when wet and to the anti-extension of "dry" when dry: for *we* use the word "dry" to mean *dry* even when we are talking *about* circumstances in which it would have meant something else, because we are not talking *in* those circumstances. If so, T2a and T2b do not express necessary truths. Similarly, perhaps the sentence "Mars was always either dry or not dry" could have failed to express a truth even though Mars was always either dry or not dry, since "always" could have meant *never*. On this reading, T1 does not express a necessary truth. We should not assume that a useful notion of aboutness would transfer across merely contingent biconditionals. Perhaps we can instead interpret T1, T2a, and T2b as expressing necessary truths by individuating linguistic expressions so that their semantic properties are essential to them; whether that requires treating the quoted expressions as necessary existents is a delicate matter. In any case, some theorists of vagueness have denied even the actual truth of biconditionals such as T1, T2a, and T2b; they might respond to the original question in one way and to the explicitly metalinguistic questions in another.[4] Thus the questions are not pragmatically, dialectically or methodologically equivalent within the context of debates on vagueness. For present purposes, we need not resolve the status of the disquotational biconditionals, because we have already seen that the sense in which they make the original question implicitly about words is too indiscriminate to be useful.

We can argue more directly that the original question is not implicitly about the word "dry" by appeal to a translation test. For consider the translation of the original question into another language, such as Serbian:

Da li je Mars uvek bio suv ili nije bio suv?

The Serbian translation is not implicitly about the English word "dry." But since the questions in the two languages mean the same, what they are implicitly about (in the same context) should also be the same. Therefore, the original question is not implicitly about the word "dry." By similar reasoning, it is not about any word of English or any other language. Of course, given the informality of the notion of implicit aboutness, the argument is not fully rigorous. Nevertheless, the translation test emphasizes how far one would have to water down the notion of reference in order to reach a notion of implicit aboutness on which the original question would be implicitly about a word.

---

[4]   A recent example of a supervaluationist rejecting such disquotational equivalences for borderline cases is Keefe (2000: 213–20). For further discussion see Williamson (1994a: 162–4) and McGee and McLaughlin (2000).

The translation test does not show that the original question is not implicitly about a *concept*, something like the meaning of a word rather than the word itself, for the English word "dry" and its Serbian synonym "suv" both express the concept *dry*. But what basis is there for the claim that the original question is implicitly about the concept *dry*? We might argue that the original question is in some sense equivalent to a metaconceptual question:

Did Mars always belong either to the extension of the concept *dry* or to the anti-extension of *dry*?

For we might apply the notions of extension and anti-extension to concepts by means of biconditionals similar to T2a and T2b respectively:

(TC2a)   For any time *t*, Mars belongs to the extension of *dry* at *t* if and only if Mars is dry at *t*.

(TC2b)   For any time *t*, Mars belongs to the anti-extension of *dry* at *t* if and only if Mars is not dry at *t*.

TC2a and TC2b can express necessary truths more easily than T2a and T2b can, for the apparently contingent relation between words and their meanings has no straightforward analogue for concepts. Concepts are individuated semantically: rather than merely having meanings, they *are* meanings, or something like them.[5] Nevertheless, the argument that the original question is implicitly about the concept *dry* in virtue of being equivalent to the metaconceptual question wildly overgeneralizes, just like the argument that the original

---

[5] Even if a word retains its linguistic meaning, its reference may shift with the context of utterance ("I," "now," "here"). If "dry" undergoes such contextual shifts, T2a and T2b may fail when interpreted as generalizations about utterances of "dry" in contexts other than the theorist's own. It might be argued that concepts can also undergo contextual shifts in reference: you use the concept *I* to refer (in thought) to yourself but I use the same concept to refer to myself; at noon we use the concept *now* to think of noon but at midnight we use the same concept to refer to midnight; at the North Pole we use the concept *here* to refer to the North Pole but at the South Pole we use the same concept to refer to the South Pole. If so, TC2a and TC2b may also fail when interpreted as generalizations about uses of the concept *dry* in contexts other than the theorist's own.

question is implicitly about the word "dry" in virtue of being equivalent to the metalinguistic question. For parallel reasoning would lead to the conclusion that the unphilosophical question "Was Mars always either uninhabited or not dry?" is implicitly about the concept *dry*, and likewise for any other unphilosophical question. Since those questions are not about concepts in any distinctive sense, the original reasoning does not show that the original question is about concepts in any distinctive sense. Even if the equivalences did show that the original question was in some sense implicitly about thought, they can be read in both directions: they would also equally show that the explicitly metaconceptual questions were in an equally good sense implicitly not about thought.

A Fregean might argue: the original question is *explicitly* about the concept *dry*, because it contains the predicate ". . . is dry" (in the past tense), which refers to the concept *dry*. In that sense, the question "Was Mars always either uninhabited or not dry?" would also be explicitly about the concept *dry*. However, the Fregean is not using the word "concept" with its contemporary meaning, on which concepts are something like mental or semantic representations, closer to the realm of sense than to that of reference. The Fregean referent of a predicate (a Fregean concept) is simply the function that maps everything to which the predicate applies to the true and everything else to the false: it could be treated as the extension of the predicate, except that in Fregean terms it is a function rather than an object. If the predicate refers to the property of dryness or to the set of dry things, then the original question is about the property of dryness or the set of dry things, but that has no tendency to show that it is about thought. Similarly, the Fregean claim has no tendency to show that the question is about thought, for the Fregean concept is in the realm of reference, not in the realm of thought. Like the property and the set, it is no sense but something to which a sense may determine reference. Since it is no sense, it is no constituent of a thought, on the Fregean view, nor is it a concept in the current sense of "concept."

Thought and talk are not always about thought or talk. To judge by its overt compositional structure, the original question in particular is not about thought or talk. It is no metalinguistic or metaconceptual question. We have seen no reason to regard its overt structure as at all misleading in that respect. Our provisional conclusion must therefore be that the original question, although at least proto-philosophical, is not about thought or language in any distinctive sense. It does not support the linguistic or conceptual turn, interpreted as a conception of the subject matter of philosophy.

2

If the original question, read literally, had too obvious an answer, either positive or negative, that would give us reason to suspect that someone who uttered it had some other meaning in mind, to which the overt compositional structure of the question might be a poor guide. But competent speakers of English may find themselves quite unsure how to answer the question, read literally, so we have no such reason for interpreting it non-literally.

It is useful to look at some proposals and arguments from the vagueness debate, for two reasons. First, they show why the original question is hard, when taken at face value. Second, they show how semantic considerations play a central role in the attempt to answer it, even though it is not itself a semantic question.

The most straightforward reason for answering the original question positively is that "Mars was always either dry or not dry" is a logical truth, a generalization over instances of the law of excluded middle ($A \lor \neg A$, "It is either so or not so") for various times. In my view, that reasoning is sound. However, many think otherwise. They deny the validity of excluded middle for vague terms such as "dry."

The simplest way of opposing the law of excluded middle is to deny outright when Mars is a borderline case that it is either dry or not dry, and therefore to answer the original question in the negative. For instance, someone may hold that Mars was either dry or not dry at time t only if one can know (perhaps later) whether it was dry at t, given optimal conditions for answering the question (and no difference in the history of Mars): since one cannot know, even under such conditions, whether it is dry when the case is borderline, it is not either dry or not dry. One difficulty for this negative response to the original question is that it seems to imply that in a borderline case Mars is neither dry nor not dry: in other words, both not dry and not not dry. That is a contradiction, for "not not dry" is the negation of "not dry."

Intuitionistic logic provides a subtler way to reject the law of excluded middle without denying any one of its instances. Intuitionists ground logic in states of increasing but incomplete information, rather than a once-for-all dichotomy of truth and falsity. They deny that anything can be both proved and refuted, but they do not assert that everything can be either proved or refuted. For intuitionists, the denial of an instance of excluded middle ($\neg$(A $\vee \neg$A), "It is not either so or not so") entails a contradiction ($\neg$A & $\neg\neg$A, "It is both not so and not not so"), just as it does in classical logic, and contradictions are as bad for them as for anyone else. Thus they cannot assert that Mars was once not either dry or not dry ($\exists$t $\neg$(Dry(m, t) $\vee \neg$Dry(m, t))), for that would imply that a contradiction once obtained ($\exists$t ($\neg$Dry(m, t) & $\neg\neg$Dry(m, t)), "Mars was once both not dry and not not dry"), which is intuitionistically inconsistent. However, although intuitionists insist that proving an existential claim in principle involves proving at least one instance of it, they allow that disproving a universal claim need not in principle involve disproving at least one instance of it. The claim that something lacks a property is intuitionistically stronger than the claim that not everything has that property. Thus one might assert that Mars was not always either dry or not dry ($\neg\forall$t (Dry(m, t) $\vee \neg$Dry(m, t))), on the general grounds that there is no adequate procedure for sorting all the times into the two categories, without thereby committing oneself to the inconsistent existential assertion that it was once not either dry or not dry. Hilary Putnam once proposed the application of intuitionistic logic to the problem of vagueness for closely related reasons.[6] Thus one might use intuitionistic logic to answer the original question in the negative.

On closer inspection, this strategy looks less promising. For a paradigm borderline case is the worst case for the law of excluded middle (for a term such as "dry" for which threats to the law other than from vagueness are irrelevant), in the sense that both proponents and opponents of the law can agree that it holds in a paradigm borderline case only if it holds universally. In symbols, if Mars was a paradigm borderline case at time τ: (Dry(m, τ) $\vee \neg$Dry(m, τ)) $\rightarrow$

---

[6] For intuitionist logic in general see Dummett (1977). For its application to the problem of vagueness see Graff and Williamson (2002: 473–506) and Chambers (1998).

∀t (Dry(m, t) ∨ ¬Dry(m, t)) ("If Mars was either dry or not dry at time τ, then Mars was always either dry or not dry"). But on this approach the law does not hold always hold in these cases (¬∀t (Dry(m, t) ∨ ¬Dry(m, t)), "Mars was not always either dry or not dry"), from which intuitionistic logic allows us to deduce that it does not hold in the paradigm borderline case (¬(Dry(m, τ) ∨ ¬Dry(m, τ)), "Mars was not either dry or not dry at τ"), which is a denial of a particular instance of the law, and therefore intuitionistically inconsistent (it entails ¬Dry(m, τ) & ¬¬Dry(m, τ), "Mars was both not dry and not not dry at τ"). Thus the intuitionistic denial of the universal generalization of excluded middle for a vague predicate forces one to deny that it has such paradigm borderline cases. The latter denial is hard to reconcile with experience: after all, the notion of a borderline case is usually explained by examples.

The problems for the intuitionistic approach do not end there. One can show that the denial of the conjunction of any finite number of instances of the law of excluded middle is intuitionistically inconsistent.[7] The denial of the universal generalization of the law over a finite domain is therefore intuitionistically false too. If time is infinitely divisible, the formula ∀t (Dry(m, t) ∨ ¬Dry(m, t)) generalizes the law over an infinite domain of moments of time, and its denial is intuitionistically consistent, but the possibility of infinitely divisible time is not crucial to the phenomena of vagueness. We could just as well have asked the original question about a long finite series of moments at one-second intervals; it would have been equally problematic. The classical sorites paradox depends on just such a finite series: a heap of sand consists of only finitely many grains, but when they are carefully removed one by one, we have no idea how to answer the question "When did there cease to be a heap?" To deny that Mars was dry or not dry at each moment in the finite series is intuitionistically inconsistent. Thus intuitionistic logic provides a poor basis for a negative answer to the original question.

Other theorists of vagueness refuse to answer the original question either positively or negatively. They refuse to assert that Mars was always either dry or not dry; they also refuse to assert that it was not always either dry or not dry.

---

[7] One proves by mathematical induction on n that if **An** is the conjunction of n instances of excluded middle then ¬**An** is intuitionistically inconsistent.

A simple version of this approach classifies vague sentences (relative to contexts) as true (T), false (F) or indefinite (I); borderline sentences are classified as indefinite. The generalized truth-tables of a three-valued logic are used to calculate which of these values to assign to a complex sentence in terms of the values assigned to its constituent sentences. The negation of **A**, ¬**A**, is true if **A** is false, false if **A** is true and indefinite if **A** is indefinite:

A	¬A
T	F
I	I
F	T

A conjunction **A** & **B** ("A and B") is true if every conjunct is true; it is false if some conjunct is false; otherwise it is indefinite. A disjunction **A** ∨ **B** ("Either A or B") is true if some disjunct is true; it is false if every disjunct is false; otherwise it is indefinite:

A	B	A & B	A ∨ B
T	T	T	T
T	I	I	T
T	F	F	T
I	T	I	T
I	I	I	I
I	F	F	I
F	T	F	T
F	I	F	I
F	F	F	F

A universal generalization is treated as if it were the conjunction of its instances, one for each member of the domain: it is true if every instance is true, false if some instance is false, and otherwise indefinite. An existential generalization is treated as if it were the disjunction of the instances: it is true if some instance is true, false if every instance is false, and otherwise indefinite. The three-valued tables generalize the familiar two-valued ones in the sense that one recovers the latter by deleting all lines with "I."

Let us apply this three-valued approach to the original question. If Mars is definitely dry or definitely not dry at *t* (the time denoted by **t**), then **Dry(m, t)** is true or false, so the instance of excluded middle

Dry(m, t) ∨ ¬**Dry(m, t)** is true. But if Mars is neither definitely dry nor definitely not dry at t, then **Dry(m, t)** is indefinite, so ¬**Dry(m, t)** is indefinite too by the table for negation, so **Dry(m, t)** ∨ ¬**Dry(m, t)** is classified as indefinite by the table for disjunction. Since Mars was once a borderline case, the universal generalization ∀t (**Dry(m, t)** ∨ ¬**Dry(m, t)**) has a mixture of true and indefinite instances; hence it is classified as indefinite. Therefore its negation ¬∀t (**Dry(m, t)** ∨ ¬**Dry(m, t)**) is also indefinite. Thus three-valued theoreticians who wish to assert only truths neither assert ∀t (**Dry(m, t)** ∨ ¬**Dry(m, t)**) nor assert ¬∀t (**Dry(m, t)** ∨ ¬**Dry(m, t)**). They answer the original question neither positively nor negatively.

Three-valued logic replaces the classical dichotomy of truth and falsity by a three-way classification. Fuzzy logic goes further, replacing it by a continuum of degrees of truth between perfect truth and perfect falsity. According to proponents of fuzzy logic, vagueness should be understood in terms of this continuum of degrees of truth. For example, "It is dark" may increase continuously in degree of truth as it gradually becomes dark. On the simplest version of the approach, degrees of truth are identified with real numbers in the interval from 0 to 1, with 1 as perfect truth and 0 as perfect falsity. The semantics of fuzzy logic provides rules for calculating the degree of truth of a complex sentence in terms of the degrees of truth of its constituent sentences. For example, the degrees of truth of a sentence and of its negation sum to exactly 1; the degree of truth of a disjunction is the maximum of the degrees of truth of its disjuncts; the degree of truth of a conjunction is the minimum of the degrees of truth of its conjuncts. For fuzzy logic, although the three-valued tables above are too coarse-grained to give complete information, they still give correct results if one classifies every sentence with an intermediate degree of truth, less than the maximum and more than the minimum, as indefinite.[8] Thus the same reasoning as before shows that fuzzy

---

[8]   This point does not generalize to the semantics of conditionals in fuzzy logic, given the popular rule that if the consequent is lower than the antecedent in degree of truth then the degree of truth of the conditional falls short of 1 by the amount by which the consequent falls short of the antecedent in degree of truth; otherwise the degree of truth of the conditional is 1. Hence if **A** has a higher degree of truth than **B** but both are indefinite then **A → B** is indefinite while **B → A** is perfectly true. Thus the information that the antecedent and consequent are indefinite does not determine whether the conditional is indefinite.

logicians should answer the original question neither positively nor negatively.

Although three-valued and fuzzy logicians reject both the answer "Yes" and the answer "No" to the original question, they do not reject the question itself. What they reject is the restriction of possible answers to "Yes" and "No." They require a third answer, "Indefinite," when the queried sentence takes the value I. More formally, consider the three-valued table for the sentence operator Δ, read as "definitely" or "it is definite that":

A	ΔA
T	T
I	F
F	F

Even for fuzzy logicians this table constitutes a complete semantics for Δ, since the only output values are T and F, which determine unique degrees of truth (1 and 0). A formula of the form $\neg\Delta A$ & $\neg\Delta\neg A$ ("It is neither definitely so nor definitely not so") characterizes a borderline case, for it is true if A is indefinite and false otherwise. In response to the question A?, answering "Yes" is tantamount to asserting A, answering "No" is tantamount to asserting $\neg A$, and answering "Indefinite" is tantamount to asserting $\neg\Delta A$ & $\neg\Delta\neg A$. On the three-valued and fuzzy tables, exactly one of these three answers is true in any given case; in particular, the correct answer to the original question is "Indefinite."

On the three-valued and fuzzy approaches, to answer "Indefinite" to the question "Is Mars dry?" is to say something about Mars, just as it is if one answers "Yes" or "No." It is not a metalinguistic response. For Δ is no more a metalinguistic operator than $\neg$ is. They have the same kind of semantics, given by a many-valued truth-table. Just as the negation $\neg A$ is about whatever A is about, so are ΔA and $\neg\Delta A$ & $\neg\Delta\neg A$. Thus the answer "Indefinite" to the original question involves no semantic ascent to a metalinguistic or metaconceptual level. It remains at the level of discourse about Mars.

The three-valued and fuzzy approaches have many suspect features. For instance, they treat any sentence of the form ΔA as perfectly precise, because it always counts as true or false, never as indefinite, whatever the status of A; thus $\Delta\Delta A \vee \Delta\neg\Delta A$ ("It is definite whether it is definitely so") is always true. This result does not fit the intended interpretation of Δ. For "Mars is definitely wet" is not perfectly precise. Just as no moment is clearly the last on which Mars was wet or the first on which it was not, so no moment is clearly the last on which it was definitely wet or the first on which it was not definitely wet. Just as it is sometimes unclear whether Mars is wet, so it is sometimes unclear whether it is definitely wet. This is one form of the notorious problem of higher-order vagueness: in other words, there are borderline cases of borderline cases, and borderline cases of borderline cases of borderline cases, and so on. The problem has never received an adequate treatment within the framework of three-valued or fuzzy logic; that it could is far from obvious.[9]

Some philosophers, often under the influence of the later Wittgenstein, deny the relevance of formal semantic theories to vague natural languages. They regard the attempt to give a systematic statement of the truth conditions of English sentences in terms of the meanings of their constituents as vain. For them, the formalization of "Mars was always either dry or not dry" as $\forall t \, (\mathbf{Dry(m, t)} \vee \neg \mathbf{Dry(m, t)})$ is already a mistake. This attitude suggests a premature and slightly facile pessimism. No doubt formal semantics has not described any natural language with perfect accuracy; what has not been made plausible is that it provides no deep insights into natural languages. In particular, it has not been made plausible that the main semantic effects of vagueness are not susceptible to systematic formal analysis. In any case, for present purposes the claim that there can be no systematic theory of vagueness is just one more theory of vagueness, although – unless it is self-refuting – not a systematic one; it does not even answer the original question. Even if that theory were true, the other theories of vagueness, however false, would still exist, and would still have been accepted by some intelligent and linguistically competent speakers.

This is no place to resolve the debate between opposing theories of vagueness. The present point is just that different theories support contrary answers to the original question. All these theories have their believers. Any answer to the original question, positive, negative, or indefinite, is contentious. Of course, if everyone found their own answer obvious, but different people found different answers obvious, then we might suspect that they were interpreting the question in

---

[9]   See Graff and Williamson (2002: 279–351) on higher-order vagueness.

different ways, talking past each other. But that is not so: almost everyone who reflects on the original question finds it difficult and puzzling. Even when one has settled on an answer, one can see how intelligent and reasonable people could answer differently while understanding the meaning of the question in the same way. If it has an *obvious* answer, it is the answer "Yes" dictated by classical logic, but those of us who accept that answer can usually imagine or remember the frame of mind in which one is led to doubt it. Thus the original question, read literally, has no unproblematically obvious answer in any sense that would give us reason to suspect that someone who asked it had some other reading in mind.

Without recourse to non-literal readings, some theorists postulate ambiguity in the original question. For example, some three-valued logicians claim that "not" in English is ambiguous between the operators $\neg$ (strong negation) and $\neg\Delta$ (weak negation): although $\neg A$ and $\neg\Delta A$ have the same value if A is true or false, $\neg\Delta A$ is true while $\neg A$ is indefinite if A is indefinite. While $A \vee \neg A$ ("It is so or not so") can be indefinite, $A \vee \neg\Delta A$ ("It is so or not definitely so") is always true. On this view, the original question queries $\forall t\ (Dry(m, t) \vee \neg Dry(m, t))$ on one reading, $\forall t\ (Dry(m, t) \vee \neg\Delta Dry(m, t))$ on another; the latter is true (Mars was always either dry or not definitely dry) while the former is indefinite. Thus the correct answer to the original question depends on the reading of "not." It is "Indefinite" if "not" is read as strong negation, "Yes" if "not" is read as weak negation. Although the three-valued logician's reasoning here is undermined by higher-order vagueness, that is not the present issue.[10]

If "not" were ambiguous in the way indicated, it would still not follow that the dispute over the original question is merely verbal. For even when we agree to consider it under the reading of "not" as strong negation, which does not factorize in the manner of $\neg\Delta$, we still find theories of vagueness in dispute over the correct answer. We have merely explained our terms in order to formulate more clearly a difficult question about Mars.

Still, it might be suggested, the dispute between different theories of vagueness is verbal in the sense that their rival semantics characterize different possible languages or conceptual schemes: our choice of which of them to speak or think would be pragmatic, based on

[10]   See Williamson (1994a: 193–5).

considerations of usefulness rather than of truth. Quine defended a similar view of alternative logics (1970: 81–6).

To make sense of the pragmatic view, suppose that the original vague atomic sentences are classifiable both according to the bivalent scheme as true or false and according to the trivalent scheme as definitely true, indefinite or definitely false, and that the truth-tables of each scheme define intelligible connectives, although the connective defined by a trivalent table should be distinguished from the similar-looking connective defined by the corresponding bivalent table. Definite truth implies truth, and definite falsity implies falsity, but indefiniteness does not discriminate between truth and falsity: although all borderline atomic sentences are indefinite, some are true and others false. As Mars dries, "Mars is dry" is first false and definitely false, then false but indefinite, then true but indefinite, and finally true and definitely true. However, this attempted reconciliation of the contrasting theories does justice to neither side. For trivalent logicians, once we know that a sentence is indefinite, there is no further question of its truth or falsity to which we do not know the answer: the category of the indefinite was introduced in order not to postulate such a mystery. Similarly, for fuzzy logicians, once we know the intermediate degree of truth of a sentence, there is no further question of its truth or falsity to which we do not know the answer: intermediate degrees of truth were introduced in order not to postulate such a mystery. In formal terms, trivalent and fuzzy logics are undoubtedly less convenient than bivalent logic; the justification for introducing them was supposed to be the inapplicability of the bivalent scheme to vague sentences. If a bivalent vague language is a genuinely possible option, then the trivalent and fuzzy accounts of vagueness are mistaken. Conversely, from a bivalent perspective, the trivalent and fuzzy semantics do not fix possible meanings for the connectives, because they do not determine truth conditions for the resultant complex sentences: for example, the trivalent table for ¬ does not specify when ¬A is true in the bivalent sense. It would, therefore, be a fundamental misunderstanding of the issue at stake between theories of vagueness to conceive it as one of a pragmatic choice of language.

We already speak the language of the original question; we understand those words and how they are put together; we possess the concepts they express; we grasp what is being asked. That semantic knowledge may be necessary if we are to know the answer to the original question.[11] It is not sufficient, for it does not by itself put one in a position to arbitrate between conflicting theories of vagueness. For each of those theories has been endorsed by some competent speakers of English who fully grasp the question.

Competent speakers may of course fail to reflect adequately on their competence. Although the proponents of conflicting theories of vagueness presumably have reflected on their competence, their reflections may have contained mistakes. Perhaps reflection of sufficient length and depth on one's competence would lead one to the correct answer to the original question. But the capacity for such more or less philosophical reflection is not a precondition of semantic competence. Philosophers should resist the professional temptation to require all speakers to be good at philosophy.

We can distinguish two levels of reflection, the logical and the metalogical. In response to the original question, logical reflection involves reasoning with terms of the kind in which the question is phrased; the aim is to reach a conclusion that answers the question. For example, one might conclude by classical logic that Mars was always either dry or not dry; one might conclude by fuzzy logic that it is indefinite whether it was always one or the other. The logical level is not purely mechanical. When the reasoning is complex, one needs skill to select from the many permissible applications of the rules one sequence that leads to an answer to the question. When the reasoning is informal, one needs good judgment to select only moves that really are permissible applications of the rules. But one is still thinking about whatever the question was about. One starts only at the metalogical level of reflection to think about the semantics of the logical connectives and other expressions one employed at the logical level. For example, at the metalogical level one may assert or deny

---

[11] Of course, monolingual speakers of another language may know whether Mars was always dry or not dry without ever hearing of the original question, which is an interrogative sentence of English; they use a synonymous sentence of their own language. They do not know whether the original English question has a positive answer. Someone may even know whether the original English question has a positive answer without understanding the question, because the knowledge can be passed along a chain of testimony; understanding of the original question is needed only at one end of the chain. These quibbles do not affect the argument.

that the sentence "Mars was always either dry or not dry" is a logical truth. The rules used at the logical level are articulated only at the metalogical level.

It must be possible to think logically without thinking metalogically, for otherwise by the same principle thinking metalogically would involve thinking metametalogically, and so *ad infinitum*: our thinking never goes all the way up such an infinite hierarchy. What can prompt ascent to the metalogical level are hard cases in which one feels unclear about the permissibility of a given move at the logical level. One's mastery of the language and possession of concepts leave one quite uncertain how to go on. In the case of the original question, a salient line of classical reasoning leads to a positive answer: it persuades some competent speakers while leaving others unconvinced. Even to discuss the contentious reasoning we must semantically ascend. We cannot hope to resolve the dispute undogmatically if we never leave the lower level.

3

The argument so far has reached two conclusions at first sight hard to reconcile with each other. First, the original question is not about thought or language. Second, to answer it adequately one must assess rival theories of vagueness in thought and language. How can that way of reaching an answer be appropriate to the original question? We might, therefore, find ourselves tempted back to the idea that somehow the original question was surreptitiously about thought or language.

On further reflection, the combination of the two conclusions is less surprising. Many non-philosophical questions that are not about thought or language cannot be resolved without inquiry into thought or language. Suppose that a court of law must decide whether Smith killed Jones. The question is not who said or thought what. Nevertheless, the crucial arguments may be over whether to trust the witnesses' testimony. How is what they say now related to what they think now or thought then? How is what they think now or thought then related to what actually happened? Are they lying or sincere? Are their memories confused or clear? Those are questions about their thought and speech. They hold the key to whether Smith killed Jones, even though that question is not about thought about language.[12] Of course, the questions about the thought or talk are not about it in isolation from what it is thought or talk about: they are relevant because they concern the relation between the thought or talk and what it is about.

The court must decide the issue on the evidence before it. In a criminal case, does the evidence put it beyond reasonable doubt that Smith killed Jones? In a civil case, does the evidence make it more probable than not? If the court is really deciding a question about testimonial evidence, that is already a question about talk.[13] But the question about the evidence arises in virtue of its bearing on the primary question, whether Smith killed Jones. Indeed, the question about the evidence is exactly a question about its bearing on the primary question. So the point stands.

Historians are often in a similar position. They want to know what happened. The way to achieve that is largely by considering documents, linguistic accounts of what happened – not in isolation, but in relation to what they represent. Most obviously, historians want to know whether the documents accurately represent what happened, but to answer that question they must in turn ask about their provenance: who produced them, when and why? Thus the history of the events of primary interest requires a history of thought and talk about those events. Those histories typically overlap, for thought or talk about some part of a complex human event is often another part of the same complex event.

Something analogous occurs in the methodology of the natural sciences. We wish to know the value of some physical quantity. We must devise apparatus to measure it. We may find ourselves in disputes over the functioning of different devices. Although the primary

---

[12]   The issue of Smith's intentions concerns his thoughts, but we may suppose that the question immediately at issue is whether Smith was even involved in Jones's death.

[13]   Non-testimonial evidence may be taken to include non-linguistic items such as a bloodied knife; this is what lawyers call "real evidence." For an argument that all evidence in an epistemologically central sense of the term is propositional see Williamson (2000a: 194–200). For example, the evidence in this sense might include the proposition that the bloodied knife was found at the scene of the crime, but not the knife itself.

question was not about those measuring devices, we cannot answer it adequately without considering them. We need a theory about the relation between the value of the quantity and the representations of it we record when we use our instruments. The scientific investigation of the physical quantity widens to include the scientific investigation of its interaction with our experimental equipment. After all, our apparatus is part of the same natural world as the primary topic of our inquiry.

These analogies make it less surprising that when we try to answer the original question, which is not a question about thought or language, our main task is to adjudicate between rival theories of vague thought and language. A theory of vagueness validates some deduction that concludes with an answer to the original question. That deduction uses but does not mention vague thought or language. It is formulated at the logical level, like the original question itself, not at the metalogical level. But discursively to justify trusting that deduction, rather than one that reaches another conclusion by other rules, one must assess the rival theories of vagueness.

That theories of vagueness conflict in their answers to the original question shows that they are not confined to claims about thought and talk. Theories such as epistemicism and supervaluationism which employ classical logic have "Mars was always either dry or not dry" as a theorem, once they are formulated in a suitably expressive language. To reiterate, that theorem is not about thought or talk.

For the three-valued and fuzzy approaches, the matter is only slightly more complicated. Their proponents assert:

(C)   It is indefinite whether Mars was always either dry or not dry.

On those approaches, C does not count as about thought or language. Strictly speaking, however, C does not follow from the three-valued or fuzzy theory of vagueness itself; for all the theory implies, there was never any liquid on Mars, in which case it would always have been either dry or not dry, even by three-valued or fuzzy standards, and so would not have been indefinite. The theory implies only a conditional theorem:

(P1)   If it was once indefinite whether Mars was dry then it is indefinite whether Mars was always either dry or not dry.

Three-valued or fuzzy theorists can combine P1 with what they regard as an empirical truth about Mars:

(P2)   It was once indefinite whether Mars was dry.

From P1 and P2 they use the rule of modus ponens (from "If P then Q" and "P" infer "Q") to infer C, the answer to the original question. Although their theorem P1 does not answer the question by itself, it is no more about thought or language than C is. Their theories are just as committed as classical ones to making claims that are not about thought or language.

In principle, just as the considerations relevant to adjudicating the dispute between theories of vagueness are relevant to answering the original question, so too may they be relevant to answering a question asked with no philosophical intention, such as "Was Mars always either uninhabited or not dry?," if it turns out to involve a borderline case. In practice, non-philosophers are often quite content to be told "It's unclear," without wondering exactly how that statement addresses the question asked; they simply drop the matter. For their purposes that may be the best thing to do. By contrast, philosophers persist; they want to know at least whether there is a right answer, even if nobody can know what it is. The difference lies not in the content of the original question but in the interests with which it is asked. Those interests can amount to a tissue of associated questions: for our original question as asked by a philosopher, the associated questions query other instances of the law of excluded middle. Given those interests, it is rational to persist with the original question, and not take an unexplained "It's unclear" for an answer. But we should not underestimate the importance outside philosophy too – in science and even in politics – of sometimes persisting with a straight question, not allowing oneself to be fobbed off with the convenient claim that no practical purpose would be served by answering it. At other times, non-philosophers in effect assume without argument a particular treatment of vagueness (not always the same one), without realizing or caring that there are alternatives. The treatment may be good enough for their purposes, or not.

In this case study, our interest in giving a clear and critically reflective answer to a simple, non-technical, non-metalinguistic, non-metaconceptual question forced us to adjudicate between complex, technical, metalinguistic, and metaconceptual theories. This phenomenon seems to have been overlooked by those who complain about the "arid" technical minuteness of much philosophy in the analytic tradition. A question may be easy to ask but hard to answer. Even if it is posed in dramatic and accessible terms, the reflections needed to select rationally between rival answers may be less dramatic and accessible. Such contrasts are commonplace in other disciplines; it would have been amazing if they had not occurred in philosophy. Impatience with the long haul of technical reflection is a form of shallowness, often thinly disguised by histrionic advocacy of depth. Serious philosophy is always likely to bore those with short attention-spans.[14]

Why should considerations about thought and language play so much more central a role in philosophy than in other disciplines, when the question explicitly under debate is not itself even implicitly about thought or language? The paradigms of philosophical questions are those that seem best addressed by armchair considerations less formal than mathematical proofs. The validity of such informal arguments depends on the structure of the natural language sentences in which they are at least partly formulated, or on the structure of the underlying thoughts. That structure is often hard to discern. We cannot just follow our instincts in reasoning; they are too often wrong (see Chapter 4 for details). In order to reason accurately in informal terms, we must focus on our reasoning as presented in thought or language, to double-check it, and the results are often controversial. Thus questions about the structure of thought and language become central to the debate, even when it is not primarily a debate about thought or language.

The rise of modern logic from Frege onwards has provided philosophers with conceptual instruments of unprecedented power and precision, enabling them to formulate hypotheses with more clarity and determine their consequences with more reliability than ever before. Russell's theory of descriptions showed vividly how differences between the surface form of a sentence and its underlying semantic structure might mislead us as to its logical relations and thereby create philosophical illusions. The development of formal

---

[14] Popularization has its place, in philosophy as in physics, but should not be confused with the primary activity.

model-theory and truth-conditional semantics by Tarski and others has provided a rigorous framework for thinking about the validity of our inferences. These theoretical advances have enormous intellectual interest in their own right. They may have made it tempting to suppose that all philosophical problems are problems of language: but they do not really provide serious evidence for that conjecture.

To deny that all philosophical questions are about thought or language is not to deny the obvious, that many are. We have also seen how in practice the attempt to answer a question which is not about thought or language can largely consist in thinking about thought and language. Some contemporary metaphysicians appear to believe that they can safely ignore formal semantics and the philosophy of language because their interest is in a largely extra-mental reality. They resemble an astronomer who thinks he can safely ignore the physics of telescopes because his interest is in the extra-terrestrial universe. In delicate matters, his attitude makes him all the more likely to project features of his telescope confusedly onto the stars beyond. Similarly, the metaphysicians who most disdain language are the most likely to be its victims. Again, those who neglect logic in order to derive philosophical results from natural science make frequent logical errors in their derivations; their philosophical conclusions do not follow from their scientific premises. For example, some supposed tensions between folk theory and contemporary science depend on fallacies committed in the attempt to draw out the consequences of common sense beliefs.

Analytic philosophy at its best uses logical rigor and semantic sophistication to achieve a sharpness of philosophical vision unobtainable by other means. To sacrifice those gains would be to choose blurred vision. Fortunately, one can do more with good vision than look at eyes.

Many have been attracted to the idea that all philosophical problems are linguistic or conceptual through the question: if the method of philosophy is *a priori* reflection, how can it lead to substantive knowledge of the world? Those who find that question compelling may propose that it informs us of relations of ideas rather than matters of fact, or that its truths are analytic rather than synthetic, or that it presents rules of grammar disguised as descriptions, or that its aim is the analysis of thought or language. In short, on this view, philosophical truths are conceptuals truths. We may suspect the presence of empiricist presuppositions in the background – or, as with Ayer, in the foreground. Not starting with such presuppositions, we should be open to the idea that thinking just as much as perceiving is a way of learning how things are. Even if one does not fully understand *how* thinking can provide new knowledge, the cases of logic and mathematics constitute overwhelming evidence that it does so. The case of the original question, which is philosophical yet queries a theorem of classical logic, shows that we cannot segregate logic from philosophy and claim that armchair thinking illuminates the former but not the latter. In particular, conceptions of logic and mathematics as (unlike philosophy) somehow trivial or non-substantial have not been vindicated by any clear explanation of the relevant sense of "trivial" or "non-substantial." Whether a given formal system of logic or mathematics is consistent is itself a non-trivial question of logic or mathematics. We know from Gödel's second incompleteness theorem that the consistency of most standard systems of elementary mathematics cannot be decided in equally elementary mathematics, unless the original system is already inconsistent. The next two chapters investigate in more depth the prospects for conceptual truth and its role in philosophy.

3
Metaphysical Conceptions of Analyticity

1

"Philosophical questions are more conceptual in nature than those of other disciplines": that can easily pass for a statement of the obvious.[1] Many philosophers consciously seek conceptual connections, conceptual necessities, conceptual truths, conceptual analyses. In effect, they present themselves as seeking far more general and less obvious analogues of "Vixens are female foxes." The suggestion is that an armchair methodology is appropriate to their quest because it concerns truths in some sense less substantial, less world-involving than those of other disciplines: in Humean terms, relations of ideas rather than matters of fact. Our conceptual or linguistic competence, retained in the armchair, is to suffice for *a priori* knowledge of the relevant truths.

As already argued, philosophical truths are not generally truths *about* words or concepts. However, analytic truths are not supposed to be always about words or concepts, even if words or concepts are supposed to play a special role in explaining their truth. The sentence "Vixens are female foxes" is in no useful sense about the word

---

[1] To give just one example, even Jack Smart, whose work robustly engages the nature of the non-linguistic, non-conceptual world and who described metaphysics as "a search for the most plausible theory of the whole universe, as it is considered in the light of total science" (1984: 138), could also write that philosophy is "in some sense a *conceptual* inquiry, and so a science can be thought of as bordering on philosophy to the extent to which it raises within itself problems of a conceptual nature" (1987: 25), although he admits that he "cannot give a *clear* account of what I have meant when earlier in this essay I have said that some subjects are more concerned with "conceptual matters" than are others" (1987: 32).

"vixen" or any other words; it is about vixens, if anything. Its meaning is not to be confused with that of the metalinguistic sentence " 'Vixens are female foxes' is true." Similarly, the thought *vixens are female foxes* is not about the concept *vixen* or any other concepts; it too is about vixens, if anything. It is not to be confused with the metaconceptual thought *the thought VIXENS ARE FEMALE FOXES is true.*

How can a sentence which comes as close as "Vixens are female foxes" does to being a definition of "vixen" be about vixens rather than about the word "vixen"? Uttering it in response to the question "What does 'vixen' mean?" normally enables the questioner to work out the answer to the question, by pragmatic reasoning, even though the literal meaning of the sentence does not directly answer the question, just as does uttering "That is a gnu" while pointing at one in answer to the question "What does 'gnu' mean?." If core philosophical truths are analytic, they may *exhibit* significant features of words or concepts without *describing* them.

Does the conception of philosophical truths as analytic or conceptual vindicate a form of the linguistic or conceptual turn without misrepresenting the subject matter of philosophy as itself linguistic or conceptual? The case study in the previous chapter gave no support to such a conjecture. Nevertheless, let us examine the matter more systematically.

Many philosophically relevant truths are clearly not conceptual truths in any useful sense. For instance, in arguing against subjective idealism, a defender of common sense metaphysics says that there was a solar system millions of years before there was sentient life. Similarly, a defender of common sense epistemology says that he knows that he has hands; that he knows that he has hands is no conceptual truth, for it is consistent with all conceptual truths that he lost them in a nasty accident. Some philosophers of time argue that not only the present exists by appeal to Special Relativity. Philosophers of mind and language dispute whether there is a language of thought; whatever the answer, it is no conceptual truth. Naturalists and anti-naturalists dispute whether there is only what there is in space and time; again, the answer is unlikely to be a conceptual truth. Moral and political philosophers and philosophers of art appeal to empirically discovered human cognitive limitations, and so on. Such philosophical arguments cannot be dismissed on general methodological grounds. One must engage with them on their merits, in the normal way of philosophy.

Despite such examples, philosophy may be thought to have a central core of truths which are all conceptual; perhaps the rest of philosophy counts as such through its relation to the central core. Let us charitably read this restriction into the appeal to analyticity or conceptual truth in the epistemology of philosophy.

Notoriously, the idea of analyticity has been under a cloud ever since Quine argued that "a boundary between analytic and synthetic statements simply has not been drawn" (1951: 34). Nevertheless, the idea is still active in contemporary philosophy, often under the less provocative guise of "conceptual truth." The terms "analytic" and "conceptual" will henceforth be used interchangeably.

Quine's arguments are generally found much less compelling than they once appeared. Although he may succeed in showing that "analytic" is caught in a circle with other semantic terms, such as "synonymous," he does not adequately motivate his jump from that point to the conclusion that the terms in the circle all lack scientific respectability, as opposed to the contrary conclusion that they all have it. Given any science, someone may insist that it define its terms, and the terms used to define them, and so on until it is driven round in a circle. By itself, that hardly demonstrates the illegitimacy of the science. Every discipline must use undefined terms somewhere or other. "Two Dogmas of Empiricism" does not explain why we should regard the undefined terms of semantics as worse off than the undefined terms of other disciplines, except by dogmatic charges of unclarity. After all, semantics is now a thriving branch of empirical linguistics. It is not to be trashed without very good reason.[2]

Some terms may be so unclear by ordinary working standards that no circle of definitions will render them scientifically useful. But semantic terms are not like that. By ordinary working standards, the word "synonymous" is quite clear enough to be useful. Although it is not perfectly precise – surely it has borderline cases – its degree of vagueness seems no worse than that of undefined terms in many other

---

[2]   The overall criticism of Quine's procedure goes back to Grice and Strawson (1956). Sober (2000) argues that Quine violates his own methodological naturalism in criticizing semantic notions on foundational grounds without considering their use in science.

sciences. When clarification is needed in some specific respect, it can be achieved by stipulation or otherwise, as elsewhere in science. Indeed, few contemporary philosophers feel special qualms in using the term "synonymous." Thus any objection they have to "analytic" can hardly be based on Quine's arguments, since his only objection to defining "analytic" in terms of "synonymous" is to the use of "synonymous" (1951: 24, 35).

The feeling remains that "analytic," unlike "synonymous," carries obsolescent philosophical baggage. For "analytic," unlike "synonymous," was once a central term in philosophical theorizing, notably in the work of logical positivists, such as Carnap, and of postwar linguistic philosophers, such as Strawson. The reason why it cannot recover that position lies not in Quine's critique, which no longer seems compelling, but rather in Kripke's widely accepted clarification of the differences between analyticity, apriority and necessity. Kripke did not deny that there is a boundary between the analytic and the synthetic; he merely distinguished it from other boundaries, such as the epistemological boundary between the *a priori* and the *a posteriori* and the metaphysical boundary between the necessary and the contingent (Kripke 1980: 39). He stipulated that "analytic" entails both "*a priori*" and "necessary." Since he argued that neither of "*a priori*" and "necessary" entails the other, he was committed to denying that either of them entails "analytic" (by the transitivity of entailment).[3] Thus "analytic" does neither the purely epistemological work of "*a priori*" nor the purely metaphysical work of "necessary." Its current role inevitably looks less central than the one it occupied when "*a priori*" and "necessary" were treated as pretty much

---

[3]   Given Kripke's arguments, defining "analytic" as the conjunction of "*a priori*" and "necessary" does not yield a natural notion, since a disjunction of an *a priori* contingency with an unrelated *a posteriori* necessity will then count as analytic: it is *a priori* because its first disjunct is and necessary because its second disjunct is. One does somewhat better by defining "analytic" as "*a priori* necessary," which excludes that example, although the point of such a combination of epistemological and metaphysical elements remains to be explained. The arguments below apply to this notion too. Of course, Kripke's main concern is the difference between the *a priori* / *a posteriori* and the necessary/contingent distinctions; he clarifies their differences from the analytic/synthetic distinction in passing. Nevertheless, the differentiation between the first two distinctions forces the demotion of the third from that of trying to play both the first role and the second.

interchangeable and "analytic" was taken to do the work of both. But that does not yet imply that no work remains for it to do.

If we try to sort sentences as "analytic" or "synthetic" in the manner of chicken-sexers, we can usually achieve a rough consensus. Of course borderline cases will occur, but so they do for virtually every distinction worth making: perfect precision is an unreasonable demand. The issue is what theoretical significance, if any, attaches to the rough boundary thus drawn. Even if "analytic" is defined in terms of "synonymous" and other expressions under better control than "analytic," we should not assume without checking that it has any of the consequences sometimes associated with it. In particular, we should not assume that analytic truths are insubstantial in any further sense.

Nothing in this book challenges the legitimacy of familiar semantic terms such as "synonymous." They will be used without apology, and they permit various senses of "analytic" to be defined. But none of them makes sense of the idea that analytic truths are less substantial than synthetic ones, or that core philosophical truths are less substantial than the truths of most other disciplines. There is something robust about "Two Dogmas of Empiricism": insights remain even when its skepticism towards meaning is stripped away.

On some conceptions, analytic sentences are true simply in virtue of their meaning, and analytic thoughts simply in virtue of their constituent concepts. They impose no constraint on the world, not even on that part of it which consists of words and concepts. That is why it is unnecessary to get up out of one's armchair to investigate whether such a constraint is met. Analytic truths are less substantial than synthetic ones because the latter do impose constraints on the world, which it may or may not meet. This is another way of putting the idea that analytic truths are true in virtue of meaning alone while synthetic truths are true in virtue of a combination of meaning and fact, for if analytic truths did impose constraints on the world, they would be true partly in virtue of the fact that the world met those constraints, and so not true in virtue of meaning alone. Call such conceptions of analyticity *metaphysical*. Other conceptions dispense with the idea of truth in virtue of meaning, and treat analyticity as a privileged status in respect of knowledge or justification which a sentence or thought has in virtue of the conditions for understanding its constituent words or possessing its constituent concepts. Although the privileged truths impose constraints on the world, the task of checking that they are met is somehow less substantial than for other truths, for those who understand the relevant words or possess the relevant concepts. Call such conceptions of analyticity *epistemological*.[4]

This chapter examines a variety of attempts to develop a metaphysical account of analyticity. Some depend on misconceptions about meaning or truth. Others yield intelligible notions of analyticity, by watering down the traditional account to a point where it loses most of its usually supposed implications. They provide no reason to regard analytic truths as in any way insubstantial.[5] Even if core philosophical truths are analytic in such a sense, that does not explain how we can know or justifiably believe them.[6] At best it reduces the problem to the epistemology of another class of truths, such as necessary truths or logical truths. The next chapter will examine attempts to develop an epistemological account of analyticity, also with negative results. The overall upshot is that philosophical truths are analytic at most in senses too weak to be of much explanatory value or to justify conceiving contemporary philosophy in terms of a linguistic or conceptual turn.

The conclusion is not best put by calling purportedly analytic truths "substantial," because in this context the term "substantial" is hopelessly vague. Rather, appeals in epistemology to a metaphysical conception of analyticity tend to rely on a *picture* of analytic truths as imposing no genuine constraint on the world, in order to

---

[4] See Boghossian (1997) for the distinction between metaphysical and epistemological accounts of analyticity, and Tappenden (1993: 240) for a somewhat similar distinction.

[5] Etchemendy (1990: 107–24) contrasts "substantive" generalizations with logical ones. The idea is widespread. It occurs in different forms in Wittgenstein's *Tractatus Logico-Philosophicus* and in Locke's "Of trifling propositions" (*An Essay Concerning Human Understanding*, Book IV, Chapter viii).

[6] Since analytic truths are standardly taken to be sentences, the term "true" will sometimes be applied to sentences, as well as to thoughts and propositions; where required, the context makes clear what kind of truth-bearer is intended. Talk of knowing or believing a sentence should be understood as elliptical for talk of having knowledge or belief which one can express with the sentence (on its standard meaning). Thus someone who knows "Grass is green" knows that grass is green and can express that knowledge by saying "Grass is green"; this is not to be confused with the metalinguistic knowledge that the sentence "Grass is green" is true.

explain the supposed fact that knowing them poses no serious cognitive challenge. If that account could be made good, it would provide a useful sense for "insubstantial," which would refer to the pictured property, epistemological not in its nature but in its explanatory power. Substantial truths would be the ones that lacked this property. But the account cannot be made good. The metaphysical picture cannot be filled in so as to have the required explanatory power in epistemology. Thus "substantial" and "insubstantial" are not provided with useful senses. The negation of a picture is not itself a picture. That is a problem for appeals to metaphysical analyticity, not for the present critique.

2

The distinction between analytic truth and synthetic truth does not distinguish different *senses* of "true": analytic and synthetic truths are true in the very same sense of "true." That should be obvious. Nevertheless, it is hard to reconcile with what many logical positivists, Wittgensteinians and others have said about analytic truths. For they have described them as stipulations, implicit definitions (partial or complete), disguised rules of grammar and the like. On such a conception, enunciating an analytic truth is not stating a fact but something more like fixing or recalling a notation: even if talk of truth as correspondence to the facts is metaphorical, it is a bad metaphor for analytic truth in a way in which it is not for synthetic truth. In the face of this conception, we should remind ourselves why "truth" is quite unequivocal between "analytic truth" and "synthetic truth."

We can start by considering a standard disquotational principle for truth (where both occurrences of "P" are to be replaced by a declarative sentence):

(T)   "P" is true if and only if P.

If "true" is ambiguous between analytic truth and synthetic truth, (T) must itself be disambiguated. Nevertheless, the left-to-right direction holds for both notions:

(Talr)   "P" is analytically true only if P.
(Tslr)   "P" is synthetically true only if P.

Obviously, "Bachelors are unmarried" is analytically true only if bachelors are unmarried, just as "Bachelors are untidy" is synthetically true only if bachelors are untidy. The exact parallelism of (Talr) and (Tslr) already casts doubt on the supposed ambiguity. Indeed, they are jointly equivalent to a single principle about the disjunction of analytic truth and synthetic truth ("simple truth"):

(Taslr)   "P" is analytically true or synthetically true only if P.

Worse, the right-to-left direction fails for both notions:

(Tarl)   "P" is analytically true if P.
(Tsrl)   "P" is synthetically true if P.

For (Tarl) has a false instance when a synthetic truth is substituted for "P"; (Tsrl) has a false instance when an analytic truth is substituted for "P." There are no natural substitutes for the right-to-left direction of (T) in the form of separate principles for analytic truth and synthetic truth. Rather, the natural substitute for the right-to-left direction disjoins the two notions:

(Tasrl)   "P" is analytically true or synthetically true if P.

But (Tasrl) reinstates simple truth as the theoretically important characteristic.

One cannot avoid the problem by qualifying "true" in (T) with "analytic" for "the relevant kind of sentence" and with "synthetic" for the rest. For the sentences of the relevant kind are presumably just the analytic truths and analytic falsehoods. Thus the schemas for analytic and synthetic truth amount to these:

(Ta)   If "P" is analytically true or analytically false, then "P" is analytically true if and only if P.
(Ts)   If "P" is neither analytically true nor analytically false, then "P" is synthetically true if and only if P.

But (Ta) and (Ts) follow from (Taslr), (Tasrl) and the analogue for falsity of (Taslr):[7]

(Faslr)   "P" is analytically false or synthetically false only if not P.

Thus the information in (Ta) and (Ts) is in effect just information about the disjunction of analytic truth and synthetic truth. The attempt to treat analytic truth and synthetic truth separately just confuses the theory of "true." The same happens for other theoretically important applications of "true."

Consider the standard two-valued truth-table for the material conditional:

A	B	A → B
T	T	T
T	F	F
F	T	T
F	F	T

If "true" is ambiguous between analytic truth and synthetic truth, what does "T" mean in that table? We might try subscripting it as $T_{analytic}$ and $T_{synthetic}$, multiplying the possibilities in the first two columns accordingly and adding the appropriate subscript in the third column. "F" will require corresponding subscripts too. Since the possibilities $T_{analytic}$, $T_{synthetic}$, $F_{analytic}$ and $F_{synthetic}$ arise for both **A** and **B**, the new truth-table will have sixteen lines. Worse, consider this case:

---

[7]   Proof: Assume (Taslr), (Faslr) and (Tasrl). To derive (Ta), note that it is equivalent to the conjunction of two claims: (i) if "P" is analytically true, then "P" is analytically true if and only if P; (ii) if "P" is analytically false, then "P" is analytically true if and only if P. Now (i) is logically equivalent to the claim that "P" is analytically true only if P, which follows from (Taslr). Moreover, by (Faslr) "P" is analytically false only if not P; as just seen "P" is analytically true only if P, so "P" is analytically false only if "P" is not analytically true; thus if "P" is analytically false then both sides of the biconditional in the consequent of (ii) fail, so (ii) holds. To derive (Ts), first note that "P" is synthetically true only if P by (Taslr). Conversely, if P then "P" is analytically true or synthetically true by (Tasrl); since by the antecedent of (Ts) it is not analytically true, it is synthetically true. Incidentally, by themselves (Ta) and (Ts) are weak in other ways too; in particular, they do not entail that nothing can be both analytically true and synthetically true.

A	B	A → B
$T_{synthetic}$	$T_{synthetic}$	$T_?$

What subscript is appropriate for the third column? Suppose that Barbara is a barrister, and therefore a lawyer. Of the following four sentences, (1), (2) and (4) are synthetic while (3) is analytic (with "if" read as →):

(1) Barbara is a barrister.
(2) Barbara is a lawyer.
(3) If Barbara is a barrister, Barbara is a lawyer.
(4) If Barbara is a lawyer, Barbara is a barrister.

Since Barbara could easily not have been a lawyer at all, (1) and (2) are synthetic. If there are analytic truths, (3) is one of them; "barrister" simply means a lawyer with certain qualifications. Thus we cannot put "synthetic" for the missing subscript in that line of the truth-table, for that gives the wrong result when we read **A** as (1) and **B** as (2). Since Barbara could easily have been a lawyer without being a barrister, by being a solicitor, (4) is synthetic too. Thus we also cannot put "analytic" for the missing subscript, since that gives the wrong result when we read **A** as (2) and **B** as (1). Therefore the truth-table cannot be completed. Whether a material conditional is analytically true and whether it is synthetically true are not a function of whether its antecedent is analytically true, whether its antecedent is synthetically true, whether its consequent is analytically true and whether its consequent is synthetically true.

The best we can do is to put the disjunction of $T_{analytic}$ and $T_{synthetic}$ in the third column. But then in order to apply the truth-table iteratively, when one occurrence of → is embedded inside another, we shall need further lines in which such disjunctions appear in the first two columns as well as the third. In effect, we have merely recovered a single sense of "true," applicable to both analytic truths and synthetic truths, albeit awkwardly defined by a disjunction. The same conclusion can be reached by looking at combinations of other logical constants, such as conjunction and negation. What does the central work in the compositional semantics is that indiscriminate notion of truth, not the more specific notions of analytic truth and synthetic truth.

A corresponding result holds for the theory of logical consequence. Valid arguments preserve truth from premises to conclusion. What can we say if "truth" must be disambiguated between analytic truth and synthetic truth? A valid argument whose premise is a synthetic truth may have either a synthetic truth or an analytic truth as its conclusion. For example, the conjunction of a synthetic truth with an analytic truth is itself a synthetic truth, and has each conjunct as a logical consequence. For logic, the significant generalizations concern the indiscriminate disjunction of analytic truth with synthetic truth, not either disjunct separately.[8]

Analytic truths and synthetic truths are true in exactly the same central sense of "true." That is compatible with their being true in very different ways, just as being a mother and being a father are two very different ways of being a parent; "parent" is not ambiguous between mothers and fathers. But truth-conditional semantics undermines even that idea. For how are (3) and (4) true in very different ways? Each is a material conditional; the antecedent and consequent of each are true in relevantly the same way as the antecedent and consequent of the other respectively. Their compositional semantic evaluation proceeds in parallel. Yet (3) is analytic, (4) synthetic. From the perspective of compositional semantics, the analytic-synthetic distinction is no distinction between different ways of being true; it is just a distinction between some truths and others.

3

On the metaphysical conception, analytic truths differ from synthetic ones by being true "in virtue of meaning." The intended contrast seems to be this. A synthetic truth is true because it means what it does and things are as that meaning requires. For example, "Barbara is a barrister" is true because it means that Barbara is a barrister, and Barbara *is* a barrister. For an analytic truth, the second conjunct drops out. "Barristers are lawyers" is true simply because it means that barristers are lawyers. Nothing else is needed. But the contrast is unconvincing. For that explanation of the truth of "Barristers are lawyers" works only when we take for granted that barristers *are*

---

[8]   For related arguments see Williamson (1994b: 141–2) and Tappolet (1997).

lawyers. It is no good to say "Never mind whether barristers *are* lawyers; 'Barristers are lawyers' is true simply because it means that barristers are lawyers." For any true sentence *s* whatsoever, a canonical explanation of the truth of *s* takes the overall form "*s* means that P, and P."[9] To use the obscure locution "in virtue of," every true sentence is true in virtue of both its meaning and how things are. This is another way of making the point that analytic truths and synthetic truths are not true in radically different ways.[10]

We can ask "in virtue of" questions about non-metalinguistic matters too. In virtue of what are vixens female foxes? To use another obscure locution, what makes it the case that vixens are female foxes? An appeal to semantic or other facts about the words "vixen," "female" and "fox" in answer to those questions would confuse use and mention. Vixens would have been female foxes no matter how we had used words. Presumably, vixens are female foxes in virtue of whatever female foxes are female foxes in virtue of; what makes it the case that vixens are female foxes is whatever makes it the case that female foxes are female foxes. Some may argue that female foxes are not female foxes in virtue of anything; nothing makes it the case that female foxes are female foxes. The suggestion may be that analytic truths require no truthmaker, unlike synthetic truths. An alternative suggestion is that analytic truths require truthmakers of a different kind from those of synthetic truths. Such suggestions are too unconstrained to be tractable for assessment. Still, two points stand out. First, they seem to conflict with general principles of

[9] See Boghossian (1997: 335–6). Quine says that we can say that the logical truth "Everything is self-identical" depends for its truth "on an obvious trait, viz., self-identity, of its subject matter, viz., everything." However, he claims that it makes no difference whether we say that or say that it depends for its truth "on traits of the language (specifically on the usage of "="), and not on traits of its subject matter" (1966: 106).

[10] Another problem for the supposed contrast is that it seems to equivocate on "means." When we explain why "Barbara is a barrister" is true by saying "It means that Barbara is a barrister, and Barbara *is* a barrister," "means" can be paraphrased as "expresses the proposition"; what proposition a sentence expresses may depend on the context in which it is uttered, if indexicals are present. By contrast, the appeal to meaning in the case of analytically true sentences is not to the proposition expressed on some particular occasion but rather to the linguistic meaning of the sentence, which is invariant across contexts, even if indexicals are present.

truthmaker theory (in the unlikely event that such a theory is needed). For instance, what makes a disjunction true is what makes one of its disjuncts true. Thus whatever makes (2) ("Barbara is a lawyer") true also makes both (5) and (6) true:

(5)   Barbara is a lawyer or Barbara is not a lawyer.
(6)   Barbara is a lawyer or Barbara is a doctor.

But (5) is a simple logical truth, while (6) is a straightforward synthetic truth. Second, no connection has been provided between truthmaker theory and epistemology. Knowing a truth need not involve knowing its truthmaker; one can know (6) without knowing which disjunct is true (Barbara works in a building where only lawyers and doctors work). No account has been given as to why it should be easy from an armchair to know a truth with no truthmaker, or a truthmaker only of the special sort supposedly appropriate to analytic truths.

Nevertheless, at least one clear difference between paradigms of "analytic" and paradigms of "synthetic" is in the vicinity. For meaning that barristers are lawyers is sufficient for being true, whereas meaning that Barbara is a barrister is not. More generally, call a meaning *sufficient for truth* just in case necessarily, in any context any sentence with that meaning is true.[11] Thus the meaning of "Barristers are lawyers" is sufficient for truth; the meaning of "Barbara is a barrister" is not. One proposal is to explicate "analytic truth" as "truth whose meaning is sufficient for truth." Call this "modal-analyticity."[12] For non-skeptics about meaning and necessity, the

---

[11]   To handle ambiguity, treat it as homonymy: distinct sentences with the same superficial form. The reification of meanings in the definition can be eliminated at the cost of circumlocution. Note also that the utterance of a modal-analytic truth may be false if the context shifts during the utterance: consider "If it is now exactly noon then it is now exactly noon." Similarly, an utterance of "If John is a bachelor then John is unmarried" may express a falsehood if the wedding ceremony is completed between the utterance of the antecedent and the utterance of the consequent. Taking such complications into account would not help friends of analyticity.

[12]   The notion of modal-analyticity is similar to the notion of deep necessity in Evans (1979), where the truth of the sentence does not depend on any contingent feature of reality.

notion of modal-analyticity is quite intelligible. But what are its consequences?

Consider any non-indexical sentence s that expresses a necessarily true proposition. Necessarily, in any context, any sentence with the actual meaning of s expresses that necessary truth and is therefore true. Thus s is a modal-analytic truth, because its meaning is sufficient for truth. In that sense, it is true in virtue of meaning. But how little has been achieved in so classifying it! Nothing has been done to rule out the hypothesis that it expresses a profound metaphysical necessity about the nature of the world, knowable if at all only through arduous *a posteriori* investigation, for instance. No reason has been provided to regard s as "merely verbal" or "insubstantial" in a pretheoretic sense, unless one already had independent reason to regard all necessities as merely verbal or insubstantial. Similarly, mathematical truths count as modal-analytic; their so counting is by itself no reason to regard them as merely verbal or insubstantial. Indeed, for all that has been said, even "Water contains H_2O" is modal-analytic, given that "water" has a different meaning as used on Twin Earth to refer to XYZ, a different substance with the same superficial appearance.

To make the point vivid, call a meaning *temporally sufficient for truth* just in case at all times, in any context any sentence with that meaning is true. Read the quantifiers "at all times" and "in any context" non-modally, so they do not range outside the actual world. Thus any sentence which expresses, in a time-independent way, an eternally true proposition, however contingent, has a meaning temporally sufficient for truth. For example, the meaning of "No hotel ever has a billion rooms" is presumably temporally sufficient for truth. We can call the sentence "temporal-analytic" if we like, but that in no way implies that it is somehow insubstantial, because there is no background connection between eternity and some sort of insubstantiality. Similarly, calling a sentence "analytic" in the sense of modal-analyticity does not imply that it is somehow insubstantial, in the absence of a background connection between necessity and some sort of insubstantiality. Yet the account of analyticity was what was supposed to substantiate the claim of insubstantiality. If we already had a background connection between necessity and insubstantiality, there would be little to gain from invoking modal-analyticity in order to argue that core philosophical truths are insubstantial, since we could do it more simply just by arguing that true philosophical sentences in the core express necessarily true propositions.

Admittedly, not all modal-analytic true sentences express necessarily true propositions. Examples of the contingent *a priori* such as "It is raining if and only if it is actually raining" are modal-analytic, since the truth of "It is raining" as uttered in a given context is necessarily equivalent to the truth of "It is actually raining" as uttered in that context, because "actually" refers rigidly to the world of the context, but the biconditional does not express a necessary truth, since the weather could have been relevantly different, in which case it would have been not raining if and only if it is actually raining. Thus modal-analyticity violates Kripke's constraint that analyticity implies necessity; in this respect it may diverge from the traditional conception. Conversely, not all sentences that express necessarily true propositions are modal-analytic: consider examples of the necessary *a posteriori* such as "I am not Tony Blair." Nevertheless, such examples seem marginal to the envisaged conception of core philosophical truths, most of which will both express necessarily true propositions and be modal-analytic.

A core of philosophical truths may indeed be modal-analytic. Some philosophers seek to articulate necessary truths without essential reliance on indexicals; if they succeed, the sentences they produce are modal-analytic. Even if contextualists are right, and key philosophical terms such as "know" shift their reference across contexts, the relevant sentences may still both express necessarily true propositions and be modal-analytic: consider "Whatever is known to be the case is the case." The answers to philosophical questions of the forms "Is it possible that P?" and "Is it necessary that P?" will themselves express necessary truths, given the principle of the widely accepted modal logic S5 that the possible is non-contingently possible and the necessary non-contingently necessary; if the answers can be phrased in non-indexical terms, they will then be modal-analytic. But outside the envisaged core many philosophically relevant truths will not be modal-analytic, as the examples near the start of the chapter show.

Unfortunately, even for modal-analytic philosophical truths, classifying them as modal-analytic does not unlock their epistemology, any more than classifying a truth as necessary explains how we can know it. Of course, if a sentence is modal-analytic, then one is safe from error in uttering it with its given meaning. In that sense, one's utterance is reliable. But such reliability falls well short of what knowledge requires, since otherwise any true mathematical assertion would count as an expression of knowledge, no matter how fallacious the "proof" on which it was based. "Vixens are female foxes" is utterly misleading as a paradigm for the epistemology of modal-analytic truths in general. To say that *s* is a modal-analytic truth whose constituent words and grammar we understand does very little way to explain how we can know or justifiably believe *s*.[13] In particular, it does not imply that the mere linguistic understanding of *s*, which every competent speaker possesses, provides any insight into the truth of *s*, or constitutes more than the minimal starting-point for inquiry it does for ordinary synthetic truths.

4

Issues related to those just raised for modal-analyticity arise for what is sometimes called "Frege-analyticity."[14] A sentence is Frege-analytic just in case it is synonymous with a logical truth. For example, "All furze is furze" is a logical truth, roughly speaking because everything of the form "All F is F" is true. "All furze is gorse" is not a logical truth, because not everything of the form "All F is G" is true ("All fungus is grease" is false). However, "All furze is gorse" is Frege-analytic, because it is synonymous with the logical truth "All furze is furze," since "furze" is synonymous with "gorse." In "Two Dogmas," Quine admits the notion of logical truth, and therefore allows that if "synonymous" were legitimate, so would be "analytic" in the sense of Frege-analyticity. By present standards, the notion of Frege-analyticity is quite intelligible. But what are its consequences?

Trivially, every logical truth is Frege-analytic, because it is synonymous with itself. Clearly, this alone does nothing to show that logical truths are somehow insubstantial in any metaphysical, epistemologically explanatory sense (see the end of Section 1). For instance, it is compatible with the hypothesis that there are truths of second-order logic which characterize the necessary structure of reality in profound

---

[13]   See n. 6 for this terminology.
[14]   The term "Frege-analytic" is from Boghossian (1997), with reference to §3 of Frege (1950) (as Boghossian suggests, the interpretation of the passage is not entirely clear). He classifies the notion of Frege-analyticity as neither epistemological nor metaphysical but semantic (1997: 363); for convenience, it is treated here under the heading of metaphysical notions of analyticity.

ways and can never be known by any mind. *A fortiori*, nothing has been done to show that Frege-analytic truths are insubstantial.[15]

To make the point vivid, call a sentence "Einstein-analytic" just in case it is synonymous with a truth once uttered by Einstein. Trivially, every truth once uttered by Einstein is Einstein-analytic. That does nothing to show that truths once uttered by Einstein are in any sense insubstantial; *a fortiori*, nothing has been done to show that Einstein-analytic truths are somehow insubstantial. Of course, if we had independent reason to regard all logical truths as somehow insubstantial, that would presumably give us reason to regard all Frege-analytic truths as insubstantial in some related way, but the mere definition of "Frege-analytic" provides no such reason. Quine devoted some of his most powerful early work to arguing that logical truths are not analytic in a less trivial sense (Quine 1936).

To explain why "All furze is furze" is a logical truth while "All furze is gorse" is not, use was made of Tarski's standard model-theoretic account of logical consequence as truth-preservation under all interpretations which preserve logical form, and in particular of logical truth as truth under all such interpretations (Tarski 1983b). It lends no support to any conception of logical truths as somehow insubstantial. The truth of a sentence under all interpretations which preserve its logical form in no way make its truth under its intended interpretation insubstantial.[16] To use a style of argument from Section 2, consider this simple logical truth (with "if" read as the material conditional):

(7)   If Barbara is a barrister, Barbara is a barrister

Its compositional semantic evaluation proceeds in parallel to that for the non-logical analytic truth (3) and the synthetic truth (4); each is true because it is a material conditional with a true antecedent and a true consequent. All three are true in the same way. From the perspective of compositional semantics, logical truths are true in the same way as other truths.

In one good sense, sentences of the form "P if and only if actually P" are logical truths, and therefore Frege-analytic, because true in

---

[15]   Quine (1966: 111) notes that so-called truth by definitions ("Every vixen is a female fox") depends on prior logical truths ("Every female fox is a female fox").

[16]   Note that the epistemological issue is not how we can know that *s* is a logical truth; it is how, given that *s* is a logical truth, we can know the simple truth of *s*.

every model (Davies and Humberstone 1980, Kaplan 1989). Nevertheless, they can express contingent truths on the same reading; it is not necessary for me to be my actual height. Although we could add a modal qualification to the definition of logical truth in order to exclude such examples, by requiring logical truths to be true at every world in every model, this mixing together of the modal dimension with the world dimension is bad taxonomy; perspicuous basic notions keep such different dimensions separate. Thus Frege-analyticity, like modal-analyticity, violates Kripke's constraint that analyticity implies necessity. In this respect Frege-analyticity too may diverge from the traditional conception.

The mathematical rigor, elegance, and fertility of model-theoretic definitions of logical consequence depend on their freedom from modal and epistemological accretions. As a result, such definitions provide no automatic guarantee that logical truths express necessary or *a priori* propositions. This is no criticism. As a theoretical discipline, logic only recently attained maturity. Tarski's model-theoretic notion of logical consequence has turned out to be a key theoretical notion. To reject it on the basis of preconceived extraneous constraints would subvert the autonomy of logic as a discipline. Pretheoretic conceptions of logical consequence are in any case too confused to provide much guidance on subtle issues.[17] Still, those who do have a non-standard account of logical truth can feed it into the definition of "Frege-analytic" if they like.

"All furze is furze," unlike many logical truths, is obvious. That does not justify the idea that it imposes *no* constraint on the world, rather than one which, by logic, we easily know to be met (Wittgenstein, *Tractatus Logico-Philosophicus*, 4.461–4.4661 and 6.1–613). What case does the constraint exclude? That not all furze is furze, of course. To complain that "Not all furze is furze" does not express a genuine case is to argue in a circle. For it is to assume that a genuine constraint must exclude some logically consistent case. Since substantiality was being understood to consist in imposing a genuine constraint, that is tantamount to assuming that no logical truth is substantial, the very point at issue. Concentration on obvious logical truths obscures this circularity.

---

[17] For more discussion and further references to the controversy over the nature of logical consequence see Williamson (2000b).

We may hope, given an epistemology for logical truths, to extend it to an epistemology for Frege-analytic truths. That task will not be trivial, for cognitive differences may arise between synonymous expressions, even for those who understand them. For example, Kripke (1979) has argued persuasively that a competent speaker of English can understand the synonymous expressions "furze" and "gorse" in the normal way without being in a position to know that they refer to the same thing. Such a speaker will assent to the logical truth "All furze is furze" while refusing assent to the Frege-analytic truth "All furze is gorse." Similarly, on standard theories of direct reference, coreferential proper names such as "Hesperus" and "Phosphorus" are synonymous, so an astronomically ignorant competent speaker may assent to the logical truth "If Hesperus is bright then Hesperus is bright" while refusing assent to the Frege-analytic truth "If Hesperus is bright then Phosphorus is bright."

The epistemological consequences of such examples are contested. According to some direct reference theorists, the proposition that if Hesperus is bright then Phosphorus is bright *is* the proposition that if Hesperus is bright then Hesperus is bright, so whoever knows that if Hesperus is bright then Hesperus is bright *ipso facto* knows that if Hesperus is bright then Phosphorus is bright.[18] However, even granted that view of propositional attitude ascriptions, that speaker is in no position to know that if Hesperus is bright then Phosphorus is bright under the guise of the sentence "If Hesperus is bright then Phosphorus is bright," but only under the guise of the sentence "If Hesperus is bright then Hesperus is bright." In a sense the speaker cannot express their knowledge by using the merely Frege-analytic sentence, even though it expresses the content of that knowledge: if they do use the sentence, their utterance will not be causally connected to their knowledge state in the right way. In elliptical terms, the speaker knows "If Hesperus is bright then Hesperus is bright" without being in a position to know "If Hesperus is bright then Phosphorus is bright"; they know the logically true sentence without being in a position to know the merely Frege-analytically true sentence.

If propositions are individuated in that coarse-grained direct reference way, what matters for progress in philosophy is less which propositions we know than which sentential guises we know them under. Suppose, just for the sake of argument, that some form of

18   See Salmon (1986), especially 133–5.

physicalism is true, and pain is in fact identical with π, where "π" is a name whose reference is fixed by a neuroscientific description. According to a hard-line direct reference theory, "pain" and "π" are synonymous. The hypothesis "Pain is π" becomes a focus of philosophical controversy. On some direct reference theories, everyone knew all along that pain is π, because they knew all along that pain is pain and the proposition that pain is π just is the proposition that pain is pain. If that view is correct, it just shows that such attitude ascriptions constitute the wrong level of description for understanding philosophical activity. What matters is that although everyone knew the proposition under the guise of the logical truth "Pain is pain," they did not know or even believe it under the guise of the merely Frege-analytic truth "Pain is π." In elliptical terms, they knew "Pain is pain" but not "Pain is π." Perhaps such physicalist theories are false, but we can hardly expect philosophy to be a discipline in which there are no informative identities; the moral of the example stands. The need for such finer-grained descriptions of propositional attitudes is even more urgent if propositions as the objects of knowledge and belief are identified with sets of possible worlds, for then all necessary truths are identical with the set of all possible worlds: anyone who knows one necessary truth knows them all (Lewis 1996, Stalnaker 1999: 241–73). Thus a coarse-grained account of attitude ascriptions does not trivialize the problem of extending an epistemology for logical truths to an epistemology for Frege-analytic truths.

Opponents of direct reference theories usually hope to make synonymy a more cognitively accessible relation for competent speakers. However, the prospects for making it perfectly accessible are very dubious. Pairs such as "furze" and "gorse" are pre-theoretically plausible cases of synonymous expressions that speakers can understand in the ordinary way without being in a position to know them to be synonymous.[19] The extension of an epistemology for logical truths to an epistemology for Frege-analytic truths will probably have to allow for significant cognitive obstacles that cannot be overcome simply by speakers' ordinary linguistic competence.

[19] See Kripke (1979). This contradicts Dummett's claim that "It is an undeniable feature of the notion of meaning – obscure as that notion is – that meaning is *transparent* in the sense that, if someone attaches a meaning to each of two words, he must know whether these meanings are the same (1978: 131). For more general theoretical considerations against such claims see Williamson (2000a: 94–107). See also Horwich (1998: 100–1).

Even for sentential guises, identity and distinctness are not guaranteed to be transparent to speakers: someone may be confused as to whether "Paderewski," the name of the politician, is the same name as "Paderewski," the name of the pianist (Kripke 1979). A single speaker at a single time may associate different mental files with the same word of a natural language, or the same mental file with different words of the language. Speakers may also be confused as to whether they are calling on two mental files or one. What needs to be found is not the mythical level of description at which perfect transparency to the subject is guaranteed but rather a perspicuous level of description at which the relevant cognitive phenomena are individuated in a way that is neither so coarse-grained that the most relevant distinctions cannot be drawn nor so fine-grained that they are drowned out by a crowd of irrelevant ones. Since philosophical debates involve many interacting individuals, sentential guises usually provide an appropriate level of description.

We also need an epistemology for logical truths in the first place. To that, the notion of Frege-analyticity contributes nothing. In particular, that a sentence is Frege-analytic does not imply that mere linguistic competence provides any insight into its truth, or constitutes more than the minimal starting-point for inquiry it does for ordinary synthetic truths.

How many philosophical truths are Frege-analytic? As a simple example, take the true sentence "Persons are not events" (if you think that persons are events, take "Persons are events" instead). It is not itself a logical truth, on any standard conception of logic. In particular, "person" and "event" seem not to be logical constants, and the logical form "Ps are not Es" has false instances such as "Parisians are not Europeans." What logical truth could "Persons are not events" be synonymous with? "Persons who are not events are not events" is a logical truth, but not synonymous with the original. Granted, "persons" and "persons who are not events" have the same intension (function from circumstances of evaluation to extension) in every context of utterance.[20] Still, they are not literally synonymous, for whatever the semantic structure of "persons," it is finite, and

---

[20]   The contexts of utterance and circumstances of evaluation here are not restricted to the actual world. If the content of an expression has a structure which reflects the grammatical structure of the expression, then sameness of intension does not imply sameness of content, and sameness of intension in every context does not entail

therefore a proper part of the semantic structure of "persons who are not events"; thus the two expressions differ in semantic structure. One can try to construct non-circular analyses of "person" and "event" or both whose substitution into the sentence would yield a logical truth: "To be a person is to be a *QRS*." However, "person" and "*QRS*" are unlikely to be literally synonymous. Almost certainly, someone will produce a purported counterexample to the analysis: "Such-and-such would be a person but not a *QRS*" or "So-and-so would be a *QRS* but not a person." Direct reference theorists will tend to expect just such counterexamples to the claim that the apparently simple term "person" and the complex description "*QRS*" have the same intension; direct reference theories partly originate from Kripke and Putnam's counterexamples to a host of similar descriptivist claims. Opponents of direct reference may be less pessimistic about the prospects for a complex description with the same intension as "person." However, on their finer-grained views of meaning, on which synonymy is as transparent as possible to competent speakers, a purported counterexample need not be correct to defeat the claim of synonymy: what counts is that its proponent is neither linguistically incompetent nor fundamentally irrational. Contemporary proponents of a descriptivist view of meaning as a rival to direct reference theory usually envisage a loose semantic connection with a cluster of descriptions rather than strict synonymy with a single description. Whichever side of the debate one takes, there are good grounds for skepticism about the supposed synonymy of "person" and "*QRS*." The best bet is that "Persons are not events" is not Frege-analytic. The point does not depend on peculiarities of the example; it could be made just as well for most other philosophical claims.[21] In contemporary philosophy, few who propose complex analyses claim synonymy for them.[22]

One might react by loosening the relation of synonymy to some equivalence relation that would have a better chance of holding

---

sameness of character, that is, sameness of content in every context. See Kaplan (1989) for relevant background.

[21] Boghossian argues that many *a priori* truths are not Frege-analytic (1997: 338–9).

[22] This point is related to the paradox of analysis: how can a conceptual analysis be both correct and informative? The paradox goes back to Langford (1942).

between the *analysandum* and the *analysans* in philosophically significant analyses. Call the looser equivalence relation "metaphysical
equivalence." A wider class of philosophical truths might be transform-
able into logical truths by the substitution of metaphysically equivalent
terms. Call the truths in the wider class "quasi-Frege-analytic." The
poor track record of philosophical analysis does not suggest that
the class of quasi-Frege-analytic truths will be very much wider than
the class of Frege-analytic truths.[23] In any case, the looser metaphysical
equivalence is, the more problematic it will be to extend an epistemology for logical truths to an epistemology for quasi-Frege-analytic
truths. The aim of the loosening is to permit some distance between the
meaning of the *analysandum* and the meaning of the *analysans*; that
will tend to make even the coextensiveness of the *analysandum* and
analysans less cognitively accessible. There will be a corresponding
tendency to make the material equivalence of the original quasi-
Frege-analytic truth to the logical truth less cognitively accessible too.

For instance, one might define "metaphysical equivalence" as
sameness of intension in every context. The question is then how the
sameness of intension in every context of the substituted terms could
enable one to advance from knowing or justifiably believing the
logical truth to knowing or justifiably believing the merely quasi-
Frege-analytic truth. No guarantee has been provided that we can
know or justifiably believe the universally quantified biconditional of
the substituted terms. By hypothesis, that biconditional will in fact
express a necessary truth in every context; the problem merely shifts
to how such truths can be known, just as in the case of modal-
analyticity. If that problem were already solved, there would be little
to gain from appealing to quasi-Frege-analyticity in order to explain
how core philosophical truths can be known.

Even if many philosophical truths are quasi-Frege-analytic, it does
not follow that we can gain cognitive access to them simply on the
basis of our logical and linguistic competence.

Yet another proposal is to consider as (metaphysically) analytic just
the logical consequences of true (or good) semantic theories. It is presumably in the spirit of this proposal to interpret semantic theories not
as stating straightforwardly contingent, *a posteriori* facts about how
people use words but as somehow articulating the essential structure
of semantically individuated languages; in this sense, the word "green"

---

[23]   See Fodor (1998: 69–87) and Williamson (2000a: 31–3) for further discussion.

could not have meant anything but *green* in English. Even so, the definition does nothing to trace any special cognitive access that speakers have to semantic facts about their own language to any special metaphysical status enjoyed by those facts. It also counts every logical truth as analytic, since a logical truth is a logical consequence of anything, without illuminating any special cognitive access we may have to logical truths. Of course, *if* someone knows the relevant semantic truths about their own language and is logically proficient, then they are also in a position to know the analytic truths as so defined. But, on this definition, we do nothing to explain how the semantics and logic are known in the first place by saying that they are analytic. As in previous cases, the account of analyticity merely shifts the burden from explaining knowledge of analytic truths to explaining knowledge of some base class of necessary or logical or semantic or other truths. Once the analyticity card has been played to effect this shift of the explanatory burden, it cannot be played again to explain knowledge of the base truths, by saying that they are analytic, for they count as analytic simply because they belong to the relevant base class, and the question remains how we know truths in the base class.

5

Unless one is a skeptic about meaning or modality, one can define several notions of analyticity in semantic and modal terms, but none of them provides any reason to regard the truths to which it applies as somehow insubstantial, or as posing no significant cognitive challenge. That upshot may seem puzzling. Surely we sometimes make a sentence true by stipulative definition. For example, I might introduce the term "zzz" (pronounced as a buzz) by saying "A zzz is a short sleep" and thereby make "A zzz is a short sleep" true. What prevents us from using such cases as paradigms to fix a semantic notion of analyticity on which analytic truths are insubstantial?

We can see the problems for the proposal more clearly by distinguishing the semantic from the metasemantic. Semantics facts are facts of the kind we attempt to systematize in giving a systematic compositional semantic theory for a language, facts as to what its expressions mean. Metasemantic facts are the nonsemantic facts on which the semantic facts supervene. The distinction is rough but clear enough to be workable. Thus the fact that "horse" applies to horses is semantic, not metasemantic; the fact that utterances of "horse" are often caused by horses is metasemantic, not semantic.[24] Similarly, the fact that "zzz" means a short sleep is semantic, while the fact that it was introduced by someone saying "A zzz is a short sleep" is metasemantic. The semantic theory takes no notice of the act of stipulation, only of its outcome – that a given expression has a given meaning. The act of stipulation makes the sentence true by making it have a meaning on which it is, in the quite ordinary way, true. My saying "A zzz is a short sleep" did not make a zzz be a short sleep, because that would be to make a short sleep be a short sleep, and my saying "A zzz is a short sleep" certainly did not make a short sleep be a short sleep. In particular, since there were many short sleeps before I was born, there were many zzzes before I was born, independently of my later actions. At best, my saying "A zzz is a short sleep" made "zzz" mean a short sleep, and therefore "A zzz is a short sleep" mean that a short sleep is a short sleep. This is simply the standard semantic contribution of meaning to truth, just as for synthetic truths. The peculiarity of the case is all at the metasemantic level; the use of stipulative definitions as paradigms does not yield a *semantic* notion of analyticity. Making "zzz" mean a short sleep helps make "A zzz is a short sleep" true only because a short sleep is a short sleep. "A short sleep is a short sleep" is a logical truth, but we have still been given no reason to regard logical truths as somehow insubstantial. The use of stipulative definitions as paradigms of analyticity does not justify the idea that analytic truths are in any way insubstantial.

My stipulation may smooth my path from knowing the logical truth "A short sleep is a short sleep" to knowing the Frege-analytic truth "A zzz is a short sleep," but of course that does not explain how I know "A short sleep is a short sleep" in the first place.

The metaphysics and semantics of analytic truths are no substitute for their epistemology. If their epistemology is as distinctive as is often supposed, that is not the outcome of a corresponding distinctiveness in their metaphysics or semantics. It can only be captured by confronting their epistemology directly. We therefore turn to epistemological accounts of analyticity.

---

[24]   For helpful discussion see the essays in Part IV of Stalnaker (2003). He sometimes use the terminology of "descriptive semantics" and "foundational semantics" rather than "semantics" and "metasemantics" respectively.

4

Epistemological Conceptions of Analyticity

1

As observed in the previous chapter, metaphysical conceptions of analyticity do not themselves imply that linguistic or conceptual competence constrains one's attitudes to analytic sentences or thoughts. If our interest is in such constraints, we had best consider them directly. We can then assess what role, if any, they play in explaining the armchair methodology of philosophy.

If someone is unwilling to assent to the sentence "Every vixen is a female fox," the obvious hypothesis is that they do not understand it, perhaps because they do not understand the word "vixen." The central idea behind epistemological conceptions of analyticity is that, in such cases, failure to assent is not merely *good evidence* of failure to understand; it is *constitutive* of such failure. Of course, it is not by itself constitutive of failure to understand the word "vixen", since someone who understands that word may nevertheless not assent to the sentence, for example because they do not understand the word "fox"; a monolingual speaker of another language may understand "vixen" through the testimony of a bilingual without understanding any other word of English. Rather, failure to assent to the sentence can by itself only be constitutive of failure to understand the whole sentence An unqualified link from understanding to assent is this:

(UAl) Necessarily, whoever understands the sentence "Every vixen is a female fox" assents to it.

One proposal is to generalize UAl to define an epistemological notion of analyticity: a sentence *s* is analytic just in case, necessarily, whoever understands s assents to s. We could go further, by articulating an explicitly constitutive and not merely modal connection, but for present purposes the question is whether even this proposed necessary connection holds.

Three obvious glosses on UAl must be taken as read throughout. First, it concerns "Every vixen is a female fox" with its current meaning, for of course if the phonetically individuated sentence had meant something different, someone might easily have understood it and refused to assent. Second, assent is dispositional, for of course we are not actively assenting to any sentence whenever we understand it. Third, assent is a mental attitude, not a merely verbal one, for someone might easily understand "Every vixen is a female fox" while refusing to give it overt assent, for example because overt assent to a triviality looks uncool. We could speak of belief rather than assent, but the latter term sounds more natural in relation to inference rules, to which the notion of analyticity will be generalized.

A corresponding notion of analyticity can be defined for thoughts: a thought t is analytic just in case necessarily, whoever grasps t assents to t. If the thought *every vixen is a female fox* is analytic in this sense, then:

(UAt)   Necessarily, whoever grasps the thought *every vixen is a female fox* assents to it.

On the simplest view, thinking a thought with any attitude towards it suffices for grasping it. Friends of principles like UAt should beware of straying too far from that simple view, by claiming that "full grasp" of a thought requires much more than the ability to think it (Peacocke 1992: 29–33, Bealer 1998: 221–2). For such a defence of UAt risks trivializing it, by in effect writing the consequent into the antecedent by hand. At any rate, grasp of a thought should be a matter of normal conceptual competence, just as understanding of a sentence is a matter of normal linguistic competence. We shall return to these issues below.

Call UAl and UAt "understanding-assent links" for language and thought respectively. The picture is that grasping a thought consists of grasping its constituent concepts and the way in which they have been put together just as understanding a sentence consists of understanding its constituent expressions and syntax.

Assent is no metalinguistic or metaconceptual attitude: normally, in actively assenting to "Grass is green," one is saying or thinking that grass is green, not that the sentence "Grass is green" or the thought *grass is green* is true. However, thinking *grass is green* cannot be uncontentiously equated with thinking that grass is green. For thinking that grass is green presumably has as its object the proposition that grass is green. On a Russellian view, that proposition is made up of grass and greenness themselves, not of the concepts *grass* and *green*. Thus the thought *grass is green*, which is composed of concepts, must be distinguished from the proposition that grass is green. The thought is something like a mental vehicle for the proposition. Moreover, the same proposition can have different vehicles. For example, on this Russellian view, the proposition that Hesperus, if it exists, appears in the evening *is* the proposition that Phosphorus, if it exists, appears in the evening. The friend of conceptual connections is still likely to distinguish the concept *Hesperus* from the concept *Phosphorus*, and the thought *Hesperus, if it exists, appears in the evening* from the thought *Phosphorus, if it exists, appears in the evening*, on the grounds that the former embodies a conceptual connection while the latter does not. Thus understanding-assent links for thought must be articulated in terms of thoughts rather than propositions, in case there is a difference (for Fregeans, the proposition is the thought). Assenting to the thought *grass is green* is something like judging that grass is green under the guise of that thought. Similarly, assenting to the sentence "Grass is green," for someone who understands it, is something like believing that grass is green under the guise of that sentence. More generally, in a context in which the sentence *s* expresses the proposition *p*, assenting to *s*, for someone who understands it, is something like believing *p* under the guise of *s*. For you, assenting to "I am hungry" is something like believing that you are hungry under the guise of the sentence "I am hungry," since in your context that sentence expresses the proposition that you are hungry, not the proposition that I am hungry. Similarly, in a context in which the thought *t* expresses the proposition *p*, assenting to *t* is something like believing *p* under the guise of *t*.

The notion of an understanding-assent link can be generalized from individual sentences or thoughts to arguments at the level of language or thought. For example, if someone is unwilling to assent to the inference from "This is red and round" to "This is red," the obvious hypothesis is that they do not understand one of the sentences, most probably because they do not understand the word "and." For epistemological conceptions of analyticity, failure to assent in such cases is again not merely good evidence of failure to understand but constitutive of such failure. Gerhard Gentzen introduced the idea that some rules of his natural deduction systems of logic have definitional status. Following him, a tradition which includes Dag Prawitz, Michael Dummett, Per Martin-Löf, Christopher Peacocke, Robert Brandom, Paul Boghossian and many others has developed in various ways the conception of acceptance of such inference rules as playing a constitutive role in understanding the logical constants, and therefore in understanding the sentences in which they occur. For many of these thinkers, this is one step towards a quite general "inferentialist" account of meaning and understanding for expressions in terms of their conceptual roles.[1]

Understanding-assent links, or something like them, are also commonly thought to play a leading role in the understanding of theoretical terms in science: if you don't assent to some core sentences of electron theory, in which the word "electron" occurs, you don't understand the word, and therefore don't understand those sentences.

A natural project is therefore to try to explain the armchair methodology of philosophy as based on something like understanding-assent links: our sheer linguistic and conceptual competence mandates assent to some sentences or thoughts and inferences, which form the starting-point for philosophical inquiry. This chapter assesses the prospects for such a project.

The envisaged method cannot accurately be characterized as "reflection on our own concepts." For that description specifies the method only as "reflection," which applies to virtually all forms of philosophy. Moreover, it specifies the subject matter as "our own concepts," whereas the envisaged method involves reflection *with* our own concepts, and is therefore reflection *on* whatever our concepts

---

[1]   The case of deductive logic is a useful reminder that many short, trivial steps of no apparent philosophical significance can be chained together into a long, non-trivial argument of obvious philosophical significance. The short steps were not really philosophically insignificant after all: no apologies for concentrating on them here.

happen to refer to – in most cases, not concepts. The idea is rather to exploit whatever epistemic assets we have simply in virtue of our linguistic and conceptual competence. Suppose that a philosopher arrives at a theory about understanding, reference, and concepts by employing a battery of general armchair techniques that rely on far more than mere linguistic and conceptual competence. Say, for definiteness, that the theory gives a crude "best fit" account of reference, and entails that justice is whatever best fits our beliefs about justice. Pretend that the theory is true. Even so, it does not follow that "Justice is whatever best fits our beliefs about justice" is epistemologically analytic. For it was not reached on the basis just of linguistic and conceptual competence. Similarly, a definition of "conceptual truth" as "truth of the theory of concepts" is unhelpful for present purposes, since it merely raises the question how the truths of the theory of concepts are known ("metaconceptual truth" would be less misleading terminology).

In what follows, we will consider more rigorously what is epistemically available simply on the basis of linguistic and conceptual competence. To a first approximation, the answer is: nothing.

2

We start with a provisional sketch of some obstacles to extracting epistemological consequences from understanding-assent links and of some attempts to overcome them. Then we turn in Section 3 to the main argument: that understanding-assent links simply do not hold.

Our concern is knowledge or justification, not just belief or assent. On the most optimistic view, understanding-assent links generate understanding-knowledge links like these:

(UKl)   Necessarily, whoever understands the sentence "Every vixen is a female fox" knows "Every vixen is a female fox."

(UKt)   Necessarily, whoever grasps the thought *Every vixen is a female fox* knows *Every vixen is a female fox.*

Here, knowing "Every vixen is a female fox" amounts to knowing that every vixen is a female fox under the guise of the sentence "Every vixen is a female fox," and knowing *every vixen is a female fox* amounts to knowing that every vixen is a female fox under the guise of the thought *every vixen is a female fox*. Since knowing something entails assenting to it (we may assume), UKl and UKt entail UAl and UAt respectively. But since assenting to something does not entail knowing it, how are understanding-knowledge links to be extracted from understanding-assent links? UAl and UAt do not entail UKl and UKt in any obvious way.

An even more elementary problem arises. Knowledge is factive. Thus understanding-knowledge links entail corresponding understanding-truth links:

(UTl)   Necessarily, someone understands the sentence "Every vixen is a female fox" only if it is true.

(UTt)   Necessarily, someone grasps the thought *Every vixen is a female fox* only if it is true.

Thus if understanding-assent links somehow imply the corresponding understanding-knowledge links, *a fortiori* they also imply the understanding-truth links. Perhaps UTl and UTt hold because the sentence "Every vixen is a female fox" and the thought *every vixen is a female fox* are necessarily true. But in other cases the question of truth becomes more urgent.

Consider theoretical terms from discredited theories. If an understanding-assent link holds for "phlogiston," and understanding "phlogiston" necessitates assent to a core of phlogiston theory, how could it follow that someone understands sentences of phlogiston theory only if a core of it is true? Didn't proponents of phlogiston theory understand their own theory, despite its untruth? The example is not completely straightforward, for at least two reasons. First, it requires the untruth of the core of phlogiston theory in the understanding-assent links, not just of phlogiston theory as a whole. Some will treat a universal generalization of the form "All phlogiston is . . ." as vacuously true if phlogiston does not exist. Second, if there is nothing for "phlogiston" to refer to, one might alternatively treat sentences in which it occurs as failing to express propositions, in which case it is unclear that genuine understanding of phlogiston theory is possible. For the sake of the example, however, we may suppose that a core claim of phlogiston theory is of the form "Phlogiston plays role R," that a necessary condition of understanding the term "phlogiston" is assenting to that claim, and that the claim is untrue, because nothing plays role R. Suppositions of this kind will be questioned later.

We are sometimes advised to drop various ordinary terms, on the grounds that obsolete and false folk theories are built into them. Those who offer such advice may be assuming that understanding-truth links fail for some critical sentences of the folk theory in which those terms occur while the corresponding understanding-assent links hold (if so, they presumably do not count themselves as fully understanding the folk theory). For if we can understand the critical sentences of the folk theory without assenting to them, in what sense is the theory built into the key terms? For example, we could use them to assert the negations of central principles of the theory.[2]

Some understanding-assent links might even be to logically inconsistent sentences or thoughts. For example, the ordinary notion of truth is sometimes held to be incoherent, on the grounds that a necessary condition for understanding "true," and so for understanding sentences in which it occurs, is assent to a disquotational principle for "true" which the Liar paradox shows to be inconsistent. Tarski's description of natural languages as "inconsistent" in virtue of the paradox (1983a: 164–5) may involve such a view, for if we can understand "true" in English without assenting to the troublesome instances of the disquotational principle, what prevents us from using English consistently?[3] Similarly, Prior's connective "tonk" has mismatched introduction and elimination rules; the introduction rule licenses the inference from "P" to "P tonk Q," while the elimination rule licenses the inference from "P tonk Q" to "Q" (Prior 1960). By putting these rules together, one can derive any conclusion "Q" from any premise "P." If assent to instances of those rules is necessary for understanding them, because necessary for understanding "tonk," it hardly follows that the rules are truth-preserving (in the context of someone who understands "tonk"); they are so only if either every

---

[2] In effect, Horwich (1998: 131–53) allows understanding-belief links for which the understanding-truth links fail.
[3] See Eklund (2002) for a defense of the idea of inconsistent languages.

sentence or no sentence of the language is true (including atomic sentences, in which "tonk" does not occur).[4]

Such examples can be interpreted in diverse ways. Nevertheless, they show at least that to advance from understanding-assent links to understanding-truth links, let alone to understanding-knowledge links, is no trivial task.

One response to the examples is to stop trying to link understanding to knowledge and truth in this way, and try only to establish links to justification, conceived as non-factive. The hope would be to reach understanding-justification links like these:

(UJl)   Necessarily, whoever understands the sentence "Every vixen is a female fox" is justified in assenting to it.

(UJt)   Necessarily, whoever grasps the thought *Every vixen is a female fox* is justified in assenting to it.

But this retreat from knowledge and truth to justification does less than full justice to the examples. Imagine a dogmatic proponent of phlogiston theory, who continues to accept it long after the accumulating negative evidence has made this unjustifiable. Suppose that "phlogiston" does indeed provide a counterexample to the putative entailment from the understanding-assent link to the understanding-truth links. Thus although understanding a core of phlogiston theory necessitates assent to that core, because understanding the core necessitates understanding the term "phlogiston" and understanding "phlogiston" necessitates assent to the core of phlogiston theory, someone can understand the core despite its untruth. But if anyone can understand the core of phlogiston theory, its proponents can. Moreover, they do not stop understanding it when they unjustifiably refuse to take seriously the mounting negative evidence. Thus our last-ditch defender of phlogiston theory understands its core but is unjustified in assenting to it: the understanding-justification links fail too. For more blatantly defective concepts, the assent mandated by understanding-assent links may be unjustifiable from the start, as with "tonk." In

---

[4]   An example in which understanding is more clearly possible: Dummett (1973: 397, 454) claims that the rules for pejorative terms such as "Boche" suffer from a related kind of incoherence; Brandom (1994: 126; 2000: 69–70) and Boghossian (2003: 241–2), among others, have relied on his description of the practice of using such terms. I argue that it is mistaken in Williamson (2003a and 2008b), and suggest an alternative.

such cases too, an understanding-assent link which lacks the under-standing-truth link also lacks the understanding-justification link.

Could one defend versions of UJt and UJl by qualifying the justi-fication as *prima facie*? Consider someone who is introduced to a long list of mutually inconsistent theories of combustion, including phlogiston theory. Their content is explained without any assurance that there was ever any serious evidence for any of them. Irrationally, this person plumps for phlogiston theory and assents to its principles (unbeknownst to him, he is being influenced by happy associations from early childhood of the sound of the word "phlogiston"). By ordinary standards, he is linguistically competent with the sentences of phlogiston theory and grasps the corresponding thoughts, but he is not even *prima facie* justified in assenting to them, since he has no evidence, even by testimony, of their truth.

The examples do not motivate a retreat from knowledge and truth to non-factive justification. Rather, if they work, they show that some understanding-assent links have no positive epistemological upshot at all.

A different response to the examples is that they do not work: either the understanding-assent link fails or the understanding-truth link holds.

Since the relevant sentences or thoughts in the examples are clearly untrue, the understanding-truth link can hold in them only vacuously. That is, in such pathological cases, understanding is impossible: no meaning or concept is there to be grasped.[5] This response seems plausible for "tonk," for any serious attempt to apply the "tonk" rules would lead to almost immediate disaster. The envisaged response also makes the links from understanding to truth and any positive epistemic status hold vacuously. Where there is no understanding, we can hardly expect much of a positive epistemological upshot from a constraint on understanding. A trickier question is whether such pos-sibilities of an illusion of understanding have negative epistemological repercussions for cases of genuine understanding, since a skeptical doubt can arise for the subject in the latter cases too as to whether the understanding is not an illusion. If it could avoid such repercus-sions, this response might maintain a general entailment from under-standing-assent links to understanding-knowledge links and the rest.

---

[5]   See Peacocke (1992: 21) and Boghossian (2002).

However, the response is less plausible for "phlogiston" and some of the other examples than for "tonk," since communities used the rules for "phlogiston" and "true" for years before running into any trouble.[6] There does seem to be some sort of difference between understanding the word "phlogiston" and not understanding it. Although speakers cannot know the reference of a term if it has none, they can attain some sort of ordinary linguistic competence with it, and in that attenuated sense understand it. If such understanding of theoretical terms requires understanding-assent links in general, it is unclear why it should fail to do so for the term "phlogiston" in particular. Similarly, even if sentences with "phlogiston" fail to express propositions, because "phlogiston" fails to refer, there is still an attenuated sense in which some speakers have the empty concept *phlogiston*, an empty mental vehicle, while others do not. If such possession of theoretical concepts requires understanding-assent links in general, it is unclear why it should fail to do so for the concept *phlogiston* in particular.

Alternatively, someone might maintain that the understanding-assent links in these examples fail, but that understanding-assent links for other sentences or thoughts hold; the examples involve genuine understanding. On this view, understanding-assent links may still be held to entail the corresponding understanding-knowledge links. It claims that the examples picked the wrong candidates for understanding-assent links. Either such links hold only for non-defective words or concepts or for those defective cases they hold only for cautiously circumscribed sentences or thoughts. For instance, rather than the core of phlogiston theory itself, we might have the conditional "If phlogiston exists then . . .," with that core filling in the dots. Arguably, however, since "phlogiston" fails to refer, that conditional too fails to express a proposition, so even this more cautious sentence is not true, although it is also not false. A more general objection is that this response treats our practices as though they are bound to have anticipated from the start all problems that could subsequently arise for them. Presumably, if understanding-assent links hold, they do so because they are built into the linguistic or conceptual practices at issue. Consider, for instance, the

---

[6]   Boghossian (2003: 242–3), which represents a change of view from Boghossian (2002).

hypothesis that understanding "true" necessitates assent to a disquotational principle carefully and ingeniously modified to avoid all the semantic paradoxes. Since they scarcely ever arise in ordinary life, why was our ordinary practice with the word "true" tailored in advance to avoid them? Indeed, the puzzlement they cause suggests quite the opposite. That such precautions are part of every possible linguistic or conceptual practice is even less likely. If understanding-assent links hold for some other reason than that they are built into the linguistic or conceptual practices at issue, what is that other reason? Even if one moderates the approach by substituting understanding-justification links for understanding-knowledge links, a version of the objection still applies. If our linguistic or conceptual practices can make assent to inference rules a precondition of understanding, nothing seems to stop bad practices from requiring assent to rules, like those for "tonk," that generate consequences not involving the original word or concept at issue. Such consequences may include arbitrary pernicious dogmas (such as racist ones) for which no justification is provided. More cautious fallbacks need not even implicitly have been provided; the practice simply breaks down once the dogma is abandoned. So this alternative way of maintaining a general entailment from understanding-assent links to understanding-justification links, let alone understanding-knowledge links, is unpromising. The objections tell equally against the putative understanding-knowledge or understanding-justification links, even if no attempt is made to *derive* them from understanding-assent links.

A more moderate response concedes that defective practices give rise to understanding-assent links without corresponding links to truth or any positive epistemological status, but maintains that understanding-assent links for non-defective practices do yield such links. For instance, one might try to tell a story on which understanding-assent links for non-defective practices constrain the reference of the relevant words or concepts so that the sentences or thoughts in the links come out true (for some defective practices, this constraint cannot be met). Under such conditions, understanding-assent links generate understanding-truth links. Thus assent to those sentences or thoughts (while understanding or grasping them) is, completely reliably, assent to truths. One might hope to squeeze understanding-knowledge links out of such reliability considerations, perhaps when enhanced by an argument that the reliability is not completely hidden from the subject. Clearly, much work would be needed to vindicate such a programme.[7]

A lazy alternative simply postulates understanding-knowledge or understanding-justification links for non-defective practices without attempting to derive them from understanding-assent links. But this has little explanatory value. I understand "Every vixen is a female fox," and it has some positive epistemic status for me. How does it get that status? How do I know "Every vixen is a female fox"? Why am I justified in assenting to it? The lazy theorist may try to dismiss the question, saying that it is simply part of our linguistic practice that "Every vixen is a female fox" has that positive epistemic status for whoever understands it. But the examples of defective practices show that it is not simply up to linguistic practices to distribute positive epistemic status as they please. That the practice is to treat a given sentence as having some positive epistemic status for competent speakers of the language does not imply that it really has that epistemic status for them. Their belief may be untrue and unjustified, however much the practice deems otherwise. Thus the only plausible way to make the relevant practice guarantee the putative link from understanding to the positive epistemic status is by making absence of the epistemic status constitute absence of understanding, just as absence of assent was supposed to do. On this account, whoever does not know "Every vixen is a female fox" or is not justified in assenting to it *thereby* fails to understand it. But this direction of explanation does not trivialize the positive epistemic status, to which it assigns the role of constituter, not constituted. Thus the lazy theorist cannot simply dismiss the question: how does "Every vixen is a female fox" gets its positive epistemic for whoever understands it? Positing direct links from understanding to knowledge or justification does not remove the need for substantive epistemology here. Indeed, it makes the armchair nature of understanding problematic. Even when the relevant sentence or thought has the positive epistemic status at issue, the reason is not simply that the linguistic or conceptual practice deems it to be so – which of course is not to say that the practice is

---

[7]   The treatment of the issue in Boghossian (2003) is of this general kind. For detailed criticism see Williamson (2003a).

irrelevant to its epistemic status. In any case, if understanding-assent links fail, as is argued below, then *a fortiori* so do understanding-knowledge links, and understanding-justification links turn out to fail for similar reasons.

Let us consider understanding-assent links in more depth. If they hold, with or without normative consequences, they should cast some light on the actual practice of philosophy. For if an understanding-assent link holds for a philosophically significant sentence, and we do understand it, then we do assent to it, whether or not we are justified in doing so. But the next sections argue that understanding-assent links fail even for paradigms of "analyticity." The main focus will be on the simplest cases, since those are the ones for which understanding-assent links have the best chance: if they fail there, they fail everywhere. We will start by examining unqualified understanding-assent links, beginning at the level of language. They fail. We then consider various ways of loosening them.

3

In their classic response to Quine's critique of the analytic-synthetic distinction, Grice and Strawson give the sentence "My neighbor's three-year-old child is an adult" as an example of a sentence that we could not understand someone using with its ordinary literal meaning to make an assertion (1956: 150–1). That suggests an understanding-assent link for the sentence "No three-year-old child is an adult": necessarily, whoever understands it assents to it. But the link fails. Someone may believe that normal human beings attain physical and psychological maturity at the age of three, explaining away all the evidence to the contrary by *ad hoc* hypotheses or conspiracy theories (many three-year-olds pretend to be eighteen-year-olds in order to vote, the abnormally polluted local water slows development, and so on). However foolish those beliefs, they do not constitute linguistic incompetence. Friends of analyticity will reply that the example was badly chosen. It is therefore best to start with the most elementary examples possible.

Here is an elementary logical truth:

(1)   Every vixen is a vixen.

Few quantified logical truths are simpler than (1), in either syntactic complexity or the number of steps needed to derive them in a standard system of natural deduction rules.[8]

One may be tempted to endorse understanding-assent links for (1):

(UAl')   Necessarily, whoever understands the sentence "Every vixen is a vixen" assents to it.

(UAt')   Necessarily, whoever grasps the thought *every vixen is a vixen* assents to it.

Are UAl' and UAt' true? Consider two native speakers of English, Peter and Stephen.

Peter's first reaction to (1) is that it seems to presuppose:

(2)   There is at least one vixen.

On reflection, Peter comes to the considered view that the presupposition is a logical entailment. He regards the truth of "There is at least one F" as a necessary condition for the truth of "Every F is a G" quite generally, and the falsity of "There is at least one F" as a sufficient condition for the falsity of "Every F is a G"; he takes universal quantification to be existentially committing. More formally, he holds that "Every F is a G" is true if and only if (i) there is a value of the variable "x" for which "x is an F" is true and (ii) there is no value of the variable "x" for which "x is an F" is true while "x is a G" is not, and that "Every F is a G" is false if and only if it is not true. Of course, Peter does not always think in such theoretical, metalinguistic terms, but he resorts to them in rationalizing and defending his

---

[8] Parenthetical numerals such as "(1)" are taken throughout to refer to sentences rather than to thoughts. On a standard formalization of (1) as $\forall x(Vx \rightarrow Vx)$, one proves it by starting from an instance of the rule of assumption, $Vx \vdash Vx$, applying the standard introduction rule for $\rightarrow$, conditional proof, to discharge the premise, giving $\vdash Vx \rightarrow Vx$, followed by the standard introduction rule for $\forall$, universal generalization, to reach $\vdash \forall x(Vx \rightarrow Vx)$ (no logical truth can be derived by the usual quantifier and structural rules alone, since none of them permits the discharge of all assumptions). A formalization of (1) closer to the English original uses a binary quantifier: $\vdash (EVERYx(Vx; Vx))$ is derivable from $Vx \vdash Vx$ in a single step by an appropriate introduction rule for **EVERY**.

pattern of assent and dissent to individual sentences. Peter also has the weird belief that (2) is false. For he spends far too much time surfing the Internet, and once came across a site devoted to propagating the view that there are no foxes, and therefore no vixens, and never have been: all the apparent evidence to the contrary has been planted by MI6, which even organizes widespread fox-hallucinations, so that people will protest about fox-hunting rather than the war in Iraq. Being a sucker for conspiracy theories, Peter accepted this one. Since he denies (2) and regards it as a logical consequence of (1), he also denies (1), and so does not assent to it.[9]

Stephen has no time for Peter's pet theories. What worries him is vagueness. He believes that borderline cases for vague terms constitute truth-value gaps. Like many truth-value gap theorists (such as Soames (1999)), he generalizes classical two-valued semantics by treating the gap as a third value ("indefinite") and using Kleene's three-valued "strong tables" (1952: 334), along the lines explained in Chapter 2. On Stephen's view, for "Every F is a G" to be true is for the conditional "x is an F $\rightarrow$ x is a G" to be true for every value of the variable "x"; for "Every F is a G" to be false is for "x is an F $\rightarrow$ x is a G" to be false for some value of "x." On his semantics, for a conditional sentence with "$\rightarrow$" to be true is for either its antecedent to be false or its consequent to be true, and for it to be false is for its antecedent to be true and its consequent false. Stephen also believes that some clearly female evolutionary ancestors of foxes are borderline cases for "fox" and therefore for "vixen." Consequently, for such an animal as the value of "x," "x is a vixen" is neither true nor false, so the conditional "x is a vixen $\rightarrow$ x is a vixen" is also neither true nor false, by the strong Kleene table for $\rightarrow$. Hence "Every vixen is a vixen" is not true; it is also not false, because the conditional is not false for any value of "x." Thus Stephen treats (1) as a truth-value gap. Of course, his initial reaction when presented with (1) is not to go through this explicit metalinguistic reasoning; he just says "What

---

[9]   Alternatively, one can imagine that Peter thinks that foxes were only recently hunted to extinction, but that his presentist conception of time implies that (2) is true only if there is now at least one vixen. Yet another alternative is that Peter is a metaphysician who denies (2) on the grounds that putative macroscopic objects such as foxes do not exist, for if they did they would have vague boundaries, which are metaphysically impossible (compare Horgan (1998)).

about borderline cases?" But his refusal to assent to (1) as true is firm.[10]

We may assume that Peter and Stephen are wrong about (1), at least on its standard reading: it is in fact a logical truth. It is true however we interpret its only non-logical syntactically atomic constituent, "vixen," given classical logic and two-valued semantics. If not, we can change the example, describing new characters who are deviant with respect to some sentence that really is an elementary logical truth. Peter and Stephen do not assent to (1). Thus, according to UAI', Peter and Stephen do not understand (1) (with its standard English meaning). If so, they presumably misunderstand at least one of its constituent words or modes of combination. Is that the impression one would have in conversing with them?

Both Peter and Stephen treat "vixen" as synonymous with "female fox." Stephen's popular but mistaken theory of vagueness does not prevent him from understanding "vixen," "female," "fox" or their mode of combination. Even Peter's conspiracy theory, however silly, involves no semantic deviation, just as religious fanatics who assert that there were never any dinosaurs do exactly that: they use the words "There were never any dinosaurs" to assert that there were never any dinosaurs, thereby expressing their belief that there were never any dinosaurs. Their problem is not that they misunderstand the word "dinosaur," but that they have silly beliefs about evolution. Peter, like Stephen, understands the word "vixen."

The best candidate for a word or mode of composition in (1) that Peter and Stephen misunderstand is "every." Is it a good enough candidate? Peter's not uncommon conception of the existential commitments of universal quantification makes little difference in practice, for when sentences of the form "Every F is a G" occur in conversation, "There is at least one F" tends to be common ground among the participants anyway. It is (usually, not always) a pragmatic presupposition in the sense of Stalnaker (1999). Pragmatically, Peter adjusts his conversation to a society that obstinately retains its belief in the existence of foxes much as members of many other small

---

[10]   Note that while Peter assents to the conditional "If there are vixens, then every vixen is a vixen," Stephen does not, because it has a true antecedent and an indefinite consequent, and is therefore itself indefinite on the Kleene semantics. Given the qualifications in Boghossian (2003), this makes Stephen more problematic than Peter for Boghossian's program.

sects with unpopular beliefs have learned to adjust to an unenlightened world. Stephen's deviation is less localized than Peter's, because his Kleene-inspired semantics turns many universal generalizations with empirical predicates into truth-value gaps. In practice, however, he often manages to ignore the problem by focusing on a small domain of contextually relevant objects among which there are no borderline cases for the noun or complex phrase which complements "every." Occasionally he cannot avoid the problem and sounds pedantic, as many academics too, but that hardly constitutes a failure to understand the words at issue. When Peter and Stephen are challenged on their logical deviations, they defend themselves fluently. In fact, both have published widely read articles on the issues in leading refereed journals of philosophy, in English. They seem like most philosophers, thoroughly competent in their native language, a bit odd in some of their views.

Someone might insist that Peter and Stephen appear to be using the word "every" in its standard sense because they are really using it in senses very similar to, but not exactly the same as, the standard one. Indeed, it may be argued, their non-standard senses were explained above, since in each case a truth-conditional semantics for the relevant fragment of English was sketched on which (1) is not true, whereas by hypothesis (1) is true on the standard semantics of English. But matters are not so simple. Peter and Stephen are emphatic that they intend their words to be understood as words of our common language, with their standard English senses. They are not making unilateral declarations of linguistic independence. They use "every" and the other words in (1) as words of the public language. Each of them believes that his semantic theory is correct for English as spoken by others, not just by himself, and that if it turned out to be (heaven forbid!) incorrect for English as spoken by others, it would equally turn out to be incorrect for English as spoken by himself. Giving an incorrect theory of the meaning of a word is not the same as using the word with an idiosyncratic sense – linguists who work on the semantics of natural languages often do the former without doing the latter. Peter and Stephen's semantic beliefs about their own uses of "every" may be false, even if they sometimes rely on those beliefs in conscious processes of truth-evaluation. Indeed, we may assume that Peter and Stephen do not regard the elaborate articulations of truth-conditions and falsity-conditions for "Every F is a G" above as

capturing the way in which they or other English speakers conceptual-
ize the meaning of "every," which they regard as a semantically
unstructured determiner for which a homophonic statement of
meaning would be more faithful: even for us "Every F is a G" is not
strictly synonymous with "There is no F that is not a G," since the
former does not contain negation. For Peter and Stephen, the more
elaborate articulations are simply convenient records of important
logical facts about "every." Only in tricky cases do they resort to their
non-standard semantic theories in evaluating non-metalinguistic
claims such as (1) expresses. Their non-metalinguistic unorthodoxy
as to when every F is a G is not ultimately derived by semantic descent
from metalinguistic unorthodoxy as to when "Every F is a G" is true;
rather, their metalinguistic unorthodoxy is ultimately derived by
semantic ascent from their non-metalinguistic unorthodoxy.

Of course, the intention to use words with their normal public
meanings does not guarantee success: it can fail in cases of sufficiently
gross and extensive error. But that does not suggest that the intention
is *irrelevant* to whether someone is using the words with those meanings. The intention is normally successful, in the absence of special
defeating circumstances, just as the intention to use a proper name
with the same reference as it has in the rest of the community is normally successful. The question is whether Peter and Stephen's eccentricities are sufficiently gross and extensive to constitute defeating
circumstances. By ordinary standards, they are not. Although they
look gross enough when seen in isolation, they are compensated for
by Peter and Stephen's normality in other respects.

Peter and Stephen are native speakers who learned English in the
normal way. They acquired their non-standard views as adults. At
least before that, nothing in their use of English suggested semantic
deviation. Surely they understood (1) and its constituent words and
modes of construction with their ordinary meanings then. But the
process by which they acquired their eccentricities did not involve
forgetting their previous semantic understanding. For example, on
their present understanding of (1), they have no difficulty in remembering why they used to assent to it. They were young and foolish
then, with a tendency to accept claims on the basis of insufficient
reflection. By ordinary standards, Peter and Stephen understand (1)
perfectly well. Although their rejection of (1) might on first acquaintance give an observer a defeasible reason to deny that they under-

stood it, any such reason is defeated by closer observation of them. They genuinely doubt that every vixen is a vixen. Nor are Peter and Stephen marginal cases of understanding: their linguistic competence is far more secure than that of young children or native speakers of other languages who are in the process of learning English. They joined the club of "every"-users; since they haven't resigned or been expelled, they are still members.

If some participants in a debate have an imperfect linguistic understanding of one of the key words with which it is conducted, they need to have its meaning explained to them before the debate can properly continue. But to stop our logical debate with Peter and Stephen in order to explain to them what the word "every" means in English would be irrelevant and gratuitously patronizing. We cannot understand them better if we translate their word "every" by some non-homophonic expression, or treat it as untranslatable. The understanding they lack is logical, is not semantic. Their attitudes to (1) manifest only some deviant patterns of belief. Since there clearly could have been, and perhaps are, people such as Peter and Stephen, we have counterexamples to UAl'.

The argument that Peter and Stephen mean what we mean by their words exemplifies two interlocking themes: Quine's epistemological holism, on which the epistemological status of a belief constitutively depends on its position in the believer's whole system of beliefs, and Putnam and Burge's semantic externalism (discussed in more detail below), on which the content of a belief constitutively depends on the believer's position in a society of believers. Epistemological holism explains how unorthodoxy on one point can be compensated for by orthodoxy on many others, so that overall Peter and Stephen's usage of the key terms is not beyond the pale of social acceptability; since they remain participants in the relevant linguistic practice, semantic externalism then explains how they can still use the terms with their normal public senses. But neither epistemological holism nor semantic externalism figured as *premises* of the argument. Rather, the argument appealed to features of the relevant systems of belief that make epistemological holism plausible, and to features of our ascription of beliefs that make semantic externalism plausible.

To try to save UAl' by restricting it to rational agents would be pointless. By ordinary standards, Peter and Stephen are rational agents. Although they fall short of some high standards of rationality, so do most humans. Understanding-assent links that do not apply to most humans would be of limited epistemological interest. The picture was that those who appear to reject analytic sentences can be excluded from the discussion because they lack the linguistic competence to engage in it; but we cannot exclude humans who reject such sentences on those grounds if the connection between rejecting them and lacking competence holds only for super-humans, not for humans.

The problem for UAI' is clearly not specific to sentences of the form "Every F is an F" Let us see how it generalizes to rules of inference.

It is often claimed that assent to arguments by modus ponens of the form "If A then B; A; therefore B" is a precondition for understanding the word "if" (Boghossian 2003, for instance). Indeed, this is a standard example in the literature. However, Vann McGee, a distinguished logician, has published purported counterexamples to modus ponens for the indicative conditional in English. Here is one of them; the others are similar:

> Opinion polls taken just before the 1980 election showed the Republican Ronald Reagan decisively ahead of the Democrat Jimmy Carter, with the other Republican in the race, John Anderson, a distant third. Those apprised of the poll results believed, with good reason:
>   If a Republican wins the election, then if it's not Reagan who wins it will be Anderson.
>   A Republican will win the race.
> Yet they did not have reason to believe:
>   If it's not Reagan who wins, it will be Anderson. (McGee 1985: 462)

With reasonable confidence, they combined assent to both premises of an argument by modus ponens with dissent from the conclusion, so they rejected the argument.[11] If McGee's examples are counterexamples to modus ponens, they are also counterexamples to the claim that assent to instances of modus ponens is necessary for understanding "if." But let us assume, with the majority, that modus ponens is

[11]   The formulation in the text is intended to distinguish the case from examples in which speakers' confidence in each premise of a modus ponens argument is just above a probabilistic threshold which their confidence in the conclusion is just below. In McGee's case, speakers are sufficiently confident of the conjunction of the two premises.

valid, so McGee's examples are not in fact counterexamples.[12] Perhaps the conclusion was true, because Reagan won; although the poll was not misleading, our usual methods for evaluating conditionals lead us astray in this case. A currently popular objection to the examples is that they depend on an illicit shift of context, perhaps in the treatment of "If it's not Reagan who wins, it will be Anderson" between the consequent of the first premise and the conclusion.[13] But even if some such confusion *causes* the pattern of assent and dissent to the premises and conclusion, the *effect* is that McGee and his envisaged speakers end up accepting the premises and rejecting the conclusion in a single context, when they look back on all three sentences.[14] They genuinely reject a genuine instance of modus ponens.[15] Such reactions do not manifest the superimposition of a perverse semantic or logical theory on native speaker intuitions; they flow from native speaker intuitions themselves in a fairly natural way, despite being mistaken.

[12]   For early critical reactions to McGee's examples see Sinnott-Armstrong, Moor, and Fogelin (1986), Lowe (1987) and Over (1987). But some authors have accepted the examples (Lycan 2001: 66–7).

[13]   Recent examples of context-shifting charges include Nolan (2003: 264) and Gauker (2005: 86).

[14]   Contrast McGee's example with instances of modus ponens such as "I know that I have hands; if I know that I have hands then I know that I'm not a brain in a vat; therefore, I know that I'm not a brain in a vat." Many people accept the premises and reject the conclusion when they encounter them in that order. However, once they have rejected the conclusion, they are typically inclined to retract their acceptance of the first premise, not out of concern for modus ponens but because it no longer looks plausible to them in its own right, in the new context that arises once the skeptical possibility becomes relevant. For contextualists in epistemology, this is a paradigm case of context-shifting (Stine (1976), Cohen (1988), DeRose (1995), Lewis (1996); see Hawthorne (2004), Stanley (2005) and Williamson (2005b) for some critical discussion and more references). By contrast, the premises of McGee's argument continue to look plausible to those who reject the conclusion.

[15]   Edgington (2001: 408) suggests that McGee's example is not a genuine instance of modus ponens on the grounds that the first premise has a misleading surface form; on her view, conditionals do not express propositions, so what look like conditionals with conditional antecedents or consequents must be reinterpreted. It is doubtful that such a view is consistent with a systematic account of the structure of English sentences, which permits a wide variety of such embeddings, for example, "If it is the case that if it's not Reagan who wins it will be Anderson, then a Republican will win the race."

Does McGee not understand the English word "if"? In conversation, he appears to understand it perfectly well. By ordinary standards, he *does* understand it. Before he had theoretical doubts about modus ponens, he understood the word "if" if anyone has ever understood it. Surely his theoretical doubts did not make him cease to remember what it means. Moreover, his doubts derive from taking at face value a natural pattern of native speaker reactions to an ingeniously chosen case. If he counts as not understanding "if," so do millions of other native speakers of English.

Could we invoke the division of linguistic labor (Putnam 1975: 228), and say that making any given inference by modus ponens is a precondition only for *full* understanding of "if," the kind of understanding characteristic of the expert rather than the layman? The trouble is that McGee *is* an expert on conditionals. He publishes on them in the best journals. He does not defer in his use of "if" to any higher authorities. He may lack some theoretical understanding of conditionals, just as experts on neutrinos may lack some theoretical understanding of neutrinos, but none of that amounts to any lack of linguistic competence with "if" or "neutrino" at all.

Are only some arguments by modus ponens such that assent to them is a precondition for understanding "if"? Presumably, McGee will accept most arguments by modus ponens. However, any particular such argument might be rejected by another expert on conditionals, on the basis of a subtle theoretical argument. By hypothesis, the expert would be mistaken, but making a subtle theoretical error does not constitute linguistic incompetence.

The problem is not just the vagueness of natural languages. Similar problems arise for carefully constructed formal languages. Consider modus ponens for the material conditional →, explained by the standard truth-table. It is equivalent to disjunctive syllogism: from **A** and ¬**A** ∨ **B** derive **B**. Technically competent relevance logicians and dialetheists such as Graham Priest reject disjunctive syllogism (Priest 1995: 5). According to him, the best account of paradoxes such as the Liar is that in special circumstances a sentence can be both true and false; one can be on different lines of the truth-table simultaneously. When **A** is true and false while **B** is merely false, the premises of disjunctive syllogism are true (for **A** is true; since **A** is also false, ¬**A** is true, so ¬**A** ∨ **B** is true), while its conclusion is straightforwardly false. Whatever the errors underlying the rejection of modus ponens for →, they do not arise from a lack of linguistic competence with → on the part of relevance logicians and dialetheists.

As a final example, consider the natural deduction rules for conjunction. Instances of the introduction rule are arguments of the form "A; B; therefore A and B." Instances of the elimination rule are arguments of the converse forms "A and B; therefore A" and "A and B; therefore B." These are just about the simplest rules for a non-trivial binary connective. One must formulate what acceptance of the introduction rule requires with particular care, since the probability of a conjunction may be less than the probability of either conjunct. Iterations of the introduction rule yield the Lottery and Preface paradoxes. Given a lottery known to have at most a million tickets and only one winner, each premise of the form "Ticket i will lose" is overwhelmingly probable, even though their conjunction is known to be false. The author of a book may endorse each individual statement in it, yet admit in the preface that, despite all her efforts, it is bound to contain errors, and on those grounds reject the conjunction of the individual premises. Of course, these paradoxes do not show that the introduction rule fails to preserve truth, although they might be used as grounds for rejecting the rule by a theorist who (mistakenly) used a probabilistic criterion for acceptance. The elimination rule does not suffer from these problems, since the probability of a conjunction is never higher than the probability of any given conjunct.

Let us therefore concentrate on the elimination rule for conjunction, as having the best chance of being non-discretionary for competent speakers.[16] Consider Simon, whose view of vagueness resembles Stephen's, except that Simon's practice conforms to a semantics with Kleene's weak three-valued tables rather than his strong ones. On these tables, a conjunction is indefinite (neither true nor false) if at least one conjunct is, irrespective of the value of the other conjunct; the same principle is applied to disjunction, the material conditional and negation (Kleene 1952: 334). Furthermore, Simon regards both

---

[16] In discussion, Boghossian suggested conjunction elimination as a fallback example of a non-discretionary rule if modus ponens fails. Peacocke writes of the possession-condition for the concept of conjunction, "On any theory, this possession-condition will entail that thinkers must find the transition from A and B to A compelling, and must do so without relying on any background information" (2004: 172).

truth and indefiniteness as designated (acceptable) semantic values for an assertion: what matters is to avoid falsity. In a borderline case, some speakers say "Jack is bald," others with equal vehemence say "Jack is not bald"; they may persist even when they recognize that the dispute cannot be resolved. According to Simon, both assertions are acceptable. In answer to the question "Is Jack bald?," even the answer "He is and he isn't" is acceptable. Although Simon does not assign the value "T" to "Jack is bald," that metalinguistic reservation is consistent with assenting to the sentence, that is, with believing that Jack is bald under the guise of that very sentence (similarly, supervaluationists about vagueness reject the disquotational inference from " 'Jack is bald' is not true" to "Jack is not bald"). The joint implication of Simon's principles is that any complex sentence formed by the application of the specified operators to simpler sentences, at least one of which is borderline, has a designated value – of course, on Simon's view, most such sentences should not be uttered, on the pragmatic grounds that they violate the conversational maxim of relevance (Grice 1989: 27). Suppose that "A" is simply false while "B" is borderline. Consequently, for Simon, "B" is indefinite, so "A and B" is also indefinite. Thus the corresponding instance of conjunction elimination – "A and B; therefore A" – has a designated premise and an undesignated conclusion. On these grounds, Simon rejects the conclusion of that instance while accepting its premise (although he points out that asserting the premise would be pragmatically misleading in most contexts, since "B" is irrelevant to its status). In other cases, he treats the premise merely as a supposition, but still rejects the deduction from it to the conclusion. Once again, this need not reflect incompetence with the English language. Conjunction elimination is no exception to the general pattern. Arguably, violations of conjunction elimination are actual, not just possible, in the Conjunction Fallacy, a much-studied, widespread and robust psychological phenomenon in which subjects assign a higher probability to a conjunction than to one of its conjuncts.[17]

---

[17]   The seminal paper is Tversky and Kahneman (1983). See also Kahneman and Frederick (2002), Sides, Osherson, Bonini, and Viale (2002) and Jönsson and Hampton (2006).We can also imagine speakers who reject instances of conjunction elimination through muddling truth and conversational appropriateness. "Did she take the money and give it back? Yes. Did she take the money? No, she took-the-money-and-gave-it-back."

No given argument or statement is immune from rejection by a linguistically competent speaker. Quine's epistemological holism in "Two Dogmas" undermines his notorious later claim about the deviant logician's predicament: "when he tries to deny the doctrine he only changes the subject" (1970: 81).

Understanding words in a natural language has much to do with the ability to use them in ways that facilitate smooth and fruitful interaction with other members of the community. That ability can be realized in indefinitely various forms. Speakers can compensate for their deviance on one point by their orthodoxy on others, their ability to predict the reactions of non-deviant speakers, their willingness in the long run to have their utterances evaluated by public standards. As we have seen, such compensation is often possible when the deviance results from localized interference in the normal practice of using a word by high-level theoretical concerns. Thus there is no litmus test for understanding. Whatever local test is proposed, someone could fail it and still do well enough elsewhere with the word to count as understanding it. Could an inferentialist reply that such objections trade on a loose everyday sense of "understanding" that must be replaced by something more precise for theoretical purposes? It is far from clear that a stricter sense would do a better job. The relevant features of the ordinary conception of understanding are not mere unreflective sloppiness. Rather, they are an appropriate response to an important constraint on a theory of linguistic meanings: that there is little point in talking about them unless they can be shared across significant differences in belief, between different individuals at the same time or the same individual at different times. They can survive factual learning and factual disagreement. Although inferentialist accounts respect the letter of that constraint, they violate its underlying spirit, by setting inflexible limits to the scope for genuine disagreement. The more holistic ordinary notion of understanding permits localized disagreement at virtually any point.

Cases of logical deviance hint at ways in which the failure of individualist accounts of meaning go deeper than the immediate lessons of the original anti-individualist arguments of Putnam (1975) and Burge (1979). Their cases are often analyzed in terms of a distinction between experts with full understanding and lay-people with partial understanding who defer to the experts, in virtue of which one may correctly ascribe to them attitudes to the contents that experts determine.[18] Such asymmetries are postulated by Putnam's Hypothesis of the Universality of the Division of Linguistic Labor:

> Every linguistic community . . . possesses at least some terms whose associated "criteria" are known only to a subset of the speakers who acquire the terms, and whose use by the other speakers depends upon a structured cooperation between them and the speakers in the relevant subsets. (Putnam 1975: 228)

But, as we have seen, experts themselves can make deviant applications of words as a result of theoretical errors and still count as fully understanding their words. Although they defer to nobody on the matters at issue, they are more than adequately integrated members of the speech community with respect to those very words. Their assignments of meaning to those words are not parasitic on the assignments that more privileged individuals make. Rather, each individual uses words as words of a public language; their meanings are constitutively determined not individually but socially, through the spectrum of linguistic activity across the community as a whole. The social determination of meaning requires nothing like an exact match in use between different individuals; it requires only enough connection in use between them to form a social practice. Full participation in that practice constitutes full understanding. That is why there is no litmus test for understanding.[19]

---

[18]   An example is Peacocke's discussion of deference-dependent propositional attitude ascriptions (1992: 29–33). Burge (1986) extends his earlier arguments in ways related to the arguments of this chapter, in his account of the understanding of words such as "sofa," and argues for such a deeper lesson. Goldberg (2000) replies on behalf of Burge to Bach (1988) and Elugardo (1993).

[19]   For a related conclusion concerning lexical competence in a shared language see Marconi (1997: 56). For the relevance of the model of full understanding as full induction into a practice to the theory of vagueness see Williamson (1994a: 211–12). It is not implied that no similar issue could arise for understanding on the part of a single isolated individual, for such an individual's meanings and concepts are constitutively determined, at least in part, by their dispositions over a range of counterfactual circumstances; those dispositions and their bearings may be hard to survey from the limited standpoint of the actual circumstances.

4

Peter and Stephen understand (1) without assenting to it; UAI' fails. Someone sympathetic to the spirit of understanding-assent links might concede that much while arguing that its upshot is only a superficial loosening of those links. If the deviance results only from erroneous theorizing that overlays an ordinary understanding of the terms, may not the links still hold at the underlying level?

However, we have already seen reason to doubt that deviance can only arise from theorizing extrinsic to speakers' ordinary understanding of the words. Vann McGee's examples exert an intuitive pull on native speakers, irrespective of and even contrary to their theoretical predilections. We can also imagine untheoretical native speakers whose unreflective patterns of assent and dissent to non-metalinguistic sentences are those which Peter, Stephen, and Simon respectively recommend, although they lack the reflective capacity to rationalize those patterns by appeal to formal semantic theories. They too would be able to fit in well enough with the rest of the linguistic community, to engage smoothly in useful communication and adjust to their differences with other speakers in order not to attract too much attention. They too would use their words as words of the public language, rather than declaring unilateral linguistic independence. How do we know that there are not in fact many such native speakers of English around us? Once we concede that Peter, Stephen, and Simon are competent speakers, we can hardly refuse the same classification to other speakers merely on grounds of their unacquaintance with formal semantics.

What might be claimed, in the case of both theoretical and untheoretical deviant native speakers, is that the deviance is some kind of performance error which leaves their underlying competence intact: at some basic level they have the required dispositions, which they fail to manifest as a result of interfering factors, such as computational limitations, conflicting dispositions to take cheap and dirty intellectual short-cuts, and so on. On this view, Peter and Stephen still have a disposition to assent to (1), masked by their later theorizing; they use "every" and other words and modes of construction with the same senses as the rest of us because they have the same underlying inferential dispositions as the rest of us.[20] At some deep level, they have a disposition to accept (1) as true. That disposition is prevented from manifesting itself by conscious reflection at an overlying level of theory-construction, just as someone's pet views about grammar might interfere with their performance in speech while having no effect on the syntactic competence which they possess in virtue of their underlying linguistic competence. For untheoretical speakers, the interfering factors are unconscious, but the effect is similar. UAl' and UAt' might therefore be watered down as follows:

(UDAl')   Necessarily, whoever understands the sentence "Every vixen is a vixen" has a disposition to assent to it.

(UDAt')   Necessarily, whoever grasps the thought *every vixen is a vixen* has a disposition to assent to it.

Having a disposition to assent does not entail assenting. Thus UDAl' and UDAt' are consistent with the denials of UAl' and UAt'. Do Peter and Stephen have the disposition to assent to (1) despite happening not to assent to it? If understanding is linked to such dispositions to assent in these cases, one might even try to use that to explain how it is also linked to dispositions to know, along lines similar to those sketched in Section 2. But are UDAl' and UDAt' true?

There are two salient ways to fill out the dispositional story: at the *personal level* or the *sub-personal level*. At the personal level, the postulated dispositions require something like counterfactual conditionals to the effect that sufficient conscious reflection and exposure to further arguments would bring the person to assent. Thus Peter and Stephen would assent to (1) if only they thought about it more and talked to more experts. By contrast, at the sub-personal level, the postulated dispositions are grounded in something like an unconscious reasoning module, even if the personal-level counterfactual conditionals are false. Thus the default outcome of Peter and Stephen's underlying competence is assent to (1), even if stable dispositions from other sources irreversibly override that default.

---

[20]   Eklund (2002: 262) defends such a view of logical deviance. See Martin (1994), Lewis (1997), Martin and Heil (1998), Bird (1998), and Mumford (1998) for some basic issues about masked dispositions. Harman (1999: 213) relies on defeasible inferential dispositions in his conceptual role semantics.

An analogous contrast arises for syntax. As a standard example, native speakers of English tend to reject (3) at first sight as ill-formed:

(3)   The horse raced past the barn fell.

They want to insert "and" between "barn" and "fell." But they tend to change their minds about (3) when asked to consider the result of inserting "that was" between "horse" and "raced" instead: they realize that the original string was well-formed after all; "the horse" is the object, not the subject, of "raced." Conversely, native speakers often unreflectively accept ill-formed strings as well-formed, for example when a plural verb is separated from its singular subject by a long intervening string that includes a plural noun, but can be brought to acknowledge their mistake, as when a draft is corrected. On a personal level account, such conscious reflective judgments, actual or counterfactual, are constitutive of well-formedness. On the contrasting sub-personal level account, those judgments play a merely evidential role: what constitutes well-formedness is the structure of the syntactic component of the unconscious language module, even if the person's conscious reflective judgment is irreversibly contrary as a result of extraneous factors, such as their dogmatic commitment to a pet theory of syntax.

The personal level account fails to shield UDAl′ and UDAt′ from the counterexamples of Peter and Stephen. For, by hypothesis, their refusal to assent to (1) is stable under conscious reflection, exposure to further arguments and so on. Like many people, not least philosophers, they are obstinate in defense of their favorite views, willing to make whatever *ad hoc* moves are needed to retain them. One knows in advance that the task of dissuading them is hopeless, however good one's objections: a common experience in philosophy. As Peter and Stephen became comfortable with their deviant theories they gradually ceased to feel even an initial temptation to assent to (1), we may assume, although they still remember what it was like to feel such a temptation. They assimilate the change to one in which education gradually eradicates the tendency to make a particular false assumption. Perhaps years of browbeating or social ostracism would cause them to change their minds, but that applies to almost any belief; it is poor evidence that an underlying disposition to assent was present all along. Would Peter and Stephen assent to (1) if they lacked their conscious theoretical commitments? Perhaps not, but that counterfactual would show little. The possibility of untheoretical analogues of Peter and Stephen has already been raised. They lack the conscious theoretical commitments but still do not assent to (1). If it is objected that the untheoretical analogues, unlike Peter and Stephen, do not understand (1) with its normal English sense because they lack the required unconscious cognitive structures, that is in effect to switch to the subpersonal version of the dispositional account. On the personal level account, Peter and Stephen are *not* disposed to assent to (1). If that makes them irrationally obstinate, they are no more so than many philosophers and non-philosophers in defense of a favorite view.

The sub-personal level story has more room for maneuver in defense of UDAl' and UDAt'. It can insist that although Peter and Stephen's personal refusal to assent to (1) is stable under conscious reflection and exposure to further arguments, they retain a disposition to assent to (1) in virtue of features of their unconscious logic rules. This requires the postulated rules to be encased in some sort of psychological module, for if they consisted only in general habits of reasoning, Peter and Stephen's earlier habits could eventually be erased by their later ones, and the disposition to assent to (1) would disappear. The module must include rules for deduction, since that is the kind of reasoning relevant to (1). This module may be a component of an overall semantic module (after all, we are considering (1) as a candidate for analyticity). If the grounds for assent to (1) were merely inductive – that we have never observed a vixen that was not a vixen – people who understood (1) could reasonably refuse to assent to it on the grounds that they had observed too few vixens to be in a position to judge. A *prima facie* attractive conjecture is that the deductive rules would include analogues for natural language connectives of the introduction and elimination rules in a Gentzen-style system of natural deduction. But do humans have a module that includes unconscious logic rules of the required sort?

One might suppose the primary adaptive value of a cognitive module to be its capacity to perform a specific type of useful information processing quickly and reliably enough for the purposes of action in a changing environment. Its design can exploit special features of the type of task to which it is dedicated, in order to achieve efficiencies that would be impossible for a general purpose central processing unit. A diversion through higher mental processes, in particular through consciousness, would be slower and less reliable. Thus one might expect unconscious modular deductive reasoning to pay its way by the speed and reliability of its results, just as modules for vision and natural language processing seem to do. Naturally, performance would tail off as the complexity of problems increased, but there should be good performance over a worthwhile range of non-trivial problems. Is that prediction borne out?

Evidence from empirical psychology, amassed over several decades, suggests that most humans are strikingly bad at even elementary deductive reasoning, a finding which should not surprise those who have taught introductory logic. For example, in the combined results of over 65 large-scale experiments by different researchers on simple conditional reasoning, although 97 percent (not 100 percent!) of subjects endorsed modus ponens, only 72 percent endorsed modus tollens (if A then B; not B; therefore not A), while as many as 63 percent endorsed the fallacy of affirming the consequent (if A then B; B; therefore A) and 55 percent endorsed the fallacy of denying the antecedent (if A then B; not A; therefore not B). When the antecedent is negative, affirming the consequent overtakes modus tollens in popularity.[21] In some cases, when a further premise of the form "If C then B" is added to modus ponens only a minority endorses the inference (Byrne 1989).[22] Similar phenomena arise for elementary syllogistic reasoning.

Performance greatly improves when the conditional premise in a reasoning task has a realistic deontic content, such as "If you use a second class stamp, then you must leave the envelope unsealed" (Manktelow and Over 1987, Wason and Shapiro 1971). In general, the real-life credibility or otherwise of premises and conclusion strongly influences judgments of validity and invalidity.

---

[21]   See Schroyens and Schaeken (2003); the percentages are as summarized by Oaksford (2005: 427).

[22]   Is it still modus ponens if there is an extra redundant premise? If not, then humans apply modus ponens only in the most artificial circumstances, since in practice we always have further information. Moreover, people without formal education tend to do *worst* in reasoning tasks with artificial premises from which all background information has been screened out (see Harris (2000: 94–117) for discussion). Such a restriction would make a disposition to assent to modus ponens a rather artificial test for understanding "if."

For simple problems in formal deductive reasoning, when the specific subject matter provides no helpful clues, success is significantly correlated with intelligence, in whatever sense it is measured by IQ tests, SAT scores or the like (Stanovich and West 2000). For some simple tasks, success is rare except among those with the intelligence of able undergraduates (Newstead *et al.* 2004; the samples in the experimental literature tend to consist of university students, since they are the most easily available subjects). Contrast this with the efficient success which humans typically show in judging whether short strings of words constitute well-formed sentences of their native language, for example. There is little sign of anything modular that contains formal rules to subserve conscious deduction, whether conceived as part of a language module or as part of a reasoning module.

Of course, there may be sub-personal processes whose inner workings can conveniently be represented as employing deductive rules, just as there may be sub-personal processes whose inner workings can conveniently be represented as employing differential equations, for example to process perceptual input, in even the most mathematically ignorant subjects. But that is not quite the issue. We are questioning the existence of a sub-personal basis for an unmanifested disposition to assent, that is, to perform an action at the personal level. The problem is that the data of normal performance tell against the hypothesis of a set of deductive rules (semantic or not) unconsciously employed as the primary route to conscious assent in the relevant normal cases.

A widespread, although not universal, view among psychologists of reasoning is that humans have two reasoning systems. In the terminology of Stanovich and West, System 1 is associative, holistic, automatic, relatively undemanding of cognitive capacity, relatively fast, and acquired through biology, exposure, and personal experience; its construal of reasoning tasks is highly sensitive to personal, conversational, and social context. System 2 is rule-based, analytic, controlled, demanding of cognitive capacity, relatively slow, and acquired by cultural and formal tuition; its construal of reasoning tasks is rather insensitive to personal, conversational, and social context.[23] System 1 lacks the formal rules that enable deductive rea-

---

[23]   See Stanovich and West (2000: 659), where a list is also provided of earlier authors who have proposed similar views.

soning to succeed in the absence of helpful clues from the content of premises and conclusion. Although defeasible and only moderately reliable, it performs an important role in tasks of the kind for which it presumably evolved, such as integrating new information from perception or testimony with standing beliefs. System 1 is not a system for formal deductive reasoning. A suitably educated, highly intelligent person can achieve success in formal deductive reasoning by means of System 2, but it is not sealed off in an unconscious module.

How does this picture apply to Peter and Stephen? With respect to System 1, they fall within the normal range of human variation. They are slightly unusual with respect to System 2, which is in any case much more sensitive than System 1 to specific features of the individual's intelligence and education. But neither high intelligence nor a good education is needed to understand simple sentences like (1). Any System 2 differences at issue between Peter or Stephen and average speakers of English are wholly consistent with Peter and Stephen's competence in their native language. If Peter and Stephen do have any underlying disposition to accept (1) as true, it concerns their System 1. But aversion to universal generalizations with empty subject terms or borderline cases seems to be within the normal range of System 1 reasoning among native speakers. On the two systems picture, there is no reason to assume that all linguistically competent speakers have an underlying disposition to assent to (1).

The two systems picture has not been conclusively established; it may turn out to need modification. Nevertheless, it throws into relief the empirical speculations on which the sub-personal understanding-disposition-to-assent links depend, and their clash with much current thinking in the psychology of reasoning. If the two systems picture is right to even a first approximation, the sub-personal links are in trouble.

How can System 1 or any other system evaluate deductive arguments without using formal rules for reasoning with logical constants in natural language, even if their effect is almost swamped by associations, heuristics, and other pragmatic factors?[24] There are alternatives. For example, one of the main psychological theories of deductive

---

[24]   For such an approach see Braine and O'Brien (1991), criticized by Evans and Over (2004: 56–9).

reasoning is currently the *mental models* approach. Two of its leading proponents write:

> The evidence suggests that it [the reasoning mechanism] is *not* equipped with logical rules of inference, which it sometimes uses correctly and sometimes misuses, misapplies or forgets. This analogy with grammar, which has seduced so many theorists, is a mistake. The reasoning mechanism constructs a mental model of the premises, formulates a putative conclusion, and tests its validity by searching for alternative models in which it is false. The search is constrained by the meta-principle that the conclusion is valid only if there are no such models, but it is not governed by any systematic or comprehensive principles. (Johnson-Laird and Byrne 1993: 178)

Thus subjects may erroneously classify an invalid argument as valid, because the unrepresentative sample of models they have examined includes no counter-model, and they wrongly treat it as representative. They may erroneously classify a valid argument as invalid, because they leave the process of constructing a counter-model incomplete, under the misapprehension that there is no obstacle to completing it. Background beliefs about the specific subject matter of an argument influence its classification because they influence which mental models are constructed. Johnson-Laird and Byrne argue that their theory gives the best fit to the empirical data.

On the mental models approach, the nearest one normally comes to employing deductive rules of inference is in the procedures for evaluating sentences (premises or conclusions) with respect to a given model, itself conceived as a mental representation.[25] But that process does not involve deductive reasoning in a natural language. Nor would natural deduction rules for the natural language connectives be very relevant; it is more like the construction of a truth-table. For example, in calculating the truth-value of a conditional in a model, one does not apply the rule of conditional proof to that very conditional if one already has the rules for constructing truth-tables.[26]

---

[25]   Mental models need not be visualized (Johnson-Laird and Byrne 1993: 182). Johnson-Laird and Byrne also claim that human reasoning is a semantic rather than a syntactic process (*ibid.*: 180), but the significance of this claim is not entirely clear, since they treat reasoning as a manipulation of representations.

[26]   Standard proofs of formalizations of (1) use conditional proof.

Evaluating a sentence in a model might involve something closer to an imaginative analogue of the processes that issue in complex perceptual judgments such as "Everybody over there is wearing a hat." Not all such universally quantified conclusions are reached by deduction from further premises. One might employ this argument:

A is wearing a hat.
B is wearing a hat.
C is wearing a hat.
Everybody over there is A, B, or C.
Therefore:
Everybody over there is wearing a hat.

But of course the final premise "Everybody over there is A, B, or C" is itself a universally quantified perceptual judgment. To suppose that it too was reached as the conclusion of a deductive argument is to start a futile regress.

Although the mental models theory does not apply to all human reasoning – for example, to the System 2 kind some humans learn to carry out in logic classes – it may apply to a high proportion of it. The theory is a salutary reminder that reasoning with logical constants need not be formal deductive reasoning, and that the empirical evidence suggests that in humans it usually is not.

One remaining concern is that logical skills must play some role in linguistic competence because logical features play a role in determining well-formedness. An example is the category of negative polarity items. Consider these sentences:

(4)   If she ate any of the cake, she was hungry.
(5)*   If she was hungry, she ate any of the cake.

"Any" is a negative polarity item. To a first approximation, the reason why "she ate any of the cake" is acceptable as the antecedent of the conditional but not as the consequent is that the antecedent is in a downward entailing (negative) context while the consequent is instead in an upward entailing (positive) context. A context C is upward entailing just in case whenever A entails B, C(A) entails C(B); C is downward entailing just in case whenever A entails B, C(B) entails C(A). Thus recognition of the logical features of contexts seems to be needed in order to distinguish between well-formed and ill-formed sentences. But things are not so simple. Consider these sentences:

(6)   Exactly four people in the room were of any help.
(7)   Few people in the room were of any help.

Logically, "few" creates a downward entailing context; "exactly four" does not. However, (6) is acceptable provided that in the context it is taken to imply (7), but not generally otherwise. Thus the phenomenon involves a significant pragmatic element: which contexts are suitable for "any" cannot be determined on purely logico-linguistic grounds. If we disagree with the speaker of (6) about how many people were in the room or what proportion of them could have been expected to help, we may find her use of "any" inappropriate without regarding her as *linguistically* incompetent. Similarly, if a speaker has deviant views as to which contexts are downward entailing, but uses "any" in just those contexts that she treats as downward entailing, we might find her deviant use of "any" inappropriate without regarding her as linguistically incompetent, precisely because the deviation in use is explained by logical rather than linguistic unorthodoxy. Thus the role of logical knowledge in such cases does not make it part of purely linguistic competence. All our knowledge is potentially relevant to judging the appropriateness of a given use of "any."[27]

Suppose, nevertheless, that our classification of strings such as (4)–(7) as well- or ill-formed does depend on some prior classification of contexts as downward entailing or not. The question remains: is that classification available for unconscious reasoning that would issue in conscious assent to supposedly analytic sentences? To identify

---

[27]   Ladusaw (1996: 325–37) surveys issues concerning negative polarity. Strictly speaking, the context of the antecedent of a counterfactual conditional is not downward entailing on standard logics of such conditionals, according to which strengthening of the antecedent fails; for example, although "It rained hard" entails "It rained," "If it had rained, it would not have rained hard" does not entail "If it had rained hard, it would not have rained hard." Nevertheless, negative polarity items are felicitous in the antecedent of counterfactual conditionals: "If you had taken any of that arsenic, you would have died" (see van Rooij (2006) for discussion).

a context as downward entailing involves a more sophisticated logical insight than identifying a particular argument as valid, since it requires the validation of an abstract pattern of argument. For example, identifying negation as a downward entailing context requires checking this schema, for arbitrary sentences "A" and "B": If "A" entails "B" then "It is not the case that B" entails "It is not the case that A." That is just the kind of abstract formal reasoning task on which humans perform worst. Contrast that with our high level of reliability in determining whether strings with negative polarity items are well-formed. Thus the evidence suggests that the unconscious logic in question is not at the service of the cognitive processes that normally produce conscious assent to sentences like (1). Such cases therefore fail to support a modification of the conclusions reached so far.

One special sort of case deserves separate discussion. Some meta-linguistic sentences or thoughts look analytic for distinctive reasons. As observed in Chapter 2, even when a philosophical question is not itself metalinguistic, metalinguistic considerations can still help us to answer it.

Consider theoretical terms. We can understand the word "phlo-giston" without believing phlogiston theory. Might we do so because we still believe that "phlogiston" is generally associated with that theory, just as one can understand a natural kind such as "gorilla" without believing the associated stereotype ("Gorillas are ferocious") because one still believes that "gorilla" is generally associated with that stereotype (Putnam 1975)? However, such sociolinguistic beliefs are no more immune than logical beliefs from the challenge of theoretical unorthodoxy without change of meaning. If T is any version of phlogiston theory, someone can understand "phlogiston" and associate it with T without believing that it is generally associated with T, in the belief that "phlogiston" is and was generally associated not with T but with somewhat different versions of phlogiston theory. This is clear if T is a strong version of the theory. Even if T is a weak version, they may believe that the word is generally associated with a stronger version, and deny that it is *ipso facto* associated with T. On such grounds, they may even disbelieve that they themselves associate the word with T. Let such sociolinguistic beliefs be false; nevertheless, holding them is quite consistent with understanding "phlogiston." It is futile to multiply disjuncts and restrictive clauses in the hope of formulating a sociolinguistic claim so anodyne that anyone who understands "phlogiston" *must* accept it. The result will just be a complex theoretical claim that ordinary speakers can legitimately doubt, on the grounds that such matters are hard to determine.

A more minimalist line of argument for metalinguistic analyticities appeals to the connection between understanding and knowledge of reference. Suppose that someone understands this sentence:

(8)   "Tree" applies to all and only trees.

Then they understand its constituent words, in particular "tree." So they know what "tree" means. For common nouns, knowledge of meaning requires knowledge of application conditions. Consequently, they know that "tree" applies to all and only trees. Moreover, since knowledge entails belief, they also believe that "tree" applies to all and only trees. Thus, it seems, they should knowledgeably assent to (1). The argument generalizes to a large class of disquotational claims (the identity of the expression mentioned on the left-hand side with the one used on the right-hand side is crucial, since if they were distinct understanding of the latter would not entail knowledge about the former).

Nevertheless, those who understand (8) may refuse assent to it. Stephen is an example, since on his view a universally quantified biconditional with borderline cases for both sides is not definitely true. Indeed, some supervaluationists about vagueness even deny such disquotational principles for vague terms, such as "tree". However erroneous such theories of vagueness, holding them is consistent with ordinary linguistic understanding of (8). If understanding really does involve tacit propositional knowledge of meaning, that knowledge may contradict conscious beliefs.

Let us grant for the sake of argument that understanding (8) entails knowing both that "tree" applies to all and only trees and that (8) means that "tree" applies to all and only trees. How then can one understand (8) without assenting to it? We lack direct conscious access to whatever tacit knowledge linguistic understanding is supposed to consist in, otherwise semantics as a branch of empirical linguistics would be much easier than it actually is. We consciously entertain the proposition that "tree" applies to all and only trees as presented by sentence (8), or by the corresponding conscious thought *"tree" applies to all and only trees*. In tacitly knowing that "tree" applies to all and only trees (if we do), we may tacitly entertain that proposition under a quite different unconscious mode of presentation. Thus understanding-assent links fail for sentences of natural language and conscious thoughts:

(UAl*)   Necessarily, whoever understands the sentence "'Tree' applies to all and only trees" assents to it.

(UAt*)   Necessarily, whoever grasps the thought *"tree" applies to all and only trees* assents to it.

For if linguistic understanding involves tacit propositional knowledge of meaning, it presumably involves tacit assent to the relevant propositions under modes of presentation of some sort. Any tacit assent to the proposition that "tree" applies to all and only trees need not be to it under the modes of presentation that UAl* and UAt* require. The same difficulty arises even if we require only a disposition to assent, as in UDAl' and UDAt'.[28]

To determine in exactly what sense of "tacit knowledge," if any, understanding does involve tacit propositional knowledge of meaning lies beyond the scope of this book. According to Gareth Evans (1985: 338–9):

> Tacit knowledge of the syntactic and semantic rules of the language are [sic] not states of the same kinds as the states we identify in our ordinary use of the terms "belief" and "knowledge." Possession of tacit knowledge is exclusively manifested in speaking and understanding a language; the information is not even potentially at the service of any other project of the agent, nor can it interact with any other beliefs of the agent (whether genuine beliefs or other tacit "beliefs") to yield further beliefs. Such concepts as we use in specifying it are not concepts we need to suppose the subject to possess, for the state is inferentially insulated from the rest of the subject's thoughts and beliefs.

Even if the contrast is less extreme than Evans argues, the lack of inferential integration is real, and crucial here. Of course, the

---

[28]   See also Soames (1995) for relevant considerations.

ordinary notions of knowledge and belief may well provide appropriate templates for the construction of new notions of "tacit knowledge" and "tacit belief" of value to cognitive psychology. It can be theoretically rewarding to exploit the similarities between tacit knowledge and ordinary knowledge, but for present purposes it is the differences that matter.

Whatever the nature of tacit assent and dissent, no reflective intellectual discipline operates at the level of such assent and dissent, even if such a tacit level is necessary for its operation. Thus linguists' tacit knowledge of their native language does not already satisfy the goal of linguistics. Similarly, philosophy as a discipline operates at the level of conscious reflection and public discussion, whatever their unconscious underpinnings. For present purposes, we may therefore restrict assent to conscious assent and maintain the generalization that there are no necessary links from understanding to assent, or even to dispositions to assent.

To summarize: The case for treating lack of a disposition to assent to (1) as lack of linguistic competence depends on the status of (1) as an elementary truth of deductive logic. But human deductive competence is far more sensitive than linguistic competence to high intelligence and advanced education. Deductive competence is a reflective skill, often painfully acquired and under one's personal control. It is not insulated from one's conscious theorizing. Thus deductive proficiency is not a precondition of linguistic competence. Links from linguistic understanding to assent or to dispositions to assent fail.

5

The argument of the last two sections was at the level of language, not thought. It was directed primarily against UAl' and UDAl', not UAt' and UDAt'. Could a theorist of thought maintain UAt' or UDAt' while acknowledging Peter and Stephen as counterexamples to UAl' and UDAl'?

For the sake of argument, thoughts are being individuated by a cognitive criterion fine enough to suit an epistemological conception of analyticity, so we may assume that when a speaker understands a sentence, they associate it with a unique thought, in the intimate way in which we associate the sentence "Grass is green" with the thought *grass is green*. In particular, the speaker assents to the sentence if and only if they assent to the thought. Consider Stephen (the argument is parallel for Peter). Since Stephen understands "Every vixen is a vixen," he associates it with a unique thought t. Thus Stephen assents to "Every vixen is a vixen" if and only if he assents to t. But Stephen is an acknowledged counterexample to UAl'; he does not assent to the sentence "Every vixen is a vixen." Therefore he does not assent to t. Consequently, if t is the thought *every vixen is a vixen*, Stephen does not assent to the thought *every vixen is a vixen*, in which case he is also a counterexample to UAt'. Thus if Stephen is not a counterexample to UAt', the thought he associates with the sentence "Every vixen is a vixen" is not the thought *every vixen is a vixen*.

There is a parallel argument for dispositions. Stephen is an acknowledged counterexample to UDAl'; he understands "Every vixen is a vixen" while having no disposition to assent to it. We may therefore assume that he is relevantly stable; thus in all relevant situations t is the unique thought he associates with the sentence. Thus Stephen has a disposition to assent to "Every vixen is a vixen" if and only if he has a disposition to assent to t. Therefore he has no disposition to assent to t. Consequently, if t is the thought *every vixen is a vixen*, Stephen has no disposition to assent to the thought *every vixen is a vixen*, in which case he is also a counterexample to UDAt'. Thus if Stephen is not a counterexample to UDAt', the thought he associates with the sentence "Every vixen is a vixen" is not the thought *every vixen is a vixen*.

The upshot is that theorists of thought can maintain links from understanding to assent or dispositions to assent at the level of thought while abandoning them at the level of language only if they deny that the thought Peter or Stephen associates with the sentence "Every vixen is a vixen" is the thought *every vixen is a vixen*. They may either deny that Peter and Stephen grasp the thought *every vixen is a vixen* at all or assert that they grasp the thought by some means other than that sentence and assent to it, or at least have a disposition to assent.

The thought *every vixen is a vixen* is the thought *we* associate with (1). Thus the envisaged theorist of thought is claiming that the thought we associate with (1) differs from the thoughts Peter and Stephen associate with it, even though all of us understand (1) with its usual meaning in English.[29] This need not imply that (1) is indexical, expressing different propositions in the contexts of different speakers, for thoughts are not being identified with propositions. You might use the sentence "He is hungry" (pointing at me), which you associate with a demonstrative thought *he is hungry* to express the very proposition I express using the sentence "I am hungry," which I associate with the distinct thought *I am hungry*; you associate the sentence "I am hungry" with the same thought but use it to express a different proposition, that you are hungry. For all that has been said, Peter and Stephen use (1) to express the same proposition as we do. But on what basis are the thoughts Peter and Stephen associate with (1) being distinguished from the thought we associate with (1)?

One could simply use the word "thought" subject to the stipulation that the inferential differences between Peter, Stephen, and us *constitute* differences between the thoughts we associate with (1). But what is the point of such a stipulation? As seen above, the linguistic understanding of (1) we share with Peter and Stephen already suffices for them and us to articulate our disagreements in rational discourse; we are not merely talking past one another. In its small way, (1) determines a piece of the common intellectual heritage of mankind, something we share with Peter and Stephen in our very capacity to disagree over it. To insist that the thought we associate with (1) nevertheless differs from the thoughts Peter and Stephen associate with (1) is to undermine Frege's requirement of the publicity of senses, and in particular thoughts.

If Peter and Stephen associate (1) with different thoughts from ours, should we not understand them better by translating their idiolects non-homophonically into ours? Presumably we should seek sentences other than (1) that we associate with the very thoughts they associate with (1), or at least sentences we associate with thoughts

---

[29]   Neo-Fregeans such as Evans (1982: 40) sometimes claim that different speakers can achieve linguistic competence with the same proper name by associating it with different concepts (modes of presentation) of the same object. On the view envisaged in the text, phrases such as "the thought *every vixen is a vixen*" or "the concept *every*" presumably are indexical, since they refer to the thought or concept that the speaker associates with the italicized expression. Discussions of concept possession tend to use such phrases freely, without attention to such indexicality. On the envisaged view, they may require consequent revision.

more similar to the thoughts they associate with (1) than is the thought we associate with (1), and translate the dissent from (1) in their mouths as dissent from those other sentences in our mouths. But the use of such a translation scheme would be intellectually disreputable, just because it would involve a refusal to acknowledge the full challenge that Peter and Stephen have issued to (1) in our mouths, not just in theirs. However mistaken their challenge, it is real. They are quite explicit that they are challenging the thought we associate with (1), and that we should apply no non-homophonic translation scheme when interpreting their dissent from (1). To insist on applying such a non-homophonic translation scheme to them in the teeth of their protests would be to treat them less than fully seriously as human beings, like patients in need of old-fashioned psychiatric treatment, whose words are merely symptoms. The claim that Peter and Stephen associate (1) with different thoughts from ours repackages our disagreement with them in a way that makes it sound less threatening than it really is. It misleadingly bundles together logical and semantic differences, without any genuine unification of the two categories. To call the logical disagreement a difference in associated "thoughts" is an advertising trick. Since a homophonic reading of (1) in the mouths of Peter and Stephen is more faithful to their intentions than is any non-homophonic reading, they associate (1) with the same thought as we do in any relevant sense of "thought."

Naturally, when Peter dissents from "Every F is a G," we may decide in the light of his logical unorthodoxy to store only the information that either not every F is a G or there are no Fs. But this is not a non-homophonic *translation*, any more than it is when someone notorious for exaggeration says "At least six thousand people went on the march" and we decide to store only the information that at least one thousand people went on the march. By "six thousand" the speaker did not mean what we mean by "one thousand." If exactly one thousand people went on the march he spoke falsely, not truly, for he was speaking English. Since we do not fully trust him, when he asserted one thing we stored only something weaker. Similarly, since we do not fully trust Peter, we do not store exactly what he asserts. If there were no Fs, he spoke falsely, not truly, for he was speaking English. Our lack of trust in Peter and Stephen's logic skills is quite consistent with reading their utterances homophonically.

Peter and Stephen are counterexamples to UAt' and UDAt'. The links from understanding to assent, or even to dispositions to assent, fail for thought as they do for language.

6

How do the considerations of preceding sections apply to traditional paradigms of analyticity? Consider:

(9)   Every vixen is a female fox.

Given that "vixen" is synonymous with "female fox," (9) results from substituting synonyms for synonyms in the logical truth (9). Hence (9) is synonymous with (1): it is Frege-analytic but not itself a logical truth. We can expect the arguments of previous sections against links from understanding to assent or dispositions to assent for examples like (1) to work at least as strongly for examples like (9). Let us check this.

We may try to reduce discussion of (9) to discussion of (1), on the grounds that the concept *vixen* just is the concept *female fox*. Thus the thought *every vixen is a female fox* just is the thought *every vixen is a vixen* (since thoughts are composed of concepts). To grasp, assent to or know a thought is just to have a relation to that thought. Consequently, to grasp, assent, or know *every vixen is a female fox* just is to grasp, assent, or know *every vixen is a vixen*. At the level of thought, the previous discussion carries over automatically. For example, in being counterexamples to the understanding-assent link for the thought *every vixen is a vixen*, Peter and Stephen are *ipso facto* counterexamples to the understanding link for the thought *every vixen is a female fox*.

At the level of language, the reduction is slightly more complicated: "vixen" and "female fox" are distinct expressions even if they are associated with the same concept. Someone can understand "female fox" without understanding "vixen." Conversely, someone can understand "vixen" without understanding "female fox": for instance, a native speaker of another language who is learning English understands "vixen," because she was taught it as a synonym for a word in her native language, but has not yet encountered "female" and "fox." If she has mastered the construction "Every . . . is a −," she can understand (1) without being in a position to understand (9). Someone who understands neither (1) nor (9) can assent to one of them without assenting to the other, on the testimony of someone else who tells him that the former is true without telling him that the latter is true. Nevertheless, we might try arguing that whoever understands (9) will take just the same attitudes to it as to (1).

The argument is this. Suppose that someone understands (9) (as always, with its normal English meaning). Thus she associates it with the thought *every vixen is a female fox*. Consequently, she takes an attitude Al (such as assent or knowledge) to (9) if and only if she takes the corresponding attitude At to the thought *every vixen is a female fox* at the level of thought (in preceding sections, Al and At were equated). Our speaker also understands (1), because it is composed entirely out of words ("vixen") and modes of construction ("every . . . is a −") which she understands in understanding (9). Thus she associates (1) with the thought *every vixen is a vixen*. Consequently, she takes Al to (9) if and only if she takes At to the thought *every vixen is a vixen*. For the reason already given, the thought *every vixen is a vixen* is the thought *every vixen is a female fox*. Therefore she takes At to the thought *every vixen is a vixen* if and only if she takes At to the thought *every vixen is a female fox*. It follows that she takes Al to (9) if and only if she takes Al to (1). Thus, with respect to speakers who understand (9), discussion of (9) reduces to discussion of (1).

Whether or not the concept *vixen* is the concept *female fox*, the reduction succeeds for Peter and Stephen, since they use the concepts interchangeably and do understand (9). They are counterexamples to epistemological analyticity for (9) just as much as they are for (1), at the levels of both thought and language.

The assumption that the concept *vixen* is the concept *female fox* is controversial. Burge (1978) has built on a point of Mates (1952) to argue that synonyms cannot always be substituted for synonyms *salva veritate* in belief ascriptions. Thus someone under the misapprehension that the term "vixen" also applies to immature male foxes may believe that every vixen is a vixen without believing that every vixen is a female fox. Burge argues powerfully against attempts to reconstrue such beliefs as metalinguistic. Does this speaker assent to the thought *every vixen is a vixen* without assenting to the thought *every vixen is a female fox*? If so, the thoughts are distinct (which is compatible with the identity of the proposition that every vixen is a vixen with the proposition that every vixen is a female fox), and the concept *vixen* is not the concept *female fox*.

To make a case more like those of Peter and Stephen, we can imagine that our speaker is quite familiar with the dictionary definition of "vixen" as "female fox." He also knows that dictionaries give a second definition of "vixen" as "quarrelsome woman." However, unlike most of us, he does not believe that these are two senses of "vixen." Rather, he thinks that "vixen" in its primary sense applies to both female foxes and quarrelsome women. He may defend his view with sophisticated arguments from the philosophy of language, although this is not essential. He denies (9), intending "vixen" in the public sense in which it applies at least to female foxes.

Our imaginary speaker is not so different from actual natives speakers of English who deny that a man who has lived with a partner for several years without getting married is a bachelor, or assert that someone who underwent a sex-change operation after giving birth is a mother without being a female parent.[30] Suppose that they are in fact mistaken; "bachelor" has the same intension as "unmarried man" and "mother" has the same intension as "female parent." Thus they are mistaken about the meaning of the English words "bachelor" and "unmarried." Nevertheless, they fall well within the range of permissible variation for linguistically competent speakers. They are only giving more weight than others to an inclination that most speakers feel in some degree to classify the cases that way. Without regarding them as having spoken parrot-fashion, we report their beliefs using the words "bachelor" and "unmarried." We classify them as believing that some unmarried men are not bachelors and that some mothers are not female parents because we interpret them as having used the words with their normal English meanings, despite their errors. That is how they intend to be interpreted, not as using the words with idiosyncratic senses.[31] If we believe that all unmarried

---

[30]   Compare Harman (1999: 151) on problems in analyzing "bachelor" as "unmarried adult male" and Nozick (2001: 135–6) on the non-synonymy of "mother" and "female parent."

[31]   One problem with interpreting speakers as all speaking their own idiolects is that it tends to undermine testimonial knowledge: if Y gets some knowledge from X and passes it on to Z in the same words, they do not mean in Y's mouth what they meant in X's.

men are bachelors and all mothers are female parents, we therefore classify their beliefs in question as untrue, for the belief that some unmarried men are not bachelors is true if and only if some unmarried men are not bachelors, and the belief that some mothers are not female parents is true if and only if some mothers are not female parents. Given that we correctly interpret them as using the words with their normal English meanings, they understand the words in the relevant sense of "understand." Although they are ignorant of some facts about the normal English meanings of the words, such ignorance is quite compatible with linguistic competence (which is why native speakers of English take university courses in the semantics of English). Arguably, their error is not primarily semantic: they have the semantic belief that the word "bachelor" does not apply to all unmarried men because they have the non-semantic belief that some unmarried men are not bachelors and the semantic knowledge that "bachelor" applies only to bachelors; they have the semantic belief that the word "mother" does not apply only to female parents because they have the non-semantic belief that some mothers are not female parents and the semantic knowledge that the word "mother" applies to all mothers.

Such cases also help answer the objection to examples such as those in this chapter that the awkward subject who consciously denies that P also has unconscious, semantically derived knowledge (or belief) that P. When a competent native speaker denies that every unmarried man is a bachelor, the postulation of unconscious knowledge (or belief) that every unmarried man is a bachelor serves no good explanatory purpose. The speaker tends to apply "bachelor" to something once they have applied "unmarried" and "man" to it, but the tendency is defeasible. Such defeasible connections can be explained without postulation of unconscious belief in a universal generalization. In such cases, there need be no hint of the cognitive dissonance or tension that one might expect from a direct contradiction between conscious and unconscious beliefs. Given that there is no contradicted unconscious knowledge in these simple cases, it is not clear what better reason there is supposed to be in postulating it for more complex cases either.

Suppose, given the considerations above, that the concept *vixen* is not the concept *female fox*. Then the claim of epistemological analyticity is even worse off for (9) than it is for (1), at the levels of both thought and language. Logically orthodox subjects can understand (9) and grasp the thought *every vixen is a female fox* while refusing to assent. In that case, they will also reject the corresponding inference rule with instances of the form "*a* is a vixen; therefore *a* is a female fox" (and conversely); likewise at the level of thought.[32]

The underlying style of argument against links from understanding to assent or dispositions to assent is quite general. For each candidate one must still find appropriate counterexamples: since they are most convincing when unorthodoxy on the point at issue is amply compensated by orthodoxy on related points, no one counterexample will suit all cases. Nevertheless, with a little ingenuity one always succeeds.[33]

---

[32]   Peter and Stephen assent to the conclusion of this inference rule whenever they assent to its premise. For some subtler problems it raises for them see Williamson (2006b: 33–4).

[33]   Another application of the present style of reasoning is to claims that sorites paradoxes reveal incoherence in vague concepts. Thus Dummett (1975a) argues that observational predicates in natural language are governed by rules that infect the language with inconsistency: for example, to understand "looks red" one must be willing to apply a tolerance principle by which one can infer from "*x* is visually indiscriminable from *y*" and "*x* looks red" to "*y* looks red," which generates sorites paradoxes because visual indiscriminability is non-transitive. More recently, Roy Sorensen (2001) has argued that linguistic competence with vague terms involves willingness to make inferences such as that from "*n* seconds after noon is noonish" to "*n* + 1 seconds after noon is noonish," which commits us to inconsistent conclusions by sorites reasoning (given our other commitments, such as "Noon is noonish" and "Midnight is not noonish"). Matti Eklund (2002) defends a similar account of both sorites and semantic paradoxes. There are no such requirements on linguistic competence and concept possession. An ordinary speaker of English who understands "looks red" and "noonish" and has the concepts *looks red* and *noonish* in the normal way but then rejects the relevant tolerance principles in the light of the sorites paradoxes does not thereby cease to understand those expressions or to have those concepts. She might treat the premises of the tolerance principles as providing good defeasible evidence for their conclusions, without even being *disposed* to expect long chains of such reasoning to preserve truth; this attitude seems to be less than Dummett, Sorensen, and Eklund require for competence, since it is insufficient to render sorites paradoxes puzzling. In any case, even if a whole community of speakers is disposed to treat tolerance principles as obviously fallacious, it can still have terms like "looks red" and "noonish" that are just as vague as ours; speakers' acceptance of tolerance principles is quite inessential to vagueness.

In principle, we could also explore putative links from understanding of one sentence to (dispositions to) assent to another sentence or a thought, or from grasp of one thought to (dispositions to) assent to another thought. In practice, such candidates fall to objections very similar to those already raised. Details are therefore omitted.

7

Old theories tend to survive refutation in the absence of new theories to take their place. Despite all the evidence against the existence of links from understanding to assent or dispositions to assent, it can be hard to resist the idea that there *must* be such links, otherwise the distinction between understanding and not understanding would dissolve: speakers who all understood the same term might have nothing substantive in common to constitute its shared meaning. For example, in the case of moral vocabulary, which he treats as representative, Frank Jackson (1998: 132) writes:

> Genuine moral disagreement, as opposed to mere talking past one another, requires a background of shared moral opinion to fix a common, or near enough common, set of meanings for our moral terms. We can think of the rather general principles that we share as the commonplaces or platitudes or constitutive principles that make up the core we need to share in order to count as speaking a common moral language.[34]

---

[34]   Jackson's application of the Ramsey-Carnap-Lewis method for defining theoretical terms to moral vocabulary (and more generally in his program of conceptual analysis) requires not merely some agreed role for moral terms but an agreed role specific enough to be uniquely instantiated: this further assumption is criticized at Williamson (2001: 629–30). Jackson's reply on this point (2001: 656) reiterates something like the assumption in the quoted passage. He also misunderstands the objection by falsely supposing that the claim that we can mean the same by a word and disagree radically about its application restricts the disagreement to what occupies the roles, rather than the roles themselves, however one imagines the latter as demarcated. For criticism of the application of the Ramsey-Carnap-Lewis method in Boghossian (2003) see Williamson (2003a). In general, if the platitudes are weak, as we have every reason to expect, many different candidates will satisfy them. Call these the *admissible candidates*. For simplicity, think of them as properties (more accurately, they are n-place sequences of properties and relations, where n is the number

Jackson's only argument for these claims is failure to see an alternative.

The notion of a shared language is vague (Jackson does not suggest otherwise). There can be sorites series of speakers in which each seems to be speaking the same language as the next but the first is clearly not speaking the same language as the last.[35] One reaction is that there is no such thing as a shared language, a conclusion endorsed in some form by both Noam Chomsky and Donald Davidson. Similarly, Margaret Thatcher once claimed "There is no such thing as society," and one can certainly construct sorites series in her support. But almost everything looks vulnerable to sorites series; they are a poor way to establish non-existence. Whatever exactly shared languages are, they are no mere illusion. We can follow Jackson in asking how they are possible. But there is an alternative to his answer.

---

of primitive predicates to which the method is being applied). The conjunction or disjunction of these admissible candidates will often not itself be an admissible candidate. Schematic example: let the platitudes be "All Fs are electrons," "Some electrons are Fs" and "Some electrons are not Fs," where the method is being applied to "F"; the conjunction of the admissible candidates is the empty property, which does not satisfy the second platitude and so is inadmissible; their disjunction is the property of being an electron, which does not satisfy the third platitude and so is inadmissible. The non-uniqueness problem for the Ramsey-Lewis-Carnap *definiens*, in effect "the property that satisfies the platitudes," is *not* that it is vague which property it denotes but that it definitely fails to denote any property at all, since many properties definitely satisfy the platitudes; neither supervaluationism nor any other theory of vagueness rescues the definition. A modified description such as "the most natural property that satisfies the platitudes" may still not solve the problem – perhaps several admissible candidates are equally natural and more natural than any others, or for every admissible candidate there is a more natural one – and in any case raises the question why the Ramsey-Carnap-Lewis method is being applied to some terms but not to the highly theoretical term "natural" itself (otherwise the problem simply recurs for "natural"). It is a mistake to assume that such problems are really problems for the linguistic practice itself rather than for the appeal to platitudes, for that is to assume that the platitudes exhaust what the practice does to secure reference for the predicate. Uses of the predicate to make controversial claims may also play a role in determining its reference, although not a naïvely descriptivist role (the account in Chapter 8 will permit this). The method of platitudes rashly throws such information away.

[35]   Williamson (1990: 137–41) discusses sorites series for languages.

What binds together uses of a word by different agents or at different times into a common practice of using that word with a given meaning? This is an instance of a more general type of question: what binds together different events into the history of a single complex object, whether it be a stone, a tree, a table, a person, a society, a tradition, or a word? In brief, what makes a unity out of diversity? Rarely is the answer to such questions the mutual similarity of the constituents. Almost never is it some invariant feature, shared by all the constituents and somehow prior to the complex whole itself – an indivisible soul or bare particular. Rather, it is the complex interrelations of the constituents, above all, their causal interrelations. Although we should not expect a precise non-circular statement of necessary and sufficient conditions for the unity in terms of those complex interrelations, we have at least a rough idea of what it takes. The similarity of the constituents is neither necessary nor sufficient; different constituents can play different but complementary roles in constituting the unity: both events in the head and events in the heart help constitute the life of a person. The idea that a shared understanding of a word requires a shared stock of platitudes depends on the assumption that uses of a word by different agents or at different times can be bound together into a common practice of using that word with a given meaning only by an invariant core of beliefs. But that assumption amounts to one of the crudest and least plausible answers to the question of what makes a unity out of diversity. In effect, it assumes that what animates a word is a soul of doctrine.[36]

As Kripke and Putnam argued, different speakers can make asymmetric contributions to binding together different uses of a word into a common practice of using it with a given meaning. The paradigm is their description of the role of scientific experts in fixing the reference of natural kind terms. Even if they oversimplified the relation between natural kind terms in natural language and scientific theory, a more refined account will still respect the division of linguistic labor, for distinctions between levels of expertise are observable even within the pre-scientific use of natural kind terms. Contrary to some of Putnam's less careful formulations, no canonical list of "criteria"

---

[36] A similar point is made in Schroeter and Schroeter (2006). More generally, the research program that these authors are pursuing has points in contact with the ideas of the present chapter.

for the application of the term need be available even to the most expert members of the community. Speakers may simply differ from each other in various ways in their ability to distinguish between members and non-members of the relevant kind.

The underlying insight is relevant far beyond the class of natural kind terms, as Burge observed. Even where we cannot sensibly divide the linguistic community into experts and non-experts, the picture of a natural language as a cluster of causally interrelated but constitutively independent idiolects is still wrong, because it ignores the way in which individual speakers defer to the linguistic community as a whole. They use a word as a word of a public language, allowing its reference in their mouths to be fixed by its use over the whole community.[37] No asymmetries in sociolinguistic status between individual speakers are required. For instance, if I classify a shade close to orange as "red" but subsequently discover that it is classified as "not red" by most native speakers of English whose eyesight is as good as mine, I may rationally admit that I was wrong without conceding that either I misunderstood the word "red" or my visual system was abnormal or malfunctioning. One can know that "red" means *red* without being infallible as to exactly which shades count as shades of red. Even if I obstinately insist that I am right and the rest are wrong in this particular case, my assumption that "red" in my mouth is inconsistent with "not red" in theirs shows that I intend my use of "red" to be treated as the use of a word of a public language. That its reference is fixed by the pattern of use over the whole community does not entail that the majority must be right in any given case: reference can supervene on underlying facts in ways far from transparent to native speakers.

The unity of a linguistic practice, like the unity of other complex objects, has both synchronic and diachronic aspects. As usual, causal continuity is necessary but not sufficient for diachronic unity. Anaphoric pronouns constitute one paradigm of such unity: the reference of later tokens is parasitic on the reference of earlier tokens; the identity of reference results from collusion, not coincidence. Over a longer timescale, the historical chains that preserve the reference of names represent a similar form of diachronic unity. Written testi-

---

[37] If the term is indexical, what is fixed by use over the whole community is not the content but the character in the sense of Kaplan (1989). For the bearing of this on communication in a vague language see Williamson (1999b: 512–14).

mony and verbal testimony preserved in memory depend on such reference-preserving links. As usual, the intention to preserve reference is not guaranteed to succeed, but success is the default (Kripke 1980).

Such diachronic links can hold non-trivially even for the linguistic or conceptual practice of an isolated individual. Contrary to some readings of Wittgenstein's private language argument, what seems right to the isolated individual need not be right, given their overall use dispositions: even at the individual level, reference can supervene on underlying facts in ways far from transparent to the subject. The point of the social determination of meaning is not that meaning can never be determined individually, but that, when an individual does use a shared language as such, individual meaning is parasitic on social meaning.

A complex web of interactions and dependences can hold a linguistic or conceptual practice together even in the absence of a common creed that all participants at all times are required to endorse. This more tolerant form of unity arguably serves our purposes better than would the use of platitudes as entrance examinations for linguistic practices.

Evidently, much of the practical value of a language consists in its capacity to facilitate communication between agents in epistemically asymmetric positions, when the speaker or writer knows about things about which the hearer or reader is ignorant, perhaps mistaken. Although disagreement is naturally easier to negotiate and usually more fruitful against a background of extensive agreement, it does not follow that any particular agreement is needed for disagreement to be expressed in given words. A practical constraint on useful communication should not be confused with a necessary condition for literal understanding. Moreover, the practical constraint is holistic; agreement on any given point can be traded for agreement on others. The same applies to principles of charity as putatively constitutive conditions on correct interpretation: imputed disagreement on any given point can be compensated for by imputed agreement on others.[38]

---

[38]   Davidson famously endorses a holistic principle of charity while rejecting the analytic-synthetic distinction (2001: 144–9). See Chapter 8 for more discussion of charity. Of course, he takes the notion of a shared language less seriously than here (Davidson 1986).

It is far easier and more rewarding to discuss the existence of true contradictions with a dialetheist such as Graham Priest than creationism with a Christian fundamentalist or Holocaust denial with a neo-Nazi.[39] The difficulty of engaging in fruitful debate with fundamentalists or neo-Nazis is not plausibly attributed to some failure of linguistic understanding on their part (or ours); it arises from their willful disrespect for the evidence. Such difficulty as there is in engaging in fruitful debate with dialetheists provides no significant reason to attribute to them (or us) a failure of linguistic understanding. Competence with the English language no more requires acceptance of some law of non-contradiction or any other logical law than it requires acceptance of the theory of evolution or the historical reality of the Holocaust.

We cannot anticipate all our disagreements in advance. What strike us today as the best candidates for analytic or conceptual truth some innovative thinker may call into question tomorrow for intelligible reasons. Even when we hold fast to our original belief, we can usually find ways of engaging rationally with the doubter. If a language imposes conditions of understanding that exclude such a doubt in advance, as it were in ignorance of its grounds, it needlessly limits its speakers' capacity to articulate and benefit from critical reflection on their ways of thinking. Such conditions are dysfunctional, and natural languages do not impose them.[40] Similarly, conceptual practices do better not to restrict in advance their capacity for innovation.

There is, of course, a distinction between understanding a word and not understanding it. One can lack understanding of a word through lack of causal interaction with the social practice of using that word, or through interaction too superficial to permit sufficiently fluent engagement in the practice. But sufficiently fluent engagement in the practice can take many forms, which have no single core of agreement.[41]

---

[39]   For examples of rational debate for and against a law of non-contradiction see Priest, Beall, and Armour-Garb (2004).

[40]   W. B. Gallie's intriguing account of the positive function of "essentially contested concepts" is relevant here; his examples are "the concepts of a religion, of art, of science, of democracy and of social justice" (1964: 168).

[41]   Someone who understands a word without being disposed to utter it (perhaps because they find it obscene or unpronounceable) can still count as sufficiently

If we picture speaking the same language in this way, how should we picture meaning the same thing? There is no quick generalization from the former to the latter. Different uses of the same word must be causally related, at least indirectly.[42] Creatures who are causally unrelated to us cannot use our word "not"; at best they can use a word exactly like our word in its general syntactic, semantic, and phonetic properties. But, on the usual view, their word can in principle be synonymous with ours. Synonymy does not entail causal relatedness.

Expressions are synonymous when they have exactly the same semantic properties. Fortunately, the tradition of truth-conditional semantics provides us with a rich store of such properties, if we take it seriously as a branch of linguistics and put aside Quinean reservations.

Two paradigms of a semantic property are the extension of a predicate, the set of things to which it applies, and its intension, the function that takes each circumstance of evaluation (say, an ordered pair of a world and a time) to the extension of the predicate with respect to that circumstance. For the purposes of compositional semantics, this approach can be generalized to expressions of other grammatical categories, so that they have intensions too. Thus synonymy entails at least sameness of intension. That is still a rather coarse-grained criterion, since it does not reflect internal compositional structure: "5 + 7" and "9 + 3" have the same intension. We can go more fine-grained by associating expressions with trees whose nodes correspond to their semantically significant constituents, each node being decorated with the content of the corresponding constituent; the branching structure of the tree encodes the constituency structure of the expression. Thus synonymy entails at least sameness of associated tree. This criterion is similar to Carnap's notion of intensional isomorphism (1947: 56). In this sense not even "vixen" and "female fox" are synonymous, since they differ in semantically significant structure, unless the account can be applied at a level of deep logical form at which they turn out to have the same constituents. Something like intensional isomorphism can serve as a criterion for sameness of content expressed in a given context of utterance.

---

engaged in the practice of using it. The account should also be read so as to allow for understanding of dead languages.

[42] On the metaphysics of words see Kaplan (1990).

An expression brings its linguistic meaning to a context rather than having that meaning made up in the context. Thus "I" as used by TW does not have the same linguistic meaning as "TW," even though they have the same content (since they are unstructured rigid designators of the same object). Rather, "I" as used by TW is identical in linguistic meaning with "I" as used by any other competent speaker of English. Thus a better approximation to the linguistic meaning of an expression is its character in the sense of Kaplan (1989), the function taking each context of utterance to the content of the expression in that context.

We might go still further. For instance, so far "and" and "but" come out synonymous, since they are simple expressions that make the same contribution to truth-conditions. We might distinguish their meanings by adding as further semantic properties conventional implicatures, themselves individuated like characters.

Even without conventional implicatures, once content is individuated by intensional isomorphism, the conception of linguistic meaning as character is already exquisitely fine-grained. Nevertheless, if semantic theory discovers a need to attribute still more semantic properties, or to revise the framework already sketched, sameness with respect to the newly identified semantic properties will be required for synonymy. In any case, we need not try to circumscribe in advance exactly what properties semantic theory will need to recognize.

The point is methodological. Whether an expression in one language is synonymous with an expression in another language is not a matter of whether the two speech communities associate similar beliefs with the expressions. Rather, the practices of each community (including their beliefs) determine the semantic properties of its expressions. Synonymy is the identity of the properties so determined, irrespective of similarities in belief. It is consistent with large differences in belief (just as very different distributions can have the same mean), and non-synonymy is consistent with much smaller differences in belief (just as very similar distributions can have different means). In particular, synonymy is consistent with the total absence of shared platitudes.

The synonymy of two expressions does not entail that competent speakers treat them interchangeably, as noted in chapter 3. Someone can understand "furze" and "gorse" by learning them from ostension of different samples without appreciating their synonymy. In some cases, even competent speakers who know two expressions to be synonymous will not treat them interchangeably. For example, the slang word "gob" means the same as "mouth," but competent speakers are normally sensitive to whether the social context makes "gob" (but not "mouth") inappropriate. Such differences in register are linguistic but not semantic. Consequently, knowing the meaning of an expression does not automatically qualify one for full participation in the practice of using it. Someone who acquires the word "gob" just by being reliably told that it is synonymous with "mouth" knows what "gob" means without being fully competent to use it. One does not achieve full competence with a sentence of a foreign language by learning its meaning from a phrasebook without knowing which constituent contributes what to that meaning. For a less obvious case, consider empty terms. Arguably, "phlogiston" fails to refer with respect to any circumstance of evaluation (since it designates rigidly, if at all) and any context of utterance (since it is non-indexical); it is semantically atomic and has no conventional implicatures. Those facts may completely determine its semantics, strictly speaking. Nevertheless, knowing them alone does not qualify one to participate in the linguistic practice of using "phlogiston," since they do not distinguish it from empty terms associated with other failed theories. Although no particular piece of knowledge is necessary for participation, such abject ignorance is not sufficient. We should resist the temptation to build all qualifications for participation in the practice of using a term into its meaning, on pain of turning semantic theory into a ragbag of miscellaneous considerations (even the inclusion of conventional implicature is marginal).

What of concepts? Presumably, thinkers causally unrelated to us could have the concept *not*. Hence sameness of concept does not entail causal relatedness; it is closer to sameness of meaning than it is to sameness of word. If so, the concept *furze* may well just be the concept *gorse*. If thoughts are composed of concepts in the obvious way, then the thought *all furze is gorse* just is the thought *all furze is furze*, and whoever assents to the latter *ipso facto* assents to the former. We may sometimes be unable to determine whether we are employing two concepts or one. That makes the individuation of thoughts and concepts less accessible to the thinker than many theorists of thought have wished. For the sake of greater (but still imperfect) accessibility, they might therefore switch to individuating concepts more like words than like meanings. In any case, the argument against epistemological analyticity at the level of thought has already been explained, in Section 5.

8

At this point, a friend of epistemological analyticity may suspect that the mistake was to go for the idea that understanding is somehow *psychologically* sufficient for assent. Instead, the suggestion is, we should go for the idea that understanding is somehow *epistemologically* sufficient for assent.[43] Externally, Peter and Stephen are in a position to know (or to assent with justification). They seem to be willfully and perversely turning their backs on knowledge that is available to them. It is there for the taking, but they are psychologically blocked from taking it.

We must be careful about the source of the blockage. Suppose that it is lack of logical insight. Although Peter and Stephen grasp the thought *every vixen is a vixen*, they lack the logical insight to know *every vixen is a vixen*. Other people just like Peter and Stephen except for having more logical insight do know *every vixen is a vixen*. Anyone who grasps the thought *every vixen is a vixen* and has a modicum of logical insight can know *every vixen is a vixen*. That story assigns no special role to grasp of concepts, beyond the usual role that grasping any thought plays as a precondition for knowing it: the decisive role is assigned to logical competence, not conceptual competence. For conceptual competence to play the decisive role, something like this is needed:

(KUt′)   Whoever knows *every vixen is a vixen* in the normal way does so simply on the basis of their grasp of the thought.

(Understand "on the basis of" more like "by an exercise of" than like "by inference from.") Similarly, for semantic competence to play the decisive role, something like this is needed:

---

[43] Some rationalist defenders of intuition seem to have something like this in mind.

(KUl')   Whoever knows "Every vixen is a vixen" in the normal way
          does so simply on the basis of their understanding of the
          sentence.

KUt' and KUl' may be plausible at first sight. They do not imply that
whoever understands the sentence or grasps the thought has a disposition to assent to it, let alone to know it.

What do the definite descriptions "their grasp of the thought" in
KUt' and "their understanding of the sentence" in KUl' denote? There
are thick and thin candidates. The thin candidates are the mere fact
that they grasp the thought and the mere fact that they understand
the sentence respectively. The thick candidates are the underlying
facts that constitute the respective thin candidates, the facts that
realize this particular subject's understanding at this particular time.
The thin candidates are exactly similar for any two people who grasp
the thought or understand the sentence, since they have the same
property of grasping the thought or understanding the sentence. The
thick candidates may differ between any two people who grasp the
thought or understand the sentence, since different underlying facts
can constitute their doing so. These characterizations are schematic,
but will do for present purposes.

Suppose that the definite descriptions in KUt' and KUl' denote the
thick candidates. KUt' and KUl' remain somewhat plausible on this
reading. Then, given the holistic picture of concept possession and
linguistic understanding in previous sections, KUt' and KUl' have
much less epistemological significance than might have been hoped.
The facts that constitute your understanding of a given sentence
include various cognitive capacities that are not in general necessary
for understanding that sentence, but help to make up your particular
competence with it. For example, the facts that constitute Peter's
understanding of (1) include his logical capacities; the facts that constitute Stephen's understanding of (1) include his rather different
logical capacities. The bases cited in KUl' and KUt' include cognitive
capacities that are not in general necessary for understanding the
sentence or grasping the thought. Thus the thick candidates are too
thick to yield bases for analyticity; they involve cognitive capacities
that are not semantic or conceptual in any relevant sense.

Suppose instead that the definite descriptions in KUt' and KUl'
denote the thin candidates. But they are not the bases in any useful

sense for knowing *every vixen is a vixen* or "Every vixen is a vixen" in the normal way, although confusion with the thick candidates may suggest otherwise. The thin candidates imply no specific logical capacity at all, as Peter, Stephen and others show. It is not as though in such cases the subject's understanding quietly tells them to assent but they override the advice; it is providing no such advice to be overridden. For the imagined overridden advice is a metaphor for the hypothesis of overridden dispositions to assent, dispositions necessary for understanding; that hypothesis was rejected in Section 4. By itself, thin understanding cannot guide our assent. Consequently, understanding in the thin sense provides no basis for assent to anyone. Of course, understanding is a precondition for knowing, and in that sense may be *part* of the basis for knowing, but that point is quite general; it is neutral between the analytic and the synthetic. Although the combination of understanding in the thin sense with the right bit of elementary but not universal logical competence is a basis for knowing (1), that point neither explains why logical knowledge is available in the armchair nor makes it distinctively conceptual or semantic. By themselves, the thin candidates are too thin to be bases for knowledge.

We could try eliminating the talk of bases, for instance in formulations like these:

(AJt′)   Whoever grasps the thought *every vixen is a vixen* and assents to it does so with justification.

(AJl′)   Whoever understands the sentence "Every vixen is a vixen" and assents to it does so with justification.[44]

But such principles are false, since someone who assents because his father told him not to does so without even defeasible justification. The obvious way to avoid such counterexamples and make the connection with conceptual or semantic competence is to qualify "assents to it" by "on the basis of that grasp [understanding]." But that returns us to the difficulties of KUt′ and KUl′.

---

[44]   The intended differences between assenting with justification in AJt′ and AJl′ and being justified in assenting in UJt and UJl are that (i) the former but not the latter entails assent and (ii) the assent in the former must be appropriately sensitive to the justification.

The problem is general. The idea that, in the cases at issue, under-standing is epistemologically sufficient for assent is the idea that assent on the basis of understanding has the desired positive epistemic status. But once we disambiguate "understanding" between thick and thin candidates, we can see that the thin candidates are too thin to be bases for assent while the thick candidates are not purely semantic or conceptual. The attempt to base the epistemology of obvious truths such as (1) and (9) on preconditions for understanding them rests on a false conception of understanding.

Linguistic competence plays the same role when we know "Vixens are female foxes" as when we know "There is a vixen in the garden." It does not gain a role just because perception loses one. The contri-bution of linguistic competence amounts to this: you won't get very far if you conduct your inquiry in a language you don't understand. Of course, that goes for *any* inquiry.

The following chapters develop a quite different account of the nature of at least some philosophical knowledge, on which linguistic and conceptual competence play only this background role, and philosophical beliefs are much less distinctive in nature than many philosophers like to think. We start with knowledge of metaphysical possibility and necessity.

5
Knowledge of Metaphysical Modality

1

Philosophers characteristically ask not just whether things are some way but whether they could have been otherwise. What could have been otherwise is *metaphysically contingent*; what could not is *metaphysically necessary*. We have some knowledge of such matters. We know that Henry VIII could have had more than six wives, but that three plus three could not have been more than six. So there should be an epistemology of metaphysical modality.

The differences between metaphysical necessity, contingency, and impossibility are not mind-dependent, in any useful sense of that frustrating phrase. Thus they are not differences in actual or potential psychological, social, linguistic, or even epistemic status (Kripke (1980) made the crucial distinctions). One shortcut to this conclusion uses the plausible idea that mathematical truth is mind-independent. Since mathematics is not contingent, the difference between truth and falsity in mathematics is also the difference between necessity and impossibility; consequently, the difference between necessity and impossibility is mind-independent. The difference between contingency and non-contingency is equally mind-independent; for if C is a mind-independently true or false mathematical conjecture, then one of C and its negation conjoined with the proposition that Henry VIII had six wives forms a contingently true conjunction while the other forms an impossible conjunction, but which is which is mind-independent. To emphasize the point, think of the mind-independently truth-valued conjecture as evidence-transcendent, absolutely undecidable, neither provable nor refutable by any means. Thus the epistemology of metaphysical modality is one of mind-independent truths.

Nevertheless, doubts begin to arise. Although philosophers attribute metaphysical necessity to mathematical theorems, what matters mathematically is just their truth, not their metaphysical necessity: mathematics does not need the concept of metaphysical necessity. Does metaphysical modality really matter outside philosophy? Even if physicists care about the physical necessity of the laws they conjecture, does it matter to physics whether physically necessary laws are also metaphysically necessary? In ordinary life, we care whether someone could have done otherwise, whether disaster could have been averted, but the kind of possibility at issue there is far more narrowly circumscribed than metaphysical possibility, by not prescinding from metaphysically contingent initial conditions. He could not have done otherwise because he was in chains, even though it was metaphysically contingent that he was in chains. Does "could have been" ever express metaphysical possibility when used non-philosophically?

If thought about metaphysical modality is the exclusive preserve of philosophers, so is knowledge of metaphysical modality. The epistemology of metaphysical modality tends to be treated as an isolated case. For instance, much of the discussion concerns how far, if at all, conceivability is a guide to possibility, and inconceivability to impossibility (Gendler and Hawthorne (2002) has a sample of recent contributions to this debate). The impression is that, outside philosophy, the primary cognitive role of conceiving is propaedeutic. Conceiving a hypothesis is getting it onto the table, putting it up for serious consideration as a candidate for truth. The inconceivable never even gets that far. Conceivability is certainly no good evidence for the restricted kinds of possibility we mainly care about in natural science or ordinary life. We easily conceive particles violating what are in fact physical laws, or the man without his chains. On this view, conceiving, outside philosophy, is no faculty for distinguishing truth from falsity in some domain, but rather a preliminary to any such faculty. Although there are truths and falsehoods about conceivability and inconceivability, they concern our mental capacities, whereas metaphysical modalities are supposed to be mind-independent. They are not contingent on mental capacities, because not contingent on anything (at least if we accept the principles of the modal logic S5, that the necessary is necessarily necessary and the possible necessarily possible). When philosophers present conceiving as a faculty for distinguishing between truth and falsity in the domain of metaphysical modality, that looks suspiciously like some sort of illicit projection or unacknowledged fiction: at best, attributions of metaphysical modality would lack the cognitive status traditionally ascribed to them (compare Blackburn (1987), Craig (1985), Wright (1989), and Rosen (1990)). The apparent cognitive isolation of metaphysically modal thought makes such suspicions hard to allay. Presenting it as *sui generis* suggests that it can be surgically removed from our conceptual scheme without collateral damage. If it can, what good does it do us? In general, the postulation by philosophers of a special cognitive capacity exclusive to philosophical or quasi-philosophical thinking looks like a scam.

Humans evolved under no pressure to do philosophy. Presumably, survival and reproduction in the Stone Age depended little on philosophical prowess, dialectical skill being no more effective then than now as a seduction technique and in any case dependent on a hearer already equipped to recognize it. Any cognitive capacity we have for philosophy is a more or less accidental byproduct of other developments. Nor are psychological dispositions that are non-cognitive outside philosophy likely suddenly to become cognitive within it. We should expect the cognitive capacities used in philosophy to be cases of general cognitive capacities used in ordinary life, perhaps trained, developed, and systematically applied in various special ways, just as the cognitive capacities that we use in mathematics and natural science are rooted in more primitive cognitive capacities to perceive, imagine, correlate, reason, discuss ... In particular, a plausible non-skeptical epistemology of metaphysical modality should subsume our capacity to discriminate metaphysical possibilities from metaphysical impossibilities under more general cognitive capacities used in ordinary life.

I will argue that the ordinary cognitive capacity to handle counterfactual conditionals carries with it the cognitive capacity to handle metaphysical modality. Section 2 illustrates with examples our cognitive use of counterfactual conditionals. Section 3 sketches an epistemology for such conditionals. Section 4 explains how they subsume metaphysical modality. Section 5 assesses the consequences for the distinction between *a priori* and *a posteriori* knowledge. Section 6 discusses some objections. Section 7 briefly raises the relation between metaphysical possibility and the restricted kinds of possibility that seem more relevant to ordinary life. Philosophers' ascriptions of metaphysical modality are far more deeply rooted in our ordinary cognitive practices than most skeptics about it realize.

2

Our overall capacity for somewhat reliable thought about counterfactual possibilities is hardly surprising, for we cannot know in advance exactly which possibilities are or will be actual. We need to make contingency plans. In practice, the only way for us to be cognitively equipped to deal with the actual is by being cognitively equipped to deal with a wide variety of contingencies, most of them counterfactual. Our present task is to understand some of the more specific cognitive value to us of thinking with those conditional constructions labeled "counterfactual."

We can usefully start with a well-known example which proves the term "counterfactual conditional" misleading. As Alan Ross Anderson pointed out (1951: 37), a doctor might say:

(1) If Jones had taken arsenic, he would have shown just exactly those symptoms which he does in fact show.

Clearly, (1) can provide abductive evidence by inference to the best explanation for its antecedent (see Edgington (2003: 23–7) for more discussion):

(2) Jones took arsenic.

If further tests subsequently verify (2), they confirm the doctor's statement rather than in any way falsifying it or making it inappropriate. If we still call subjunctive conditionals like (1) "counterfactuals," the reason is not that they imply or presuppose the falsity of their antecedents. In what follows, we shall be just as concerned with conditional sentences such as (1) as with those whose premises are false, or believed to be so.

Of course, what (2) explains is not the trivial necessary truth that Jones shows whatever symptoms he shows. What is contingent is that Jones shows exactly those symptoms which he does in fact show – he could have shown other symptoms, or none – and, given (1), (2) explains that contingent truth.

While (1) provides valuable empirical evidence, the corresponding indicative conditional does not (Stalnaker 1999: 71):

(1I)   If Jones took arsenic, he shows just exactly those symptoms which he does in fact show.

We can safely assent to (1I) without knowing what symptoms Jones shows, since it holds whatever they are. Informally, (1) is non-trivial because it depends on a comparison between independently specified terms, the symptoms Jones would have shown if he had taken arsenic and the symptoms he does in fact show; by contrast, (1I) is trivial because it involves only a comparison of his symptoms with themselves. Thus the process of evaluating the "counterfactual" conditional requires something like two files, one for the actual situation, the other for the counterfactual situation, even if these situations turn out to coincide. No such cross-comparison of files is needed to evaluate the indicative conditional. Of course, when one evaluates an indicative conditional while disbelieving its antecedent, one must not confuse one's file of beliefs with one's file of judgments on the supposition of the antecedent, but that does not mean that cross-referencing from the latter file to the former can play the role it did in the counterfactual case. One logical manifestation of this difference is that any indicative conditional $A \rightarrow @A$ is a logical truth, where @ is the "actually" operator (@A is true at any given world just in case A is true at the actual world), whereas the counterfactual conditional $A \mathrel{\Box\!\!\rightarrow} @A$ is false if A is contingently false. For instance, I can trivially assert "If the coin landed heads, it actually landed heads," without checking how it landed, but "If the coin had landed heads, it would have actually landed heads" is false if the coin actually landed tails, because it implies that if the coin could have landed heads, it actually did so (Williamson (2006a) has more discussion).

The sentence (1I) works differently from the non-trivial habitual:

(1H)   If Jones takes arsenic, he shows just exactly those symptoms which he does in fact show.

The latter can be false when both (1) and (1I) are true, for example because Jones's symptoms are not those he would normally show on arsenic poisoning but those he would show given that he had, unusually, been fasting for the previous 72 hours, a fact the doctor took into account. Since habituals in some sense characterize "normal" cases while counterfactual conditionals can depend on abnormal features of the current case, habituals are not in general adequate substitutes for counterfactual conditionals. Of course, the truth conditions of habituals themselves involve counterfactual cases.

Since (1) constitutes empirical evidence, its truth was not guaranteed in advance. If Jones had looked suitably different, the doctor would have had to assert the opposite counterfactual conditional:

(3)   If Jones had taken arsenic, he would not have shown just exactly those symptoms which he does in fact show.

From (3) we can deduce the falsity of its antecedent. For modus ponens is generally agreed to be valid for counterfactual conditionals. Thus (2) and (3) entail:

(4)   Jones does not show just exactly those symptoms which he does in fact show.

Since (4) is obviously false, we can deny (2) given (3).

The indicative conditional corresponding to (3) is:

(3I)   If Jones took arsenic, he does not show just exactly those symptoms which he does in fact show.

To assert (3I) is like saying "If Jones took arsenic, pigs can fly." Although a very confident doctor might assert (3I), on the grounds that Jones certainly did not take arsenic, that certainty may in turn be based on confidence in (3), and therefore on the comparison of actual and counterfactual situations.

Could a Bayesian account dispense with the counterfactual conditionals in favor of conditional probabilities? Consider the simple case in which we completely trust the doctor who asserts (1). Before the doctor speaks, we are certain what symptoms Jones shows but agnostic over the characteristic symptoms of arsenic poisoning. We want to update our probability for his having taken arsenic on evidence from the doctor, in Bayesian terms by conditionalizing on it. The doctor cannot simply tell us what probability to assign, because we may have further relevant evidence unavailable to the doctor, for example about Jones's character. We need the doctor to say something that we can use as evidence; (1) exactly fits the bill (of course, our evidence also includes the fact that the doctor asserted (1), but in the circumstances we can treat (1) itself as the relevant part of our evidence). It may even do better than a non-modal generalization such as "Jones showed exactly those symptoms which everyone who takes arsenic shows": for the symptoms may vary with bodily characteristics of the victim, and through long experience the doctor may be able to judge what symptoms Jones would have shown if he had taken arsenic without being able to articulate a suitable generalization. If he were to say "Jones showed exactly those symptoms which everyone relevantly like him who takes arsenic shows," he might easily have to do so without knowing of any instance of this contextually restricted generalization other than the one at hand; in such cases belief in the restricted generalization is epistemically based on the counterfactual conditional, not *vice versa*. Any Bayesian account depends on an adequately varied stock of propositions to act as bearers of probability, as evidence or hypotheses. Sometimes that range has to include counterfactual conditionals.

We also use the notional distinction between actual and counterfactual situations to make evaluative comparisons:

(5)   If Jones had not taken arsenic, he would have been in better shape than he now is.

Such counterfactual reflections facilitate learning from experience; one may decide never to take arsenic oneself. Formulating counterfactuals about past experience is empirically correlated with improved future performance in various tasks.[1]

Evidently, counterfactual conditionals give clues to causal connections. This point does not commit one to the ambitious program of

---

[1]   The large empirical literature on the affective role of counterfactuals and its relation to learning from experience includes Kahneman and Tversky (1982), Roese and Olson (1993, 1995) and Byrne (2005).

analyzing causality in terms of counterfactual conditionals (Lewis (1973b), Collins, Hall, and Paul (2004)), or counterfactual conditionals in terms of causality (Jackson 1977). If the former program succeeds, all causal thinking is counterfactual thinking; if the latter succeeds, all counterfactual thinking is causal thinking. Either way, the overlap is so large that we cannot have one without much of the other. It may well be over-optimistic to expect either necessary and sufficient conditions for causal statements in counterfactual terms or necessary and sufficient conditions for counterfactual statements in causal terms. Even so, counterfactuals surely play a crucial role in our causal thinking (see Harris (2000: 118–39) and Byrne (2005: 100–28) for some empirical discussion). Only extreme skeptics deny the cognitive value of causal thought.

At a more theoretical level, claims of nomic necessity support counterfactual conditionals. If it is a law that property P implies property Q, then typically if something were to have P, it would have Q. If we can falsify the counterfactual in a specific case, perhaps by using better-established laws, we thereby falsify that claim of lawhood. We sometimes have enough evidence to establish what the result of an experiment would be without actually doing the experiment: that matters in a world of limited resources.

Counterfactual thought is deeply integrated into our empirical thought in general. Although that consideration will not deter the most dogged skeptics about our knowledge of counterfactuals, it indicates the difficulty of preventing such skepticism from generalizing implausibly far, since our beliefs about counterfactuals are so well-integrated into our general knowledge of our environment. I proceed on the assumption that we have non-trivial knowledge of counterfactuals.

3

In discussing the epistemology of counterfactuals, I assume no particular theory of their compositional semantics. Although I sometimes use the Stalnaker-Lewis approach for purposes of illustration and vividness, I do not assume its correctness or that of any other specific semantic account of counterfactuals, within or without the framework of possible worlds. That evasion of semantic theory might seem dubious, since it is the semantic facts which determine what has to be known. However, we can go some way on the basis of our pretheoretical understanding of such conditionals in our native language. Moreover, the best developed formal semantic theories of counterfactuals use an apparatus of possible worlds or situations at best distantly related to our actual cognitive processing. While that does not refute such theories, which concern the truth conditions of counterfactuals, not how subjects attempt to find out whether those truth conditions obtain, it shows how indirect the relation between the semantics and the epistemology may be. When we come to fine-tune our epistemology of counterfactuals, we may need an articulated semantic theory, but at a first pass we can make do with some sketchy remarks about their epistemology while remaining as far as possible neutral over their deep semantic analysis. Although I formalize the counterfactual conditional with the usual sentence operator □→, I do not assume that that exactly reflects the structure of the corresponding natural language sentences.[2] As for the psychological study of the processes underlying our assessment of counterfactual conditionals, it remains in a surprisingly undeveloped state, as recent authors have complained (Evans and Over 2004: 113–31).

Start with an example. You are in the mountains. As the sun melts the ice, rocks embedded in it are loosened and crash down the slope. You notice one rock slide into a bush. You wonder where it would have ended if the bush had not been there. A natural way to answer the question is by visualizing the rock sliding without the bush there, then bouncing down the slope into the lake at the bottom. Under suitable background conditions, you thereby come to know this counterfactual:

(6)   If the bush had not been there, the rock would have ended in the lake.

You could test that judgment by physically removing the bush and experimenting with similar rocks, but you know (6) even without performing such experiments. Logically, the counterfactual about the

---

[2]   Lewis (1975) treats "if" in some occurrences as a restrictor on quantifiers rather than a sentential connective. This approach was generalized to all occurrences of "if" in Kratzer (1986).

past is independent of claims about future experiments (for a start, the slope is undergoing continual small changes).

Somehow, you came to know the counterfactual by using your imagination. That sounds puzzling if one conceives the imagination as unconstrained. You can imagine the rock rising vertically into the air, or looping the loop, or sticking like a limpet to the slope. What constrains imagining it one way rather than another?

You do not imagine it those other ways because your imaginative exercise is radically informed and disciplined by your perception of the rock and the slope and your sense of how nature works. The default for the imagination in its primary function may be to proceed as "realistically" as it can, subject to whatever deviations the thinker imposes by brute force: here, the absence of the bush. Thus the imagination can in principle exploit all our background knowledge in evaluating counterfactuals. Of course, how to separate background knowledge from what must be imagined away in imagining the antecedent is Goodman's old, deep problem of cotenability (1954). For example, why don't we bring to bear our background knowledge that the rock did not go far, and imagine another obstacle to its fall? Difficult though the problem is, it should not make us lose sight of our considerable knowledge of counterfactuals: our procedures for evaluating them cannot be too wildly misleading.

Can the imaginative exercise be regimented as a piece of reasoning? We can undoubtedly assess some counterfactuals by straightforward reasoning. For instance:

(7)   If twelve people had come to the party, more than eleven people would have come to the party.

We can deduce the consequent "More than eleven people came to the party" from the antecedent "Twelve people came to the party," and assert (7) on that basis. Similarly, it may be suggested, we can assert (6) on the basis of inferring its consequent "The rock ended in the lake" from the premise "The bush was not there," given auxiliary premises about the rock, the mountainside and the laws of nature.

At the level of formal logic, we have the corresponding plausible and widely accepted closure principle that, given a derivation of C from $B_1, \ldots, B_n$, we can derive the counterfactual conditional $A \,\square\!\!\rightarrow C$ from the counterfactual conditionals $A \,\square\!\!\rightarrow B_1, \ldots, A \,\square\!\!\rightarrow B_n$; in other words, the counterfactual consequences of a supposition **A** are closed under logical consequence (Lewis (1986: 132) calls this "Deduction within Conditionals"). With the uncontroversial reflexivity principle **A** □→ **A**, it follows that, given a derivation of **C** from **A** alone, we can derive **A** □→ **C** from the null set of premises.

We cannot automatically extend the closure rule to the case of auxiliary premises, for since we can derive an arbitrary conclusion **C** from an arbitrary premise **A** with **C** as auxiliary premise, we could then derive **A** □→ **C** from the auxiliary premise **C** alone: but that implies the invalid principle that any truth is a counterfactual consequence of any supposition whatsoever. The truth of "Napoleon lost at Waterloo" does not guarantee the truth of "If Grouchy had marched towards the sounds of gunfire, Napoleon would have lost at Waterloo." Auxiliary premises cannot always be copied into the scope of counterfactual suppositions (this is the problem of cotenability again). Even with this caution, the treatment of the process by which we reach counterfactual judgments as inferential is problematic in several ways.

First, a technical problem: not every inference licenses us to assert the corresponding counterfactual, even when the inference is deductive and the auxiliary premises are selected appropriately. For the consequent of (1) is a logical truth (count it vacuously true if Jones shows no symptoms):

(8)   Jones shows just exactly those symptoms which he does in fact show.

Thus (8) follows from any premises, including (2), the antecedent of (1); but we cannot assert (1) on the basis of that trivial deduction alone, independently of *which* symptoms Jones does in fact show. Formally, although **A** ≡ **@A** is always a logical truth, **B** □→ (**A** ≡ **@A**) may be false. Similarly, although **@A** is always a logical consequence of **A**, **A** □→ **@A** may be false. This is related to Kaplan's (1989) point that the rule of necessitation fails in languages with terms such as "actually." The logical truth of (8) does not guarantee the logical truth, or even truth, of (9):

(9)   It is necessary that Jones shows just exactly those symptoms which he does in fact show.

For it is contingent that Jones shows just exactly those symptoms which he does in fact show.[3] But let us assume that this technical problem can be solved by a restriction on the type of reasoning from antecedent to consequent that can license a counterfactual, and on the closure principle above, like the restriction on the type of reasoning that licenses the necessitation of its conclusion.

A more serious problem is that the putative reasoner may lack general-purpose cognitive access to the auxiliary premises of the putative reasoning. In particular, the folk physics needed to derive the consequents of counterfactuals such as (6) from their antecedents may be stored in the form of some analogue mechanism, perhaps embodied in a connectionist network, which the subject cannot articulate in propositional form. Normally, a subject who uses negation and derives a conclusion from some premises can at least entertain the negation of a given premise, whether or not they are willing to assert it, perhaps on the basis of the other premises and the negation of the conclusion. Our reliance on folk physics does not enable us to formulate its negation. More generally, the supposed premises may not be stored in a form that permits the normal range of inferential interactions with other beliefs, even at an unconscious level. This strains the analogy with explicit reasoning.

The third problem is epistemological. Normally, someone who believes a conclusion on the sole basis of inference from some premises knows the conclusion only if they know the premises. This principle must be applied with care, for often a thinker is aware of several inferential routes from different sets of premises to the same conclusion. For example, you believe that a and b are F; you deduce that something is F. If you know that a is F, you may thereby come to know that something is F, even if your belief that b is F is false, and so not knowledge. Similarly, you may believe more premises than you need to draw an inductive conclusion. The principle applies only to essential premises, those that figure in all the inferences on which the relevant belief in the conclusion is based. However, folk physics is an essential standing background premise of the supposed inferences

---

[3] The phrase "does in fact show" is read throughout as inside the scope of the counterfactual conditional or modal operator, but as rigid, like "actually shows." See Williamson (2006a) for discussion.

from antecedents to consequents of counterfactuals like (6), as usually conceived, so the epistemological maxim applies. Folk physics in this sense is a theory whose content includes the general principles by which expectations of motion, constancy, and the like are formed online in real time; it is no mere collection of memories of particular past incidents. But then presumably it is strictly speaking false: although many of its predictions are useful approximations, they are inaccurate in some circumstances; knowledge of the true laws of motion is not already wired into our brains, otherwise physics could be reduced to psychology. Since folk physics is false, it is not known. But the conclusion that no belief formed on the basis of folk physics constitutes knowledge is wildly skeptical. For folk physics is reliable enough in many circumstances to be used in the acquisition of knowledge, for example that the cricket ball will land in that field. Thus we should not conceive folk physics as a premise of that conclusion. Nor should we conceive some local fragment of folk physics as the premise. For it would be quite unmotivated to take an inferential approach overall while refusing to treat this local fragment as itself derived from the general theory of folk physics. We should conceive folk physics as a locally but not globally reliable method of belief formation, not as a premise.

If folk theories are methods of belief formation rather than specific beliefs, can they be treated as patterns of inference, for example from beliefs about the present to beliefs about the future? Represented as a universal generalization, a non-deductive pattern of inference such as abduction is represented as a falsehood, for the relevantly best explanations are not always correct. Nevertheless, we can acquire knowledge abductively because we do not rely on every abduction in relying on one; we sometimes rely on a locally truth-preserving abduction, even though abduction is not globally truth-preserving. The trouble with replacing a pattern of inference by a universal generalization is that it has us rely on all instances of the pattern simultaneously, by relying on the generalization. Even if the universal generalization is replaced by a statement of general tendencies, what we are relying on in a particular case is still inappropriately globalized. Epistemologically, folk "theories" seem to function more like patterns of inference than like general premises. That conception also solves the earlier problem about the inapplicability of logical operators to folk "theories," since patterns of inference cannot themselves be negated or made the antecedents of conditionals (although claims of their validity can).

Once such a liberal conception of patterns of inference is allowed, calling a process of belief formation "inferential" is no longer very informative. Just about any process with a set of beliefs (or suppositions) as input and an expanded set of beliefs (or suppositions) as output counts as "inferential." Can we say something more informative about the imaginative exercises by which we judge counterfactuals like (6), whether or not we count them as inferential?

An attractive suggestion is that some kind of simulation is involved: the difficulty is to explain what that means. It is just a hint of an answer to say that in simulation cognitive faculties are run offline. The cognitive faculties that would be run online to evaluate A and B as free-standing sentences are run offline in the evaluation of the counterfactual conditional $A \, \square\!\!\rightarrow B$.[4] This suggests that the cognition has a roughly compositional structure. Our capacity to handle $A \, \square\!\!\rightarrow B$ embeds our capacities to handle A and B separately, and our capacity to handle the counterfactual conditional operator involves a general capacity to go from capacities to handle the antecedent and the consequent separately to a capacity to handle the whole conditional. Here the capacity to handle an expression comprises more than mere linguistic understanding of it, since it involves ways of assessing its application that are not built into its meaning. But it virtually never involves a decision procedure that enables us always to determine the truth-values of every sentence in which the expression principally occurs, since we lack such decision procedures. Of course, we can sometimes take shortcuts in evaluating counterfactual conditionals. For instance, we can know that $A \, \square\!\!\rightarrow A$ is true even if we have no idea how to determine whether A is true. Nevertheless, the compositional structure just described seems more typical.

How do we advance from capacities to handle the antecedent and the consequent separately to a capacity to handle the whole conditional? "Offline" suggests that the most direct links with perception have been cut, but that vague negative point does not take us far.

---

[4] Matters become more complicated if A or B itself contains a counterfactual condition, as in "If she had murdered the man who would have inherited her money if she had died, she would have been sentenced to life imprisonment if she had been convicted," but the underlying principles are the same.

Perceptual input is crucial to the evaluation of counterfactuals such as (1) and (6).

The best developed simulation theories concern our ability to simulate the mental processes of other agents (or ourselves in other circumstances), putting ourselves in their shoes, as if thinking and deciding on the basis of their beliefs and desires (see for example Davies and Stone (1995), Nichols and Stich (2003)). Such cognitive processes may well be relevant to the evaluation of counterfactuals about agents. Moreover, they would involve just the sort of constrained use of the imagination indicated above. How would Mary react if you asked to borrow her car? You could imagine her immediately shooting you, or making you her heir; you could even imagine reacting like that from her point of view, by imagining having sufficiently bizarre beliefs and desires. But you do not. Doing so would not help you determine how she really would react. Presumably, what you do is to hold fixed her actual beliefs and desires (as you take them to be just before the request); you can then imagine the request from her point of view, and think through the scenario from there. Just as with the falling rock, the imaginative exercise is richly informed and disciplined by your sense of what she is like.

How could mental simulation help us evaluate a counterfactual such as (6), which does not concern an agent? Even if you somehow put yourself in the rock's shoes, imagining first-personally being that shape, size, and hardness and bouncing down that slope, you would not be simulating the rock's reasoning and decision-making. Thinking of the rock as an agent is no help in determining its counterfactual trajectory. A more natural way to answer the question is by imagining third-personally the rock falling as it would visually appear from your actual present spatial position; you thereby avoid the complex process of adjusting your current visual perspective to the viewpoint of the rock. Is that to simulate the mental states of an observer watching the rock fall from your present position?[5] By itself, that suggestion explains little. For how do we know what to simulate the observer seeing next?

That question is not unanswerable. For we have various propensities to form expectations about what happens next: for example, to

[5]   See Goldman (1992: 24), discussed by Nichols, Stich, Leslie, and Klein (1996: 53–9).

project the trajectories of nearby moving bodies into the immediate future (otherwise we could not catch balls). Perhaps we simulate the initial movement of the rock in the absence of the bush, form an expectation as to where it goes next, feed the expected movement back into the simulation as seen by the observer, form a further expectation as to its subsequent movement, feed that back into the simulation, and so on. If our expectations in such matters are approximately correct in a range of ordinary cases, such a process is cognitively worthwhile. The very natural laws and causal tendencies our expectations roughly track also help to determine which counterfactual conditionals really hold. Thus some reliability in the assessment of counterfactuals is achieved.

However, talk of simulating the mental states of an observer may suggest that the presence of the observer is part of the content of the simulation. That does not fit our evaluation of counterfactuals. Consider:

(10)   If there had been a tree on this spot a million years ago, nobody would have known.

Even if we visually imagine a tree on this spot a million years ago, we do not automatically reject (10) because we envisage an observer of the tree. We may imagine the tree as having a certain visual appearance from a certain viewpoint, but that is not to say that we imagine it as appearing to someone at that viewpoint. For example, if we imagine the sun as shining from behind that viewpoint, by imagining the tree's shadow stretching back from the tree, we are not obliged to imagine either the observer's shadow stretching towards the tree or the observer as perfectly transparent.[6] Nor, when we consider (10),

<hr>

[6]   The question is of course related to Berkeley's claim that we cannot imagine an unseen object. For discussion see Williams (1966), Peacocke (1985) and Currie (1995b: 36–7). Gaut (2006: 116–21) describes the role of art in facilitating the evaluation of counterfactuals by means of the imagination. He disavows commitment to the view, which he credits to Currie (1995a) (ch. 5), that "imagination is a kind of 'offline' running of cognitive processes, and that this is a source of knowledge of psychological states," appealing instead to the tradition of Vico and Weber, on which the relevant role of imagination is in *verstehen*, in understanding oneself and others (Gaut 2006: 121). However, it is doubtful that this tradition can (or wants to) explain knowledge of counterfactuals that do not concern mental states.

are we asking whether if we had believed that there was a tree on this spot a million years ago, we would have believed that nobody knew.[7] It is better not to regard the content of the simulation as referring to anything specifically *mental* at all. It is just that visual imagining reuses offline some of the very same cognitive resources that visual perceiving uses online.

Of course, for many counterfactuals the relevant expectations are not hardwired into us in the way that those concerning the trajectories of fast-moving objects around us may need to be. Our knowledge that if a British general election had been called in 1948 the Communists would not have won may depend on an offline use of our capacity to predict political events. Still, where our more sophisticated capacities to predict the future are reliable, so should be corresponding counterfactual judgments. In these cases too, simulating the mental states of an imaginary observer seems unnecessary.

The offline use of expectation-forming capacities to judge counterfactuals corresponds to the widespread picture of the semantic evaluation of those conditionals as "rolling back" history to shortly before the time of the antecedent, modifying its course by stipulating the truth of the antecedent and then rolling history forward again according to patterns of development as close as possible to the normal ones to test the truth of the consequent (compare Lewis (1979)).

The use of expectation-forming capacities may in effect impose a partial solution to Goodman's problem of cotenability, since they do not operate on information about what happened after the time treated as present. In this respect indicative conditionals are evaluated differently: if I had climbed a mountain yesterday I would remember

---

[7]   A similar problem arises for what is sometimes called the Ramsey Test for conditionals, on which one simulates belief in the antecedent and asks whether one then believes the consequent. Goldman (1992: 24) writes "When considering the truth value of 'If X were the case, then Y would obtain,' a reasoner feigns a belief in X and reasons about Y under that pretence." What Ramsey himself says is that when people "are fixing their degrees of belief in q given p" they "are adding p hypothetically to their stock of knowledge and arguing on that basis about q" (1978: 143), but he specifically warns that "the degree of belief in q given p" does not mean the degree of belief "which the subject would have in q if he knew p, or that which he ought to have" (1978: 82; variables interchanged). Of course, conditional probabilities bear more directly on indicative than on subjunctive conditionals.

it today, but if I did climb a mountain yesterday I do not remember it today. The known fact that I do not remember climbing a mountain yesterday is retained under the indicative but not the counterfactual supposition.

Our offline use of expectation-forming capacities to unroll a counterfactual history from the imagined initial conditions does not explain why we imagine the initial conditions in one way rather than another – for instance, why we do not imagine a wall in place of the bush. Very often, no alternative occurs to us, but that does not mean that the way we go adds nothing to the given antecedent. We seem to have a prereflective tendency to minimum alteration in imagining counterfactual alternatives to actuality, reminiscent of the role that similarity between possible worlds plays in the Lewis-Stalnaker semantics.

Of course, not all counterfactual conditionals can be evaluated by the rolling back method, since the antecedent need not concern a particular time: in evaluating the claim that space-time has ten dimensions, a scientist can sensibly ask whether if it were true the actually observed phenomena would have occurred. Explicit reasoning may play a much larger role in the evaluation of such conditionals.

Reasoning and prediction do not exhaust our capacity to evaluate counterfactuals. If twelve people had come to the party, would it have been a large party? To answer, one does not imagine a party of twelve people and then predict what would happen next. The question is whether twelve people would have constituted a large party, not whether they would have caused one. Nor is the process of answering best conceived as purely inferential, if one has no special antecedent beliefs as to how many people constitute a large party, any more than the judgment whether the party is large is purely inferential when made at the party. Rather, in both cases one must make a new judgment, even though it is informed by what one already believes or imagines about the party. To call the new judgment "inferential" simply because it is not made independently of all the thinker's prior beliefs or suppositions is to stretch the term "inferential" beyond its useful span. At any rate, the judgment cannot be derived from the prior beliefs or suppositions purely by the application of general rules of inference. For example, even if you have the prior belief that a party is large if and only if it is larger than the average size of a party, in order to apply it to the case at hand you also need to have a belief as to what the average size of a party is; if you have no prior belief as to that, and must form one by inference, an implausible regress threatens, for you do not have the statistics of parties in your head. Similarly, if you try to judge whether this party is large by projecting inductively from previous judgments as to whether parties were large, that only pushes the question back to how those previous judgments were made.

In general, our capacity to evaluate counterfactuals recruits *all* our cognitive capacities to evaluate sentences. A quick argument for this uses the assumption that a counterfactual with a true antecedent has the same truth-value as its consequent, for then any sentence A is logically equivalent to $T \,\square\!\!\rightarrow A$, where T is a trivial tautology; so any non-logical cognitive work needed to evaluate A is also needed to evaluate the counterfactual $T \,\square\!\!\rightarrow A$.[8] For if we could evaluate that counterfactual without doing the non-logical work, we could also evaluate A without doing it, by first evaluating the counterfactual, then deriving its equivalence to A and finally extending the evaluation of the former to the latter. Any logical work needed to evaluate A will also be needed to evaluate $T \,\square\!\!\rightarrow A$ when T is chosen to be irrelevant to A.

There is no uniform epistemology of counterfactual conditionals. In particular, imaginative simulation is neither always necessary nor always sufficient for their evaluation, even when they can be evaluated. Nevertheless, it is the most distinctive cognitive feature of the process of evaluating them, because it is so much more useful for counterfactuals than for most non-counterfactual contents, whereas reasoning, perception, and testimony are not generally more useful for counterfactuals than for non-counterfactual contents.

We can still schematize a typical overall process of evaluating a counterfactual conditional thus: one supposes the antecedent and

---

[8]   Lewis (1986: 26–31) defends the assumption; Nozick (1981: 176) rejects it to make the fourth condition in his analysis of knowledge non-trivial. Bennett (2003: 239–40) also rejects it. The point can be made independently of that assumption, using the rigidifying "actually" operator @. For @A entails $B \,\square\!\!\rightarrow$ @A for any B and therefore $T \,\square\!\!\rightarrow$ @A in particular; conversely, $T \,\square\!\!\rightarrow$ @A entails @A by modus ponens. Since A is logically equivalent to @A, it is logically equivalent to $T \,\square\!\!\rightarrow$ @A. Thus any cognitive capacities needed to assess A will also be needed to assess the more complex $T \,\square\!\!\rightarrow$ @A (modulo those needed to recognize the equivalence).

develops the supposition, adding further judgments within the supposition by reasoning, offline predictive mechanisms, and other offline judgments. The imagining may but need not be perceptual imagining. All of one's background knowledge and beliefs are available from within the scope of the supposition as a description of one's actual circumstances for the purposes of comparison with the counterfactual circumstances (if we know **B**, we can infer **A** □→ @**B** for any **A**; in this respect the development differs from that of the antecedent of an indicative conditional). Some but not all of one's background knowledge and beliefs are also available within the scope of the supposition as a description of the counterfactual circumstances, according to complex criteria (the problem of cotenability). To a first approximation: one asserts the counterfactual conditional if and only if the development eventually leads one to add the consequent.

An over-simplification in that account is that one develops the initial supposition only once. In fact, if one finds various different ways of imagining the antecedent equally good, one may try developing several of them, to test whether they all yield the consequent. For example, if in considering (10) one initially imagines a palm tree, one does not immediately judge that if there had been a tree on this spot a million years ago it would have been a palm tree, because one knows that one can equally easily imagine a fir tree. One repeats the thought experiment. Robustness in the result under such minor perturbations supports a higher degree of confidence.

What happens if the counterfactual development of the antecedent **A** does not robustly yield the consequent **C**? We do not always deny **A** □→ **C**, for several reasons. First, if **C** has not emerged after a given period of development the question remains whether it will emerge in the course of further development, for lines of reasoning can be continued indefinitely from any given premise. To reach a negative conclusion, one must in effect judge that if the consequent were ever going to emerge it would have done so by now. For example, one may have been smoothly fleshing out a scenario incompatible with the consequent with no hint of difficulty. Second, even if one is confident that **C** will not robustly emerge from the development, one may suspect that the reason is one's ignorance of relevant background conditions rather than the lack of a counterfactual connection between **A** and **C** ("If I were to follow that path, it would lead me out of the forest"). Thus one may remain agnostic over **A** □→ **C**.

The case for denying A □→ C is usually strongest when the coun-terfactual development of A yields ¬C. Then one asserts the opposite counterfactual, A □→ ¬C. The default is to deny a counterfactual if one asserts the opposite counterfactual, moving from A □→ ¬C to ¬(A □→ C). The move is defeasible; sometimes one must accept opposite counterfactuals together. For example, deductive closure generates both (B & ¬B) □→ B and (B & ¬B) □→ ¬B. Normally, if the counterfactual development of A robustly yields ¬C and robustly fails to yield C then one denies A □→ C, but even this connection is defeasible, since one may still suspect that C (as well as ¬C) would emerge given more complex reasoning or further background information.

Sometimes a counterfactual antecedent is manifestly neutral between contradictory consequents: consider "If the coin had been tossed it would have come up heads" and "If the coin had been tossed it would have come up tails." In such cases one will clearly never be in a position to assert one conditional, and thus will never be in a position to use it as a basis for denying the opposite conditional. Whether the symmetry permits one to deny both conditionals is controversial.[9]

The epistemological asymmetry between asserting and denying a counterfactual conditional resembles an epistemological asymmetry in practice between asserting and denying many existential claims. If I find snakes in Iceland, without too much fuss I can assert that there are snakes in Iceland. If I fail to find snakes in Iceland, I cannot deny that there are snakes in Iceland without some implicit or explicit assessment of the thoroughness of my search: if there were snakes in Iceland, would I have found some by now? But we are capable of making such assessments, and sometimes are in a position to deny such existential claims. Similarly, if I find a counterfactual connection

---

[9]   On the Lewis semantics, both A □→ C and A □→ ¬C are false when there is a tie for the closest A worlds to the actual world and some but not all of the joint winners are C worlds. Thus we may truly assert both ¬(A □→ C) and ¬(A □→ ¬C). On the Stalnaker semantics, "Conditional Excluded Middle" (A □→ C) ∨ (A □→ ¬C) is a logical law, because a unique A world must be selected, but sometimes neither disjunct is determinately true, because it is indeterminate which A world is selected. In such cases, neither disjunct is determinately false, so we cannot truly assert either ¬(A □→ C) or ¬(A □→ ¬C); we must simply reject both A □→ C and A □→ ¬C as not definitely true.

between **A** and **C** (my counterfactual development of **A** robustly yields C) without too much fuss I can assert **A** $\Box\!\!\rightarrow$ C. If I fail to find a counterfactual connection between **A** and **C** (my counterfactual development of **A** does not robustly yield C), I cannot deny **A** $\Box\!\!\rightarrow$ C without some implicit or explicit assessment of the thoroughness of my search: if there were a counterfactual connection, would I have found it by now? But we are capable of making such assessments, and sometimes are in a position to deny counterfactual conditionals.

For both assertions and denials of counterfactuals, the reliability of our cognitive faculties in their online applications across a wide range of possible circumstances induces reliability in their offline applications too. Offline reliability is achieved even with respect to counterfactual circumstances in which we would not be around to apply those faculties ("If there had been no sentient beings . . ."), for online reliability is often best achieved by tracking robust underlying trends (in nature, in logic, . . .) that hold irrespective of the presence of an observer.

The preceding remarks are the merest sketch of an epistemology of counterfactuals. Nevertheless, they will serve for purposes of orientation in what follows.

Despite its discipline, our imaginative evaluation of counterfactual conditionals is manifestly fallible. We can easily misjudge their truth-values, through background ignorance or error, and distortions of judgment. But such fallibility is the common lot of human cognition. Our use of the imagination in evaluating counterfactuals is moderately reliable and practically indispensable. Rather than cave in to skepticism, we should admit that our methods sometimes yield knowledge of counterfactuals.

4

How does the epistemology of counterfactual conditionals bear on the epistemology of metaphysical modality? We can approach this question by formulating two plausible constraints on the relation between counterfactual conditionals and metaphysical modalities. Henceforth, "necessary" and "possible" will be used for the metaphysical modalities unless otherwise stated.

First, the strict conditional implies the counterfactual conditional:

NECESSITY $\Box(A \rightarrow B) \rightarrow (A \,\Box\!\!\rightarrow B)$

Suppose that **A** could not have held without **B** holding too; then if **A** had held, **B** would also have held. In terms of possible worlds semantics for these operators along the lines of Lewis (1973) or Stalnaker (1968): if all **A** worlds are **B** worlds, then any closest **A** worlds are **B** worlds. More precisely, if all **A** worlds are **B** worlds, then either there are no **A** worlds or there is an **A** world such that any **A** world at least as close as it is to the actual world is a **B** world.

Second, the counterfactual conditional transmits possibility:

POSSIBILITY $(A \,\Box\!\!\rightarrow B) \rightarrow (\Diamond A \rightarrow \Diamond B)$

Suppose that if **A** had held, **B** would also have held; then if **A** could have held, **B** could also have held. In terms of worlds: if any closest **A** worlds are **B** worlds, and there are **A** worlds, then there are also **B** worlds. More precisely, if either there are no **A** worlds or there is an **A** world such that any **A** world at least as close as it is to the actual world is a **B** world, then if there is an **A** world there is also a **B** world.

Together, NECESSITY and POSSIBILITY sandwich the counterfactual conditional between two modal conditions. But they do not squeeze it very tight, for $\Diamond A \rightarrow \Diamond B$ is much weaker than $\Box(A \rightarrow B)$: although the latter entails the former in any normal modal logic, the former is true and the latter false whenever **B** is possible without being a necessary consequence of **A**, for example when **A** and **B** are modally independent.

Although NECESSITY and POSSIBILITY determine no necessary and sufficient condition for the counterfactual conditional in terms of necessity and possibility, they yield necessary and sufficient conditions for necessity and possibility in terms of the counterfactual conditional.

We argue thus. Let $\bot$ be a contradiction. As a special case of NECESSITY:

(11) $\Box(\neg A \rightarrow \bot) \rightarrow (\neg A \,\Box\!\!\rightarrow \bot)$

By elementary modal logic (specifically, the weakest normal modal logic K, used throughout), since a truth-functional consequence of something necessary is itself necessary:

(12) $\Box A \to \Box(\neg A \to \bot)$

From (11) and (12) by transitivity of the material conditional:

(13) $\Box A \to (\neg A \,\Box\!\!\to \bot)$

Similarly, as a special case of POSSIBILITY:

(14) $(\neg A \,\Box\!\!\to \bot) \to (\Diamond\neg A \to \Diamond\bot)$

By elementary modal logic, since the possibility of a contradiction is itself inconsistent, and necessity is the dual of possibility (being necessary is equivalent to having an impossible negation):

(15) $(\Diamond\neg A \to \Diamond\bot) \to \Box A$

From (14) and (15) by transitivity:

(16) $(\neg A \,\Box\!\!\to \bot) \to \Box A$

Putting (13) and (16) together:

(17) $\Box A \equiv (\neg A \,\Box\!\!\to \bot)$

The necessary is that whose negation counterfactually implies a contradiction. Since possibility is the dual of necessity (being possible is equivalent to having an unnecessary negation), (17) yields a corresponding necessary and sufficient condition for possibility, once a double negation in the antecedent of the counterfactual has been eliminated.

(18) $\Diamond A \equiv \neg(A \,\Box\!\!\to \bot)$

The impossible is that which counterfactually implies a contradiction; the possible is that which does not. In (17) and (18), the difference between necessity and possibility lies simply in the scope of negation.

Without assuming a specific framework for the semantics of counterfactuals (in particular, that of possible worlds), we can give a simple semantic rationale for (17) and (18), based on the idea of vacuous truth. That some true counterfactuals have impossible antecedents is clear, for otherwise $A \square\!\!\rightarrow A$ would fail when A was impossible. Make two widely accepted assumptions about the distinction between vacuous and non-vacuous truth: (a) $B \square\!\!\rightarrow C$ is vacuously true if and only if B is impossible (this is almost a definition of "vacuously" for counterfactuals); (b) $B \square\!\!\rightarrow C$ is non-vacuously true only if C is possible. The truth of (17) and (18) follows, given normal modal reasoning. If $\square A$ is true, then $\neg A$ is impossible, so by (a) $\neg A \square\!\!\rightarrow \bot$ is vacuously true; conversely, if $\neg A \square\!\!\rightarrow \bot$ is true, then by (b) it is vacuously true, so by (a) $\neg A$ is impossible, so $\square A$ is true. Similarly, if $\lozenge A$ is true, then A is not impossible, so by (a) $A \square\!\!\rightarrow \bot$ is not vacuously true, and by (b) not non-vacuously true, so $\neg(A \square\!\!\rightarrow \bot)$ is true; if $\lozenge A$ is not true, then A is impossible, so by (a) $A \square\!\!\rightarrow \bot$ is vacuously true, so $\neg(A \square\!\!\rightarrow \bot)$ is not true.

Given that the equivalences (17) and (18) and their necessitations are logically true, metaphysically modal thinking is logically equivalent to a special case of counterfactual thinking. Thus, modulo the implicit recognition of this equivalence, the epistemology of metaphysically modal thinking is tantamount to a special case of the epistemology of counterfactual thinking. Whoever has what it takes to understand the counterfactual conditional and the elementary logical auxiliaries $\neg$ and $\bot$ has what it takes to understand possibility and necessity operators.

The definability of necessity and possibility in terms of counterfactual conditionals was recognized long ago. It is easy to show from the closure and reflexivity principles for $\square\!\!\rightarrow$ in Section 3 that $A \square\!\!\rightarrow \bot$ is logically equivalent to $A \square\!\!\rightarrow \neg A$. Thus (17) and (18) generate two new equivalences:

(19) $\square A \equiv (\neg A \square\!\!\rightarrow A)$
(20) $\lozenge A \equiv \neg(A \square\!\!\rightarrow \neg A)$

The necessary is that which is counterfactually implied by its own negation; the possible is that which does not counterfactually imply its own negation. Stalnaker (1968) used (19) and (20) to define necessity and possibility, although his reading of the conditional (with a different notation) was not exclusively counterfactual. Lewis (1973a: 25) used (17) and (18) themselves to define necessity and possibility in terms of the counterfactual conditional. However, such definitions seem to have been treated as convenient notational economies, their potential philosophical significance unnoticed (Hill (2006) is a recent exception).

If we permit ourselves to quantify into sentence position ("propositional quantification"), we can formulate another pair of variants on (17) and (18) that may improve our feel for what is going on.[10] On elementary assumptions about the logic of such quantifiers and of the counterfactual conditional, $\neg A \; \square\!\!\rightarrow A$ is provably equivalent to $\forall p \, (p \; \square\!\!\rightarrow A)$: something is counterfactually implied by its negation if and only if it is counterfactually implied by everything. Thus (19) and (20) generate these equivalences too:

(21) $\quad \square A \equiv \forall p \, (p \; \square\!\!\rightarrow A)$
(22) $\quad \Diamond A \equiv \exists p \; \neg(p \; \square\!\!\rightarrow \neg A)$

According to (21), something is necessary if and only if whatever were the case, it would still be the case (see also Lewis 1986: 23). That is a natural way of explaining informally what metaphysically necessity is. According to (22), something is possible if and only if it is not such that it would fail in every eventuality.

We can plausibly treat NECESSITY and POSSIBILITY as axiom schemas of a joint logic of modality and counterfactuals, susceptible in the usual way to necessitation and the analogous closure principles for counterfactuals. Then (17)–(22) will be theorems, and susceptible to the same rules. Consequently, the result of substituting the left-hand for the right-hand side of any of these biconditionals or *vice versa* anywhere in any formula built up out of atomic sentences using

---

[10]   This quantification into sentence position need not be understood substitutionally. In purely modal contexts it can be modeled as quantification over all sets of possible worlds, even if not all of them are intensions of sentences that form the supposed substitution class, although this modeling presumably fails for hyperintensional contexts such as epistemic ones. A more faithful semantics for it might use non-substitutional quantification into sentence position in the metalanguage. Such subtleties are inessential for present purposes.

the modal operators, the counterfactual conditional, and truth-functors will be logically equivalent to the original (see also Appendix 1; the restrictions on necessitation and the closure principles discussed there are not relevant here).

Since the right-hand sides of (17), (19), and (21) are not strictly synonymous with each other, given the differences in their semantic structure, they are not all strictly synonymous with □A. Similarly, since the right-hand sides of (18), (20), and (22) are not strictly synonymous with each other, they are not all strictly synonymous with ◊A. Indeed, we have no sufficient reason to regard any of the equivalences as strict synonymies. That detracts little from their philosophical significance, for failure of strict synonymy does not imply failure of logical equivalence. The main philosophical concerns about possibility and necessity apply equally to anything logically equivalent to possibility or necessity. A non-modal analogy: ¬A is logically equivalent to A → ⊥, but presumably they are not strictly synonymous; nevertheless, once we have established that a creature can handle → and ⊥, we have established that it can handle something logically equivalent to negation, which answers the most interesting questions about its ability to handle negation. We should find the mutual equivalence of (17), (19), and (21), and of (18), (20), and (22) reassuring, for it shows the robustness of the modal notions definable from the counterfactual conditional, somewhat as the equivalence of the various proposed definitions of "computable function" showed the robustness of that notion.

If we treat (17) and (18) like definitions of □ and ◊ for logical purposes, and assume some elementary principles of the logic of counterfactuals, then we can establish the main principles of elementary modal logic for □ and ◊. For example, we can show that what follows from necessary premises is itself necessary. Given that counterfactual conditionals obey modus ponens (or even weaker assumptions), we can show that what is necessary is the case. We can also check that the principles NECESSITY and POSSIBILITY, which we used to establish (17) and (18), do indeed hold under the latter characterizations of necessity and possibility. Under much stronger assumptions about the logic of the counterfactual conditional, we can also establish much stronger principles of modal logic, such as the S5 principle that what is possible is necessarily possible. Such connections extend to quantified modal logic. The logic of counterfactual conditionals smoothly generates the logic of the modal operators (Appendix 1 gives technical details).

In particular, the proposed conception of modality makes quantification into the scope of modal operators tantamount to a special case of quantification into counterfactual contexts, as in (23) and (24):

(23) Everyone who would have benefited if the measure had passed voted for it.

(24) Where would the rock have landed if the bush had not been there?

Thus challenges to the intelligibility of claims of *de re* necessity are tantamount to challenges to the intelligibility of counterfactuals such as (23) and (24). But (23) and (24) are evidently intelligible.

Other properties of metaphysical modality follow from corresponding properties of counterfactual conditionals. For instance, if this is identical with that then what would have been the case of this in given counterfactual circumstances is what would have been the case of that in those circumstances; thus $x = y$ and the triviality $x \neq y \ \square\!\!\rightarrow x \neq y$ yield $x \neq y \ \square\!\!\rightarrow x \neq x$; hence $x = y$ entails $x \neq y \ \square\!\!\rightarrow x \neq x$; since $x \neq x$ entails $\bot$, $x = y$ entails $x \neq y \ \square\!\!\rightarrow \bot$ and therefore $\neg\Diamond x \neq y$, which is a form of the law of the necessity of identity.[11] Again, consider the Kripkean conception of the essentiality of origin, on which, very roughly, an object could not have originated otherwise than it actually did. It follows from the plausible assumption that if something in any circumstance had originated otherwise than a given object actually did, it would not have been that very object. By contrast, objects could easily have ended otherwise than they actually did. That temporal asymmetry seems to be related to more general temporal asymmetries in the evaluation of counterfactual conditionals by the "rolling back" procedure mentioned above, which involves holding fixed an initial segment of the past but not a final segment of the future.

---

[11] In his 1961 dissertation, Dagfin Føllesdal was already clear that problems of quantifying in and substitution of coreferential terms arise for counterfactual conditionals just as they do for modal operators, although the direct connection he envisaged was through an analysis of counterfactuals in terms of natural necessity (2004: 14, 99).

Given (17) and (18), we should expect the epistemology of metaphysical modality to be a special case of the epistemology of counterfactuals. Despite the non-synonymy of the two sides, our cognitive capacity to evaluate the counterfactual conditionals gives us exactly what we need to evaluate the corresponding modal claims too. The idea that nevertheless we evaluate them by some quite different means is highly fanciful, since it indicates a bizarre lack of cognitive economy and has no plausible explanation of where the alternative cognitive resources might come from. Furthermore, as we shall see, characteristic features of the epistemology of modality are well explained by subsumption under corresponding features of the epistemology of counterfactuals. Far from being *sui generis*, the capacity to handle metaphysical modality is an "accidental" byproduct of the cognitive mechanisms that provide our capacity to handle counterfactual conditionals. Since our capacity for modal thinking cannot be isolated from our capacity for ordinary thinking about the natural world, which involves counterfactual thinking, skeptics about metaphysical modality cannot excise it from our conceptual scheme without loss to ordinary thought about the natural world, for the former is implicit in the latter.

A useful comparison is with the relation between logical consequence and logical truth. Consider some agents who reason in simple ways about themselves and their environment, perhaps using rules of inference formalizable in a Gentzen-style natural deduction calculus, perhaps in some less sophisticated way. The practical value of their reasoning skill is that they can move from ordinary empirical premises to ordinary empirical conclusions in ways that always preserve truth, thereby extending their knowledge of mundane matters (see Schechter 2006 for discussion). In doing so, they need never use logically true sentences. Nevertheless, the cognitive capacity that enables them to make these transitions between empirical sentences also enables them, as a special case, an "accidental" byproduct, to deduce logical truths from the null set of premises. Highly artificial moves would be needed to block these bonus deductions; such *ad hoc* restrictions would come at the price of extra computational complexity for no practical gain. Likewise at the semantic level: the simplest compositional semantics that enables us to negate and conjoin empirical sentences also enables us to formulate logical truths and falsehoods, even if we have hitherto lacked any interest in doing so. By good fortune, everything is already in place for the logician to evaluate logical truths and falsehoods (at least in first-order logic, since it is complete). The philosopher's position with respect to metaphysical modality is not utterly different.

Discussions of the epistemology of modality often focus on imaginability or conceivability as a test of possibility while ignoring the role of the imagination in the assessment of mundane counterfactuals. In doing so, they omit the appropriate context for understanding the relation between modality and the imagination. For instance, scorn is easily poured on imagination as a test of possibility: it is imaginable but not possible that water does not contain oxygen, except in artificial senses of "imaginable" that come apart from possibility in other ways, and so on. Imagination can be made to look cognitively worthless. Once we recall its fallible but vital role in evaluating counterfactual conditionals, we should be more open to the idea that it plays such a role in evaluating claims of possibility and necessity. At the very least, we cannot expect an adequate account of the role of imagination in the epistemology of modality if we lack an adequate account of its role in the epistemology of counterfactuals.

On the rough sketch in Section 3, we assert $A \: \Box\!\!\rightarrow B$ when our counterfactual development of the supposition A robustly yields B; we deny $A \: \Box\!\!\rightarrow B$ when our counterfactual development of A does not robustly yield B (and we do not attribute the failure to a defect in our search). Correspondingly, by (17), we assert $\Box A$ when our counterfactual development of the supposition $\neg A$ robustly yields a contradiction; we deny $\Box A$ when our counterfactual development of $\neg A$ does not robustly yield a contradiction (and we do not attribute the failure to a defect in our search). Similarly, by (18), we assert $\Diamond A$ when our counterfactual development of the supposition A does not robustly yield a contradiction (and we do not attribute the failure to a defect in our search); we deny $\Diamond A$ when our counterfactual development of A robustly yields a contradiction. Thus our fallible imaginative evaluation of counterfactuals has a conceivability test for possibility and an inconceivability test for impossibility built in as fallible special cases.

Such conceivability and inconceivability will be subject to the same constraints, whatever they are, as counterfactual conditionals in general, concerning which parts of our background information are held fixed. If we know enough chemistry, our counterfactual development of the supposition that gold is not the element with atomic number 79 will generate a contradiction. The reason is not simply that we know that gold is the element with atomic number 79, for we can and must vary some items of our knowledge under counterfactual suppositions. Rather, part of the general way we develop counterfactual suppositions is to hold such constitutive facts fixed.

A nuanced account of our handling of counterfactuals is likely to predict that we are more reliable in evaluating some kinds than others. For example, we may well be more reliable in evaluating counterfactuals whose antecedents involve small departures from the actual world than in evaluating those whose antecedents involve much larger departures. We may be correspondingly more reliable in evaluating the possibility of everyday scenarios than of "far-out" ones, and extra caution may be called for in the latter case. At the limit, actuality is often the best argument for possibility. But current philosophical practice already shows some sensitivity to such considerations. Many philosophers are more confident in their judgments about more or less realistic thought experiments in epistemology and moral philosophy than about more radically strange ones in metaphysics. More explicit consideration of the link between modal thought and counterfactual thought may lead to further refinements of our practice.

The considerations of this chapter will not resolve every fraught dispute about metaphysical modality, such as whether zombies (unconscious physical duplicates of us) are possible. For suppose that the source of such a dispute really is the failure of our usual methods for resolving modal issues to issue a clear verdict in the case at hand – rather than, say, the unsolvability of a non-modal problem about the nature of consciousness. Then since the present account characterizes our usual method, rather than proposing an alternative, it cannot be expected to resolve the dispute. For all that has been argued here, we may in many cases be incapable of coming to know whether a given hypothesis is metaphysically possible. Philosophical controversy will naturally make the unclear cases salient. That should not blind us to the wide range of clear cases (talking donkeys are possible). General skepticism in the epistemology of metaphysical modality without general skepticism in the epistemology of counter-factuals is unmotivated. The use of imagination to evaluate philosophical claims of possibility and necessity is just as legitimate in principle, and sometimes just as effective in practice, as is its use to evaluate mundane counterfactuals.

5

What does the envisaged assimilation of modality to counterfactual conditionals imply for the status of modal judgments as knowable *a priori* or only *a posteriori*?

Some counterfactual conditionals look like paradigms of *a priori* knowability: for example (7), whose consequent is a straightforward deductive consequence of its antecedent. Others look like paradigms of what can be known only *a posteriori*: for example, that if I had searched in my pocket five minutes ago I would have found a coin. But those are easy cases.

Standard discussions of the *a priori* distinguish between two roles that experience plays in cognition, one *evidential*, one *enabling*. Experience is held to play an evidential role in my visual knowledge that this shirt is green, but a merely enabling role in my knowledge that all green things are colored: I needed it only to acquire the concepts *green* and *colored*, without which I could not even raise the question whether all green things are colored. Knowing *a priori* is supposed to be incompatible with an evidential role for experience, or at least with an evidential role for sense experience, so my knowledge that this shirt is green is not *a priori*. By contrast, knowing *a priori* is supposed to be compatible with an enabling role for experience, so my knowledge that all green things are colored can still be *a priori*. However, in our imagination-based knowledge of counterfactuals, sense experience can play a role that is neither strictly evidential nor purely enabling. For, even without surviving as part of our total evidence, it can mold our habits of imagination and judgment in ways that go far beyond a merely enabling role.

Here is an example. I acquire the words "inch" and "centimeter" independently of each other. Through sense experience, I learn to make naked eye judgments of distances in inches or centimeters with moderate reliability. When things go well, such judgments amount to knowledge: *a posteriori* knowledge, of course. For example, I know *a posteriori* that two marks in front of me are at most two inches apart. Now I deploy the same faculty offline to make a counterfactual judgment:

(25)   If two marks had been nine inches apart, they would have been at least nineteen centimeters apart.

In judging (25), I do not use a conversion ratio between inches and centimeters to make a calculation. In the example I know no such ratio. Rather, I visually imagine two marks nine inches apart, and use my ability to judge distances in centimeters visually offline to judge under the counterfactual supposition that they are at least nineteen centimeters apart. With this large margin for error, my judgment is reliable. Thus I know (25). Do I know it *a priori* or *a posteriori*? Sense experience plays no direct evidential role in my judgment. I do not consciously or unconsciously recall memories of distances encountered in perception, nor do I deduce (25) from general premises I have inductively or abductively gathered from experience: Section 3 noted obstacles to assimilating such patterns of counterfactual judgment to the use of general premises. Nevertheless, the causal role of past sense experience in my judgment of (25) far exceeds enabling me to grasp the concepts relevant to (25); the weakness of the conditions for concept possession was noted in the previous chapter. Someone could easily have enough sense experience to understand (25) without being reliable enough in their judgments of distance to know (25). Nor is the role of past experience in the judgment of (25) purely enabling in some other way, for example by acquainting me with a logical argument for (25). It is more directly implicated than that. Whether my belief in (25) constitutes knowledge is highly sensitive to the accuracy or otherwise of the empirical information about lengths (in each unit) on which I relied when calibrating my judgments of length (in each unit). I know (25) only if my offline application of the concepts of an inch and a centimeter was sufficiently skilful. Whether I am justified in believing (25) likewise depends on how skilful I am in making such judgments. My possession of the appropriate skills depends constitutively, not just causally, on past experience for the calibration of my judgments of length in those units. If the calibration is correct by a lucky accident, despite massive errors in the relevant past beliefs about length, I lack the required skill.[12]

If we knew counterfactual conditionals by purely *a priori* inference from the antecedent and background premises to the conclusion, our knowledge might count as *a priori* if we knew all the background premises *a priori*, and otherwise as *a posteriori*. However, it was argued above that if the process is inferential at all, the relevant inferences are themselves of just the kind for which past experience plays a role that is neither purely enabling nor strictly evidential, so the inferential picture does not resolve the issue.

Suppose that we classify my knowledge of (25) in the envisaged circumstances as *a priori*, because sense experience plays no strictly evidential role; perhaps we insist on counting the role of such experience in knowledge of (25) as enabling. Then the danger is that far too much will count as *a priori*. Long-forgotten experience can mold my judgment in many ways without playing a direct evidential role, for example by calibrating my skilful application of concepts and conditioning me into patterns of expectation which are called on in my assessment of ordinary counterfactual conditionals. How we know (25) may turn out to be quite similar to how many of us know (26):

(26)   If two marks had been nine inches apart, they would have been further apart than the front and back legs of an ant.

Sense experience need play no direct evidential role in knowledge of (26). One can know (26) without remembering any occasion on which one perceived an ant, and without having received any testimony about the size of ants. The ability to imagine accurately what an ant would look like next to two marks nine inches apart suffices. Doubtless (25) is necessary and (26) contingent. But that metaphysical difference does not imply any epistemological difference between how we know (25) and how we know (26). It does not justify the claim that (25) is known *a priori* and (26) *a posteriori*. Yet (26) is not usually supposed to be known or even knowable *a priori*.

Suppose, on the other hand, that we classify my knowledge of (25) as *a posteriori*, because experience plays more than a purely enabling

---

[12]   Yablo (2002) has a related discussion of the concept *oval*.

role; perhaps we insist on counting the role of sense experience in knowledge of (26) as evidential. Then the danger is that the same verdict will apply to many philosophically significant modal judgments too. The assumption that they are known or even knowable *a priori* will be undercut. Of course, Kripke has argued strongly for a category of necessary truths knowable only *a posteriori*, such as "Gold is the element with atomic number 79"; "It is necessary that gold is the element with atomic number 79" would then be knowable only *a posteriori* too. The present suggestion is intended far more widely than that. For example:

(27)   It is necessary that whoever knows something believes it.
(28)   If Mary knew that it was raining, she would believe that it was raining.
(29)   Whoever knew something believed it.

Although (28) is not general and (29) is not modal, our way of knowing them is similar to our way of knowing (27); we do not learn (28) by analysis of Mary's individual psychology or (29) by enumerative induction. Knowledge of truths such as (27)–(29) is usually regarded as *a priori*, even by those who accept the category of the necessary *a posteriori*. The experiences through which we learned to distinguish in practice between belief and non-belief and between knowledge and ignorance play no strictly evidential role in our knowledge of (27)–(29). Nevertheless, their role may be more than purely enabling. Many philosophers, native speakers of English, have denied (27) (Shope (1983: 171–92) has a critical survey). They are not usually or plausibly accused of failing to understand the words "know" and "believe." Why should not subtle differences between two courses of experience, each of which sufficed for coming to understand "know" and "believe," make for differences in how test cases are processed, just large enough to tip honest judgments in opposite directions? Whether knowledge of (27)–(29) is available to one may thus be highly sensitive to personal circumstances. Such individual differences in the skill with which concepts are applied depend constitutively, not just causally, on past experience, for the skillfulness of a performance depends constitutively on its causal origins.

   In a similar way, past experience of spatial and temporal properties may play a role in skilful mathematical "intuition" that is not directly evidential but far exceeds what is needed to acquire the relevant mathematical concepts. The role may be more than heuristic, concerning the context of justification as well as the context of discovery. Even the combinatorial skills required for competent assessment of standard set-theoretic axioms may involve offline applications of perceptual and motor skills, whose capacity to generate knowledge constitutively depends on their honing through past experience that plays no evidential role in the assessment of the axioms.

If the preceding picture is on the right lines, should we conclude that modal knowledge is *a posteriori*? Not if that suggests that (27)–(29) are inductive or abductive conclusions from perceptual data. In such cases, the question "*A priori* or *a posteriori*?" is too crude to be of much epistemological use. The point is not that we cannot draw a line somewhere with traditional paradigms of the *a priori* on one side and traditional paradigms of the *a posteriori* on the other. Surely we can; the point is that doing so yields little insight. The distinction is handy enough for a rough initial description of epistemic phenomena; it is out of place in a deeper theoretical analysis, because it obscures more significant epistemic patterns. We may acknowledge an extensive category of *armchair knowledge*, in the sense of knowledge in which experience plays no strictly evidential role, while remembering that such knowledge may not fit the stereotype of the *a priori*, because the contribution of experience was far more than enabling. For example, it should be no surprise if we turn out to have armchair knowledge of truths about the external environment.[13]

6

It is time to consider objections to the preceding account.

Objection: Knowledge of counterfactuals cannot explain modal knowledge, because the former depends on the latter. More specifically, in developing a counterfactual supposition, we make free use

---

[13]   This problem for the *a priori/a posteriori* distinction undermines arguments for the incompatibility of semantic externalism with our privileged access to our own mental states that appeal to the supposed absurdity of *a priori* knowledge of contingent features of the external environment (McKinsey 1991). It also renders problematic attempts to explain the first dimension of two-dimensional semantics in terms of *a priori* knowability, as in Chalmers (2006). Substituting talk of rational reflection for talk of the *a priori* does not help, since it raises parallel questions.

of what we take to be necessary truths, but not of what we take to be contingent truths. Thus we rely on a prior or at least independent stock of modal knowledge or belief. The principle NECESSITY above illustrates how we do this.

Reply: Once we take something to be a necessary truth, of course we can use it in developing further counterfactual suppositions. But that does nothing to show that we have any special cognitive capacity to handle modality independent of our general cognitive capacity to handle counterfactual conditionals. If we start only with the latter, just as envisaged above, it will generate knowledge of various modal truths, which can in turn be used to develop further counterfactual suppositions, in a recursive process. For example, we need not judge that it is metaphysically necessary that gold is the element with atomic number 79 *before* invoking the proposition that gold is the element with atomic number 79 in the development of a counterfactual supposition. Rather, projecting constitutive matters such as atomic numbers into counterfactual suppositions is part of our general way of assessing counterfactuals. The judgment of metaphysical necessity originates as the output of a procedure of that kind; it is not an independently generated input.

What if our general cognitive capacity to handle counterfactuals has as a separate constituent a special cognitive capacity to handle metaphysical modality? Consider the cognitive resources sketched in Section 3 for the evaluation of counterfactual conditionals: most distinctively, imaginative simulation; less distinctively, reasoning, memory, testimony, perception. The question is whether they require supplementation by an additional capacity for the evaluation of counterfactuals of the special form $A \mathbin{\square\!\!\rightarrow} \perp$. They do not. Although we often cannot *perceptually* imagine the truth of A, not all imagining is perceptual imagining. "Imagine that there is a barber who shaves all and only those who do not shave themselves" is not radically different from the instruction "Suppose that there is a barber who shaves all and only those who do not shave themselves." In imaginatively and inferentially developing a counterfactual supposition, one may or may not run into a contradiction. Of course, we often find claims of metaphysical possibility or necessity hard to evaluate. But that is not the point. There is no evidence whatsoever that we are *better* at evaluating claims of metaphysical modality than we would be if we had just the sorts of cognitive capacity listed above for evaluating counterfactual conditionals, with no additional separate capacity for evaluating claims of metaphysical modality. Therefore the postulation of such an additional capacity is unwarranted.

Objection: The account associates metaphysical modality with counterfactual conditionals of a very peculiar kind: in the case of (17) and (18), those with an explicit contradiction as their consequent. Why should a capacity to handle ordinary counterfactuals confer a capacity to handle such peculiar ones too?

Reply: That is like asking why a capacity to handle inferences between complex empirical sentences should confer a capacity to handle inferences involving logical truths and falsehoods too. There is no easy way to have the former without the latter. More specifically, developing a counterfactual supposition includes reasoning from it, and we cannot always tell in advance when such reasoning will yield a contradiction (there are surprises in logic). The undecidability of logical truth for first-order logic implies that there is no total mechanical test for the consistency even of first-order sentences. Thus the inconsistent ones cannot be sieved out in advance (consider "In the next village there is a barber who shaves all and only those in that village who do not shave themselves"). Consequently, a general capacity to develop counterfactual suppositions must confer in particular the capacity to develop those which subsequently turn out inconsistent. Although the capacity may not be of uniform reliability, as already noted, the variation is primarily with the *antecedent* of the counterfactual (the supposition under development), not with its consequent (which is what is exceptional in (17) and (18)). In deductive inference, our reasoning to contradictions (as in proof by reductio ad absurdum) is not strikingly more or less reliable than the rest of our deductive reasoning. We can reach many conclusions about metaphysical modality without overstretching our imaginative resources. For instance, whenever we can deny a counterfactual A □→ B, we can assert ◊A, because A □→ ⊥ entails A □→ B. Again, the argument in Section 4 for a version of the necessity of identity employed only straightforward reasoning in the logic of counterfactuals. It is not an objection to the present account that our use of the imagination in evaluating counterfactuals may be unreliable for some with far-out antecedents.

Objection: The assumption about vacuous truth on which the account relies is wrong (Nolan 1997). For some counterpossibles (counterfactuals with metaphysically impossible antecedents) are false, such as (30), uttered by someone who mistakenly believes that he answered "13" to "What is 5 + 7?"; in fact he answered "11":

(30) If 5 + 7 were 13 I would have got that sum right.

Thus, contrary to (17), □A may be true while ¬A □→ ⊥ is false. In the argument for (17) in Section 3, the objectionable premise is NECESSITY. If some worlds are metaphysically impossible, and A is true at some of them but false at all metaphysically possible worlds, then every metaphysically possible A world is a B world, even if the closest A worlds are not B worlds.[14] Similar objections apply to the other purported equivalences (18)–(22).

Reply: Suppose that *all* counterpossibles are false. Then ◊A is equivalent to A □→ A, for the latter will still be true whenever A is possible; correspondingly, □A is equivalent to the dual ¬(¬A □→ ¬A) and one can carry out the program of Section 3 using the new equivalences. But that is presumably not what the objector has in mind. Rather, the idea is that the truth-value of a counterpossible can depend on its consequent, so that (30) is false while (31) is true:

(31) If 5 + 7 were 13 I would have got that sum wrong.

However, such examples are quite unpersuasive.

First, they tend to fall apart when thought through. For example, if 5 + 7 were 13 then 5 + 6 would be 12, and so (by another eleven steps) 0 would be 1, so if the number of right answers I gave were 0, the number of right answers I gave would be 1. We prefer (31) to (30) because the argument for (31) is more obvious, but the argument for (30) is equally strong.

---

[14]   Technically, NECESSITY fails on a semantics with similarity spheres for □→ that include some impossible worlds (inaccessible with respect to □). Conversely, POSSIBILITY fails on a semantics with some possible worlds excluded from all similarity spheres (see Lewis (1986: 16) on universality). Inaccessible worlds seem not to threaten POSSIBILITY. For suppose that an A world w but no B world is accessible from a world v. Then if A □→ B holds at v on the usual semantics, there is an A world x such that every A world as close as x is to v is a B world. It follows that w is not as close as x is to v and that x is inaccessible from v, which contradicts the plausible assumption that any accessible world is at least as close as any inaccessible world.

Second, there are general reasons to doubt the supposed intuitions on which such examples rely. We are used to working with possible antecedents, and given the possibility of **A**, the incompatibility of **B** and **C** normally implies that **A** □→ **B** and **A** □→ **C** cannot both be true. Thus by over-projecting from familiar cases we may take the uncontentious (31) to be incompatible with (30). The logically unsophisticated make analogous errors in quantificational reasoning. Given the evident truth of "Every golden mountain is a mountain," they think that "Every golden mountain is a valley" is false, neglecting the case of vacuous truth. Since the logic and semantics of counterfactual conditionals is much less well understood, even the logically sophisticated may find similar errors tempting. Such errors may be compounded by a tendency to confuse negating a counterfactual conditional with negating its consequent, given the artificiality of the constructions needed to negate the whole conditional unambiguously ("it is not the case that if . . ."). Thus the truth of **A** □→ ¬**B** (with **A** impossible) may be mistaken for the truth of ¬(**A** □→ **B**) and therefore the falsity of **A** □→ **B**. If we must choose between (30) and (31), it is clear which we should choose; but the impression that we must choose is an illusion.

Some objectors try to bolster their case by giving examples of mathematicians reasoning from an impossible supposition **A** ("There are only finitely many prime numbers") in order to reduce it to absurdity. Such arguments can be formulated using a counterfactual conditional, although they need not be. Certainly there will be points in the argument at which it is legitimate to assert **A** □→ **C** (in particular, **A** □→ **A**) but illegitimate to assert **A** □→ ¬**C** (in particular, **A** □→ ¬**A**). But of course that does not show that **A** □→ ¬**A** is false. At any point in a mathematical argument there are infinitely many truths that it is not legitimate to assert, because they have not yet been proved (Lewis (1986: 24–6) pragmatically explains away some purported examples of false counterfactuals with impossible antecedents). Similarly, this reply could just as well have begun "If all counterpossibles were false, ◊**A** would be equivalent to **A** □→ **A**." Read "the antecedent" in such a way that it is impossible. Then it would have been equally true to say "If all counterpossibles were false, ◊**A** would not be equivalent to **A** □→ **A**." But that would not have mattered, for only the former counterfactual is assertable in a context in which for dialectical purposes the possibility of the antecedent is not excluded, and that is what the argument requires.

We may also wonder what logic of counterfactuals the objectors envisage. If they reject elementary principles of the pure logic of counterfactual conditionals, that is an unattractive feature of their position. If they accept all those principles, then they are committed to operators characterized as in (17) and (18) that exhibit all the logical behavior standardly expected of necessity and possibility. What is that modality, if not metaphysical modality?

A final problem for the objection is this. Here is a paradigm of the kind of counterpossible the objector regards as false:

(32)   If Hesperus had not been Phosphorus, Phosphorus would not have been Phosphorus.

Since Hesperus is Phosphorus, it is metaphysically impossible that Hesperus is not Phosphorus, by the necessity of identity. Nevertheless, the objectors are likely to insist that in imaginatively developing the counterfactual supposition that Hesperus is not Phosphorus, we are committed to the explicit denial of no logical truth, as in the consequent of (32). According to them, if we do our best for the antecedent, we can develop it into a logically coherent though metaphysically impossible scenario: it will exclude "Phosphorus is not Phosphorus." But they will presumably accept this trivial instance of reflexivity:

(33)   If Hesperus had not been Phosphorus, Hesperus would not have been Phosphorus.

In general, however, coreferential proper names are intersubstitutable in counterfactual contexts. For example, the argument from (34) and (35) to (36) is unproblematically valid:

(34)   If the rocket had continued on that course, it would have hit Hesperus.
(35)   Hesperus = Phosphorus.
(36)   If the rocket had continued on that course, it would have hit Phosphorus.

Similarly, the argument from (33) and (35) to (32) should be valid. But (33) and (35) are uncontentiously true. If the objector concedes that (32) is true after all, then there should be an explanation of the felt resistance to it, compatible with its truth, and we may reasonably expect that explanation to generalize to other purported examples of false counterpossibles. On the other hand, if the objector rejects (32), they must deny the validity of the argument from (33) and (35) to (32). Thus they are committed to the claim that counterfactual conditionals create opaque contexts for proper names (the same argument could be given for other singular terms, such as demonstratives). But that is highly implausible. (34) and (36) are materially equivalent because their antecedents and consequents concern the same objects, properties, and relations: it matters not that different names are used, because the counterfactuals are not about such representational features (if the substitution of coreferential names in propositional attitude ascriptions does not preserve truth value, the reason is that such ascriptions are about representational features). But then exactly the same applies to (32) and (33). Their antecedents and consequents too concern the same objects, properties, and relations. That the antecedent of (32) and (33) is in fact metaphysically impossible does not radically alter their subject matter. The transparency of the counterfactual conditional construction concerns its general semantic structure, not the specific content of the antecedent.

Under scrutiny, the case for false counterpossibles looks feeble. The logic of quantifiers was confused and retarded for centuries by unwillingness to recognize vacuously true universal generalizations; we should not allow the logic of counterfactuals to be similarly confused by unwillingness to recognize vacuously true counterpossibles.[15]

Objection: Counterfactuals are desperately vague and context-sensitive; equivalences such as (17) and (18) will infect $\square$ and $\lozenge$, interpreted as metaphysical modalities, with all that vagueness and context-sensitivity.

Reply: Infection is not automatic. For instance, within a Lewis-Stalnaker framework, different readings or sharpenings of $\square \rightarrow$ may

---

[15] For an account of metaphysical modality in terms of counterfactuals that does admit false counterpossibles see Kment (2006). See also Lange (2005).

differ on the similarity ordering of worlds while still agreeing on what worlds there are, so that the differences cancel out in the right-hand sides of (17) and (18). Whether a given supposition counterfactually implies a contradiction may be unclear to us; that does not imply that there is no right answer.

On some dynamic accounts, the semantics of counterfactuals involves a more systematic interaction with context, because one normal effect of the antecedent is to update the context to one in which the horizon of contextually relevant worlds includes some in which the antecedent is true; the truth of the sentence is then equivalent to the truth of the consequent in *all* the relevant worlds in the updated context (von Fintel 2001). The present account can be adapted to such an account, if it is allowed that updating can fail to provide a world in which the antecedent is true when there is no such world, for then the counterfactual is vacuously true: its consequent is true in every relevant world in which its antecedent is true. Even if, less plausibly, the counterfactual is "undefined" in such cases (a view with awkward consequences for many informal mathematical proofs by reductio ad absurdum involving counterfactuals), metaphysical impossibility and the other modalities can still be recovered from the counterfactual, since "$\Diamond A$" will be equivalent to "It is defined whether ($A \mathbin{\Box\!\!\rightarrow} A$)."

Objection: It has been argued that counterfactual conditionals lack truth-values (Edgington 2003, Bennett 2003: 252–6). If so, the assimilation of claims of metaphysical possibility and necessity to counterfactuals will deprive such claims of truth-values.

Reply: The issues are too complex to discuss properly here, but the readily intelligible occurrence of counterfactual conditionals embedded in the scope of other operators as in (23) and (24) is hard to make sense of without attributing truth-values to the embedded occurrences. Here is another example:

(37)   Every field that would have been flooded if the dam had burst was ploughed.

(37) can itself be intelligibly embedded in more complex sentences in all the usual ways; for example, it can be negated or made the antecedent of another conditional. In order to understand how such embeddings work, we must assign truth conditions to (37); *ad hoc*

treatments of a few particular embeddings are not enough. For (37) to have truth conditions, "field that would have been flooded if the dam had burst" must have application-conditions. Thus there must be a distinction between the fields to which "would have been flooded if the dam had burst" applies and those to which it does not. But that is just to say that there must be a distinction between the values of "x" for which "If the dam had burst, x would have been flooded" is true and those for which it is false. That it is somewhat obscure what the truth conditions of counterfactual conditionals are, and that we sometimes make conflicting judgments about them, hardly shows that they do not exist. The requirement that counterfactual conditionals have truth conditions is one way in which the preceding discussion has not been perfectly neutral on their semantics.

7

The counterfactual conditional is of course not the only construction in ordinary use that is closely related to metaphysical modality. Consider comments after a swiftly extinguished fire in an explosives factory:

(38) There could have been a huge explosion.
(39) There could easily have been a huge explosion.

The truth-value of both (38) (on a natural reading) and (39) depends on the location of the fire, the precautions in place, and so on. The mere metaphysical possibility of a huge explosion is insufficient to verify either (38) (so interpreted) or (39). The restricted nature of the possibility is explicit in (39) with the word "easily"; it is implicit in the context of (38).[16] To discover the truth-value of (38) or (39), we need background information. We may also need our imagination, in attempting to develop a feasible scenario in which there is a huge explosion. We use the same general cognitive faculties as we do in evaluating related counterfactual conditionals, such as (40):

[16] On easy possibility see Sainsbury (1997), Peacocke (1999: 310–28) and Williamson (2000a: 123–30). On the idea that natural language modals such as "can" and "must" advert to contextually restricted ranges of possibilities see Kratzer (1977).

(40)   If the fire engine had arrived a minute later, there would have been a huge explosion.

Judgments of limited possibility such as (38) (interpreted as above) and (39) have a cognitive value for us similar to that of counterfactual conditionals such as (40). Both (38) and (39) entail (41), although not *vice versa*:

(41)   It is metaphysically possible that there was a huge explosion.

This is another way in which our ordinary cognitive capacities enable us to recognize that something non-actual is nevertheless metaphysically possible. But we cannot reason from the negation of (37) or of (38) to the negation of (41).

Can metaphysical possibility be understood as the limiting case of such more restricted forms of possibility? Perhaps, but we would need some account of what demarcates the relevant forms of possibility from irrelevant ones, such as epistemic possibility. It also needs to be explained how, from the starting-point of ordinary thought, we manage to single out the limiting case, metaphysical modality. The advantage of counterfactual conditionals is that they allow us to single out the limiting case simply by putting a contradiction in the consequent; contradictions can be formed in any language with conjunction and negation. Anyway, the connections with restricted possibility and with counterfactual conditionals are not mutually exclusive, for they are not being interpreted as rival semantic analyses, but rather as different cases in which the cognitive mechanisms needed for one already provide for the other.

The epistemology of metaphysical modality requires no dedicated faculty of intuition. It is simply a special case of the epistemology of counterfactual thinking, a kind of thinking tightly integrated with our thinking about the spatio-temporal world. To deny that such thinking ever yields knowledge is to fall into an extravagant skepticism. Here as elsewhere, we can do philosophy on the basis of general cognitive capacities that are in no deep way peculiarly philosophical.

6

Thought Experiments

1

Of all the armchair methods of philosophy, one of the most conspicuous is the thought experiment. Much of the philosophical community allows that a judicious act of the imagination can refute a previously well-supported theory. In natural science, one might expect, to imagine obtaining a negative outcome to a crucial experiment may be to imagine refuting the theory at issue, but imagining refuting a theory no more actually refutes it than imagining killing a tyrant actually kills him. Why should philosophy be any different? If the idea of a crucial experiment is too crude to describe the workings of real science, that merely reinforces skepticism about crucial thought experiments in philosophy.

Such an objection to thought experiments is facile, as their seminal role in physics immediately suggests, most famously in the work of Galileo and Einstein. Of course, philosophy-hating philosophers (a common breed) claim that philosophical thought experiments are profoundly unlike those in natural science, in ways which make the former bad and the latter good, but we should be suspicious of such claims of philosophical exceptionalism. We have already seen the imagination play a mundane but vital role in the evaluation of counterfactual conditionals, from the most ordinary empirical ones to those equivalent to statements about metaphysical modality. We shall see it play a corresponding role in thought experiments.

The canonical example in the literature on philosophical thought experiments is Edmund Gettier's use of them to refute the traditional analysis of knowledge as justified true belief (Gettier 1963). The background working hypothesis is that his thought experiments are paradigmatic, in the sense that if any thought experiments can succeed in philosophy, his do: thus to determine whether Gettier's thought experiments succeed is in effect to determine whether there can be successful thought experiments in philosophy. Even if we do not afford them quite that status, they provide a convenient focus for discussion. Moreover, they demonstrate the cognitive weight analytic philosophers rest on thought experiments. Sociologically, the phenomenon is remarkable. Gettier had no previous publications and was unknown to most of the philosophical profession; he did not write as an established authority. For the theory he was attacking, a neat and at the time widely accepted analysis of the central concept of epistemology, he cited well-known books by two leading philosophers of his time (Ayer 1956, Chisholm 1957) and, more tentatively, Plato (*Theaetetus* 201, *Meno* 98).[1] His three-page article turns on two imaginary examples.[2] Yet his refutation of the justified true belief analysis was accepted almost overnight by the community of analytic epistemologists. His thought experiments were found intrinsically compelling.

This chapter analyzes the logical structure of Gettier-style thought experiments. The discussion can be generalized to many imaginary counterexamples that have been deployed against philosophical analyses and theories in ways more or less similar to Gettier's. Far more extensive investigation would be needed to warrant the claim that all philosophical thought experiments work in that way, but one must start somewhere. The main overall aim is to subsume the epistemology of thought experiments under the epistemology of counterfactual conditionals and metaphysical modality developed in the previous chapter, and thereby to reveal it as an application of quite ordinary ways of thinking, not as something peculiarly philosophical. A related subsidiary aim is to achieve a finer-grained understanding of the structure of the arguments that underlie thought experiments, both

---

[1]   Shope (1983: 12–19) discusses whether Plato endorsed the justified true belief analysis of knowledge and argues that Kant did in the *Critique of Pure Reason* at A822, B850.

[2]   Russell (1912) gave examples with a structure very similar to Gettier's, but used them only to draw the conclusion that "a true belief is not knowledge when it is deduced from a false belief" (in the chapter on "Knowledge, error and probable opinion").

for its own sake and in order to test the overall account by developing it in detail.

2

We can extract from Gettier's paper an argument that makes no obvious appeal to thought experiments. According to the target analysis, a necessary and sufficient condition for knowing something is that it is true, one believes it and one is justified in believing it; for short, one has justified true belief.[3] Now in the sense of "justified" in which being justified in believing something is necessary for knowing it, Gettier argues, one can be justified in believing what is in fact false (the truth component of the justified true belief analysis is not redundant). But if one is justified in believing something, and correctly deduces from it something else, one is justified in believing the latter proposition on that basis (deduction is a way of transmitting justification from the premises to the conclusion of an argument). Since any truth is deductively entailed by various falsehoods, one can believe a truth on the basis of having correctly deduced it from a falsehood one is justified in believing, and thereby be justified in believing the deduced truth too; thus one has justified true belief in the latter. Nevertheless, one does not know, for one's belief in the truth, no matter how justified, is essentially based on a false lemma; one's conclusion cannot be epistemically better off than one's premises. Therefore, justified true belief is insufficient for knowledge.

One disadvantage of the abstract argument is that it rests on several very general claims for which we might find adequate support hard to provide. In particular, it assumes that a belief essentially based on a false belief does not constitute knowledge. Can we take that for granted? How do we know that a belief essentially based on a false belief never constitutes knowledge even in *recherché* cases? Fortunately, the universal generalization is more than Gettier needs in order to refute the target analysis. He needs only some particular instance in which the belief essentially based on a false lemma clearly

---

[3] In a sense, one can believe something and be justified in believing it without having a justified belief in it, because the available justification is not the reason for which one believes. What follows does not depend on this distinction.

fails to constitute knowledge, whether or not all other cases go the same way. As Gettier proceeds, the verdict that the subject lacks knowledge in the particular case has epistemic priority over the general diagnosis that a true belief essentially based on a false one never constitutes knowledge. In this account, the primary direction of support is abductive, from particular verdict to general principle (by inference to the best explanation), rather than deductive, from general principle to particular verdict (by universal instantiation). Gettier's own focus is on the particular verdicts, and that is how his counterexamples have usually been understood as working. In any event, his examples *can* be used in that way, and methodologically it is best to start with the simplest case, in which the particular verdict has priority. A similar point applies to Gettier's explicit assumption that justification is closed under deduction: what matters for his immediate purposes is just that the assumption clearly holds in his chosen cases, whether or not it holds in all more *recherché* ones. The need for examples is also implicit in Gettier's claim that one can be justified in believing a falsehood, for how could he adequately support the claim without appeal to examples? In effect, he provides a general recipe for developing any example of justified false belief into a counterexample to the justified true belief analysis.

Gettier's assumption that there can be justified false belief is not unquestionable, for any belief which does not constitute knowledge is *ipso facto* defective, and so in some sense not fully justified, even if it is fully excusable. That objection clearly does not invoke a standard of justification on which it is unnecessary for knowledge, nor does it give any succor to skepticism. However, it does invoke a concept of justification which is not prior to the concept of knowledge, and so risks making the analysis of knowledge as justified true belief circular (Williamson 2000a: 184–5, Sutton 2007). The analysis of knowledge as justified true belief loses much of its intended explanatory power if justification has to be understood by reference to knowledge. It is dialectically legitimate for critics of the analysis to work, as Gettier does, with the view of justification on which its proponents rely. On such a view, my justification for believing that I have hands is equally good whether I am an ordinary human with hands or a brain in a vat which merely seems to itself to be an ordinary human with hands: since my belief is justified in the former case, on pain of skepticism, it is equally justified in the latter case, when it is false. In what follows, we assume a sense of "justified" in which one can be justified in believing falsehoods.

Gettier presents his specific counterexamples to the target analysis through short fictional narratives, in the present tense indicative, with fictional uses of proper names ("Smith" and "Jones"), all introduced by "suppose that." Beyond their conformity to the abstract pattern just explained, their details do not concern us. Let us construct another example to the same pattern. A clever bookseller fakes evidence which appears to show conclusively that a particular book once belonged to Virginia Woolf; convinced, Orlando pays a considerable sum for the book. He has a justified false belief that this book of his once belonged to Virginia Woolf. On that basis alone, he forms the existential belief that he owns a book which once belonged to Virginia Woolf. The latter belief is in fact true, because another of his books in fact once belonged to her, although he does not associate that one with her in any way. Thus Orlando has a justified true belief that he owns a book which once belonged to Virginia Woolf, but he does not know that he owns a book which once belonged to Virginia Woolf. What we need to understand is how such fictional narratives can present counterexamples to philosophical analyses.

On Gettier's account, the target analysis is a claim of necessary and sufficient conditions for knowing. Let us formalize this as the claim that, necessarily, for any subject x and proposition p, x knows p if and only if x has a justified true belief in p.[4] Symbolically:

(1) $\Box \forall x \forall p \, (K(x, p) \equiv JTB(x, p))$

This does not say that knowledge is identical with justified true belief, nor does it entail that the word "knowledge" is synonymous with the phrase "justified true belief" or that the concept *knowledge* is identical with the concept *justified true belief*. But if any of those further claims is true, so too is (1). Thus a refutation of (1) automatically refutes each of those further claims too, although not conversely.

For present purposes, in formalizing Gettier's argument against (1), we can ignore most of the structure specific to his cases, and

[4]   The assumption that propositions are the objects of knowledge is convenient, but inessential to the underlying argument.

concentrate on the logical structure they share with most other imaginary counterexamples to philosophical analyses. Suppose that we fix on a particular Gettier-style story (the one about Orlando would do), henceforth "the Gettier case," told in neutral terms, without prejudice to the target analysis. For instance, it is not explicitly part of the story that Orlando does not know that he owns a book which once belonged to Virginia Woolf. Since the story contains fictional singular terms, such as "Orlando" and "this book," it is arguably just a pretence that its constituent sentences express propositions. However, we can treat such fictional singular terms as picturesque substitutes for variables. Replacing them by variables, we can represent the Gettier-style story by an open sentence $GC(x, p)$, where the variables "x" and "p" occupy the positions for, respectively, the believer and the content of the justified true belief. Although one could attempt an analysis of thought experiments that took their fictional aspect more seriously, their relevance to fictional claims such as (1) is most easily understood in this more literal-minded way.

If the Gettier case were impossible, it would pose no obvious threat to the claim of necessity (1). We therefore make the putative possibility of the case explicit:

(2) $\Diamond \exists x \exists p \; GC(x, p)$

Someone could stand in the relation described in the Gettier story to some proposition. In order to complete the argument against (1), we need the verdict that the subject in the Gettier case has justified true belief without knowledge. To a first approximation, we can formalize that as the claim that, necessarily, anyone who stands in the Gettier relation to a proposition has justified true belief in that proposition without knowledge:

(3) $\Box \forall x \forall p \; (GC(x, p) \rightarrow (JTB(x, p) \; \& \; \neg K(x, p)))$

By elementary modal reasoning, a necessary consequence of something possible is itself possible. Therefore, as a logical consequence of (2) and (3), someone could have justified true belief in a proposition without knowledge:

(4) $\Diamond \exists x \exists p \; (JTB(x, p) \; \& \; \neg K(x, p))$

But (4) is straightforwardly inconsistent with (1), in particular with its right-to-left direction. Justified true belief is insufficient for knowledge. Consequently, (2) and (3) suffice as premises for a deductive argument against the target analysis.

This objection to (1) relies essentially on its modal content. If (1) were replaced by a non-modal universally quantified biconditional, thought experiments would not refute it, for an imaginary case in which two things fail to coincide is quite compatible with their coincidence over all actual cases. The function of the thought experiment is to show that a certain case could arise, and that if it did, the two things would come apart, from which it follows that the two things could come apart. That refutes the modal claim that they could not come apart, but not the non-modal claim that they never in fact come apart.

That (3) is the best representation of the verdict on the Gettier case is doubtful. In philosophy, examples can almost never be described in complete detail. An extensive background must be taken for granted; it cannot all be explicitly stipulated. Although many of the missing details are irrelevant to whatever philosophical issues are in play, not all of them are. This applies not just to highly schematic descriptions of examples, such as the initial abstract Gettier schema, but even to the much richer stories Gettier and other philosophers like to tell. For example, in the Gettier case, if the subject's inference to the true belief **p** from the false belief **q** bizarrely happens to trigger awkward memories or apparent memories that cast doubt on **q**, the effect may be to lose justification for **q** rather than to gain it for **p**. Without specifically addressing the question, we do not envisage the Gettier case like that. Nor do we worry about whether our verdicts would hold even if mad scientists were interfering with the subject's brain processes in various ways; those possibilities do not normally occur to us when we assess Gettier examples. Similarly, when moral philosophers assess imaginary examples, one can almost always fill out the case with unintended but morally relevant additions that would reverse the verdict. Any humanly compiled list of such interfering factors is likely to be incomplete.

Instead of asking whether justified true belief without knowledge is a necessary consequence of the Gettier case, one might more naturally ask whether, if there *were* an instance of the Gettier case, it *would* be an instance of justified true belief without knowledge. The verdict that it would constitutes a counterfactual conditional, which is much weaker than the strict conditional (3).[5] In very rough terms, it requires justified true belief without knowledge only in the closest realizations of the Gettier case, not in all possible realizations. By using the counterfactual conditional, we in effect leave the world to fill in the details of the story, rather than trying to do it all ourselves. For present purposes the counterfactual can be symbolized thus (its formalization will be discussed in detail later):

(3*) $\exists x \exists p \; GC(x, p) \; \Box\!\!\rightarrow \; \forall x \forall p \; (GC(x, p) \rightarrow (JTB(x, p) \; \& \; \neg K(x, p)))$

The counterfactual conditional in (3*) takes widest possible scope. If there were an instance of the Gettier case, it would be an instance of justified true belief without knowledge. For the time being, let us simply assume that (3*) correctly formalizes Gettier's major premise. That assumption will be evaluated in later sections.

Let us reconstruct the logic of the argument against (1). Informally, why do (2) and (3*) entail (4)? Given (2), (3*) cannot hold vacuously. Thus, given (2) and (3*), (3*) holds non-vacuously. Therefore its antecedent and consequent hold together in some possible world. That must be a possible world in which someone has justified true belief without knowledge. Thus (4) is true, so (1) is false.

We can make the reasoning rigorous without reliance on possible worlds. First, consider the logical relations between the non-modal constituents of the argument. Let **A** be $\exists x \exists p \; GC(x, \; p)$ ("Someone stands in the Gettier relation to something"), **B** be $\forall x \forall p \; (GC(x, p) \rightarrow (JTB(x, p) \; \& \; \neg K(x, p)))$ ("Whoever stands in the Gettier relation to something has justified true belief in it without knowledge") and **C** be $\exists x \exists p \; (JTB(x, p) \; \& \; \neg K(x, p))$ ("Someone has justified true belief in something without knowledge"). Thus (2) is $\Diamond A$, (3*) is $A \; \Box\!\!\rightarrow \; B$ and (4) is $\Diamond C$. Obviously, **C** is a logical conse-

---

[5]   Similarly, in describing one of his famous examples to motivate the causal theory of perception, Grice writes "if, unknown to me, there were a mirror interposed between myself and the pillar, it would certainly be incorrect to say that I saw the first pillar, and correct to say that I saw the second" (1961, section 5); the counter-factual conditional here reads completely naturally (although one might object to his dressing up a fact about perception as, in his words, a "linguistic fact"). Sorensen (1992) formalizes the arguments underlying thought experiments using counterfactual conditionals; for discussion of his proposal see Häggqvist (1996: 92–103).

quence of **A** and **B**: in symbols, **A**, **B** ⊨ **C**. By the principle that the counterfactual consequences of a given supposition are closed under logical consequence (CLOSURE), we therefore have **A** □→ **A**, **A** □→ **B** ⊨ **A** □→ **C**.[6] Since everything counterfactually implies itself (REFLEXIVITY), the first premise is a logical truth: ⊨ **A** □→ **A**. Thus we can simplify to **A** □→ **B** ⊨ **A** □→ **C**. By the principle POSSIBILITY from the previous chapter, a counterfactual consequence of a possibility is itself a possibility, which yields ◊**A**, **A** □→ **C** ⊨ ◊**C**. Combining these two results gives ◊**A**, **A** □→ **B** ⊨ ◊**C**, in other words, (2), (3*) ⊨ (4), as required. Thus weakening the major premise from a strict to a counterfactual implication leaves the validity of the argument intact. The extra strength of strict implication was an unnecessary commitment.

This account of the use of imaginary counterexamples in refuting philosophical analyses extends far beyond Gettier cases. It also generalizes to their use in refuting philosophical claims of necessity which lack the form of an analysis, such as one-way strict implications.

Preview: Section 3 makes some observations about the epistemology of the argument just analyzed. Section 4 assesses (3*) as a formalization of the counterfactual (Appendix 2 considers another alternative). Section 5 asks whether the right counterfactual was selected for formalization. The final section considers whether Gettier's argument concerns counterfactual possibility at all. The foregoing account survives all these tests, at least as an adequate approximation.

3

On our account, a thought experiment such as Gettier's embodies a straightforward valid modal argument for a modal conclusion. The role of the imagination is in verifying the premises.[7]

---

[6]   As noted in the previous chapter, CLOSURE cannot be applied to cases when the original argument preserves truth at the actual world of every model but not at counterfactual worlds. Since **C** is an ordinary first-order logical consequence of **A** and **B**, this problem does not arise here.

[7]   There is a debate as to whether thought experiments in science reduce to arguments (Norton 1991, 2004) or contain an irreducible imaginative element (Gendler

The major premise (3*) is a counterfactual conditional; the imagination is used in verifying it just as it is used in verifying many everyday counterfactuals, such as "If the bush had not been there, the rock would have landed in the lake." There is nothing peculiarly philosophical about the way in which the counterfactual is assessed. The antecedent and consequent express empirical conditions. Is the connection between them endorsed on distinctively "conceptual" grounds? The epistemological idea of conceptual connections turned out in earlier chapters to be a myth. Here, two points are enough. First, if what warranted the counterfactual conditional (3*) was that its antecedent conceptually entailed its conclusion, then that would also warrant the strict implication (3); but we have seen that the strict implication is not warranted. Second, native English speakers sometimes dispute the Gettier verdict, and so by implication reject the counterfactual. In doing so, they show poor epistemological judgment but not linguistic incompetence: they are not usually accused of failing to understand the relevant words of English; it would be inappropriate to send them off to language school for retraining. Some of them have had no exposure to philosophy; others are professional epistemologists.[8] We assent to (3*) on the basis of an offline application of our ability to classify people around us as knowing various truths or as ignorant of them, and as having or as lacking other epistemologically relevant properties. That classificatory ability goes far beyond mere linguistic understanding of "know" and other words.

The minor premise (2) is a claim of possibility. For standard Gettier cases it is quite uncontentious. They constitute mundane practical possibilities; nobody doubts that they could arise: (2) is not where the philosophical action is. What skeptics about Gettier's thought experiments doubt is not (2) but (3*). They call into question "the Gettier intuition," that the case is one of justified true belief without knowledge: it corresponds to (3*), not (2), for the English original of (2) does not even contain "know" or cognate terms. In

---

1998, 2004). The present account of thought experiments in philosophy goes some way towards reconciling the two sides: thought experiments do constitute arguments, but the imagination plays an irreducible role in warranting the premises.

[8]   Shope (1983: 26–33) discusses some attempts by professional epistemologists to argue that the Gettier problem is not genuine. See Weinberg, Stich, and Nichols (2001) for lay denials.

any case, the previous chapter showed how the ordinary epistemology of counterfactual conditionals applies to possibility claims such as (2).

For other philosophical thought experiments, the possibility premise corresponding to (2) may be far more contentious: a bizarre science fiction possibility, perhaps involving a brain swap or even a disembodied mind. Whether the possibility premise is warranted depends on the details of the case, but there is no reason in principle why it should not be. In general, we have a trade-off between the uncontentiousness of the major premise and the uncontentiousness of the minor premise. The more we pack into the description of the case (such as $GC(x, p)$), the more firmly we can secure the major premise, the desired verdict, but the less obvious we make the minor premise, the possibility claim. By packing less into the description, we can make the possibility claim more obvious, but risk loosening our grip on the desired verdict. However, such trade-offs are a commonplace of abstract argument; they do not mean that we cannot make both premises simultaneously plausible enough for our purposes.

Do we know the premises (2) and (3*) a priori? Presumably, we do so if and only if we also know the conclusion (4) a priori, given that we believe it just on the basis of this logically valid deduction. However, in the previous chapter we saw reason to doubt the significance of the distinction between a priori and a posteriori knowledge. The considerations there apply to the present case too. We accept (2) and (3*) on the basis of a capacity for applying epistemological concepts that goes far beyond what it takes to possess the concepts in the first place, since someone with a distorted epistemological outlook may reject (3*), yet still possess the relevant concepts: they genuinely believe that the subject of the Gettier case would not have justified true belief without knowledge. Past experience contributed to the acquisition of those classificatory epistemological skills that go far beyond possession of the relevant concepts. That experience included sense experience. For example, we learn to recognize perceptually conditions of observation under which observers can gain perceptual knowledge of various features of their environment. Again, our skill in discriminating justification from its absence is developed in observation of other thinkers. In our acceptance of (3*), sense experience is not confined to a purely enabling role, for example by providing

the opportunity to acquire those concepts or to encounter philosophical arguments about them. It is more directly implicated than that.
It plays a positive role in helping to tip judgment one way rather than
the other when one imagines the Gettier case instantiated as such that
the subject's inference extends justification from the false premise
to the true conclusion, rather than as such that the inference undermines justification for the premise. Which way one goes depends on
what one finds normal or natural, which partly depends on the past
course of one's sense experience. Thus knowledge of (3*) does not
conform to the usual stereotype of *a priori* knowledge. Typically,
however, past experience plays no strictly evidential role in knowledge of (3*): for example, we need not invoke past instances of lack
of knowledge as inductive evidence for lack of knowledge in the
Gettier case. The experience of performing the thought experiment
itself is not sense experience as usually understood. Thus knowledge
of (3*) fails equally to conform to the usual stereotype of *a posteriori*
knowledge. Although we might try to resolve the issue by stipulation,
doing so would yield little insight into the nature of knowledge such
as we have of (3*). To gain such insight, we must focus on the ways
in which that knowledge differs both from the stereotype of *a priori*
knowledge and from the stereotype of *a posteriori* knowledge.

One manifestation of the influence of past experience on epistemological judgments may be cross-cultural variation in verdicts on
thought experiments, including the Gettier case.[9] Such variation, if it
occurs, may result from cross-cultural variation in the meaning of
"know" or other epistemological terms, but it need not. It may occur
between sub-communities of English speakers who all use the words
as part of a single common vocabulary, but disagree in their applications of them, just as different communities may disagree in their
applications of the word "justice" while still using it with a single
shared meaning. Cross-cultural disagreement over the theory of evolution is compatible with a common meaning of the word "evolution" between the cultures. In the present cases, the variation between
individuals within a single group is just as striking as the statistical

[9]   For some evidence see Weinberg, Stich, and Nichols (2001), critically discussed by
Sosa (2005). The rationale for the use of thought experiments in philosophy which
Weinberg, Stich and Nichols attack is very different from that defended in this
book.

variation between groups: the data do not suggest a clash of mono-lithic cultures, but rather some variation in the proportion of the population who respond in a given way.

Much of the evidence for cross-cultural variation in judgments on thought experiments concerns verdicts by people without philosophi-cal training. Yet philosophy students have to learn how to apply general concepts to specific examples with careful attention to the relevant subtleties, just as law students have to learn how to analyze hypothetical cases. Levels of disagreement over thought experiments seem to be significantly lower among fully trained philosophers than among novices. That is another manifestation of the influence of past experience on epistemological judgments about thought experiments.

We should not regard philosophical training as an illegitimate contamination of the data, any more than training natural scientists how to perform experiments properly is a contamination of their data. Although the philosophically innocent may be free of various forms of theoretical bias, just as the scientifically innocent are, that is not enough to confer special authority on innocent judgment, given its characteristic sloppiness. Training in any intellectual discipline whatsoever has some tendency to instill unquestioning conformity to current basic assumptions in that discipline, and a consequent slow-ness to recognize errors in those assumptions. That is inevitable, for no progress is made when everything is put simultaneously into ques-tion. Fully trained practitioners can still obtain experimental results that undermine currently accepted theories. That can happen with philosophical thought experiments too, as the example of Gettier shows.[10]

The residual levels of disagreement in judgments between trained philosophers do not warrant wholesale skepticism about the method of thought experiments. Naturally, philosophical debates focus on points of disagreement, not on points of agreement. Most intellectual disciplines have learned to live with significant levels of disagreement between trained practitioners, concerning both theory and observa-tion: philosophy is not as exceptional in this respect as some pretend.

---

[10]   Contrast Goldman (2005), discussed in Kornblith (2007). Goldman's interest is in the analysis of "pretheoretic concepts," but theoretical innocence often causes people to misapply their own concepts.

Notoriously, eye-witnesses often disagree fundamentally in their descriptions of recent events, but it would be foolish to conclude that perception is not a source of knowledge, or to dismiss all eye-witness reports. To ignore the evidence of thought experiments would be a mistake of the same kind, if not of the same degree. Disagreement can provide a reason to be somewhat more cautious than we might otherwise have been, in our handling both of eye-witness reports and of thought experiments; such caution is commonplace in philosophy. There is no need to be panicked into more extreme reactions.

This account has emphasized the epistemological continuity between verdicts on philosophical thought experiments and other judgments. That emphasis is supported by cases in which observations of real life do the same epistemological work as philosophical thought experiments. For instance, not all Gettier counterexamples are imaginary: sometimes a stopped watch really does show the right time. To make the point vivid, I have occasionally created Gettier cases for lecture audiences. For example, I have begun a lecture by apologizing for not giving a power-point presentation; I explained that the only time I gave a power-point presentation it was a complete disaster. Since my listeners had no reason to distrust me on a claim so much to my discredit, they acquired through my testimony the justified belief that the only time I gave a power-point presentation it was a complete disaster. They competently deduced that I had never given a successful power-point presentation. Thus they acquired the justified belief that I had never given a successful power-point presentation. That belief was true, but the reason was that I had never given a power-point presentation at all (and still do not intend to). My assertion that the only time I had given a power-point presentation it was a complete disaster was a bare-faced lie.[11] Thus they were basing their justified true belief that I had never given a successful power-point presentation on their justified false belief that the only time I had given a power-point presentation it was a complete disaster. Consequently, they did not know that I had never given a successful power-point presentation. The original audience encountered the case by living through it, others do so by reading my testimony, which is more similar to encountering a case by reading a fictional narrative. Either way, this actual Gettier case is a counterexample to

[11]   Someone commented "You can't believe the first thing he says."

the non-modal principle that knowledge coincides with justified true belief in all actual cases; since actuality entails possibility ($A \vDash \Diamond A$), it is also a counterexample to the modal principle (1) that knowledge coincides with justified true belief in all possible cases.

What is striking about real life Gettier cases is how little difference they make. They are not markedly more or less effective as counter-examples to the target analysis than imaginary Gettier cases are. Those who found the imaginary counterexamples convincing find the real life ones more or less equally convincing. Unless one is a skeptic about the external world, the reliance on empirical methods is no reason for serious doubt.[12] Conversely, those who were suspicious of the imaginary counterexamples are more or less equally suspicious of the real life ones.

It might be replied that the process of classifying a real life instance of the Gettier case as an instance of justified true belief without knowledge involves a modal judgment, because it can be factorized into a deduction from the non-modal premise that this is an instance of the Gettier case and the modal premise that if something were an instance of the Gettier case it would be an instance of justified true belief without knowledge. However, such factorization is deeply problematic. Note first that the modal element in it is quite gratu-itous; the deduction works just as well with the non-modal second premise that every (actual) instance of the Gettier case is an instance of justified true belief without knowledge. Furthermore, we have no good reason to insist on factorization here but not for utterly ordi-nary ascriptions of epistemological predicates, as when someone says that John does not know that the meeting has been cancelled. Nor have we any good reason to insist on it for ascriptions of epistemo-logical predicates and not for ascriptions of other empirical predi-cates. But if factorization is ubiquitous, an infinite regress occurs. The process of classifying this as an instance of the Gettier case is itself factorized into a deduction from the non-modal premise that this is an instance of F and the modal premise that if something were an instance of F it would be an instance of the Gettier case. The process of classifying this as an instance of F would in turn be factorized into

---

[12] In principle, someone could react to a real life Gettier case by judging it to be possible without judging it to be actual, and reject (1) on the former basis alone. It is implausible that most people take that unnatural route.

a deduction from the non-modal premise that this is an instance of E and the modal premise that if something were an instance of E it would be an instance of F, and so on. Plainly, no such infinite regress of inferences occurs in us. At some point, we simply apply our concepts to what confronts us, without relying on an inference from further premises. Why should that not happen with the original epistemological classification of the real life instance of the Gettier case? No doubt epistemological facts supervene on non-epistemological facts (so that the non-epistemological facts in a suitable instance of the Gettier case determine that it is an instance of justified true belief without knowledge), but of course that does not entail that our epistemological beliefs are derived from non-epistemological beliefs. Our epistemological beliefs are certainly not inferred from our beliefs about microphysics, even if epistemological facts supervene on microphysical facts. Why should our epistemological beliefs be inferred from some other putative supervenience base? Most people have scarcely any idea how to formulate even approximately sufficient conditions in informative non-epistemological terms for epistemological conclusions. Even if they do happen to speculate along such lines, their speculations are far less secure epistemically than are their ordinary applications of epistemological concepts, so the latter do not depend on the former. The factorization hypothesis has little independent plausibility. Moreover, even if the factorization hypothesis were true, it would apply equally to non-philosophical applications of epistemological predicates in ordinary life and natural science, and so would indicate nothing distinctive about their applications in real-life instances of Gettier cases.

Removing the tricky apparatus of thought experiments and modal judgments does not reassure those who doubted that the subjects of Gettier's original examples lacked knowledge: whatever their rhetoric, their doubts did not really concern the method of thought experiments. Rather, they concerned the reliability of our epistemological judgments, whether modal or non-modal, in particular of our applications of the concepts of knowledge and justification.[13] The switch

---

[13] *Objection*: Nozick (1981: 172–96) analyzes knowledge in counterfactual terms; on his view, any judgment about knowledge implicitly involves judgments concerning counterfactual conditionals. *Reply*: First, the objection does not fully generalize, since it depends on a specific analysis of knowledge. Second, Nozick's analysis does not make philosophers' ascriptions of knowledge or of its absence any more modal than

from an "*a priori*" to an "*a posteriori*" method here makes very little practical difference. We manifest recognition of this underlying cognitive similarity when we refuse to treat real life and fictional Gettier cases as mutually independent evidence against the justified true belief account of knowledge to a much greater extent than we treat two fictional Gettier cases as mutually independent evidence.

4

Let us now consider more carefully the fine structure of the major premises of the arguments which underlie philosophical thought experiments.

What is sometimes called "the Gettier intuition" has been expressed by a counterfactual conditional in English, roughly:

(5)   If a thinker were Gettier-related to a proposition, he/she would have justified true belief in it without knowledge.[14]

This was in turn symbolized by the formula (3*). Later, we will assess some alternative expressions of the Gettier intuition in English. For the time being, let us treat (5) as faithfully expressing the Gettier intuition, and ask whether (3*) faithfully enough formalizes (5).

We might query (3*) as a formalization of (5) on grounds of syntactic structure. Where (5) has the anaphoric pronouns "he/she" and "it," (3*) repeats the material $GC(x, p)$ and applies universal quantification. In fact, (5) is a case of "donkey anaphora." It is similar to (6):

(6)   If a farmer owned a donkey, he would beat it.

---

non-philosophers' ascriptions are. Third, skeptics about epistemological thought experiments typically make no appeal to counterfactual analyses of knowledge. After all, the way in which Nozick reaches his conclusions exemplifies the very methodology about which they are skeptical. Nor would they regard their skepticism as undermined by growing evidence that counterfactual analyses of knowledge are incorrect (Williamson 2000a: 147–63). Their skepticism is intended to get its grip irrespective of whether ascriptions of knowledge as such involve modal thinking.

[14]   To be Gettier-related here is to be related as specified in the given Gettier scenario, not merely to be related as in some Gettier scenario or other.

This is just the "subjunctive" analogue of the classic indicative donkey sentence (7):

(7) If a farmer owns a donkey, he beats it.

The standard first-order formalization of (7) is (8):

(8) $\forall x \forall y$ ((Farmer(x) & Donkey(y) & Owns(x, y)) $\rightarrow$ Beats(x, y))

The main challenge is to explain how (7) can have the truth conditions of (8) in terms of a compositional semantics for (7), given the mismatch in syntactic structure between (7) and (8).[15] For present purposes, however, what matters most is just getting the right truth conditions, up to logical equivalence. We might expect that if (7) has the same truth conditions as (8), then (6) will have the same truth conditions as the result of replacing the material conditional in (8) by a counterfactual conditional:

(9) $\forall x \forall y$ ((Farmer(x) & Donkey(y) & Owns(x, y)) $\square\!\!\rightarrow$ Beats(x, y))

The analogous formalization of (5) is not (3*) but (10):

(10) $\forall x \forall p$ (GC(x, p) $\square\!\!\rightarrow$ (JTB(x, p) & $\neg$K(x, p)))

In the indicative case, (8) is logically equivalent to the donkey analogue of (3*):

(11) $\exists x \exists y$ (Farmer(x) & Donkey(y) & Owns(x, y)) $\rightarrow$
       $\forall x \forall y$ ((Farmer(x) & Donkey(y) & Owns(x, y)) $\rightarrow$ Beats(x, y))

---

[15] Elbourne (2005) is a recent discussion of the topic with further references. Some will judge "If John had a dime, he would put it in the meter" true if in the relevant counterfactual circumstances John has two dimes and puts one in the meter. They may also have to judge "If John had a dime, he would put it in his piggybank" simultaneously true by parity of reasoning. There is no corresponding true reading of "If John had a dime, he would put it in the meter and put it in his piggybank." All that is clearly true in the envisaged case is "If John had a dime, he would put one in the meter."

For since (8) is the consequent of (11), (8) obviously entails (11), and conversely, if the antecedent of (11) is false then (8) is vacuously true, so (11) entails (8). However, the corresponding equivalence fails in the counterfactual case: (9) is not equivalent to (12).

(12) $\exists x \exists y$ (Farmer(x) & Donkey(y) & Owns(x, y)) $\square\!\!\rightarrow$
       $\forall x \forall y$ ((Farmer(x) & Donkey(y) & Owns(x, y)) $\rightarrow$ Beats(x, y))

For (12) is true and (9) false in the following circumstances. In the actual world (and, if you like, in all close ones) some farmer owns some donkey and every farmer who owns a donkey beats it. Farmer Giles could have owned this donkey, although he does not own it in the actual world (or in any close one). If he owned it, he would not beat it. Similarly, (10) is not equivalent to (3*). For (3*) is true and (10) false in the following circumstances. In the actual world (and, if you like, in all close worlds) someone is Gettier-related to some proposition and everyone who is Gettier-related to a proposition has justified true belief in it without knowledge. That woman could have been Gettier-related to that proposition, although she is not Gettier-related to it in the actual world (or in any close world). If she had been Gettier-related to it, she would have lacked justified belief in it (perhaps because making the relevant inference would have caused her to lose justification for the premise rather than gain it for the conclusion). Thus if (5) and (6) respectively have the same truth conditions as (10) and (9), then they have different truth conditions from (3*) and (12). One might therefore conclude that (3*) does not capture the truth conditions of (5).

However, there is reason to doubt that (5) and (6) respectively do have the same truth conditions as (10) and (9). Consider another sentence of the same form:

(13) If an animal escaped from the zoo, it would be a monkey.

The formalization of (13) corresponding to (9) and (10) is (14):

(14) $\forall x$ ((Animal(x) & Escapedzoo(x)) $\square\!\!\rightarrow$ Monkey(x))

Consider an elephant; (14) implies that if it had escaped from the zoo, it would have been a monkey. Thus (14) is trivially false. But

(13) is not trivially false; it may well be true. Thus (13) does not have the same truth conditions as (14). For similar reasons, (5) and (6) respectively seem to differ in truth conditions from (10) and (9). Indeed, the very examples used to establish that (3*) and (12) respectively differ in truth conditions from (10) and (9) tell in favor of (3*) and (12) rather than (10) and (9) as formalizations of (5) and (6), on at least one reading. Suppose that in the actual world (and, if you like, in all close ones) some farmer owns some donkey and every farmer who owns a donkey beats it; Farmer Giles could have owned this donkey, although he does not own it in the actual world (or in any close one); if he owned it, he would not beat it. In these circumstances, (6) seems to be true on at least one reading, and thereby to have the same truth-value as (12) rather than (9). Similarly, suppose that in the actual world (and, if you like, in all close worlds) someone is Gettier-related to some proposition and everyone who is Gettier-related to a proposition has justified true belief in it without knowledge; that woman could have been Gettier-related to that proposition, although she is not Gettier-related to it in the actual world (or in any close world); if she had been Gettier-related to it, she would have lacked justified belief in it. In these circumstances, (5) seems to be true on at least one reading, and thereby to have the same truth-value as (3*) rather than (10).[16]

We can formalize (13) along the lines of (3*) and (12):

(15) $\exists x \, (\text{Animal}(x) \,\&\, \text{Escapedzoo}(x)) \,\square\!\!\rightarrow$
$\forall x \, ((\text{Animal}(x) \,\&\, \text{Escapedzoo}(x)) \rightarrow \text{Monkey}(x))$

This deals with the elephant problem. For (15) is true if, had some animal escaped, only monkeys would have escaped; it does not entail that if the elephant had escaped, it would have been a monkey.

The example of (13) also supports the use of universal quantification in the consequents of (3*) and (12). For suppose that, if some animal had escaped, both a monkey and an elephant would have escaped: then (13) is not true. It is not the case *both* that if an animal escaped it would be a monkey *and* that if an animal escaped it would

---

[16]   As can easily be checked, placing **Farmer(x)** & **Donkey(x)** in (9) and **Animal(x)** in (14) outside the scope of $\square\!\!\rightarrow$ makes no serious difference to the argument.

be an elephant. Thus (13) is not equivalent to the result of replacing universal quantification in the consequent of (15) by existential quantification:

(16) ∃x (Animal(x) & Escapedzoo(x)) □→
        ∃x (Animal(x) & Escapedzoo(x) & Monkey(x))

In sloppy terms, what is wrong with (16) as a formalization of (13) is that it does not require the escaping animal with which we started to be a monkey; it is satisfied if some other escaping animal is a monkey. That is not enough to vindicate (13). Analogous points apply to (5) and (6). For purposes of deriving (4), we could have used (17) in place of (3*):

(17) ∃x∃p GC(x, p) □→ ∃x∃ p (GC(x, p) & JTB(x, p) & ¬K(x, p))

But (17) does not entail (5). In sloppy terms, what is wrong with (17) as a formalization of (5) is that it does not require the instance of the Gettier case with which we started to be an instance of justified true belief without knowledge; it is satisfied if some other instance of the Gettier case is an instance of justified true belief without knowledge. That is not enough to vindicate (5). Formalizing (5) as (3*) avoids this problem.[17]

Henceforth, we assume that (3*) adequately formalizes the English counterfactual sentence (5).[18] But does (5) adequately express "the Gettier intuition"?

---

[17] Such truth conditions emerge naturally from accounts that analyze anaphoric pronouns in terms of (not obligatorily singular) definite descriptions (Davies 1981: 166–76, Neale 1990: 180–91); Elbourne (2005) develops a related approach within a framework of situation semantics. It may be less straightforward for alternative approaches to donkey anaphora (such as those based on discourse representation theory or dynamic semantics, for example van Rooij (2006)) to deliver appropriate truth conditions for the relevant sentences: but perhaps it can be done.

[18] For an alternative approach to formalizing the Gettier argument, see Appendix 2.

5

One might worry that the counterfactual claim (5) overstates the Gettier intuition, just as the claim of strict implication (3) turned out to do. If the actual world happens to contain an abnormal instance of the Gettier case that is not an instance of justified true belief, however many normal instances it also contains that are instances of justified true belief without knowledge, the counterfactual (5) is still false. It is false too if, although the actual world contains no instance of the Gettier case, it happens to be such that if there had been instances, they would have included an abnormal one which was not an instance of justified belief. If it is still possible to have normal instances of the Gettier case which are instances of justified true belief without knowledge, the Gettier intuition might be regarded as still correct, and therefore as not adequately formalized by the false counterfactual (5). Why make the premise of the Gettier argument unnecessarily strong?

We might alleviate the problem by understanding the quantifiers in the formalization (3*) of (5) as restricted by the conversational context. For example, it might sometimes exclude instances of the Gettier case on Alpha Centauri. However, such restrictions are unlikely to provide a complete solution. For even the contextually relevant domain may happen to betray our expectations.

Here is a simple example. Hank is better at logic than at geography. He wants to refute someone's claim that it is impossible validly to deduce a true conclusion from a false premise. Since he falsely believes that Glasgow is in England, he presents a thought experiment in which "Glasgow is in England or Glasgow is in France" is deduced from "Glasgow is in France." Contextual restrictions do not save Hank. What should we say about this case?

As it stands, Hank's counterexample does not work, and his belief that it works is mistaken. But when the mistake is pointed out, he has no difficulty in repairing it. The easiest repair is simply to substitute "Scotland" for "England." Alternatively, he might stipulate that in his thought experiment Glasgow is in England. One mild disadvantage of the latter stipulation is that it makes the thought experiment depend on an assumption about the contingency of national boundaries which is irrelevant to the logical point at issue. What would be childish on Hank's part would be to insist that his original thought experiment already constituted a correct counterexample, before he made the stipulation, because he *believed* that Glasgow was in England, and it could have been, so the thought experiment could have been realized in line with his beliefs and, if it had been, it would have been a case of a valid deduction from a false premise to a true conclusion. Although Hank may insist that Glasgow was in England in the case which he had in mind, that was just not the "counterexample" which he actually presented. He spoke falsely when he first said "Someone who infers "Glasgow is in England or Glasgow is in France" from "Glasgow is in France" has validly deduced a true conclusion from a false premise." Similarly, suppose that someone says "Every man in the room is wearing a tie"; I look around, see a man not wearing a tie, misidentify him as Dave (who is in fact wearing a tie), and say "Dave isn't." When it is pointed out to me that Dave is wearing a tie, I deceive myself if I insist that my original reply was correct because the man whom I had in mind was not wearing a tie; that was just not the "counterexample" I actually presented. I spoke falsely when I said "Dave isn't." Even if the audience shares the speaker's false belief that Glasgow is in England or that the man over there is Dave, a third party overhearing the conversation can know that the "counterexample" as it stands is incorrect. For a thought experiment to constitute a counterexample, it is not sufficient that some counterfactual filling out of it, no matter how far-fetched, constitutes a counterexample.

Many philosophers have the common human characteristic of reluctance to admit to having been wrong. We should not distort our account of thought experiments in order to indulge that tendency. Often purported counterexamples fail for accidental reasons and can easily be repaired. To attempt to build into the counterexample in advance all repairs which might conceivably be needed is a futile exercise. It loads the purported counterexample with complexity and in the process weakens it in other respects. The repairs need not articulate qualifications that were in some obscure sense implicit in the thought experiment from the beginning. Rather, they genuinely modify the thought experiment, but the similarity of the new thought experiment to the old one is evidence that the old one was not far wrong.

An example is this. If one is working in the modal system S5, one can weaken the counterfactual premise (3*) to its mere possibility:

(3**)　◊(∃x∃p GC(x, p) □→
　　　　　　　　　∀x∀p (GC(x, p) → (JTB(x, p) & ¬K(x, p))))

The reason is that in S5, given the necessity of the POSSIBILITY principle, one can reason from ◊A and ◊(A □→ B) to ◊B. For since POSSIBILITY allows the move from A □→ B to ◊A → ◊B, it also allows the move from ◊(A □→ B) to ◊(◊A → ◊B). But in S5 the application of ◊ and □ to fully modalized formulas such as ◊A → ◊B is redundant (modal matters are not themselves contingent), so ◊(◊A → ◊B) entails ◊A → ◊B. Consequently, ◊(A □→ B) entails ◊A → ◊B. In particular, we can deduce (4) from (2) and (3**). Thus one might be tempted to weaken the counterfactual premise to (3**). But that move has its costs too. For it makes thought experiments depend on the soundness of the characteristic principles of S5, whereas the original analysis in terms of (3*) rather than (3**) involved no such commitment.[19] Moreover, it is strained to attribute the commitment to S5 to people who have never considered the matter when their reasoning can readily be rationalized without it, as before.

　Another watering down of the counterfactual premise is to its dual, the negation of the opposite counterfactual:

(3***)　¬(∃x∃p GC(x, p) □→
　　　　　　　　　¬∀x∀p (GC(x, p) → (JTB(x, p) & ¬K(x, p))))

Indeed, from (3***) one can reason to (4) without invoking (2) as a separate premise.[20] Roughly speaking, (3***) says that if the Gettier case had an instance, it *might* be an instance of justified true belief without knowledge, rather than that it *would* be. But (3***) falls

---

[19]　Strictly speaking, one must check that that the inference schema from ◊(A □→ B) to ◊A → ◊B *requires* the characteristic S5 schema, ◊□A → □A. But substituting ¬A for A and the contradiction ⊥ for B in the inference schema gives the inference from ◊(¬A □→ ⊥) to ◊¬A → ◊⊥. Since ¬A □→ ⊥ is just the counterfactual equivalent of □A from the previous chapter and ◊¬A → ◊⊥ is equivalent to □A by normal modal logic, that is tantamount to the inference from ◊□A to □A, which is equivalent to the S5 schema, as required.

[20]　From the negation of (4) one infers □∀x∀p (JTB(x, p) → K(x, p)) and thence □(∃x∃p GC(x, p) → ¬∀x∀p (GC(x, p) → (JTB(x, p) & ¬K(x, p)))) by standard quantified modal logic; the negation of (3***) follows by the NECESSITY principle in the previous chapter. Similarly, the negation of (3***) follows from the negation of (2). Thus both (2) and (4) follow from (3***).

short of normal standards of adequacy for thought experiments. Suppose that a slow-witted philosopher wants to test the hypothesis that the objective probability of a false belief cannot be greater than 99 percent. He imagines himself having bought one ticket in a fair lottery of a thousand tickets with only one winner, believing before the draw that his ticket will lose. He notes that the objective probability of his belief would be greater than 99 percent. However, he has not yet considered whether the scenario is to be one in which his ticket wins. By normal standards, he has not yet determined a counterexample to the hypothesis, although he will have done so once he specifies that in the scenario his ticket wins.[21] Yet presumably the analogue of (3***) already holds for his unspecific scenario. It is not true that if the unspecific scenario were realized, his ticket would lose – it *might* win. Normal standards of adequacy for thought experiments require something much more like (3*) than like (3***). A similar objection applies to (3**) too.

At the limit, it may be suggested that the role of the Gettier thought experiments is to supply not premises for the conclusion (4) but instead something more like a causal basis for assenting to (4). However, such an undifferentiated account fails to capture what is rational about our rejection of the target analysis. It does not articulate the evidential role of the Gettier case. In most valid deductions, the premises are collectively stronger than the conclusion: that is, the conclusion does not entail every premise. Therefore, they are unnecessarily strong in a purely logical sense. But that sense is not the one that matters. Epistemically and dialectically, the "unnecessarily strong" premises may be exactly what we need. Although their extra strength sometimes leads to trouble, and revision is required, we should not try to cross all such bridges right now, before we come to them; many of them we shall never need to cross.

In any field, arguments are subject to inessential problems of various kinds. Once such problems are identified, they can be fixed without too much difficulty or damage to the original purpose of the argument. We may well be warranted in continuing to attribute the "essential insight" for the argument to its originator, despite his or her minor slips, as we might for the proof of a mathematical theorem. Where reasoning is most explicit, in logic and mathematics, the

[21] For the sake of a simple example, issues about the open future are ignored.

history of mistakes and corrections is often easily documented. Where reasoning is less explicit, as in philosophy, there is more scope for cover-ups. Nevertheless, we should expect that the same process of fine-tuning occurs for philosophical thought experiments as elsewhere. We should not confuse subsequent fallbacks with the original claims. Unnatural formulations such as (3**) and (3***) are far more likely to be the fallbacks than to be the original claims. But even when lacunae are identified in a thought experiment, the most likely response in practice is just to add further stipulations to the specification of the case, as it were simply to replace **GC(x, p)** by **GC⁺(x, p)**, so as to preserve the original structure of argument.[22] We resort to the likes of (3**) and (3***) only in exceptional circumstances.

One may even wonder whether the move to the counterfactual conditional (3*) from the strict conditional (3) represents another such fallback. Perhaps: but the question "If there had been an instance of this case, would it have been an instance of justified true belief without knowledge?" seems quite a natural way of articulating what is at stake with a Gettier counterexample. The corresponding questions for (3**) and (3***) seem less natural. Moreover, counterfactual questions arise continually in everyday thought, whereas questions of metaphysical necessity rarely arise outside philosophy, so the burden of proof is on those who claim that our initial questions about a hypothetical case are metaphysically modal rather than simply counterfactual in nature. We may, therefore, treat a counterfactual analysis of the arguments underlying philosophical thought experiments as the default. In particular, we may continue to view the Gettier argument as something like the argument from (2) and (3*) to (4).

6

In the original paper, Gettier presents his cases as indicative suppositions. He uses no "subjunctive" conditionals. Although he describes

---

[22]   Merely adding the stipulation that **x** and **p** constitute a normal instance of the Gettier case is unlikely to solve the problem, for the relevant notion of normality is an epistemological one that violates the supposed neutrality of the initial description of the case.

his target as an attempt "to state necessary and sufficient conditions for someone's knowing a given proposition" (1963: 121), not as an attempt to analyze the concept of knowledge, we cannot take it for granted that his concern was the metaphysical possibility of justified true belief without knowledge rather than its possibility in some other senses. He wrote before Kripke made the relevant distinctions salient.

Gettier's intentions aside, why should we not interpret his examples in terms of some non-metaphysical notion of possibility? For instance, we might read the target analysis as the claim that it is conceptually necessary that knowledge coincides with justified true belief. We should then read premise (2) and the conclusion (4) as saying respectively that the Gettier case and justified true belief without knowledge are conceptually possible. If we read (3) as saying that it is conceptually necessary that every instance of the Gettier case is an instance of justified true belief without knowledge, the argument from (2) and (3) to (4) should be valid.

Unfortunately for this reading, the claim that every instance of the Gettier case is an instance of justified true belief without knowledge is unlikely to be conceptually necessary in any useful sense, even if we bracket the general doubts in previous chapters about conceptual modalities. The reason is very similar to that for which we weakened the strict implication premise (3) to the counterfactual conditional premise (3*). On any reasonable understanding of the phrase "conceptually possible," it is conceptually possible that some abnormal instance of the Gettier case is not an instance of justified true belief. However, we cannot simply replace the claim of conceptual necessity by the counterfactual premise (3*). For the argument from (2) and (3*) to (4) is invalid if the possibility operator in (2) and (4) is understood as conceptual. The POSSIBILITY principle that a counterfactual conditional transmits possibility from its antecedent to its consequent holds for metaphysical but not for conceptual possibility. For instance, friends of conceptual possibility typically think that it is conceptually possible that Hesperus is not Phosphorus but not conceptually possible that Phosphorus is not Phosphorus. But we saw in the previous chapter that the counterfactual conditional "If Hesperus was not Phosphorus, Phosphorus would not be Phosphorus" follows by the logic of identity and counterfactuals from the true identity statement "Hesperus is Phosphorus."

If the argument from (2) and (3*) to (4) is to be reworked in terms of conceptual possibility, we need a conditional for (3*) that stands to conceptual possibility as the counterfactual conditional stands to metaphysical possibility. It is doubtful that the ordinary indicative conditional will do, for "If Hesperus is not Phosphorus, Phosphorus is not Phosphorus" also seems to follow by the logic of identity from "Hesperus is Phosphorus" and the triviality "If Hesperus is not Phosphorus, Hesperus is not Phosphorus."

Even if we succeeded in cooking up a suitable conditional for (3*) in respect of conceptual possibility, the reinterpreted argument would show little of philosophical interest. The conclusion would be that it is conceptually possible to have justified true belief without knowledge. That does not refute the hypothesis that knowledge just is justified true belief, of metaphysical necessity, any more than the conceptual possibility of something with atomic number 79 that is not gold refutes the hypothesis that gold just is the element with atomic number 79, of metaphysical necessity. The primary concern of epistemology is with the nature of knowledge, not with the nature of the concept of knowledge. If knowledge were in fact identical with justified true belief, that would be what mattered epistemologically, irrespective of the conceptual possibility of their non-identity. Presumably, if the concept of knowledge were the concept of justified true belief, that identity of concepts would entail the identity of natures, but the converse fails: the non-identity of concepts does not entail the non-identity of natures.

The result of a Gettier thought experiment, interpreted in terms of mere conceptual possibility, would be of significance primarily to theorists of concepts, not to epistemologists. Similarly, the result of a thought experiment in moral philosophy, interpreted in terms of mere conceptual possibility, would be of significance primarily to theorists of concepts, not to moral philosophers. The same would apply to thought experiments in other branches of philosophy. But the use of thought experiments is not confined to the theory of concepts; it flourishes in most branches of philosophy. Consequently, we need an interpretation of them where the possibility at issue is not merely conceptual. The sort of possibility most relevant to the nature of the phenomena under investigation is metaphysical. That fits the approach of this chapter. Nor should we forget how badly the idea of conceptual modality fared under examination in earlier chapters.

The present reflections reinforce the earlier conclusion that it is not a fit instrument for understanding philosophical inquiry.

Related criticisms would apply to the interpretation of philosophical thought experiments in terms of epistemic modalities other than conceptual possibility and necessity. The upshot of a thought experiment in the philosophy of X would be the epistemic possibility (in some sense) of some state of affairs concerning X, not the metaphysical possibility of that state of affairs. That would teach us about the epistemology of beliefs about X, not directly about the nature of X itself. Of course, the epistemology of beliefs about X may indirectly teach us something about the nature of X itself. Indeed, for X = knowledge, the epistemology of beliefs about knowledge is a special case of the philosophy of knowledge, although hardly a representative one. But philosophy does not in general take the diversion of studying X through studying the epistemology of beliefs about X. A more direct approach is feasible. Thus the interpretation of philosophical thought experiments in terms of epistemic possibility is typically inappropriate. Although we may occasionally wish to use them to learn about the epistemology of the object of our study, often we wish to learn more directly about the object of our study itself, in which case a different interpretation of thought experiments is required. The possibility we need then is metaphysical, not epistemic. Thus the non-epistemic approach of this chapter is more widely applicable. Paradigm thought experiments in philosophy are simply valid arguments about counterfactual possibilities.

7

Evidence in Philosophy

1

In most intellectual disciplines, assertions are supposed to be backed by evidence. Mathematicians have proofs, biochemists have experiments, historians have documents. You cannot just say whatever you happen to believe. Is philosophy an exception? That hardly fits the emphasis many philosophers place on *arguing* for one's claims. When they cannot provide a deductive argument, they still offer supporting considerations. Often they cite phenomena which, they suggest, their theory best explains: they provide abductive arguments. Indeed, in the last three sentences I gave evidence that philosophers give evidence; so philosophers *do* sometimes give evidence. Of course, philosophers who give evidence that evidence is relevant in philosophy can be accused of begging the question. But let us proceed on the working hypothesis that evidence plays a role in philosophy not radically different from its role in all other intellectual disciplines. Without such a role, what would entitle philosophy to be regarded as a *discipline* at all?

To describe mathematics, biochemistry, and history as evidence-based disciplines is obviously not to subscribe to any extreme foundationalism. Particular appeals to proofs, experiments, and documents can all be questioned. The same goes for philosophy.

In any evidence-based discipline, it is good for an assertion to be consistent with the evidence. The alternative is inconsistency with the evidence, which is bad. Since consistency and inconsistency are relations among truth-evaluable items, evidence will be treated as consisting of such items, in particular, of propositions. In this sense, the historical evidence is not the physical document itself but various propositions about it, for example that it is signed "John." The bio-chemical evidence is not the experiment as an event but, for example, the proposition that it was carried out with such-and-such results. The mathematical evidence is not the proof as a sequence of steps but, for example, the proposition that the sequence is a correct proof of this claim. This propositional conception of evidence fits the discursive nature of philosophy. When philosophers produce evidence, they produce something truth-evaluable.[1]

Why is it bad for an assertion to be inconsistent with the evidence? A natural answer is: because then it is false. That answer assumes that evidence consists only of *true* propositions. For if an untrue proposition p is evidence, the proposition that p is untrue is true but inconsistent with the evidence. Using "fact" for "true proposition," we may say that evidence consists only of facts. That helps explain the point of conforming one's beliefs to the evidence.

Although all evidence is true, not all truths are evidence. Some sort of epistemic accessibility is required. Internalists about evidence require the accessibility to be independent of the environment external to the thinker; externalists about evidence reject that requirement. This difference generates a further difference as to what sorts of facts are capable of being evidence. These issues will be considered later.

Since all evidence is true, whatever the evidence entails is also true. The evidence can still support a false proposition non-deductively. If you have not yet heard the result of the lottery, your evidence strongly supports the proposition that your ticket lost, even if in fact it won. Your evidence consists of truths about the lottery available to you at the time.

How can all evidence be true when sometimes the evidence offered turns out to be false? The document was mistranscribed; it was signed "Joan," not "John." But the claim that it was signed "Joan" was not really inconsistent with the evidence before the mistranscription was recognized. It was only inconsistent with what was then taken to be the evidence. It was consistent with the fact that the document was transcribed as signed "John." No evidence was lost when the mistranscription was recognized, and the claim that the document was

---

[1] Williamson (2000a: 194–200) argues in more detail that propositionality is essential to the functional role of evidence (for the purposes of this chapter, little turns on the choice between sentences and propositions).

signed "Joan" is consistent with the present evidence, so it was consistent with the past evidence. Similarly, biochemists who rely on the misreported results of an experiment are mistaken in saying that part of their evidence for a theory is that the experiment was performed with such-and-such results. Mathematicians who overlook a fallacy in a proof are mistaken in saying that their evidence for the purported theorem is that this sequence of steps is a correct proof of it. Practitioners of any discipline sometimes mistake the extent of their evidence. What is offered as evidence is not always evidence.

Since we can mistake the extent of our evidence, it can be controversial whether a given proposition is evidence. When evidence is not recognized as such, it cannot play its proper role in inquiry. If its status as evidence is controversial, it is not part of the common ground in debate. Relying on a premise one's opponents have already refused to accept tends to be dialectically useless. They will probably deny that it constitutes evidence; one's argument will make no headway. As far as possible, we want evidence to play the role of a neutral arbiter between rival theories. Although the complete elimination of accidental mistakes and confusions is virtually impossible, we might hope that whether a proposition constitutes evidence is *in principle* uncontentiously decidable, in the sense that a community of inquirers can always in principle achieve common knowledge as to whether any given proposition constitutes evidence for the inquiry. Call that idea *Evidence Neutrality*. Thus in a debate over a hypothesis **h**, proponents and opponents of **h** should be able to agree whether some claim **p** constitutes evidence without first having to settle their differences over **h** itself. Moreover, that agreement should not be erroneous: here as elsewhere, "decidable" means correctly decidable. Barring accidents, if they agree that **p** constitutes evidence, it does; if they agree that **p** does not constitute evidence, it does not.

One problem for Evidence Neutrality is that the nature of evidence is itself philosophically controversial, as may already be obvious. For example, suppose that a philosophical theory T entails that every mathematical theorem is evidence, while another philosophical theory T* entails that no mathematical theorem is evidence. When proponents of T debate with proponents of T*, whether a given mathematical theorem is evidence is in principle uncontentiously decidable neither positively (since proponents of T* are committed to saying that it is not) nor negatively (since proponents of T are committed to saying that it is). This objection has the faint air of a self-reflexive paradox, however; perhaps it is an isolated singularity. We turn to more general problems for Evidence Neutrality.

Arguing from the Gettier proposition that the subject in a Gettier case lacks knowledge, I conclude that knowledge is not equivalent to justified true belief. Now I meet someone who thinks the Gettier proposition a mere cultural prejudice, not itself evidence. In this context, it is not in principle uncontentiously decidable that the Gettier proposition is evidence. Thus the only way to satisfy Evidence Neutrality is by ruling that the Gettier proposition does not constitute evidence. To argue that knowledge is not equivalent to justified true belief, I must go back a step to less contentious premises. What can they be? My opponent allows that I *believe* the Gettier proposition, and may even admit to feeling an inclination to believe it too (I am not merely idiosyncratic), while overriding it on theoretical grounds. Thus Evidence Neutrality tempts one to retreat into identifying evidence with uncontentious propositions about psychological states, that I believe the Gettier proposition and that both of us are inclined to believe it. How much that helps is questionable. For now I face the challenge of arguing from a psychological premise, that I believe or we are inclined to believe the Gettier proposition, to an epistemological conclusion, the Gettier proposition itself. That gap is not easily bridged.

The example depends on no special feature of the Gettier proposition. Any such premise can be questioned and usually is, by skeptics of one sort or another. The dialectical nature of philosophical inquiry exerts general pressure to psychologize evidence, and so distance it from the non-psychological subject matter of the inquiry.

Attempts have been made to close the gap by psychologizing the subject matter of philosophy. If we are investigating our own concepts, our applications of them must be relevant evidence. But this proposal makes large sacrifices for small gains. As seen in earlier chapters, the subject matter of much philosophy is not conceptual in any distinctive sense. Many epistemologists study knowledge, not just the ordinary concept of knowledge. Metaphysicians who study the nature of identity over time ask how things persist, not how we think or say they persist. In such inquiry, the gap between belief and truth is of the same kind as in most non-philosophical inquiry, and the proposal offers little help. Even when one of our own concepts is our subject matter, our inclination to apply it in a given case by no means guarantees that the application is correct. Cultural prejudices really do sometimes wear the mask of self-evident truth. More generally, the problem with attempts to defend the philosophies of mind and language on the grounds that beliefs about mind and language have a special epistemic status, because they help to constitute their own subject matter, is not just that to extend the argument to other branches of philosophy is to succumb to the usual idealist fallacies. The argument is weak even for the philosophies of mind and language, since our beliefs about our own mind and language can be false for any number of reasons.[2] The gap between belief and truth never completely disappears.

Evidence Neutrality has no more force in philosophy than in other intellectual disciplines: philosophers are lucky if they achieve as much certainty as the natural sciences, without quixotic aspirations for more. If Evidence Neutrality psychologizes evidence in philosophy, it psychologizes it in the natural sciences too. But it is fanciful to regard evidence in the natural sciences as consisting of psychological facts rather than, for example, facts about the results of experiments and measurements. When scientists state their evidence in their publications, they state mainly non-psychological facts (unless they are psychologists); are they not best placed to know what their evidence is? The psychologization of evidence by Evidence Neutrality should be resisted in the natural sciences; it should be resisted in philosophy too. Moreover, not even psychologizing evidence suffices to meet the demands of Evidence Neutrality. For ascriptions of beliefs or inclinations to belief are contestable too, in ways sketched later in this chapter.

Evidence Neutrality is false. Having good evidence for a belief does not require being able to persuade all comers, however strange their views, that you have such good evidence. No human beliefs pass that test. Even in principle, we cannot always decide which propositions constitute evidence prior to deciding the main philosophical issue; sometimes the latter is properly implicated in the former. Elsewhere, I have argued on more general grounds that we are not always in a position to know whether a proposition constitutes evidence (Williamson 2000a: 93–113, 147–83; 2008a). That argument implies

---

[2] Hintikka (1999) argues that philosophical appeals to "intuitions" were inspired by the paradigm of Chomsky's linguistics.

the same conclusion, for when it cannot be known whether **p** constitutes evidence, it is not in principle uncontentiously decid-able whether **p** constitutes evidence. Of course, we can *often* decide whether a proposition constitutes evidence prior to deciding the main issue, otherwise the notion of evidence would be useless. But the two sorts of question cannot be kept in strict isolation from each other.

In this respect, philosophy is no different in principle from inquiry in other areas. Since comprehensive physical theories have implications for the reliability of various forms of observation and measurement, they are not neutral as to which reports of such processes constitute evidence. Which axioms of set theory are legitimately assumed in mathematical proofs is itself a mathematical question. Most of the evidence historians cite can be disputed on the basis of perverse conspiracy theories, which are themselves historical theories, however bad. Although philosophy is unusually tolerant of challenges to evidence, no discipline can afford to exclude them altogether, on pain of fatal gullibility.

How much do failures of Evidence Neutrality threaten the conduct of philosophy? From an internal perspective, they make consensus harder. Each of many conflicting theories may be the one best supported by the evidence by its own lights. The role of evidence as a neutral arbiter is undermined. From an external perspective, both the good fortune of being right and the misfortune of being wrong are magnified. If your theory is true, so are its consequences for which propositions constitute evidence; it will be a reliable methodological guide in your further theorizing. If your theory is false, it may have false consequences for which propositions constitute evidence and be an unreliable guide in your further theorizing (if you are very lucky, its falsity is confined to other areas). Although both internal and external effects are damaging, neither is fatal if the failures of Evidence Neutrality are limited enough. The predicament is not special to philosophy, although it may be worse there than elsewhere. It is not in practice fatal to other disciplines; it is not in principle fatal to philosophy.

Unfortunately, the difficulties consequent on failures of Evidence Neutrality are compounded by unawareness of them in much philosophical writing. That unawareness does more than distort philosophers' descriptions of philosophy. It alters their first-order philosophizing, because the regulation of philosophical debate must be informed by a conception of its nature. For example, the popular but unclear accusation of "question-begging" is leveled on the basis of assumptions about the scope and purpose of philosophical argument.[3] Philosophers under the influence of Evidence Neutrality tend to reject evidence which is not in principle uncontentiously recognizable as such.

These questions are explored below in more detail. They arise with particular urgency from talk of "intuitions." When contemporary analytic philosophers run out of arguments, they appeal to intuitions. It can seem, and is sometimes said, that any philosophical dispute, when pushed back far enough, turns into a conflict of intuitions about ultimate premises: "In the end, all we have to go on is our intuitions." Thus intuitions are presented as our evidence in philosophy.

I have heard a professional philosopher argue that persons are not their brains by saying that he had an intuition that he weighed more than three pounds. Surely there are better ways of weighing oneself than by intuition. But such inapposite appeals to intuition should not be dismissed as mere idiosyncratic misjudgments. They are clues to the role of the term "intuition" in contemporary analytic philosophy. Its use may reflect the tacit influence of Evidence Neutrality.

That philosopher knew that if he had simply said that he weighed more than three pounds, rather than that he had an intuition that he weighed more than three pounds, he would have been accused of naïvely begging the question against those who identify persons with their brains. Their theory of personal identity may commit them to denying that he weighed more than three pounds, but not to denying the psychological claim that he had the intuition that he weighed more than three pounds. Thus he used the term "intuition" in an attempt to formulate a psychological premise, not directly about the subject matter of the dispute, which his opponents would concede. Had he been more artful, he might have said that his body weighed more than three pounds, and that he had the intuition that he weighed the same as his body, since they might have conceded both those premises too, and the latter "intuition" has a less empirical flavor.

---

[3] See Sinnott-Armstrong (1999) for some of the complexities. Naïve attempts to define "begging the question" typically count all deductively valid arguments as question-begging (if you reject the conclusion, you cannot consistently accept the premises).

The point of such maneuvers is primarily dialectical, to find common ground on which to argue with the opponent at hand. The rest of us can be still more confident that he weighed more than three pounds than that he had an intuition that he weighed more than three pounds – he had more chance of deceiving himself or others on the latter point than on the former. But even the dialectical value of such maneuvers is dubious. For if his opponents concede that he has the intuition, they will challenge him to argue from the occurrence of the intuition to its truth: how is he to do that? The simple premise that he weighs more than three pounds at least has the merit of bearing directly on the subject matter of the dispute. Nor need his opponents even concede that he has an intuition that he weighs more than three pounds. They may argue that he is reporting an intuition with some other content, or something other than an intuition.

"Intuition" plays a major role in contemporary analytic philosophy's self-understanding. Yet there is no agreed or even popular account of how intuition works, no accepted explanation of the hoped-for correlation between our having an intuition that P and its being true that P. Since analytic philosophy prides itself on its rigor, this blank space in its foundations looks like a methodological scandal. Why should intuitions have any authority over the philosophical domain?

2

What are intuitions supposed to be, anyway? Let us start by considering a minimalist answer. For David Lewis, "Our 'intuitions' are simply opinions" (1983a: x). For Peter van Inwagen, "Our 'intuitions' are simply our beliefs – or perhaps, in some cases, the tendencies that make certain beliefs attractive to us, that 'move' us in the direction of accepting certain propositions without taking us all the way to acceptance" (1997: 309; he adds parenthetically "Philosophers call their philosophical beliefs intuitions because 'intuition' sounds more authoritative than 'belief'"). If all beliefs or tendencies to belief count as intuitions, then reliance on intuitions is in no way distinctive of philosophy. No scientific progress can be made without reliance on some beliefs and tendencies to belief: simultaneous universal doubt is a dead-end.

In the metaphilosophical debate, that the subject in a Gettier case lacks knowledge is standardly taken as the content of a paradigmatic philosophical intuition. The account of this example in the previous chapter fits indiscriminate characterizations of intuition like Lewis's and van Inwagen's. Our belief in the Gettier proposition (3*) depends on our capacity to apply epistemological concepts online to encountered instances, our general capacity to apply concepts we can apply online offline too, in the imagination, and our capacity to use such imaginative exercises to evaluate counterfactual conditionals. Far from the brute simplicity which the term "intuition" may suggest, that basis involves complexities absent from the basis of the corresponding judgment about a perceptually encountered Gettier case. For most philosophical purposes, however, the differences between fictional and real-life instances of the Gettier case turned out to be unimportant; what matter are the relevant applications of epistemological concepts, whether offline or online. Nor were those applications especially intimately connected to grasp of the relevant concepts, as some rationalists suggest (Bealer 1998, 2002). Many people grasp the concepts in question without feeling inclined to assent to the Gettier proposition. What they lack is a skill in applying those concepts which goes beyond mere possession. Those who respond correctly to the Gettier case, presented in imagination or perception, do so on the basis of skill in applying the concepts; possessing them is insufficient. None of this encourages the use of the Gettier "intuition" as an exemplar to pick out a special psychological or epistemological kind to which the term "intuition" could helpfully applied.

Epistemologically, the most significant feature of the example may be that many of us *know* the truth of the Gettier proposition. But those trying to demarcate a distinctive category of intuition usually insist that there are false intuitions as well as true ones; they do not project truth from the Gettier example to other cases (for example, Sosa 2006).

George Bealer conceives (rational) intuitions as intellectual seemings (1998: 207; 2002: 73). Background information can defeat our inclination to take perceptual or intellectual seemings at face value. Although we are tempted to believe that one line is longer than the other in the Müller-Lyer illusion, we resist the temptation when we know better. Similarly, the Naïve Comprehension principle for sets, by which any predicate has a set as its extension, seems true, although we know it to be false, since it is inconsistent by Russell's paradox. But intellectual seemings typically lack the rich phenomenology of perceptual seemings. In its perceptually appearing that something is so, normally in the same event much else perceptually appears too: that various things have various specific shapes and sizes, colors, sounds, tastes, textures, smells . . . Even very primitive sensations have a specific quality of their own. By contrast, in the moment of its intellectually appearing that something is so, often nothing much else intellectually appears. Although mathematical intuition can have a rich phenomenology, even a quasi-perceptual one, for instance in geometry, the intellectual appearance of the Gettier proposition is not like that. Any accompanying imagery is irrelevant. For myself, I am aware of no intellectual seeming beyond my conscious inclination to believe the Gettier proposition. Similarly, I am aware of no intellectual seeming beyond my conscious inclination to believe Naïve Comprehension, which I resist because I know better. I can feel such an inclination even if it is quite stably overridden, and I am not in the least danger of giving way to temptation (just as one can feel the inclination to kick someone without being in the least danger of giving way). Of course, dwelling introspectively for long on *any* belief or inclination to believe has its characteristic phenomenology, but that is the phenomenology of the dwelling, not of what is dwelt upon. These paradigms provide no evidence of intellectual seemings, if the phrase is supposed to mean anything more than intuitions in Lewis's or van Inwagen's sense.

Can we at least restrict intuitions to non-inferential beliefs or inclinations to believe? The belief that one weighs more than three pounds is inferential. So is the belief that there either was or wasn't a cat on this spot exactly five hundred years ago. Yet philosophers often count such beliefs as intuitive, and rejection of them as counterintuitive. If there is a narrower sense of "intuitive," it is often not the operative one when appeal is made in practice to the intuitiveness of some theories as a virtue and the counterintuitiveness of others as a vice.

Does a belief or inclination to believe with an inappropriate causal origin, such as wishful thinking, count as an intuition? We do not want such beliefs or inclinations to believe to carry weight in philosophy. But that is explicable quite independently of whether we classify them as intuitions. Wishful thinking is as relevant to the epistemology of intuition as misperception is to the epistemology of perception.

Should we restrict philosophical intuitions to those whose basis is grasp of the relevant thought? That is just a variant on the epistemological conceptions of analyticity that were seen to fail in the final section of Chapter 4. The thin grasp of the thought is no basis for assent. The thick grasp of the thought is a basis for assent, but it involves cognitive capacities that are not exclusively conceptual, because they are not necessary for the thin grasp; on such a criterion, intuitions again lose their distinctiveness.

Although we could decide to restrict the term "intuition" to states with some list of psychological or epistemological features, such a stipulation would not explain the more promiscuous role the term plays in the practice of philosophy. This emerges more clearly in appeals to intuition in disputes over actual cases.

Some revisionary metaphysicians deny that, strictly and literally, there are mountains.[4] They deny a proposition of the sort for which G. E. Moore stood up in his defense of common sense (1925). For example, they may argue that although, if there were such a thing as a mountain, it would be a vague object, it is logically impossible for an object to be vague, so there is no such thing as a mountain. Alternatively, they may appeal to ontological economy, and argue that since all the appearances can be explained in terms of the microscopic objects, postulating macroscopic ones in addition is unnecessary and unjustifiable. And so on. The revisionists may concede that microscopic events occur in the joint presence of which it is usual to believe that a mountain is present, but they count that belief false. They hold that although the ordinary use of the word "mountain" has utility, because it registers genuine discriminations between different cases in which different actions are appropriate, it also embodies a mistaken metaphysical theory as to what the difference between those cases consists in (skeptics who doubt that there are mountains may

---

[4]   Van Inwagen (1995) and Horgan (1995) defend related views. They allow that the sentence "There are mountains" may express a truth in some loose or non-literal way, for example when the quantifier is not taken at face value, but in this book "There are mountains" is to be understood strictly and literally. The text presents a metaphysical view of a familiar general type without attempting to follow any one metaphysician in detail.

also be committed to doubting that there are words or beliefs; for the sake of argument we ignore such complications, just as the skeptics tend to do). The claim that there are no mountains is usually regarded as counterintuitive. Even its proponents may concede that it is counterintuitive, arguing that the cost to intuition is worth paying for the overall gain in simplicity, strength, logical coherence, and consonance with science they attribute to their total metaphysical system, which entails the claim. If their system also entails that there could not have been mountains, it contradicts the modal "intuition" that there could have been mountains. But even without the claim of necessity, the non-modal claim that there are no mountains is already counterintuitive as many philosophers use the term, because it contradicts the common sense judgment that there are mountains, for example in Switzerland. Thus the term "intuition" may even be applied to the inferential belief that there are mountains, when based on the belief that there are mountains in Switzerland and elsewhere. Whether or not they agree that there are no mountains, many contemporary metaphysicians would find it philosophically naïve to dismiss a revisionary metaphysical system by appeal to our elementary geographical knowledge that there are mountains in Switzerland. Thus doubts about "intuition" arise for straightforward empirical judgments, even for perceptual judgments: (pointing in the Alps) "Those are mountains."

Someone could of course stipulate that the only "intuition" in their sense around here is conditional in form: if matter is arranged mountain-wise, then there is a mountain. They would then need to explain what they mean by "mountain-wise." If they mean *so that it constitutes a mountain*, the purported intuition is an obvious quasilogical truth: trivially, if matter is arranged so that it constitutes a mountain, then there is a mountain. Perhaps the content of the intuition is supposed to be more like this: if matter is so arranged that *according to the mountain-story* it constitutes a mountain, then there is a mountain. But what exactly is the mountain story? Hard theoretical work is needed to clarify the content of the purported conditional intuition. Once that is done, if it can be, perhaps common sense will be brought to accept the conditional, although it feels more like the conclusion of a plausible argument than the premise. In any case, it lacks the immediate attraction of whatever makes us describe the denial that there are mountains as counterintuitive.

The application of "intuition" and cognate terms in philosophical practice is scarcely more restricted than Lewis and van Inwagen suggest. In general, the objection "That's only an intuition" is ill-posed in the same way as the objection "That's only a judgment." Some judgments are indeed objectionable, but the mere fact that a proposition is judged is not even a *prima facie* reason for doubting it.

Philosophers might be better off not using the word "intuition" and its cognates. Their main current function is not to answer questions about the nature of the evidence on offer but to fudge them, by appearing to provide answers without really doing so. If so, what is really at issue in disputes over the legitimacy of intuitions in philosophy?

3

Perhaps skepticism about intuition consists not in skepticism about a special kind of judgment but in a special kind of skepticism about any judgment. That skepticism does not target the distinctive features of perception, memory, testimony, or inference. Rather, it targets our practices of applying concepts in judgment. Call it *judgment skepticism*. For example, it does not question the existence of an external world to which we are causally related in the ways appropriate to perception – at least, not until the concepts of causation and perception themselves come under scrutiny. Indeed, many judgment skeptics are naturalists, their rhetoric scientistic. They present themselves as identifying ways in which our conceptual practices need, or may need, revision in the light of scientific advances those practices failed to anticipate. They doubt that we should go on in the same way.

Few judgment skeptics advocate skepticism about all judgments. Total judgment skepticism would result in total intellectual paralysis. Call "judgment skeptics" those skeptical in the way just sketched about some contextually relevant judgments. For example, in a context that concerns folk psychological ascriptions of belief and desire, Paul Churchland and other eliminativists about such mental states are judgment skeptics. In a context that concerns ordinary geographical judgments, Terry Horgan and other eliminativists about mountains are judgment skeptics. Such skeptics question our standards for applying ordinary concepts both in experience and in thought: the concept of a mountain, the concept of belief, the concept of knowledge, the concept of possibility, the concept of the counterfactual conditional, and so on. Philosophers tend to call judgments "intuitive" when they are considered as the primary targets of judgment skepticism. Thus the term is applied even to the perceptual demonstrative judgment "Those are mountains" or the inferential judgment "There are mountains," derived by existential generalization – although, for obvious reasons, the primary targets of judgment skepticism are more usually the premises rather than the conclusion of an inference.

Like other skeptics, judgment skeptics construct scenarios to explain how we might make the judgments in question even if they were false. The debunking explanation aims to make massive error a genuine possibility. Scenarios for judgment skepticism are often distinctive in attempting to verify the scientific image of the world while falsifying the manifest image, common sense, or what passes for it in our culture. Sometimes they allow that the ability to apply the key terms of ordinary language (such as "mountain") in the ordinary way confers an evolutionary advantage, because it helps us communicate to each other genuine but misarticulated differences. The disposition to apply such terms immediately on the basis of casual observation contributes to practical efficiency. Such unreflective discriminations have survival value in harsh environments, where quick decisions are needed. We are here because our ancestors could make them before discovering the true theory of reality. Although the physical theory embedded in our intuitions has to be approximately correct in its predictions over a limited range of practically important cases, we do not expect it to match or even resemble the true physics in representation of the underlying reality. Why should we expect other parts of folk theory to do much better? The cheapest, fastest, and easiest conceptual route for us to making useful discriminations may run through intellectually dirty shortcuts that presuppose false but convenient metaphysics.

In other cases, skeptics may regard a conceptual practice as of merely local value, or even as doing more harm than good. Thus if standards for applying the term "know" vary radically with cultural background, an evolutionary-biological explanation of my current standard is less plausible.[5] The skeptic may tell a different, more sociological story about the cultural role of knowledge ascriptions, detaching them from their truth conditions. The story might imply that such ascriptions nevertheless fulfill a positive social function to which their cultural variability adapts them. But we can also envisage more sinister stories, on which they serve as instruments of intellectual repression.

Like other skeptics, judgments skeptics ask for independent evidence that favors the piece of common sense at issue over their skeptical hypothesis. The "scientific" flavor of their alternative scenario disguises the resemblance to more traditional forms of skepticism. However, there is one significant difference.

Traditional skeptics argue that we do not know that we are not in a skeptical scenario. They do not positively argue that we are in such a scenario; their point is that we cannot know what our situation really is. For them, the claim that we are in the common sense scenario is no better in epistemic status, but also no worse, than the claim that we are in the skeptical scenario. By contrast, judgment skeptics often argue that we actually are in their skeptical scenario, for example in which there are no mountains, or no beliefs.[6] If they hold that we can recognize that their argument is sound, they must also hold that we can deduce that we are actually in their skeptical scenario. That involves them in no immediate inconsistency, for their skepticism is intended to be partial; they might compare it to skepticism about superstition. Some present their views as superior to "common sense" judgments in compatibility with the results of the natural sciences. They take for granted that those results have some positive epistemic status. Indeed, they often treat them as scientific knowledge. They feel a crisis of confidence in common sense, not in scientific method. For others, it is metaphysical reasoning rather than natural science that trumps common sense.

Despite this more positive aspect of judgment skepticism, judgment skeptics often fall back on traditional skeptical strategies. For instance, they try to put defenders of a piece of common sense into the position

---

[5] Kornblith (2002) treats knowledge as a natural kind.
[6] Of course, once we stop believing that there are mountains we can no longer be in the full skeptical scenario in which one falsely believes that there are mountains.

of arguing for it over the judgment skeptical scenario from a starting point neutral between the two alternatives, just as skeptics about the external world do.

Judgment skeptics need not puritanically insist that nobody should ever say things like "There are mountains in Switzerland." Some of their debunking explanations imply that in everyday contexts those are good, useful things to say: outside the metaphysics seminar, utterances of "There are mountains in Switzerland" have more desirable effects than utterances of "There are no mountains in Switzerland." Discovering the true theory of metaphysics will not change that. Even revisionary metaphysicians can continue to say such things, just as they can continue to say "The sun will rise at 6 a.m. tomorrow." But, they hold, those things are not strictly and literally true: the sun will not strictly and literally *rise* at 6 a.m. tomorrow; there are not strictly and literally any *mountains* in Switzerland. If we want to think what is *really* true, we must think with the learned; for many purposes it is enough to say what is *to all appearances* true, and speak with the vulgar. We can live most of our lives on the basis of a fiction; only when we take a more scientific attitude are we forced to recognize the fiction for what it is.

For judgment skeptics, appeals to intuition are nothing more than the last resort of dogmatic conservativism, in its desperate attempt to hold back the forward march of scientific and metaphysical progress. But how can such skeptics prevent their arguments for skepticism from applying as far as the sciences themselves?

Judgment skeptical arguments apply to standard perceptual judgments, on which the natural sciences systematically depend: microscopes, telescopes, and other scientific instruments enhance ordinary perception but do not replace it, for we need ordinary perception to use the instruments. If the contents of those perceptual judgments concern ordinary macroscopic objects, they are vulnerable to judgment skepticism about common sense ontology. If so, the empirical evidence for scientific theories is threatened. To assume that the evidence can be reformulated without relevant loss in ontologically neutral terms, in the absence of any actual such reformulation, would be optimistic to the point of naïvety.

Even if that problem could be solved, a more pressing one would remain. Given judgment skeptical arguments, what is the status of scientists' evidential judgments? For example, suppose that they judge that a given complex body of evidence of various kinds supports one theory against another, because the former theory explains the evidence better than the latter does. The concept of a better explanation is an informal one, rooted in ordinary ways of thinking, even if scientists' particular applications of it are informed by their background knowledge. A question typical of judgment skepticism arises: what evidence is there that our rankings of explanations are reliable? If the evidence for the hypothesis that our rankings of explanations are reliable is that it provides the best explanation of something else (such as the survival of our species), the charge of question-begging can hardly be ignored. Thus when scientists apply standard concepts of epistemic appraisal, they are not immune to judgment skeptics' styles of argument. In particular, judgment skeptics who judge that our empirical evidence tells against the reliability of some folk theory are vulnerable to judgment skepticism about the elements of folk epistemology on which they are relying.

Although in practice judgment skeptics are often skeptical about only a few judgments or concepts at a time, the underlying forms of argument are far more general. We may suspect that judgment skepticism is a bomb which, if it detonates properly, will blow up the bombers and those whom they hope to promote together with everyone else. But it does not follow that we can dismiss judgment skepticism as self-defeating. That the revolutionary movement would be incapable of establishing a stable new government of its own does not show that it cannot bring the old government down. At worst, judgment skeptics are troublemakers who put on the table arguments we find powerful and in need of a proper response, irrespective of their dubious motives for putting them there.[7]

The similarity between some arguments for judgment skepticism and traditional arguments for traditional forms of skepticism already gives us grounds for suspicion of the arguments for judgment skepticism. If the skeptic about the external world wears the traditional garb of the philosopher while the judgment skeptic dresses up in a scientist's white coat, that should not blind us to the underlying structural similarity of their arguments. A judgment skeptic argues that our evidence is neutral between the ordinary hypothesis that there are mountains and the skeptical hypothesis that there are no

---

[7]   Compare Feyerabend (1978: 143).

mountains, but instead only complex microphysical events the human brain usefully but untruthfully classifies as mountains, and concludes that we cannot know and are not justified in believing that there are mountains. A skeptic about the external world argues that our evidence is neutral between the ordinary hypothesis that there are mountains and the skeptical hypothesis that there are no mountains, but instead only mental states indiscriminable from the inside from perceptions of mountains, and concludes that we cannot know and are not justified in believing that there are mountains. Most people are confident that an argument like the latter for skepticism about the external world is unsound, much less confident as to where exactly it goes wrong. That position is quite reasonable. Similarly, it is fallacious to assume that if one cannot put one's finger on the mistake in an argument for judgment skepticism, one must accept the conclusion, however implausible.

Still, we do want to identify the mistake. Let us therefore consider the epistemological position in more detail, while remembering that the diagnosis of the error in a skeptic's argument may be far less obvious than the fact that it contains an error somewhere.

4

Different kinds of skepticism distinguish themselves from each other by questioning some things while leaving others unquestioned. The skeptic about induction grants that all emeralds observed so far were green, in order to question the distinctively inductive step to the conclusion that all emeralds will always be green. The skeptic about deduction grants the premises that if P then Q and that P of an inference by modus ponens, in order to question the distinctively deductive step to its conclusion that Q. The skeptic about testimony grants that someone has said that it was raining, but questions whether she spoke the truth. The skeptic about memory grants that my experience is as of remembering that it was raining, but questions whether I really remember that it was raining. The skeptic about perception grants that my experience is as of seeing that it is raining, so that it visually appears to me that it is raining, but questions whether the experience is veridical. In each case, the skeptic concedes an evidential base, in order to accuse us of going illegitimately beyond it. For the judgment skeptic, sometimes the only evidential base to hand short of the disputed proposition itself is the conscious inclination to assent to that proposition, to make the judgment.

If judgment skepticism is treated by analogy with skepticism about perception, its evidential base will be described as intellectual seemings, somehow analogous to perceptual seemings. As we saw, Bealer has defended just such an account of intuitions as intellectual seemings. Its intellectually or perceptually seeming to one that P is a psychological state one can be in whether or not P, even if the default outcome of being in the state is judging that P. Whether intellectual seemings are more than conscious inclinations to believe we found reason to doubt.

Skepticism about perception typically narrows one's evidential base to one's present internal mental state. When I can see and hear and feel that it is raining, I suppose my total evidence to include the fact that it is raining, available for assessing hypotheses, for example the hypothesis that the grass will grow. By contrast, the skeptic about perception insists that I have as evidence only the fact that it perceptually appears to me that it is raining, for sometimes what perceptually appears to me is not so. From the fact about my present mental state I am challenged to reason legitimately outwards to the conclusion about my external environment that it really is raining. The skeptic about perception asks by what right I treat the fact that it perceptually appears to me that it is raining as good evidence that it is raining. Judgment skepticism narrows and internalizes our evidential base in a similar way without going as far as skepticism about perception, since typically it treats other people on a par with oneself, and other times on a par with the present. After reading Gettier's article, I suppose my total evidence to include the fact that the subject in a Gettier case lacks knowledge. But the judgment skeptic insists that I have as evidence at most the fact that it non-perceptually appears to me and others that the subject in a Gettier case lacks knowledge, for sometimes what non-perceptually appears to me is not so. From the fact about our mental states we are challenged to reason legitimately outwards to the conclusion that the subject in a Gettier case really does lack knowledge. The judgment skeptic asks by what right we treat the fact that it non-perceptually appears to us that the subject in a Gettier case lacks knowledge as good evidence that the subject in a Gettier case does lack knowledge.

Behind the skeptic about perception's rhetorical question lies an assumption like this: one should be confident that P (on the basis of perception) only if its (perceptually) appearing that P is good evidence that P. Similarly, behind the judgment skeptic's rhetorical question lies an assumption like this: one should be confident that P (on the basis of common sense) only if its appearing (by the standards of common sense) that P is good evidence that P. Call such principles *appearance principles*. They have some initial plausibility. For example, suppose that although whenever I am about to toss a coin either it appears to me that it will come up heads or it appears to me that it will come up tails, such appearances turn out to be correlated no better than chance with the actual results. Its appearing to me that the coin will come up heads is no evidence that it will come up heads. Then I should not take those appearances at face value. Although it appears to me that the coin will come up heads, I should not be confident that it will come up heads.

To discipline the assessment of appearance principles, let us think probabilistically. Say that **q** *would be evidence for* **p** just if **q** raises the probability of **p**, that is, the conditional probability of **p** on **q** is higher than the unconditional probability of **p**, $\text{Prob}(p) < \text{Prob}(p \mid q)$.[8] That it appears to me that the coin will come up heads does not raise the probability that the coin will come up heads, so the former proposition would not be evidence for the latter, and I should not be confident that the coin will come up heads on the basis of that appearance, by the relevant appearance principle. More generally, the appearance of **p** is *truth-indicative* just if it would be evidence for **p** ($\text{Prob}(p) < \text{Prob}(p \mid Ap)$), and *falsity-indicative* just if it would be evidence against **p** ($\text{Prob}(\neg p) < \text{Prob}(\neg p \mid Ap)$, equivalently $\text{Prob}(p) > \text{Prob}(p \mid Ap)$). An appearance principle implies that one should be confident in **p** only if the appearance of **p** is truth-indicative

---

[8]   The conditional probability $\text{Prob}(p \mid q)$ is usually defined as the ratio of unconditional probabilities $\text{Prob}(p \ \& \ q)/\text{Prob}(q)$ for $\text{Prob}(q) > 0$. The reason for the "would be" is that, in the sense defined, it may happen that q would be evidence for p even though q is itself unknown or even false: the relation between p and q is purely conditional. Compare Williamson (2000a: 187). In order to keep the conditional probabilities that are relevant to this chapter uncontentiously well-defined, we allow some metaphysical impossibilities to have non-zero probabilities (for example, according to some judgment skeptics, it may well be metaphysically impossible that there are mountains).

(for specified types of sentence and appearance). A weaker principle says that one should be confident in **p** only if the appearance of **p** is not falsity-indicative. Note that appearance principles merely purport to give *necessary* conditions for when one should be confident, not sufficient conditions.

On some views, if the prior probability of **p** is high enough, we should be confident of **p** even if its probability is somewhat lowered by **Ap**. The judgment skeptic regards such a defence of disputed philosophical propositions as unacceptably dogmatic, having the advantages of theft over honest toil. Let us concentrate on the unrestricted appearance principles.

What kind of probability should we use to interpret "Prob"? The appearance of **p** must not be certain, for if Prob(**Ap**) = 1 then automatically Prob(**p** | **Ap**) = Prob(**p**), making truth-indicativeness and falsity-indicativeness uselessly indiscriminate as tests: trivially, the appearance of **p** is neither truth-indicative nor falsity-indicative. Thus purely subjective probabilities (credences, degrees of belief) are unsuitable, for the subject may always have been subjectively certain of the appearance of **p**. Purely objective probabilities (chances) are also unsuitable, for in a deterministic world with the appearance of **p** the appearance of **p** is objectively certain. A kind of evidential epistemic probability intermediate between subjective and objective extremes is most relevant.[9] Assume, for the sake of argument, that we have fixed on such probabilities: the discussion below is neutral on their exact nature.

It appears that there are mountains in Switzerland, in a liberal sense of "appears" correlative with the liberal sense of "counterintuitive" in which the claim that there are no mountains in Switzerland is counterintuitive. Presumably, this appearance is truth-indicative, even if significant epistemic probability is assigned to the suggestion of a judgment skeptic that mountains are metaphysically impossible. For there is still a nonzero epistemic probability that mountains are metaphysically possible; conditional on that non-skeptical hypothesis, the appearance that there are mountains in Switzerland surely raises the epistemic probability that there are mountains in Switzerland (for Switzerland might have been a plain), whereas, conditional

---

[9] Williamson (2000a: 209–37) describes such an intermediate kind of epistemic probability.

on the skeptical hypothesis, the appearance merely leaves the probability unchanged rather than lowering it. Overall, therefore,
the appearance that there are mountains in Switzerland raises
the epistemic probability that there are mountains in Switzerland.[10]
Some philosophically contested "intuitive" propositions are
truth-indicative.

However, let SS be the judgment skeptic's scenario in which it
falsely appears that there are mountains in Switzerland, because folk
geography misinterprets joint microscopic events as the presence of
mountains in Switzerland when in fact mountains are metaphysically
impossible. Add to the specification of SS that each trivially necessary
condition of there being mountains in Switzerland appears (in the
liberal sense) to hold. Since SS is set up as a scenario in which there
are no mountains in Switzerland, a trivially necessary condition of
there being mountains in Switzerland is that SS does not obtain.
Consequently, in SS, it appears that SS does not obtain. Since that is
built into the background logic, it is certain, conditional on its not
appearing that SS does not obtain, that SS does not obtain. Thus
$Prob(\neg s \mid \neg A\neg s) = 1$, where s says that SS obtains. It can be shown
to follow that $Prob(\neg s \mid A\neg s) \leq Prob(\neg s)$, that is, that the appearance
that SS does not obtain is not truth-indicative.[11] It is not evidence
that SS does not obtain. By the stronger appearance principle, one
should not be confident that SS does not obtain.

The judgment skeptic can go further. As already noted, the appearance in question must not be certain, otherwise truth-indicativeness
and falsity-indicativeness are trivialized. Thus we may assume
$Prob(A\neg s) < 1$. Moreover, those with even the slightest sympathy for
judgment skepticism will allow that it is not certain that we are not
in SS: $Prob(s) > 0$. These two further assumptions entail that the
appearance that SS does not obtain is falsity-indicative: it actually

---

[10]   Formally, where m says that there are mountains in Switzerland and s that mountains are metaphysically impossible, if all the probabilities are well-defined as ratios
and $Prob(m \mid \neg s) < Prob(m \mid \neg s \ \& \ Am)$ and $Prob(m \mid s) = Prob(m \mid s \ \& \ Am) = 0$ then
$Prob(m) < Prob(m \mid Am)$. Although there are cases of $\neg s \ \& \ Am \ \& \ \neg m$, they are
outweighed by cases of $\neg s \ \& \ Am \ \& \ m$.

[11]   *Proof*: If $Prob(\neg s \mid \neg A\neg s) = 1$
then $Prob(\neg s \mid A\neg s) = Prob(A\neg s).Prob(\neg s \mid A\neg s) + (1 - Prob(A\neg s)).Prob(\neg s \mid A\neg s)$
$\leq Prob(A\neg s).Prob(\neg s \mid A\neg s) + Prob(\neg A\neg s).Prob(\neg s \mid \neg A\neg s) = Prob(\neg s)$.
The weaker assumption $Prob(\neg s \mid A\neg s) \leq Prob(\neg s \mid \neg A\neg s)$ also suffices.

lowers the probability that SS does not obtain.[12] Its appearing that SS does not obtain is evidence that SS *does* obtain. Therefore, even by the weaker appearance principle, one should not be confident that SS does not obtain.

That there are mountains in Switzerland obviously entails that SS does not obtain. Consequently, one's confidence that there are mountains in Switzerland should be no higher than one's confidence that SS does not obtain: if **p** entails **q** and subjective probabilities obey the standard probability axioms then the subjective probability of **p** is no higher than the subjective probability of **q**. By the appearance principle, one's confidence that SS does not obtain should be low. So one's confidence that there are mountains in Switzerland should also be low, even though the appearance that there are mountains in Switzerland is truth-indicative. We therefore face an argument for a sweeping form of judgment skepticism.

The form of argument is not specific to judgment skepticism. It applies equally to skepticism about the external world. We need only replace SS by a skeptical scenario of a more traditional kind. Let **p** be a description of the external world acceptable to the judgment skeptic, perhaps in terms of particle physics. Let SS* be a scenario in which **p** is false but an evil demon makes each trivially necessary condition for the truth of **p**, including the truth of **p** itself, appear to hold. By the same reasoning as before, it is certain, conditional on its not appearing that SS* does not obtain, that SS* does not obtain. Thus $\text{Prob}(\neg s^* \mid \neg A\neg s^*) = 1$, where s* says that SS* obtains. It follows that the appearance that SS* does not obtain is not truth-indicative; it is not evidence that SS* does not obtain. By the relevant appearance principle, one should not be confident that SS* does not obtain. The skeptic will further argue that the appearance that SS* does not obtain is falsity-indicative; it is evidence that SS* *does* obtain. Since **p** obviously entails that SS* does not obtain, one's confidence in **p** should be no higher than one's confidence that SS* does not obtain. By the appearance principle, one's confidence that SS* does not obtain should be low. So one's confidence in **p** should

---

[12]   *Proof:* $0 < \text{Prob}(s) = \text{Prob}(A\neg s).\text{Prob}(s \mid A\neg s) + \text{Prob}(\neg A\neg s).\text{Prob}(s \mid \neg A\neg s) = \text{Prob}(A\neg s).\text{Prob}(s \mid A\neg s)$ because $\text{Prob}(s \mid \neg A\neg s) = 0$. Therefore $0 < \text{Prob}(s \mid A\neg s)$, so $\text{Prob}(\neg s \mid A\neg s) < 1 = \text{Prob}(\neg s \mid \neg A\neg s)$. Since $0 < \text{Prob}(\neg A\neg s)$, $\text{Prob}(\neg A\neg s).\text{Prob}(\neg s \mid A\neg s) < \text{Prob}(\neg A\neg s).\text{Prob}(\neg s \mid \neg A\neg s)$, so the inequality in the previous footnote is strict.

also be low, even if its appearance is truth-indicative. We therefore face an argument for a sweeping form of skepticism about the external world, more specifically, the external world as described in terms the judgment skeptic would accept.

Few judgment skeptics would be consoled by the idea that one's confidence in **p** need only be low in contexts in which, since SS* has been considered, one must fix a level of confidence in the proposition that SS* does not obtain. For they would be unimpressed by a defense of common sense based on the idea that confidence in it is legitimate provided that one refuses to consider their skeptical scenarios. They will insist that head-in-the-sand strategies are futile. They are asking how confident we can be that SS* does not obtain, not whether we are capable of ignoring the proposition altogether.

It is unsurprising that if an argument for traditional skepticism works, so does an argument for judgment skepticism. But that is not the kind of success most judgment skeptics seek. They want a more selective skepticism, which for example does not undermine the results of fundamental physics, even though the latter are in the target area for skepticism about the external world. Consequently, they should not use appearance principles as premises in their reasoning, since such principles generate traditional skepticism as well as judgment skepticism. At least in some cases, one can be legitimately confident in a proposition even though its apparent truth is no evidence for its truth, and is even evidence for its falsity.

An observation reinforces that moral. Let **t** be any ordinary tautology. The standard probability axioms entail that **t** has probability 1, conditional on anything. Then no appearance of **t** in any sense is truth-indicative, for Prob(**t** | A**t**) = 1 = Prob(**t**). Since **t** is also not falsity-indicative, this observation might be met by weakening the requirement of the corresponding appearance principle from truth-indicativeness to lack of falsity-indicativeness. But that misses the intended point of appearance principles. After all, the appearance to me that the coin will come up heads is not falsity-indicative. It does as well as chance, but no better. A different kind of epistemological diagnosis is needed; truth-indicativeness and falsity-indicativeness are just not the relevant criteria.

The problem is not that the definitions of truth-indicativeness and falsity-indicativeness mention only one aspect of appearances, the apparent truth of the proposition **p** directly at issue. The arguments work just the same if we ask whether the totality of appearances (in the relevant sense) would be evidence for **p**, given a skeptical scenario SS** in which **p** is false but the totality of appearances matches the actual totality of appearances and all the trivially necessary conditions for the truth of **p** appear to hold. For it is certain, conditional on the absence of that totality of appearances, that SS* does not obtain. By the same reasoning as before, the totality of appearances is not evidence that SS** does not obtain, and is even evidence that SS** does obtain.

Nor is the problem that the arguments were framed in terms of appearances rather than psychological states such as beliefs or dispositions to belief. They work equally well in the latter terms (just substitute **B** for **A**).

Rather, the problem concerns a more abstract issue about the structure of confirmation. Let **e** be a body of evidence that raises the probability of a hypothesis **h** to a value close to 1 without quite making **h** certain, so $Prob(h) < Prob(h \mid e) < 1$. The material conditional **e** → **h** is a logical consequence of **h**, and therefore at least as probable as **h**; in fact, $Prob(e \rightarrow h \mid e) = Prob(h \mid e)$. However, **e** is evidence against **e** → **h**, for $Prob(e \rightarrow h) > Prob(e \rightarrow h \mid e)$, simply because **e** → **h** is true in all those possibilities which **e** eliminates (**e** → **h** is a logical consequence of ¬**e**).[13] Clearly, all of this is compatible with a high degree of legitimate confidence in both **h** and **e** → **h**. Whenever evidence makes some hypothesis more probable than before without making it certain, that evidence makes some logical consequence of that hypothesis less probable than before. Similarly, whenever a hypothesis is certain on some evidence, that evidence makes some logical consequence of that hypothesis no more probable than before (of course, it does not make any such consequence less probable than before, since they all become or remain certain). What this reveals is a fallacy in the tactic of criticizing confidence in a theory by identifying a logical consequence of the theory (not itself a logical

---

[13] *Proof*: $Prob(e \rightarrow h) = 1 - Prob(e \ \& \ \neg h) = 1 - (Prob(e).Prob(e \ \& \ \neg h \mid e) + Prob(\neg e).Prob(e \ \& \ \neg h \mid \neg e) = 1 - Prob(e).Prob(e \ \& \ \neg h \mid e) > 1 - Prob(e \ \& \ \neg h \mid e) = Prob(e \rightarrow h \mid e)$. The assumption here that $Prob(e).Prob(e \ \& \ \neg h \mid e) < Prob(e \ \& \ \neg h \mid e)$ holds because $Prob(e) < 1$ (otherwise $Prob(h \mid e) = Prob(h)$, contrary to hypothesis) and $Prob(e \ \& \ \neg h \mid e) > 0$ (otherwise $Prob(h \mid e) = 1$, contrary to hypothesis).

truth) whose probability is not raised by the evidence. Call that the *consequence fallacy.*

Consider the deductively valid argument from (1) and (2) to (3):

(1)   Physical events occur that folk geography takes to constitute the presence of mountains in Switzerland.
(2)   If physical events occur that folk geography takes to constitute the presence of mountains in Switzerland, then there are mountains in Switzerland.
(3)   There are mountains in Switzerland.

We may assume that the defender of folk geography is committed to both the premises and the conclusion. In particular, premise (2) is a logical consequence of the common sense conclusion (3) (read the conditional as material). A judgment skeptic may hold that our evidence raises the probability of (1) but not of (2). However, to argue on that basis that, given our evidence, we are not entitled to high degrees of confidence in (2) and (3) is to commit the consequence fallacy.

Similarly, consider the valid argument from (1*) and (2*) to (3*):

(1*)   The Gettier case has features that folk epistemology takes to constitute the subject's lack of knowledge.
(2*)   If the Gettier case has features that folk epistemology takes to constitute the subject's lack of knowledge, then the subject in the Gettier case lacks knowledge.
(3*)   The subject in the Gettier case lacks knowledge.

We may assume that the defender of folk epistemology is committed to both the premises and the conclusion. In particular, premise (2*) is a logical consequence of the common sense conclusion (3*). A judgment skeptic may hold that our evidence raises the probability of (1*) but not of (2*). However, to argue on that basis that, given our evidence, we are not entitled to high degrees of confidence in (2*) and (3*) is again to commit the consequence fallacy.

Finally, consider the valid argument from (1**) and (2**) to (3**):

(1**)   It appears to me that I have hands.
(2**)   If it appears to me that I have hands, then I have hands.
(3**)   I have hands.

As before, the defender of common sense is committed to both the premises and the conclusion. A skeptic about the external world may hold that our evidence raises the probability of (1**) but not of (2**). However, to argue on that basis that, given our evidence, we are not entitled to high degrees of confidence in (2**) and (3**) is once again to commit the consequence fallacy.

The point is doubtless connected to the role of the assumption in some skeptical arguments that knowledge is closed under competent deduction: if I cannot know that I am not a handless brain in a vat that appears to itself to have hands, how can I know that I have hands?[14] However, the arguments in this section have been framed in terms not of knowledge but of legitimate degrees of confidence, conceived as answerable to the standard axioms of probability. In this setting, closure is much less contentious.[15]

5

Although judgment skepticism, like other forms of skepticism, easily falls into the consequence fallacy, it would be complacent to assume that it loses all its force once the consequence fallacy has been identified and abjured. We saw in Section 1 the temptation, under the influence of Evidence Neutrality, to conceive the evidence in philosophy as consisting of psychological facts, such as the fact that we believe that there are mountains in Switzerland, not the fact that there are mountains in Switzerland. Since psychological evidence has no obvious bearing on many philosophical issues, judgment skepticism is also encouraged in ways that do not depend on the consequence fallacy. For now the issue is not whether our evidence is evidence for some devious consequence of our theory but whether it is evidence

---

[14]   Seminal works are Dretske (1970), Stine (1976) and Nozick (1981). More recent discussions of closure include DeRose (1995) and Hawthorne (2004); see the latter for more references.
[15]   See Williamson 2005c for more discussion of skepticism in relation to truth-indicativeness, and Williamson 2000a: 164-83 for more on traditional skepticism.

for our theory as a whole. And even if our evidence does raise the probability of the whole theory somewhat, is it raised high enough for confidence, in particular, to a higher level than its skeptical alternatives?

Traditional skepticism exploits Evidence Neutrality to achieve a similar psychologization of evidence: only the fact that it appears to me that I have hands is evidence, not the fact that I have hands. How does that happen? Since evidence is true, the false proposition that I have hands is not evidence in a skeptical scenario in which it falsely appears to me that I have hands. Thus the proposition that I have hands is evidence only if I am not in the skeptical scenario. But in the presence of a real or notional skeptic it is contentious that I am not in the skeptical scenario. So it is contentious that the proposition that I have hands is evidence, hence not in principle uncontentiously decidable that it is evidence. Therefore, by Evidence Neutrality, that I have hands is not evidence, even if I am in fact in the common sense scenario in which I have hands and all my perceptual faculties are working properly. Only the proposition that it appears to me that I have hands is evidence. Since both the common sense scenario and the skeptical scenario are consistent with all my evidence, so conceived, the question arises: with what right do I regard the former scenario as more probable than the latter?

Both traditional skepticism and judgment skepticism reflect the tendency of Evidence Neutrality to narrow our evidence base. One result is the uneasy conception many contemporary analytic philosophers have of their own methodology. They think that, in philosophy, ultimately our evidence consists only of intuitions (to use their term for the sake of argument). Under pressure, they take that to mean not that our evidence consists of the mainly non-psychological putative facts which are the contents of those intuitions, but that it consists of the psychological facts to the effect that we have intuitions with those contents, true or false.[16] On such a view, our evidence in philosophy amounts only to psychological facts about ourselves.

---

[16]   A recent example is Brian Weatherson (2003: 27), who, despite showing far more sophistication in these matters than most philosophers do, still assumes that the argument from Gettier cases against the traditional analysis has the premise "Intuition says that Gettier cases are not cases of knowledge" rather than the simpler "Gettier cases are not cases of knowledge." His considered view may not be the one described in the text.

Nevertheless, they do not want the psychological fact that we have an intuition that P to be perfectly neutral with respect to the non-psychological question whether P, for that leads to skepticism about philosophy. If we merely seek the best explanation of our having the intuitions, without any presumption in favor of their truth, we may find a psychological theory to explain them, but how are we to answer the questions about a mainly non-psychological universe that grip many metaphysicians and other philosophers? In explaining why we have intuitions, analytic philosophy has a preference for explanations that make those intuitions true over explanations that make them untrue, but the justification for that preference remains unclear. Even if we have an intuition that the former sort of explanation is better than the latter, why should we give that intuition a special privilege over others by adopting a methodology that assumes its truth? That our evidence in philosophy consists of facts about intuitions and that explanations of those facts on which the intuitions come out true are better (*ceteris paribus*) than explanations on which they do not are themselves epistemological rather than psychological claims. Taken far enough, the psychologization of philosophical method becomes self-defeating. Psychologism is no more a psychological theory than the Pythagorean doctrine that everything consists of numbers is a mathematical theory.[17]

Not even psychological facts really meet the demands of Evidence Neutrality. Whatever Descartes thought, facts about one's own present consciousness are not always cognitively accessible to one. For example, on any reasonable view, intuitions vary in strength. An adequately fine-grained theory of intuitions would have to distinguish weaker ones from stronger ones in evidential impact. If the strength of intuitions is taken into account, the evidence will be recorded in something like the form "I have an intuition of strength s that P." The strength parameter s will have to be specified according to some common scale, in order to permit the comparisons between the strengths of sometimes conflicting intuitions which the theory of evidence will need to make. But that will give plenty of scope both for

---

[17] Pust (2001) argues carefully that the following principle is self-defeating: "Aside from propositions describing the occurrence of her judgements, S is justified in believing only those propositions which are part of the best explanation of S's making the judgements that she makes." Contrast Goldman and Pust (1998).

misjudging the strength of one's intuitions and for being accused by others of having done so. After all, philosophers have a powerful vested interest in persuading themselves and others that the intuitions which directly or indirectly favor their position are stronger than they really are. The stronger those intuitions, the more those who appeal to them gain, psychologically and professionally. Given what is known of human psychology, it would be astonishing if such vested interests did not manifest themselves in some degree of wishful thinking, some tendency to overestimate the strength of convenient intuitions and underestimate the strength of inconvenient ones. In trying to compensate for such bias, one may undercompensate or overcompensate; the standpoint of consciousness gives one no privileged access to whether one has succeeded, for bias does not work by purely conscious processes. Its effects are much easier to observe in others than in oneself. A further obstacle to classifying one's intuitions is that some philosophers with a tin ear for natural language seem to misarticulate their own strong intuitions, using forms of words that do not express what they really want. There is sometimes controversy as to whether this has happened. It would be naïve to suppose that all these obstacles can be overcome just by "trying harder." Restricting evidence to psychological facts, even to those about present conscious intuitions, does not satisfy Evidence Neutrality. It is often not in principle uncontentiously decidable whether someone has an intuition of a given degree of strength that P.

Radical eliminativists about the mind are another source of contentiousness. They say "Research in neurophysiology has shown that folk psychology is a false theory; its ascriptions of mental states and acts are never strictly and literally true, however convenient they may have been" (even if they do not believe what they say). At least some of them will classify "S has the intuition that P" and "S has the belief that P" together as ascriptions of folk psychological mental states (perhaps not the same one). On their view (itself a form of judgment skepticism), humans never have the intuition that P. In particular, consistent radical eliminativists will not even concede that their theory is counterintuitive, or that we have the intuition that we have beliefs and desires. To find common ground with radical eliminativists, one must rigorously depsychologize one's evidence. I am better off showing them my brain scans than describing my intuitions. For other philosophers, brain scans no more exist than mountains do.

Does a more pragmatic attitude to evidence finesse these difficulties? On a pragmatic view, what permits a fact to serve as evidence in a given context is that it happens to be uncontroversial in that context, not that it is uncontroversial in all contexts, or foundational in any deeper sense. The dialectical standard does not favor the use of psychological facts as evidence in contexts in which such facts are controversial. Currently undisputed non-psychological truths can be used as evidence too. We get by with agreement on particular pieces of evidence without any context-independent standard for evidence. This dialectical conception of evidence makes sense even for a single thinker: in isolation one can still play rival theories against each other in one's head; virtual opponents suffice for much philosophical thinking.

We should not assume too readily that a dialectical standard of evidence is always appropriate. It works well when both sides show moderation and restraint. But the adversarial system of inquiry has limits. By accepting the dialectical standard unconditionally, we lay ourselves open to exploitation by ruthless opponents – such as skeptics. It allows them to rule our best evidence out of court simply by issuing a peremptory challenge to that evidence. A debate conducted in that spirit is unlikely to converge on the truth. The common ground is too narrow to form an adequate evidence base. Testing one's beliefs that way is a dangerous game; we should expect unreliable results. For example, if one uses only premises and forms of inference that a skeptic about perception will allow one, and therefore only premises that are true and forms of inference that are valid even if one is a brain in a vat, one has little prospect of reaching the conclusion that one has hands. But that does not show that we should not be confident that we have hands. To be warranted, confidence need not be recoverable from an impoverished skeptical starting-point. After all, if one uses only premises and forms of inference that skeptics about reason will allow one, one cannot reach the conclusion that there are good reasons. For since such skeptics doubt that there are good reasons, they allow one neither the premise that there are good reasons nor any form of reasoning with which to reach that conclusion from some other starting-point. It would be frivolous to conclude, from that trivial point, that we do not know that there are good reasons. Indeed, even skeptics about reason must deny that conclusion to follow, since they deny that anything follows from anything.

Sometimes, in self-defense, one must abandon skeptics to their fate. Some skepticism, like skepticism about reason, is so radical that it leaves too little unchallenged for what remains as shared evidence to be an appropriate basis for evaluating the claims under challenge. When one is warranted in refusing to play the skeptic's dialectical game, the dialectical standard of evidence becomes irrelevant. In refusing, one does not abandon one's claims to knowledge and reason, for the appropriate standard of evidence is non-dialectical. By that standard, the skeptic's peremptory challenge fails to disqualify the challenged fact as evidence. To neglect such evidence would be to violate the requirement of total evidence.[18] One continues to assert propositions of the disputed kind on the basis of evidence, without expecting to find arguments for them that use only premises and forms of inference acceptable to the skeptic. Since escape from the radical skeptical predicament is impossible, one must take good care not to get into it in the first place.

Is this attitude a legitimate response to judgment skepticism? For instance, may one take the fact that the subject in a Gettier case lacks knowledge or the fact that there are mountains in Switzerland as evidence, even though the judgment skeptic challenges one's right to such evidence? In reaching one's views, one does not restrict oneself to premises and forms of inference acceptable to judgment skeptics, for one regards their restricted evidence base as too willfully impoverished to constitute a reasonable starting-point for inquiry. Such skeptics have not shown that the facts they allow as evidence are really more certain than the facts they disallow. In particular, it is quite insufficient for them to point out that it is possible to judge that there are mountains in Switzerland even if there are no mountains in Switzerland, for a parallel objection can be made to any evidence worth having in the sciences.

Even if (let us pretend) facts about our intuitions were in some sense more certain for us than all other facts, it would not follow that we should restrict our evidence to facts about our intuitions. For the extra information in a wider evidence base may be worth a cost in reliability. If logical truths were more certain than all other facts,

---

[18]   "[I]n the application of inductive logic to a given knowledge situation, the total evidence available must be taken as a basis for determining the degree of confirmation" (Carnap 1950: 211; compare Hempel 1965: 63–7). See also Williamson (2000a: 189–90).

it would not follow that we should restrict our evidence to logical truths: that would eliminate most of our knowledge. It would be skepticism about everything except reason. Similarly, if facts of some other special kind were more certain than all other facts, it would not follow that we should restrict our evidence to facts of that special kind.

Isn't this short way with the judgment skeptic contrary to the open spirit of philosophical discussion? The skeptic has thoughtful, recognizably philosophical concerns: don't they deserve a fair hearing? How can they be given such a hearing if the very propositions the skeptic challenges are taken as evidence? Skeptics of any principled kind can indeed expect more tolerance in philosophy than in other disciplines. One can discuss their skepticism with them without stepping outside the bounds of philosophy. In talking to them, it is futile to offer for their acceptance arguments with premises they have already refused to accept. In particular, it seems unphilosophical to refuse to discuss judgment skepticism with its proponents. In conversation with them, it is dialectically pointless, rude, to offer as evidence propositions one knows they do not accept. But the issue remains: what implications, if any, does the outcome of such a conversation have for the epistemic status of belief in the propositions the skeptic questions? Faced with a skeptic about reason, or everything except reason, many philosophers would be willing to start a conversation, out of politeness, curiosity, competitiveness, or the desire to save a soul. But their inability to achieve a dialectical triumph over such a resourceful opponent does not oblige them to become skeptics about reason, or everything except reason, themselves. There is no bad faith in continuing to claim (and have) knowledge of the contested truths. For the anti-skeptic is not obliged to treat dialectic as the measure of all things. Indeed, the claim that dialectic is the measure of all things faces self-defeat, for it cannot triumph dialectically over its denial; even if it appeared to be getting the better of the argument, would not taking that to establish its truth beg the question? Similarly, even if one cannot establish dialectically, in dispute with a judgment skeptic, that the subject in a Gettier case lacks knowledge or that there are mountains in Switzerland, without bad faith one can still claim to know that the subject in a Gettier case lacks knowledge or that there are mountains in Switzerland, and use those facts as evidence.

What prevents astrologers from using this approach to defend astrology by arguing that the fact that astrological predictions have an excellent track record constitutes good evidence for astrological theory? Nothing prevents astrologers from *saying* such things, although they will presumably be speaking falsely, since astrological predictions have no such excellent track record. Similarly, nothing prevents astrologers from *saying* that astrology meets the strictest methodological standards of natural science, although again they will be speaking falsely. In both cases, there will be excellent evidence that they are speaking falsely, which they will not accept as evidence of that. There is a persistent temptation to assume that a good account of methodology should *silence* astrologers and other cranks, by leaving them in a position where they can find nothing more to say. That assumption is naïve. They always find more to say. Of course an account of methodology should specify respects in which good intellectual practices are better than bad ones. But that does not mean that if devotees of a bad intellectual practice endorse the account, they will abandon the practice; more likely they will convince themselves that their practice triumphantly conforms to its precepts. No methodology is proof against misapplication by those with sufficiently poor judgment.

None of the foregoing arguments provides any guarantee that judgment skepticism is not correct for some types of judgment; "common sense" is sometimes wrong. But if it is accepted in such cases, that should be on the basis of evidence specific to those types of judgment, not on the basis of general skeptical fallacies.

6

Our evidence in philosophy consists of facts, most of them non-psychological, to which we have appropriate epistemic access. Consequently, there is a one-sided incompleteness to descriptions of philosophical methodology, and attempts to justify or criticize it on that basis, if formulated in terms neutral over the extent of that evidence. For instance, in describing some philosophers as believing or having the intuition that P, one fails to specify whether their evidence includes the fact that P.

A simple attempt to justify common sense as a starting point for philosophy on the basis of such a neutral description appeals to the principle of *Epistemic Conservativism*: one has a defeasible right to one's beliefs, which may be defeated by positive reasons for doubt, but not by the mere absence of independent justification.[19] Thus one's belief that there are mountains in Switzerland gives one the defeasible right to rest arguments on the premise that there are mountains in Switzerland. Whether or not the belief constitutes knowledge, it confers the right.

Our beliefs are what we start from, the boat we find ourselves in. Even if we can progressively replace them, we cannot distance ourselves from all of them at once, for we have nowhere else to stand. Epistemic Conservativism elevates the practical necessity of starting from where one is, wherever that is, to normative status, subject to the proviso on defeaters. Although the principle is not perfectly neutral on the epistemic status of the belief, since the notion of a defeater is epistemologically normative, it is neutral on how much evidence, if any, the subject has. Justifying a philosophical method by appeal only to Epistemic Conservativism ignores crucial epistemological distinctions concerning the relevant beliefs: it is like justifying scientific methodology without giving any information as to what evidence is required in its application. Even if Epistemic Conservativism is true, it is radically incomplete as a basis for an account of the epistemic status of philosophical beliefs.

If philosophical "intuitions" are simply beliefs, they fall within the domain of Epistemic Conservativism. That is less clear if "intuitions" include inclinations to belief. Someone inclined to believe **p** may nevertheless not believe **p**; inclinations conflict. This difference matters for Epistemic Conservativism.

Justin has been brought up to believe that knowledge is equivalent to justified true belief. He is confronted for the first time with a Gettier case. He might have immediately and confidently judged that the subject has justified true belief without knowledge, and abandoned his old belief that knowledge is equivalent to justified true belief. Presumably, Epistemic Conservativism would then have switched sides and started supporting the new belief that knowledge is not equivalent to justified true belief. Instead, Justin is more cau-

---

[19]   See Harman (1986: 29–42) for a defense of epistemic conservativism, and Vahid (2004) for a recent critical survey of its varieties. For simplicity and generality, subtleties in the formulation of the principle have been glossed over.

tious, not wanting to assent too readily to anything tricky. Although he is consciously inclined to judge that the subject has justified true belief without knowledge, he does not immediately give in to that inclination or abandon his ingrained belief that knowledge is equivalent to justified true belief. Does Epistemic Conservativism counsel abandoning his ingrained belief in this situation? If Justin is asked "What reason have you to doubt your analysis?," he cannot answer "The subject in this possible case has justified true belief without knowledge," since he does not yet believe that. He must say something else. The answer "I am inclined to believe that the subject in this possible case has justified true belief without knowledge" would be relevant if the function of the prefix "I am inclined to believe that" were to signal tentative assent to what follows, but Justin's commitment to his analysis inclines him to resist even tentative assent to a putative counterexample. If the function of the prefix "I am inclined to believe that" is instead to report his psychological state of being inclined to believe the proposition expressed by the embedded sentence, as its literal compositional semantics suggests, the relevance of that answer to the original question is far from obvious, for he has not yet assented even tentatively to a counterexample.

Can Epistemic Conservativism be extended to the claim that one has a defeasible right to believe whatever one is inclined to believe? Such an extension is less clearly motivated than the original principle by the idea that, since one must start from where one is, one has at least a defeasible right to be there. A right to be where I am is a right to have the beliefs and inclinations I have. That does not obviously include a right to follow those inclinations to new places, especially when the beliefs I already have imply that those are bad destinations, for example, when the inclinations are to believe things inconsistent with what I currently believe. As Gettier counterexamples show, intuition can be revolutionary as well as conservative. If I currently believe **p**, I am currently committed to the belief that any inclination to believe something inconsistent with **p** is an inclination to believe something false. I am not committed to the beliefs I am merely inclined to have in the way I am committed to my current beliefs. I am merely inclined to commit myself to them in that way. After all, a right to be where I am is of limited practical use unless it involves a right to stay where I am, to continue believing, at least for a while, what I currently believe.

7

Many philosophers recognize their philosophical activity in the more dynamic notion of reflective equilibrium, described by Nelson Goodman and John Rawls.[20] Our initial set of general theories and particular intuitions is inconsistent; each side is revised in the light of the other, by an iterative process, until they are brought into harmony. There is a debate whether the beliefs that emerge from this process are thereby justified. But a prior question is whether such descriptions of the process yield an adequate conception of a philosophical method, good or bad. The question is not whether philosophers engage in the mutual adjustment of general theory and judgments about specific cases – they manifestly do – but whether such descriptions of it are sufficiently informative for epistemological purposes.

A process generally acknowledged as at least superficially analogous to the attainment of reflective equilibrium in philosophy is the mutual adjustment of theory and observation in natural science.[21] Imagine a description of it in which the word "observation" is used simply as a label for judgments with non-general content, irrespective of origin; it ignores the perceptual process. Such a description misses the point of the natural scientific enterprise. It provides no basis for an epistemological assessment. The nature of scientists' evidence has been left unspecified. Similarly, one has no basis for an epistemological assessment of the method of reflective equilibrium in philosophy without more information about the epistemological status of the "intuitions." In particular, it matters what kind of evidence "intuitions" provide. The previous account of thought experiments is consistent with the idea that the Gettier proposition and its like are evidence. Indeed, since real life counterexamples will sometimes do in place of imaginary ones, observed facts are sometimes relevant evidence. Talk of reflective equilibrium fails to address such issues.

---

[20]   See Goodman (1955: 65–8) and Rawls (1951, 1971: 20). David Lewis (1983a: x) describes philosophers' task as the identification of such equilibria. Two recent critiques of the method are Cummins (1998) and Stich (1998); a recent defense is DePaul (1998).

[21]   For such an analogy see Rawls (1951).

One factor obscuring the descriptive inadequacy of standard accounts of reflective equilibrium is the already noted tendency to conceive evidence in philosophy as the mere having of "intuitions": it is easy to slip into the illusion that our epistemic access to such psychological facts is unproblematic. Thus attention is distracted away from the epistemic status of the "intuitions" themselves. Even if we revise an "intuition," our evidence may still include the fact that we had it. But the epistemic status of the original "intuition," however much the model ignores it, must be relevant to the epistemic value of revising general theories in line with its content.

The reflective equilibrium account, as usually understood, already assigns a proto-evidential role to at least one kind of non-psychological fact. For it treats philosophers as relying on logical relations between theories and intuitions, in particular their consistency and inconsistency. Can one retell the story in purely psychological terms, with beliefs about logical relations in place of actual logical relations? That move is doubly problematic. It reduces explanatory power unless the assumption is added that beliefs about logical relations are reliable, for otherwise the account no longer explains any tendency to bring theory and intuition into mutual consistency, but at best a tendency to believe that one has done so. Moreover, the beliefs about logical relations are explanatorily redundant. Consider the theory (4) and the "intuition" (5):

(4)   Every F is a G.
(5)   This F is no G.

In order to explain, without appeal to the inconsistency of (4) with (5), why philosophers do not simply retain both, we merely say that they believe (6):

(6)   (4) and (5) are jointly inconsistent.

Philosophers do not in fact fix belief in all of (4), (5), and (6). But the envisaged strategy does not understand that in terms of a proto-evidential role for (7):

(7)   (4), (5), and (6) are jointly inconsistent.

It no more assumes that (7) is evidence than it assumes that (6) is. To invoke the fact of belief in (7) as evidence is merely to take another backwards step on an infinite regress. But if the strategy relies on a brute unwillingness to believe all three of (4), (5), and (6), it might as well have relied on a brute unwillingness to believe both of (4) and (5) in the first place; they are already inconsistent. Without proto-evidential backing from the inconsistency of (4) and (5), the unwillingness to believe both of (4) and (5) looks irrational.

If the reflective equilibrium story assigns a proto-evidential role to some logical facts even though all logical facts are philosophically contestable, as we saw in earlier chapters, why not allow a similar role to other philosophically contestable facts? If no other philosophically contestable facts can play such a role that is something we need to know, and have not yet been given any good reason to believe. If other philosophically contestable facts can play a proto-evidential role, that too is something we need to know and which the reflective equilibrium story leaves unacknowledged.

To say that mathematicians or biochemists or historians strive to bring their opinions into equilibrium would be sadly inadequate as even a summary description of their method of research. It omits the constraining evidence that makes their opinions worth listening to, their research worth funding. Is philosophy so different that in its case such a description will suffice? If so, it should give up any claim to be an evidence-based discipline. Such pessimism is unwarranted once we accept the contestability of evidence. Thought experiments do provide evidence, in the shape of mainly non-psychological facts. That philosophers sometimes disagree as to what evidence they provide is only to be expected.

8

Knowledge Maximization

1

In philosophy, as elsewhere, one can easily experience conflict between one's role as a believer and one's role as an appraiser of oneself as a believer. I cannot *simply* regard my belief in **p** as a psychological phenomenon. For **p** implies that **p** is true, and therefore that whoever believes **p** does so truly. In believing **p**, I am committed by that implication to the belief that a belief in **p** is true, and that to continue believing truly on the matter I must continue believing **p** (if the truth-value of **p** is atemporal). Similarly, **p** implies that its negation ¬**p** is false, and therefore that whoever believes ¬**p** has a false belief in ¬**p**. In believing **p**, I am committed by that implication to the belief that a belief in ¬**p** is false.[1] Neutrality is not an option for believers. One is bound to think any given belief of one's own superior in truth-value to the contrary beliefs of others. But sometimes we step back from our beliefs and regard them as psychological phenomena on a par with the beliefs of others, in equal need of both psychological explanation and epistemological criticism. I may see my beliefs as the product of my social and cultural background, your beliefs as the product of your social and cultural background, and wonder what objective reason there is to prefer mine to yours. As argued in the previous chapter, that third-person stance can involve a refusal to take crucial knowledge seriously, just because someone disputes it; sometimes we must take a first-person present tense stance. But

---

[1] The exact status of the implications depends on delicate issues about disquotational principles for truth and falsity, but whatever their outcome the point in the text will hold in some form.

sometimes the third-person stance is the right one to take. This chapter explores some general aspects of the tension between one's role as a believer and one's role as an appraiser of oneself as a believer in philosophy.

Some anti-skeptical commitment is built into the role of believer. If I believe **p**, I am thereby committed to the belief that I do not falsely believe **p**. This commitment can be generalized in two ways. First, the content of the hypothetical commitment can be generalized. If I believe **p**, I am thereby committed to the belief that no one falsely believes **p**. Similarly, given that propositional truth is atemporal, if I believe **p**, I am thereby committed to the belief that I shall never falsely believe **p** (since propositional truth is not amodal, there is no corresponding modal generalization: if I believe **p**, my commitments may allow that **p** could have been false and still believed). Second, the whole conditional can be generalized, on personal, temporal, and modal dimensions. Necessarily, anyone who ever believes **p** is thereby committed to the belief that they do not falsely believe **p**. All these generalizations can be combined: necessarily, anyone who ever believes **p** is thereby committed to the belief that no one ever falsely believes **p**.

Nevertheless, this anti-skeptical commitment is very limited. For if I believe **p**, my commitments may allow that just about everyone else falsely believes ¬**p** at all times in all circumstances, that I falsely believe ¬**p** at just about all other times in all circumstances, and that I would now have falsely believed ¬**p** in just about all counterfactual circumstances: true belief with respect to **p** in the current case contrasts with error on the same question in just about all other cases. I might take skeptical scenarios to prevail almost everywhere while insisting that I happen not to be currently in one. Such a response to skepticism would be unimpressive, perhaps unstable. The admitted frequency of skeptical scenarios in nearby situations constitutes an urgent reason for doubting one's own beliefs. One should beware of regarding oneself as too happy an exception to sadly general trends. Sometimes the tension between one's role as a believer and one's role as an appraiser of oneself as a believer becomes unbearable, and the belief in question is abandoned.

Few of us regard ourselves as highly exceptional in having currently escaped the worst scenarios for skepticism about perception. We think them rare in worlds like ours. We find the brain in a vat scenario far-fetched; while dreams are common, dreams with the sustained coherence of waking life are very rare. The environment as we perceive it is full of creatures in regular perceptual contact with it. No special luck or skill is needed to avoid envatment: it has never been a big danger for humans. Of course, skeptics will say that such claims about our environment merely beg the question; their truth is part of what is at stake. But the claims were not addressed to skeptics, in a futile attempt to persuade them out of skepticism. Instead, they figure in our appraisal of skeptical arguments, from our current non-skeptical point of view.[2] Not yet having suspended our ordinary beliefs, we must decide whether the acknowledged bare metaphysical possibility of skeptical scenarios gives us good reason to suspend those beliefs – not just momentarily in an epistemology seminar, but for the rest of our lives. Most of us find the reason inadequate. Bare possibilities of error, however picturesque, constitute no imminent threat; the threat is not nearly urgent enough to warrant the drastic and costly precautions skeptics recommend. For most purposes, we do not take the skeptical possibilities seriously.

Our tendency to ignore skeptical possibilities is not explained by their making no practical difference; many of them make such a difference. If you are a brain in a vat, not really interacting with other people, much of your altruistic behavior is futile. Again, in some skeptical scenarios you feel unremitting horrible pain for years, starting tomorrow, unless you immediately do what appears to you exactly like going out and buying ten copies of the same newspaper: I bet you do not take even that elementary precaution. Of course, in other skeptical scenarios you feel unremitting horrible pain for years, starting tomorrow, if you immediately do what appears to you exactly like going out and buying ten copies of the same newspaper. If one takes all possibilities equally seriously, they tend to cancel each other out for practical purposes. But that does not imply that we are left back where we were before skeptical possibilities occurred to us. If everything except present consciousness is utterly unknown, why not simply indulge in sweet dreams?

For the thorough skeptic, that you have hands is no more probable (epistemically) than that you are in a skeptical scenario in which you merely appear to have hands: will you therefore reject a bet on which you win 10 euros if you have hands and lose 100 euros otherwise on the grounds that its expected utility is negative, since $10/2 - 100/2 = -45$? If skepticism makes you doubt the enforceability of the bet, that is no reason to accept it. Surely it is a good bet, even when you happen to be in an epistemology seminar. We ignore radical skeptical possibilities in practice, even when they are drawn to our attention, because we do not rate them as epistemically serious possibilities. We make that epistemic assessment from our non-skeptical perspective.

When we judge that in our world radical skeptical scenarios present no imminent danger to anyone, we do so on the basis of our own beliefs, but that judgment depends on the specific content of those beliefs; it is not automatic. We have a rich conception of ourselves and our environment on which brains in vats are very far-out physical possibilities, and even long-term coherent dreams are highly unlikely. That conception also enables us to give specific answers to the question "How do you know?" as it arises on specific occasions, for example by indicating relevant processes of perception, memory, testimony, and inference, although of course the conception need not figure among premises from which the more specific knowledge was inferred, since the latter need not have been inferred at all. None of this amounts to a detailed dissection of the flaws in particular skeptical arguments. Rather, it provides the appropriate background to our confidence that such flaws must be there.

How imminent a threat do scenarios for judgment skepticism pose? Skepticism about perception starts with actual perceptual errors and imaginatively radicalizes them until it reaches brains in vats. Similarly, judgment skepticism starts with actual errors about witchcraft, oracles, and magic and imaginatively radicalizes them until it reaches the nonexistence of mountains. In both cases, there is a trade-off between how remote the skeptical scenarios are (judged from our current perspective) and how far-reaching a skepticism they motivate. The set of very close possibilities motivates only a very limited skepticism; a wider range of possibilities motivates a more general skepticism. The closer the possibility, the more seriously it deserves to be taken. For skepticism about perception, we know at least roughly what makes the more radical scenarios remote, the enormous practical obstacles to setting up all the requisite causal mechanisms, not to mention the shortage of motivation for doing so. For judgment skepticism, what corresponds to those obstacles? Do we even believe that the actual world is not full of apt scenarios for judgment skepticism?

Suppose that most ordinary beliefs in most other cultures are false, because somehow laden with false theories.[3] Then the possibility that, for similar reasons, most ordinary beliefs in our own culture are also false is too close to home to be dismissed as fanciful or far-fetched. Judgment skepticism gets a grip. A satisfying response would put such skeptical scenarios far from other cultures, not just far from one's own.

Given empirical evidence for the approximate intertranslatability of all human languages and a universal innate basis of human cognition, we may wonder how "other" any human culture really is. If we believe **p** and believe that others believe **p** too, then we are committed to the belief that the others' belief in **p** is true. But if human beliefs tend to be true merely as an accidental by-product of our DNA, and other galaxies are rife with nonhuman persons most of whose beliefs are false, because laden with false theories, then scenarios for judgment skepticism are still dangerously close to home. Even if such scenarios are rare or absent in the actual universe, but only by good luck, it remains uncomfortable for opponents of judgment skepticism. If we are to refuse in good conscience to take seriously the radical scenarios for judgment skepticism, we must do so from a perspective on which there is a quite general tendency for beliefs to be true. Anything less than that will look like special pleading on our own behalf. But why should there be any such tendency? What we believe is one question, what is true another.

2

Some naturalists argue on evolutionary grounds that beliefs tend to be true, for creatures with too many false beliefs are unfit to survive. True beliefs tend to cause one to get what one wants in a way in which false beliefs do not. Truth conduces to success. That is not to deny that some false beliefs have survival value; the suggestion is only that on the whole truth is more conducive than falsity to survival. Since we are arguing from our current perspective, on which our

---

[3] For present purposes, how finely cultures are individuated matters little.

world is governed by regularities extending over past, present, and future, we need not worry overmuch about scenarios for inductive skepticism on which generalizations with only true instances up to some future time t have false instances thereafter (in any case, judgment skepticism is not skepticism about induction). We can take past success as some guide to future success.

How do true beliefs tend to cause success in action? This principle seems central to the nature of belief and desire:

(1)   If an agent desires that P, and believes that if it does A then P, then *ceteris paribus* it does A.

The "*ceteris paribus*" clause in (1) covers possibilities of irrationality, alternative means to the same end, countervailing desires, and so on. If an agent desires that P, believes that if it does A then P, and does A, then P if the belief is true, so its desire is realized. If its belief is not true, then it may well not happen that P. Of course, that P may not help the agent if it is not good for the agent that P. The argument might therefore be taken to support a stronger conclusion: that evolution favors creatures who both believe what is true and desire what is good for them. "Good for them" here means good for them collectively, since evolution sometimes favors altruistic behavior which benefits one's relatives to one's individual disadvantage; for simplicity, this qualification is left tacit in what follows.[4]

An agent has some idea of the act A in believing that if it does A then P. If it does A without believing itself to be doing so, then the natural link between antecedent and consequent in (1) is broken. For example, if you go north while believing that you are going south,

---

[4]   If for them to desire that P were for them to believe that it is good for them that P, the tendency to desire what is good for them might be subsumed under the tendency to believe what is true. However, in whatever sense of "good for them" evolution can be assumed to favor creatures that get what is good for them, for them to believe that it is good for them that P seems to be neither necessary nor sufficient for them to desire that P. For example, they may believe that it is good for them in that sense that there be a cull of the unfit without desiring one, and they may desire that cigarettes be more readily available without believing that it is good for them in that sense that cigarettes be more readily available. But if in some relevant sense desiring that P can be equated with believing that it is good that P, so much the better for the argument in the text.

your action is not explained just by your desire to reach the oasis and belief that if you go north then you will reach the oasis, (1) notwithstanding. Perhaps the explanation is that, in addition, you desire even more strongly to avoid your enemy and believe that he is at the oasis. Although such examples do not refute (1), since the *"ceteris paribus"* clause absorbs their shock, they indicate that the rationale for (1) takes for granted that beliefs about what one is doing tend to be true, which is a special case of the very phenomenon that we are trying to understand. Therefore, in order not to assume what needs to be explained, let us revise (1) thus:

(2)   If an agent desires that P, and believes that if it does A then P, then *ceteris paribus* it acts so that it believes that it does A.

A natural variant of (2) would have "on the intention to do A" in place of "so that it believes that it does A." The argument below could be reformulated in terms of this variant, but for simplicity let us stick with (2), to minimize the number of types of propositional attitude under consideration.

Given that you want to avoid your enemy, and believe that if you go south then you will avoid him, (2) helps explain why you act so that you believe that you go south, even though in fact you go north. But the reason for taking (2) rather than (1) as basic for present purposes is not that anything is wrong with (1) as a *ceteris paribus* generalization in its own right. Rather, the point is just that (1) is too close to what we are trying to explain to be an appropriate starting point for an illuminating explanation.

Starting from (2) rather than (1), one can still explain why it is good for an agent to have true beliefs and desires for what is good for it. For if it desires that P, believes that if it does A then P, and acts so that it believes that it does A, then P if both beliefs are true, which is good for it if its desire is for what is good for it. Unfortunately, such a derivation explains much less than it appears to. For, given (2), one can show in the same way for infinitely many deviant properties true* and good* that the combination of true* beliefs and desires for what is good* for one yields (*ceteris paribus*) what is good (not just good*) for one.

To see this, consider an arbitrary mapping on propositions, taking the proposition that P to the proposition that ^P, subject to the constraint that it commutes with logical operations, in the sense that the proposition that $^\wedge$(not P) is the proposition that not $^\wedge$P, the proposition that $^\wedge$(if P then Q) is the proposition that if $^\wedge$P then $^\wedge$Q, and so on. In other respects, the mapping is arbitrary: for example, the proposition that $^\wedge$(I am going north) can be the proposition that you are eating slowly.

If a proposition is just the set of possible worlds in which it is true, then we can construct such a mapping for any permutation π of possible worlds (a one-one mapping of the possible worlds onto the possible worlds) by stipulating that each world w belongs to the proposition that $^\wedge$P if and only if $\pi(w)$ belongs to the proposition that P. The mapping commutes with negation, for example, because, for any world w, the following are equivalent: w belongs to the proposition that $^\wedge$(not P); $\pi(w)$ belongs to the proposition that not P; $\pi(w)$ does not belong to the proposition that P; w does not belong to the proposition that $^\wedge$P; w belongs to the proposition that not $^\wedge$P. For similar reasons the mapping commutes with other logical operations, such as the truth-functional conditional.

Alternatively, if propositions have quasi-syntactic structure, we can take an arbitrary permutation of their atomic constituents and extend it recursively to complex propositions in the natural way. The mapping automatically commutes with logical operations because the commutativity clauses are built into its inductive definition.

Now define "true*" and "good*" by these equivalences:

(3)   That P is true* if and only if that $^\wedge$P is true.
(4)   That P is good* for an agent if and only if that $^\wedge$P is good for it.

Suppose that an agent desires that P, believes that if it does A then P, and acts so that it believes that it does A. Suppose further that both beliefs are true*. By (3), since the proposition that if it does A then P is true*, the proposition that $^\wedge$(if it does A then P) is true. Since the mapping commutes with logical operations, in particular with the truth-functional conditional employed (by stipulation) in (1) and (2), the proposition that $^\wedge$(if it does A then P) is the proposition that if $^\wedge$(it does A) then $^\wedge$P. Thus the proposition that if $^\wedge$(it does A) then $^\wedge$P is true. By (3) again, since the proposition that it does A is true*, the proposition that $^\wedge$(it does A) is true. Since truth is closed under modus ponens, the proposition that ^P is true. Suppose finally that what the agent desires is good* for it. So that P is good* for it; therefore, by (4), that ^P is good for it. In other words, something (that ^P) good for the agent obtains: together, true* belief and desire for what is good* for one yield (*ceteris paribus*) what is good (not just good*) for one.

From (2), we cannot conclude that the combination of true belief and desire for what is good for one is any better for one than the combination of true* belief and desire for what is good* for one. Yet, despite all the evolutionary pressures, we have no special tendency to believe what is true* or to desire what is good* for us. For example, that I am going north may be true* if and only if you are eating slowly, and that I reach the oasis may be good* for me if and only if it is good for me that you read your book. I have no special tendency to believe that I am going north only if you are in fact eating slowly or to desire that I reach the oasis only if it is in fact good for me that you read your book. If we start theorizing without any reason to expect a correlation between belief and truth, considerations of survival will not make the connection for us.

We can envisage schemes for interpreting creatures under which they tend to believe the true* and desire the good* for them, rather than to believe the true and desire the good for them. Suppose that we are trying to understand some aliens. We already have an extremely plausible interpretation Int of their beliefs and desires, under which they tend to believe the true and desire the good for them. We define a new interpretation Int* by specifying that, under Int*, an alien believes that ^P if and only if, under Int, it believes that P, and, under Int*, it desires that ^P if and only if, under Int, it desires that P.[5] Thus Int* ascribes a true belief just where Int ascribes a true* belief; Int* ascribes a desire for what is in fact good for one just where Int ascribes a desire for what is in fact good* for one. Int* attributes bizarre contents to the aliens: under Int*, their beliefs about their environment have no tendency to be true, their bodily movements no tendency to bring about the satisfaction of their desires. For example,

[5] The definition of Int* assumes that the proposition that ^P is the proposition that ^Q if and only if the proposition that P is the proposition that Q; this condition is easily met. Int* is also stipulated to ascribe to the aliens only beliefs and desires of the form that ^P.

under Int, an alien desires that it will be cool and believes that if it jumps into the lake then it will be cool; it jumps into the lake and will be cool. Under Int*, it desires that ^(it will be cool) and believes that ^(if it jumps into the lake then it will be cool), in other words, that if ^(it jumps into the lake) then ^(it will be cool); it jumps into the lake and will be cool. For definiteness, let that ^(it will be cool) and that ^(it jumps into the lake) be that you were tall and that you went to bed respectively. Thus, under Int*, the alien desires that you were tall and believes that if you went to bed then you were tall; it jumps into the lake and will be cool. Under Int, when it jumps into the lake it also believes that it jumps into the lake and that it will be cool. Thus, under Int*, when it jumps into the lake it believes that you went to bed and that you were tall. Int* make the aliens' mental lives formally as rational and coherent in propositional content as Int does; but Int* radically disconnects their mental lives from what is happening around them and from what they are physically doing, whereas Int connects them in the normal way. Moreover, Int* postulates no special mechanism to help explain the strange disconnection. Surely Int* misinterprets the aliens. Even if such radical disconnection is not metaphysically impossible, it would occur only under highly abnormal circumstances. The nature of mental content seems to favor Int over Int* in some constitutive way.

We could try to rule out Int* by proposing more specific constraints on the internal interconnections of propositional attitudes for Int* to fail. But that approach is unpromising; it misses the point of the problem. The deviant interpretation Int* can meet even more specific constraints on the internal structure of the agent's system of propositional attitudes while still attributing mental lives radically disconnected from the environment and bodily behavior. For the mapping ^ preserves the main structural features of propositions, and could be tailored to preserve even finer-grained structure.

It may be objected that truth* and goodness* are less natural properties than truth and goodness, just as grue and bleen are less natural than green and blue (Lewis 1983b). Although green will coincide with grue until some future moment, we have evolved a tendency to react differentially to green rather than to grue (even when they diverge) because green is a more natural property than grue, so a mechanism sensitive to green can develop far more easily than a mechanism sensitive to grue. Evolutionary selection does not have a completely free hand; it is constrained by the available material and its causal powers. Why not explain the tendency to believe the true and desire the good for one through the combination of constraints of internal coherence such as (2) with considerations of naturalness?

A difficulty for the proposal is that truth* and goodness* need not be much more unnatural than truth and goodness. For we can define the mapping ^ of propositions in quite natural ways, while still preserving constraints of internal coherence. For example, suppose that propositions are sets of possible worlds. Then the permutation π of possible worlds used to define ^ might be a rotation of the similarity spheres of worlds about some counterfactual world. Thus each proposition that ^P would have the same shape in similarity space as the proposition that P, and their locations would be systematically related. Alternatively, if propositions have quasi-syntactic structure, we could replace all atomic predicative constituents of the proposition that P by their negations in constructing the proposition that ^P. Although such mappings may involve some loss of naturalness, it is comparatively slight. Indeed, we may even gain naturalness by selecting more natural entities than the "right" ones out of which to construct the "wrong" propositions. Yet the proposition that ^P will differ in truth-value from the proposition that P in very many cases; truth* is very poorly correlated with truth, and goodness* with goodness. Thus some wildly deviant interpretations Int* are approximately as natural as or even more natural than the non-deviant interpretation Int. Moreover, the propositions we ordinarily entertain do not concern only *very* natural objects, properties and relations, for we do not ordinarily think in terms that figure in the fundamental laws of the universe. The proposition that this car is green does not cut nature at its most fundamental joints; this car is not a very natural object and greenness is not a very natural property. Nor are the properties of believing truly and desiring what is good for one very natural. At best, propositional attitude ascriptions proceed at a level of moderate naturalness. Thus the combination of constraints of internal coherence with considerations of naturalness is quite insufficient to explain why Int* is a hopeless interpretation.

Of course, evolution *does* to some extent favor believing what is true and desiring what is good for one. But one cannot understand

why it does so simply by appeal to internal constraints and considerations of naturalness. For that understanding, one must start with
a richer conception of belief and desire. More specifically, we need
external constraints on the relation between mental life and the
non-mental world. Much contemporary philosophy consists of
attempts to provide such constraints.

3

Attempts to impose external constraints on the relation between
mental life and the non-mental world may be roughly divided into
the molecular and the holistic.[6] Molecularists analyze mental contents
into constituents, and try to specify conditions for employing each
constituent in thought. For example, a simple theory of possession
conditions for concepts says that to possess the concept *mountain*
one must, under optimal conditions specified without ascription of
that very concept, be willing to judge *here is a mountain* if and only
if a mountain is present. A simple verificationist theory of meaning
states necessary and sufficient conditions for the sentence "Here is a
mountain" to be canonically verified (or assertable). A simple causal
theory of reference says that a thought token refers to mountains if
and only if it is causally related in a specified way to mountains. And
so on. More complex and sophisticated accounts can be developed
in the same spirit.

If a molecularist account could be made to work, it might support
many of the conclusions of this chapter. However, molecularist
accounts face major obstacles. For instance, it is hard for an account
that is intended to provide non-circular necessary conditions for
concept possession to say anything non-trivial about what the agent
does in non-optimal conditions, where ignorance and error are rife
even among those who possess the concepts at issue; yet it is hard
for an account to provide non-circular sufficient conditions for
concept possession if it says nothing non-trivial about what the
subject does in non-optimal conditions.

---

[6]   The terminology of "holism" and "molecularism" is hijacked from Dummett
(1975b) to make a slightly different distinction.

It is also hard to screen out the effects of the subject's background theory without circularity. As seen in earlier chapters, radical unorthodoxy is compatible with concept possession and linguistic understanding. For example, if the optimal conditions are specified without ascription of the concept *mountain*, then they can presumably be met when a revisionary metaphysician, a native English speaker with good eyesight and open eyes, dissents in good visibility from the sentence "Here is a mountain" in the middle of the Alps. The danger is that a molecularist possession condition would count her as lacking the concept *mountain*, a highly implausible result. By any reasonable standard she had the concept *mountain* before she developed her revisionary metaphysics; since she fully understood the English word "mountain," she knew that it meant *mountain*. Developing her revisionary metaphysics did not make her cease to understand the word "mountain"; she understands the word in the normal way as used by other speakers, and therefore knows that it means *mountain*; she still has the concept *mountain*. When she denies that there are mountains, she is consciously disagreeing with common sense, not talking past it. Similar problems plague verificationist theories of meaning. Not even causal theories of reference are free of such problems. Mountains may cease to cause tokenings of "mountain" in speakers with unorthodox background beliefs who continue to understand the word "mountain." Nor are causal connections always needed. Even for mountains, a community might think about them without ever having had any causal contact with them, by having causal contact with hills and envisaging mountains like hills, only bigger. As usual, attempts to preserve the necessity of the alleged condition for concept possession or linguistic understanding tend to undermine its non-circular sufficiency.

The history of molecularist programs gives little ground for optimism that such obstacles will eventually be overcome. That is not to imply that all molecularist claims are hopelessly false. Many of them seem to be true "for the most part." What is doubtful is that they can be replaced by strictly true claims within the spirit of a molecularist program.

The alternative to molecularism is holism. Although holism need not deny that thoughts have constituent structure, its constraints on thinking given thoughts apply at the level of the subject's total system of thoughts, not at the level of individual constituents; they are global rather than local. The most salient holistic proposal is Donald Davidson's principle of charity. According to Davidson (1974: 197): "Charity is forced on us; whether we like it or not, if we want to understand others, we must count them right in most matters." He argues that methodologically good interpretation imputes agreement in the main between interpreter and interpreted; there is no obstacle in principle to a methodologically good omniscient interpreter, agreement with whom guarantees truth; since the omniscient interpreter's interpretation is by hypothesis correct, correct interpretation imputes truth in the main (1977: 200–1). Thus, by Davidson's lights, revisionary metaphysicians are bad interpreters if they interpret ordinary people as in massive error, for example over the existence of mountains. Of course, a revisionary metaphysician might claim that ordinary people do not really believe that there are mountains, but that seems to be an even worse misinterpretation. Davidson's account directly implies a tendency for beliefs to be true.

Davidson's principle of charity evokes massive disagreement. However, it is not wholly to blame for the contentious conclusions that Davidson uses it to draw. It figures in his notorious argument against the very idea of mutually incommensurable conceptual schemes, alien ways of thought or untranslatable languages (1974). But that argument also makes both the verificationist assumption that other creatures have beliefs only if we can have good evidence that they have beliefs and the constructivist assumption that we can have good evidence that they have beliefs only if we can have good evidence as to which beliefs they have. Neither assumption follows from the principle that beliefs tend to be true. Neither assumption is warranted, for we are far from omniscient interpreters (compare Nagel 1986: 93–9). The aliens may be able to interpret each other even if we cannot interpret them. More generally, Davidson's application of the methodology of radical interpretation to the philosophy of language embodies a kind of ideal verificationism, on which agents have just the intentional states that a methodologically good interpreter with unlimited access to non-intentional data would ascribe to them. However, we could, as David Lewis (1974: 110–11) recommends, treat the predicament of the radical interpreter as merely a literary device for dramatizing the question: how do the intentional states of agents supervene on the non-intentional states of the world? The sense in which that question concerns the determination of content is metaphysical, not epistemological. In this spirit, we could consistently accept a principle of charity while allowing that alternative conceptual schemes are possible.[7]

If the role of the radical interpreter is inessential, so too is that of agreement between interpreter and interpreted. Truth is prior to agreement: the metaphysical version of Davidson's principle of charity requires that agents have mostly true beliefs. Other things equal, interpretation should maximize the ascribed proportion of true beliefs. That is in effect a constraint on reference for the constituents of beliefs or of the sentences that express them. Agreement is secondary; two agents with mostly true beliefs do not mostly disagree with each other, although they may have few beliefs in common, if they have different concerns, and may even tend to disagree over their limited common concerns.

Davidson's principle of charity is too loose to figure in an algorithm for reducing the intentional to the non-intentional. But present purposes do not force us to engage in the heroically ambitious quest for such a reduction. What we need are correct non-trivial principles about propositional attitudes that somehow link belief and truth, metaphysically rather than epistemologically. Such principles can fall far short of reducing the intentional to the non-intentional, even of fixing the supervenience of the former on the latter.

Even in its de-epistemologized, non-reductive version, Davidson's principle of charity remains highly contentious. Massive error seems genuinely possible for a brain envatted only months ago.[8] Some have responded by formulating revised principles that allow one to interpret another as in massive error when one would have been in massive error oneself in her circumstances. For example, Richard Grandy (1973: 443) proposes "as a pragmatic constraint on translation" a *principle of humanity*: "the condition that the imputed pattern of relations among beliefs, desires, and the world be as similar to our own as possible." Even if we treat the principle of humanity as a metaphysical constraint on what makes an ascription of content

---

[7] By contrast, McGinn (1986) treats radical interpretation as an epistemological problem. He explicitly allows for uninterpretable believers (367). For a recent discussion of Davidson on radical interpretation see McCulloch (2003: 94–108).

[8] Klein (1986) discusses of Davidson's treatment of skeptical scenarios. McCulloch (2003: 126–40) is a recent discussion of the difficulty of interpreting brains in vats.

correct, rather than an epistemological guide to plausible translation, it says nothing directly about any tendency for beliefs to be true. However, since each of our beliefs commits us to regarding it as true, and therefore as having that relation to the world, one could argue that the principle of humanity requires the beliefs of others to tend to have the same relation to the world, and therefore to be true too. Perhaps humanity implies at least a limited version of charity, although the vagueness of "similarity" between patterns of relations makes it hard to tell. But the anthropocentrism of the metaphysical principle of humanity is suspect. After all, humans are prone to peculiar logical and statistical fallacies: once we recognize a quirky design fault in ourselves, it would be perverse to prefer, on metaphysical principle, interpretations of non-human aliens that attribute the same design fault to them. Although humans are the clearest examples of rational agents with which we are familiar, we are also clear that there could be far more rational agents than we are. On their metaphysical reading, anthropocentric principles of charity implausibly imply that the very nature of content militates against the possibility of superhuman rationality.

Other principles of charity put a premium on rationality or coherence, conceived as conditions internal to the agent. But they do not explain the superiority of the sensible interpretation Int over the silly Int* above. Even those which enjoin the minimization of *inexplicable* error or ignorance rely on there being further principles, so far unspecified, for explaining error and ignorance when they are legitimately attributed: whatever those further principles are, they will do much of the work in specifying the relations between mind and world. We need to make a new start.

4

Suppose that Emanuel has an ill-founded faith in his ability to discern character and life-history in a face. On that basis he forms elaborate beliefs about passers-by, in which he is confident enough to bet large sums when the opportunity offers, which it rarely does. By sheer luck he has won such bets so far, which has increased his confidence in his powers, although many other beliefs he has formed in this way are in fact false. Now Emanuel sees a stranger, Celia, standing some distance away. Looking at her face, he judges "She is F, G, H, . . ."; he ascribes a character and life-history in considerable detail. In fact, none of it fits Celia. By pure coincidence, all of it fits someone else, Elsie, whom Emanuel has never seen or heard of. Does the pronoun "she" as used by Emanuel in this context refer to Celia or to Elsie? Which of them does he use it to express beliefs about? He accepts "She is standing in front of me," which is true if "she" refers to Celia but false if it refers to Elsie. However, he also accepts "She is F," "She is G," "She is H, . . . ," all of which are false if "she" refers to Celia but true if it refers to Elsie. We may assume that the latter group far outweighs the former. A principle of charity that crudely maximizes true belief or minimizes error therefore favors Elsie over Celia as the referent of the pronoun in that context. But that is a descriptive theory of reference gone mad. Emanuel has no beliefs about Elsie. He has many beliefs about Celia, most of them false. In virtue of what is Emanuel thinking about Celia rather than Elsie?

A causal theorist of reference will point out that Emanuel's use of "she" in this context is causally related to Celia. Of course, it may be causally related to Elsie too – she may have saved Celia's life by performing the plastic surgery on Celia's face that helped cause Emanuel's beliefs – but not in the right way for reference, whatever that is. In this case, the specific link is that Emanuel is perceptually attending to Celia and using "she" as a perceptual demonstrative. But to say that he is using "she" as a perceptual demonstrative is to say little more than that he is using it so as to refer to what he is perceptually attending to, and we may hope to say something more useful about what sets up this link between perception and reference. If the notion of perceptual attention is purely causal, and does not involve the notion of thinking about, in virtue of what is Emanuel thinking about that to which he has this causal relation? If, on the other hand, the notion of perceptual attention is not purely causal, and does already involve the notion of thinking about, in virtue of what is Emanuel perceptually attending to Celia? Although it is somewhat obscure just what such "in virtue of" questions are demanding, we do not simply want to meet them with silence.

A natural idea is this. The perceptual link from Celia to Emanuel matters because it is a channel for *knowledge*. If "she" refers to Celia, then, in the circumstances, Emanuel expresses knowledge when he says "She is standing in front of me," although of course not when he says "She is F," "She is G," "She is H, . . . ," since they are false. If "she" refers to Elsie, then of course Emanuel does not express knowledge when he says "She is standing in front of me," since it is false, but he also fails to express knowledge when he says "She is F," "She is G," "She is H, . . . ," even though they are true. Emanuel is in a position to know of Celia that she is standing in front of him; he is not in a position to know of Elsie that she is F, G, H, . . . The same contrast holds, more fundamentally, at the level of thought. The assignment of Elsie as the referent in Emanuel's beliefs gains no credit from making them true because it does not make them knowledge. The assignment of Celia wins because it does better with respect to knowledge, even though it does worse with respect to true belief.

Such examples are of course just the analogue for demonstrative pronouns of examples Kripke and Putnam used to refute descriptive cluster theories of reference for proper names and natural kind terms. In effect, such theories are special cases of a truth-maximizing principle of charity. One fundamental error in descriptive theories of reference is to try to make true belief do the work of knowledge.

As for causal theories of reference, the postulated link between knowledge and reference suggests a schematic explanation of both their successes and their failures. Roughly: a causal connection to an object (property, relation, . . .) is a channel for reference to it if and only if it is a channel for the acquisition of knowledge about the object (property, relation, . . .). Often, a causal connection is a channel for both. Equally, a non-causal connection, such as a definite description, to an object (property, relation, . . .) is a channel for reference to it if and only if it is a channel for the acquisition of knowledge about the object (property, relation, . . .). Sometimes, a non-causal connection is a channel for both. It was in any case clear that causal theories of reference and causal theories of knowledge were closely linked in their successes and failures. Both faced the problem of deviant causal chains, of specifying which causal chains carry the relevant intentional link. Both faced the problem of mathematics, which appears to exhibit both non-causal reference to abstract objects and non-causal knowledge about them.

The proposal is to replace true belief by knowledge in a principle of charity constitutive of content. But how can doing so help with the objection that massive error is possible? Presumably knowledge implies true belief. Unless the agent is inconsistent, any case of massive error is also a case of massive ignorance. At first sight, the objection only makes the problem worse. However, it is independently obvious that our knowledge is dwarfed by our ignorance. The right charitable injunction for an assignment of reference is to maximize knowledge, not to minimize ignorance (which is always infinite).[9]

Suppose that under some assignment of reference a brain in a vat has mainly true beliefs about electrical impulses in the computer that controls it. If we are still disinclined to accept the assignment, a natural reason to give is that the brain is not in a position to know about the electrical impulses. If we are inclined to accept the assignment, we probably think that the brain is in a position to know about them.

Here is a simpler case. A fair coin was tossed and landed heads. The agent cannot see or otherwise know which way up it landed, but is easily convinced by what are really just his own guesses. He sincerely asserts "Toda." Is a point in favor of interpreting "Toda" to mean "It landed heads" rather than "It landed tails" that it has him speaking and believing truly rather than falsely? Surely not. The true belief would no more be knowledge than the false belief would be. Although Davidson's principle of charity does not imply that "Toda" cannot mean "It landed tails," since data from other cases might outweigh the current data, it does imply that this case provides a defeasible consideration in favor of interpreting "Toda" as "It landed heads" rather than "It landed tails," which it does not. The point extends to less irrational beliefs. If we interpret someone as judging on purely probabilistic grounds that ticket n did not win the lottery, our interpretation gains or loses no credit dependent on whether ticket n did in fact win, since either way the agent in the circumstances could not have known that it did not win.[10]

Is knowledge maximization in danger of absurdly imputing knowledge of quantum mechanics to Stone Age people? They were in no

[9] The substitution of knowledge for truth in a principle of charity is proposed in connection with a knowledge-based account of assertion by Williamson (2000a: 267).
[10] An interpretation on which the agent believes that ticket n did not win might do better than one on which the agent believes that ticket n won, even though neither constitutes knowledge, if the former attributes more knowledge of chances to the agent than the latter does.

position to know about quantum mechanics, so even on an interpretation on which they referred to quantum mechanical properties and relations they would not know about those properties and relations. Objective limits on what subjects are in a position to know appropriately constrain the maximization of knowledge by the assignment of reference. Unless it is raining, one does not know that it is raining. Even if it is raining, one may lack the kind of causal contact with the rain one needs in order to know that it is raining. The compositional structure of sentences and thoughts further constrains the ascription of knowledge, because the inferential processes in which subjects engage are sensitive to that structure: to interpret those processes as yielding knowledge, one must interpret them as valid inferences. Knowledge maximization need not make the ascription of knowledge come too cheap. By contrast, Davidson's principle of charity gives good marks to an interpretation for having Stone Age people assent to many truths of quantum mechanics, if it happens to fit the compositional structure of their language.

One might still fear that the knowledge maximization principle is over-charitable. Suppose, for example, that I can see only a small part of a ball, the rest of which is hidden by some obstacle. I judge of the ball "It is red." Unknown to me, the rest of the ball is green, so that the ball as a whole does not qualify as red. I falsely believe, and do not know, that the ball is red; at best I know that the visible part of the ball is red. Does knowledge maximization imply, falsely, that the visual demonstrative "it" refers to just the presently visible part of the ball rather than to the whole ball? Ask first why the visual demonstrative does not refer to the ball part. One answer is that since the ball is a more natural object than the ball part, it is a more eligible referent; I refer to the ball by default because I have done nothing special to divert reference to the ball part. Equally, then, I have failed to do the individuative work required to know anything about the ball part. By contrast, I can express some knowledge about the ball, for example, by "It is there," if "it" refers to the ball. An alternative answer is that I have positively individuated the ball, for example because my basic judgment was "That thing is red," in a thick sense of "thing" applicable to the ball but not to the ball part, from which in effect I derived "It is red" using the identity "It is that thing." But then "It is red" expresses knowledge only if "That thing is red" and "It is that thing" express knowledge and the inference is valid, so "it" and "that thing" remain constant in reference across premises and conclusion. But if "it" refers to the ball part on both occurrences, then both premises are false, since "that thing" refers to the ball, so the conclusion fails to express knowledge. By contrast, if "it" refers anaphorically on "that thing" to the ball, "It is that thing" expresses knowledge, even though the other premise and the conclusion are false. Of course, there are further possibilities. But it is already appreciable that the holistic character of the considerations gives plenty of scope for the knowledge maximization principle to get the right answer, arguably for the right reasons.

Another doubt about knowledge maximization concerns variants of the Celia/Elsie case above in which Emanuel knows independently that Elsie is F, G, H, . . . However, he can still use "she" as a visual demonstrative to refer to Celia in judging "She is F," "She is G," "She is H, . . . ," thereby expressing false beliefs about Celia rather than knowledge about Elsie, because those judgments are not causally based on his independent knowledge of Elsie, and therefore fail to express that knowledge. Of course, in a further variant of the case, Emanuel makes the identity judgment "She is Elsie," and then judges "She is F," "She is G," "She is H, . . . ," on the basis of inference from the identity judgment and the premises "Elsie is F," "Elsie is G," "Elsie is H, . . . ," so that his independent knowledge of Elsie is causally active in his reaching the conclusions. Even in that case, knowledge maximization still does not warrant assigning Elsie as the referent of the visual demonstrative "she." If knowledge is sensitive to differences in mode of presentation, and "she" is associated with a visual mode of presentation, then the judgment "She is Elsie" does not constitute knowledge; consequently, the further judgments derived from it also fail to constitute knowledge. On the other hand, if knowledge is not sensitive to differences in mode of presentation, then assigning Elsie as the referent of "she" merely makes the judgments "She is F," "She is G," "She is H, . . . ," express the same knowledge as "Elsie is F," "Elsie is G," "Elsie is H, . . . ," already express; no knowledge is gained. Moreover, that assignment also makes judgments such as "She is standing in front of me" fail to constitute knowledge, whereas they do constitute knowledge on the assignment of Celia as the referent of "she." Hence the correct assignment (Celia) involves the ascription of more knowledge than the incorrect one

(Elsie) does. Thus knowledge maximization is consistent with a correct interpretation of such cases.

Perhaps the underlying worries about knowledge maximization can be captured in a more abstract form. Knowing is itself an intentional state. As already emphasized, the present aim is not to reduce the intentional to the non-intentional. But to explain reference by appeal to the intentional features of knowledge states – which objects, properties, and relations they are about – is in effect to explain reference in terms of itself. In order to avoid such trivialization, we must avoid helping ourselves to those intentional features, and instead concentrate on the imputed reliability of the subject (in some appropriate sense) under various assignments of reference (where such assignments assign reference across many possible worlds). But if that is what we have to maximize, surely the winner is likely to be some artificial cooked-up assignment quite different from what is pretheoretically correct. For example, a highly context-sensitive assignment may make the Stone Age people reliable about matters of quantum mechanics. Similarly, some assignment will make the victim of a skeptical scenario come out thinking reliably about their own brain states rather than unreliably about the wider world. And so on. How can knowledge maximization avoid such false consequences without collapsing into triviality?

We take such assignments of reference to be incorrect because we take them to be gerrymandered, unnatural, insensitive to the underlying similarities and differences, not cutting at the joints. The corresponding ascriptions of knowledge make it an equally artificial attitude. In response to such examples, we should therefore insist that the relation to be maximized is a natural one: doubtless not a *perfectly* natural one, for the most basic structure of the world is not mental, but natural by the standards of mentality. Such a bias towards naturalness in the objects of reference has independent support (Lewis 1983b, Weatherson 2003, Hawthorne 2006: 53–69). Here it is extended to the relation of reference itself, by inheritance from the relation of knowledge. It holds the anti-skeptical effect of knowledge maximization within reasonable limits.

The more abundant ontology is, the more objects, properties, and relations there are, the more scope there is for an assignment of reference under which we know. Conversely, the sparser ontology is, the fewer objects, properties, and relations there are, the greater the danger that we do not know under any assignment. But the correlation is imperfect, for a sparse ontology sometimes facilitates knowledge by reducing the number of wrong answers clustered around the right one and hard to distinguish from it. Knowledge maximization tilts the playing field in our favor without guaranteeing us victory.

Is it surprising that reference maximizes knowledge? Reference concerns what mental states and acts are about. Knowledge is one mental state among many. Why should it play a privileged role in determining what all of them are about? One answer is that knowledge is not just one mental state among many. A creature that is not aware of anything at all has no mental life. It lacks genuine intelligence. Although intelligent life does not consist solely of awareness, it is intelligent only because appropriately related to awareness of something. But to be aware is to know: one is aware *that* P if and only if one knows that P, and one could hardly be aware *of* anything without some capacity to know *that* something is the case. Intelligent life is life appropriately related to intelligent action, and intelligent action is action appropriately related to knowledge. In a paradigm of intelligent action, given a desire that P, one knowingly does A, knowing that if one does A then P. One can believe that one does A and that if one does A then P, even truly, without knowing, but the action is defective in such cases; they are to be understood in relation to non-defective cases. The function of intelligent action involves the application of knowledge to realize the agent's ends. In unfavorable circumstances, only mere beliefs are available, and intentional action does not function properly, although with good luck it may still achieve the desired end, just as other defective processes sometimes issue in the intended product.[11]

---

[11]   Williamson (2000a) has more on the associated conception of mind and knowledge. The idea that all thinking qualifies as such by being appropriately related to knowing was advocated by another Wykeham Professor of Logic, John Cook Wilson (1926, vol. I: 35–40, also for the view that knowledge is indefinable). He defends a neo-Aristotelian version of common sense realism on which ordinary language has a central role in metaphysics. Of the "examination of the meaning of grammatical forms" and the consideration of "certain distinctions of the kind called metaphysical" he says "The two investigations are necessarily connected with one another; for since the sentence or statement describes the nature of objects and not any attitude of ours to the objects described, in the way of apprehension or opinion, its meaning is wholly objective, in the sense that we have already given to objective. That is, it is about

When conditions are unfavorable, the agent is in no position to know anything much, just as a victim of total paralysis may be in no position to do anything much. Intentional action may be limited to pursuing a line of thought. For a brain in a vat, both knowledge and action may shrink to the internal: but that pathological case does not reveal their underlying nature, for it does not show them to be equally shrunken in more normal cases. Rather, the pathological cases are parasitic on the normal ones.

Given the central role of knowledge in intelligent life, the intimate relation between knowledge and reference is hardly surprising. Reference maximizes knowledge because its role is to serve knowledge, not to impose any independent limitation on it. Although maximizing knowledge is not equivalent to maximizing true belief, the nature of reference grounds a general, highly defeasible tendency for beliefs to constitute knowledge, and therefore to be true.

5

On a more internalist proposal, the nature of reference is to maximize justified belief rather than knowledge, where justified beliefs can be false; charity is often presented as a principle of rationality maximization. But such internalism makes the bearing of reference on justification obscure. Suppose that I have a few factual memories of a brief acquaintance, which I express using the pronoun "he." The assignment of one reference rather than another to "he" seems to make no difference to the internalist justification of my memory beliefs; it makes an obvious difference to whether they constitute knowledge. Similarly, internalist considerations of justified belief are much less likely than externalist considerations of knowledge to explain why the silly interpretation Int* in Section 2 is worse than the sensible

---

something apprehended, in the case of knowledge for instance, and not about our apprehension of it" (1926, vol. I: 149). In respect of the fundamental role assigned to knowing, both Williamson (2000a) and the present book belong to a tradition that runs from Cook Wilson to Prichard and others, then to J.L. Austin and later to John McDowell; see Marion (2000). That there are also very significant differences between these philosophers hardly needs saying.

connection Int, for the permutation of contents preserves internal coherence but not knowledge.

On an uneasy compromise, what matters for reference is neither knowledge nor internalist justification but an intermediate standard of non-factive externalist justification. That still gets it wrong, because the failure of a brain in a vat to refer to a new object in its external environment is far better explained by its incapacity for knowledge of it than by its incapacity for justified (and perhaps true) beliefs about it, for on the supposition that it has beliefs about the object there need be no further obstacle to classifying them as justified in the relevant sense By contrast, the full-blooded external involvement of knowledge exactly suits it to constrain reference.

Can the semantic significance of knowledge be understood within Davidson's framework? He tries to recover a plausible epistemology by extracting epistemological consequences from his principle of charity by appeal to the immunity from massive error that it is supposed to grant. That immunity is holistic: it is consistent with the falsity of almost any given one of our beliefs, given enough compensating truth elsewhere in the system. For example, my belief that I have hands enjoys no immunity from error. The supposed general immunity from massive error does not explain how I know that I have hands: likewise for most of what we ordinarily take ourselves to know. Davidson adds an appeal to causal constraints on reference in simple cases, but formulates the constraints too crudely to permit any straightforward connection with knowledge (Davidson 1991: 196–7). Even if my belief that P is caused by what it is about, I may fail to know that P because the causal chain is somehow deviant. When Davidson tries to explain how his principle of charity yields knowledge, he appears to rely on something like the pre-Gettier assumption that justified true belief is knowledge.[12]

---

[12] "There is at least a presumption that we are right about the contents of our own minds; so in the cases where we are right, we have knowledge" (Davidson 1991: 194); "Anyone who accepts perceptual externalism knows he cannot be systematically deceived about whether there are such things as cows, people, water, stars, and chewing gum. Knowing why this is the case, he must recognize situations in which he is justified in believing he is seeing water or a cow. In those cases where he is right, he knows he is seeing water or a cow" (Davidson 1991: 201). See also Davidson (1983).

A subtler attempt to extract knowledge from Davidson's principle of charity exploits beliefs that one knows. Very often, when one believes that P, one also believes that one knows that P.[13] If one believes truly that one knows that P, then one does know that P. Does maximizing true belief therefore indirectly maximize knowledge too? The detour through second-order belief is unpromising. First, it depends on the assumption that the relevant agents are to be interpreted as believing that they know. Of course, *we* often believe that we know; for that matter, we often know. But the aim was to derive the conclusion that agents in general often know from a truth-maximizing principle of charity; that agents in general often believe that they know has not been derived from such a principle. Second, even granted that agents believe that they know, Davidson's principle attributes no special status to beliefs of that form; an interpretation might sacrifice them all as false and still maximize true belief overall by making enough other beliefs true. Third, the account does not generate attributions of knowledge to simple creatures who lack the concept of knowledge and therefore cannot believe that they know; surely they can have knowledge without having the concept of knowledge.[14] Truth maximization lacks most of the epistemological rewards of knowledge maximization.

Quine endorses as a canon of translation the epistemological-sounding maxim "Save the obvious" (1970: 82; compare 1960: 59): do not interpret the natives as dissenting from obvious truths. On that

[13]   The principle cannot be exceptionless, otherwise having any belief involves having infinitely many beliefs of increasing complexity.

[14]   Davidson might have denied that one can have knowledge without the concept of knowledge, for he denies that one can have beliefs without the concept of belief: "Someone cannot have a belief unless he understands the possibility of being mistaken, and this requires grasping the contrast between truth and error – true belief and false belief" (1975: 170). Whether or not he would extend it to knowledge, Davidson's argument is unconvincing, for it conflates *de re* and *de dicto* readings. Grant for the sake of argument that, to believe that P, one must grasp the contrast between the state of affairs that P, which is in fact the condition for the belief to be true, and the state of affairs that not P, which is in fact the condition for the belief to be false (the *de re* reading). Even so, Davidson does not explain why one must grasp it *as* the contrast between the condition for the belief to be true and the condition for it to be false (the *de dicto* reading), which is what he needs. Thus he leaves it obscure why a creature with the concept of negation could not have a belief without the concept of belief.

basis he argues that apparent deviations in logic are mere artifacts of bad translation. Although this appears to invoke a knowledge-related standard of charity, like the principle of knowledge maximization, Quine insists on interpreting "obvious" behavioristically rather than epistemologically.[15] His intended maxim is that translation should preserve general assent. Without further argument, we cannot conclude that sentences that enjoy general assent are true, for we can assume neither that every sentence to which speakers of another language assent can be translated into English nor that every sentence to which speakers of English assent is true – naturally, it is harder for us, as speakers of English, to produce a counterexample. Like Grandy's principle of humanity, Quine's maxim on its behavioral reading tends to project our design faults onto others. For example, it discourages us from translating a sentence to which the natives universally assent by a simple logical truth from which many speakers of English dissent through intellectual confusion. On an epistemological reading of "obvious," the maxim is not vulnerable to that criticism, for confused speakers can dissent from what is obvious.

We do better to start with the notion of knowledge in the explanatory order.

6

A picture of the mind has been sketched, with the broadest strokes, on which the nature of reference nudges belief towards the status of knowledge, and therefore of truth. That helps put the burden of proof on judgment skeptics to argue that their radical scenarios deserve to be taken more seriously than do the radical scenarios for skepticism about perception. Although we can allow that scenarios of both sorts are metaphysically possible, much more than that is needed to justify serious doubt. The burden of proof on the judgment skeptic is particu-

---

[15]   "I must stress that I am using the word 'obvious' in an ordinary behavioral sense, with no epistemological overtones. When I call '1 + 1 = 2' obvious to a community I mean only that everyone, nearly enough, will unhesitatingly assent to it, for whatever reason; and when I call 'It is raining' obvious in particular circumstances I mean that everyone will assent to it in those circumstances" (Quine 1970: 82).

larly heavy when the proposed scenarios make vast ranges of common beliefs false or at least not knowledge, as many of them do.[16]

A judgment skeptic might respond: "Granted, when we believe **p**, we often – but not always – know **p**. That we believe **p** should therefore be treated as good but defeasible evidence for **p**. It is just one more part of the total body of evidence on which philosophical theories should be evaluated." This response depends on the fallacy, diagnosed in the previous chapter, of psychologizing evidence. It perversely ignores the evidential role of **p** itself, as opposed to that of the fact that we believe **p**. After all, if we do know **p**, would it not be negligent not to use that knowledge in evaluating a philosophical theory to which it is relevant? Philosophy is hard enough already: why make it even more difficult by forbidding ourselves to bring some of our knowledge to bear? You are not obliged to fight with one arm tied behind your back.[17]

The judgment skeptic might reply that, if we know **p** without knowing that we know **p**, the knowledge does not really help. But that response is doubly inadequate. First, it gives no more reason to deny that we know that we know **p** than to deny that we know **p** in the relevant cases. Although we cannot expect to have infinitely many iterations of knowledge, for more than computational reasons (Williamson 2000a: 114–34), that general point merely shows that we must sometimes simply apply our knowledge, without first checking whether we know, for otherwise we get stuck in an infinite regress of checks. That is the second problem for the judgment skeptic's envisaged reply. It gave us no evidence that we are entitled to rely on the premise **p** in philosophical discussion only if we know that we know **p**.

When we know, there is something non-trivial to be said about how we know. But we may know **p**, and even know that we know **p**, without knowing how we know **p**. For instance, we may know that we know the truth of some logical or mathematical axioms without knowing how we know their truth. Similarly, the epistemic role of elegance and simplicity in theoretical physics seems as indis-

---

[16]   The case of folk physics does not constitute a straightforward skeptical scenario, for folk physics plays a role in generating much knowledge of particular facts about our environment.

[17]   See Williamson (2000a: 184–208) for defense and development of the conception of our total evidence as everything that we know.

pensable as it is hard to explain. But for many philosophically contentious facts, the question "How do you know?" is not unusually puzzling. There is no distinctive mystery as to how we know that there are mountains in Switzerland. We can explain how we know, typically by describing the process by which we acquired the knowledge, without having to convince the skeptic who doubts that we know.

Even those who know **p** can sometimes be too dogmatic about **p** in this sense: their summary dismissal of objections to **p** manifests general cognitive dispositions whose overall tendency is to limit their knowledge and increase their error, by preventing them from learning from experience or criticism.[18] But that does not show that they acted wrongly in treating **p** as evidence in this particular case. There will always be cases in which bad dispositions produce right actions and good dispositions produce wrong ones; since philosophers question fundamental assumptions, they are particularly liable to get themselves into such cases.

The knowledge maximization principle is not itself intended as an answer to the question "How do you know?" The knowledge maximized may have been acquired by quite familiar means of perception, memory, testimony, inference, and imagination. The proper response to judgment skepticism is not to postulate a separate means to knowledge to underpin all the others but rather to challenge the skeptical idea that they need such underpinning. The supposed function of the underpinning would be to rule out the scenarios that motivate judgment skepticism. But a good answer to the question "How do you know **p**?" need not specifically address far-fetched skeptical scenarios for **p**, since knowing **p** does not require specifically addressing them. Knowledge maximization is a factor, typically unnoticed by judgment skeptics, that makes their scenarios more far-fetched than they realize.

More naturalistically inclined judgment skeptics try to induce a crisis of confidence in present common sense by pointing towards a present or future scientific outlook that stands to present common sense as the latter stands to a Stone Age outlook. But the analogy rebounds against judgment skepticism. For although it is plausible

[18] One can know p and acquire counter-evidence to p that is significant, but not significant enough to make one cease to know p.

that Stone Age people had many false beliefs about the general nature of the world, it is at least as plausible that they had significant knowledge of their local environment. Knowledge maximization implies that our ancestors had some primitive knowledge as soon as they had some primitive beliefs; it is not as though archaeology suggests otherwise. Again, if it is plausible that some non-human animals have primitive beliefs, it is equally plausible that they have some primitive knowledge.

Consider this analogue for observational evidence of the judgment skeptic's response to knowledge maximization: "Granted, when we have a perceptual belief in **p**, we often – but not always – know **p**. That we have a perceptual belief in **p** should therefore be treated as good but defeasible evidence for **p**. It is just one more part of the total body of evidence on which scientific theories should be evaluated." What this response perversely ignores is the evidential role of **p** itself, as opposed to that of the fact that we have a perceptual belief in **p**. After all, if we do know **p**, would it not be negligent not to use that knowledge in evaluating a scientific theory to which it is relevant? It would not advance science to insist that scientists' evidence cannot include the fact that 19 out of 20 rats fed the substance died within 24 hours, but only the fact that the scientist had the perceptual belief that 19 out of 20 rats fed the substance died (only the former fact leads itself to statistical analysis). Such claims about past beliefs are not peculiarly foundational. Indeed, they are less amenable to public checking by the scientific community than are claims about the actual outcomes of experiments. Of course, it may later turn out that a disgruntled lab technician fed the rats the wrong substance, but the proper response to such remote possibilities is to backtrack if one of them is found to obtain, not to make a futile attempt in advance to identify evidence for which backtracking will never be required in even the remotest eventualities.

In philosophy as in natural science, our evidence consists of ordinary human knowledge. We have no general guarantee that we know everything we think we know. Our evidence is more contested in philosophy than in natural science. The philosopher's predicament is somewhat like that which would face natural scientists if accusations of falsified evidence were vastly more common in science than they currently are. Whatever the discipline, when someone disputes the evidence, it is often better to look for common ground on which to pursue the argument than to ride roughshod over the objections. For that temporary purpose, we may refrain from treating the disputed evidence as evidence; that does not entail that it should never have been treated as evidence in the first place. Moreover, as we have seen, the search for common ground can be taken too far, especially with a reckless opponent who does not scruple to challenge any inconvenient evidence. An indiscriminate skeptic can challenge whatever we offer as evidence, by always demanding a proof; that should not drive us to suspend all our evidence. At some point we are entitled to hold on to what we know, and apply it.

Our evidence in philosophy consists of a miscellaneous mass of knowledge, expressed in terms of all kinds, some from ordinary language, some from the theoretical vocabulary of various disciplines. Some of it consists of knowledge about our own mental states; most of it does not. Whatever we know is legitimate evidence. Inevitably, we make mistakes, treating as known what is unknown, or as unknown what is known. The principle of knowledge maximization helps our practice survive our critical reflection, by reassuring us that knowing is a natural state for believers, not an anomalous achievement. In general, our practice makes sense, which of course does not excuse us from meeting particular challenges on their merits. This messy epistemological predicament in which philosophers find themselves is not deeply different from the messy epistemological predicament of all human inquiry.

Afterword
Must Do Better

Imagine a philosophy conference in Presocratic Greece. The hot question is: what are things made of? Followers of Thales say that everything is made of water, followers of Anaximenes that everything is made of air, and followers of Heraclitus that everything is made of fire. Nobody is quite clear what these claims mean; some question whether the founders of the respective schools ever made them. But among the groupies there is a buzz about all the recent exciting progress. The mockers and doubters make plenty of noise too. They point out that no resolution of the dispute between the schools is in sight. They diagnose Thales, Anaximenes, and Heraclitus as suffering from a tendency to over-generalize. We can intelligibly ask what bread is made of, or what houses are made of, but to ask what *things in general* are made of is senseless, some suggest, because the question is posed without any conception of how to verify an answer; language has gone on holiday. Paleo-pragmatists invite everyone to relax, forget their futile pseudo-inquiries, and do something useful instead.

The mockers and doubters had it easy, but we know now that in at least one important respect they were wrong. With however much confusion, Thales and the rest were asking one of the best questions ever to have been asked, a question that has painfully led to much of modern science. To have abandoned it two and a half thousand years ago on grounds of its conceptual incoherence or whatever would have been a feeble and unnecessary surrender to despair, philistinism, cowardice, or indolence. Nevertheless, it is equally clear that the methods of investigation used by the Presocratics were utterly inadequate to their ambitions. If an intellectual tradition applied just those methods to those questions for two and a half millennia, which is far from unimaginable, it might well be very little the wiser at the end. Much of the progress made since the Presocratics consists in the development of good methods for bringing evidence to bear on questions that, when first asked, appear hopelessly elusive or naïve. Typically, of course, making progress also involves refining and clarifying the initial question: but the relevant refinements and clarifications cannot all be foreseen at the beginning. They emerge in the process of attempting to answer the original rough question, and would not emerge otherwise.

The Presocratics were forerunners of both modern philosophy and modern natural science; they did not distinguish natural science from philosophy. For positivists, the moral of the story is that natural science had to be separated from philosophy, and marked out as the field for observation, measurement, and experiment, before it could make serious progress. There is doubtless something right about that moral, although as it stands it hardly does justice to the significance of armchair methods in natural science, such as the use of mathematics and of thought experiments, for example by Galileo and Einstein. Moreover, the positivist moral misses a deeper methodological point. The case of the Presocratics shows that one cannot always tell in advance which questions will be fruitful to pursue. Even if a community starts with no remotely adequate idea of how to go about answering a question, it does not follow that the question is meaningless or not worth addressing. That goes for the questions we now classify as philosophical as much as it does for those we now classify as empirical or natural-scientific.

The opponents of systematic philosophical theorizing might reply that they are not judging philosophical questions in advance; they are judging them after two and a half millennia of futile attempts to answer them. Of course, it is an important issue how similar our philosophical questions are to those of ancient Greece, or even to those of Enlightenment Europe. Nevertheless, philosophy has been going too long as an intellectual tradition separate from natural science (although sometimes interacting with it) for the question "How much progress has it made?" to be simply dismissed as premature.

We should not be too pessimistic about the answer, at least concerning the broad, heterogeneous intellectual tradition we conveniently label "analytic philosophy." In many areas of philosophy, we know much more in 2007 than was known in 1957; much more was known in 1957 than in 1907; much more was known in 1907 than was known in 1857. As in natural science, something can be collectively known in a community even if it is occasionally denied by eccentric members of that community. Although fundamental disagreement is conspicuous in most areas of philosophy, the best theories in a given area are in most cases far better developed in 2007 than the best theories in that area were in 1957, and so on. Much of the knowledge is fairly specific in content. For example, we know far more about possibility and necessity than was known before the development of modern modal logic and associated work in philosophy. It is widely known in 2007 and was not widely known in 1957 that contingency is not equivalent to *a posteriority*, and that claims of contingent or temporary identity involve the rejection of standard logical laws. The principle that every truth is possibly necessary can now be shown to entail that every truth is necessary by a chain of elementary inferences in a perspicuous notation unavailable to Hegel (every instance of the schema $A \rightarrow \Box A$ is derivable from instances of the schema $A \rightarrow \Diamond\Box A$ in the weak modal system T). We know much about the costs and benefits of analyzing possibility and necessity in terms of possible worlds, even if we do not yet know whether such an analysis is correct.[1]

Another example: Far more is known in 2007 about truth than was known in 1957, as a result of technical work by philosophical and mathematical logicians such as Saul Kripke, Solomon Feferman, Anil Gupta, Vann McGee, Volker Halbach, and many others on how close a predicate in a language can come to satisfying a full disquotational schema for that very language without incurring semantic

---

[1]   This guarded optimism about philosophical progress is consistent with the pessimism in Williamson (2000a) about the prospects for the post-Gettier program of analyzing the concept of knowledge and similar programs of analyzing other philosophically significant concepts. Such programs did make progress in clarifying the relations between the concepts under study (and between the things to which those concepts refer). What they failed to make plausible was that the eventual outcome of such progress would be anything like an analysis in the intended sense (necessary and sufficient conditions stated in non-circular terms, perhaps meeting further conditions). Take any concept that is indefinable in the relevant sense: the vain program of analyzing it in terms of more basic concepts, if conducted by able and honest people over several decades, would lead to some progress of this kind.

paradoxes. Their results have significant and complex implications, not yet fully absorbed, for current debates concerning deflationism and minimalism about truth (see Halbach (2001) for a recent example). One clear lesson is that claims about truth need to be formulated with extreme precision, not out of knee-jerk pedantry but because in practice correct general claims about truth often turn out to differ so subtly from provably incorrect claims that arguing in impressionistic terms is a hopelessly unreliable method. Unfortunately, much philosophical discussion of truth is still conducted in a programmatic, vague, and technically uninformed spirit whose products inspire little confidence.

In 1957, Michael Dummett was about to open his campaign to put the debate between realism and anti-realism, as he conceived it, at the centre of philosophy. The campaign had a strong methodological component. Intractable metaphysical disputes (for example, about time) were to be resolved by being reduced to questions in the philosophy of language about the proper form for a semantic theory of the relevant expressions (for example, tense markers). The realist's semantic theory would identify the meaning of an expression with its contribution to the truth conditions of declarative sentences in which it occurred. The anti-realist's semantic theory would identify the meaning with the expression's contribution to the assertability conditions of those sentences. Instead of shouting slogans at each other, Dummett's realist and anti-realist would busy themselves in developing systematic compositional semantic theories of the appropriate type, which could then be judged and compared by something like scientific standards. But that is not what happened.

True, over recent decades truth-conditional semantics for natural languages has developed out of philosophical logic and the philosophy of language into a flourishing branch of empirical linguistics. Frege already had the fundamental conception of compositional truth-conditional semantics, in which expressions refer to items in the mostly non-linguistic world, the reference of a complex expression is a function of the reference of its constituents, and the reference of a sentence determines its truth value. But Frege was more concerned to apply that conception to ideally precise and perspicuous artificial languages than to messy natural ones. The systematic application of compositional truth-conditional semantics to natural languages goes back to Richard Montague (under the influence of

Carnap) in its intensional form and has been mediated in linguistics by Barbara Partee and others. In its extensional form, it goes back to Donald Davidson (under the influence of Tarski) and has been mediated in linguistics by Jim Higginbotham and others. Needless to say, that crude schema does no justice to the richness of recent work and the variety of contributors to it (in both departments of philosophy and departments of linguistics), which one can check by looking at any decent handbook of contemporary semantic theory as a branch of linguistics. Surprisingly, however, most participants in the Dummett-inspired debates between realism and anti-realism have shown little interest in the success of truth-conditional semantics, judged as a branch of empirical linguistics. Instead, they have tended to concentrate on Dummett's demand for "non-circular" explanations of what understanding a sentence with a given truth condition "consists in," when the speaker cannot verify or falsify that condition. That demand is motivated more by preconceived philosophical reductionism than by the actual needs of empirical linguistics. Thus the construction and assessment of specific truth-conditional semantic theories has almost disappeared from sight in the debate on realism and anti-realism.

As for assertability-conditional semantics, it began with one more or less working paradigm: Heyting's intuitionistic account of the compositional semantics of mathematical language in terms of the condition for something to be a proof of a given sentence. The obvious and crucial challenge was to generalize that account to empirical language: as a first step, to develop a working assertability-conditional semantics for a toy model of some small fragment of empirical language. But that challenge was shirked. Anti-realists preferred to polish their formulations of the grand program rather than getting down to the hard and perhaps disappointing task of trying to carry it out in practice. The suggestion that the program's almost total lack of empirical success in the semantics of natural languages might constitute some evidence that it is mistaken in principle would be dismissed as crass.

Some participants in the debate denied any need for anti-realists to develop their own semantic theories of a distinctive form. For, it was proposed, anti-realists could take over truth-conditional semantic theories by interpreting "true" to mean assertable or verifiable at the limit of inquiry, or some such epistemic account of truth (Wright

1993: 403–25). But that proposal is quite contrary to Dummett's original arguments. For they require the key semantic concept in the anti-realistic semantics, the concept in terms of which the recursive compositional clauses for atomic expressions are stated, to be decidable, in the sense that the speaker is always in a position to know whether it applies in a given case. That is what allows anti-realists to claim that, unlike realists, they can give a non-circular account of what understanding a sentence consists in: a disposition to assert it when and only when its assertability condition obtains. But it is supposed to be common ground between realists and anti-realists that truth is not always decidable. A speaker may understand a sentence without being in a position either to recognize it as true or to recognize it as not true. I can understand the sentence "There was once life on Mars," even though I have neither warrant to assert "There was once life on Mars" nor warrant to assert "There was never life on Mars." The point is particularly clear in the intuitionistic semantics for mathematical language. The key concept in the compositional semantics is the concept p *is a proof of* s, which is decidable on the intuitionistic view because to understand a sentence is to associate it with an effective procedure for recognizing whether any given putative proof is a proof (in some canonical sense) of it. By contrast, what serves as the intuitionistic concept of truth is not the dyadic concept p *is a proof of* s nor even the monadic concept s *has been proved* but the monadic concept s *has a proof* or s *is provable*. According to intuitionists, we understand many mathematical sentences (such as "There are seven consecutive 7s in the decimal expansion of π") without having a procedure for recognizing whether they are provable. We understand them because we can recognize of any given putative proof, once presented to us, whether it is indeed a proof of them. Nor can we replace "true" in a truth-conditional semantics by "has been proved" (treated as decidable), because that would reduce the semantic clause for negation (that the negation of a sentence s is true if and only if s is not true) to the claim that the negation of s has been proved if and only if s has not been proved, which is uncontroversially false whenever s has not yet been decided.

Dummett's requirement that assertability be decidable forces assertability-conditional semantics to take a radically different form from that of truth-conditional semantics. Within this tradition, anti-realists have simply failed to develop natural language semantics in that form, or even to provide serious evidence that they could so develop it if they wanted to.[2] They proceed as if Imre Lakatos had never promulgated the concept of a degenerating research program.

Dummett's posing of the issue between realism and anti-realism provides a case study of an occasion when the philosophical community was offered a new way of gaining theoretical control over notoriously elusive issues, through the development of systematic semantic theories. The community spurned the opportunity, if that is what it was. Those who discussed realism and anti-realism on Dummett's terms tended to concentrate on the most programmatic issues, which they debated with no more clarity or conclusiveness than was to be found in the traditional metaphysical reasoning that Dummett intended to supersede. The actual success or lack of it in applying the rival semantic programs to specific fragments of natural language was largely ignored. Far from serving as a beacon for a new methodology, the debate between realism and anti-realism has become notorious in the rest of philosophy for its obscurity, convolution, and lack of progress.

Of course, one may reject Dummett's attempted reduction of issues in metaphysics to issues in the philosophy of language. As seen in earlier chapters, not all philosophical questions are really questions about language or thought. However, as we also saw, that a question is non-semantic does not imply that semantics imposes no useful constraints on the process of answering it. To reach philosophical conclusions one must reason, usually in areas where it is very hard to distinguish valid from invalid reasoning. To make that distinction reliably, one must often attend carefully to the semantic form of the premises, the conclusion, and the intermediate steps. That requires implicit semantic beliefs about the crucial words and constructions. Sometimes, those beliefs must be tested by explicit semantic theorizing. Philosophers who refuse to bother about semantics, on the grounds that they want to study the non-linguistic world, not our

---

[2]   Perhaps some work in contemporary formal semantics can be interpreted as assertability conditional rather than truth conditional in spirit: for instance, probability semantics for conditionals and other constructions, some forms of speech act theory, some theories of dynamic semantics. It is doubtful that much of this work conforms to Dummett's anti-realist constraints, or even makes a serious attempt to do so.

talk about that world, resemble scientists who refuse to bother about the theory of their instruments, on the grounds that they want to study the world, not our observation of it. Such an attitude may be good enough for amateurs; applied to more advanced inquiries, it produces crude errors. Those metaphysicians who ignore language in order not to project it onto the world are the very ones most likely to fall into just that fallacy, because their carelessness of the structure of the language in which they reason makes them insensitive to subtle differences between valid and invalid reasoning.

Explicit compositional semantic theories for reasonable fragments of particular natural languages also have the great methodological advantage of being comparatively easy to test in comparatively uncontentious ways, because they make specific predictions about the truth conditions (or assertability conditions) of infinitely many ordinary unphilosophical sentences. The attempt to provide a semantic theory that coheres with a given metaphysical claim can therefore constitute a searching test of the latter claim, even though semantics and metaphysics have different objects.

Discipline from semantics is only one kind of philosophical discipline. It is insufficient by itself for the conduct of a philosophical inquiry, and may sometimes fail to be useful, when the semantic forms of the relevant linguistic constructions are simple and obvious. But when philosophy is not disciplined by semantics, it must be disciplined by something else: syntax, logic, common sense, imaginary examples, the findings of other disciplines (mathematics, physics, biology, psychology, history, . . .) or the aesthetic evaluation of theories (elegance, simplicity, . . .). Indeed, philosophy subject to only one of those disciplines is liable to become severely distorted: several are needed simultaneously. To be "disciplined" by X here is not simply to pay lip-service to X; it is to make a systematic conscious effort to conform to the deliverances of X, where such conformity is at least somewhat easier to recognize than is the answer to the original philosophical question. Of course, each form of philosophical discipline is itself contested by some philosophers. But that is no reason to produce work that is not properly disciplined by anything. It may be a reason to welcome methodological diversity in philosophy: if different groups in philosophy give different relative weights to various sources of discipline, we can compare the long-run results of the rival ways of working. Tightly constrained work has the merit that even those who reject the constraints can agree that it demonstrates their consequences.

Much contemporary analytic philosophy seems to be written in the tacit hope of discursively muddling through, uncontrolled by any clear methodological constraints. That may be enough for easy questions, if there are any in philosophy; it is manifestly inadequate for resolving the hard questions with which most philosophers like to engage. All too often it produces only eddies in academic fashion, without any advance in our understanding of the subject matter. Although we can make progress in philosophy, we cannot expect to do so when we are not working at the highest available level of intellectual discipline. That level is not achieved by effortless superiority. It requires a conscious collective effort.

We who classify ourselves as "analytic" philosophers tend to fall into the assumption that our allegiance automatically grants us methodological virtue. According to the crude stereotypes, analytic philosophers use arguments while "continental" philosophers do not. But within the analytic tradition many philosophers use arguments only to the extent that most "continental" philosophers do: some kind of inferential movement is observable, but it lacks the clear articulation into premises and conclusion and the explicitness about the form of the inference that much good philosophy achieves. Again according to the stereotypes, analytic philosophers write clearly while "continental" philosophers do not. But much work within the analytic tradition is obscure even when it is written in everyday words, short sentences and a relaxed, open-air spirit, because the structure of its claims is fudged where it really matters.

If the high standards that make philosophy worth doing are often absent even in analytic philosophy, that is not because they are a natural endowment found only in a brilliant elite. Even if Frege's exceptional clarity and rigor required innate genius – although they undoubtedly also owed something to the German mathematical tradition within which he was educated – after his example they can now be effectively taught. Some graduate schools communicate something like his standards, others notably fail to do so.

Of course, we are often unable to answer an important philosophical question by rigorous argument, or even to formulate the question clearly. High standards then demand not that we should ignore the question, otherwise little progress would be made, but that we should be open and explicit about the unclarity of the question and the inconclusiveness of our attempts to answer it, and our dissatisfaction with both should motivate attempts to improve our methods. Moreover, it must be sensible for the bulk of our research effort to be concentrated in areas where our current methods make progress more likely.

We may hope that in the long term philosophy will develop new and more decisive methods to answer its questions, as unimaginable to us as our methods were to the Presocratics. Indeed, the development of such methods is one of the central challenges facing systematic philosophy. Paul Grice once wrote "By and large the greatest philosophers have been the greatest, and the most self-conscious, methodologists; indeed, I am tempted to regard this fact as primarily accounting for their greatness as philosophers" (Grice 1986: 66). Nevertheless, we must assume, in the short term philosophy will have to make do with something like currently available methods. But that is no reason to continue doing it in a methodologically unreflective way. A profession of very variable standards can help the higher to spread at the expense of the lower, by conscious collective attention to best practice.

One might think that methodological consciousness-raising is unnecessary, because on any particular issue good arguments will tend to drive out bad in the long run, by a reverse analogue of Gresham's Law. But that is over-optimistic. Very often – not least in debates between realists and anti-realists – a philosopher profoundly *wants* one answer rather than another to a philosophical question to be right, and is therefore predisposed to accept arguments that go in the preferred direction and reject contrary ones. Where the level of obscurity is high, wishful thinking may be more powerful than the ability to distinguish good arguments from bad, to the point that convergence in the evaluation of arguments never occurs.

Consider a dispute between rival theories in natural science. Each theory has its committed defenders, who have invested much time, energy, and emotion in its survival. The theories are not empirically equivalent, but making an empirical determination between them requires experimental skills of a high order. We may predict that if the standards of accuracy and conscientiousness in the community are high enough, truth will eventually triumph. But if the community is slightly more tolerant of sloppiness and rhetorical obfuscation, then each school may be able to survive indefinitely, claiming empirical vindication and still verbally acknowledging the value of rigor, by protecting samples from impurities a little less adequately, describing experimental results a little more tendentiously, giving a little more credit to *ad hoc* hypotheses, dismissing opposing arguments as question-begging a little more quickly, and so on. Each tradition maintains recruitment by its dominance and prestige in some departments or regions. A small difference in how carefully standards are applied can make the large difference between eventual convergence and ultimate divergence.

It seems likely that some parts of contemporary analytic philosophy just pass the methodological threshold for some cumulative progress to occur, however slowly, while others fall short of the threshold. For example, a reasonable fear is that debates over realism and anti-realism fall short. That is not to condemn every piece of work in such areas individually – which would surely be unfair – but to say that collectively the community of participants has not held itself responsible to high enough methodological standards. Perhaps these debates raise even more difficult issues than are encountered elsewhere in philosophy: if so, all the more reason to apply the very highest standards available. As already noted, that appears not to have happened.

How can we do better? We can make a useful start by getting the simple things right. Much even of analytic philosophy moves too fast in its haste to reach the sexy bits. Details are not given the care they deserve: crucial claims are vaguely stated, significantly different formulations are treated as though they were equivalent, examples are under-described, arguments are gestured at rather than properly made, their form is left unexplained, and so on. A few resultant errors easily multiply to send inquiry in completely the wrong direction. Shoddy work is sometimes masked by pretentiousness, allusiveness, gnomic concision, or winning informality. But often there is no special disguise: producers and consumers have simply not taken enough trouble to check the details. We need the unglamorous virtue of patience to read and write philosophy that is as perspicuously structured as the difficulty of the subject requires, and the austerity to be dissatisfied with appealing prose that does not meet those standards. The fear of boring oneself or one's readers is a great enemy of truth. Pedantry is a fault on the right side.

Precision is often regarded as a hyper-cautious characteristic. It is importantly the opposite. Vague statements are the hardest to convict of error. Obscurity is the oracle's self-defense. To be precise is to make it as easy as possible for others to prove one wrong. That is what requires courage. But the community can lower the cost of precision by keeping in mind that precise errors often do more than vague truths for scientific progress.

Would it be a good bargain to sacrifice depth for rigor? That bargain is not on offer in philosophy, any more than it is in mathematics. No doubt, if we aim to be rigorous, we cannot expect to sound like Heraclitus, or even Kant: we have to sacrifice the stereotype of depth. Still, it is rigor, not its absence, that prevents one from sliding over the deepest difficulties, in an agonized rhetoric of profundity. Rigor and depth both matter: but while the continual deliberate pursuit of rigor is a good way of achieving it, the continual deliberate pursuit of depth (as of happiness) is far more likely to be self-defeating. Better to concentrate on trying to say something true and leave depth to look after itself.

Nor are rigor and precision enemies of the imagination, any more than they are in mathematics. Rather, they increase the demands on the imagination, not least by forcing one to imagine examples with exactly the right structure to challenge a generalization; cloudiness will not suffice. They make imagination consequential in a way in which it is not in their absence. The most rigorous and precise discussion often involves the most playfulness and laughter: toying with subtly different combinations of ideas yields surprising scenarios. Humorless solemnity masks sloppiness and confusion.

Beyond rigor and precision, mathematics has less obvious values to teach. In particular, a mathematical training makes one appreciate the importance of the aesthetics of definitions. Experience shows that a mathematician or logician with no ability to discriminate between fruitful and unfruitful definitions is unlikely to achieve much in research. Such discriminations involve a sort of aesthetic judgment. The ugly, convoluted, ramshackle definitions of concepts and theses that philosophers seem to feel no shame in producing are of just the kind to strike a mathematician as pointless and sterile. Of course, it is notoriously hard to explain *why* aesthetic criteria are a good methodological guide, but it would be dangerously naïve to abandon them for that reason.

In addition to the humdrum methodological virtues, we need far more reflectiveness about how philosophical debates are to be subjected to enough constraints to be worth conducting. For example, Dummettian anti-realism about the past involved, remarkably, the abandonment of two of the main constraints on much philosophical activity. In rejecting instances of the law of excluded middle concerning past times, such as "Either a mammoth stood on this spot a hundred thousand years ago or no mammoth stood on this spot a hundred thousand years ago," the anti-realist rejected both common sense and classical logic. Those constraints are simultaneously abandoned in many contemporary philosophical debates too, for example over vagueness. Neither constraint is methodologically sacrosanct; both can intelligibly be challenged, even together. But when participants in a debate are allowed to throw out both simultaneously, methodological alarm bells should ring: it is at least not obvious that enough constraints are left to frame a fruitful discussion. Yet such qualms surface remarkably little (although Dummett himself did not ignore the methodological issues).

Part of the problem is that it is often left unclear just how extensively a constraint is being challenged. A philosopher treats the law of excluded middle as if it carried no authority whatsoever but implicitly relies on other logical principles (perhaps in the metalanguage): exactly which principles of logic are supposed to carry authority? A philosopher treats some common sense judgment as if it carried no authority whatsoever but implicitly relies on other judgments that are found pre-philosophically obvious: exactly which such judgments are supposed to carry authority?

When law and order break down, the result is not freedom or anarchy but the capricious tyranny of petty feuding warlords. Similarly, the unclarity of constraints in philosophy leads to authoritarianism. Whether an argument is widely accepted depends not on publicly accessible criteria that we can all apply for ourselves but on the say-so of charismatic authority figures. Pupils cannot become autonomous from their teachers because they cannot securely learn the standards by which their teachers judge. A modicum of willful unpredictability in the application of standards is a good policy for a professor who does not want his students to gain too much independence. Although intellectual deference is not always a bad thing, some debates have seen far too much of it. We can reduce it by articulating and clarifying the constraints.

Philosophy can never be reduced to mathematics. But we can often produce mathematical models of fragments of philosophy and, when we can, we should. No doubt the models usually involve wild idealizations. It is still progress if we can agree what consequences an idea has in one very simple case. Many ideas in philosophy do not withstand even that very elementary scrutiny, because the attempt to construct a non-trivial model reveals a hidden structural incoherence in the idea itself. By the same token, an idea that does not collapse in a toy model has at least something going for it. Once we have an unrealistic model, we can start worrying how to construct less unrealistic models.

Philosophers who reject the constraints mentioned above can say what constraints they would regard as appropriate. Of course, those who deny that philosophy is a theoretical discipline at all may reject the very idea of such constraints. But surely the best way to test the theoretical ambitions of philosophy is to go ahead and try to realize them in as disciplined a way as possible. If the anti-theorists can argue convincingly that the long-run results do not constitute progress, that is a far stronger case than is a preconceived argument that no such activity could constitute progress. On the other hand, if they cannot argue convincingly that the long-run results do not constitute progress, how is their opposition to philosophical theory any better than obscurantism?

Unless names are invidiously named, sermons like this one tend to cause less offence than they should, because everyone imagines that they are aimed at other people. Those who applaud a methodological platitude usually assume that they comply with it. I intend no such comfortable reading. To one degree or another, we all fall short not just of the ideal but of the desirable and quite easily possible. Certainly this afterword exhibits hardly any of the virtues that it recommends, although with luck it may still help a bit to propagate those virtues (do as I say, not as I do). Philosophy has never been done for an extended period according to standards as high as those that are now already available, if only the profession will take them seriously to heart. None of us knows how far we can get by applying them systematically enough for long enough. We can find out only by trying.

In making these comments, it is hard not to feel like the headmaster of a minor public school at speech day, telling everyone to pull their socks up after a particularly bad term. It is therefore appropriate to end with a misquotation from Winston Churchill. This is not the end of philosophy. It is not even the beginning of the end. But it is, perhaps, the end of the beginning.

Appendix 1
Modal Logic within Counterfactual Logic

This appendix sketches the development of logics of possibility and necessity as subsystems of logics of the counterfactual conditional, on suitable definitions of the former in terms of the latter. No particular formal semantic account of the counterfactual conditional is assumed, although various sorts of model theory are occasionally used in auxiliary roles. The emphasis is on questions of deducibility from principles plausible on an informal reading of the counterfactual conditional.

For most purposes our object language is L, which has countably many propositional variables **p, q, r, . . .** , the propositional constant ⊥ (a logical falsehood) and two binary connectives, → (the material conditional) and □→ (the counterfactual conditional). Other truth-functional operators are introduced as metalinguistic abbreviations in the usual way; for example, ¬A is A →⊥. The metalinguistic variables "A," "B," "C," . . . range over all formulas.

Except when otherwise specified, we work in the following axiomatic system (⊦ means theoremhood):

PC	If **A** is a truth-functional tautology then ⊦ **A**
REFLEXIVITY	⊦ **A** □→ **A**
VACUITY	⊦ (¬**A** □→ **A**) → (**B** □→ **A**)
MP	If ⊦ **A** → **B** and ⊦ **A** then ⊦ **B**
CLOSURE	If ⊦ (B_1 & . . . & B_n) → **C** then
	⊦ ((**A** □→ B_1) & . . . & (**A** □→ B_n)) → (**A** □→ **C**)
EQUIVALENCE	If ⊦ **A** ≡ **A*** then ⊦ (**A** □→ **B**) ≡ (**A*** □→ **B**)

These axiom schemas and inference rules constitute a weak subsystem of David Lewis's "official" logic of counterfactuals, VC (1986:

132). PC, REFLEXIVITY, and VACUITY are his axiom schemas (1), (3), and (4) respectively, and MP is his rule of Modus Ponens (for →). CLOSURE is his rule of Deduction within Conditionals (unlike Lewis, we allow $n = 0$, interpreting this case as the rule that if ⊢ C then ⊢ A □→ C; but that special case is anyway derivable from CLOSURE for $n = 1$ and REFLEXIVITY). EQUIVALENCE is a special case of Lewis's rule of Interchange of Logical Equivalents (incorrectly omitted from the original 1973 edition (1986: ix)); Interchange of Logical Equivalents in its full generality for all sentential contexts in L is derivable from EQUIVALENCE, CLOSURE, PC, and MP (proof: by induction on the construction of formulas).

PC and MP simply encapsulate the background classical logic. REFLEXIVITY reflects the triviality that in developing a counterfactual supposition we can start with that supposition itself. The point of VACUITY is that ¬A is the "worst" antecedent for A as consequent; if A is forthcoming even in that case, it is forthcoming in every case. To think of it another way, ¬A □→ A can be true only by being vacuously true, in which case A is true in every eventuality. CLOSURE means that in developing a counterfactual supposition, we can include any logical consequence of the results obtained so far. EQUIVALENCE goes with the idea that differences between logically equivalent counterfactual suppositions are in effect differences only in the mode of presentation of the way things are being supposed to be.

One way in which the present subsystem of Lewis's system is weak is that it lacks his irredundant "centering" axiom schema (7) (A & B) → (A □→ B), for, unlike the principles above, it is invalid when □→ is reinterpreted as strict implication in S5. It also lacks his "weak centering" axiom schema (6) (A □→ B) → (A → B), the addition of which will be considered later. Finally, our subsystem lacks the axiom schema (5) for whose length and obscurity Lewis apologizes:

(A □→ ¬B) ∨ (((A & B) □→ C) ≡ (A □→ (B → C)))

(Lewis 1986: 133). Unlike (6) and (7), (5) is part of Lewis's core system V. We can check that (5) is irredundant in Lewis's axiomatization by considering an unintended semantics on which it is invalid but all his other axiom schemas are valid and his rules preserve validity. Specifically, suppose that each model supplies a set of worlds and a function f from formulas **A** and worlds w to sets of worlds f(**A**, w) satisfying the constraints (i) **A** is true at every world in f(**A**, w); (ii) f(**A**, w) is empty only if **A** is true at no world; (iii) if **A** is true at w then f(**A**, w) = {w}; (iv) if **A** and **B** are true at exactly the same worlds then f(**A**, w) = f(**B**, w). The semantic clause for □→ is then that **A** □→ **B** is true at w if and only **B** is true at every world in f(**A**, w). One easily checks by induction on the length of proofs that all Lewis's other axiom schemas are true at every world in every model under this semantics, and that his rules preserve this property. However, schema (5) fails. Consider a set of four worlds {0, 1, 2, 3}, let the atomic formula **p** be true at 1, 2 and 3 only, **q** be true at 1 and 2 only, **r** be true at 1 only; if **A** is true at w let f(**A**, w) be {w}; if **A** is false at w let f(**A**, w) be the set of all worlds at which **A** is true, except when w is 0 and **A** is true at 1 and 2 only, in which case f(**A**, w) is {1}. These stipulations obviously satisfy (i)–(iv). Now **p** □→ ¬**q** is false at 0, because f(**p**, 0) is {1, 2, 3} and ¬**q** is false at 1 and 2, and **p** □→ (**q** → **r**) is false at 0 because **q** → **r** is false at 2, but (**p** & **q**) □→ **r** is true at 0, because f(**p** & **q**, 0) is {1} and **r** is true at 1. Consequently, (**p** □→ ¬**q**) ∨ (((**p** & **q**) □→ **r**) ≡ (**p** □→ (**q** → **r**))) is false at 0. In this setting, we therefore cannot apply most of Lewis's results about derived modal logics within counterfactual logics (1986: 137–42), because they depend on completeness theorems for his counterfactual logics with respect to classes of models with respect to which the present systems are incomplete. Not that any reason has been provided to regard Lewis's extra schemas as informally invalid on their intended natural language readings (if we do not already assume the correctness of Lewis's semantic theory); the point is just that their informal validity on those readings is hard to assess, so it is better to derive modal logic from counterfactual logic without them.

   CLOSURE and EQUIVALENCE are not quite as straightforward as they look. In a language with a rigidifying "actually" operator @, **p** ≡ @**p** is arguably a logical truth. But if it is a theorem, each of CLOSURE and EQUIVALENCE separately (when combined with REFLEXIVITY) yields the theorem **p** □→ @**p**, which is false on many interpretations: "If it had rained, it would have actually rained" is false if it did not rain. In the terminology of Davies and Humberstone (1980), CLOSURE and EQUIVALENCE preserve general validity (truth at every world of every model) but not real world validity (truth at the actual world of every model). Thus CLOSURE and EQUIVALENCE must be restricted to theorems derived solely by appeal to axioms and rules that preserve general validity. A similar restriction is needed on the standard Rule of Necessitation (RN) in modal logic, that if **A** is a theorem so is □**A**, for even if **p** → @**p** is logically true, □(**p** → @**p**) may be false. For present purposes we can ignore this complication, since the languages under consideration lack operators such as "actually" (see Williamson (2006a) for further discussion).

For our immediate purposes, we expand L to the language L+ by adding propositional quantifiers. That is, if **p** is a propositional variable and **A** is a formula of L+, ∀**p A** is also a formula of L+. We extend the axiomatization by a corresponding axiom schema and rule (where **A[B/p]** is the result of substituting the formula **B** for all free occurrences of **p** in **A**, on the assumption that no variable free in **B** thereby becomes bound):

UINST   If **p** is any propositional variable then ⊢ ∀**p A** → **A[B/p]**
UGEN   If **p** is any propositional variable not free in **A**, and
⊢ **A** → **B** then ⊢ **A** → ∀**p B**

This system, like that for L, satisfies the rule of substitution of proved material equivalents, in the sense that if ⊢ **B** ≡ **B*** then ⊢ **A[B/p]** ≡ **A[B*/p]** for any formula **A** and propositional variable **p** (proof: by induction on the complexity of **A**). Thus proved material equivalents are interchangeable in all relevant contexts. In the setting of possible worlds semantics, UINST and UGEN are sound when the propositional quantifiers are interpreted as ranging over all subsets of the set of possible worlds associated with the given model, but they will not yield a complete system, since they do not guarantee the existence of maximally specific possible propositions, true in exactly one world (for example, one cannot derive ∃**p** (**p** & ∀**q** (**q** → □(**p** → **q**)))).[1] For present purposes, those stronger assumptions are unnecessary.

---

[1]   See the pioneering works of Fine (1970) and Kaplan (1970) for more technical detail on propositional quantification in modal logic. Williamson (1999a) discusses its interpretation: interpreting it by means of quantification into name position in the metalanguage, over sets of possible worlds or anything else, is arguably only a rough approximation to its philosophically most significant interpretation, which involves ineliminable quantification into sentence position.

Our first task is to show that three candidate definitions of □A in L+ are mutually equivalent: (i) ∀ p (p □→ A) (where **p** is not free in A); (ii) ¬A □→ A; (iii) ¬A □→ ⊥. First we establish the equivalence of (i) and (ii):

(1) ∀ p (p □→ A) → (¬A □→ A)   UINST
(2) (¬A □→ A) → (p □→ A)   VACUITY
(3) (¬A □→ A) → ∀ p (p □→ A)   2, UGEN
(4) ∀ p (p □→ A) ≡ (¬A □→ A)   1, 3, PC, MP

Now we establish the equivalence of (ii) and (iii):

(1) (A & ¬A) → ⊥   PC
(2) ((¬A □→ A) & (¬A □→ ¬A)) → (¬A □→ ⊥)   1, CLOSURE
(3) ¬A □→ ¬A   REFLEXIVITY
(4) (¬A □→ A) → (¬A □→ ⊥)   2, 3, PC, MP
(5) ⊥ → A   PC
(6) (¬A □→ ⊥) → (¬A □→ A)   5, CLOSURE
(7) (¬A □→ A) ≡ (¬A □→ ⊥)   4, 6, PC, MP

Thus (i), (ii), and (iii) are mutually interchangeable in all relevant contexts. It matters little which of them we use to define □A. However, the complexities of propositional quantification are best avoided when not needed, and (iii) is marginally simpler than (ii), so we treat □A as a metalinguistic abbreviation for ¬A □→ ⊥. We therefore return to the propositional language L, and omit the quantifier rules. As usual in modal logic we treat ◊A as a metalinguistic abbreviation for ¬□¬A, which in our case is ¬(¬¬A □→ ⊥), which is equivalent by EQUIVALENCE to ¬(A □→ ⊥).

The next task is to check the status on our definitions of two principles used in the main text:

NECESSITY   ⊢ □(A → B) → (A □→ B)
POSSIBILITY ⊢ (A □→ B) → (◊A → ◊B)

We prove them in our system as follows. First, NECESSITY:

(1) □(A → B) → (¬(A → B) □→ ⊥)   DEF□, PC
(2) (¬(A → B) □→ ⊥) → (¬(A → B) □→ (A → B))   PC, CLOSURE

(3) $(\neg(A \rightarrow B) \;\square\!\!\rightarrow (A \rightarrow B)) \rightarrow$ VACUITY
     $(A \;\square\!\!\rightarrow (A \rightarrow B))$
(4) $\square(A \rightarrow B) \rightarrow (A \;\square\!\!\rightarrow (A \rightarrow B))$ 1, 2, 3, PC, MP
(5) $((A \;\square\!\!\rightarrow (A \rightarrow B)) \;\&\; (A \;\square\!\!\rightarrow A))$ PC,
     $\rightarrow (A \;\square\!\!\rightarrow B)$ CLOSURE
(6) $(A \;\square\!\!\rightarrow (A \rightarrow B)) \rightarrow (A \;\square\!\!\rightarrow B)$ 5, REFLEXIVITY, PC,
     MP
(7) $\square(A \rightarrow B) \rightarrow (A \;\square\!\!\rightarrow B)$ 4, 6, PC, MP

Then, POSSIBILITY:

(1) $\neg\Diamond B \rightarrow (\neg\neg B \;\square\!\!\rightarrow \bot)$ DEF$\Diamond$, PC
(2) $(\neg\neg B \;\square\!\!\rightarrow \bot) \rightarrow (\neg\neg B \;\square\!\!\rightarrow \neg B)$ PC, CLOSURE
(3) $(\neg\neg B \;\square\!\!\rightarrow \neg B) \rightarrow (A \;\square\!\!\rightarrow \neg B)$ VACUITY
(4) $\neg\Diamond B \rightarrow (A \;\square\!\!\rightarrow \neg B)$ 1, 2, 3, PC, MP
(5) $((A \;\square\!\!\rightarrow B) \;\&\; (A \;\square\!\!\rightarrow \neg B))$ PC, CLOSURE
      $\rightarrow (A \;\square\!\!\rightarrow \bot)$
(6) $((A \;\square\!\!\rightarrow B) \;\&\; \neg\Diamond B) \rightarrow (A \;\square\!\!\rightarrow \bot)$ 4, 5, PC, MP
(7) $(\neg\neg A \;\square\!\!\rightarrow \bot) \rightarrow \neg\Diamond A$ DEF$\Diamond$, PC
(8) $(A \;\square\!\!\rightarrow \bot) \rightarrow (\neg\neg A \;\square\!\!\rightarrow \bot)$ PC, EQUIVALENCE
(9) $((A \;\square\!\!\rightarrow B) \;\&\; \neg\Diamond B) \rightarrow \neg\Diamond A$ 6, 7, 8, PC, MP
(10) $(A \;\square\!\!\rightarrow B) \rightarrow (\Diamond A \rightarrow \Diamond B)$ 9, PC, MP

We now turn to deriving some basic principles of modal logic within counterfactual logic. The weakest normal modal logic is K, which is axiomatized by PC, MP, and the following axiom schema and rule:

K $\vdash \square(A \rightarrow B) \rightarrow (\square A \rightarrow \square B)$
RN   If $\vdash A$ then $\vdash \square A$

We derive K in our system thus:

(1) $\square A \rightarrow (\neg A \;\square\!\!\rightarrow \bot)$ PC, DEF$\square$
(2) $\square A \rightarrow (\neg A \;\square\!\!\rightarrow A)$ 1, PC, CLOSURE, MP
(3) $\square A \rightarrow (\neg B \;\square\!\!\rightarrow A)$ 2, VACUITY, PC, MP
(4) $\square(A \rightarrow B) \rightarrow (\neg B \;\square\!\!\rightarrow (A \rightarrow B))$ Like 3
(5) $((\neg B \;\square\!\!\rightarrow (A \rightarrow B)) \;\&\; (\neg B \;\square\!\!\rightarrow A))$ PC, CLOSURE
     $\rightarrow (\neg B \;\square\!\!\rightarrow B)$
(6) $(\square(A \rightarrow B) \;\&\; \square A) \rightarrow (\neg B \;\square\!\!\rightarrow B)$ 3, 4, 5, PC, MP

(7)   (¬B □→ B) → (¬B □→ ⊥)   REFLEXIVITY,
                                                                CLOSURE, PC, MP

(8)   (¬B □→ B) → □B   7, DEF□

(9)   □(A → B) → (□A → □B)   6, 8, PC, MP

Here is a derivation of RN:

(1)   A   Theorem by assumption
(2)   ¬A → ⊥   1, PC, MP
(3)   (¬A □→ ¬A) → (¬A □→ ⊥)   2, CLOSURE
(4)   ¬A □→ ⊥   3, REFLEXIVITY, PC, MP
(5)   □A   4, DEF□

Thus all theorems of K are theorems of our system, under our definition of □.

We can prove something stronger: the modal principles derivable
in our current system are *just* those derivable in K. More precisely,
let $L_\square$ be the language of propositional modal logic, built up from
the propositional variables, ⊥, → and □ (treated as primitive). Let *
be the mapping from $L_\square$ to L that corresponds to our definition of
□:

*p = p for each propositional variable p
*⊥ = ⊥
*(A → B) = *A → *B
*□A = ¬*A □→ ⊥

Then for any formula A of $L_\square$, *A is a theorem of our system (⊢ *A)
if and only if A is a theorem of K (⊢ₖ A). We have in effect already
proved that if ⊢ₖ A then ⊢ *A. The converse is trickier, because the
proof of *A in our system may involve formulas such as p □→ q that
are not of the form *B for any formula B of $L_\square$. We define an auxiliary "unintended" mapping ^ back from L to $L_\square$:

^p = p for each propositional variable p
^⊥ = ⊥
^(A → B) = ^A → ^B
^(A □→ B) = □(^A → ^B)

We note two easy lemmas.

(I)   For any formula **A** of L, if ⊢ **A** then ⊢$_k$ ^**A**. Proof: by induction on the length of proofs in our system.

(II)   For any formula **A** of L$_□$, ⊢$_k$ **A** ≡ ^***A**. Proof: by induction on the complexity of **A**.

Now suppose that **A** is a formula of L$_□$ and ⊢ ***A**. By (I), ⊢$_k$ ^***A**. By (II), ⊢$_k$ **A** ≡ ^***A**. Therefore ⊢$_k$ **A**, as required. Thus ⊢ ***A** if and only if ⊢$_k$ **A**.

The system K is far too weak to be an adequate logic of metaphysical possibility and necessity. The most saliently missing principle is that what is necessarily so is so:

T   ⊢ □**A** → **A**

We can derive T in our system by adding Lewis's "weak centering" principle (schema (6) in his official logic of counterfactuals (1986: 132); it is also axiom schema (a6) in Stalnaker 1968), which corresponds to modus ponens for the counterfactual conditional given the logic of the material conditional:

MP□→   ⊢ (A □→ B) → (A → B)

T is an immediate consequence of MP□→:

(1)   (¬A □→ ⊥) → (¬A → ⊥)   MP□→
(2)   (¬A □→ ⊥) → A   1, PC, MP
(3)   □A → A   2, DEF□

By a proof along just the same lines as for K (with the same mappings), we can show that for any formula **A** of L$_□$, ***A** is a theorem of our system extended by MP□→ if and only if **A** is a theorem of KT, the result of extending K (as axiomatized above) by T. Thus PC, REFLEXIVITY, VACUITY, MP□→, MP, CLOSURE, and EQUIVALENCE induce the simple logic KT for metaphysical modality.

MP□→ is an immensely plausible principle. If we discover that *e* happened without *f*, doesn't that refute the claim that if *e* had happened, f would have happened?[2] Nevertheless, it is worth observing that the full strength of MP□→ is not needed to derive T. For if we merely add T itself to our original system (read by means of DEF□), we cannot derive MP□→. We can show this by giving an unintended model theory that validates PC, REFLEXIVITY, VACUITY, T, MP, CLOSURE, and EQUIVALENCE but not MP□→. It is a "possible worlds" semantics, but with the natural numbers playing the role of the worlds. The clause for □→ is this: **A** □→ **B** is true at all worlds iff either **A** is false at all worlds or **B** is true at the least world at which **A** is true ("least" in the sense of the usual ordering of the natural numbers; recall that every nonempty set of natural numbers has a least member); otherwise **A** □→ **B** is false at all worlds. Everything else is standard. It is routine to check (by induction on the length of proofs) that every formula of L derivable from PC, REFLEXIVITY, VACUITY, T, MP, CLOSURE, and EQUIVALENCE is true at all worlds in all such models. For example, in the case of T, suppose that □**A** is true at a world, which is to say that ¬**A** □→ ⊥ is true at that world; since ¬**A** □→ ⊥ cannot be non-vacuously true, it must be vacuously true; thus **A** is true at every world. But not all instances of MP□→ are true at all worlds in all such models. For example, let **p** be true at 0 but false at every other world. Then ¬**p**□→ **p** is true at every world, while ¬⊥ → **p** is false at 1.

A more controversial but still plausible principle about metaphysical modality is the characteristic axiom schema of the modal system S5, known as E:

E   ⊢ ◇A → □◇A

KTE is simply S5; in that system, matters of possibility and necessity are always non-contingent. We can also derive in it the characteristic principle of S4:

---

[2]   One can accept a counterfactual when rationally unwilling to apply modus ponens to it, in the sense that on learning its antecedent one would reject the counterfactual rather than accept its consequent. For example, I accept "If Oswald had not shot Kennedy, Kennedy would not have been shot," but if I come to accept "Oswald did not shoot Kennedy," I will not conclude "Kennedy was not shot." But that is no threat to the validity of modus ponens. In circumstances in which both "If Oswald had not shot Kennedy, Kennedy would not have been shot" and "Oswald did not shoot Kennedy" are true, so is "Kennedy was not shot."

4S   ⊢ □A → □□A

(Hughes and Cresswell (1996) provides appropriate background in modal logic.) If we read E directly in terms of our counterfactual definitions of the modal operators, □◊A becomes a counterfactual conditional with a (negated) counterfactual conditional in its antecedent, which is quite hard to get a feel for. Lewis adds axioms involving such intractable counterfactuals to his system to obtain S5. Here is a more natural equivalent of E in counterfactual conditional terms:

ES   ⊢ (A □→ (B □→ ⊥)) → ((A □→ ⊥) ∨ (B □→ ⊥))

The embedded counterfactual conditional has been moved into the consequent, where such embeddings occur somewhat more naturally. Informally, ES says that embedding one possible counterfactual hypothesis inside another cannot lead to an impossibility: even if **B** is incompatible with **A**, counterfactually supposing **B** within the counterfactual supposition of **A** takes one back out of the **A** worlds into the **B** worlds, not to an impossibility.

   The generalization of ES to arbitrary sentences in place of the logical falsehood is much less plausible:

ES+   ⊢ (A □→ (B □→ C)) → ((A □→ C) ∨ (B □→ C))

If I had been a French grocer then I would have been such that if I had been a philosopher I would have been a French philosopher; but it is not the case that if I had been a French grocer I would have been a French philosopher, nor is it the case that if I had been a philosopher I would have been a French philosopher. In terms of Lewis's similarity semantics, suppose that **p** holds only at the counterfactual world w, **q** holds only at the actual world and a third world x, closer to w than the actual world is, and **r** holds only at x. Then w is a **q** □→ **r** world, because the closest **q** world to w is x, which is an **r** world; thus the actual world is a **p** □→ (**q** □→ **r**) world, since w is the closest **p** world to the actual world; but the actual world is neither a **p** □→ **r** world (since the closest **p** world to the actual world, w, is not an **r** world) nor a **q** □→ **r** world (since the closest **q** world to the actual world is the actual world itself, which is not an **r** world). Thus

ES+ is invalid in Lewis's semantics. By contrast, ES holds on Lewis's semantics provided that all worlds form a single similarity space (compare Lewis's uniformity condition (1986: 120–1)). For then B □→ ⊥ is false at every world if B is true at some world; thus if B □→ ⊥ is false at a world, so B is true at some world, then B □→ ⊥ is true at exactly the same worlds as ⊥, so A □→ (B □→ ⊥) and A □→ ⊥ have the same truth-value at all worlds; thus ES holds (consequently, ES does not entail ES+). The plausibility of ES depends on the occurrence of a logical falsehood in the consequent. Although we will not attempt to determine here whether ES should ultimately be accepted, it at least gives us a new perspective on the status of S5 (Salmon 1982: 238–40, 1989, and 1993 argue that S4 and therefore S5 are invalid for metaphysical modality; Williamson 1990: 126–43 and 2000a: 119–20 reply).

We still have to establish the equivalence of ES with E. First, we argue from ES to E in our original system:

(1)	((¬¬A □→ ⊥) □→ (¬¬A □→ ⊥)) →	ES
	(((¬¬A □→ ⊥) □→ ⊥) ∨ (¬¬A □→ ⊥))	
(2)	((¬¬A □→ ⊥) □→ ⊥) ∨ (¬¬A □→ ⊥)	1, REFLEXIVITY, MP
(3)	¬(¬¬A □→ ⊥) →	2, EQUIVALENCE,
	(¬¬ (¬¬A □→ ⊥) □→ ⊥)	PC, MP
(4)	◊A → □◊A	3, DEF◊, DEF□

Now we establish the converse, again in our original system:

(1)	◊B → □◊B	E
(2)	¬(B □→ ⊥) → (¬¬(B □→⊥) □→ ⊥)	1, EQUIVALENCE,
		PC, MP, DEF◊, DEF□
(3)	(¬¬(B □→ ⊥) □→ ⊥) →	CLOSURE, MP, PC
	(¬¬(B □→ ⊥) □→ ¬(B □→ ⊥))	
(4)	¬(B □→ ⊥) → (¬¬(B □→ ⊥)	2, 3, MP, PC
	□→ ¬(B □→ ⊥))	
(5)	¬(B □→ ⊥) → (A □→ ¬(B □→ ⊥))	4, VACUITY, MP, PC
(6)	((A □→ (B □→ ⊥)) & (A □→ ¬(B □→ ⊥)) →	
	(A □→ ⊥)	CLOSURE, MP, PC
(7)	(A □→ (B □→ ⊥)) →	5, 6, MP, PC
	((A □→ ⊥) ∨ (B □→ ⊥))	

Although PC, REFLEXIVITY, VACUITY, MP□→, ES, MP, CLOSURE, and EQUIVALENCE together yield the full strength of S5, they still constitute a rather weak logic of counterfactuals. For example, they do not yield axiom schema (a7) from Stalnaker (1968), a strengthening of EQUIVALENCE:

(a7)   ⊢ ((A □→ B) & (B □→ A)) → ((A □→ C) → (B □→ C))

To check independence, consider another deviant semantics in which the possible worlds are the natural numbers. Let A □→ B be true at a world w if and only if three conditions hold: (i) if A is true at w then B is true at w; (ii) if A is true at exactly one world then B is also true at that world; (iii) if A is true at a world x and at some world y such that $x > y$ then B is true at x. In particular, therefore, A □→ ⊥ is true at all worlds if A is false at all worlds; otherwise A □→ ⊥ is false at all worlds. Everything else is standard. It is routine to check that all theorems of our system are true in all such models. But (a7) fails: for if **p** is true at just 1 and 2, **q** at just 0, 1 and 2 and **r** just at 2, then **p** □→ **q**, **q** □→ **p** and **p** □→ **r** are true but **q** □→ **r** false at 2 (since **q** is true and **r** false at 1, which is not the least world at which **q** is true). The same semantics shows that the complex axiom schema (5) of Lewis's official system VC (1986: 132) is not derivable in our system (since (**q** & **p**) □→ **r** is true but **q** □→ (**p** → **r**) is false at 2). We might wish to add some of these further principles to our system.

Moderately natural counterfactual equivalents of other modal principles can also be provided. For example, the 4 schema ⊢ □A → □□A is equivalent to this schema:

4S   ⊢ (A □→ ⊥) → (B □→ (A □→ ⊥))

Similarly, the B schema ⊢ A → □◊A is equivalent to this schema:

BS   ⊢ (A □→ (B □→ ⊥)) → (B → (A □→ ⊥))

The proofs are similar to some already given. The observations in this appendix merely begin the work of exploring the modal subsystems of logics of the counterfactual conditional. With luck, they will encourage others to explore the matter more thoroughly.

Appendix 2
Counterfactual Donkeys

This appendix experiments with an alternative way of formalizing the anaphora in the major premises of the arguments underlying philosophical thought experiments, by permitting the conditional in them to bind variables. Thus we formalize (5), (6) and (13) in Chapter 6 respectively as:

(A1) $GC(x, p) \, \square\!\!\rightarrow_{x,p} (JTB(x, p) \, \& \, \neg K(x, p))$

(A2) $(Farmer(x) \, \& \, Donkey(y) \, \& \, Owns(x, y)) \, \square\!\!\rightarrow_{x,p} Beats(x, y)$

(A3) $(Animal(x) \, \& \, Escapedzoo(x)) \, \square\!\!\rightarrow_x Monkey(x)$

These give a less unnatural treatment of the anaphora in (5), (6) and (13) than (3*), (12) and (15) do, without repeating material or pulling a universal quantifier out of a hat. Of course, much depends on the semantics of this variable-binding conditional.

The natural strategy is to build on the preferred semantics for the conditional without variable-binding. Suppose, for a simple example, that we have a crude version of possible worlds semantics for $\square\!\!\rightarrow$ (allowing, as usual, for vacuous truth):

$[\square\!\!\rightarrow]$ $A \, \square\!\!\rightarrow B$ is true at a world w if and only if B is true at the most similar worlds (if any) to w at which A is true.

Now think of assignments as assigning values both to the explicit variables and to a tacit world variable. Define an assignment s^* to be an $x, \ldots, y, w$-variant of an assignment s just in case s^* differs from s at most over the values of the explicit variables $x, \ldots, y$ and of the world variable w. Then the modified semantic clause is this:

[□→$_{x,…,y}$]   A □→$_{x,…,y}$ B is true under an assignment s if and only if
B is true at the most similar x, . . . , y, w-variants of s
(if any) to s at which A is true.

In effect, [□→$_{x,…,y}$] replaces comparative similarity of worlds in
[□→] with comparative similarity of assignments, conceived as something like cases. Evidently, many more refined semantic clauses for
□→ could be modified in corresponding ways.

Clause [□→$_{x,…,y}$] corresponds to semantic clauses for variable-
binding possibility and necessity operators:

[◊$_{x,…,y}$]   ◊$_{x,…,y}$ A is true under an assignment s if and only if A is
true at some x, . . . , y, w-variant of s.

[□$_{x,…,y}$]   □$_{x,…,y}$ A is true under an assignment s if and only if A is
true at every x, . . . , y, w-variant of s.

The target analysis is expressible in this notation:

(A4)   □$_{x,p}$ (K(x, p) ≡ JTB(x, p))

We could then rework the Gettier argument from (2) and (3*) to (4)
as an argument from (A1) and (A5) to (A6):

(A5)   ◊$_{x,p}$ GC(x, p)
(A6)   ◊$_{x,p}$ (JTB(x, p) & ¬K(x, p))

Together, [□→$_{x,…,y}$] and [◊$_{x,…,y}$] validate the required analogue of
the POSSIBILITY principle. The conclusion (A6) is inconsistent with
the target analysis (A4), as expected.

Here is one advantage of formalizing (5) as (A1), understood in
terms of a semantic clause like [□→$_{x,…,y}$], rather than as (3*), understood in terms of a semantic clause like [□→]. As noted in Chapter
6, section 5, (3*) may be false in unexpected ways. For example,
suppose that the Gettier case has many instances in the actual world;
most of them are instances of justified true belief without knowledge,
but a few abnormal instances are not instances of justified belief.
Then (3*) is false, because its antecedent is true and its consequent
false in the actual world, even though most actual instances of the
Gettier case are genuine counterexamples to the target analysis. In

such circumstances, is Gettier's argument really unsound? By contrast, (A1) understood in terms of $[\square \rightarrow_{x,\ldots,y}]$ may avoid this problem, because the assignments which correspond to the normal instances may be closer to the assignment s with which we started than are the assignments which correspond to the abnormal instances. It is not implausible that they would be if we started with an assignment of ordinary objects to the explicit variables and the actual world to the world variable. Even abnormal instances in the actual world may be trumped in the overall similarity ranking by more ordinary realizations in counterfactual worlds. Although we could achieve some of the same effect by reading the quantifiers in (3*) as contextually restricted, speakers may not know in advance how much restriction is needed, whereas $[\square \rightarrow_{x,\ldots,y}]$ does not require any restriction to be specified in advance, and permits a flexible trade-off between similarity in the values of explicit variables and similarity in the value of the world variable.

The preceding remarks highlight an unusual feature of $[\square \rightarrow_{x,\ldots,y}]$ as a semantic clause. Normally, the semantic clause for an operator O binding explicit variables has the effect that a closed formula with O as its main operator is true under all assignments if it is true under any. For example, on standard clauses for quantifiers, the truth-value of a closed quantified formula is independent of the assignment. Thus $\forall x \forall x$ A and $\exists x \forall x$ A are equivalent to $\forall x$ A in any nonempty domain. By contrast, even when $x, \ldots, y$ exhaust the variables in A $\square \rightarrow_{x,\ldots,y}$ B, $[\square \rightarrow_{x,\ldots,y}]$ allows it to be true under some assignments and false under others. In this it behaves with respect to both explicit variables and the world variable as counterfactual conditionals do with respect to the world variable in the absence of explicit variable-binding: a semantic clause like $[\square \rightarrow]$ allows A $\square \rightarrow$ B to be true at some worlds and false at others. Similarly, $\square\square$A and $\lozenge\square$A are not equivalent to $\square$A in many modal logics. Although the sensitivity of A $\square \rightarrow_{x,\ldots,y}$ B in truth-value to the initial values of $x, \ldots, y$ creates no purely technical problem, it does raise the question where the explicit variables are to get their default values from. The context of utterance smoothly provides the world of the context as the default value of the world variable, but how is it to provide corresponding default values for the explicit variables?

It is in any case unlikely that a variable-binding operator in the object-language will give us everything we want, since the anaphora in formulations of the Gettier argument can run across sentences, as in this wooden dialogue:

John: A person and a proposition could have stood in the Gettier relation.
Mary: If they had, they would have been an instance of justified true belief without knowledge.

The interaction of anaphora with intensional contexts creates notoriously thorny problems, which we obviously cannot attempt to solve here (for some of the issues see Roberts 1996). They do not show that the arguments underlying philosophical thought experiments are not to be understood in terms of counterfactual conditionals such as (5). They reveal some subtle obstacles to articulating a perfectly faithful formal analysis of those arguments, but for all they show the argument from (A1) and (A5) to (A6) (or from (2) and (3*) to (4)) is a perfectly adequate approximation for almost all metaphilosophical purposes.

Part II

9

Widening the Picture

9.1 How Did We Get Here from There? The Transformation of Analytic Philosophy

Opponents of analytic philosophy often associate it with logical positivism. From a historical point of view, it is clear that one main strand in the development of the broad tradition known as "analytic philosophy" was indeed the logical positivism of the Vienna Circle, with its austerely verificationist principle of significance and its exclusion of metaphysics as cognitively meaningless. Another main strand in the development of the analytic tradition, ordinary language philosophy, tended to be almost equally suspicious of the ways in which metaphysicians made free with ordinary words, far from the everyday contexts of use on which their meaning was supposed to depend. Despite that history, however, recent decades have seen the growth and flourishing of boldly speculative metaphysics within the analytic tradition. Far from being inhibited by logical positivist or ordinary language scruples, such analytic metaphysics might be described by those unsympathetic to it as *pre-critical*, ranging far outside the domain of our experience, closer in spirit to Leibniz than to Kant.

How did a species of philosophy with so much anti-metaphysics in its gene pool evolve so quickly to the opposite extreme? Enough time has passed for us now to start achieving the historical perspective necessary to answer the question in a systematic way. That project is too extensive to be properly carried out in less than a book. In this section, I attempt no more than to make some informal and unsystematic remarks on the transformation of analytic philosophy. Especially in Section II, I write as someone who lived through the latter stages of the process, and concentrate on the parts of which

I have the closest knowledge. That will at least provide some sense of what it was like to experience the transformation at the time, from a broadly sympathetic point of view. I close with a few sketchy remarks on the historiography of recent analytic philosophy, in Section III.

I

The central, most influential figure in the development of analytic metaphysics over the final quarter of the twentieth century, and the contemporary philosopher most cited within recent analytic philosophy, is undoubtedly David Lewis, also known as "the machine in the ghost" for his eerie computational power, mechanical diction, faint air of detachment from ordinary life, and beard from another era (by contrast with "the ghost in the machine," Gilbert Ryle's summary description of the immaterial Cartesian ego in the clockwork Cartesian body). The prize specimen of Lewis's speculative metaphysics is in turn his notorious doctrine of *modal realism*, according to which there are infinitely many possible worlds, mutually disconnected spatiotemporal systems each as real and concrete as our own actual world (Lewis 1986a). For Lewis, strictly and literally there are talking donkeys, because there *could have been* talking donkeys (as we may all agree), so some possible world contains talking donkeys, which are just as real, alive, and made of flesh and blood as any donkey you have ever seen. Of course, those other worlds are not open to our observation; there are no trans-world telescopes. Lewis postulates them because they follow from his modal realism, which he regards as the best theory of possibility, necessity, and related phenomena, in respect of simplicity, strength, elegance, and explanatory power: to use C. S. Peirce's term broadly, Lewis's argument for modal realism is *abductive*. In a way, Lewis takes non-actual possible worlds even more seriously than did Leibniz, for whom they are merely unrealized ideas in the mind of God. Leibniz's God realized only the best of all possible worlds, whereas *all* of Lewis's possible worlds are equally realized. We can take Lewis's modal realism as a case study for the resurgence of speculative metaphysics in contemporary analytic philosophy.

Some philosophers treat any appeal to possible worlds at all as a metaphysical extravagance. But that is a mistake, for some theories treat possible worlds as merely abstract objects or representations, harmlessly built from this-worldly materials. Indeed, Rudolf Carnap, the logical positivist anti-metaphysician *par excellence*, explicitly compared to Leibniz's possible worlds his state-descriptions, maximal consistent classes of sentences used in his semantics for languages with modal operators such as "possibly" and "necessarily." He also compared them with the possible states of affairs in Wittgenstein's *Tractatus Logico-Philosophicus* (Carnap 1947: 9). For Carnap, necessity is a purely intra-linguistic matter of truth guaranteed by meaning, and possibility is a correspondingly semantic form of consistency. Lewis's modal realism has always been a minority view, even amongst those analytic metaphysicians who work with possible worlds of some sort. It is an example of extreme metaphysics.

Where did Lewis's modal realism come from? It already appears in one of his earliest published papers (Lewis 1968). Exciting developments in modal logic, culminating in the work of Saul Kripke, had already made the idea of possible worlds central to the understanding of languages with modal operators (Kripke 1963). "Necessarily" is understood as "in every possible world" and "possibly" as "in some possible world." For technical mathematical reasons, it turned out to be more fruitful not to equate possible worlds with Carnap's state-descriptions, or other such representational entities, but instead to leave their nature unconstrained when characterizing models for the modal language (Williamson 2013a: 81–4). That did not enforce a more metaphysically speculative conception of possible worlds, but it made space for one.

Another significant factor was the development of tense logic, above all by Arthur Prior. He was acutely aware of the strong structural analogies between modal logic and tense logic, with possible worlds playing the same role in the modal case as moments of time play in the temporal case (Prior 1957). An orthographically identical operator could be read as "necessarily" in modal logic and as "always" (or "always in the past" or "always in the future") in tense logic. When one read formulas of the logic in temporal terms, they expressed blatantly metaphysical principles about the structure of time and of existence in time. Those readings provided templates for more metaphysical readings of the same formulas in modal terms, on which they expressed analogous metaphysical principles about the structure of possibility and of possible or necessary existence. Carnap's intra-linguistic modalities could then be replaced by Kripke's metaphysical modalities, which concern how things really could have been.

But developments within modal logic alone cannot fully explain Lewis's modal realism. For Kripke and other leading modal logicians did not go down the modal realist road. Indeed, Lewis's modal realist semantics for modal languages introduces messy complications that from a purely technical point of view are quite unmotivated, even by Prior's analogy between time and modality. In particular, Lewis postulates that no individual exists in more than one world, the analogue of the highly implausible postulate that no individual exists for more than one moment. In order to make sense of the common sense idea that one could have acted differently, Lewis then has to introduce an elaborate theory of counterparthood relations between distinct but similar individuals in different possible worlds. Those complications were motivated by Lewis's prior commitments.

At this point, one must note that Lewis's doctoral supervisor at Harvard in the mid-1960s was Willard van Orman Quine, the leading critic of modal logic. Quine was especially critical of quantified modal logic, as developed by Carnap and Ruth Barcan Marcus, which allows one in effect to reason about the properties and relations that particular individuals could have, as opposed to just the general states of affairs that could obtain. Originally, Quine had tried to prove that quantified modal logic is technically flawed to the point of incoherence, that it collapses the modal distinctions between possibility, necessity, and actuality. As it became clear that his purely formal arguments were technically flawed, Quine gradually switched his line of attack to the informal intelligibility of quantified modal formulas. His standard of intelligibility in logic was austere: first-order non-modal logic, roughly, that of the logical constants "not," "and," "or," "everything," "something," and "is." For Quine, logic *is* first-order non-modal logic. Lewis assumed modal realism because it permits the reduction by translation of a quantified modal language to a first-order non-modal language in which one talks about worlds and individuals in those worlds. Crucially, Lewis's modal realism gave him a way of informally explaining what a possible world is in non-modal terms: roughly, a spatiotemporal system; the individuals in such a system are spatiotemporally connected to each other and to nothing outside the system. Lewis thereby aimed to make quantified modal logic intelligible by his teacher's standards. Since much ordinary discourse in natural language involves expressive resources at least as great as those of quantified modal logic – "can" and "must" are common words, to say the least – Lewis's procedure is also motivated by a principle of charity (Lewis 1974), which Quine explicitly endorsed: prefer an interpretation of a natural language on which speakers are being sensible to one on which they are being silly (Quine 1960: 59). Possible worlds other than our own and their inhabitants are needed to make true ordinary statements about what could have been but isn't. Lewis gave an ingenious solution to the Quinean problem of charitably interpreting quantified modal discourse, on its own Quinean terms, even though Quine rejected the gift.

Quine's lack of interest in modal realism was no anti-metaphysical stance. He did as much as anyone to put ontology as a branch of metaphysics on the map of analytic philosophy, and his conception of philosophy as continuous with natural science overtly involved a naturalistic approach to metaphysical theorizing. One might rather be tempted to suggest that he rejected modal realism because it lacked support from natural science. However, Quine did not require each point of a metaphysical theory to receive its own specific support from natural science. For instance, although he took mathematics – with its ontological commitment to abstract objects such as sets or numbers – to be holistically justified by its applications in natural science, he was well aware that the power of the standard axioms of set theory goes far beyond the needs of natural science, but still regarded them as a legitimate rounding out of the fragment actually used in scientific applications, justified by its simplicity, elegance, and other such virtues. Thus Quine's justification of mathematics is abductive, in a similar spirit to Lewis's justification of modal realism. No doubt, if Quine had felt some tension between modal realism and current natural scientific theory, he would have treated that as a good reason to reject modal realism, but so might Lewis himself. However, neither of them seems to have felt such a tension. In my view, there *is* in fact such a tension, or inconsistency, but the argument for it must be made with some delicacy and was not generally recognized at the time (Williamson 2013a: xii, 17, 2014c: 744–6). Perhaps

Quine simply gave modal realism the same "incredulous stare" that so many other analytic metaphysicians have given it (Lewis 1986a: 133–5). Moreover, Quine encountered modal realism at a stage of his career when he was not disposed to accept radical revisions of his views from outside; publicly retracting his well-entrenched signature skepticism about quantified modal logic would have been a bitter pill to swallow. He showed a similar lack of interest even in the purely technical development of the model theory of modal logic, and in particular of quantified modal logic, by Kripke and others, which is a piece of regular mathematics, no more vulnerable to Quine's concerns about intelligibility than any other piece of mathematics.

The example of Quine is a salutary reminder that the analytic tradition, as normally understood, has never been a metaphysics-free zone. Before Quine, Bertrand Russell was a major figure in the analytic tradition blatantly engaged in metaphysical theorizing. Indeed, F. H. Bradley may well be right that critiques of metaphysics themselves depend on contentious metaphysical assumptions (Bradley 1893: 1–2). Nevertheless, the role and status of metaphysics have changed in significant ways over the history of the analytic tradition, and our concern is with those ways.

Lewis's case for his modal realism itself evolved over time. In the original 1968 paper, the emphasis is on the relation between modal and non-modal languages, and the clarity to be achieved in modal logic by translating the modal language into the non-modal language of Lewis's counterpart theory (the precursor of his modal realism). His postulates for counterpart theory are used to validate elementary principles of modal logic, but they also clarify the metaphysical picture. For instance, the postulate that nothing is in two worlds has the advantage, according to Lewis, that it answers the question of the identity of individuals across possible worlds at a stroke, with a uniform negative. That is his answer to Quine's complaints about the obscurity of trans-world individuation (he cites Quine 1960: 245). By the time he wrote what became the canonical case for modal realism, his book *On the Plurality of Worlds* (Lewis 1986b), based largely on his 1984 John Locke lectures at Oxford, Lewis's perspective had changed. He talks much less about linguistic matters, and much more about the abductive advantages of modal realism as a theoretical framework for explaining a variety of phenomena, many of them non-linguistic. Faced with some objections to specific translation schemes between the language of quantified modal logic (in effect, a formalization of ordinary modal language) and the language of counterpart theory, he tells us not to worry about the details, but instead to abandon the language of quantified modal logic and do our metaphysical theorizing directly in the more perspicuous language of counterpart theory (Lewis 1986a: 12–13). Clearly, from 1968 to 1986 the balance of power in Lewis's work swung towards metaphysics and away from the philosophy of language.

Writing in 1981, Lewis described "a reasonable goal for a philosopher" as bringing one's opinions into stable equilibrium. The trouble with losing "our moorings in everyday common sense," according to him, is not that common sense is infallible but that we do not achieve stable equilibrium, since we keep reverting to something like our everyday opinions (Lewis 1983a: x). He requires the equilibrium to be stable under theoretical reflection. In principle, this is not radically different from a Quinean methodology for philosophy and science together of adjustments to ease tensions in one's web of beliefs (Quine 1951). For Lewis, modal realism does better than other theories of modal metaphysics with respect to stability under reflection, given our other beliefs. Of course, many philosophers would insist that to adopt modal realism *is* to lose one's moorings in everyday common sense, but Lewis was adept at interpreting the putative deliverances of everyday common sense in ways that made them consistent with modal realism, often by postulating large measures of tacit contextual restriction in the utterances that gave them voice. Although he admitted some disagreements between modal realism and common sense, for instance on whether (speaking unrestrictedly) there are talking donkeys, he managed to steer the disagreements into abstruse areas that might plausibly be regarded as of low priority for common sense. Whereas critics condemned Lewis for his extravagant departures from common sense, he saw his modal realism as part of his defense of common sense – just the way Berkeley saw his subjective idealism.

In practice, the process of bringing one's opinions into stable equilibrium will involve extensive reflection on what one's opinions actually are. Since one's general beliefs are typically presented to one as expressed by sentences, whose underlying semantic structure is not perfectly transparent, in reflecting on what it is one believes one is drawn into semantic reflection on one's own language – or, as some would have it, reflection on one's own conceptual system.

A natural comparison is between Lewis's Quinean or at least post-Quinean methodology and the methodology of Peter Strawson, Quine's leading opponent from the tradition of ordinary language philosophy. By the late 1950s, however, "ordinary language philosophy" was no longer an apt phrase for what Strawson was doing. He was working in a far more abstract and systematic way than that phrase suggests. His concern was with very general structural features of ordinary thought and talk, such as the distinction between subject and predicate, rather than with the fine detail of ordinary usage. In 1959 he published *Individuals*, subtitled *An Essay in Descriptive Metaphysics*, a major monograph widely felt at the time to mark a turning-point in the rehabilitation of metaphysics within analytic philosophy. Strawson contrasted descriptive metaphysics with the wilder *revisionary metaphysics*, which despite its "partial vision" is nevertheless useful when "at the service of descriptive metaphysics" (Strawson 1959: 9). Revisionary metaphysics can help at the periphery of our thinking, but goes astray when it tries to revise "a massive central core of human thinking which has no history" because "there are categories and concepts which, in their most fundamental character, change not at all" (ibid.: 10). What descriptive metaphysics is supposed to describe are the conceptual connections that constitute the structure of that central core. In Strawson's view, that structure is not hierarchical, as envisaged by programs of conceptual analysis with their non-circular definitions by necessary and sufficient conditions. Rather, the descriptive metaphysician traces conceptual interconnections on the same level, going round in complex closed curves: the exploration is horizontal rather than vertical.

How different in kind is Strawsonian metaphysics, which may revise the margins but must only describe the core of ordinary thinking, from Lewisian metaphysics, which must not lose its moorings in everyday common sense in its attempt to steer one's opinions into equilibrium? At this point, it may be worth recalling that Lewis attended lectures by Strawson, amongst others, when he spent the academic year 1959–1960 as a visiting student from Swarthmore College at Oxford, tutored by Iris Murdoch, a year that resulted in his momentous decision to major in Philosophy rather than, as he had previously intended, Chemistry. Of course, Strawson's characterization of descriptive metaphysics as the tracing of conceptual connections relies on some form of the analytic-synthetic distinction, which he had defended with his old teacher Paul Grice against Quine's massively influential critique (Quine 1951, Grice and Strawson 1956). Indeed, the complex closed curve of definitions that Quine traced from "analytic" round to other semantic terms and back again in his attempt to show that none of them could be satisfactorily explained was just the sort of explanation the descriptive metaphysician sought. But on this issue Lewis sided with his earlier teacher against his later one. Lewis's first book concluded with an attempt to rehabilitate analyticity as truth in all possible worlds (Lewis 1969: 208), to Quine's regret in the book's Foreword (Quine 1969: xii). Although both Strawson and Lewis accepted an analytic-synthetic distinction, in their philosophical practice neither of them had much tendency to use it as the sort of glib conversation-stopper it so often becomes in less resourceful hands. Admittedly, Strawson was more prone than Lewis to characterize philosophical questions as questions about words or concepts, or as questions about *how we must think about* a subject matter, rather than about the subject matter itself. But Lewis himself frequently went metalinguistic, as we have already seen, and Strawson was quite willing to speak in a ground-level metaphysical idiom, as with remarks such as "A person is not an embodied ego, but an ego might be a disembodied person" (Strawson 1959: 103). They both moved easily between object-language and meta-language, as it were, depending on the argumentative needs of the moment.

Quine insisted on continuity between philosophy and natural science in a way that Strawson did not. In this respect, Lewis was closer to Quine than to Strawson. In practice, however, natural science played only a very minor role in the metaphysics of all three philosophers. A good test is their treatment of the dispute between the three-dimensionalist Aristotelian metaphysics of enduring continuants and the four-dimensionalist metaphysics of occurrents composed of successive time-slices, often associated with Einstein's theory of special relativity. Predictably, Strawson is a three-dimensionalist while Quine and Lewis are four-dimensionalists. But what is striking is how little Quine and Lewis made of special relativity in their cases for four-dimensionalism. In *Word and Object*, Quine emphasized the advantages in logical smoothness of treating space and time on a par (Quine 1960: 170–2). He adds only as a convenient afterthought that Einstein's discovery of special relativity "leaves no reasonable alternative to treating time as spacelike," but then immediately points out that the logical benefits of doing so "are independent of Einstein's principle" and adds, with references, "the idea of paraphrasing tensed sentences into terms of eternal relations of things to times was clear enough before Einstein" (ibid.: 172). In *On the Plurality of Worlds*, Lewis's case for four-dimensionalism does not mention Einstein or depend on modern science at all; it just relies on rather shaky old-fashioned purely metaphysical reasoning about temporary intrinsic properties, such as shapes (Lewis 1986a: 202–5). Presumably, Lewis was not convinced that special relativity really did leave no reasonable alternative to treating time as spacelike, otherwise he would have mentioned such impressive support for his conclusion. Since the specifics of Lewis's argumentation fail to take seriously an approach that treats temporal operators as explanatorily basic, it is hard to avoid the impression that what was really decisive with him was a somewhat Quinean preconception about the proper sort of language for doing metaphysics in, something close to the language of mathematics. Of course, glancing through the pages of *On the Plurality of Worlds*, one sees them filled with formula-free English prose, just like the pages of *Individuals*. Nevertheless, the systematicity at which Lewis aims is modeled on that of a scientific theory articulated in a mathematical language. The systematicity at which Strawson aims is different; it is that of a satisfying general account in English itself, or some other natural language. The sort of formal logical smoothness that Quine and Lewis valued so highly, Strawson regarded as a trap. In this less standard sense, despite the similarities, and even in their metaphysics, Strawson remained at heart an ordinary language philosopher, and Lewis at heart an ideal language philosopher. Each of them was reluctant to disagree extensively with common sense (or natural science, for that matter), but left some room for maneuver by acknowledging a belt of revisable opinions on the periphery of common sense. As a result of quite a subtle difference in intellectual values, they ended up with radically different theories.

What if Strawson is right, in that Lewis's views conflict with the unchanging core of ordinary thought? Then those views fail by Lewis's own criterion, since no totality of his opinions that includes them will be stable under theoretical reflection, for it will also include the unchanging core of ordinary thought. We cannot expect to keep questions about the general methodological position in a philosophical debate clinically isolated from questions about who is right and who is wrong on the specific matters at issue within the debate (see 212–16, this volume).

We can refine our sense of the intellectual options by comparing both Strawson and Lewis with Kripke. In the 1970s, Kripke and Lewis were often paired as leaders of the "possible worlds revolution." Kripke's essentialism and his defense of quantified modal logic were radical in relation to Quinean orthodoxy. It took time for them to be understood as articulations of quite ordinary ways of thinking, so *not* radical in relation to common sense. Of course, the connection between essentialism and Aristotle already noted by Quine was a clue, since Aristotle always had a strong claim to be the founder of common sense philosophy. Strawson names Aristotle and Kant as the great descriptive metaphysicians (1959: 9). Kripke's arguments in *Naming and Necessity* tend to be based on common sense examples, and he explicitly rejects Lewis's modal realism, in favor of a more deflationary conception of possible worlds as possible states of affairs (Kripke 1972). His metaphysics is arguably not revisionary in Strawson's sense. This feature of it may have been obscured by his technical achievements in quantified modal logic, based on the mathematical apparatus of "possible worlds semantics," even though it is in itself no more metaphysically problematic than any other piece of mathematics (Williamson 2013a: 81–4).

Although Kripke's metaphysics initially could seem more revisionary than it really was, his methodology could initially seem more linguistic than it really was. His titles yoked together semantic and metaphysical terms: *Naming and Necessity* (1972) and *Reference and Existence* (2013 – the book of his John Locke Lectures given at Oxford in 1973 under the same title). Of course, it was Kripke who played the central role in distinguishing metaphysical from epistemic or semantic modalities, through his famous examples of contingent truths knowable *a priori* and of necessary truths knowable only *a posteriori*, which made trouble for the then-popular Humean slogan "All necessity is verbal necessity." Even so, there was a diffuse but influential impression in the 1970s that Kripke had somehow managed to derive apparently substantial metaphysical conclusions about the specific essential properties of individuals and kinds, from his semantic analysis of modal language, in particular his insight that names are rigid designators (their designation remains constant while different possible worlds are considered). Nathan Salmon published a detailed monograph *Reference and Essence* (1982) to refute that impression. The title uses "and" to separate the semantic term from the metaphysical one, rather than to join them together. The front cover showed a rabbit being pulled from a hat. Salmon demonstrated that Kripke had relied on metaphysical premises to derive his metaphysical conclusion (Kripke himself had not claimed otherwise). That did not make Kripke's argument merely question-begging, for the plausibility of the premises could still be more immediate than the plausibility of the conclusion. Salmon's point was widely accepted. That contributed to an increasingly popular conception of metaphysics as separate from the philosophy of language.

Just as it was a mistake to regard Kripke's metaphysics as derived from his semantics, it would be a mistake to regard them as simply orthogonal to each other. For misconceptions in semantics often induce misconceptions in metaphysics, by causing fallacious metaphysical arguments to be treated as valid, so that coherent metaphysical views are incorrectly dismissed as confused or inconsistent. Quine's early critique of quantified modal logic is an example. It was crucial to get straight about the semantics of modal language in order to see one's way through to defending metaphysical theses of essentialism. Thus Kripke's semantic theory of rigid designators was after all relevant to his essentialist metaphysics, but its role was negative, in driving off arguments *against* essentialism, not positive, in driving forward arguments *for* essentialism.

There is a more general moral here about the famous "linguistic turn," a phrase that has looked less and less appropriate as a description of mainstream analytic philosophy over recent decades. Nevertheless, although analytic philosophers are ceasing to regard their central questions as linguistic or even conceptual in any sense that would distinguish them from questions asked in other disciplines, the traces of the linguistic turn are not simply being erased. For it has left a rich legacy of methodological sophistication. In testing the soundness of arguments about non-linguistic matters, analytic philosophers regularly draw on work in both semantics and pragmatics (48–9, this volume). Kripke's work on quantified modal logic is a good example with respect to semantics.

With respect to pragmatics, the prime exhibit is the work of Strawson's teacher, Paul Grice, on conversational implicature (1961, 1975). If you comment after my lecture "Williamson was sober this afternoon," you *imply* that I am often drunk in the afternoon, even though that is not a precondition for the *truth* of what you said: it is even true if I am a scrupulous teetotaller. Grice developed a powerful theoretical apparatus for analyzing such effects. Although this work emerged from within the Oxford of ordinary language philosophy, it made an important contribution to undermining the methodology of such philosophy. For ordinary language philosophy involved a focus on "what we would say" in various conversational contexts. By analyzing the diversity of reasons for which an utterance might be conversationally inappropriate, Grice demonstrated the limitations to what can be concluded from such data. But his theory of conversation was not just a factor in the implosion of ordinary language philosophy; it has a far more lasting and positive value. It is massively cited by linguists, because it is the starting-point for much contemporary work in pragmatics. But it also continues to play a vital negative role in contemporary analytic philosophy.

Analytic epistemology provides a good case study of the philosophical application of Gricean pragmatics outside the philosophy of language. Analytic epistemologists today typically regard the object of their study as knowing (or justified believing) itself, as opposed to the corresponding words or concepts. In reflecting on knowledge or justified belief, they work through example after example of epistemologically suggestive situations, often of quite everyday sorts. In determining how to describe such situations, they frequently have to ask themselves whether a proposed description is false or, by contrast, true but conversationally misleading because it has a false conversational implicature. They use Grice's theory of conversation to filter out contaminated data. They also have to engage with semantics as well as pragmatics, since some of the leading contender theories are contextualist, in the sense that they postulate shifts in the reference of epistemic terms according to the context in which they are used. Despite all that, the epistemologists' underlying object of study is knowing itself, not the verb "to know" or the concept of knowing. They sound like ordinary language philosophers, and in a loose enough sense they *are* ordinary language philosophers, even when ordinary language plays no special role in their epistemological aims (Hawthorne 2004, Stanley 2005 are good examples). In that respect, ordinary language has returned to its origins. For the classic manifesto for ordinary language philosophy, at least in its Oxford form, appeared in J. L. Austin's paper "A plea for excuses" (1956–1957). But much of Austin's discussion of philosophical method there appears strongly influenced by similar comments in the work of John Cook Wilson, Wykeham Professor of Logic at Oxford from 1889 until his death in 1915, founder of an Oxford tradition of realist metaphysics and knowledge-centered epistemology, and by no means a linguistic philosopher as the term is usually understood. For instance, Cook Wilson's remark "Distinctions current in language can never be safely neglected" (1926: 46) is echoed in Austin's emphasis on the value of starting with distinctions robust enough to have survived in ordinary language. Cook Wilson's ideas and writings still loomed large in the Oxford philosophy of Austin's student days, not least through the influence of his star pupil H. A. Prichard, the White's Professor of Moral Philosophy from 1927 to 1937, whose lectures Austin attended as an undergraduate – despite Prichard's attempt to ban him for asking too many questions. Thus many contemporary analytic philosophers pay close attention to linguistic subtleties, without treating their primary subject matter as in any way linguistic.

The foregoing sketch suggests no easy moral, except that the closer one looks at the history of anything, the less it lends itself to easy morals. But I can add some color to the picture, and another perspective on the transition, by going back to my own experience of it at Oxford.

II

I arrived as an undergraduate at Oxford in 1973, to study Mathematics and Philosophy. Logic played a central role in the course, to my lasting benefit; its centrality is relevant to the point of view from which I observed the scene. I received my undergraduate degree in 1976 and began to study for a doctorate. Originally I hoped to formalize Leibniz's principle of sufficient reason, but I soon switched to Karl Popper's idea of verisimilitude, on which science can progress through a succession of theories that get closer and closer to the truth without ever quite reaching it. I left Oxford in 1980, to start my first proper job, as a lecturer in philosophy at Trinity College Dublin, and received my doctorate in 1981.

In 1973, the two senior professors of theoretical philosophy at Oxford were A. J. (Freddie) Ayer, Wykeham Professor of Logic from

1959 to 1978, and P. F. (Peter) Strawson, Waynflete Professor of Metaphysics from 1968 to 1987. Austin had died in 1960 and Prior in 1969, both prematurely; Grice had left for Berkeley in 1967. One could schematically associate Ayer and Strawson with the two main strands of mid-century analytic philosophy: logical positivism and ordinary language philosophy respectively. Ayer had studied with the Vienna Circle and his first book, *Language, Truth and Logic* (1936) contained much logical positivist doctrine, including a critique of metaphysics based on the verification principle, although he traced his genealogy further back: "The views which are put forward in this treatise derive from the doctrines of Bertrand Russell and Wittgenstein, which are themselves the logical outcome of the empiricism of Berkeley and David Hume" (1936: 31). The book had been notorious for its advocacy of expressivism about morality and religion. Its cheeky, provocative style is conveyed by the title of the last chapter, "Solutions of outstanding philosophical problems." Whereas Ayer was a follower of Russell, Strawson's most famous article (1950) was a critique of Russell's prize contribution to philosophy, his theory of descriptions, and Strawson's first book argued more generally that such applications of modern logic did no justice to the subtleties of ordinary language (1952). In live discussion, Ayer used rapid fire, Strawson elegant rapier play. Ayer was better known to the general public, as a radio personality; Strawson was more highly rated by professional philosophers, as more original. Strawson had been a candidate for the Wykeham Chair of Logic; when Ayer was elected, through the votes of the non-philosophers on the committee, Austin and Ryle resigned in protest. Asked that evening by a colleague whether he felt very disappointed not to have been elected, Strawson replied "Not disappointed, just unappointed."

By 1973, it was no longer strictly appropriate to classify Ayer as a logical positivist, or Strawson as an ordinary language philosopher. It was closer to the mark to describe Ayer as a Humean, and Strawson as a Kantian: the contrast between them was no less marked for that. Strawson's development into a systematic metaphysician has already been noted. Ayer had retreated from his early radicalism, including the verificationist critique of metaphysics. He commented that the trouble with *Language, Truth and Logic* was that all its main doctrines were false. In 1976, on the fortieth anniversary of its first publication, he gave a series of lectures about what remained of his original view. In the book, he had quoted as an example of an unverifiable pseudo-proposition of metaphysics "the Absolute enters into, but is itself incapable of, evolution and progress," which he describes as "A remark taken at random from *Appearance and Reality*, by F. H. Bradley" (1936: 36). In his lecture, he admitted that, far from having taken the remark at random, he had searched through *Appearance and Reality* for hours to find something suitably nonsensical-sounding. It is a salutary reminder of the intelligibility by ordinary standards of much metaphysical discourse – especially when not torn out of context in the way he presented the passage from Bradley.

To younger philosophers in 1973, Ayer appeared quite old-fashioned philosophically. So too, though to a lesser extent, did Strawson. The underlying reason was in large part their relation to modern formal logic in philosophy. Officially, Ayer was for it and Strawson against it, but neither of them knew much about it. They had received their philosophical education at a time when such logic did not loom large in Oxford. Philosophers of that generation sometimes referred to formal logic as "sums," the primary school word for elementary arithmetic. The effect of Ayer and Strawson's lack of facility with modern formal logic was that they were poorly placed to deal with the new wave of philosophy of language sweeping across the Atlantic, led by Kripke and Lewis (who was at least as much a philosopher of language as a metaphysician in the 1970s), and other philosophers and linguists such as Donald Davidson, Hilary Putnam, David Kaplan, Robert Stalnaker, Keith Donnellan, Richard Montague, and Barbara Hall Partee. New-wave philosophy of language involved the application of formal semantics, based on modern logic, to natural languages.

Ayer had never had a detailed interest in the philosophy of language. His resentment of the new wave focused on Kripke's case for the necessary *a posteriori* and the contingent *a priori*, in effect because those categories violated Hume's supposedly exhaustive distinction between matters of fact (contingent and *a posteriori*) and relations of ideas (necessary and *a priori*). An annual ritual took place in Ayer's "Informal Instruction," his class open to all comers, where a short presentation of some recently published work would kick off the discussion. Many of the brightest graduate students attended, even though they had joined the new wave, for Ayer was good at creating an atmosphere conducive to discussion. But every year he would read a short paper purporting to refute Kripke on the necessary *a posteriori* and the contingent *a priori*, in fact based on exactly the confusions Kripke had done so much to clear up. When he had finished, the graduate students would by implication plead with Ayer not to misunderstand Kripke – in vain. Strawson was much more of a philosopher of language than Ayer, but even his perception of new-wave philosophy of language was distorted by the old-fashioned lens of an exaggerated contrast between, in effect, ordinary language philosophy attentive to speakers' actual use of natural language in all its complexity and ideal language philosophy trying to project the simple logical structure of a formal language onto natural language, in abstraction from its speakers, with Procrustean effect (Strawson 1971). What he never properly appreciated was the new-wave conception of the two projects as mutually complementary rather than in competition, so that interpreting a natural language in terms of a comparatively simple formal truth-conditional semantics would make the best sense of the complexities of speakers' actual use of the language (Lewis 1975a). That Strawson's criticisms of new-wave philosophy of language were widely felt to miss the point contributed to his looking like a figure from the past too.

In effect, new-wave philosophy of language achieved a surprising reconciliation between elements from the two main competing strands of mid-twentieth century analytic philosophy, logical positivism and ordinary language philosophy. From logical positivism it took the rigorous use of formal languages with precisely and systematically described syntax and semantics, as found in modern logic, to model meaning. From ordinary language philosophy it took most of its data about use to be explained, as well as ideas about the nature of the relation between meaning and use, in order to bring the formal models to bear on the data. An encouraging precedent was Noam Chomsky's success in explaining subtle, apparently messy complexities in the surface syntax of English in terms of formal models of a postulated underlying deep structure (Chomsky 1957). What new-wave philosophers of language hoped to do for the semantics of natural languages seemed analogous to what Chomsky and others were already doing for syntax – despite Chomsky's own skepticism about the scientific status of semantics. Indeed, it was natural to expect a tight relation between the semantic and syntactic structure of an expression, at least at the level of deep structure or logical form. For it was a fundamental tenet of new-wave philosophy of language, coming through Carnap from Gottlob Frege, that the semantics must be *compositional*, in the sense that the meaning of a complex expression is determined by the meanings of its constituents; how else to explain our ability to understand sentences we have never previously encountered, if made up of familiar words in familiar types of combination? The initial hypothesis must surely be that the requisite semantic articulation of sentences into their semantic constituents matches their syntactic articulation into syntactic constituents at some deep enough level. The compositionality constraint exerted a powerful force in the direction of systematicity. In practice, the only semantic theories to exhibit (rather than merely claim) such a compositional structure were those for formally specified languages. Without such a formal semantics, a philosophy of language looked badly undeveloped to new wavers. It was partly for this reason that Austin was barely mentioned in Oxford philosophy of language by 1973, since he had no formal semantics to offer. The same went for his *protégé* and in some respects intellectual heir John Searle, whose major work *Speech Acts* looked out of date from an Oxford perspective almost as soon as it was published in 1969. Although Austin and Searle continued to exert a significant influence, it was mainly outside the new wave.

New-wave semantics came in two main varieties, though methodologically the differences between them were minor compared to their shared differences from their predecessors. One variety was possible worlds semantics, which went back to Carnap and by 1973 was associated with philosophers of language such as Kripke, Lewis, Kaplan, Stalnaker, and Montague. In "English as a formal language" (1970), "The proper treatment of quantification in ordinary English" (1973), and other papers, Montague showed how it could provide a rigorously working compositional semantics for large fragments of a natural language. His work had a major influence on Barbara Hall Partee and has been seminal for a major tradition of intensional semantics as a branch of linguistics. The other main variety of new-wave semantics was extensional, under the influence of Quine. Chastened by his skepticism about meanings, it approached the semantic realm less directly, through theorizing explicitly about reference and truth rather than meaning itself. Nevertheless, its emphasis on the constraint of compositionality was just as strong. Formally, it took inspiration from Tarski's theory of truth. Its main proponent was Donald Davidson

(1967a). It too had a significant impact on linguistics, most notably through Davidson's semantics for verbs and adverbs in natural
language, which postulated tacit quantifiers over events (Davidson
1967b). A leading Davidsonian linguist was James Higginbotham.

I first encountered new-wave philosophy of language in my first
term as an undergraduate, when my tutor encouraged me to attend
the John Locke lectures, to be given by the rising young star of American philosophy, Saul Kripke. I was hugely impressed by his clarity,
informal rigor, pointed examples, common sense, and humor. The
lectures were mostly non-technical, but one both sensed and independently knew of his easy technical mastery of the subject. Although I
did not think of it this way at the time, Kripke combined and recon-
ciled the virtues of ideal language philosophy with those of ordinary
language philosophy. At that stage, of course, I knew very little of the
background in the philosophy of language to what he was saying, and
was in no position to follow everything that went on in the lectures
and the discussion that followed them. Nevertheless, Kripke became
the nearest I had to a model of how to do philosophy.

Although Kripke's work was widely discussed in Oxford at that
time, especially by younger philosophers, the dominant variety in
town of new-wave semantics was extensional rather than intensional.
Davidson had given the John Locke lectures in 1970. The two most
admired young theoretical philosophers in Oxford, Gareth Evans and
John McDowell, somehow combined Davidson with Frege as the
packed audiences at their joint classes looked on. It was the moment
of the "Davidsonic boom" – although people tended to utter the Tarskian mantra "The sentence 'Snow is white' is true in English if and
only if snow is white" in a rather slow and quiet voice. If you wanted
to write on the philosophy of X, whatever X was, then you were supposed to start by writing a truth theory for a language for talking
about X. I found the atmosphere of reverence for Davidson unhealthy,
not to say sickening. It was fine for him to choose a speculative and
controversial extensionalist starting point for his program for the philosophy of language, and to take it as far as he could from there, but
the project cried out to be undertaken in a scientific spirit, as a test of
its assumptions. Instead, they were treated – especially by those lower
in the hierarchy – as dogmas of mysterious but compelling power,
an attitude encouraged by Davidson's elliptical and slightly evasive
style. It was recognized that Davidson's program had to meet the

challenge of providing a compositional semantics for various apparently non-extensional constructions in natural language, for ascribing beliefs and desires or possibility and necessity, for example, but the discussion of alternative proposals muffled the issues with a lack of openness and clarity about the rules of the game. Philosophers, some with only a rather tenuous grasp of technical matters, would invoke obscurely motivated technical constraints – a ban on substitutional quantification, say, or a requirement of finite axiomatizability – to exclude rival hypotheses. Kripke's critique of Davidsonians' objections to substitutional quantification (1976) has been condemned as cruel, but to me it came as a breath of fresh air; I can attest to the presence at the time of the sort of atmosphere about which he complained.[1] By contrast, intensional semantics seemed to be conducted in a more open, scientific spirit, though Davidsonians objected, darkly, to its possible worlds as creatures of darkness.

Davidsonians did not expect the philosophy of language to be independent of metaphysics. Davidson (1977) explicitly motivated an ontology of events by a Quine-inspired principle of charity in interpretation, through the semantics of adverbs. This was not so different from Lewis's original motivation of his ontology of possible worlds, in effect by the principle of charity, through the semantics of modal operators. But Davidson gave his metaphysics a turn reminiscent of Strawson, with a transcendental argument to show that it was not really possible to think differently (Davidson 1974). As so often with transcendental arguments, it turns out to depend on concealed verificationist assumptions (see the later remarks on Wittgenstein's Private Language Argument). More recent metaphysics has been much less tempted by transcendental arguments.

Amongst the important features shared by the extensional and intensional varieties of new-wave semantics was truth-conditionality: they both treated the meaning of a declarative sentence as in some sense the condition for it to be true. By contrast, the senior Oxford philosopher properly to engage new-wave philosophy of language, Michael Dummett, opposed such truth-conditional semantics in favor of assertibility-conditional semantics, which treated the meaning of a

---

[1] My first article to be accepted for publication, though not my first to be published, protested against the Davidsonian dogma that theories of truth *qua* theories of meaning had to be finitely axiomatizable (Williamson 1984).

declarative sentence as the condition for it to be assertible, or verifiable, rather than true. Assertibility-conditional semantics was inspired by the proof-conditional semantics for mathematical language developed by Heyting, Prawitz, and other intuitionists, which equated the meaning of a sentence in the language of mathematics with the condition for something to be a proof of it. The plan was to generalize this semantics to the whole of language by treating mathematical proof as a special case of verification. This may be seen as a descendant of a logical positivist conception of the meaning of a sentence as its method of verification, although Dummett did not present it as such.

Unlike the logical positivists, Dummett saw the subversive threat that verification-centered semantics posed to classical logic, given the compositionality constraint which he accepted, in line with new-wave philosophy of language. For example, the natural compositional semantic clause for disjunctive sentences of the form "A or B" says that "A or B" is verified if and only if either "A" is verified or "B" is verified. But that makes immediate trouble for the classical law of excluded middle, "A or not A." For the special case of the semantic clause where "B" = "not A" says that "A or not A" is verified if and only if either "A" is verified or "not A" is verified. But often we cannot verify a sentence and cannot verify its negation. For instance, we cannot verify "Napoleon had an even number of hairs at his death" nor can we verify "Napoleon had an odd number of hairs at his death." Thus, by the semantic clause, we cannot verify "Napoleon had an odd or even number of hairs at his death."

In these ways, Dummett saw the philosophy of language as calling into question a realist metaphysical conception of reality as how it is quite independently of our capacity to find out how it is, and pointing towards an alternative anti-realist metaphysics. In his view, the role of the philosophy of language here is not merely evidential, to give us reasons to believe one metaphysical theory and not another. Rather, he saw alternative theories of meaning as giving something like the cash-value of alternative metaphysical pictures. Methodologically, he proposed to replace futile quarrels between metaphysical pictures by comparisons between the corresponding theories of meaning as the only scientific way to resolve the issue. For him, metaphysical disputes are not senseless; nor are they what they seem, since they are implicitly disputes in the philosophy of language. One might compare Dummett's understanding of metaphysics with Strawson's. For both of them, metaphysical questions turn into questions about the structure and limits of coherent thought, to be answered by systematic inquiry. But Dummett was more open to revisionary metaphysics than Strawson was, because he took seriously the danger of fundamental incoherence in our current ways of thinking (as with our acceptance of the law of excluded middle), which Strawson did not. Dummett also differed from Strawson in regarding modern logic as a decisive advance over its predecessors, including its capacity to provide formal methods and model formal languages for use in the philosophy of language: he was adept himself in such methods. In that sense too, he was a new-wave philosopher of language.

Dummett laid out his program early on in his career (1959). The year Kripke gave the John Locke lectures, Dummett brought out his first *magnum opus*, *Frege: Philosophy of Language* (1973), in which he engaged creatively with Frege to develop his own views. Central to Oxford philosophy in my student days was the dispute between, on one side, realism and truth-conditional semantics, represented by the Davidsonians, and, on the other side, anti-realism and assertibility-conditional semantics, represented by Dummett. My sympathies were strongly with realism, though not with Davidsonianism. Dummett supervised me for the last year of my doctoral studies (1979–1980), at the start of his period as Wykeham Professor of Logic (1979–1992), the first holder of that chair with a deep knowledge of modern logic. He was remarkably tolerant of the strident realism of my thesis, which effectively presupposed the futility of his life's work and pursued other issues from that starting-point. I cannot resist a couple of memories from that period.

When I told other philosophers at Oxford that I was working on the idea of approximation to the truth as applied to scientific theories, their reaction was always to ask "Is that something to do with vagueness?" For vagueness was a big issue in Oxford then, being conceived as a major challenge to realism, truth-conditional semantics, and other forms of orthodoxy (Dummett 1975a, Fine 1975, Wright 1975). I always found that reaction annoying, because I thought it betrayed a myopic obsession with the philosophy of language. I would reply that my thesis had nothing at all to do with vagueness, pointing out that, of two perfectly precise but false scientific theories, one may be a better approximation to the truth than the other (I also enjoyed shocking people by saying that I found Popper more interesting than

Davidson). On the narrow issue I was right, but my later trajectory suggests that my interlocutors were not completely wrong about the direction of my interests (Williamson 1994a). Indeed, one of my main reasons for later working on vagueness was that it was generally regarded as a paradigm of a phenomenon in need of anti-realist treatment. I wanted to strike at what was supposed to be the safest fortress of anti-realism.

Another memory comes from a supervision with Dummett. We were discussing an argument that I thought one of the best in my thesis, and he thought one of the worst; it later became the kernel of the only publication that emerged from my doctoral studies (Williamson 1988). After a while, Dummett reflected and said "The difference between us is that you think that inference to the best explanation is a legitimate method of argument in philosophy, and I don't." I realized that his characterization of the difference was right, although I was a little shocked at his outright rejection of inference to the best explanation in philosophy. His view was something like this: the deep philosophical issue will be about which of the theories that yield the putative explanations is so much as meaningful; that issue must be settled first before we can judge the value of those putative explanations; but once it has been settled, nothing much is left for inference to the best explanation to do. I still favor inference to the best explanation and an abductive methodology in philosophy (Williamson 2013a: 423–9). Indeed, it is hard to see how the kind of positive, systematic, general theory that Dummett sought in the philosophy of language could be established by any other means. He was optimistic about the long-run prospects of settling philosophical issues in a decisive, systematic way, just as he took to happen in science (Dummett 1978). But if one tries to establish the meaningfulness of a theory by an argument more decisive than abduction, won't one have to first establish the meaningfulness of that argument by a further argument more decisive than abduction? There starts an infinite regress. Dummett's dislike of inference to the best explanation may help to explain why his discussion of assertibility-conditional semantics never really got beyond the programmatic stage to the nitty-gritty of properly developing models of such semantics for non-trivial fragments of non-mathematical language. Even if such models had worked well (a tall order), they would at best have provided him with some sort of abductive argument in favor of his program, whereas he wanted something more decisive. In the long run, the failure of his program to develop such working models has been a major reason for its marginalization, especially when combined with its radically revisionary and implausible consequences for logic and metaphysics.

Dummett presented his views on the relationship between the philosophy of language and metaphysics in his William James Lectures at Harvard in 1976, the same year that Hilary Putnam gave the John Locke Lectures at Oxford. A book soon grew out of Putnam's lectures, showing signs of Dummett's influence in some rather unfortunate arguments against something called "metaphysical realism" (Putnam 1978). But it was not long before the anti-realist Dummett was replaced by the realist (if not metaphysical realist) J. L. Austin as the main Oxford presence in Putnam's work (Putnam 1994). Dummett's lectures took much longer to appear in print, as *The Logical Basis of Metaphysics* (Dummett 1991). For a key work of a major philosopher, it had comparatively little impact. One problem was that its discussion of proof theory as the foundation of semantics was informal, often elliptical, digressive, or vague, with philosophical and purely technical matters all mixed together, making it excessively and unnecessarily hard for logicians to extract and perhaps answer the purely technical questions raised. Moreover, the generalization of the semantics to non-mathematical language still remained at a tentative, programmatic stage, not conducive to applications in linguistics. A more general problem for Dummett was that by 1991 the philosophical *zeitgeist* was even less receptive to anything like Dummett's program than it had been earlier. He did not engage with the new paradigms of metaphysics, such as the work of David Lewis. There was no obvious way to interpret the new metaphysical theories as picturesque guises for views in the theory of meaning, nor did the new generation of metaphysicians wish to do so. Metaphysics itself had grown in self-confidence and felt no need to present itself as anything else. Incidentally, despite its title, my own book *Modal Logic as Metaphysics* (2013a) is very far from a return to Dummett's understanding of the relationship between logic and metaphysics. As a first approximation, "logic" in Dummett's title means something like "philosophical reflection on the meaning of the logical constants," while in mine it means "generalizing about the world in terms just of the logical constants." For Dummett, logic is metalinguistic, for me it is not.

By the 1990s, few readers felt in danger of being compelled, against their wills, by Dummett's convoluted arguments, even when they understood them. One of several reasons was that he discussed the mind in ways that still carried behaviorist baggage from a philosophy of mind widely rejected by younger generations since the collapse of behaviorist psychology and its replacement by cognitive psychology in the 1960s. Such baggage is detectable in remarks like this about knowledge of meaning: "we should [...] not be content with saying *what* is known, without saying what it is to have that knowledge, that is, how it is manifested by one who has it" (Dummett 1991: 104–5), where the manifestation is in observable behavior. In this respect, Dummett can be compared to Quine, who was influenced by his Harvard colleague Skinner's behaviorism in psychology. One might think that behaviorism about language had been outdated since the publication of Chomsky's famously destructive review of Skinner's *Linguistic Behavior* (1959), but digestion can be a slow process. I remember sophisticated young philosophers of language at Oxford in the late 1970s still talking of children learning their native language by being "drilled" in it by adults. In Dummett's case, his behaviorist tendencies came from his reading of Wittgenstein rather than Skinner, and were correspondingly subtler and less eliminativist than Quine's. Nevertheless, the differences should not be exaggerated. An anecdote from late in Dummett's career: A group of younger Oxford philosophers were discussing what he meant, in the great man's silent presence. Suggestion after suggestion was rejected because it would attribute to him "crude old-fashioned behaviorism." Eventually, someone turned to him and asked "So what *is* your view, Michael?" Dummett replied "I *think* it's the one you've been calling 'crude old-fashioned behaviorism.'"

For Dummett, as for other British philosophers of his generation, Wittgenstein's central contribution to the philosophy of mind was his Private Language Argument. Its interpretation was disputed, but it was widely supposed to show *something* very deep about the need for talk about mental states to involve observable criteria (in some sense) for attributing them to others. The putative insight had widespread repercussions for the philosophy of language, concerning not just the semantics of mental state ascriptions but the nature of the mental states in play for speakers and hearers of any speech act, and in particular the nature of understanding. Dummett's preference for assertibility-conditions over truth-conditions in the theory of meaning was rooted in the close linkage of assertibility-conditions to the observable use of the language, which realist truth-conditions lacked, since users of the language might have no idea whether they obtained. He combined this Wittgenstein-inspired focus on use with a Frege-inspired insistence on the need for a systematic, compositional theory of meaning, modeled on the semantics of a formal language. In thus uniting elements of the two previous traditions of analytic philosophy, ordinary language philosophy and ideal language philosophy, Dummett resembled the younger new-wave philosophers of language, although his selection of elements to combine differed from theirs.

At this point something must be said more generally about the influence of Wittgenstein on British philosophy in the period under discussion – as has often been remarked, his influence in North America was never as great as in Europe, one reason being the greater sway of naturalism or scientism in North America, led by Quine and others. In the case of Dummett, since he was a student at Oxford in 1950 when Wittgenstein spent some time there living in Elizabeth Anscombe's house, future historians might wonder whether there was face-to-face influence. It is therefore worth recounting the story Dummett liked to tell about his only meeting with Wittgenstein. Dummett was going for a tutorial at Anscombe's house. She kept the door unlocked. As was the practice, Dummett went in, and sat down to await her summons. An elderly man in a dressing-gown came downstairs and asked "Where's the milk?"; Dummett replied "Don't ask me." That was the extent of his conversation with Wittgenstein. What mattered instead was Anscombe's mediating role. She was probably the strongest transmitter of Wittgenstein's influence at Oxford until she left in 1970 to take up a chair at Cambridge, although of course she was always a fiercely independent-minded philosopher in her own right. Other Oxford ordinary language philosophers such as Ryle, Austin, and Grice were not molded by Wittgenstein, and the number of card-carrying Wittgensteinians at Oxford was never very high. Nevertheless, his influence was still pervasive when I was a student in the 1970s. Gordon Baker and Peter Hacker, guardians of the flame, had a large following amongst graduate students. They were later to have an ill-tempered dispute about the value of Frege's philosophy with Dummett: when their disparaging book on Frege was published, Dummett organized an emergency series of graduate classes to denounce it (Baker and

Hacker 1984, Dummett 1984). It is easy to list many Oxford philosophers of the time whose work showed significant Wittgensteinian
influence to varying extents, even though it would be crass to classify
them simply as Wittgensteinians: Dummett, Strawson, Philippa Foot,
Iris Murdoch, David Pears, Anthony Kenny, of a younger generation
John McDowell and Crispin Wright, and so on. What may be less
obvious is how wary even those who barely mentioned him were of
plainly saying that he was wrong about something. One knew that
doing so incurred the automatic charge of shallow misinterpretation.
It was best to step quietly around, and let sleeping dogs lie.

Wittgenstein's main influence at that time was through his later
work, although few of those under the influence imitated his style of
philosophizing in that work. Most engaged in overt theorizing of a
more or less systematic kind. The citadel was the Private Language
Argument, from which he exerted his power over the philosophy of
mind and the philosophy of language. The growing external threat to
that power from cognitive psychology was surprisingly little felt in
1970s British philosophy. But there was also an internal threat. For
how exactly was the Private Language Argument supposed to work?
Wittgenstein's presentation was notoriously Delphic. The simplest
and clearest reconstructions had the argument rest on a verificationist
premise to the effect that one couldn't *be* in a mental state unless some
independent *check* was possible on whether one was in that state. But
it was generally agreed that *if* the argument rested on a verificationist
premise *then* it was not compelling, because verificationism could not
just be assumed without argument. Defenders of the argument insisted that it worked without such a premise, but could not satisfactorily
explain how (a similarity with Davidson's transcendental argument
mentioned earlier). Wittgenstein's citadel was in danger from within;
his power was waning as a result. At this point an unlikely would-be
rescuer arrived: Saul Kripke. In lectures from 1976 onwards, and in
his book on the Private Language Argument and the associated considerations on rule-following (Kripke 1982), he offered a conjectural
interpretation of the argument that was clearly non-verificationist
and, if not compelling, at least powerful. The question was: did it fit
what Wittgenstein meant? The consensus amongst Wittgensteinians
was that it did not, and as a matter of historical scholarship they may
well have been right. But they seemed not to realize that in taking the
negative attitude they did, they were also rejecting their last chance to

avoid marginalization from the philosophical mainstream. The power of Wittgenstein's name resumed its decline. As for Kripke's argument in its own right, it inadvertently gave the new metaphysics an opportunity to spread its influence. For Kripke's argument took the form of a skeptical paradox, to which Kripke offered a rather unclear and unattractive radically skeptical solution. By contrast, David Lewis offered a clearer and more attractive non-skeptical solution, by means of a highly metaphysical distinction between objectively natural and objectively non-natural properties (Lewis 1983b). It was something like Lewis's solution, not Kripke's, that was widely accepted.

Here are two snapshots of the decline in Wittgenstein's standing. The first is of a meeting in about 1994 of the "Tuesday group," originally founded by Ayer on his return to Oxford in 1959 as a counterweight to Austin's Saturday morning meetings. Susan Hurley read a carefully reasoned paper against the Private Language Argument to an audience that included many leading Oxford philosophers. The audience divided by age. Roughly, those over fifty did not take the possibility seriously that Wittgenstein's argument was fundamentally flawed, although they also did not explain how it worked or what it showed; those under fifty were more sympathetic to Hurley's objections. The second snapshot is of a large graduate class on philosophical logic shortly after my return to Oxford in 2000. One student kept pressing the Wittgensteinian line that contradictions are meaningless rather than false. I kept giving the standard responses, that contradictions have true negations while the negation of what is meaningless is itself meaningless so not true, that the compositional semantics generates meanings even for contradictions, and so on, whose effect was merely to elicit variations on the same theme that did not meet the objection. Eventually I became exasperated and said "Maybe Wittgenstein was just wrong; it wouldn't be the first time." There was a collective gasp of shock. I have never again witnessed such a reaction when Wittgenstein's name was taken lightly.

Of course, the flame is kept alive by surviving groups of Old Believers. Some others, more willing to believe that there has been progress in philosophy since 1970, still find value in engaging with Wittgenstein's work. Nevertheless, his influenced has declined drastically over the past forty years. No doubt that could be roughly measured by his proportion of citations in journals. But what strikes me most forcefully is that the fear factor has gone. As a test of authority, of intellectual or other kinds, admiration tells less than fear. In the 1970s, even non-Wittgensteinian philosophers were often *afraid* to speak out against Wittgenstein. They are so no longer. Another philosopher who has ceased to elicit the fear factor is Quine. Originally, he was frightening because few could match his skill with the weapons of formal logic in philosophical debate. By the 1970s that was no longer so, but philosophers were still very nervous of relying on ordinary semantic notions such as synonymy, because they were afraid of being caught out by Quine's argument for the indeterminacy of translation. That fear too gradually evaporated in the 1970s, as Quine's behaviorist assumptions fell into disrepute.

Having said so much about the Oxford philosophical scene in the 1970s, I should continue the story into the 1980s and 1990s. It was not at all a linear extrapolation from the 1970s. Strikingly, new-wave philosophy of language receded fast (though it proved temporarily) in Oxford, less so elsewhere. One reason was tragically extrinsic: Gareth Evans died at the age of 34 in 1980. With him, the new wave in Oxford lost much of its technical panache, and detailed work in semantics dropped off. Although James Higginbotham was Professor of General Linguistics from 1993 to 2000, not much else was going on at Oxford in Davidsonian semantics for him to engage with. The Davidsonic boom had come to an odd end, morphing into moral philosophy in the work of John McDowell, David Wiggins (Wykeham Professor of Logic from 1994 to 2000, in succession to Dummett), Mark Platts, and others. The transition was made through the Davidsonian emphasis on the legitimacy of homophonic truth theories, in which a word is used to state its own reference. Contrary to appearances, it is not trivial that "round" in English applies to all and only round things, because one has that to learn in learning English. Semantic analysis cannot go on forever; eventually we reach semantic atoms, and switching to a non-homophonic semantics achieves nothing to the purpose, because the aim of semantics is not to write a textbook that one might read in order to learn the object-language from scratch, but rather to say explicitly what its expressions mean in a systematic, compositional way, to those who may already understand them implicitly. Those in the intensionalist strand of new-wave philosophy of language had to resort to homophonic lexical semantics too. The Davidsonians realized that, in particular, they could just as well give a homophonic semantics for moral language too (Wiggins 1976). For instance, "evil" in English applies to all and only evil things. Nothing in their philosophy of language made it problematic to give such an ostensibly out-and-out realist treatment of moral language. Nor did it require any further semantic analysis of moral terms; they could be treated as unanalyzable. Thus David-sonian philosophy of language found itself in the unaccustomed role of providing a protective environment for Aristotelian moral realism. By contrast, Dummett put much heavier explanatory demands on the theory of meaning, perhaps too heavy to be satisfiable.

From the late 1970s onwards, Dummett also found himself fight-ing a more global trend in analytic philosophy: a move away from the philosophy of language towards the philosophy of mind. On his picture of the history of philosophy, Descartes had made epistemol-ogy first philosophy, the engine for the rest of philosophy, then Frege had replaced epistemology by the philosophy of language as first philosophy. Analytic philosophy was philosophy downstream from that linguistic turn. But many analytic or ex-analytic philosophers were starting, heretically, to treat the philosophy of mind as more fundamental than the philosophy of language. Cognitive psychology made a far more interesting and attractive conversation partner for philosophy than behaviorist psychology had done, and had a natural interface directly with the philosophy of mind, for instance in the theory of perception. Computer models of the internal workings of the mind were also increasingly influential. Once again, many of the innovations came from North America. As behaviorism lost its au-thority, Thomas Nagel (1974) led the way in talking directly about conscious experience. Although Daniel Dennett (1981) still showed some influence from his Oxford supervisor Ryle, he engaged with psychology through the philosophy of mind, not the philosophy of language. Jerry Fodor (1975) postulated a language of thought, on the model of a computer's machine code, but it was to be studied by the methods of psychology and computer science, not those of lin-guistics. Moreover, it was not a *public* language, whereas Dummett envisaged first philosophy as the philosophy of public language, in line with the Private Language Argument.

In Oxford, the move into the philosophy of mind took a very spe-cific form, which Dummett had unintentionally facilitated. For him, much of Frege's achievement in the philosophy of language depended on his distinction between sense and reference. Sense is individuated cognitively: two senses may present the same reference in ways which count as different because they fail to render the sameness of reference transparent to the thinker. The cognitive nature of sense promised to make the connection Dummett wanted between the semantics of a language and speakers' *use* of that language. Thus "Hesperus" and "Phosphorus" differ in sense and use but not in reference. Dummett followed Frege in making sense a level of linguistic meaning distinct from the level of reference. Initially, this gave Fregean semantics a large head start over one-level referential semantics, like that associated with Russell, in explaining linguistic phenomena such as the apparent difference in truth-conditions between "Mary thinks that Hesperus is bright" and "Mary thinks that Phosphorus is bright." However, new-wave philosophy of language in North America turned against Frege, especially at the level of public language. In particular, the semantic property of a name that speakers share is its reference; as Kripke and even Frege emphasized, the name's cognitive connections may vary wildly from one speaker to another. Something similar applies to terms whose reference depends on context: the linguistic meaning of the phrase "that dog" does not encode the rich cognitive connections that it will have when used as a perceptual demonstrative by a particular speaker on a particular occasion. Most of the younger Oxford philosophers of language in the 1970s and 1980s followed Dummett in his Fregean sympathies. But, more impressed than Dummett by the work of Kripke and other North American new-wave philosophers of language, they applied the sense-reference distinction only at the level of individual users of the language, not at the level of the language as a whole. If senses are cognitively individuated determinants of reference, a proper name expresses different senses for different speakers, and a perceptual demonstrative expresses different senses on different occasions even for the same speaker. If senses are structured, much of that structure will be at the level of thought and not at the level of language. "Sense" was often glossed as "a way of thinking of the referent." This shift in focus from language to thought was already visible in the work of Evans (1982). By Dummett's standard, it meant that Evans and the others who took that turn no longer even counted as analytic philosophers.

Thus Dummett found himself fighting on the home front too, trying to reassert the primacy of language over thought in philosophical method. Although he was happy to regard philosophy as the study of thought – of *what* is thought, not the act of thinking it – he insisted that the proper way for philosophers to study thought was by studying it as expressed in public language, which the neo-Fregean philosophers of thought no longer did. Perhaps they were not in direct contravention of the Private Language Argument, because their senses could in principle be shared. Nevertheless, from Dummett's methodological perspective, they had taken a step backwards, because the study of public language gave philosophy the objective discipline it needed. To replace that discipline by the objective discipline of experimental psychology would be, from his perspective, to commit the disastrous error of psychologism, against which Frege had railed: it would involve confusing what is thought with the act of thinking.

Dummett seemed to be fighting a losing battle. Globally, the center of gravity of analytic or post-analytic philosophy moved towards the philosophy of mind in the 1980s. Logic and semantics suffered a significant loss of prestige: graduate students became less convinced of the need, intellectual or professional, to put in the hard work of learning them. Locally, neo-Fregean philosophers of thought were taking over. For instance, Strawson was succeeded as Waynflete Professor of Metaphysics by Christopher Peacocke, who held the post from 1988 to 2000. Senses became concepts (Peacocke 1992).

Since the 1980s, the philosophy of mind worldwide has continued to enjoy a far more fruitful relationship with experimental psychology than it did in the heyday of behaviorism. However, it did not become first philosophy in the way it had been expected to do. Nor did the philosophy of thought, which anyway never solidified as a recognized branch of the subject. For instance, developments in metaphysics have typically not been driven by anything in the philosophy of mind. After all, with regained confidence in metaphysics, its contemporary practitioners tend to see themselves as investigating the most general and fundamental nature of a world in which human minds play only a very minor role. Why should the philosophy of mind or the study of concepts drive metaphysics any more than it drives physics? In principle, even if it cannot contribute towards constructive metaphysical theory-building, it might help towards understanding the folk metaphysical beliefs that may obstruct our acceptance of the correct revisionary metaphysics. In practice, the philosophy of mind and the study of concepts have had little impact on recent mainstream metaphysics even in that modest negative way.

For the past several decades, *no* branch of philosophy has played the fully fledged role of first philosophy within analytic philosophy. To some extent, that reflects the increasing specialization of academic research in general. But it also concerns a change more specific to analytic philosophy (in a sense broader than Dummett's), in what philosophers take their subject matter to be. As already noted, an increasingly prevalent, broadly realist attitude is that when you are doing the philosophy of X, you are primarily interested in X itself, in its most general and fundamental aspects, and only secondarily in the word "X," or our concept of X, or our beliefs about X, or our knowledge of X. You are not surreptitiously doing the philosophy of language or thought or mind or knowledge. This reconception of the subject gives no branch of philosophy a head start over the others.

However, the situation is more complicated than those simple formulations suggest. For they might lead one to expect the philosophy of language to be just one more branch of philosophy alongside all the others, the philosophy of a phenomenon specific to humans and perhaps some other species scattered here and there over the universe. It looked like that to some in the 1980s, and taken in isolation it may still sometimes look like that. But, as already suggested, the philosophy of language also plays a more general role throughout analytic philosophy, in the evaluation of arguments. Of course, we do not need the philosophy of language to determine whether an argument is deductively valid in simple cases. But on almost any view of philosophy, it often involves arguments with a subtle illusion of validity, and other arguments that are really valid but need to be checked for such subtle illusions. The illusion may come from confusions between entailments and presuppositions or conversational or conventional implicatures, or from concealed shifts in context, or from lexical or syntactic ambiguities, or from other linguistic complexities. Any discipline that uses subtle, complex would-be deductive arguments in natural language about abstract issues is liable to such illusions, and philosophy characteristically uses arguments of that kind. That is of course not to say that it uses nothing else, or that no other discipline uses them at all; nevertheless, philosophical methodology past and present may put more weight on such arguments than does the methodology of any other discipline. The shift from a deductive to an abductive methodology makes less difference here than one might have expected, because abduction involves the assessment of – amongst other factors – a theory's strength, explanatory power, and consistency with the evidence, which in turn depend on its deductive consequences. Thus, simply using the methods of analytic philosophy critically, by contemporary standards, takes some sophistication in both semantics and pragmatics, irrespective of the subject matter under philosophical investigation. That is a robust legacy from analytic philosophy of language for all philosophy.

One day, perhaps, cognitive psychology will have developed to a point at which it can be usefully deployed to locate likely trouble spots for philosophical reasoning, for instance where framing effects may be exerting an undue influence. Some "experimental philosophers" believe that we have already reached that point. However, perhaps with a few limited exceptions, it is doubtful that purely psychological methods have yet reached an adequate level of discrimination to be usefully applied in the way that linguistic methods already can be. Just to be told that the order in which material is presented can influence our judgment is of little help, since either we ignore the material or it is presented in some order or other. For the time being, linguistics and the philosophy of language offer more help than do psychology and the philosophy of mind when we check an alleged deduction. In this limited respect, Dummett was right about the methodological danger of assigning priority to thought over language, but not for the deep and permanent reasons he envisaged.

For the evaluation of deductive arguments, the relevance of logic is even more obvious than that of the philosophy of language. Of course, some would-be deductive arguments in philosophy are cast in such seamlessly discursive form that no extant logical theory is of much use in evaluating them. Nevertheless, in most branches of contemporary analytic philosophy complex would-be deductive arguments often *are* articulated with sufficient clarity for formal logical skills to make a significant difference to the reliability with which their validity is assessed. Thus logic makes an instrumental contribution to philosophy in general similar in kind to that made by the philosophy of language, and perhaps greater in degree.

The development of formal methods in recent philosophy has also extended the scope for logic to make a more direct contribution to branches of philosophy usually conceived as "other" than logic. For instance, in epistemology, models of epistemic logic enable us to work through the consequences of epistemological claims in exactly described, appropriately simplified situations in a far more rigorous and systematic way than would otherwise be available. Something similar goes for decision theory too. The model-building methodology that has proved so successful in the natural sciences can thereby be applied in philosophy too, and provides new insights into old problems. In metaphysics, rival logics often supply powerful structural cores to rival metaphysical theories: for instance, a quantified modal logic is the structural core of any properly developed theory of modal metaphysics. Although not all of modal metaphysics is usefully treated as logic, a vital part of it is. Logic, far from displacing metaphysics as the logical positivists hoped, is at its center.

The history of philosophy makes a mockery of any limited vision of what philosophy is. It has not followed the path laid out for it by the logical positivists, nor that laid out by the ordinary language philosophy. Nor has it (perhaps with a few limited exceptions) become a branch of psychology, or of physics. Nevertheless, under all the surface turbulence, it somehow manages to extract the residue it needs from each changing fashion. Who knows where the cunning of reason will take it next?

III

History is often said to be written by the winners. In the case of analytic philosophy, however, there is a danger that history will be written predominantly by the losers. One reason is that analytic philosophy is a somewhat anti-historical tradition, especially where it most resembles a science, in aspiration or achievement. For there it tends to be oriented towards the future rather than the past, in the manner of a science – hardly surprising when progress is expected. Those who do not like history cannot complain when their history is written by people who are not like them. A second reason is that recent analytic philosophy seems to subvert the global narratives it might otherwise be tempting to tell about the history of the subject – most notably, in the resurgence of realist metaphysics, often unashamedly concerned with things in themselves. For those sympathetic to Kant or Wittgenstein or Dewey, it must be tempting to see much recent analytic philosophy as an insignificant anomaly, a passing throwback, in the long march of philosophy.

A case in point is Richard Rorty, who was admirably willing to step back, identify bold patterns in the then-recent history of analytic philosophy, and list his heroes – Kant, Hegel, Wittgenstein, Dewey, Heidegger, Sellars, Brandom, …; no wonder his racy, deliberately provocative stories have been so widely read. It is striking that the very large number of names of contemporary philosophers – villains as well as heroes – in the index to *Philosophy and the Mirror of Nature* (Rorty 1979) does not contain that of David Lewis, who had already published two much-discussed books and many articles, and been Rorty's colleague at Princeton since 1970. Rorty's radar had missed a serious threat, the central figure in analytic philosophy for the coming decades. Rorty was out of sympathy with most new-wave philosophy of language, and the metaphysics that increasingly accompanied it, because its referential approach to semantics came too close for his comfort to making language a mirror of the world. For the future, he put his money instead on the inferential approach, particularly in the neo-pragmatist form offered by Robert Brandom (1994), focused on the commitments and entitlements of speakers to make moves in the language game. Brandom himself has his own grand narrative of the history of philosophy, in which – tongue partly but not wholly in cheek – he presents himself as the natural successor to Kant and Hegel (Brandom 2009b). But his inferentialism has remained at an even more programmatic stage than Dummett's, lacking an equivalent of Dummett's connection with technical developments in proof theory by Dag Prawitz and others. As a result, inferentialism has been far less fruitful than referentialism for linguistics. In that crude sense, referentialism beats inferentialism by pragmatic standards.

Of course, we cannot expect a history of recent philosophy to remain neutral about the future. Even the driest chronicle of who published what when has implicit standards of historical significance in selecting whom and what to include. Good historical narratives discern patterns in their material more explicitly and reflectively. This section – which manifestly does not aspire to the depth or rigor of serious history – has indicated a few of the messy complexities that any history of recent analytic philosophy must try to order. Nevertheless, it does at least gesture towards some larger patterns to be made explicit and reflected on. A chronicle is not enough.

The power of fashion in philosophy already ensures that its history will exhibit some patterns, if only of the mob rushing here and there. Some of those fashions look foolish in retrospect; most of them did at the time to non-sympathizers. But fashion is powerful in all academic disciplines, even in mathematics – for instance, concerning which branches of the subject or styles of work carry most prestige. Nor is that merely an inevitable defect in any collective human enterprise. Academic fashions arise because people trained in a discipline have some respect for the judgment of others trained in the discipline as to what is good or fruitful work, worth imitating or following up. When things go well, that mechanism enables the community to concentrate its energies quickly where progress is being and will be made, to avoid wasted effort, and to raise collective standards. It is a way of learning from others. The word "fashion" is most appropriate when the level of deference to majority opinion becomes too high, stifling diversity and independence of mind, making it harder in the long run for the community to back up out of a wrong turning, since it loses its sense of the alternatives. But the rule of fashion is only an exaggerated form of something no community can do without. Even the time and energy spent on bad ideas and misconceived programs has its value, since the effect of the investment is that their limitations are properly explored and tested, so lessons are properly learnt. The history of academic fashions is the history of how things once looked to highly intelligent and knowledgeable people.

The changes in philosophy discussed in this section occurred in a period whose political, social, and cultural history is already being written. Its philosophical history needs to be properly written too, by historians of philosophy with at least enough sympathy for them to understand why what so many philosophers did seemed a good idea at the time. There are encouraging signs that such histories are just starting to be written. I look forward to reading them.

Acknowledgments

This section is a slightly corrected version of an article in the *Belgrade Philosophical Annual* (Williamson 2014a), which derived from a talk given at the Faculty of Philosophy of Belgrade University in September 2014. I thank Professor Miroslava Trajkovski for the suggestion that I might depart from my usual practice and give a talk on an historical theme, based in part on my own experience. Thanks to the audience for constructive discussion, and to Peter Vallentyne, Zhaoqing Xu, and Isaac Choi for spotting some bad typos. Additional thanks go to Professor Slobodan Perović for inviting me to write up the paper for publication in this journal. He also pointed out the thematic connection with Peter Strawson's 1977 lecture at Belgrade University on the nature of analytic philosophy, subsequently translated into Serbo-Croat (as it then was) and published in *Theoria* (Strawson 1977). On that visit to Yugoslavia, Strawson lectured in Belgrade, Zagreb, and Sarajevo. He later commented: "I registered a certain difference in atmosphere in the three places. At least in academic circles the intellectual style seemed relatively untrammeled in Belgrade and Zagreb, though the political tone was different. In Sarajevo, where I was only allowed to give one of my two scheduled lectures and had minimal contact with fellow academics, one perhaps time-serving young man in my audience suggested that my lecture revealed an essentially bourgeois outlook. I replied 'But I *am* bourgeois – an elitist liberal bourgeois.' My interpreter commented, *sotto voce*, 'They envy you'" (Strawson 1998: 14). The contrast between Strawson's account of analytic philosophy and the present one, almost forty years later, may be instructive.

9.2 Abductive Philosophy

Abduction is an informal method of non-deductive, ampliative inference and theory choice familiar from the natural sciences. Although the term goes back to Charles Sanders Peirce, I will not attempt to align my use of it exactly with any of his various characterizations of "abduction." The term is approximately equivalent to "inference to the best explanation," when "explanation" is understood to cover non-causal as well as causal explanations. I will suggest that philosophy sometimes already uses an abductive methodology and ought to use it more in the future. I will also argue that in using an abductive methodology philosophy can still remain a primarily "armchair" discipline.

1. Michael Dummett and inference to the best explanation

Using abduction in philosophy never struck me as problematic. The methodological issue became salient for me when Michael Dummett took over as my supervisor at Oxford for the final year of my doctoral studies (1979–1980). My dissertation was on Karl Popper's idea of verisimilitude – that scientific theories may approach closer and closer to the truth yet never get there. Dummett had just taken up the Wykeham Chair of Logic, which I now hold. My approach was broadly realist; he may well have felt that it presupposed the futility of his life's work in philosophy, but he made no complaint about that and simply discussed my dissertation with me on its own terms. He seemed to find it a refreshing change from supervising dozens of theses critically assessing his own writings. In one supervision, we were discussing what I regarded as one of the best arguments in my thesis and he regarded as one of the worst (it was the origin of Williamson 1988, the only publication to emerge from my dissertation). Dummett paused for a while, then said: "The difference between us about how to do philosophy is that you think that inference to the best explanation is a legitimate method of argument in philosophy, and I don't." I realized that he was right about that being the methodological difference between us. My dominant reaction was, and to some degree still is, surprise at the idea that philosophy could or should get by without something like inference to the best explanation.

Dummett's view seemed to be something roughly like this (in my words, not his): "The deepest, most important philosophical questions are about meaning. If someone proposes a philosophical theory to explain some data, there is a prior question as to whether the theory even has a coherent meaning. If not, it offers no genuine explanation. While that question remains unsettled, attempts to apply inference to the best explanation are premature. But once the question of meaning has been settled, the question of explanation will be comparatively trivial."

In response to the meaning-based argument, several points should be made. First, if one can advance a philosophical argument only after showing its terms to have coherent meanings, then in particular one can advance the latter argument for coherent meaningfulness (which will itself be philosophical) only after showing *its* terms to have coherent meanings too, and so on. Clearly, we have embarked on a vicious infinite regress. Philosophy could never get started. Second, Dummett held that we can settle general questions of meaning only by establishing a systematic *theory* of meaning. But how can we establish it if not by inference to the best explanation? The uncontested data will not entail any non-trivial systematic theory of meaning.

A more promising attitude is to apply an abductive methodology to questions of meaningfulness as well as to questions of truth. If a theory does well by abductive criteria, that is reason to take it to be coherently meaningful as well as true. After all, if a theory really had no coherent meaning, one would expect that defect to show up most quickly when one tried to put the theory to serious use.

Dummett's repudiation of the abductive method in philosophy is particularly striking since he regarded philosophy as a nascent science. He wrote (Dummett 1978: 454):

> I am maintaining that we have now reached a position where the search for such a theory of meaning can take on a genuinely scientific character; this means, in particular, that it can be carried on in such a way, not, indeed, that disputes do not arise, but that they can be resolved to the satisfaction of everyone, and, above all, that we may hope to bring the search within a finite time to a successful conclusion.

How is philosophy to achieve the eventual unanimity allegedly characteristic of mature science if it is not permitted to use a key method at least of mature natural science? Would Dummett have denied that natural science does rely on abduction?

One subtlety deserves notice. The most famous form of non-deductive inference is *enumerative induction*, whereby one infers a general conclusion "Every *F* is *G*" from many of its particular instances ("This *F* is *G*") and no counter-instances. Enumerative induction does not seem vulnerable to Dummett's skepticism, since its conclusion contains only standard logical constants that everyone needs ("every," "is") and expressions already present in the premises ("*F*," "*G*"). Thus the passage from premises to conclusion seems to incur no significant new risk of incoherence in meaning. Indeed, Dummett discusses inductive generalization in non-skeptical terms (Dummett 1991: 276–7). Thus he has at least one form of non-deductive inference at his disposal. However, enumerative induction is inadequate for systematic philosophical theorizing, which often requires introducing new distinctions at a more abstract level not given in the data. A glance at Dummett's own writings will show that he often introduces new meaning-theoretic distinctions, like that between "assertoric content" and "ingredient sense," which cannot simply be read off the data (Dummett 1991: 48). Moreover, enumerative induction itself is arguably legitimate only when it can be subsumed under inference to the best explanation (Harman 1965).

I will not go deeper into Dummett's methodological views here. The rest of this section leaves aside his rejection of abductive philosophy, to concentrate on developing a positive alternative.

2. A sketch of abduction

Before considering abduction in philosophy, we need to characterize the method in terms general enough to be applicable to philosophical theories. We may start by understanding abduction as inference to the best explanation. The following remarks are merely indicative; they do not aspire to be a full account (for something closer to which see Lipton 2004).

We can rank theories (or hypotheses) as potential explanations of our evidence. The point of the qualifier "potential" is that a false theory is not the *actual* explanation of the data; in that sense, it does not really explain them. But we need to rank theories as potential explanations before knowing whether they are true, in order then to use the ranking to guide our judgments as to which theory *is* true. A *potential* explanation of the evidence is anything that *would* explain the evidence *if it were true*. A theory T is a better potential explanation of evidence E than a theory T* if and only if T *would* explain E if T were true better than T* *would* explain E if T* were true – in brief, T would explain E better than T* would.

In the best case, T explains E by entailing E. More typically, T must be conjoined with auxiliary hypotheses to entail E. Those auxiliary hypotheses must be evaluated in turn; they may be independently plausible, or the abductive assessment may have to be of their conjunction with T. Obviously the auxiliary hypotheses should not entail E by themselves, otherwise T would be redundant. In still other cases, the connection is irremediably probabilistic: E is probable conditional on T, perhaps in conjunction with auxiliary hypotheses, which as before must themselves be evaluated, and should not render T redundant. At a bare minimum, T must be consistent with E. In brief, the closer T comes to entailing E, the better (*ceteris paribus*).

Apart from its relation to E, the more T has the intrinsic virtues of a good theory, the better (*ceteris paribus*). It should be elegant and unified, not arbitrary, gerrymandered, *ad hoc*, or messily complicated. It should be informative and general. In brief, it should combine simplicity with strength.

When a theory T scores highly enough as a potential explanation of our evidence E, and better than its rivals, we may infer T from E by inference to the best explanation. Such an inference is of course usually non-deductive: there was no suggestion that the closer E comes to entailing T, the higher T should be ranked as a potential explanation of E (*ceteris paribus*). Inference to the best explanation is obviously fallible; it can lead us from some true evidence E to a false theory T. Nevertheless, fallibility does not justify skepticism. Inference to the best explanation is a vital means to knowledge.

We use inference to the best explanation continually in both the natural sciences and ordinary life. For example, it is often the natural way to reach conclusions about past events of which we have no more direct evidence through perception, memory, testimony, or the like: think of a cosmologist concluding that the Big Bang was the origin of the universe, an archaeologist concluding that three thousand years ago a city on this spot was destroyed by enemy attack, and a hunter concluding that several deer passed this way a few hours ago going east. All do it on the basis of present evidence, which can be explained as the traces of such past events. But inference to the best explanation can also be used to arrive at general theories, not just conclusions about particular past events. Indeed, it is the archetypical means of arguing for theories in natural science. The theories may concern either the observable but unobserved, or the unobservable, or both. When two theories make the same observable predictions, inference to the best explanation may still be able to select one over the other because the former is simpler and less *ad hoc*. In taking us from the observed to the unobservable, inference to the best explanation is far more powerful than enumerative induction.

Of course, we rank only those potential explanations that have been thought of. Sometimes there is a better potential explanation that nobody has thought of. Sometimes it is the actual explanation. In such cases, inference to the best explanation may lead us astray. But, as already noted, fallibility does not justify skepticism. Consolingly, the potential explanations we have thought of will tend to be simpler than those we have not thought of, and so do better on the criterion of simplicity.

Inference to the best explanation does not directly rank potential explanations according to their probability. This does not automatically make it inconsistent with a probabilistic epistemology, for instance a Bayesian one. Inference to the best explanation may be a good heuristic to use when – as often happens – probabilities are hard to estimate, especially the Bayesian prior probabilities of theories. In such cases, inference to the best explanation may be the closest we can get to probabilistic epistemology in practice.

Nothing in this account requires the evidence propositions, the explananda, to be of some special kind. Any known truths will do (Williamson 2000a). They may be theory-free or theory-laden, particular or general. Nor does anything in the account require the explanations to be *causal*. They may be *constitutive* instead. An example of both points is the use of Kepler's laws of planetary motion as evidence for Newton's far more general laws of motion. Given that such laws are timeless, they are neither causes nor effects. Newton's laws explain but do not cause Kepler's laws, by subsuming them. Strictly speaking, of course, the explanation is only potential in this case, since Newton's laws are only approximately true, but the point is clear enough.

How wide should the evidence base be? In principle, we want the theory T to be consistent with *all* our evidence. That suggests making the evidence base E be our *total evidence*. In practice, however, we only expect a theory to explain a tiny fraction of our total evidence. If a theory is a good (potential) explanation of some key pieces of evidence, and at least consistent with the rest, we are often happy enough. Indeed, the criteria above for a good (potential) explanation do not depend on treating the relation between T and E as specifically explanatory. This suggests that we should envisage the required relation between theory and evidence in more general terms. To acknowledge that generalization, I will use Peirce's word "abduction" instead of "inference to the best explanation" (although Peirce sometimes spoke of explanation in characterizing abduction).

The foregoing sketch leaves it far from clear what makes abduction such a good method. For instance, why should aesthetic criteria such as elegance contribute to the pursuit of truth? Nevertheless, the central role of abduction in the success of the natural sciences provides good reason to think that it *is* a good method, even though we do not fully understand *why*. For the time being, we can reasonably proceed on that basis. Crucially for present purposes, nothing in the characterization of the abductive method limits its use to the natural sciences. In particular, it *can* be applied in philosophy, whether or not it *should* be.

3. Abduction in philosophy

I propose that philosophy *should* use a broadly abductive methodology. Indeed, to some extent it already does so. I propose that it should do so in a bolder, more systematic, more self-aware way.

From what evidence base should we start when applying abduction to the construction and selection of philosophical theories? As always, the answer is in principle: our total evidence. That is arguably no less than the total sum of human knowledge. It includes whatever knowledge the natural and social sciences, philosophy, and common sense have already gained. None of our knowledge is irrelevant in principle to philosophy, for any philosophical theory inconsistent with any of it is false (since what is known is true). In particular, there is no restriction to knowledge gained in some special "conceptual" or "*a priori*" or "intuitional" or "armchair" way.

A tempting retort to this view of philosophy as an abductive inquiry with an unrestricted evidence base is the claim that, if adopted, it would turn philosophy into an embryonic natural science – for good or ill. It is not just that the evidence base contains the results of all the natural and social sciences, which will require philosophy to keep up to date with new developments in them, including new experimental and observational data. On such a conception, shouldn't we also expect that sometimes the choice between rival philosophical theories will require philosophy to generate new evidence, for instance to test their consequences? In that case, won't philosophers have to start doing their own experiments and making their own observations? After all, the most salient models of successful systematic abductive inquiry are the natural sciences.

One reply is that philosophers can generate their own new data by doing thought experiments. Natural scientists themselves sometimes use thought experimentation, so why shouldn't philosophers do so too? But although the method of thought experiments is legitimate in philosophy (see Chapter 6), that reply is inadequate, for it gives no reason why the method should satisfy *all* of philosophy's needs for new data, any more than it does for the natural sciences.

Indeed, it is independently plausible that philosophical progress *does* sometimes depend on the generation of new data from real life experiments. For instance, contemporary philosophy of perception is deeply informed by recent experimental results from the psychology of perception. Sometimes the experiments most relevant to a question in the philosophy of perception will not yet have been performed, or even conceived. Of course, the execution of the experiments is better left to experimental psychologists, since they have the relevant practical expertise, rather than to philosophers acting as amateur experimentalists, but philosophers can and occasionally do play a significant and legitimate role in their design and interpretation.

There is no methodological firewall between philosophy and real life experiments. However, that does not mean that once philosophy becomes a more systematically abductive inquiry, its current methodological differences with the natural sciences will fade away altogether. For natural science is not the only form of systematic inquiry in which abduction plays a significant role. It also does so in at least one highly successful form of "armchair" inquiry: mathematics. Of course, it would be foolish to expect philosophy to adopt exactly the same methodology as mathematics, but no more foolish than expecting it to adopt exactly the same methodology as a natural science. Rather, mathematics is a useful foil to the natural sciences in exhibiting the wide range of methodologies consistent with a significant role for abduction.

Since the use of abduction in mathematics may not be obvious, it is sketched in the next section.

4. Abduction in mathematics

At first sight, mathematics looks like a paradigm of a purely *deductive* form of inquiry. Mathematical journals are filled with deductive proofs of theorems. However, those deductive proofs ultimately rely on *first principles*, principles for which no further deductive proof is expected, even on demand. Whatever one thinks of circular or infinitely regressive proofs, contemporary mathematics does not rely on them.

What are the first principles of contemporary mathematics? Admittedly, working mathematicians are often vague about that, because they can get by with a multitude of proof techniques certified by the mathematical community, whose derivation from more fundamental principles they are happy to leave to others. On a standard view, the first principles of contemporary mathematics include the axioms of a set theory such as ZFC (Zermelo-Fraenkel set theory with the Axiom of Choice), as well as the principles of classical first-order deductive logic and arguably second-order logic too. However, some set theorists deny set-theoretic axioms the status of first principles. Instead, they treat them as simply defining a class of mathematical structures, the models of the set theory at issue, about which they take themselves to be proving theorems just as they might prove theorems about other classes of mathematical structures, such as groups, rings, or fields. But that makes less difference than one might think, since in proving theorems about models of the set theory they rely on implicit principles as to what mathematical structures there are, which they treat as first principles. Indeed, those implicit principles about mathematical structures bear a striking resemblance to standard principles about sets. Principles of higher-order logic may also do some of the work otherwise done by axioms of set theory.

For present purposes it does not matter exactly what the first principles of contemporary mathematics are, and in particular whether they are general rules of logic or specifically mathematical axioms. The alternatives are at least roughly equivalent in deductive power. The question is how the first principles, whatever exactly they are, attain that status in mathematics.

It was once thought that the first principles of mathematics were all *self-evident*. However, that is no longer plausible. Although the axioms of a set theory such as ZFC can be made plausible, with a bit of hand waving, they do not all seem self-evident. One can understand them but still doubt their truth without obvious irrationality. Indeed, all contemporary set theories are very significantly shaped by the need to avoid the paradoxes of set theory, in particular Russell's and Burali-Forti's, which unexpectedly arose from simpler and seemingly more evident principles, such as Frege's notorious Basic Law V and the unrestricted comprehension principle that there is a set of all and only those things satisfying any given predicate of the mathematical language. Moreover, by Gödel's second incompleteness theorem, even the mere consistency of ZFC can be established only in a theory ZFC^+ stronger than ZFC itself. Such a consistency proof does little to quell skeptical doubts, for if ZFC *is* inconsistent then so too is ZFC^+, in which case it "proves" the consistency of ZFC because it "proves" everything. The same problem affects any other formal theory cast in the same foundational role as ZFC.

The natural alternative to self-evidence for the first principles of mathematics is an abductive justification. The first principles must be strong enough to prove all established mathematical theorems; they must not be strong enough to prove a contradiction. Subject to those constraints, we naturally want the first principles to maximize simplicity and similar virtues.

Bertrand Russell developed such a view of mathematics as early as 1907 (long before the second incompleteness theorem was proved or even conceived). He proposed first principles or foundations for mathematics in a logical rather than epistemological sense, emphasizing both the "logical simplicity" of the first principles and the nondeductive nature of their support:

... we tend to believe the premises because we can see that their consequences are true, instead of believing the consequences because we
know the premises to be true. But the inferring of premises from consequences is the essence of induction; thus the method in investigating
the principles of mathematics is really an inductive method, and is substantially the same as the method of discovering general laws in any
other science. (Russell 1907: 273–4; see also Russell 1919: 1–2)

For Russell, the first principles of logic and mathematics bear an
abductive relation to the less fundamental but more firmly established parts of mathematics, of which the most obvious are simple
arithmetical truths such as "2 + 2 = 4." We believe the first principles
because we can derive those more obvious truths from them (and cannot derive their negations). Although he wrote "induction," Russell
clearly had in mind something more general than mere enumerative
induction. For the first principles as Russell conceived them are not
expressible in the language of arithmetic; he formulates them in the
more abstract logical framework of type theory. The first principles
of logic and mathematics are not universal generalizations of truths
of arithmetic or any more concrete branch of mathematics, although
those truths (once suitably analyzed) are consequences of the first
principles. The term "abduction" better conveys that relationship.

For Russell, not even the obviousness of simple arithmetic truths
amounts to self-evidence. Rather, they in turn bear an abductive relation to observable matters such as counting sheep (Russell 1907). But
his view is not the same as Quine's idea that mathematics is confirmed
empirically by its indispensability for natural science. For Russell allows mathematics more autonomy with respect to natural science
than Quine does. Once mathematics has got started, the move to
more fundamental principles depends on abductive relations between
more fundamental and less fundamental principles *of mathematics*, for
Russell, whereas for Quine it depends on abductive relations between
mathematics and natural science as it develops. Arguably, Russell's
view makes a better fit than Quine's with the history of mathematics.
Over the past two hundred years, foundational inquiries in mathematics have generally lacked specific connections with applications of
mathematics in natural science, in part because only quite weak fragments of mathematics are needed for such applications. (Einstein's
successful application of non-Euclidean geometry to physics left little

room for the conception of geometrical axioms as self-evident truths about physical space, but the independent reconstruction of geometry as more like a branch of algebra had in any case left that conception far behind.) Instead, the most important evidence on which to base the relevant abductions for foundational inquiries in mathematics is itself mathematical – less foundational mathematics, just as Russell suggests. It consists not just of fairly trivial truths such as "2 + 2 = 4," but of the whole body of established theorems of mainstream mathematics. That is how a standard set theory such as ZFC is abductively confirmed. If a proposed alternative global framework theory for mathematics does not prove all those theorems, it is thereby deeply problematic.

The search for first principles of logic and mathematics is not a completed project. It is arguably not even a completable one. We may accept all the axioms of ZFC as first principles on abductive grounds, but some claims expressible in the language of ZFC cannot be decided on the basis of those axioms. The classic example is Cantor's Continuum Hypothesis (CH). Cantor proved that there are more real numbers (those on the continuous number line) than there are natural numbers (the finite counting numbers 0, 1, 2, 3, ...). CH says that no set has more members than the natural numbers yet fewer than the real numbers. From the work of Gödel and Paul Cohen, we know that CH is neither provable nor refutable in ZFC. Indeed, CH cannot be settled either way on the basis of currently accepted mathematical principles. But it may still be true or false, even if we are not yet in a position to know which. Some contemporary mathematicians, such as Hugh Woodin, seek more powerful new axioms for set theory that will prove or refute CH. Of course, we need good evidence for the truth of those new axioms: we cannot solve the problem trivially just by arbitrarily choosing CH itself or its negation as a new axiom. The desired sort of evidence for the new axioms is abductive: in combination with the other axioms, they should as far as possible yield a simple, elegant, natural, unified theory of sets strong enough to settle many mathematical questions left open by our current theories, yet which also makes a good fit with our current mathematical knowledge (see Maddy 2011 for more discussion of the nature of the evidence for axioms of set theory).

On an alternative view, CH is neither absolutely true nor absolutely false, but simply true of some set-theoretic universes and false of others, so the attempt to prove or refute CH rests on a confusion. If so, set theorists should be generalizing over those universes, not singling one of them out. But then we still need first meta-principles about what set-theoretic universes there are, for instance in order to prove that that CH holds in some and fails in others, and more generally to reason about the differences amongst set-theoretic universes. Those meta-principles will themselves need abductive support. Moreover, they will still be subject to Gödel's incompleteness theorems, and so leave many questions unanswered (perhaps including an analogue of CH), which we shall need new first meta-principles to decide, which will in turn require abductive support, and so on *ad infinitum*.

For present purposes, we need not pursue those mathematical issues. What matters here is that mathematics is a precedent for a successful discipline with an "armchair" methodology that still has a key role for abduction. Thus it would be myopic to assume that an abductive methodology for philosophy implies its assimilation to the experimental sciences.

Unsurprisingly, abduction in philosophy is and should be less "pure" than in mathematics. The evidence on which it does and should depend is often exogenous, generated from outside the discipline itself. It is perfectly proper for philosophers of time to appeal to Einstein's theory of special relativity, for philosophers of perception to use experimental results from the psychology of perception, and for political philosophers to consider the historical outcomes of attempts to apply various political theories.

However, philosophy does not always need other disciplines for its data. In philosophical logic, for example, an armchair methodology closer to that of mathematics is appropriate, though input from the semantics of natural languages as a branch of linguistics is sometimes illuminating. Indeed, the standard non-modal logic of quantification, predication, and identity just is the background logic for mathematics, and no more vulnerable than mathematics itself to objections from linguistics or other extraneous disciplines. Even when we extend the object-language with non-mathematical operators, the methodological repercussions may be quite mild. For instance, suppose that we introduce sentential operators for possibility and necessity (in specified senses). We then have to assess schemas like (I) and (II):

(I) Possibly (A or B) if and only if (possibly A or possibly B).

(II) Necessarily (A or B) if and only if (necessarily A or necessarily B).

Without going interdisciplinary, we can evaluate simple instances of (I) and (II) with declarative sentences substituted for the schematic letters "A" and "B," by evaluating their constituents. We find a counterexample to (II) in the left-to-right direction when we substitute "It is raining" for "A" and "It is not raining" for "B"; we find no counterexample to (I). Abductively, we conjecture that the universal generalization of (I) is true while the universal generalization of (II) is false (on their intended interpretations). Although such armchair abductive assessments of simple principles in logic are not the last word, they take us a long way. They are no more likely to be overturned by experimental data than are armchair abductive assessments of simple principles in set theory. Since I have defended an abductive methodology for philosophical logic in more detail elsewhere (Williamson 1994a: 186, 2013a: 423–9, 2017b), I will concentrate in what follows on less formal areas of philosophy.

5. What difference would an abductive methodology make to philosophy?

As just seen, an abductive methodology for philosophy does not automatically force a change in what evidence it uses, although in some circumstances such a change may be needed. That raises the question: how revisionary of contemporary philosophical method is the abductive proposal?

Of course, contemporary philosophy is far from uniform in its methods; only a near-vacuous methodological proposal would be entirely non-revisionary. In particular, some contemporary philosophers reject the conception of philosophy as a systematic truth-directed theoretical inquiry. They may instead conceive it as clarifying, creating, or subverting concepts, as critical or emancipatory, or as otherwise engaged in projects quite incommensurable with those of the sciences. Such philosophers can hardly be expected to endorse an abductive methodology in principle or conform to one in practice. This is not the place to criticize such radically alien conceptions of philosophy. A more interesting because subtler comparison is with a *deductive* methodology still used by many contemporary analytic philosophers, including many who *do* regard philosophy as a systematic truth-directed theoretical inquiry. Indeed, it may be what they have in mind when they say that analytic philosophy is distinguished from other sorts of philosophy by the imperative to *argue* for one's claims.

Deductivists argue deductively for their claims. Much competent work in contemporary analytic philosophy follows the deductive paradigm, sometimes with great skill. For negative conclusions, such a methodology can work well. Using uncontroverted principles of logic, one may succeed in showing that an opponent's universal generalization is inconsistent with an uncontroverted description of an example, or even with itself. However, if philosophy is a systematic truth-directed theoretical inquiry, one should presumably aspire to more positive conclusions too, such as informative universal generalizations of one's own. But, in non-formal areas, one typically needs informative universal premises in order to derive an informative universal conclusion. All too often, if the argument is deductively valid, opponents simply reject one of those informative universal premises as "question-begging." One can try deducing the rejected premise from further informative universal premises, but that way an infinite regress looms. To avoid the regress, one may declare the premise "self-evident," a "Moorean fact," or an "intuition," but no such talk forces a skeptic to accept one's premise. Such rules of engagement are conducive to deadlock. But in effect that outcome constitutes defeat for the argument, since in putting it forward the proponent by implication accepted the burden of proof, and failed to discharge that burden. It is so hard for an argument to succeed on those terms that the methodology puts pressure on its practitioners to water down their conclusions to a point where they can be deduced from uncontroversial premises, but that is a recipe for trivializing the discussion. When both sides follow the deductive paradigm, the usual result is stalemate.

One form of the deductivist methodology is the attempt to refute a rival theory by *reductio ad absurdum*, which often ends in deadlock as to whether the derived consequence of the theory really is absurd. There is in effect a race between proponents and opponents of a theory to derive its bad consequences. If the proponents spot a bad consequence first, they can claim it as simply "part of the view" and so no objection to it. If the opponents spot it first, they can claim it as a *reductio ad absurdum* of the view.

Of course, it is not only in philosophy that arguments rarely produce switches in allegiance between rival theories. In a famous passage quoted by Thomas Kuhn, Max Planck wrote: "a new scientific truth does not triumph by convincing its opponents and making them see the light, but rather because its opponents eventually die, and a new generation grows up that is familiar with it" (Planck 1949: 33–4, quoted at Kuhn 1970: 151). Human obstinacy and pride are potent factors in all intellectual life. Individual irrationality may even contribute to group rationality, by helping ensure that a theory's resources for dealing with problems are fully explored, so that it is not given up prematurely. The concern about the deductivist methodology in philosophy is not that it produces so few conversions, but that it channels energy in unproductive directions. For example, an *ad hoc* hypothesis with little explanatory potential may nevertheless be very hard to refute in a deductivist sense. Yet a deductive argument for any theory incompatible with that hypothesis must deductively rule out the hypothesis. Thus considerable time may be spent in trying to refute a hypothesis of no serious interest. That time would have been better used in exploring the explanatory potential of more promising theories.

An abductive methodology bypasses deductive deadlocks, by encouraging both the accumulation of more evidence of various kinds and the development of better explanations of that evidence (which may simply bring it under illuminating generalizations). There is less need to lock horns over one piece of evidence as many others become available. Discriminations between theories gradually emerge on the abductive scoresheet. Given Planck's warning, we should not expect even this abductive methodology to make diehard proponents of the losing theories renounce them. But the discipline as a whole may make progress in the usual way: new entrants to the profession, less invested in any of the competing theories, may be more sensitive to their comparative merits.

Deduction still plays a major role within abductivist inquiry, since deducing consequences from a theory (usually with some auxiliary hypotheses) is integral to the explanatory enterprise. More generally, abduction values theories of great deductive strength (at least, when they are consistent with the evidence). Indeed, the abductive methodology gives more scope to deduction, by eliminating the deductivist pressure for the premises to be uncontentious, and replacing it with pressure for them to include an informative general theory. In that sense, abduction and deduction play complementary roles – and logic is a vital part of philosophy.

Conversely, abduction often plays a significant role on the quiet within deductivist inquiry, since it may be used unofficially to support premises of the official deduction. Once that role is acknowledged, one might even wonder how much abductivism really differs from deductivism. But they do not collapse into each other. The dialectical role of deduction within the two paradigms is quite different: as just seen, deductivism exerts pressure for uncontentious premises in a way that abductivism does not. Indeed, once one is permitted to use abduction in supporting the premises of the deduction, why not use it directly to support the conclusion? The rationale for deductivism is undermined. Moreover, within the deductivist paradigm, the cases for the individual premises are normally made separately from each other, so that abduction is applied one premise at a time. By contrast, within the abductivist paradigm, it makes more sense to apply abduction to the conjunction of the premises together. For instance, each of several premises may give a nicely unified picture, while their conjunction gives a nastily disunified one. It is better to use deduction within an overall abductivist methodology than to use abduction within an overall deductivist methodology.

Contrary to some stereotypes of analytic philosophy, abduction rewards boldly speculative theories. Bolder theories are riskier but stronger, in other words more informative; they entail more and so tend to have more explanatory potential, but are easier to falsify. For the same reason, abduction rewards precise theories. Many wildly unclear, obscure, and vague theories have the air of setting off into the unknown, and so look bold, when really they are the opposite. Since it is quite unclear what they are supposed to entail, they avoid the risk of falsification, but by the same token they give up the hope of explaining anything. Such theories rank low on the abductive scale. Abduction also rewards virtues such as simplicity, elegance, generality, and unificatory power, which all tend to make for bold theories.

As already emphasized, an abductive methodology will not infrequently lead us to false theories. But the clearer those theories are, other things equal, the better able we are to discover their falsity, and so learn from our mistakes. This is another advantage of precise theories over vague ones, which are much harder to falsify.

6. *Simplicity, over-fitting, and error-fragility in the method of thought experiments*

One of the main puzzles in understanding the effectiveness of an abductive methodology, even in natural science, is its apparent reliance on simplicity, elegance, and similar factors in ranking theories. Such more or less aesthetic criteria have no obvious connection with truth: why should the truth be simple or elegant? Someone might even be tempted to think, desperately, that the use of such criteria requires a pragmatist or anti-realist understanding of natural science. These puzzles arise just as much for an abductive methodology in philosophy. Someone might likewise be tempted to think that the use of such criteria requires a pragmatist or anti-realist understanding of abductive philosophy too.

Experience of theorem-proving in logic suggests that without a strong aesthetic sense in such matters one is lost, directionless, unable to discriminate fruitful from pointless definitions, promising conjectures from dead ends. Such an aesthetic sense is surely connected to a capacity for abstract pattern recognition, though that is not yet to say very much.

We still do not fully understand the role of simplicity in science. The problem itself may have no simple solution: on closer analysis, it may turn out to involve several interacting issues. As Nelson Goodman's new riddle of induction suggests, the problem arises even at the level of enumerative induction about observable matters: why should we expect emeralds next century to be green rather than grue (Goodman 1955)? When we cross a bridge, we presumably rely on abductive reasoning. It is quite unclear that pragmatism or anti-realism has anything useful to offer in such cases.

Nevertheless, some piecemeal progress has been made, and it is compatible with a fully realist conception of science. In particular, Malcolm Forster and Elliott Sober (1994) have made a strong case that at least part of the story concerns the problem of "over-fitting" in natural science. I will suggest that their account has a significant moral for the role of simplicity in philosophy.

Consider the scientific challenge of curve-fitting, extrapolating a curve (a general equation) from the finite set of currently available data points for some given variables. By using sufficiently complex equations (such as polynomials with sufficiently many parameters) we can normally fit the available data very accurately. However, scientific experience shows that doing so leads to the problem of *over-fitting*, where such equations tend to be predictively inaccurate: although they fit present data well, they fit future data badly.

Forster and Sober (1994) point out that restricting ourselves to simple equations (such as linear or quadratic ones) helps avoid the problem of over-fitting. Although it typically leads to equations that fit present data slightly less well, they tend to be predictively more accurate, that is, to fit future data better. The reason is that they are less vulnerable to distortion by errors in the data. The restriction helps us avoid mistaking noise for signal, which we do if we fit the current data too closely. This account of the role of simplicity and similar aesthetic criteria in abductive methodology is consistent with a fully realist, non-pragmatist understanding of science.

What is meant here by "errors in the data?" Elsewhere I have defended the thesis $E = K$, that the total content of our evidence is the total content of our knowledge (Williamson 2000a). Since only truths are known, $E = K$ entails that all our evidence is true. How then can our evidence contain errors? The answer is that it does not. The "data" here are merely measurements of the values of the relevant variables. Typically, scientists do not even believe that the measurements are perfectly accurate. At best, they know what the measurements were and that they were accurate within a given margin for error. That is the limit of their evidence, but the best method in such cases is to find the simple equation that best approximates the measured values. Indeed, we are often wrong about the extent of our evidence too, thinking that something is part of our evidence when really it is not (thinking we know something when really we don't). An abductive methodology allows for the near-inevitability of some such errors.

Forster and Sober's rationale for the criterion of simplicity can be extended to philosophy, even though quantitative data are not involved. For something very like the problem of over-fitting occurs in philosophy too. Consider, for instance, the research program of reductively analyzing knowledge in response to Gettier's refutation by counterexamples (in the form of thought experiments) of the "justified true belief" analysis of knowledge, one of the main activities of analytic epistemologists. (Gettier 1963, Shope 1983). Notoriously, what happened was a cycle of proposed analysis, followed by new counterexamples (again in the form of thought experiments), followed by a revised analysis, with an extra epicycle, a new disjunct or other complication, in order to finesse both the new counterexamples and all the old ones. Just as in the quantitative case, tolerance for highly complicated, messy, gerrymandered analyses yielded a succession of proposals that fitted the current data but succumbed to new ones. Other programs for reductive analysis in philosophy, for instance of causation or meaning, have had similar track records. Strikingly, the philosophical community showed very little aversion to the multiplication of complication. A firmer preference for simplicity and elegance would have warned the community that something was going wrong. Indications of over-fitting remain quite widespread in analytic philosophy.

Of course, abductive criteria of simplicity and elegance do not license one simply and elegantly to *ignore* recalcitrant data. Rather, they encourage a more critical attitude to the data. In the case of thought experiments, we should be more willing to countenance the possibility that our verdict was mistaken, especially in unclear cases. This does not imply that it is wrong to use thought experiments in philosophy, any more than Forster and Sober's point implies that it is wrong to use quantitative data in natural science. It is just that serious inquiry requires sophistication in the handling of evidence. We need a strategy to take account of our own fallibility.

These considerations suggest a response to one of the more interesting criticisms of reliance on thought experiments, advanced by experimental philosophers. Joshua Alexander and Jonathan Weinberg (2014) have argued that the method of thought experiment is *error-fragile*, in the sense that it tends to multiply the effect on the output theories of any errors in the supposed input evidence. For instance, one misjudgment of a thought experiment could lead us to mistakenly treat it as a counterexample to a theory that is in fact true, and thereby dismiss the true theory. This is like the error-fragility of a naïve falsificationist methodology in natural science, which treats a theory as refutable by a single observation: if there is an error in the observation, we may thereby dismiss a true theory as refuted. Since all evidence is true, if our evidence really contains one counterexample to a theory then the theory is false: but inevitably we sometimes take our evidence to contain things that it does not really contain. Since we cannot keep our premises completely free of error, we need robust methods of theory choice that do not crash every time an error enters.

By giving weight to simplicity and elegance as a counterbalance to evidential fit, an abductive methodology avoids error-fragility in both the experimental sciences and philosophy.

There is another dimension to the problem. In the special sciences, such as economics, psychology, and even biology, we study systems so complex that informative exceptionless universal generalizations about them are rare. Instead of vainly seeking such laws, we can often make more progress in understanding the phenomena by building highly simplified, elegant, precise formal models of them and exploring their consequences. We do not expect the models to be perfectly accurate. We must be satisfied with a reasonable approximation instead. In such cases, at least some of the discrepancies between model and evidence are genuine. We can treat model-building as a special case of the abductive methodology in which the requirements of evidential fit are relaxed. Thinking beings, especially human beings, are paradigms of systems too complex to be best understood in terms of exceptionless universal laws; the model-building methodology is more appropriate. Many branches of philosophy focus on thinking beings, especially human beings: for instance epistemology, philosophy of mind, philosophy of language, and moral, social, and political philosophy. I have argued elsewhere that the model-building methodology is appropriate for such branches of philosophy (Section 9.3). In the case of epistemology, I have shown how combining the methods of model-building and of thought experimentation can give more robust results than either method on its own (Williamson 2013b, 2015a). In other branches of philosophy, such as philosophical logic and fundamental metaphysics, there is much more hope of informative exceptionless universal generalizations, and a more direct approach is often appropriate, with no relaxation of the requirements of evidential fit. In both kinds of case, however, the underlying methodology is abductive.

Acknowledgments

This section first appeared in an issue of *Philosophical Forum* containing papers presented to the 2015 conference on "Williamson, Logic, and Philosophy" at Peking University. Earlier versions of the material were presented in my 2013 Kim Young-Jung lectures at

Seoul National University, at a conference on "Realism and Objectivity" at Matera, at a workshop on "Philosophical Methodology" at St Andrews, and in classes and seminars at the universities of Göttingen, Michigan (Ann Arbor), Oxford, and Trnava. I thank participants in all these events for helping me develop my ideas.

9.3 Model-Building in Philosophy

One notable form of progress in the natural and social sciences over the past century has been the development of better and better *models* of the phenomena they study. The models are typically presented in mathematical terms: for instance, by differential equations for the rise and fall in population of a predator species and a prey species, interacting only with each other, or by a set of ordered pairs for the networking relations in a society.

When a system resists direct study, because it is so complex or hard to observe, model-building constitutes a key fall-back strategy. Studying a model often yields insight into the phenomena it models. When one model is replaced by another that captures more about how the phenomena work, science progresses.

Sometimes such progress is a step towards discovering universal laws of nature, non-accidentally exceptionless generalizations. However, macroscopic phenomena are typically too complex and messy to obey many informative exceptionless generalizations framed in macroscopic terms. (Some microscopic phenomena are like that too.) In such cases, the discovery of universal laws may not be a reasonable aim for those branches of science, even if there are still useful rules of thumb. It may be more realistic and more fruitful to aim at building increasingly good models instead. Special sciences such as economics and psychology are salient examples. Even in evolutionary biology, progress may consist more in the development of better models than in the discovery of universal laws.

This section argues that in philosophy, too, one form of progress is the development of better and better models – especially, but not exclusively, in those branches of philosophy, such as ethics, epistemology, and philosophy of language, which deal primarily with the human world in all its complexity and mess. Not only *can* philosophy make progress through model-building, it has been doing so for quite some time. Philosophers tend to feel embarrassed by the question "So what has philosophy discovered recently?" When we try to think of an informative generalization whose universal truth has recently come to be known through the efforts of philosophers, we may well not come up with much. We tend to assume that most of the natural and social sciences are doing far better. Surely they are indeed making progress, but this may consist much less than we suppose in the discovery of universal generalizations and much more in the development of better models. Once we look for progress of that kind in philosophy, it is not hard to find. It is there right under our noses.

What are Models?

Philosophers of science use the word "model" in a confusing variety of ways, as do scientists themselves. Clarity has not been served by a universalizing tendency in the philosophy of science to define the word in a way meant to apply to *all* scientific theories or *all* uses of the word "model" in science. For present purposes, a more helpful recent trend in the philosophy of science has been to use the term "model-building" to identify a specific recognizable type of theoretical activity that some but not all scientists engage in, some but not all of the time (Godfrey-Smith 2006a, Weisberg 2007). A scientific research group may advertise a position as a "modeler"; some but not all members of the group will be modelers. Similarly, I do *not* suggest that all philosophizing is model-building. Rather, some but not all philosophers build models, some but not all of the time.

Even on the restricted use of "model," there are different views of what models are. For the sake of simplicity and clarity, I will give my own account, but what I say could be adapted to other accounts: it is easier to agree on *whether* a scientist is presenting a model than on what sort of thing that model is.

Here, a model of something is a *hypothetical example* of it. Thus a model of predator-prey interaction is a hypothetical example of predator-prey interaction. The point of the qualification "hypothetical" is that the example is presented by an explicit description in general terms, rather than by pointing to an actual case. For instance, one writes down differential equations for the changing population sizes of the two species, rather than saying "the changing numbers of foxes and rabbits in Victorian Sussex." The description picks out a *type* of case, rather than one particular case: for instance, the type of any predator-prey interaction that obeys the given differential equations.

For the model-building methodology to work well, the description of the hypothetical example must be precise and specific enough to be formally tractable. That is, it should enable us to derive answers to many relevant questions about the example. When we explore the model, we do so on the basis of what follows from the description itself, which is designed to facilitate that process. We do not assume that the model fits the knowledge we already have of the phenomenon under study, since that is one of the main questions at issue. But if the fit turns out to be reasonably good, exploring the model becomes a way of indirectly exploring the original phenomenon. The mathematical clarity of the description helps make direct study of the model easier than direct study of the phenomenon itself.

The hypothetical example, the type picked out by the description, may or may not have actual instances. Indeed, it may or may not have *possible* instances. For example, evolutionary biology typically uses differential equations for population change, even though they treat the change in the number of group members as continuous whereas really it must be discrete; answers to "How many?" questions do not form a continuum. Strictly speaking, such a model is *impossible*; it is a type metaphysically incapable of having instances. But that does not mean that the model collapses. The differential equations are mathematically consistent; we can still make a stable tripartite distinction between what follows from them, what is inconsistent with them, and what is neither. Moreover, the mathematical consequences of the description may turn out to be similar enough to descriptions in similar terms of the observed behavior of the target real-life phenomenon for the model to provide considerable theoretical insight into the target. In advance, we might not have expected impossible models to have such cognitive value, but it has become clear that they can.

The role of formal consistency in a model-building methodology provides a link between this meaning of "model" and its meaning in mathematical logic. In the logical sense, a model of a theory (call it a "logic-model") is an interpretation of the theory on which it comes out true. The interpretation must give the purely logical expressions (such as "if" and "not") their intended interpretations but may radically reinterpret non-logical expressions (for instance, by treating the word "fox" as applying to numbers). A theory is *logically consistent* if and only if it is true on at least one such interpretation, in other words, it has a logic-model. A sentence *logically follows* from a theory if and only if it is true on every interpretation on which the theory is true, in other words, every logic-model of the theory is a logic-model of the sentence.

We can apply those logical distinctions to model-building in science by treating the description of the model as a mini-theory, and the purely mathematical expressions in the description as logical, so that their interpretation is held fixed. On its intended interpretation, the description of the model may pick out an impossible type (for instance, because it describes population growth as continuous). Nevertheless, the description is logically consistent, because it has a logic-model: it is true on some unintended interpretation.

The mathematical clarity of the description typically makes such a logic-model easy to construct, for instance by reinterpreting its non-logical terms (such as "predator" and "prey") as applying to purely mathematical entities with the right formal structure. The purely logical consequences of the description do not depend on the intended interpretations of its non-logical terms; they are determined by the whole class of intended and unintended interpretations alike. Nevertheless, the non-logical terms are not idle, for they are needed to co-ordinate comparisons with the real-life phenomenon. If we interchange the words "predator" and "prey" in the description, the comparisons go differently.

The simplified and sometimes idealized nature of models is no surprise on this account. They are typically intended to be easier to explore than the real thing; simplicity and idealization contribute to that.

A warning is in order. The talk of *building* models might suggest a constructivist philosophy of science, on which model-building is a matter of invention rather than discovery, and is not in the business of uncovering truths independent of the inquiry itself. But that would be a very naïve conclusion to draw. Rates of population change in predators and prey are not figments of the scientific imagination. If we are investigating a complex reality out there, it is not at all surprising that it is sometimes best to use a sophisticated, indirect strategy, to ask questions quite subtly related to the overall aims of the inquiry. To build a model is just to identify by description a hypothetical example which we intend to learn about in hope of thereby learning about the more general subject matter it exemplifies. Nothing in that strategy is incompatible with a full-bloodedly realist nature for the scientific inquiry. The same goes for model-building in philosophy.

On a full-bloodedly realist conception of model-building, we should expect it under favorable conditions to provide *knowledge*. But, since only what is true is known, and virtually no model description is strictly true of its real-life target, what knowledge can model-building provide? What could its content be?

When we explore a model by valid deductive reasoning from the model description, we learn necessary truths of the general conditional form "If a given case satisfies the model description, then it satisfies this other description too." That broadly logico-mathematical knowledge has the virtue of precision, but by itself is less than we want, since it says nothing unconditional about how close the original phenomenon (such as predator-prey interaction) comes to satisfying the model description. Fortunately, we can also learn unconditional though vaguer truths of the general form "This model description fits the phenomenon better than that one does in the following ways," where the fit is usually approximate. Although much more needs to be said about what such approximation consists in, for present purposes the general picture will do. Such a combination of precise conditional knowledge and vague unconditional knowledge of the target is ample reward for the work of model-building. (For a far more detailed account of model-building in science see Weisberg 2013.)

Models in Philosophy

The need for model-building is hardest to avoid where the complex, messy nature of the subject matter tends to preclude informative exceptionless universal generalizations. The paradigm of such complexity and mess is the human world. Hence the obvious places to look for model-building in philosophy are those branches most distinctively concerned with human phenomena, such as ethics, epistemology, and philosophy of language. Of course, categories like goodness and duty, knowledge and justification, meaning and communication are not restricted to humans. Even those that do not apply to non-human animals on earth can in principle apply to actual or possible non-human agents, perhaps vastly more sophisticated intellectually than we will ever be. Philosophers typically want their theories to apply to such non-human agents too. But that only makes exceptionless universal generalizations still harder to find. By contrast, pure logic supplies fertile ground for powerful exceptionless universal generalizations. One might expect the same of fundamental metaphysics too.

Although the metaphysical question of personal identity looks more complex and messy, it also looks less fundamental.

As it happens, the few extant discussions of model-building in philosophy have tended to concentrate on model-building in metaphysics (Godfrey-Smith 2006b, 2012, Paul 2012). One reason is perhaps that metaphysics has the worst press of any branch of philosophy, so the need for a new methodological defense may be felt most strongly there. Model-building is indeed sometimes used even in fundamental metaphysics. An example is the idea of *gunk*, stuff (or space itself) of which every part has a lesser part, so it has no perfectly atomic parts. Gunk may not be actual, but is it metaphysically possible? It is very tricky to work out which natural assumptions about the part-whole relation are logically consistent with gunk. Constructing mathematical models of gunk provides a good way of answering such questions (see Arntzenius 2008, Russell 2008, and Wilson 2008 for a debate).

If we turn to more obviously likely branches of philosophy, such as epistemology and philosophy of language, examples of model-building are easy to find.

In epistemology, a standard model of epistemic uncertainty is a lottery. Here is a typical description:

> There are exactly 1000 tickets in the lottery, numbered from 1 to 1000. Exactly one will win. The lottery is fair. That is all you know about it. Thus, on your evidence, each ticket has probability 1/1000 of winning.

That description involves various assumptions typically false of lotteries in real life. For instance, it assumes that it is certain on your evidence exactly how many tickets will be in the draw. Nevertheless, a good test of epistemological theories is to work out what they say about this simple case. For instance, consider the proposal that you should accept a proposition if and only if it is at least 90% probable on your evidence. If so, you should accept that the winning number will be greater than 100, and you should accept that it will be at most 900, but it is not the case that you should accept that it will be greater than 100 and at most 900. You are obliged to accept one conjunct and you are obliged to accept the other, but you are not obliged to accept their conjunction. That is at best an uneasy combination. One can show that a similar problem arises for any probabilistic threshold for acceptance more than 0% and less than 100% (varying the number of tickets when necessary). Although lottery models are elementary, they already have enough structure to make trouble for many superficially attractive ways of thinking about uncertainty. Moreover, their simple mathematical structure makes it trivial to define mathematical logic-models with that structure, so their consistency is not in doubt.

The branch of epistemology known as *formal epistemology* is much concerned with model-building. The models come from two main sources. Some, like the lottery example just discussed, are probabilistic, often in the Bayesian tradition of thinking about probability, which has been hugely influential in the natural and social sciences (see Howson and Urbach 1993). Others are models associated with epistemic logic in a rich tradition originating with Jaakko Hintikka (Hintikka 1962, Ditmarsch, Halpern, Hoek, and Kooi 2015): although not all standard logic-models of epistemic logic are models in the present sense of epistemic situations, they can all be reinterpreted in a natural way as such models. One can also add probabilities to models of epistemic logic in a natural way (Williamson 2000a). When our models exclude something observed in real life, we may build more sophisticated models to include the observed phenomenon. For instance, the simplest epistemic models exclude ignorance of one's own ignorance. But people such as holocaust-deniers are ignorant of their own ignorance. More sophisticated epistemic models include agents ignorant of their own ignorance.

Model-building in epistemic logic has found numerous applications in computer science and theoretical economics, for instance in understanding the relations between public and private knowledge. When one looks back on the vast body of results produced by model-building in formal epistemology over the past half-century, it seems idle to deny that considerable progress has been made in understanding the epistemic subtleties of many kinds of situation. Nor should one imagine that the progress is primarily mathematical. Although mathematics is usually involved, as in model-building throughout the natural and social sciences, the main interest of the models is not in their abstract mathematical structure but in their epistemic interpretation.

In the natural and social sciences, models are often tested by their predictions of measurable quantities. Models of epistemic logic typically make no such predictions, so how are they to be tested? But even in the natural and social sciences, models are often tested by their qualitative predictions (Weisberg 2013: 136). Models of epistemic logic can be tested that way too. For instance, we can ask whether they allow for ignorance of one's own ignorance. For some purposes we can legitimately abstract away from such cases. But once we become interested in the limitations of self-knowledge, such cases matter, and our models must permit them. Of course, such qualitative testing presumes that we have some model-independent knowledge of the target phenomenon, but that is equally true of quantitative testing. If we started in total ignorance of the target, we could hardly expect to learn much about it by modelling alone.

Many developments in philosophy of language can also be understood in model-building terms.

Originally, Frege and Russell introduced formal languages into philosophy as languages in which to carry out proofs more rigorously than was possible in natural languages, because the formal languages were more precise and perspicuous. That was not model-building. Later, Russell and the younger Wittgenstein argued that such formal languages articulate the covert underlying structure of ordinary thought and language. That was still not model-building.

Carnap did something different. He defined the syntax and semantics of simple, artificial examples of languages in meticulously explicit detail (Carnap 1947). He did not intend to work *in* these languages, nor did he intend them to have the expressive power of natural languages. Rather, he intended them as *models of language*, to show exactly how his intensional semantics could in principle assign meanings to all the expressions of a language. It did so *compositionally*, determining the meaning of a complex expression as a function of the meanings of its constituents, in a way that explains how we can understand new sentences we have never previously encountered by understanding the familiar words of which they are composed and the ways in which they are put together.

The key challenge was to explain how modal operators like "possibly" and "necessarily" work. They did not fit the available model for sentence operators, truth-functionality. Operators like "and," "or," and "not" are truth-functional in the sense that they are used to form complex sentences out of simpler ones, where the truth-value of the former is determined by the truth-values of the latter. For instance, the conjunction "A and B" is formed from the simpler sentences A and B; it is true if they are both true, false if one of them is false. But modal operators are not truth-functional. That A is false does not determine the truth-value of "Possibly A," which depends on whether A is contingently false or necessarily false.

Carnap solved the problem by taking as the crucial semantic property of a sentence not its *extension*, its actual truth-value, but its *intension*, its spectrum of truth-values across all possible worlds (in his terminology, "state-descriptions"). Although the extension of A does not determine the extension of "Possibly A," the intension of A *does* determine the intension of "Possibly A." For if the intension of A has truth at some possible world, then the intension of "Possibly A" has truth at *every* possible world, while if the intension of A has truth at no possible world, then the intension of "Possibly A" also has truth at no possible world.

Carnap's insight is the root of the immensely fruitful tradition of possible world semantics, which has been central to later developments in both philosophy of language and formal semantics as a branch of linguistics. Although various aspects of his account are no longer widely accepted, it still constitutes major progress. He provided a simple working model of the semantics of a language with modal operators. Much subsequent work in formal semantics has in effect provided increasingly sophisticated model languages whose expressive power comes increasingly close to that of natural languages. For instance, they predict more and more subtle effects of the way tricky words like "if" work.

Even if one thinks that formal models can never capture all the untidy complexity of natural languages, it is obscurantist to conclude that they provide no insight into the workings of natural languages, just as it would be obscurantist to claim that formal models in natural science provide no insight into the untidy complexity of the natural world. (One might even treat the later Wittgenstein's carefully described language games as partial models of language, emphasizing links to action and imperative rather than indicative utterances, intended as a corrective to over-emphasis on language's descriptive function. Presumably, he would have hated their assimilation to a scientific method.) The philosophical significance of those semantic insights extends far beyond philosophy of language. For instance, philosophers in virtually all branches of the subject ask what is possible or necessary. If they use such modal terms in their reasoning with no reflective understanding of how their meanings work, they are liable to commit logical blunders.

The future may well see radical changes in the overall theoretical frameworks within which epistemic, semantic, and other models are built. Nevertheless, it is reasonable to expect that insights embodied in current models will be preserved, refined, and deepened in models constructed within those future frameworks, just as happens in the natural and social sciences.

Perhaps, in the future, research groups in philosophy will advertise positions for modelers.

Methodological Reflections

Not all the advantages of formal methods in philosophy depend on model-building. Sometimes one formalizes the premises and conclusion of a tricky philosophical argument in order to show that the latter follows from the former in a recognized proof system for the formal language. That is progress, but it is not model-building in any distinctive sense.

Model-building is more relevant to showing that a conclusion does *not* follow from some premises. As already noted, model descriptions facilitate the construction of uncontentious logic-models with the appropriate mathematical structure. When a model description seems informally consistent with the premises but not with the conclusion of a philosophical argument, one can often construct a corresponding logic-model on which the premises are true but the conclusion false, and thereby demonstrate that the conclusion does not logically follow from the premises. As a special case, when a model description seems informally consistent with a philosophical theory, one can often construct a corresponding logic-model on which the theory is true, and thereby demonstrate that it is logically consistent: it does not logically entail a contradiction.

Of course, those logical relations are not all that matters; a logically consistent theory may still be obviously false, and a conclusion that does not follow logically from some premises alone may follow from them plus some obvious truths as auxiliary premises. But the same model-building methodology helps us track those further logical relations too. Thus one advantage of model-building – not the only one – is to make us more efficient and accurate at mapping the logical space in which we are theorizing. Without such a map, we blunder about in a fog, bumping into unexpected obstacles, falling over cliffs. It is not uncommon for elaborate philosophical theories to suffer some form of logical collapse: if not inconsistency, the erasing of vital distinctions. Many such disasters could have been avoided if the theory's proponents had thought to subject it to preliminary testing by model-building, for instance by trying to build a model yielding a non-trivial logic-model on which the theory came out true.

For the efficient mapping of logical relations, the advantages of simple models are obvious. Simplicity conduces to computational feasibility, so we can in practice derive the model's mathematical properties by deductive reasoning from its description. This is particularly important for the strategy of learning about the target phenomenon by manipulating the model, adjusting it (by varying the values of parameters or in other ways) to see what difference it makes – for instance, whether a prediction of the model is robust under such perturbations. One can gain large cognitive rewards, as well as pleasure, from playing even with a toy model, because such variations are so easy to track.

Simple models have other, less obvious advantages. One is the avoidance of arbitrary features. The more adjustable parts a model has, the more opportunities it offers the model-builder to rig the results, to gerrymander the model by setting parameters and arranging structure in *ad hoc* ways to fit preconceived prejudices. Simplicity, elegance, symmetry, naturalness, and similar virtues are indications that the results have not been so rigged. Such virtues may thus ease us into making unexpected discoveries and alert us to our errors.

Simplicity is often connected with idealization. An idealized surface is frictionless; an idealized planet is a mass at a point. Those idealizations simplify the mathematics. But idealization is also a means of abstracting from "noise," complicating factors that interfere with, and obscure, the phenomenon we are trying to understand.

Here is an instance from formal epistemology. Standard epistemic logic treats agents as *logically omniscient*: the structure of its models presupposes that if one knows some things, one also knows anything else they entail. Standard probability theory makes a similar though slightly weaker assumption: if one thing entails another, the latter is at least as probable as the former. Such models ignore the computational limits of actual agents. Even if two mathematical formulas are logically equivalent, we may accept one but not the other because we are unaware of their equivalence; mathematics is difficult. However, idealizing away such computational limits is not just a convenient over-simplification. One may be interested in the epistemological effects of our *perceptual* limits: our eyesight is imperfect, our powers of visual discrimination are limited. Since ignorance may result from either perceptual or computational limits, we must separate the two effects. A good way to do so is by studying models where the agent resembles a short-sighted perfect logician, with perceptual limits but no computational ones, whose ignorance therefore derives only from the former. For that purpose, the structure of standard models of epistemic logic is just right (Williamson 2014b). More generally, model-building allows us to isolate one factor from others that in practice always accompany it.

Although model-building already plays a significant role in philosophy, philosophers have not fully adjusted to its methodological implications. For instance, *counterexamples* play a much smaller role in a model-building enterprise than they do in traditional philosophy. The traditional philosopher's instinct is to provide counterexamples to refute the simplifications and idealizations built into a model, which rather misses the point of the exercise. A theoretical economist once remarked to me that a paper like Gettier's classic refutation of the analysis of knowledge as justified true belief by means of a couple of counterexamples (1963) would be considered unpublishable in economics. For economics is primarily a model-building discipline: since no model is expected to fit the actual phenomena perfectly, pointing out that one fails to do so is not considered newsworthy. What defeats a model is not a counterexample but a *better model*, one that retains its predecessor's successes while adding some more of its own. For reasons explained earlier, that does not mean that model-building disciplines are unconcerned with truth. They too pursue truth, but by more indirect strategies. Of course, it is unfair to suggest that Gettier missed the point of model-building, for the analyses of knowledge he was refuting were not intended as models; they were meant as statements of exceptionless necessary and sufficient conditions for knowledge, to which counterexamples were indeed apt. However, if epistemologists and other philosophers start aiming to build good models rather than provide exceptionless analyses, different forms of criticism become appropriate.

Models can also play a role in the criticism of would-be universal generalizations. If we are willing to dismiss theories on the basis of one-off negative verdicts in a single type of thought experiment, as with Gettier cases, we risk sometimes dismissing true theories because a glitch in the human cognitive system causes us to deliver mistaken verdicts in those thought experiments (Alexander and Weinberg 2014). A robust methodology should have ways of correcting such errors, even granted that thought experimentation is in general a legitimate method. After all, sense perception is a legitimate method for gaining knowledge, but we still need ways of catching and correcting perceptual errors. Elsewhere, I have argued that theoretical considerations about models of epistemic logic lead one to predict failures of the justified true belief analysis of knowledge, independently of thought experiments (Williamson 2013c, 2015a). When the methods of thought experimentation and model-building converge on the same conclusion, it has more robust support than when it relies on either method alone.

Another respect in which rigorous-minded philosophers may find the method of model-building alien is that selecting and interpreting models is an *art* – in science as well as in philosophy. It depends on good judgment, honed by experience. One must distinguish simplifications that abstract away inessential complications from those that abstract away crucial features of the phenomenon, and genuine insights from mere artefacts introduced for mathematical convenience. This raises the general issue of realism versus instrumentalism, familiar from the philosophy of science. Which aspects of a model tell us something about reality itself, and which are there only as instruments of the model-building process? We should not expect to settle all such issues in advance. Sometimes the successes of a model may indicate that what originally looked like a mere artefact should instead be regarded as a genuine insight. Although we can expect good model-builders to be reasonably articulate in explaining why they have selected one model rather than another and drawn one conclusion from it rather than another, there is no foreseeable prospect of reducing their skills and expertise to mechanical rules.

Some philosophers may continue to find the methodology of model-building mysterious, and resist. How can we learn from models that embody assumptions we know to be false? How exactly are we supposed to decide which false assumptions are legitimate? The short answer is: in the same way as the natural and social sciences. A full answer will be hard to articulate. Nevertheless, accumulating experience of model-building in philosophy provides good evidence that it does work.

Conclusion

Model-building already plays a significant role in contemporary philosophy. One neglected form of progress in philosophy over the past fifty years has been the development of better and better formal models of significant phenomena. It shares that form of progress with the natural and social sciences. Philosophy can do still better in the future by applying model-building methods more systematically and self-consciously. Although it is neither likely nor desirable for model-building to become the sole or even main philosophical method, its use enhances the power and reliability of philosophical thinking.

Note

This section originally appeared as Williamson 2017a in Russell Blackford and Damien Broderick (eds.), *Philosophy's Future: The Problem of Philosophical Progress* (Wiley). Earlier versions of the material were presented at the universities of Athens, Cologne, Michigan (Ann Arbor), Olomouc, Oxford, Peking University, Seoul National University, and the Inter University Centre in Dubrovnik; thanks to all the audiences and to Alexander Bird for helpful questions and comments.

9.4 Morally Loaded Cases in Philosophy

1. *The question*

Dialectical effectiveness in philosophy can pattern in surprising ways. For instance, when apparently morally neutral issues are debated in epistemology and metaphysics, philosophical logic and philosophy of language, morally loaded examples sometimes have greater dialectical power than morally neutral examples based on knowledge from ordinary life or natural science. One might have expected it to be the other way round, given the contested status of moral knowledge. By "morally loaded" I mean cases explicitly described in moral terms, or at least in ways which make moral matters very salient, as with Holocaust denial. Such cases seem to be so dialectically powerful *because* they are so highly emotive. That raises an obvious question: is this dialectical power legitimate, or does it involve a kind of *cheating*, getting readers or hearers worked up to a point where they are in no mood to apply subtle but necessary distinctions? We are usually supposed to be best at assessing philosophical claims in a cool hour.

2. *Three classes of example*

Before addressing the main question, we should look more closely at the phenomenon to be understood. I will sketch three classes of philosophical view which seem vulnerable to such moralizing critiques. The list is far from exhaustive.

Relativism

I have in mind full-blown relativism about truth, the idea that when you and I seem deadlocked in disagreement, the bottom line is that some things are true for me but not for you, while other things are true for you but not for me; there is no question of one of us being *really* or *absolutely* right and the other *really* or *absolutely* wrong. Such a view is hard to articulate in a coherent or even fully intelligible way, for reasons going back to Plato. Nevertheless, in more or less radical forms, it has a massive cultural presence in many contemporary societies, including our own, outside as well as inside academia. For confused reasons, many people treat relativism as the required intellectual basis for tolerance of diversity (fortunately, there are better non-relativist reasons for tolerance). Although few analytic philosophers take it seriously, most have encountered it in their students. Elsewhere in the humanities, it is widely taken as the default metatheory, however unsuited such an elusive doctrine is to informing day-to-day practice. It survives rigorous criticism by Protean shapeshifting.

Extreme relativists are often unperturbed by the usual counterexamples from common sense or natural science. "Anyone who thinks the Earth is flat is simply wrong." "That's just your point of view." They are more likely to start ducking and weaving when faced with morally loaded cases. In response to "Anyone who thinks the Holocaust never happened is simply wrong," a plain "That's just your point of view" seems to cast the relativist in the uncomfortable role of defending Holocaust deniers. Expect some convoluted special pleading. The difference in response does not come from a difference in the strength of evidence. Decisive though the evidence for the Holocaust is, it is not more decisive than the evidence for the roundness of the Earth. Rather, the difference comes from the moral wrong-footing of the relativist in one case and not the other. Few relativists rushed to the defense of US Counselor to the President Kellyanne Conway when she was widely derided for using the phrase "alternative facts" in explaining White House Press Secretary Sean Spicer's false statements about attendance numbers at Donald Trump's inauguration as President.

In the heyday of post-modern Theory, its protagonists flirted with relativism, though they may have had a commitment problem. Within that intellectual environment, the pushback to relativism came not so much from defenders of common sense or natural science as from Marxists, concerned that relativism would undermine the imperatives of political action. That concern was not morally neutral: they feared that the political effect of relativism would be to reduce the pressure to do what (they thought) ought to be done.

Although Richard Rorty disliked being described as a relativist, he was at the very least an anti-absolutist. But he was much more comfortable disparaging the absoluteness of truth than the absoluteness of justice, no doubt with an eye to the moral and political repercussions. Relatedly, in discussing Orwell's *1984*, Rorty allows him the distinction between cruelty and kindness, but dismisses his appeals to the distinctions between truth and falsity and between appearance and reality as contributing nothing of substance to his critique of to-talitarianism (1989: 173). Of course, Rorty was right that making the latter distinctions is not *sufficient* for adequately reasoned resistance to tyranny, but Orwell makes a strong case that it is *necessary*. Indeed, how effectively can we oppose cruelty, if we cannot distinguish its real absence from its apparent absence?

Skepticism

The skeptic rejects claims to knowledge, and even to epistemically justified belief, either globally or over some large domain, such as morality, about which we usually take ourselves to have significant knowledge.

What could be more academic in the pejorative sense than the problem of skepticism? What theory could be further from practical consequences? It does not interfere with a game of backgammon, even if neither player knows that the other exists. The skeptic feels comfortably at home disavowing knowledge that he has hands, that he is not dreaming, that he is not a brain in a vat. He takes the moral high ground, as the open-minded inquirer, quite willing to believe if only someone would show him a good reason to do so. But when skeptical arguments are deployed against scientific studies of climate change, the philosophical skeptic becomes uneasy. Again, the difference is not evidential. Those studies are no *more* resistant to radical skeptical scenarios than is anything else. It is just that philosophical skeptics do not want to find themselves fighting on the same side as climate change skeptics when there is a danger of their arguments being taken seriously and applied to a specific case, perhaps with the effect that policy is no longer made on the basis of (supposed) scientific knowledge. For when philosophical skeptics are off-duty, their political and scientific beliefs are very little different from those of their non-skeptical fellow-academics.

The slogan "Doubt is our product" goes back to public relations consultants on behalf of the tobacco industry (https://www.industrydocuments.ucsf.edu/tobacco/docs/#id=psdw0147). The strategy is not to try to prove that smoking has no harmful effects on health, but merely to create enough doubt in people's minds about the scientific evidence to make them feel licensed to ignore it and follow their inclination to smoke. That strategy is closely related to the "post-truth" atmosphere of current politics, which makes skepticism look a rather less benign intellectual force. Create enough confusion and doubt, and people will fall back on believing what they would anyway like to believe.

Skeptical arguments in political and commercial advertising are not somehow of a fundamentally different kind from philosophical arguments for skepticism. They make standard skeptical moves, appealing to skeptical scenarios and shifting the burden of proof to their anti-skeptical opponents, but in concrete, localized applications, which obscure the very general form of the underlying arguments.

When the United Kingdom participated in the 2003 invasion of Iraq, Tony Blair, then Prime Minister, justified the action by appeal to the existence of weapons of mass destruction (WMD) in Iraq. After it became clear that there had been no WMD there at the time, Blair said in a 2004 speech to his party conference: "I'm like any other human being – fallible. Instinct is not science. I only know what I believe" (https://www.theguardian.com/uk/2004/sep/28/labourconference. labour1). In the last sentence, was he just making the point that knowledge entails belief, so if in 2003 he lacked the belief that there were no WMD in Iraq he also lacked the knowledge? That entailment has nothing to do with fallibility. The context suggests another interpretation: all he could really know at the time was that *he believed that* there were WMD in Iraq. He could know his own current mental states, but not the states of affairs on the ground in Iraq to which they were supposed to correspond. Perhaps skepticism about the external world is not the best basis for deciding foreign policy. Of course, Blair was not really a philosophical skeptic, but as a practical politician he was able and willing to take opportunistic advantage of the cultural credibility of implicitly skeptical moves.

In brief, local skeptical moves made for bad political or commercial reasons look much more sinister than globalized versions of the same skeptical moves made for bad epistemological reasons.

Internalism

Here is a still-influential view in epistemology; for short, we may call it "internalism": The key normative status for belief is *justification*.

Whether a belief is justified at a time depends on its coherence with the internal consciously introspectible mental states of the subject at that time, especially *seemings*, and perhaps other beliefs too. Seemings are pre-doxastic; they are neither beliefs nor inclinations to believe. You have a seeming when things seem to you a certain way, either sensorily or intellectually. Seemings can be false: sometimes things seem to you to be some way even though they are not in fact that way. Still, when it seems to you that P, you are at least *prima facie* justified in believing that P. You are all-things-considered justified in believing that P when so believing also coheres with your other relevant mental states, especially your seemings. Consequently, false beliefs are sometimes justified. For example, a standard brain in a vat has a justified belief that it has hands, because that belief coheres with how things seem to the brain. The internalist regards that consequence of the view as a benefit, not a cost.

A similar consequence of internalism is that an unconscious bias can result in a bigoted false seeming and so, provided that coherence is maintained, in a bigoted but justified false belief (compare Siegel 2017). We may as well use the familiar figure of the consistent Nazi. I call him (or her) a *neo*-Nazi to emphasize that such people are alive and active, politically and criminally, in contemporary society. Of course, in practice neo-Nazis no doubt tend to be inconsistent, but the same goes for other people too. The paradox of the preface, sorites paradoxes, and Liar-like paradoxes all show that it is very hard for *anyone* to maintain consistency amongst their beliefs. Nevertheless, in principle, someone can have a mass of the most obnoxious neo-Nazi beliefs while still maintaining consistency, and indeed coherence: their beliefs are mutually supporting. In effect, difficulties about consistency are only a delaying tactic. The internalist must eventually face the question: what to say about the consistent neo-Nazi?

Suppose that it seems to the consistent neo-Nazi that he ought to kill *such people*, with reference to some totally innocent members of one of the many groups neo-Nazis target, just because they belong to that group. Moreover, that intellectual seeming perfectly coheres with all his other seemings and beliefs, thanks to the harmonizing effects of his unconscious biases. As a result, he goes ahead and forms the belief that he ought to kill such people. By internalist standards, the neo-Nazi is justified in believing that he ought to kill such people.

Of course, the internalist will emphasize, it does not follow that the neo-Nazi *in fact* ought to kill such people, for justified beliefs may be false. The point is "merely" that, by internalist standards, the neo-Nazi's belief is justified, and so possesses the key normative status for belief. For the internalist, the neo-Nazi is a moral brain in a vat. But is that really an appropriate way to view a consistent neo-Nazi? There is something dodgy about the way in which internalism of the sort described makes unconscious biases self-laundering, manufacturing the very seemings that justify the corresponding belief.

In a fascinating recent paper, "Radical Externalism," Amia Srinivasan has used related cases to argue against internalist accounts of justification (Srinivasan 2020). The titles of her three main examples convey their flavor: "Racist Dinner Table," "Classist College," and "Domestic Violence." The idea is that if internalists appeal to pre-theoretic verdicts on skeptical scenarios in support of their view, they are in trouble when pre-theoretic verdicts on Srinivasan's cases go against them. Readers can judge her cases for themselves, but for better or worse they certainly seem to derive some of their dialectical force from their moral loading.

No two of relativism, skepticism, and internalism are mutually equivalent. Nevertheless, there are structural similarities between them. They share a tendency to assign the same cognitive status in some important respect to both parties in a deadlocked dispute. For the relativist, there is no absolute truth of the matter, but each side's view is justified and true by its own lights. For the skeptic, there may be an absolute truth of the matter, but neither side knows what it is, or even has a justified belief in it. For the internalist, there is an absolute truth of the matter, but both sides may be justified in their internally consistent, mutually inconsistent beliefs as to what it is.

3. Emotive cases

Is the use of morally loaded examples against relativism, skepticism, and internalism cheap, or even cheating? In a morally heated exchange, one may well be reluctant to concede anything at all against the good guys, or in favor of the bad guys. When the red mist of righteous indignation descends on us, we lose sight of nuances. Perhaps the loaded cases gain their boost in effectiveness by illicitly bringing down moral and political opprobrium on one's opponents. They have to shift their ground to avoid guilt by association.

Autobiographical confession: I was brought up in a family that had a plentiful supply of moral outrage, usually directed not at family members but at various politicians, policies, and political arrangements. Probably, most philosophers, both now and then, would find the outrage appropriately or at least defensibly directed. However, it has left me with a lifelong suspicion of moral outrage, as likely to direct all the critical scrutiny in one direction, and to obscure the messy, paradoxical complexity of real political problems. For that reason, I give considerable weight to concerns about the philosophical use of morally loaded examples.

Nevertheless, something else may be going on. One hypothesis is that it is *moral encroachment*, roughly, the hypothesis that high moral stakes raise the standard for what it takes to know, or to have a justified belief (Moss 2018). However, that does not fit the role of morally loaded cases as counters to skepticism. For the point of mentioning climate change skepticism and attempts to create a cloud of doubt around the health hazards of smoking is to warn *against* raising epistemic standards too high. Indeed, raising the moral stakes can have the effect of *lowering* epistemic standards, at least those *perceived* as appropriate: "This is so morally urgent, we don't have time to examine the evidence carefully." By contrast, the role of morally loaded cases as counters to internalism can be to put pressure in the opposite direction: the point of mentioning the consistent neo-Nazi is to warn against setting epistemic standards so low that his terrible beliefs count as justified. Even if moral encroachment occurs, it does not provide a uniform explanation of the dialectical effectiveness of morally loaded cases. A different approach is needed.

In all three classes of example – concerning relativism, skepticism, and internalism – the morally loaded cases make salient the potential connections between an abstract philosophical issue and serious practical and political problems: how to deal with those who deny the Holocaust, man-made climate change, the health hazards of smoking, and so on. Such connections pose a threat to one popular strategy for defending what on first hearing may sound like wildly radical philosophical ideas. We may call it the strategy of *intellectual isolationism*. It involves cutting those ideas off from their apparent practical consequences. The reassuring message is: don't worry, if these philosophically radical ideas are accepted, for all practical purposes life will go on just as before (though with a better intellectual conscience, or in a more ironic spirit). Science funding will not be cut; educational policy will not be changed; you should treat other people just as you always did. This quietism may be connected to the "playful" or "ludic" aspect of some postmodern discourse: play Theory as freely as you like, because there will be no serious consequences.

The morally loaded cases call into question the supposed practical neutrality of such radical philosophical ideas. They indicate that glorious intellectual isolation has not been fully achieved. Those ideas may have practical consequences after all. The playful attitude starts to look irresponsible.

Of course, the isolationist can try to execute the strategy more completely, cutting any remaining links between theory and practice. The next section considers that approach in more detail, with special reference to internalism in epistemology.

4.   Case study: internalism and isolationism

We are considering the epistemological internalist who asserts (1), but of course denies (2) – we may assume that the internalist is not himself (or herself) a neo-Nazi:

(1) The consistent neo-Nazi is justified in believing that he ought to kill such people.
(2) The consistent neo-Nazi ought to kill such people.

The reader can substitute "Jews," "Muslims," "homosexuals," "Romani," or "disabled children" for "such people."

To fill out the case: The envisaged neo-Nazi *does* believe that he ought to kill such people, and he bases his belief on the coherence of its content with his other beliefs and seemings in the prescribed internalist way. The internalist will therefore say, in the jargon of epistemology, that (1) is true on the *doxastic* as well as the *propositional* sense of "justified" (the latter does not even require the subject to have the belief). For definiteness, "justified" in (1) will be understood in the doxastic sense.

One natural-looking way to implement the isolationist strategy is by making a clean break between the justification of belief and the justification of action. In particular, this internalist will deny (3) as well as (2):

(3) The consistent neo-Nazi is justified in killing such people.

For commensurability with (1), we may suppose that the neo-Nazi *does* kill such people, and that his action is based on his belief that he ought to kill them, and coheres with all his other beliefs and seemings. Accordingly, "justified" in (3) will be understood as applied to that token of the action type, *killing such people*, rather than to the action type in general.

How comfortable is the internalist's position? Of course, one would expect any decent person to deny (2). The issue is the tenability of the combination: asserting (1) while denying (3). For if (1) holds while (3) fails, someone can be justified in believing that they ought to do something, yet at the same time *not* justified in doing it.

Another standard distinction in epistemology between different senses of "justified" gives initial hope to this way of implementing the isolationist strategy. For epistemologists typically explain that when they apply the term "justified" to beliefs, they mean *epistemically justified*, rather than *pragmatically justified*. Pascal's Wager provides a standard example of the distinction. It is intended to give a pragmatic justification for believing that God exists, by showing that having the belief maximizes expected utility. It is not intended to give an epistemic justification for believing that God exists; it involves no attempt to provide proof or evidence of any kind that God exists. Similarly, if someone is about to undergo a medical intervention, which has a 20% chance of success for those who lack the belief that it will succeed, but a 40% chance of success for those who have the belief that it will succeed, she has a pragmatic justification for believing that it will succeed, but not an epistemic justification for so believing – even for those who have the belief, the intervention is more likely to fail than to succeed. Thus the internalist can say: "justified" in (1) means *epistemically justified*, whereas "justified" in (3) does not mean *epistemically justified*, instead it means *morally justified*, or *pragmatically justified*, or *all things considered justified*, or something else action-oriented like that; thus it is not at all surprising for (1) to be true while (3) is false.

However, merely distinguishing senses of "justification" is not enough to make the isolationist strategy work. For the distinction does not guarantee that norms of belief and norms of action are quite independent of each other. After all, the nature of a belief is that the believer is disposed to act on it. That is what makes the difference between believing a proposition and just warmly entertaining it. Given that connection with action in the nature of belief, we can expect it to be reflected in norms for belief. According to epistemological internalists, justification is the key normative status for belief; by "justification" there they normally mean *epistemic* justification. For epistemic justification to merit being the key normative status for belief, it should somehow reflect the nature of belief as that on which the agent acts.

Such a connection between belief and action is manifest in standard decision theory. One's epistemic state is taken to be encoded in one's probabilities. Those probabilities, combined with one's utilities or preferences, are then used to calculate the expected utilities of actions. When pragmatic justifications are in play, those actions include getting oneself (perhaps by indirect means) to form a belief, such as the belief that God exists, or the belief that the medical intervention will succeed. Such calculations of the expected utilities of various potential actions are in turn used to determine which of those actions are rational – and which beliefs one is pragmatically justified in getting oneself to form. Thus one's epistemic state plays a key role in determining pragmatic justification. For epistemological internalists, epistemic justification is in turn a central determinant of one's epistemic state. Thus epistemic justification is in turn a major determinant of pragmatic justification.

States of knowledge or belief play a fundamental role in other forms of decision theory too. Presumably, a central norm for belief should reflect which states are well fitted to have the connection to action that a good decision theory assigns to belief states.

Indeed, epistemic and pragmatic justification can be expected normally to go together. For, normally, if it is the case that P, then it is useful to believe that P, while if it is not the case that P, then it is not useful to believe that P. Moreover, we normally seem to be epistemically justified in believing such conditionals. Thus there is some presumption that if one is epistemically justified in believing that P, then one is epistemically justified in believing that it is useful to believe that P. Conversely, there is a similar presumption that if one is epistemically justified in believing that it is useful to believe that P, then one is epistemically justified in believing that P. Moreover, being epistemically justified in believing that it is useful to believe that P seems quite close to being pragmatically justified in believing that P. Such considerations suggest a strong correlation between epistemic and pragmatic justification. The correlation is not perfect, as the previous examples showed, but they depend on quite unusual conditions. Although the presumptions of the argument are defeasible, and some other aspects of it are not watertight, they suggest that the default is for epistemic and pragmatic justification to go together. Those considerations in favor of the default are available to the internalist.

To get more specific, such connections between belief and action are also discernible in an internalist treatment of the favored case of a brain in a vat. Why is the brain not justified in taking steps to drop its belief in the false proposition that it has hands? By internalist standards, the brain is epistemically justified in believing that it has hands. Similarly, it is epistemically justified in believing that its belief that it has hands is both true and useful, and in believing that it would be worse off without its belief that it has hands. For reasons like that, the brain is not justified in taking steps to drop its belief that it has hands.

Consider a more straightforward case of action. The brain seems to itself to see a baby drowning in a shallow pond. That all coheres with the brain's other seemings and beliefs. On that basis, it believes that it sees a baby drowning in a shallow pond. That belief is epistemically justified, by internalist standards. Presumably, the internalist also thinks that the brain is justified in trying to rescue the baby (the actual effects of its action will depend on how the mad scientist has wired up the vat). In explaining why that action is justified, the internalist will appeal to the brain's epistemically justified beliefs. Such an appeal will not be avoided by citing the brain's *pragmatically* justified beliefs, because such pragmatic justifications eventually trace back to epistemic justifications.

The envisaged internalist cannot reject the distinction between epistemic and pragmatic justification, because it is being used as the main obstacle to moving from (1) to (3). The trouble is that the internalist seems quite happy to move from (1*) to (3*), even though "justified" means *epistemically justified* in (1*) and not in (3*):

(1*) The brain is justified in believing that it ought to try to rescue the baby.

(3*) The brain is justified in trying to rescue the baby.

But the moves from (1) to (3) and from (1*) to (3*) instantiate the same relevant pattern: from "S is justified in believing that he/she/it ought to φ" to "S is justified in φing." Moreover, from an internalist perspective, nothing seems to disrupt the analogy between the consistent neo-Nazi and the consistent brain in a vat. The internalist was trying to make a clean break between the justification of belief and the justification of action, and so between (1) and (3). But presumably the internalist does not want to make the analogous clean break between (1*) and (3*). Even from the internalist perspective, the attempt to have (1) without (3) is not looking very unpromising.

Someone might argue that the word "ought" is not strong enough in meaning to force the move from "S is justified in believing that he/she/it ought to φ" to "S is justified in φing." After all, it is sometimes reasonable to say things like "I ought to go to the lecture, but I'm just too busy." However, that point will not help the internalist. For the example can simply be set up from the beginning with a stronger deontic operator in place of "ought." For instance, the consistent neo-Nazi may believe that he has an indefeasible duty of the most imperative kind to kill such people. Such a belief may fully cohere with his other beliefs and seemings, and so be epistemically justified by internalist standards. Then the relevant move is from "S is justified in believing that he/she/it has an indefeasible duty of the most imperative kind to φ" to "S is justified in φing." Perhaps the dial can be turned even higher on the content of the belief. Even if no strength of the operator can make the move purely logical, it is still hard to resist. For convenience, I will continue to use "ought," but the reader should bear in mind that it can be strengthened if required.

Suppose that the internalist gives up on the attempt to drive a wedge between the justification of belief and the justification of action, between (1) or (1*) and (3) or (3*) respectively. What if the internalist simply allows the move from "S is justified in believing that he/she/it ought to φ" to "S is justified in φing," at least in the cases at issue, and *accepts* (3), as well as (3*)? That would smooth the internalist's analogy between the consistent neo-Nazi and the consistent brain in a vat. It also looks more faithful to the internalist's underlying motivation. For the internalist picture is that justification depends solely on factors directly accessible to consciousness, the first-person present-tense perspective; hence the focus on seemings and internal coherence. That picture seems equally applicable to the justification of belief and the justification of action. To apply it to one while refusing to apply it to the other looks unmotivated.

But is it not simply outrageous for internalists to claim that the consistent neo-Nazi is justified in killing such people? Of course, they can still deny that the neo-Nazi *ought* to kill such people. They can even insist that he ought *not* to kill them. Thus the idea is that the neo-Nazi is *justified* in doing things which he is in no way *permitted* to do. The difficulty for internalists is to maintain this line without either compromising their condemnation of the neo-Nazi or marginalizing the role of justification. They can try to downplay what they have conceded in saying that the neo-Nazi is justified in killing such people by emphasizing that justification is just a matter of consistency with the agent's perspective. But what is supposed to be so good about consistency with something bad? Unless consistency with the agent's perspective is supposed to bring something *else* good with it, such consistency does not seem to be what matters most. Despite internalist claims to the contrary, it does not look like the key normative status for either belief or action. Then justification as consistency with the agent's perspective is marginalized. But if consistency with the agent's perspective *is* supposed to bring something else good with it, then in evaluating the neo-Nazi's beliefs and actions as justified, because consistent with his perspective, internalists are implying that there is something else good about the neo-Nazi's beliefs and actions, which is where they risk compromising their condemnation of those beliefs and actions.

For example, if internalists take consistency with the agent's perspective to bring *blamelessness* with it, then in evaluating the neo-Nazi's beliefs and actions as justified, because consistent with his perspective, they are implying that his beliefs and actions are blameless. But the neo-Nazi *should* be blamed for killing those innocent people, which suggests that his belief that he ought to kill them is also blameworthy. That the brain in a vat's beliefs and actions are blameworthy is much less obvious, which may suggest some underlying asymmetry between the two cases.

No doubt there is much more to be said, both for and against internalist epistemology (for some of it see Boghossian and Williamson 2020). But the challenge to produce a morally decent account of the consistent neo-Nazi has turned out to be genuinely difficult for internalists; it is not just bluff by moral grandstanding. That it turns on the stock figure of the consistent (neo-)Nazi only makes it worse for internalists, by emphasizing how long they have had to work on their defense.[1]

The case of the neo-Nazi brings out general problems for the isolationist strategy. Given the close connection between belief and action, and so between norms for action and norms for belief, it is rather unlikely that a philosophical theory will have radical implications for belief but no repercussions for action. In particular, when a dispute is assessed as involving some epistemic symmetry between the two views – which is what relativism, skepticism, and internalism in their different ways all involve – there is always the danger that a corresponding symmetry will be implied between actions based on the opposing views.

5. Conclusion

Morally loaded cases serve a legitimate and distinctive function in areas of philosophy that are not distinctively moral, such as general epistemology. They highlight potential consequences of theories in such areas for action. Where those practical consequences are objectionable, so are the theories that entail them.

---

[1] It has been suggested that non-internalist accounts of justification face similar problems in dealing with the consistent neo-Nazi. For even on views of evidence which award facts about appearances no special privilege in an agent's total evidence, the fact that it seems to the neo-Nazi that he ought to kill such people may still be thought to give him *some* evidence that he ought to kill them. But even if that point is granted, the evidential probability that he ought to kill them may still be negligible, given that evidential probability is not subjective probability (Williamson 2000a). In any case, there is a stark asymmetry between internalist views on which justification, understood as internal coherence, is the central norm of belief and hardline externalist views which endorse a knowledge norm for belief (Williamson 2017c), and in particular for belief *qua* premise in practical reasoning (Hawthorne and Stanley 2008). On that externalist view, since it is false that the neo-Nazi ought to kill such people, he does not know that he ought to kill them, so he is in no position to use the proposition that he ought to kill them as a premise in his practical reasoning.

Acknowledgments

This section originally appeared as an article in *Proceedings and Addresses of the American Philosophical Association* (Williamson 2019a), based on the 2019 Sanders Lecture, delivered at the 2019 Central Division meeting of the American Philosophical Association in Denver. Earlier versions of the material were presented at these universities: Belgrade, Canterbury (Christchurch), Düsseldorf, Edinburgh, Oxford, and Yale. I thank audiences at all these events for their questions, and Paul Boghossian, Georgi Gardiner, Rae Langton, Sarah Moss, Jennifer Nagel, Jason Stanley, and Amia Srinivasan for discussion of relevant issues, all of which has been very helpful. The section inherits an intentionally broad-brush, big-picture quality from the lecture.

9.5   Reply to Dennett and Kuznetsov on Abductive Philosophy

In "Armchair Philosophy" (Williamson 2019c), I characterized a broadly abductive methodology for philosophy. To emphasize that this need not give philosophy the character of a natural science, I cited the example of foundational inquiry within mathematics. Anton Kuznetsov (2019) objects: "Mathematics and philosophy are significantly different – the ontology of formal systems is known without a trace: we know all the basic laws of these systems." But that is not true of foundational mathematics. As Kurt Gödel and Paul Cohen proved, neither Cantor's Continuum Hypothesis (CH) nor its negation is derivable from standard set theory (given the consistency of the theory). If CH is true, it is a basic law of set theory. If CH is false, its negation is a basic law of set theory. Either way, there is a basic law of which we are ignorant. Of course, on some views there are many set-theoretic universes, with CH holding in some and failing in others. Then the more basic framework is that in which we investigate the space of all set-theoretic universes. But then we do not know all the basic laws of that more general framework, for reasons connected with Gödel's incompleteness theorems. Although there are many obvious differences between mathematics and philosophy, whether our knowledge has limits is not one of them.

Daniel Dennett (2019)'s main concern with philosophers' use of an abductive methodology is that if they take intuitions as the input, the abductively derived outputs will be no more reliable than the inputs – unless the outputs are recycled as a theory about the content of the implicit folk theory which generated the intuitions, not as a theory about whatever the intuitions themselves are about. The radical unclarity of "intuition" discussed in Section 10.5 clouds that concern too. Dennett mentions David Lewis in connection with an "intuition"-based abductive methodology, but Lewis spoke of "intuitions" just as our opinions, in describing something like the method of reflective equilibrium in philosophy, with no intention to exclude natural scientific opinions.

Dennett seems a little unfair to advocates of an "intuition"-based abductive methodology when he describes them as "taking their intuition-pumped consensus as a sure path to the 'real nature' of whatever they were talking about." His words "a sure path" suggest that they expect something like certainty from their methodology. But many of them would settle for a much weaker epistemic status, such as high rational credence. Dennett also flirts with a reading of a passage I quote from Austin as "a complacent assurance that the time-honored, well-honed home truths of the manifest image are the *last word* on anything," but in that discussion Austin explicitly proposes that ordinary language should just be the *first word* on some things; he offers no candidate for the last word.

In my view, the conception of philosophical methodology as directed towards reflective equilibrium suffers from the usual defects of internalist and coherentist epistemology. It ignores crucial questions about where our evidence comes from. To discuss the methodology of natural science as directed towards reflective equilibrium without mentioning our interactions with the external world through observation and experiment would, rather blatantly, be to miss half the picture. Although the omission is less obvious when philosophical methodology is described in terms of reflective equilibrium, it is still there. Our knowledge of the world includes many findings of natural science; it also includes much else besides. In principle, our evidence base for abduction in philosophy comprises all of that knowledge. In practice, parts coming from natural science are highly relevant to some philosophical questions; to ignore them would be foolish. But, again in practice, not all philosophical questions are like that. For example, the findings of natural science often have no distinctive relevance to abductive arguments for first principles of logic or mathematics, though there is no ban in principle on appeal to them even there. Sometimes, common sense knowledge is enough; sometimes, high-powered mathematical knowledge is needed. When things go well, we acquire knowledge (not just high rational credence) in the form of the abductive conclusions. It does not follow that the conclusions are the last word on anything. That something is known does not imply that no one is allowed to question it.

Acknowledgment

This section first appeared as part of Williamson 2019d, which was in turn part of a symposium on Williamson 2019c, a short summary of my philosophy of philosophy, in *Epistemology and Philosophy of Science* (Moscow). I thank Daniel Dennett and Anton Kuznetsov for their interesting contributions.

9.6　Reply to Kuznetsov and Stoljar on Model-Building in Philosophy

In "Armchair Philosophy" (Williamson 2019c), I proposed that philosophy, like much of natural science, often makes progress by constructing better models of matters of interest, rather than by discovering new universal laws of those matters. Of course, models in philosophy are usually not geared to making testable quantitative predictions, but the same applies to some models in natural science. For example, a model of evolution with three-sex rather than two-sex reproduction need not aim at making quantitative predictions: instead, its purpose may be to help explain why three-sex reproduction tends *not* to occur. Similarly, the purpose of models in philosophy tends to be explanation, not prediction. Anton Kuznetsov (2019) seems to have an overly predictive conception of models when he writes "Model building in science relies on empirical results and is mediated by them."

Daniel Stoljar (2019) agrees that the conception of progress as the discovery of new universal laws is far too narrow for both philosophy and natural science, but he argues that it is for a more general reason as well: "progress in both science and philosophy consists in the provision of better information about dependency structures." Such structures may involve relations of either causal or constitutive dependence.

I was certainly not suggesting that discovering new universal laws and constructing better models are the *only* forms that progress in either philosophy or natural science can take. Nor have I anything against progress in either case by providing better information about dependency structures. However, I do not see what is so special about dependency structures. Progress in philosophy or natural science might be made by providing better information about almost any general kind of relational structure, whether they involve dependency relations or relations of some other sort.

Dependency relations typically involve an *ordering*, irreflexive (x does not depend on itself), asymmetric (if x depends on y, then y does not depend on x), and transitive (if x depends on y, and y depends on z, then x depends on z). But many relations of philosophical and natural scientific interest are not dependency relations. Logical relations, such as entailment, are an example. That p entails q tells us nothing about whether p depends on q, or q depends on p, or neither. For a start, the entailment may be mutual. Of course, we can rig up an irreflexive, asymmetric, and transitive relation of *one-way entailment*, where p one-way entails q just in case p entails q but q does not entail p. But it still implies nothing about dependency. For example, "This is red and square" one-way entails "This is red," where the temptation is to say that the entailer depends on the entailed, but "This is red" one-way entails "This is red or square," where the temptation is to say that the entailed depends on the entailer. Nevertheless, better information about entailment is often highly explanatory, in both philosophy and natural science. Something similar goes for mereological relations: to say that x is a proper part of y is not yet to say whether x depends on y, or y depends on x, or neither. Yet better information about parthood can be explanatory. In philosophy, better information about the existence, identity, and distinctness of things can also be explanatorily crucial, yet it is not naturally understood as information about a dependency structure.

The significance of progress by building better models is not that it is the only alternative to progress by discovering new laws, but that it is a different, widespread, and theoretically very powerful form of progress, distinctive of advanced natural science and, as it turns out, advanced philosophy too. How much progress in advanced natural science really consists of finding out more about dependency structures?

Acknowledgment

This section first appeared as part of Williamson 2019d, which was in turn part of a symposium on Williamson 2019c, a short summary of my philosophy of philosophy, in *Epistemology and Philosophy of Science* (Moscow). I thank Anton Kuznetsov and Daniel Stoljar for their interesting contributions.

10

Experimental Philosophy

10.1 Reply to Weinberg

Experimental results can in principle undermine the procedures of any intellectual community, by revealing patterns of variation in its members' judgments that are hard to reconcile with the supposition that those judgments are even moderately reliable. It does not follow that every intellectual community should suspend its procedures until the relevant experiments have actually been done and shown to have reassuring results, otherwise all inquiry would come to a halt, since the procedures for interpreting experimental results would themselves have been suspended. In "On Doing Better, Experimental-Style" (Weinberg 2009), Jonathan Weinberg recognizes that the experimentalist challenge to the armchair methods of philosophy must do better than appeal to the mere skeptical possibility of seriously disquieting experimental results. Such results must actually have been obtained, if the challenge is to attain any urgency. According to Weinberg, such results have indeed been obtained, enough of them to remove any initial presumption in favor of the procedures of a well-established discipline like philosophy.

In the first edition, I complained about experimentalists' use of experiments on undergraduates just beginning philosophy to cast doubt on its methods as applied by highly trained practitioners (193, this volume). Weinberg responds that the existence of "real expertise" in philosophy is just another empirical hypothesis in need of experimental test. By the same token, the existence of real expertise in physics is just another empirical hypothesis in need of experimental test. As before, the question is how urgent the challenge is. Weinberg does not directly claim that any actual experimental results cast doubt on the existence of real expertise in philosophy. He does cite a paper by Shanteau (1992) as showing something about the characteristics of domains conducive to the development of real expertise.[1] It will be useful to consider whether Shanteau's work really does support Weinberg's argument.

One of Shanteau's main conclusions is that expert competence fares better where the stimuli to be evaluated are static, and worse where they are dynamic (as in making real-time judgments about unfolding events). A moving target is harder to hit. Armchair philosophy typically involves the evaluation of constant stimuli, such as the scenario of a thought experiment, often presented by a written description, so in that respect Shanteau's paper is encouraging. He also suggests that it is easier to achieve expert competence with stimuli that involve things, and harder with stimuli that involve human behavior. In that respect general metaphysics *may* be better off than moral philosophy, although it is unclear whether Shanteau would count a written description of a moral predicament as a stimulus that involves things or as one that involves human behavior.

Shanteau also argues that expert competence tends to be associated with tasks of recurrent types, on which frequent feedback is possible. Of course, intellectually taxing research in any discipline

---

[1]   In Shanteau's terms, some armchair philosophers are clearly experts in philosophy, since he in effect defines an "expert" in a field as someone generally regarded as an expert in the field by those who work in that field, and some armchair philosophers are clearly generally regarded as experts in philosophy by philosophers. Similarly, he defines "competence" in a field as what the experts in the field generally regard as competence in the field; by that standard, there is clearly competence in armchair philosophy, since some of it is clearly generally regarded by those generally regarded by philosophers as experts in philosophy as showing competence in philosophy. Reliance on such operational definitions is widespread in the literature on expertise that Weinberg cites, because non-experts often have no expert-independent way of assessing expertise. This is one of several reasons why the bearing of that literature on the status of philosophy is much less direct than Weinberg appears to suggest. For the sake of argument, I will go along with his apparent assumption that Shanteau's conclusions about the bearing of task characteristics on competence in experts apply similarly to real expertise; unless he is assuming that, it is not obvious why he cites Shanteau's paper. I concentrate on that paper because the other work that Weinberg cites from the expertise literature, Ericsson, Charness, Feltovich, and Hoffman (2006), is even less relevant to his claims.

is not wholly repetitive. Nevertheless, anyone with a PhD from a program in analytic philosophy is likely to have received feedback from their teachers on their evaluations of scores of thought experiments and arguments, many of them variations on recognizable themes. The feedback process continues throughout an academic career in philosophy in the form of reactions from colleagues, audiences, and referees. In this respect too, armchair philosophy does not seem especially badly off.[2]

Another feature of experts, according to Shanteau, is that they tend to decompose complex problems. Armchair philosophy lends itself to that process. For example, in determining whether a thought experiment provides a counterexample to a complex proposed analysis, one often decomposes the task into subtasks corresponding to the sub-clauses of the *analysans*.

The literature on expertise that Weinberg cites does not constitute even a *prima facie* challenge to the natural assumption that there is real expertise in armchair philosophy. His challenge to the assumption is not urgent. More specifically, he does not identify any respect in which he has shown the challenge to be more urgent for philosophy than it is for other academic disciplines, such as physics or psychology. It is no better than routine skepticism about the results of unspecified experiments that have not been carried out. Scientists perform only a tiny fraction of all the experiments that it would be physically possible for them to perform. Virtually any scientific theory has implications for the results of experiments that will never be performed. If scientists had to remain neutral about the results of all unperformed experiments, they would have to avoid commitment to virtually any scientific theory.

The question of expertise arose as a challenge to experimental philosophers' reliance on data about beginners in philosophy to cast doubt on work by experienced, intensively trained armchair philosophers. Since Weinberg's response to the challenge in his paper provides no evidence against the assumption that there is real expertise in philosophy, it fails to legitimize his use of such data.

---

[2] Weinberg's paradigm of an intellectual method that required abandonment rather than reform is introspectionism in psychology. The scope for feedback from others on introspective reports is notably narrower than it is on judgments in armchair philosophy.

Is Weinberg's use of other psychological data any more convincing? He cites evidence that verdicts on thought experiments are affected by factors that vary independently of the correctness of those verdicts. For instance, the verdicts sometimes show sensitivity to the order in which the thought experiments are considered, to differences in wording between logically equivalent descriptions, and to whether they are made in a clean, tidy environment or a dirty, messy one.[3] The conflicting verdicts cannot all be correct.[4] However, in using these data Weinberg ignores the difference between one-off individual judgments and consensus reached through the interaction of many participants in a public philosophical debate, conducted over several years in conferences and journals. In the course of such a debate, most participants are forced by their opponents to consider the thought experiments in orders and wordings more favorable to those opponents. Some participants consider them in clean, tidy environments, others in dirty, messy environments, many sometimes in one and sometimes in the other. Of course, these interpersonal and intrapersonal variations do not guarantee convergence on the right answer. Nevertheless, if the initial individual judgments are more accurate than chance, without being perfectly reliable, then the majority view has a higher probability of being right. Such social controls are as important in philosophy as they are in the natural sciences, and the social dimension of philosophy is frequently emphasized in the first edition, for example on the first page. Weinberg would have to work much harder to show that verdicts on thought experiments are no more accurate than chance, especially since the relevant data include uncontroversial thought experiments as well as controversial ones. Thus his appeals to such framing effects are undermined by his neglect of the psychological and social conditions of actual philosophical practice.

---

[3] The importance of order effects in verdicts on thought experiments is, of course, already emphasized in Williams (1970).

[4] Attempts to reconcile the verdicts by contextualist hypotheses about their content would be far-fetched in most of these cases. Williamson (2005b) suggests that the data used to support contextualist or subjective-sensitive invariantist hypotheses in epistemology are better explained in terms of errors induced by giving too much weight in some settings to factors that are psychologically salient in those settings.

Weinberg repeatedly cites the use of double-blind methods as a way in which science has learned to do better. So it has, but in its modest way armchair philosophy uses double-blind methods too where appropriate, most notably in the refereeing of submissions to journals. Although many such social mechanisms in philosophy are common to most academic disciplines, they are none the worse for that.

Weinberg makes no attempt to specify the psychological or social nature of armchair philosophy. He sprays his experimental data in its general direction, as though everything in the area deserves to be hit – at least by the charge of not currently deserving our confidence. Such an indiscriminate approach is peculiarly liable to shoot itself in the foot, or worse. Its targets include informal qualitative epistemological judgments, such as verdicts on Gettier cases. But Weinberg's paper is itself full of informal qualitative epistemological judgments, for example about whether we are justified in believing that armchair methods in philosophy are reliable. Nor could any current natural science proceed without such judgments. Even statistical data need to be interpreted; the judgment that they render some hypothesis untenable remains an informal, qualitative one, whatever formal and quantitative considerations it draws on. Presumably, Weinberg thinks that we are entitled to accept many informal qualitative epistemological judgments made by natural scientists, without special qualms about their reliability. He does not seem to think that we are entitled to accept many informal qualitative epistemological judgments made by armchair philosophers, without special qualms about *their* reliability. Does anything in his data justify this differential attitude?

It would not help Weinberg to say that the natural scientists' epistemological judgments are supported by empirical data while the armchair philosophers' are not. First, the relevant judgments concern the relation between data and theory, not the correctness of the data themselves. Both natural scientists and philosophers can make them in the armchair. Although natural scientists' epistemological judgments may be informed by background knowledge, the first edition shows that the same is true of verdicts on Gettier cases (187, this volume). In any case, there are real-life Gettier cases as well as imaginary ones; for epistemological purposes, it matters little which sort one uses (194–5, this volume). Second, Weinberg offers no evidence (experimental or otherwise) that informal qualitative epistemological judgments are more reliable about real-life cases than about imaginary ones.

In practice, Weinberg lays down the experimental challenge for armchair philosophy and simply fails to mention that it could be laid down for natural science too. Of course, experimental philosophers have tested for framing effects in informal qualitative epistemological judgments in armchair philosophy without testing for framing effects in informal qualitative epistemological judgments in natural science.[5] Framing effects threaten to constitute a rather general problem for human cognition, although not a wholly insuperable one. The experimental philosophers' practice of testing for them in philosophy and not elsewhere is analogous to that of a group of men who spend their time testing for framing effects in women's judgments, and find many. They never do the tests on men. They conclude that women's judgments are unreliable, and not to be trusted. When asked about men's judgments, they reply that since there is no evidence that they are unreliable, they can be trusted. Such experimental misogyny would not deceive Weinberg, but his own experimental anti-philosophy is scarcely more respectable from a scientific point of view. The experiments are not properly controlled, because the experimenter is looking for framing effects only where it suits him to find them.

Some experimental results on human judgment *are* disquieting. We really are less reliable than we thought we were. Our judgments are often influenced by irrelevant factors. We need to map out our intellectual vices, in order to manage them more effectively. Many disciplines have in effect already evolved methods that may allow them to work round some of the worst effects of the vices. We can reasonably hope that future advances in cognitive psychology will enable us to do better. The first edition is quite explicit that philosophy can learn from experiment (not just of the thought kind), and itself applies experimental work on the psychology of reasoning to philosophical issues (8, 104–8, this volume). But one point of the book is that any psychological kind that includes armchair philosophical judgments includes a mass of non-philosophical judgments too. In order to manage framing effects more successfully, we need to know

---

[5] The possibility of framing effects in natural science should hardly come as a surprise after Kuhn (1970) and much subsequent empirical work on the practice of science. Weinberg speaks of scientific practices as "unchallenged"; they are not unchallenged in general, just by experimental philosophers.

more about what the relevant psychological kinds are. There is no reason to believe that they will be restricted to psychological process-es that are dispensable in the way in which experimental philosophers may suppose armchair philosophy to be dispensable.

On the basis of the evidence that Weinberg offers, the idea that armchair philosophy is peculiarly at risk from experimental results is a bluff. The experimental critique discredits itself by confusing a scientistic spirit with a scientific one. Bad science does not make good philosophy.

Acknowledgment

This section originally appeared in *Philosophical Studies* as part of my half of a symposium on the first edition (Williamson 2009b). Thanks to Jonathan Weinberg for his interesting questions, and to participants at the Arché workshop in St Andrews which led to this exchange symposium for discussion, including Stephen Stich, who co-authored the paper with Jonathan Weinberg as presented there.

10.2   Philosophical Expertise and the Burden of Proof

1

An eye-catching feature of contemporary analytic philosophy is the argumentative weight it lays on thought experiments. This feature has been the target of an extended critique by self-described "experimental philosophers" since Jonathan M. Weinberg, Shaun Nichols, and Stephen Stich published their "Normativity and Epistemic Intuitions" in 2001. They have conducted extensive trials of some well-known philosophical thought experiments on a variety of subjects under a variety of circumstances. Their results suggest that the answers given to key questions in the thought experiments are sensitive to the ethnicity of the subjects, the order in which the questions are asked, and other factors presumably irrelevant to the truth of the answers. On this basis, experimental philosophers have argued that the use of thought experiments in philosophy should be substantially restricted, because on our current evidence they do not deserve our trust.

In the first edition, I developed an account of thought experiments in philosophy as employing deductively valid arguments with counterfactual premises that we evaluate as we evaluate other counterfactuals, using a mixture of imaginative simulation, background information, and logic. In response to the experimental philosophers' critique, I noted that their trials have been conducted not on professional philosophers but on lay subjects, typically undergraduates, with little or no philosophical training:

> Yet philosophy students have to learn how to apply general concepts to specific examples with careful attention to the relevant subtleties, just as law students have to learn how to analyze hypothetical cases. Levels of disagreement over thought experiments seem to be significantly lower among fully trained philosophers than among novices. [...] We should not regard philosophical training as an illegitimate contamination of the data, any more than training natural scientists how to perform experiments properly is a contamination of their data. Although the philosophically innocent may be free of various forms of theoret-

ical bias, just as the scientifically innocent are, that is not enough to
confer special authority on innocent judgment, given its characteristic
sloppiness. (193, this volume).

Call this way of defending the use of thought experiments in contemporary philosophy *the expertise defense.*

As the quotation makes clear, the expertise defense does not imply that a good philosophical education involves the cultivation of a
mysterious *sui generis* faculty of rational intuition, or anything of the
kind. Rather, it is supposed to improve far more mundane skills, such
as careful attention to details in the description of the scenario and
their potential relevance to the questions at issue.

In "Are Philosophers Expert Intuiters?" (2010), four experimental
philosophers – Jonathan M. Weinberg, Chad Gonnerman, Cameron
Buckner, and Joshua Alexander (WGBA) – provide the best-developed
response to the expertise defense currently available. In brief, WGBA
argue that whether philosophical training confers genuine expertise
(significantly greater reliability) in conducting thought experiments
is a squarely empirical question, to be answered by detailed empirical investigation in the light of the extensive scientific literature on
expertise, and that the burden of proof is on proponents of the expertise defense to carry out such investigations and show that they
deliver the requisite results. Since no such detailed investigations
have in fact been carried out, the four authors treat the experimental
critique as still holding the field: in their view, philosophers are not
currently justified in laying argumentative weight on thought experiments as they do.

This article is a response to WGBA.[1] I argue that they have
misconstrued the dialectical situation, which it is currently the experimental critique of professional philosophers' use of thought
experiments that lacks adequate evidential support, and that philosophers *are* currently justified in laying argumentative weight on
thought experiments. Of course, it is never completely satisfying just
to return the burden of proof to one's opponents. It would be more fun
to lay out a vast array of specific experimental evidence for the value

[1] The present article builds on points briefly made in Section 10.1, in response to
Weinberg 2009.

of philosophical training in improving performance with thought experiments. However, it will be a long time before we have strong evidence of that kind one way or the other, and in the meantime philosophers must get on with their job. They should not be expected to abandon their use of thought experiments when there is no good evidence that doing so would improve their philosophizing. Nor should philosophers be expected to suspend their current projects in order to carry out psychological investigations of their capacity as thought experimentalists, on the basis of evidence that undergraduates untrained in philosophy are bad at conducting thought experiments. After all, we do not expect physicists to suspend their current projects in order to carry out psychological investigations of their capacity as laboratory experimentalists, on the basis of evidence that undergraduates untrained in physics are bad at conducting laboratory experiments. Standards of laboratory experimentation in physics are doubtless higher than standards of thought experimentation in philosophy; nevertheless, in both cases the point remains that it would be foolish to change a well-established methodology without serious evidence that doing so would make the discipline better rather than worse.

2

WGBA describe the target of the experimentalist critique as "analytic philosophy's longstanding practice of deploying armchair intuitive judgments about cases" (331).[2] This description is a little misleading. Critics of "armchair philosophy" tend to forget that there are real life analogues of some philosophical thought experiments; stopped clocks really do show the right time twice a day (see 194–7, this volume). One can argue against the justified true belief account of knowledge just as easily with such real life Gettier cases as with the original fictions. But experimental philosophers never suggest that actualizing the scenarios of thought experiments would help solve the methodological problem. Rather, in discussion they have typically been quick to insist that their critique should be applied equally to

---

[2]   All quotations are from, and pages references to; Weinberg, Gonnerman, Buckner, and Alexander 2010 unless otherwise specified.

the analogues for the real life cases of the judgments at issue in philosophical thought experiments. Since the real life cases can be encountered far from the armchair, the word "armchair" should be deleted from WGBA's description of the target of the experimentalist critique.

Deleting "armchair" leaves "analytic philosophy's longstanding practice of deploying intuitive judgments about cases." Presumably, WGBA have nothing against deploying judgments about cases; one does not make philosophy more scientific by compelling philosophers to speak only in generalities. Thus the weight falls on "intuitive." Unfortunately, WGBA do not explain what they mean by the word. When is a judgment about a case intuitive? If I judge "You do not know how many coins I have in my pocket," is that an intuitive judgment about a case? If experimental philosophers judge "There is currently insufficient evidence to deny that there is knowledge in this Gettier case," is that an intuitive judgment about a case? WGBA give no help in answering such questions. If such examples do count as judgments we are not currently justified in trusting, then the experimentalist critique is self-destructively general. If we are currently justified in trusting such judgments about cases, what is supposed to differentiate them from those judgments in which, according to the experimentalist critique, we should not trust?

The extreme unclarity about the target of the experimentalist critique does not render the critique completely vacuous. It is clear at least that full-dress philosophical thought experiments are supposed to lie in the center of the target area; what is unclear is how far out the area is supposed to extend. That is not simply a matter to be left for further experimental investigation. For, according to the experimentalists, on *present* evidence we should already be withdrawing our trust from some "judgments about cases"; they should tell us, at least roughly, which ones. Presumably, they feel justified in assuming that their own judgments in the article fall outside the present target area. Again, when they discuss "the areas of philosophy in which appeals to intuition about cases are still central, such as epistemology and action theory" (345), they treat themselves as already having some capacity to discriminate between what is an appeal to intuition about a case and what is not.[3]

---

[3]   WGBA's concern in the quoted passage is not only with *explicit* appeals to intuitions about cases.

Having signaled this major problem with the experimentalist critique, I will not elaborate on it in what follows. Nor will I discuss objections that have been raised to details of the experimental designs, such as the wording of the questions. Moreover, I am quite willing to grant that the apparent disagreements between the answers of different subjects were genuine, so that if one answer was true another was false.[4] My concern is with the experimentalist response to the expertise defense.

I will not be questioning the expertise literature, or WGBA's interpretation of it. In one respect they sometimes misrepresent the expertise defense itself, when they speak of their opponents as claiming that a philosophical education "immunizes" one against the influence of whatever psychological factors distort the judgments of untrained subjects in their trials. It is not plausible that philosophical training will totally eradicate such influence, just as it is not plausible that historical training will totally eradicate the influence of whatever psychological factors distort the judgments of untrained subjects about historical matters. But the expertise defense requires no such extreme claim. The defense is vindicated if philosophical training substantially reduces the influence of the distorting factors, even short of total eradication. WGBA's more circumspect formulations acknowledge this obvious point: "What the purveyors of the expertise defense require is that philosophers' intuitions are *sufficiently less susceptible to the kinds of unreliability that seem to afflict the folk intuitions studied by experimental philosophers*" (333, their italics).

3

In assessing the dialectical status of the expertise defense, it is useful to start with some general points about observational evidence. Since they are near-platitudes, they are presumably points of agreement in theory between proponents and opponents of the expertise defense. The issue will be whether opponents of the defense have respected them in practice.

---

[4] WGBA provide references to several sorts of response to the experimental critique other than, although compatible with, the expertise response.

Experimentation and other systematic forms of observational evidence-gathering use scarce resources of time, energy, and money (for brevity, I will say only "experiments" in what follows). Even on a comparatively long timescale, the human race will only perform a tiny fraction of all the experiments it is humanly feasible to perform. Many possible experiments appear to lack any value; no outcome of them appears to provide significant evidence on any significant theoretical or practical question. Other possible experiments have more apparent value than that, but still deserve far lower priority than more urgent ones to which the resources should go instead.

What attitude should we take to the outcome of an unperformed experiment? It may sound laudably open-minded to insist that we should not commit ourselves as to the outcome. On reflection, however, that attitude reveals itself as a damaging form of skepticism. For let T be a scientific theory so well confirmed by a mass of experimental and theoretical considerations that it is unreasonable to continue testing T, and reasonable to commit ourselves to T. Nevertheless, we cannot have separately tested *all* the experimentally testable consequences of T, since there are infinitely many. Thus T has some experimentally testable but untested consequence O. The proposed attitude to unperformed experiments requires us not to commit ourselves to O. But since T entails O, commitment to T involves commitment to O. Thus the proposed attitude requires us not to commit ourselves to T. But, by hypothesis, it is reasonable to commit ourselves to T. Thus the attitude requires us not to do something it is in fact reasonable to do. Hence the attitude is not binding. Indeed, it is worse than that. For the argument is very general: the attitude in question forbids commitment to virtually any scientific claim, however well confirmed within the limits of human feasibility. We should not take such an attitude. The case of skepticism about global warming shows just how pernicious such an "open-minded" attitude to missing data can be. No one is more dogmatic than skeptics in their skepticism. It is sometimes reasonable to commit oneself as to the outcome of an experiment that has never been performed, and perhaps never will be. More generally, it is sometimes reasonable to commit oneself to a hypothesis (such as O) that could be tested by systematic experiment but never has been, whether or not it ever will be.

Care is needed in applying the argument. Presumably, T does not entail that the experiment will not be performed incompetently or on an unluckily unrepresentative sample. It may be unwise to assume that no misfortune or mistake will occur in the performance of the experiment. But that is not the issue. As a consequence of T, O too does not rule out such performance noise. What is reasonable is to commit oneself to O itself, which could be tested by systematic experiment but never has been. Similarly, the mere fact that the expertise defense could be tested by systematic experiment but never has been is consistent with the present reasonableness of commitment to the expertise defense. Any critique of it must be based on far more specific considerations.

For purposes of comparison, consider the hypothesis that professional physicists tend to display substantially higher levels of skill in cognitive tasks distinctive of physics than laypeople do. The hypothesis could be tested by systematic experiment. But even before that has happened, one can reasonably accept it. More generally, consider how philosophers of science (in the broadest sense) proceed when working on the philosophy of mathematics, physics, chemistry, biology, psychology, economics, linguistics, history, or almost any other academically well-established discipline with departments in most major universities across the world. They normally assume that professional academics in a discipline tend to display substantially higher levels of skill in its distinctive cognitive tasks than laypeople do. For example, they assume that professional judgments on its distinctive questions carry more weight than do the judgments of laypeople or philosophers. The assumption is defeasible: external criticism of the discipline is not forbidden, but it must be based on a body of evidence strong enough to defeat the initial presumption that the professionals are the people best placed to distinguish between good and bad work within their own discipline. In practice, that initial presumption is hard but not impossible to overturn.

Of course, professional training filters as well as educates. Professional academics in a discipline might tend to display substantially higher levels of skill in its distinctive cognitive tasks than laypeople do even if their professional training did not enhance those skills but merely selected people who already had them to a higher degree than others did. In practice, that "mere selection" hypothesis is grossly implausible for many cognitive skills in most academic disciplines. If it were true of skill in thought experimentation in philosophy, that would anyway suffice for purposes of the expertise defense, but in this section the focus is on professional academic training as an enhancer of cognitive skills in given individuals.

To some extent, the efficacy of professional training in academic disciplines as an enhancer of relevant cognitive skills is a matter of common experience. In principle, it can be assessed in more systematic ways too, but such assessment itself involves reliance on cognitive skills distinctive of an academic discipline such as psychology. Without an initial presumption that such skills are higher amongst those with relevant professional training than amongst laypeople, the assessment would be problematic. Moreover, it is hard to devise and apply credible tests of a skill in an intellectual discipline without relying on someone's already accredited skill in that very discipline. If every implicit claim to cognitive skill faced a burden of experimental proof, inquiry would grind to a halt. The defeasible presumption in favor of the relevant cognitive skills of those trained in a discipline plays a significant role in enabling intellectual progress.

From a sociological perspective, philosophy is a fairly normal academic discipline. Consequently, since thought experimentation is a cognitive task distinctive of contemporary analytic philosophy, the initial presumption should be that professional analytic philosophers tend to display substantially higher levels of skill in thought experimentation than laypeople do. Although that initial presumption is in principle open to experimental testing, it does not follow that the onus is on proponents of the expertise defense to do the testing. Rather, the burden of proof is on experimental philosophers to demonstrate that, contrary to initial expectations, professional training in analytic philosophy fails to enhance skill in one of its central cognitive tasks, and the corresponding professional qualifications do not select for such skill. They must point to specific features of our present evidence that tell against the expertise defense. What are those features?

Thoughts naturally turn to the difference in track record between philosophy and many other academic disciplines. Although it would be myopic to deny that philosophy has made *some* progress, one must admit that in most areas it has not made as much progress as the natural sciences (formal logic is an exception). The suggestion is that the comparative lack of philosophical progress is what defeats the initial presumption in favor of genuine philosophical expertise. However, this is not what WGBA intend, for it does not distinguish between different cognitive skills in philosophy. For some cognitive skills, WGBA explicitly concede that philosophical expertise is genuine. In particular, they assert that "philosophical training does typically bring a mastery of relevant literatures both contemporary and historical, and even specific technical skills such as argument evaluation and construction" (334), without providing any experimental evidence such as they require their opponents to produce for genuine expertise in thought experimentation. Similarly, they grant "philosophers' possession of such demonstrable skills as, say, the close analysis of texts, or the critical assessment of arguments, or the deployment of the tools of formal logic" (335), without explaining how such skills have been demonstrated in ways for which thought experimentation would have no analogue. In these cases, they treat the positive effect of philosophical training as obvious. Thus their objection to the expertise defense must turn on specific differences between thought experimentation and other cognitive skills in philosophy, not on the general phenomenon of philosophy's poor track record.

Thought experiments in any case constitute an unpromising scapegoat for the discipline's lack of progress, for if the category is understood narrowly enough to save the experimentalist critique from self-defeat, it has played a comparatively small role in the history of philosophy, even though one can find examples in Plato and other great philosophers. Nor was thought experimentation to blame for what experimental philosophers might regard as some of the more embarrassing episodes in the history of philosophy, such as the shift from logic to rhetoric in the Renaissance or the idealist turn in the eighteenth and nineteenth centuries (to paint with the broadest of brushes).

WGBA must therefore specify which differences between thought experiments and other cognitive tasks in philosophy are supposed to explain why the philosophical training they presume to enhance the latter cannot be presumed to enhance the former. One of the problems they face in doing so is that thought experimentation *overlaps* the skills they presume philosophical training to grant. For example, "the close analysis of texts," which WGBA describe as a "demonstrable skill" possessed by philosophers, is exactly what one needs adequately to take in and digest the description of the scenario in a thought experiment. Similarly, on many accounts of thought experiments, including that in the first edition, thought experiments employ arguments. In effect, conducting a thought experiment is a special case of "argument construction and evaluation," which WGBA describe as a "technical skill" that "philosophical training does typically bring" (334–5). WGBA appear not to notice this problem. Although they might classify the areas of overlap as somehow untypical (they would need to say why), the tasks for which they regard philosophical expertise as presumptively bogus are strikingly close to some of those for which they regard it as obviously genuine.

WGBA accuse proponents of the expertise defense of giving a merely generic argument, rather than one specific in the requisite way to skill in thought experimentation. They conjecture that we are relying on a "folk theory of expertise" according to which "expertise at one aspect of an activity is closely correlated with expertise in other aspects of that activity" (333). I rely on no such theory. It takes very little experience of teaching philosophy to know that expertise in solving logic problems is not closely correlated with expertise in reading historical texts. WGBA cite my comparison between the training of philosophers and the training of lawyers as an example of the generic approach, failing to notice that the comparison was specific to skills relevant to thought experimentation: "Philosophy students have to learn how to apply general concepts to specific examples with careful attention to the relevant subtleties, just as law students have to learn how to analyze hypothetical cases" (193, this volume). Nothing they say undermines the analogy. They neglect it just as they neglect the overlap between the skills they explicitly treat as enhanced by philosophical training and those relevant to thought experimentation.

4

WGBA do try to identify some relevant differences between thought experiments and other cognitive tasks in philosophy in terms drawn from the scientific literature on expertise. In that literature, various characteristics of training regimes have turned out to be conducive to the production of genuine expertise. WGBA maintain that these characteristics are absent from philosophical training with respect to thought experiments (and presumably not with respect to the cognitive tasks for which they take philosophical training to confer genuine expertise). We might therefore interpret WGBA as accepting the gist of the analysis in section 3 of the dialectical situation, while attempting to discharge the burden of proof on them by providing specific evidence of the relevant differences between thought experiments and other cognitive tasks in philosophy.

From WGBA's discussion of the expertise literature, one can extract three characteristics of training regimes that have turned out to be conducive to the production of genuine expertise. They are:

(a) repetitive practice with fast, accurate feedback;
(b) decomposition of the task into sub-tasks;
(c) use of external decision aids.

I accept that (a) to (c) are conducive to the production of genuine expertise, and that their absence has the opposite effect. In their published article, WGBA concentrate on arguing that training regimes in philosophy are deficient with respect to (a). Let us take each feature in turn.

(a) By the time one has a PhD in analytic philosophy, one has typically read many dozens of articles and books in which thought experiments play a key role, has thought, talked, and written about them on numerous occasions, and has received extensive feedback on one's reactions from one's teachers, much of it immediate (for example, in class). These uses of thought experiments often involve exploring many variations on the same theme (brains in vats, twin earths, Gettier cases, trolley cases). According to WGBA, the number of such occasions for a given individual is still orders of magnitude less than for a chess player practicing a given opening (342). But who ever claimed that the difference in skill at thought experimentation between a professional philosopher and an undergraduate is as dramatic as the difference in skill at chess between a grandmaster and a beginner? A more relevant comparison is with the number of occasions on which the trainee philosopher receives feedback with respect to philosophical skills for which WGBA acknowledge the efficacy of a standard training, such as the close analysis of texts and the critical assessment of arguments. Another relevant comparison is between feedback in legal and philosophical training with respect to hypothetical cases. WGBA's vague remarks ignore the more appropriate comparisons. They also confuse the issue by failing to distinguish between feedback for trainee philosophers and feedback for already trained philosophers (341–2). In short, they provide no serious evidence of deficiency with respect to (a), and so fail to shift the burden of proof on to their opponents.

(b) It is not hard to decompose the task of thought experimentation into consciously discernible sub-tasks. First, one must read and digest the description of the scenario; this is the part that corresponds to WGBA's "demonstrable skill" of "the close analysis of texts." Then one must judge what would be the case in the scenario described, which in turn often decomposes into answering several questions, such as Is it a belief? Is it true? Is it justified? Is it knowledge? One must also judge whether the scenario is really possible, for otherwise the thought experiment may not be fit for purpose. Finally, one must determine whether the premises, if verified, do entail the proposed conclusion; this part corresponds to WGBA's "technical skill" of "argument construction and evaluation."

(c) Formal methods as decision aids facilitate some, although not most, thought experiments. For example, consider the proposed law of tense logic "If P then it will be the case that it was the case that P." One can test it by a thought experiment in which one envisages a last moment of time, using formal techniques to check that the schema has a false instance in that scenario. The exercise is no merely formal one, for it concerns the intended interpretation of the tense operators. A more commonplace example is the regular use of outcome tables and other visual aids in perspicuously displaying the structure of thought experiments in decision theory. Although aids of that kind are "purely notational," a good notation can do much to facilitate understanding and insight, as mathematicians know.

On closer inspection, therefore, philosophical training with respect to thought experiments may have about two and a half of the three characteristics conducive to the production of genuine expertise, for all WGBA say. Their elaborate invocation of the expertise literature threatens to undermine their own argument.

WGBA make several points that could be construed as objections to the foregoing assessments of (a) to (c). These points must now be evaluated.

First, WGBA insist that we cannot determine from the armchair *how much* practice is needed for genuine expertise, and likewise for the other factors. That is obviously correct, but it is a quite generic point; it does not discriminate between thought experimentation and the skills WGBA acknowledge to be developed by philosophical training. For example, my comments about practice and feedback on thought experimentation could equally be applied to practice and feedback on "argument construction and evaluation" (WGBA's comments on that "technical skill" are not aimed at formal logic, and their own arguments are informal). After all, it is often the thought experiments that absorb classroom time because their vivid details grip the imagination, to the detriment of drier material on the structure of informal arguments. Since WGBA provide no evidence that thought experimentation fares worse in such respects than the other skills, they give no reason to expect philosophical training to be relevantly less efficacious for the former than for the latter.

Second, to the suggestion "that philosophers train their intuitions against other, already-certified expert intuitions," WGBA respond: "This appears to be a non-starter, since it just invites an explanatory regress: how did the purveyors of *those* intuitions develop their expertise?" (341). Such an objection might be made concerning the feedback philosophy students receive from their teachers on thought experiments, mentioned earlier under (a). Incompetent feedback is not conducive to genuine expertise. This point too is dangerously generic for WGBA's purposes. When students receive feedback from their teachers on "argument construction and evaluation" or "the close reading of texts," how did their teachers develop their expertise? The infinite regress concern would be more serious if thought experimentation did not decompose into sub-tasks, for then there might seem to be little for the feedback to consist of beyond bare verdicts. Even there, however, the teacher might also suggest other related thought experiments for purposes of comparison. Moreover, in most branches of philosophy there are many sufficiently uncontentious thought experiments, such as fictional cases of *un*justified true beliefs that do not constitute knowledge, on which beginners are often started; it is their very uncontentiousness that makes them comparatively inconspicuous. In any case, given the decomposition of the task of thought experimentation into sub-tasks, described under (b), feedback can be far more articulated. For example, the teacher can draw the student's attention to overlooked aspects of the description of the scenario. In any academic discipline, the capacity of teachers to provide correct and useful feedback depends to some extent on the teachers' expertise, but the regress need not be vicious. We sometimes have a high enough level of expertise to bootstrap ourselves to a higher level of expertise by mutual criticism without input from anyone already at the higher level. Pupils sometimes surpass their teachers without having more innate ability. WGBA provide no evidence that this does not happen for thought experimentation just as it happens for other cognitive skills.

Third, WGBA complain about a hypothesis on which trained philosophers do better than laypeople when "the correct verdict turns on a very subtle detail" that it is "not what is needed here, dialectically," because it "will not help explain away a difference in intuitions found between different groups of the folk, or between different orders of consideration of cases by the folk, that would lead us to expect philosophers not to recapitulate the same variation" (347–8). But that is to impose an unreasonable explanatory demand. The effect of education is often to increase uniformity on some cognitive task; explaining the effectiveness of the education need not involve explaining the specific patterns of variation amongst the uneducated. For example, one can explain why very few professional historians are Holocaust deniers or very few professional biologists are creationists without explaining why Holocaust denial or creationism is much commoner amongst relevantly uneducated people in some countries than in others. WGBA provide no reason to expect a different pattern in philosophical training on thought experiments.

In summary, the dialectical situation is this. The experimental critique presents evidence that philosophically untrained subjects perform poorly at thought experimentation, a cognitive task characteristic of contemporary analytic philosophy. In general, given a cognitive task characteristic of a discipline, it is unwarranted to project data about the performance at the task of subjects untrained in the discipline onto subjects trained in the discipline, without specific evidence that training in the discipline makes no substantial difference to skill at that task. WGBA's attempt to provide such specific evidence consists of a few vague and casual claims about training in philosophy and thought experimentation. They provide no significant evidence that thought experimentation is worse off in the relevant respects than the cognitive skills they acknowledge to be enhanced by training in philosophy, such as informal argumentation and the close analysis of texts. Consequently, they provide no reason to rely less on trained philosophers' skill at thought experimentation than on their skill at those other cognitive tasks.

5

The fear is sometimes expressed that philosophical training merely enforces orthodoxy in thought experiments. It socializes the malleable into eventually accepting the standard judgments, whatever their initial views. Those who stubbornly resist are excluded from the profession. They fail to get into a top graduate school, or fail to get their doctoral dissertation accepted, or fail to get a proper job in philosophy. Even if they somehow manage to sneak into the profession, referees for prestigious journals and publishers reject their article and book manuscripts. WGBA briefly raise such a possibility (351).

Of course, one can see academic training in many disciplines in such reductively sociological terms. It surely has some tendency to filter out unpopular views in all academic fields, including the natural sciences. But a view may be unpopular for good reason. By the arguments above, the onus is on those who suspect the professional consensus in philosophical thought experiments of being a merely sociological phenomenon to provide solid evidence for their suspicion, to distinguish this professional consensus from more benign ones. Otherwise the suspicion is just one more conspiracy theory. WGBA provide the skeptic with no such evidence.

We have more to rely on than that general consideration. As WGBA note, philosophical training fosters a variety of cognitive skills, which they treat as obviously genuine (close analysis of texts, argument construction and evaluation, formal logic, and so on). We might expect that if thought experimentation were a rogue pseudo-skill, orthodoxy in thought experiments would be at best poorly correlated with possession of all or most of the genuine cognitive skills in philosophy. Since a significant minority even of Western students give unorthodox responses to thought experiments, according to the experimental philosophers' own results, such responses should sometimes be combined with genuine cognitive skills in philosophy, if the latter are poorly correlated with orthodoxy. Given that highly rated performance on most dimensions can compensate for poorly rated performance on one or two in academic tests, we should not expect philosophical training to exclude all or almost all of those who deviate from orthodoxy in thought experiments, any more than it excludes all or almost all of those who are not much good at formal logic.

Furthermore, orthodoxy in thought experiments is not all or nothing. People who ascribe knowledge in a Gettier case may give orthodox answers in other thought experiments. If they fail in epistemology, they can try metaphysics or moral philosophy instead. If they are good enough in all other respects, they can still make it in the profession. Having achieved tenure and prestige, they are in a position to go back to their old grievance, deliver lectures in which they skillfully construct arguments to show that their unorthodox answer in the thought experiment fits a better overall theory, and use their reputation to have their arguments published in books and articles. After all, a powerful challenge to orthodoxy brings rich professional rewards in philosophy.

Once one seriously considers what it would take to enforce a given response to a particular thought experiment across the philosophical profession purely by a process of social exclusion, with no deeper cognitive basis, the scenario looks increasingly paranoid. It is, in any case, not the scenario most experimental philosophers had in mind.

6

The claims of this article do not entail that we should be complacent about trained philosophers' skill at thought experimentation. There are too many internal tensions between common verdicts in different cases for that.[5] But we should also not be complacent about trained philosophers' skill at the construction and evaluation of informal arguments. Given the widespread negative evaluations of the experimental philosophers' informal arguments, and the many arguments against their conclusions, experimental philosophers presumably cannot rate trained philosophers' skill in that respect very highly either. Plainly, however, the proper response is not to give up the practice of informal argumentation in philosophy. That would only make

---

[5]   See, for example, Williamson 2005b in the case of knowledge ascriptions.

things worse (*much* worse). Rather, we must try to refine the practice from within, as we do. Why should we not do the same with thought experimentation?

Psychological evidence may well have a significant role to play in refining our skill at thought experimentation. It can alert us to unexpected sources of bias and distortion in our verdicts, and help us correct for them. We are likely to have most to learn from general psychological theories of judgment that are well established on the basis of a broad range of evidence, rather than from data gathered with a specific philosophical (or anti-philosophical) agenda on complex, philosophically contested judgments. Some such work is already available.[6] That is a far more promising way forward than a wholesale ban on thought experimentation. Indeed, given the point from Section 1 that the target of the experimental critique is not just thought experimentation but the more general practice of relying on "intuitive judgments about cases," whether made in or out of the armchair (since otherwise the experimental critique would not make the intended difference), it is quite unclear what philosophy without the practice at issue would be, if such a thing is even possible.

Consider, for example, a theory of confirmation. We may hope to test it by drawing out its predictions for a range of specific counterfactual cases, kept artificially simple in order to make it as clear as possible, independent of the theory, which hypotheses would really be better confirmed than which. Those tests are thought experiments. To follow the experimentalists' advice not to use such tests is to make philosophy less scientific, not more.

Acknowledgments

This section first appeared in *Metaphilosophy* (Williamson 2011a). I thank Jonathan Weinberg for detailed written comments on related material, both him and others for useful discussion at an Arché workshop entitled "Philosophy Without Intuitions?" at St. Andrews, a graduate conference at Trinity College Dublin, the 26th International Philosophical School of the Institute for Philosophical Research of the

[6]Nagel 2008, 2010 constitute promising recent examples.

Bulgarian Academy of Sciences conference "Applied and Experimental Philosophy in Knowledge Based Society East and West" in Sofia, and meetings of philosophical societies at Oriel College Oxford and the University of Geneva, where I presented other versions of this section, and likewise participants in the December 2009 symposium marking the 40th anniversary of the founding of the journal *Metaphilosophy*, "The Future of Philosophy: Metaphilosophical Directions for the 21st Century," at the Institute of Philosophy, School of Advanced Studies, University of London.

10.3   On Joshua Alexander's *Experimental Philosophy: An Introduction*

Most philosophers accept that experimental findings can in principle bear on philosophical questions. Experimental confirmation of the theory of special relativity is relevant to the philosophy of time, as are results from experimental psychology to the philosophy of perception. The usual pattern is that experimental findings about X bear on the philosophy of X by showing something about X in real or apparent conflict with assumptions on which philosophers of X had relied. The movement calling itself "Experimental Philosophy" does not fit that pattern. The experiments it promotes as bearing on the philosophy of X are not directly about X. Rather, they are about *what people say* about X. The people surveyed are typically not experts on X. Their reactions are supposed to bear on the philosophy of X by showing something about the everyday *concept* "X," perhaps that philosophers had misunderstood its structure, or neglected its variation from one social group to another. Reconsidering the concept "X" is supposed to lead philosophers indirectly to reconsider X itself. In the philosophy of time, such a method might involve, not physicists' experiments about time, but statistical surveys (carried out by the philosophers themselves) of ordinary people's verdicts on examples from the philosophy of time, and even (if funding permits) scans of their brains as they react.

Advocates present Experimental Philosophy as a revolution in philosophy, starting about the new millennium. But the approach is older than they suggest. During the heyday of ordinary language philosophy in the 1950s, the complaint was sometimes heard that if philosophers want to discuss the ordinary uses of words, they should go out and see how ordinary people really use those words. The Norwegian philosopher Arne Næss put an early version of the approach into practice in the 1930s with questionnaires about truth. His results had very little impact. His approach was generally treated as eccentric, although quite what entitled ordinary language philosophers to dismiss it was not altogether clear. The current philosophical climate is more favorable; an atmosphere of excitement surrounds Experimental Philosophy.

Joshua Alexander, an activist in the movement, has written a clear and accessible introduction to its work. The reader obtains a good sense of what Experimental Philosophers are doing and why. The impression is conveyed that the revolution will triumph eventually, though not without an arduous struggle. Much of the book is devoted to showing how tricky the data are to interpret and to confronting critics of Experimental Philosophy (including this reviewer).

The starting-point of Alexander's account is that "philosophical intuitions," glossed as *"what we would say* or *how things seem to us"* (1, 101), play a central evidential role in much contemporary philosophy. They constitute data against which theories are measured. He discusses contrasting accounts of the nature of intuitions without settling on any, but continues on the basis that we can recognize when they are being invoked. If philosophers are indeed using *what we would say* or *how things seem to us* as data, then they should be careful to find out what we really would say or how things really do seem to us, and large-scale surveys are relevant to that enterprise. The first person plural pronouns are a clue. If I am relying on what *we* would say or how things seem to *us*, what entitles me to assume without asking that what the rest of us would say is what I would say, or that how things seem to the rest of us is how they seem to me? Anyway, who are "we?" If we include people who differ from me in race, gender, culture, or education, isn't the assumption of uniformity in the data hopelessly shaky? If we include only those who resemble me in all such respects, what value has a philosophical theory based on so narrow a range of data? The stage is set for Experimental Philosophy. Alexander illustrates the range of roles it can play in alerting us to unexpected and theoretically suggestive complexities and variations in responses, using case studies of its application in epistemology, ethics, and the philosophy of mind. His general moral is that we are not yet in a position to draw firm conclusions: more Experimental Philosophy is needed because the data so far do not point unequivocally to a single explanation.

Alexander's case studies are detailed and readable. Unfortunately, they can mislead in philosophically crucial respects. For instance, he discusses the recent debate between contextualists and subject-sensitive invariantists in epistemology (36–48). He presents contextualism as the view that the standard for knowledge varies with how salient possibilities of error are, and subject-sensitive invariantism as the view that it varies with how much is at stake. Readers unfamiliar with the debate will not realize that the fundamental difference between contextualism and subject-sensitive invariantism has nothing to do with either salience or stakes, but concerns instead the difference between the context of the ascriber of "knowledge" and the context of the subject to whom it is ascribed: according to contextualism, the truth-value of the ascription is sensitive to the ascriber's context even when the subject's context is held fixed; according to subject-sensitive invariantism, the truth-value of the ascription is sensitive not to the ascriber's context but to features of the subject's context traditionally thought to be epistemically irrelevant. Thus to hold the truth-value of "knowledge"-ascriptions sensitive to how much is at stake *for the ascriber* but not to salience is to be a contextualist rather than a subject-sensitive invariantist, while to hold it sensitive to how salient error possibilities are *for the subject* but not to stakes or the ascriber's context is to be a subject-sensitive invariantist rather than a contextualist. In an endnote, Alexander acknowledges an over-simplification in his statement of the issue, but not the crucial one; he says that the debate is really "about whether or not salience matters" (119n19). His discussion shows no care in distinguishing between the ascriber's context and the subject's. In several of his examples, error possibilities are salient in both contexts, so the experiments are not properly controlled. It is hard to design a good experiment to test a theory if you do not pay attention to what the theory says.

Another chapter illustrates the use of experimental methods to distinguish between conceptual competence and conceptual performance with examples where the application of the concept "intentional action" is apparently sensitive to normative judgments about the agent. Alexander concludes that survey methods are of little help in determining whether the influence of some factor in an application of the concept was part of conceptual competence or just of conceptual performance. "What is needed instead, for example," he proposes, "are neuroanatomical accounts of the cognitive processes and mechanisms responsible for our folk psychological judgments and evolutionary (or other teleological) accounts of the work that our folk concepts are supposed to be doing" (69). However, those accounts will be of limited use in determining the bounds of conceptual competence if "conceptual competence" is ill-defined. Alexander explains it thus: "The central idea is that certain factors (e.g., resource limitations or interference from other cognitive processes) can influence a person's use of a given concept without influencing her knowledge of that concept or being reflective of the meaning of that concept" (60). Suppose that on seeing my son spill his milk I judge that he did it intentionally. Presumably, my visual perception is not itself part of my competence with the concept "intentional action," since it involves another cognitive process, even though the latter's role is hardly just "interference." Rather, my conceptual competence is meant to be something I bring to perception. Is it some mechanism for determining whether what I perceive is an intentional action? Such accounts are suspiciously verificationist. The mechanism will be less than 100% accurate. I could change it without changing the meaning of "intentional action." Or does my conceptual competence consist in a list of analytic truths about intentional action written in my brain? The analytic-synthetic distinction is notoriously problematic and ambiguous. "Conceptual competence" as Alexander presents it is so unclear that trying to determine its parts through neuroanatomical or evolutionary investigations would be a waste of time. It is hard to design a good experiment to test an ill-defined theory.

If some Experimental Philosophers neglect traditional philosophical skills in their enthusiasm for experimental methods, that is not an essential feature of Experimental Philosophy. In principle, it could disappear as the movement matures – although the divisions between experimentalists and theoreticians in natural science hint that some trade-off between the two sorts of skill is not easily avoided. A more central worry is that the project of Experimental Philosophy, as characterized by Alexander, does not withstand scrutiny.

What the Experimental Philosophy revolution is supposed to change – systematize, restrict, or abolish – is a philosophical method: the use of philosophical intuitions as evidence. Alexander's starting-point is that such method is obviously widespread in, and distinctive of, contemporary philosophy (1, 11). The systematic deployment of elaborate hypothetical cases is indeed an eye-catching feature of much recent analytic work. But what Experimental Philosophers target is neither the systematicity nor the elaboration. Nor, officially, is it the hypothetical nature of the cases. For many of them can be replaced by real life cases. For example, hypothetical Gettier cases are famously used to refute the equation of knowledge with justified true belief. Experimental Philosophers have argued that verdicts about such cases are too culturally variable to carry weight in epistemology (although recent work by Jennifer Nagel has cast doubt on the robustness of their results). But there are also real-life Gettier cases; stopped clocks sometimes really do show the right time. Epistemologists can easily use them instead to make the same point. Unsurprisingly, that does not satisfy Experimental Philosophers. They insist that verdicts on real-life cases involve philosophical intuitions just as much as do verdicts on hypothetical cases. If so, the judgment "He does not know that it is noon" may involve a philosophical intuition just as much as does the judgment "In the hypothetical case, the agent does not know that it is noon." But "He does not know that it is noon" is not distinctively philosophical; it is a judgment in ordinary language for which there is perceptual evidence: you see him at noon setting his watch by the stopped clock.

Although philosophical intuitions are often treated as non-inferential, one must be careful about the relevant sense of "inferential." Just as the judgment "He does not know that it is noon" somehow derives from information such as "He is relying on a stopped clock," so the judgment "In the hypothetical case, the agent does not know that it is noon" somehow derives from information such as "In the hypothetical case, the agent is relying on a stopped clock." Although one normally reaches such verdicts without conscious deductive or inductive argument, the same applies to vast numbers of unproblematic judgments in natural science and everyday life, including many nonperceptual judgments. For instance, conscious deductive or inductive argument is not how scientists usually make their overall judgments as to which of several rival theories is best confirmed by a mixed body of evidence. I doubt that the reader used conscious deductive or inductive argument to reach the reasonable belief that there are no hobgoblins (I certainly didn't). Few of the statements made in Alexander's book appear to be based on conscious deductive or inductive argument. The sense in which verdicts on cases in philosophy are non-inferential covers far too much to characterize a distinctive philosophical method.

The criterion that the cases be philosophically significant is equally unhelpful. Any judgment whatsoever has potential philosophical interest, because it will be inconsistent with some whacky philosophical theories.

If the judgments that involve philosophical intuitions are in ordinary language, concern examples, and are not based on conscious deductive or inductive argument, so are vast numbers of uncontroversially unproblematic everyday and scientific judgments, including many made by Experimental Philosophers themselves. Who imagines that philosophy would be improved by a ban on examples, or an insistence that it be conducted entirely in technical jargon? Nor can all judgments in philosophy be based on conscious deductive or inductive argument; some premises are needed too.

Alexander's own gloss on "philosophical intuitions," "*what we would say* or *how things seem to us*," does no better. In both everyday and scientific situations, when I say that P, I would say that P, and (if I am sincere) it seems to me that P. If I am not idiosyncratic, we would say that P, and it seems to us that P. If I believe that I am not idiosyncratic, I believe that what we would say, and how things seem to us, is that P.

Alexander proceeds on the assumption that, even if he cannot define "philosophical intuition," we can recognize when one is being used as evidence, and thereby demarcate a tractably narrow class of cases. But although we may indeed be able to recognize when a judgment about an explicit hypothetical case is being used as evidence, that is not the point. As just seen, under dialectical pressure Experimental Philosophers have applied the term "philosophical intuition" so broadly that it fails to capture anything useful. If Experimental Philosophers want to put their activities on a proper scientific basis, they would do well to drop misleading terms like "philosophical intuition," and face up to their failure to identify any distinctive philosophical method to be transformed or overturned by their revolution.

Eliminating all the parts of Alexander's book that depend on talk of "philosophical intuitions" does not leave nothing. His case studies need not be described in such terms. If the experiments have been properly designed and conducted, they still reveal unexpected and intriguing patterns in ordinary human judgments about philosophically central matters such as knowledge, intentional action, causation, and morality. What to make of those patterns is unclear, but simply ignoring them would be imprudent and incurious. Even if they turn out to result from various kinds of bias, a philosophical training is unlikely to render one entirely immune to such bias. Understanding a source of bias is a step towards correcting for it. To be credible, the diagnosis of bias should be backed by an appropriate psychological theory, independently tested on philosophically uncontentious evidence. Such a theory is more likely to come from cognitive psychology than from

Experimental Philosophy, and to rely on experiments designed and conducted by psychologists with the requisite experience and know-how. The methodological moral for philosophers to draw will concern ways of correcting for bias of the psychologically identified kind. It will not be to avoid or reduce reliance on "philosophical intuitions," because that term does not pick out any specific psychological kind.

Alexander's reliance on the ideology of "philosophical intuition" is not the only problematic aspect of his discussion of the epistemology of philosophy. His arguments tend to instantiate all-purpose skeptical forms. His comments on evidence are an example. Consider a philosopher who uses a Gettier case to refute the theory that justified true belief is knowledge. The key premise of her refutation is that the subject does not know. One might suppose that she is using that premise as evidence against the theory. But Alexander claims that further evidence is needed for the premise. His point is that further evidence is needed to persuade those whom the premise does not initially persuade (104–7). But such an argument could be formulated about *any premise whatsoever*. The upshot would be that no premise is ever good enough to use as evidence, because further evidence would always be needed to persuade those whom it did not initially persuade. Although Alexander naturally does not endorse or even consider that conclusion, he gives no reason why his form of argument should work in the case to which he applies it but not in general.

When one puts forward a premise p, one usually hopes that one's audience will accept p. If they do not, one may use whatever further evidence one expects to carry weight with them. One may say "The Pope believes p" or "Daniel Dennett believes p," depending on circumstances. One may emphasize anything the challenger believes that favors p. But one is unlikely to get far by saying "I philosophically intuit p" or "We philosophically intuit p." Appeals to further evidence typically reflect the dialectical needs and opportunities of the moment rather than revealing the standing basis on which one believes p. Sometimes, when you fail to persuade your interlocutor, that reflects shortcomings on his part rather than on the part of your evidence. Alexander does not engage with the task of showing that it is otherwise when a philosopher uses a Gettier case as evidence.

Alexander also falls back on generic skeptical arguments in his discussion of philosophical expertise. For example, he sees an explanatory regress in the idea that students train their judgments against those of established experts, and worries that various kinds of bias may make us overconfident of the value of our training (94). Those are skeptical possibilities for any academic discipline. Alexander provides no serious evidence that they are more urgent in philosophy than elsewhere. To the suggestion that theoretical reflection may improve philosophical judgment, he responds "theoretical commitments are just as likely to contaminate as they are to clarify." The next sentence backs off from the unsubstantiated "just as likely" to a mere claim of possibility: "The fact that expert philosophical intuitions are theoretically informed doesn't ensure that they are *more* theoretically valuable than folk intuitions" (95). Indeed; but in no academic discipline does the fact that expert judgments are theoretically informed *ensure* that they are more theoretically valuable than lay judgments. Alexander also objects that "If our theoretical commitments shape our philosophical intuitions, it is hard to see how our philosophical intuitions can help us *independently* assess the accuracy of those theories" (ibid.). That is just a version of the old concern, familiar from the philosophy of science, that the theory-ladenness of observation undermines the rationality of theory testing. But a theory can get into trouble on its own terms; its influence on our observations does not entail that they will always favor it. Anyway, the theory under test need not be one of those with which our observations are laden. Alexander applies such all-purpose concerns about expertise to argue that we need Experimental Philosophy to test whether the purported experts in philosophy are any good. He does not explain why, if at all, such testing of expertise is more urgent in philosophy than in other disciplines.

Confronted with Alexander's restriction of generic forms of skepticism to philosophy, it is hard not to suspect some anti-philosophical bias. "Calls for change," he reminds the reader, "are often met with resistance, especially by those heavily invested in the orthodox" (89). But those heavily invested in revolution have their own reasons for resisting their opponents. Fortunately, Experimental Philosophy shows signs of outgrowing the sort of polemical philosophy-hating philosophizing from which it has not been entirely free. The best work reported in this book does not reflect any such anti-philosophical agenda.

Experimental Philosophers did not invent the idea of "philosophical intuition." It belonged to the ideology of one faction of the *ancien régime*. Against that faction, their use of it was dialectically legitimate.

For constructive purposes, however, it has outlived its utility. The psychological and sociological study of philosophy will make more progress once it ceases to work within a framework of obsolescent epistemology.

Acknowledgment

This section first appeared as a review of Alexander 2012 in *Philosophy* (Williamson 2013f).

10.4   Philosophical Criticisms of Experimental Philosophy

1. Introduction

The phrase "experimental philosophy" can mean many things. In a broad sense, it covers any experimental inquiry with a philosophical purpose (Rose and Danks 2013 argue for a similarly broad understanding of "experimental philosophy"). On that reading, few philosophers today object to experimental philosophy as such. For example, it is generally agreed that the philosophy of perception has much to learn from experiments on the psychology of perception. Although the experiments tend to have been conducted by psychologists for psychological rather than philosophical purposes, in principle philosophers of perception themselves could initiate and even conduct similar experiments for philosophical purposes – although in practice the results will be better if they do so in collaboration with experimental psychologists, who have more of the required know-how in designing, conducting, and interpreting experiments. Analogous considerations apply to the philosophy of space and time and experiments in physics. A few diehard Wittgensteinians may still claim that no outcome of scientific experimentation is of special relevance to philosophy, whose role they confine to dissolving conceptual confusions. This section assumes that philosophy is a theoretical discipline with more constructive ambitions than that.

In a narrower sense, "experimental philosophy" refers to a more specific kind of philosophically motivated experimental inquiry, in which verdicts on hypothetical cases relevant to some philosophical question are elicited from significant numbers of subjects, sometimes under controlled conditions, and hypotheses are tested about the underlying patterns. Again, there is no reason in principle why philosophy cannot learn from the results of such activities, though their bearing on the original philosophical questions needs to be clarified. But within experimental philosophy in the narrower sense, there is a minority movement, sometimes known as the "negative program," which has attracted attention disproportionate to its size, because its proponents' claims seem to have radical implications for philosophical methodology. The negative program offers a naturalistic critique of the non-experimental ("armchair") methods of much recent analytic philosophy, and in particular of its reliance on thought experiments (for these purposes, thought experiments do not count as experiments themselves). The well-known paper by Weinberg, Stich, and Nichols (2001) may conveniently be taken as the opening broadside of the negative program, at least in its contemporary form. The results of some of its experiments are interpreted as showing that the crucial verdicts in thought experiments on which philosophers have relied are sensitive to factors presumably irrelevant to their truth, such as the ethnicity or gender of the experimental subjects, or the order or environment in which they are presented with the thought experiments. Although most experimental philosophy even in the narrow sense is independent of that critique, this section focuses on the negative program, and criticisms of it. Nor does it concern all such criticisms. Various objections have been raised to the specific design, execution, interpretation, and repeatability of specific experiments on which proponents of the negative program have relied. This section does not discuss such objections. Rather, it concentrates on broader theoretical challenges to the negative program that arise even if the specific experiments at issue are well designed, well executed, well interpreted, and repeatable.

2. "Philosophical Intuitions"

Many proponents and many opponents of philosophical thought experiments describe them as eliciting "philosophical intuitions," corresponding to the crucial verdicts. For example, it is said to be a philosophical intuition that, in the hypothetical scenario, the subject ought to divert the trolley to save five lives at the expense of one, or does not know that it is 3 p.m. by looking at a stopped clock that happens to be showing the right time. Thus many proponents of the negative program define the overall target of their methodological critique as reliance on philosophical intuitions, or on intuitions more generally (see, e.g., Alexander and Weinberg 2007: 63). Against them, many other philosophers defend reliance on philosophical intuitions, or on intuitions more generally (Sosa 2007). Still others deny that philosophical thought experiments involve reliance on such intuitions (Deutsch 2009, Cappelen 2012).

The phrase "philosophical intuition" is obviously technical jargon, in need of explanation. Surprisingly, both proponents and opponents of the negative program tend to use the phrase as though it were self-explanatory. Alternatively, they give it a perfunctory vague gloss such as "*what we would say* or *how things seem to us*" (Alexander 2012: 1). At first sight, this does not look like much of a problem, since it seems clear enough from examples what is meant. We can recognize a philosopher's thought experiment when we see one, and the crucial verdict in it is the one the philosopher subsequently invokes. Of course, examples do not reveal the underlying psychological nature of philosophical intuitions, but we need not know that nature in order to recognize when they are being relied on.

We can start to appreciate the inadequacy of that attitude by considering real life analogues of thought experiments. In epistemology, I have sometimes played tricks on audiences to create actual Gettier cases (see 194, this volume). Instead of judging that in the hypothetical scenario the subject has justified true belief without knowledge of the given fact, audience members judged (after I revealed the trick) that they themselves had had justified true belief without knowledge. Instead of judging that the man you *imagine* relying on a stopped clock would not know that it is 3 o'clock, you can judge that the man you *observe* relying on a stopped clock does not know that it is 3 o'clock. Indeed, you can receive the description of the imaginary case in the very same words as a report of a real life case, and judge whether he knows on that basis. For epistemological purposes, such actual cases do just as well as hypothetical ones in showing justified true belief to be insufficient for knowledge.[1] If epistemologists rely on actual cases rather than hypothetical ones, are they still relying on philosophical intuitions? If the negative program's answer is "No," its critique of reliance on philosophical intuitions will be quite easy to get round in some key debates: just bring about a real life analogue of the contested thought experiments. Of course, that will often be a

---

[1] Arguably, what most epistemologists call "justified belief" is better classified as *blameless* belief (Williamson 2021a), but the experimental critique of Gettier cases concerns the denial of "know," not the application "justified," which most epistemologists use as a theoretical term, since they intend a restriction to *epistemic* (as opposed to moral or pragmatic) justification. In this section, I apply the term "justified" in the way analytic epistemologists have usually done.

laborious business, and in moral philosophy an unethical one, since lives will be lost in the non-fictional analogues of trolley cases. Nor is such an alternative available for the more science-fictional cases. Nevertheless, for some of the thought experiments which negative programmers have expended most effort resisting, their resistance would have been futile.

Understandably, negative programmers have preferred to rule that using real life cases instead of the corresponding philosophical thought experiments still counts as relying on philosophical intuitions. That ruling is not *ad hoc*. It is very plausible that the cognitive processes underlying the crucial verdicts on the imagined hypothetical cases have much in common with the cognitive processes underlying the crucial verdicts on the corresponding experienced real life cases (see 181–209, this volume). Thus it is natural for negative programmers to extend suspicion of the cognitive processing of imaginary cases to suspicion of the cognitive processing of corresponding real-life cases, since one might expect biases in the former to be inherited from similar biases in the latter. However, this extension has a price. Our fairly straightforward ability to discriminate situations where thought experiments are being performed from other situations no longer constitutes an ability to discriminate situations where *philosophical intuitions* are being used from other situations, since many situations where philosophical intuitions about real life cases are being used are situations where no thought experiment is being performed. For virtually any judgment one makes on an actual case, there is a corresponding judgment to be made on an analogous hypothetical case, and using that hypothetical case for a thought experiment may suit the dialectical purposes of some philosopher, since some other philosopher may have inadvertently proposed a theory to which it is a counterexample. The obvious danger is that the category of philosophical intuitions will be stretched so wide, encompassing virtually anything one says about actual cases, that the negative programmers' critique of reliance on philosophical intuitions will become a global skepticism, at odds with their conception of their general enterprise as a positive contribution to naturalistic inquiry.

Can negative programmers reply that what counts as a "philosophical intuition" is itself a matter for further experimental inquiry to determine, by uncovering underlying similarities? The trouble with such a reply is that negative programmers take their critique in its current state *already* to have present practical implications for philosophical methodology. They face the challenge of articulating those implications without assuming that we are already in a position to recognize a philosophical intuition when we see one. As already explained, the methodological ambitions of the negative program require us to reform our practices with respect to real life cases as well as fictional ones, but they leave it quite unclear how much they intend that category to include.

In the heady early days of the negative program, a commonly drawn moral was that philosophers should *stop relying* on philosophical intuitions, at least until substantial experimental evidence was produced of their reliability. But how can philosophers act now on that moral if they have no idea how far the category of philosophical intuitions extends? If negative programmers are banning some parts of current philosophical practice, they had better make it clear enough for present working purposes which parts they are banning. Thus, if they define those parts as the ones that involve reliance on "philosophical intuitions," they had better make it clear enough for present working purposes which situations involve reliance on philosophical intuitions. Mere appeal to the results of future experimental inquiry is not enough for present working purposes.

Since those early days, negative programmers have become more cautious, in response to both philosophical criticisms and difficulties in reproducing experimental results. As noted earlier, there is an increasing realization that the category of "philosophical intuitions" may be so broad that general skepticism about them can easily lead to hopeless global skepticism. A view something like the following is now widespread: The overall reliability of philosophical intuitions may well be quite high: non-accidentally, a reasonable proportion of them are true. However, such moderate global reliability is consistent with both extreme local unreliability here and there, and less extreme but more global unreliability more widely, resulting from bias, distortion, and sensitivity to irrelevant factors. In the background of this picture may be an evolutionary line of thought: for central, common cases our practices of applying a concept have enough causal repercussions for a propensity to serious error to have a significant cost in fitness, but in rare or marginal cases that is not so.

One might try stating the proposed methodological moral of the negative program in a more circumscribed way: we should not rely on a *specific* philosophical intuition until we have experimental evidence that *it* is widely shared. However, the difficulty remains: how can we act on that advice unless we can recognize a philosophical intuition when we see one?

The difficulty depends on the presumption that the methodological moral is not being generalized *beyond* the category of philosophical intuitions. If mad-dog naturalists make such a generalization, and insist that we should not rely on any judgment at all until we have experimental evidence that it is widely shared, it may not matter for their purposes whether the judgment counts as a philosophical intuition. But the more general moral is hopeless, because it generates an infinite regress: the experimental evidence takes the form of a report of the experiment, that report consists of the authors' judgments, on which we are told not to rely until we have experimental evidence that *they* are widely shared, and so on. Negative programmers do not endorse such mad-dog generalized morals. Their methodological moral is specific to philosophical intuitions, which is why its application depends on our ability to distinguish in practice between philosophical intuitions and other judgments.

Not all negative programmers insist that we must wait until we have experimental evidence that a philosophical intuition is widely shared before we rely on it. A more moderate moral is that we may rely on a philosophical intuition even in the absence of experimental evidence that it is widely shared, as long as no one rejects the intuition – but once someone has rejected it, we must suspend judgment on it until we get such experimental evidence. But the workability even of that more moderate moral depends on our ability to distinguish in practice between philosophical intuitions and other judgments, unless the moral is generalized to those other judgments. Once again, the generalized moral is hopelessly immoderate. It implies that we must suspend any judgment that someone has rejected until we have experimental evidence that it is widely shared. That principle would make it all too easy for a troublemaker to bring any inquiry he or she disliked to a grinding halt, simply by rejecting a key judgment on which its practitioners relied, then rejecting a key judgment in the report of the experimental evidence that the former judgment was widely shared, and so on. In particular, such a malicious critic could soon stop the negative program in its tracks.

The methodological moral can be watered down still further, so that more than one lone troublemaker is required to trigger the obligation to suspend judgment until experimental evidence is obtained. But numbers are not the issue: naturalists cannot accept any generalized methodological moral that would enable large teams of postmodernists or religious fundamentalists to bring natural scientific inquiry to a standstill just by rejecting key judgments whenever it suited them, in order to trigger a potentially infinite regress of experimental demands. Thus the point remains: the intended methodological moral of the negative program mandates some sort of special treatment for a category of "philosophical intuitions" so its present workability depends on our present ability in practice to determine when we are faced with a member of that category. Negative programmers are treating disagreement in philosophical intuitions differently from disagreement in other judgments. They cannot simply sidestep the demand for a workable demarcation of the category. What differentiates philosophical intuitions from the rest?

There is no promise in the idea of distinguishing *philosophical* intuitions by something distinctively philosophical in their *content*. The only candidate in the content of the supposed philosophical intuition "He doesn't know that it's 3 p.m." is the reference to knowledge, a philosophically interesting relation. But if the use of the ordinary term "know" for a philosophically interesting relation suffices to make "He doesn't know that it's 3 p.m." a philosophical intuition, then the discourse of experimental philosophers themselves is packed with philosophical intuitions, since they often apply ordinary terms such as "learn" (acquire knowledge) and "evidence" for philosophically interesting relations to specific cases. The problem of over-generation remains.

Intuitive judgments are often contrasted with *reflective* judgments (see, e.g., Nagel 2012: 497–503, drawing on Mercier and Sperber 2009). The difference is not that reflective judgments are based on evidence, for so are many intuitive judgments. Thus the "philosophical intuition" in a real life Gettier case "He doesn't know that it's 3 p.m." depends on evidence such as that the clock he looked at has stopped, that he is wearing no watch, and so on. In the corresponding thought experiment, "He doesn't know that it's 3 p.m." presumably relies on hypothetical evidence in a similar way, and when one steps back outside the imaginative exercise to judge "In the story, the man doesn't know that it's 3 p.m.," that does not undo the original use of evidence; it simply involves a further step of conditionalization, marked by the introduction of the operator "in the story." The difference is rather that reflective judgments are reached through something like consciously controlled reasoning, in a series of steps, whereas intuitive judgments are not. For instance, if one reasons to oneself "No one who relies on a stopped clock knows the time; he is relying on a stopped clock; therefore he does not know that it is 3 o'clock," the concluding judgment is reflective rather than intuitive. Consciously controlled reasoning has distinctive psychological features: unlike intuitive judgment, it is slow, it makes heavy demands on working memory, and it can only integrate very limited amounts of information.

By the proposed standard, the judgment about the thought experiment "In the story, the man doesn't know that it is 3 o'clock" may count as *less* intuitive than the judgment about the real life case "He doesn't know that it is 3 o'clock," since the former but not the latter involves the extra step of conditionalization noted earlier, marked by "in the story," which may well be a piece of consciously controlled reasoning. However, we can allow that there is a spectrum from intuitive judgments through increasingly reflective ones, and that here we are still close to the intuitive end. But grading intuitiveness does not mean that the negative program can confine itself to judgments that are not highly reflective. For example, having judged "He doesn't know that it is 3 o'clock," through a series of steps of consciously controlled reasoning one can conclude "A son of a child of a child of that man's great-grandmother in the maternal line has a justified true belief that it is 3 o'clock without knowing that it is 3 o'clock," which counts as a highly reflective judgment by the proposed standard. It does just as well as the original intuitive judgment for arguing against the justified true belief account of knowledge.

Clearly, the negative program needs to extend to reflective judgments derived from intuitive judgments. But what reflective judgments are *not* derived from intuitive judgments? If a reflective judgment results from several steps, what about the *first* judgment in the series? Suppose that one reflectively concludes "Socrates is mortal" by syllogistic reasoning from "All men are mortal" and "Socrates is a man." One's judgment "Socrates is a man" may well be intuitive;

if one consciously recognizes the valid pattern of the reasoning, the judgment in which one does so may also count as intuitive. If those judgments are not intuitive, others earlier in the process will be. As the distinction has been drawn, all reflective judgments rely on intuitive judgments. If intuitive judgments are the outputs of system 1 and reflective judgments of system 2, the point is that all system 2 thinking involves system 1 thinking. Thus skepticism about intuitive judgments generalizes to skepticism about *all* judgments. It is an illusion that reliance on intuitive judgments, characterized along anything like the lines sketched above, constitutes a distinctive method of armchair philosophy. In that sense of "intuitive," all human thinking relies on intuitive judgments.

Both opponents and proponents of a postulated distinctively philosophical method of "reliance on intuitive judgments" need to demarcate "intuitive judgment" much more narrowly. Another sign of this is that ordinary perceptual judgments come out as intuitive rather than perceptual, but they are far from the only non-reflective judgments that are not supposed to be at issue. Even mathematical reasoning ultimately relies on non-reflective pattern recognition. But it is quite unclear how this required narrower type of "intuitive judgment" is supposed to be demarcated.

Unfortunately, the terms "intuition" and "intuitive" continue to be used by all sides in debates on philosophical methodology without remotely adequate clarification. This is a significant obstacle to progress. A more hopeful sign is that some negative programmers have seen the need for a much more nuanced and qualified characterization of the target of their methodological critique, one that puts little or no weight on the category of philosophical intuition. Such a redefinition of the terms of debate should facilitate progress. The next section discusses the redefined debate.

3. *Proper Domains for the Application of Concepts*

For definiteness, I will concentrate on a paper by Edouard Machery (2011) that argues for the combination of moderate global reliability with local unreliability in the setting of the negative program. To his credit, Machery avoids the term "intuition" altogether, so the concerns of Section 2 do not arise directly for him.

Machery is sympathetic to what he calls "the Ordinary Judgment Proposal," that "the judgments elicited by thought experiments are underwritten by the psychological capacities that also underlie the judgments we make about everyday situations" (2011: 194). What he calls "the Parity Defense of Thought Experiments" argues from the Ordinary Judgment Proposal to the conclusion that one cannot challenge the "reliability and thus trustworthiness" of the judgments elicited by thought experiments "without also challenging the reliability and thus trustworthiness of all our judgments – a price too high to pay for even the most ardent critics of thought experiments" (2011: 196). Machery attacks the Parity Defense, and indeed argues that the Ordinary Judgment Proposal has skeptical implications for philosophical thought experiments (2011: 197).

According to Machery, "the main criticism of the Parity Defense" is that we have reason to believe that philosophical thought experiments involve the application of concepts in situations outside the proper domain of the psychological capacities underlying our application of those concepts, where the proper domain of a psychological capacity is defined to comprise the circumstances in which it is reliable (2011: 201). Machery is obviously right that the Ordinary Judgment Proposal does not *entail* the Parity Defense. It is logically consistent to hold that the psychological capacities underlying our application of a given concept are reliable in everyday situations but unreliable in philosophical thought experiments. The question is whether we have any reason to believe that combination of claims, and in particular whether the Ordinary Judgment Proposal gives us any reason to believe it.

The mere atypicality of the circumstances does not give us good reason to believe that we are outside the proper domain of the relevant concept. Atypicality does not imply unreliability. For example, some people have exceptionally good memories; they are good to a rare, atypical degree. That does not give us reason to believe that we are outside the proper domain of the concept of remembering when we apply it to them. Although atypicality may tend to increase the chance of unreliability, it does not in general do so enough to warrant agnosticism. After all, situations of danger tend to be atypical in various ways; we are in trouble if our cognitive systems fail whenever we need them most.

Machery himself is sometimes quite liberal about proper domains. "At an abstract level," he says, the situations described in science fiction novels "are clearly very similar to everyday situations, and we thus have reason to believe that they belong to the proper domains of the relevant psychological capacities" underlying our judgments about those science fictional situations (2011: 202 n11). In Machery's view, the most important characteristic of philosophical thought experiments in giving us reason to believe that they fall outside the proper domains of the relevant concepts is that they "typically pull apart the features that go together in everyday life" (2011: 203). As he points out, if the imagined cases have this characteristic, then their real life counterparts will share it.

Machery's first example is that in a standard thought experiment from moral philosophy (pushing a fat man off a footbridge to save five other people), "using physical violence and doing more harm than good are pulled apart," whereas using physical violence and doing more harm than good supposedly go together in everyday life. Thus, his argument goes, we have reason to believe that the psychological capacities underlying our application of moral concepts are unreliable in such cases, and therefore to be skeptical about our initial moral judgment. But consider a woman who fights off her would-be rapist, kicking him in the groin and having him arrested. We judge that her action was morally permissible, indeed right. But this too is a case of using physical violence without doing more harm than good, and therefore pulls apart the features that go together in everyday life. According to Machery's argument, therefore, we have reason to believe that the psychological capacities underlying our application of moral concepts are unreliable in this case too, and therefore to be skeptical about our initial judgment that the woman's action was morally permissible. Surely this skepticism is unwarranted, and potentially pernicious. More generally, although professors at top universities may rarely encounter at first-hand situations in which physical violence is the only effective form of self-defense or defense of innocent people, such situations have been quite common in human experience. Thus Machery's argument as he states it severely over-generates skepticism about moral judgment. No doubt it is rare to be able to save many people by killing one, but to characterize the supposedly problematic feature of the case so narrowly would smack of special pleading.

The treatment of epistemologists' thought experiments is similar. According to Machery (2011: 204):

When people fail to know something, their beliefs are typically false, unjustified, and the products of unreliable methods. When people know something, their beliefs are typically true, justified, and the product of reliable methods. By contrast, Gettier cases sever truth and justification from the reliability of the methods of belief formation since they describe situations where truth comes about by luck. [Footnote: Here the method is not the tendency to endorse one's perceptual experience (which is a reliable method) but the use of a broken clock.] Thus, one has a reason to believe that the situations described by Gettier cases are beyond the proper domain of our everyday capacity to ascribe knowledge.

Here Machery seems to assume that we have a reason to believe that any situation where the three features of truth, justification, and reliability of the methods of belief formation fail to go together is beyond the proper domain of our everyday capacity to ascribe knowledge (or its absence). Therefore we should be skeptical about our initial judgment that the protagonist of the Gettier case lacks knowledge. Now consider a man who irrationally forms beliefs simply on his guru's authority. The guru makes assertions at random; a few of them are true, so the follower forms some true beliefs. Those cases sever truth from justification and the reliability of the methods of belief formation. Therefore, by the principle on which Machery seems to be relying, we have a reason to believe that the situation of the follower's true beliefs is beyond the proper domain of our everyday capacity to ascribe knowledge or its absence. Therefore we should be skeptical about any initial judgment we may have made that the follower lacks knowledge. Again, this skepticism is surely unwarranted. Thus Machery's argument severely over-generates skepticism about epistemological judgment.[2]

Machery's takes the same line about the sort of thought experiment that Kripke (1980) uses to refute descriptivist theories of reference for proper names (2011: 204):

---

[2] The complaint that the counterexamples in the text differ from philosophical thought experiments in being clear cases assumes what the negative program is trying to establish. By current philosophical standards, Gettier cases are clear cases of not knowing.

Situations involving proper names associated with a single description that happens to be false of the original bearer of the name are probably beyond the proper domain of our capacity to identify the reference of proper names since in everyday circumstances many of the numerous descriptions associated with a proper name tend to be true of the original bearer of the name.

But it is just false that in everyday circumstances numerous descriptions are always associated with a proper name. Think of the proper names we picked up when half-attending to lessons in schools, the conversations of others, the television, or the internet, and subsequently forgot the source (as often happens to me). Kripke's examples are of an utterly familiar type, slightly schematized only to make the point clearer. For instance, someone uninterested in sport may associate only the description "professional soccer player" with the name "Toby Flood" and falsely believe "Toby Flood is a professional soccer player"; in fact, "Toby Flood" refers to a professional rugby union player (meta-linguistic descriptions like "the person called 'Toby Flood'" need special discussion, which Kripke (1980) gives them). Such cases occur frequently in everyday circumstances. Here Machery's argument over-generates skepticism about semantic judgment.

Although the psychological capacities underlying our application of ordinary concepts are doubtless unreliable in some circumstances, Machery's diagnostics for falling outside their proper domain are far too weak to provide good evidence of unreliability. They severely underestimate the range of variation amongst the cases with which we need to deal reliably in everyday life. Animals need minds in order to deal flexibly and appropriately with the somewhat complex, novel situations they not infrequently find themselves in. A high proportion of ordinary cases are complex enough to fit Machery's diagnostics. For instance, he gives this example of a reliable everyday judgment about knowledge: "judging by her answer to the test, one of my undergraduate students does not know what the DN account of explanation is" (2011: 195–6). By the loose standards Machery applies in assessing philosophical thought experiments, the features of lacking elementary knowledge in an academic field and of never having taken a course on it "typically" go together in everyday life, but they pull apart in this case, so we have reason to believe that the psychological capacities underlying his judgment that his student does not know what the DN account of explanation is are being applied outside their proper domain, and we should be skeptical of his judgment. Once again, his style of argument severely over-generates skepticism. Far more exacting criteria would be needed to provide serious reason to expect unreliability in a given case. Machery does not offer such criteria. Since the Ordinary Judgment Proposal is in no way committed to his easy-going criteria that over-generate skepticism about judgment, Machery's claim that it implies skepticism about philosophical thought experiments is unfounded.

Like Machery, Joshua Alexander and Jonathan Weinberg (2014) defend a qualified version of the negative program. Unlike him, they still make frequent use of the unclarified term "intuition." Concerned to avoid global skepticism, they envisage intuitions as moderately reliable in general but subject to various potential sources of error over which, they claim, only experimental methods will give us control.

Alexander and Weinberg propose some specific features of thought experiments that we might take as danger signals of a potential error source. For instance, they suggest as such a danger signal that the reader of many epistemological thought experiments is supplied with more information about their protagonists' mental states than is typically available in everyday life. That is true; philosophers supply such information in hopes of making their thought experiments as watertight as possible. However, Alexander and Weinberg give no evidence that supplying less information would make a significant difference to the outcome. For example, the man who truly believes that it is 3 p.m. by looking at a stopped clock can be described from the perspective of an external observer watching the man. That does not reverse the verdict that he does not know that it is 3 p.m.

Alexander and Weinberg suggest that the "subtle" or "unusual and marginal sorts of cases that are popular with epistemologists" are prime candidates for local unreliability, although they also allow that some sources of bias may be present in more ordinary cases too, and that our "intuitions" may sometimes withstand experimental tests even in extraordinary cases. They do not expand on what it takes for a case to be "subtle" or "marginal." As for "unusual," their use of the term is vulnerable to the problem of generality. Any case whatsoever falls under many descriptions, some more specific than others, and so belongs to many sorts. The narrowest sorts to which it belongs will be highly unusual ones; however ordinary the case, a sufficiently fine-grained description of it will apply to few or no actual cases. At the other extreme, the broadest sorts to which the case belongs will be very usual ones; however extraordinary the case, a sufficiently coarse-grained description of it will apply to many actual cases. In Machery's phraseology, at an abstract enough level the situations described in epistemological thought experiments are clearly very similar to every-day situations, just as the situations described in science fiction novels are. At a less abstract level, in practice every application of a concept is made in a situation different in some respects from all previous situations. The action is in the sorting of cases in the first place, which Alexander and Weinberg fail to discuss. The sorts need to be individuated in such a way that the differences between them may reasonably be expected to correlate with differences in the reliability of the relevant psychological capacities. Without such a principle of individuation, the emphasis on the rarity of the sorts of cases to which epistemologists appeal is just the kind of generic skeptical move that will discredit the experimental philosophers' critique.[3]

One consequence of this failure to provide useful danger signals of unreliability is that it remains unclear what methodological moral philosophers are supposed to draw from the negative critique. "Avoid unusual, marginal, or subtle cases!" is not very helpful advice. After all, compared to everyday life, a carefully controlled experiment looks like an unusual, marginal, and subtle sort of case, but presumably we are allowed to apply ordinary epistemological concepts such as "evidence" and "learning" to it. One challenge to the negative program is to provide a much clearer, more workable and less generic specification of what are supposed to be the serious danger signals.

4. Further Questions about the Parity Defense

Machery (2011) raises several other interesting issues about the Parity Defense of Thought Experiments, which this section will discuss.

Machery reasonably points out that if psychological capacities underlying the application of a concept are unreliable in everyday life, the Ordinary Judgment Proposal suggests that they will be unreliable

---

[3] Note that the problem of the comparison class here primarily concerns the application of "usual," not the application of "reliable".

in thought experiments too. We cannot normally expect imagination to do better than observation. So far so good. Moreover, he argues, "everyday causal judgments in the social domain are biased, and they are unlikely to be reliable" (a sweeping generalization for which he provides minimal evidence). He concludes that "causal judgments elicited by thought experiments provide no evidence for the premises of philosophical arguments when the judgments bear on whether an agent caused an outcome" (2011: 200).[4]

Once again, Machery's argument severely over-generates skepticism. Consider this thought experiment:

> Life has not advanced beyond stone-age technology. A community has been living on an island for many years without communicating with the rest of the world. A woman there utters a word. A second later, a man ten thousand miles away utters another word. Did her utterance cause his utterance?

Presumably, we judge that the answer is "No." That judgment "bears on whether an agent caused an outcome." Therefore, given Machery's conclusion, that judgment should not be relied on in philosophical argument. This seems rather extreme. To vary the example, consider Machery's own case (quoted earlier) of a *reliable* everyday judgment: judging by her answer to the test (he uses the female pronoun), he judges that one of his undergraduate students does not know what the DN account of explanation is. That judgment is in the social domain, and it depends on the causal judgment that her bad answer was caused by her ignorance rather than by her determination to get a bad grade in order to win a bet. Should we therefore reclassify the judgment as unreliable? Presumably not. What all this really shows is again that one must take much greater care to avoid more or less generic skepticism about judgment.

What Machery calls his least important criticism of the Parity Defense is that some philosophical thought experiments have no counterparts in everyday life because they involve matters that lay people do not consider (2011: 197–8). That may be so. For example, some thought experiments about reference may involve a more

---

4 Machery makes these claims after considering cases involving the apportionment of blame, but does not restrict his claim to such cases.

theoretically constrained reading of "reference" than is employed in everyday life – and they may be none the worse for that, if the theoretically constrained reading is clear.

Machery's own example of the point is Burge's arthritis thought experiment (Burge 1979). We are to imagine two situations, in which the medically untrained protagonist (Oscar) is in all the same internal physical states and sincerely says "I have arthritis in my thigh." The underlying difference between the two situations is in how the rest of Oscar's speech community uses the word "arthritis." In situation S1, they apply it as in the actual world only to arthritis, an ailment of the joints but not of the thighs. In situation S2, they apply it much more broadly, to both ailments of the joints and ailments of the thighs. Burge argues that Oscar's beliefs differ in content between the two situations – in S1 but not in S2 Oscar believes that he has arthritis – and therefore that the contents of propositional attitudes do not always supervene on internal physical states, but may depend on the external social environment. Machery complains that since lay people do not consider the individuation of the content of propositional attitudes, the psychological capacities used in everyday life do not support Burge's thought experiments. We can certainly grant Machery that asking theoretical questions about the individuation of content is no part of everyday life. But that is far less damaging to Burge's thought experiment than Machery assumes. Note first that Oscar does not have arthritis in his thigh in either S1 or S2, since it is a medical fact that one cannot have arthritis in one's thigh. After all, Oscar does not have arthritis in his thigh in the straightforward situation S1, and he is in exactly the same medical state in S2 as in S1, so he does not have arthritis in his thigh in S2. Note second that in S1 Oscar believes that he has arthritis in his thigh. This is an everyday propositional attitude ascription, reporting the sort of ordinary medical error to which non-experts are prone. Machery himself describes Oscar in S1 as "convinced that he has arthritis in his thigh" (2011: 197). Therefore, if Oscar believes in S2 what he believes in S1, Oscar believes in S2 that he has arthritis in his thigh. In that case, however, he believes *falsely* in S2 that he has arthritis in his thigh, since in S2 he does *not* have arthritis in his thigh. But there is no reason whatsoever to impute error to Oscar in S2. In S2, he is using the word "arthritis" correctly; it does apply to the ailment in his thigh. Since Oscar does not believe falsely in S2 that he has arthritis in his thigh, Oscar does not believe in S2 that he has arthritis in his thigh.[5] Therefore, in S1 but not in S2 Oscar believes that he has arthritis in his thigh, which is exactly Burge's point. Of course, the argument as just laid out uses explicit though fairly elementary deductive logic, which is untypical of everyday life. But it also makes essential use of the thought experiment, to establish the premises of the reasoning, in part by rather easy applications of the psychological capacities underlying our everyday ascriptions of propositional attitudes. Despite the residual opposition of some philosophers with internalist commitments in the philosophy of mind, there is no good reason for skepticism about the argument.

The arthritis example also brings out one role for philosophical expertise in some thought experiments: in this case, broadly logical expertise acquired through training in logic, a form of philosophical expertise which even experimental philosophers seem willing to grant. Such expertise is relevant not only to constructing the explicit argument, but also to avoiding various confusions to which the folk may be vulnerable. For instance, if one is careless about the use-mention distinction, one may be tempted to think that in S2 Oscar *does* have arthritis in his thigh, because the *word* "arthritis" as used in S2 does correctly apply to the ailment in Oscar's thigh. Some ordinary subjects may indeed give false verdicts on Burge's thought experiment as a result of such undergraduate errors. They warrant no more skepticism than other undergraduate errors do. Alas, however, not even a PhD in philosophy *guarantees* immunity to use-mention confusions.[6]

5. Acts of Judging and Evidence

Machery (2011) assumes that the main evidence for the truth of the key judgment in a thought experiment is the act of judging itself (even if it is poor evidence). For example, the main evidence that in the Gödel-Schmidt case "Gödel" refers to Gödel is that (some) subjects

---

[5] A few loose ends need to be tied up, for example to ensure that Oscar in S2 does not have some other word that refers to arthritis and so does not apply to the ailment in Oscar's thigh. They do not affect the point in the text.

judge that in the Gödel-Schmidt case "Gödel" refers to Gödel. Is this epistemological claim correct?

Machery justifies his assumption by analogy with ordinary judgments: "If I judge of an object that it is a chair, my judgment that it is a chair is evidence that it is a chair because I am reliable at sorting chairs from nonchairs" (2011: 194). This remark blurs a crucial distinction between two issues. First, is the act of making the judgment evidence for its truth from the standpoint of a third party? Second, is the act of making the judgment evidence on which that very judgment is based? Clearly, these two questions can have different answers. Suppose that initially I know nothing about an object o except that there is such an object. I have the background information that Machery is reliable at sorting chairs from nonchairs. Now I learn just that Machery judges that o is a chair. Obviously, the probability that o is a chair on my evidence goes up considerably. In that sense, Machery's act of judging that o is a chair can of course be evidence for me that o is a chair. But that does not mean that his act of judging was evidence on which that very judgment of his was originally based. It could not have been, for his act of judging was not available as evidence until the judgment had already been made. Typically, he knows that o is a chair much more directly, by *seeing* that o is a chair. If he needs further evidence, he has much better and more direct evidence from perception: he can see that o has legs, a seat, a back, and so on. Even when o is no longer in sight, he can remember that o has legs, a seat, and a back. For Machery to go instead by the fact that he once judged that o was a chair would be a pointlessly indirect detour. And if for some reason he starts doubting that his original judgment that o was a chair was correct, the consideration that he did indeed make that judgment is unlikely to reassure him. It is unclear why anyone would attribute a special evidential role to the fact of judging itself,

---

[6]   See Machery 2011: 206–12, and 2015, and Section 10.2 (this volume), and references therein, for discussion of a more general defence of philosophical thought experiments by appeal to the phenomenon of philosophical expertise. I have not focused on this defense here for two reasons. First, many of the issues it raises are specific experimental ones of the sort with which this section is not concerned. Second, most of the arguments from experimental philosophy discussed in this section can be rebutted without appeal to the phenomenon of philosophical expertise.

except under the influence of the psychologization of evidence, which I have criticized elsewhere (see 236–40, this volume).

Parallel considerations apply to thought experiments. Suppose that initially I know nothing about a situation GS except that there is such a counterfactual situation. I have the background information that Kripke is reliable at doing thought experiments. Now I learn just that Kripke judges that in GS "Gödel" refers to Gödel. Obviously, the probability that in GS "Gödel" refers to Gödel on my evidence goes up considerably. In that sense, Kripke's act of judging that in GS "Gödel" refers to Gödel can of course be evidence for me that in GS "Gödel" refers to Gödel. But that does not mean that his act of judging was evidence on which that very judgment of his was originally based. It could not have been, for his act of judging was not available as evidence until the judgment had already been made. Presumably, Kripke knows that in GS "Gödel" refers to Gödel much more directly, by considering GS appropriately in his imagination. If he needs further evidence, he has much better and more direct evidence from noting the stipulated features of GS itself: he knows that in GS there is a stipulated historical connection of a certain kind between "Gödel" and Gödel (which is good *evidence* that the former refers to the latter on any reasonable theory of reference for proper names). For Kripke later to go instead by the fact that he once judged that in GS "Gödel" refers to Gödel would be a pointlessly indirect detour. And if for some reason he starts doubting that his original judgment that in GS "Gödel" refers to Gödel was correct, the consideration that he did indeed make that judgment is unlikely to reassure him. Again, it is unclear why anyone would attribute a special evidential role to the fact of judging itself, except under the influence of the psychologization of evidence.

According to Machery (2011: 194 n4): "it is hard to see what other kind of evidence [than the act of judging] could be put forward to support the claim that, e.g., in the situation described by the Gödel case 'Gödel' refers to Gödel." This incomprehension seems to be related to the error, against which Section 2 warned, of regarding the crucial judgments in thought experiments as involving no role for ordinary evidence, which comes of forgetting how those judgments correspond to evidence-based judgments about observed cases.[7]

6. Error-fragility

The use of elaborate imaginary cases *is* a distinctive methodological feature of much contemporary philosophy, even though our verdicts on them do not form a psychological kind. Despite all that has been said, we might still reasonably hope for some independent corroboration of those verdicts. Even when verdicts on many different thought experiments corroborate each other, we might still hope for some independent corroboration of the lot of them. One can take that view while regarding the method of thought experiments as evidentially quite respectable. Compare Whewell's idea of the consilience of inductions: a conclusion supported by one sort of inductive evidence is much better off if it is supported by other sorts of inductive evidence too.

Still, if thought experimentation can yield *knowledge* of a fact, why should more support be needed? That is like asking: if naked-eye vision can yield knowledge of a fact, why should more support be needed? Methodological questions are not just about the epistemology of a one-off situation. They concern what general epistemic policies we should follow, for instance in philosophy. Although naked-eye vision without further checks can yield knowledge, a general policy of relying on naked-eye vision without further checks must be expected to yield errors too, since the faculties we use in naked-eye vision are fallible. Similarly, although thought experimentation without further checks can yield knowledge, a general policy of relying on thought experimentation without further checks must be expected to yield errors too, since the faculties we use in thought experimentation are fallible.

The point is reinforced by what Alexander and Weinberg (2014) call "error-fragility." A method is error-fragile if it multiplies error: pursuing it tends to make one error produce many more. Pure deduction is an error-fragile method. Although genuine deductions preserve truth, an imperfect logician applying a purely deductive method will occasionally mistake fallacies for genuine deductions, with potentially disastrous consequences. By contrast, simple induction is not very error-fragile, when based on more or less independent observations.

---

[7]   That one may have both direct evidence for a proposition by perception or imagination and also indirect evidence for it by knowing that others believe it does not undermine the points in the text.

Requiring a consilience of inductions makes it even less error-fragile. Pure falsificationist methods are also error-fragile, since they involve rejecting a theory on the basis of a single counterexample. If the supposed counterexample is erroneous, one may reject a true theory. But analytic philosophers have typically used thought experiments in applying just such a falsificationist method. For instance, a proposed analysis of knowledge is rejected when one thought experiment is judged to yield a counterexample. Thus a single erroneous verdict on a thought experiment might eliminate the true analysis of knowledge (if there were one).

Evidently, we need some system of checks on thought experiments. That does not imply their marginalization. After all, mathematics has an adequate system of checks on the error-fragile method of deduction without marginalizing it at all. One mathematician's proof is checked by others, and in the long run even if a fallacy in the proof passes unnoticed a false "theorem" is likely to be found incompatible with true ones. To some degree, a method based mainly on thought experiments has analogues of those error-correcting mechanisms. But does it have them to a high enough degree? We might reasonably hope for a more robust philosophical methodology where the method of falsification by thought experiment is checked and balanced by other methods. But which other methods should they be?

Experimental philosophers will of course propose experimental methods. For these purposes, it does not matter whether philosophers were involved in designing and conducting the experiments. As noted in Section 1, experimental science already has an important input to several branches of philosophy. But it is unclear how much it can offer to constructive theorizing in those branches where the experimental critique of thought experiments has been most salient, especially moral philosophy and epistemology. Results about what lay people think about goodness or knowledge is only very indirect evidence about which theory of goodness or knowledge is true. Nevertheless, it is not unlikely that received verdicts on some thought experiments *do* reflect cognitive bias of some kind, for instance when high stakes are involved, and we may hope that, in the long run, experimental methods will help us filter out such cases. And, of course, cognitive psychology will surely contribute much to epistemology through experimental studies of perception, memory, and reasoning, although one must not imagine that popularizing such work is an adequate substitute for properly epistemological theorizing.[8]

Some branches of philosophy, such as philosophical logic, have far more to gain from formal methods than from experimental ones.[9] We should not assume that moral philosophy and epistemology are nothing like that. Moral philosophy learns from mathematical decision theory and game theory. Epistemology learns from probability theory and epistemic logic. Of course, moral philosophy and epistemology cannot be reduced to branches of mathematics, on pain of losing their connection to their subject matter. Formal models of moral or epistemic phenomena need informal motivation. Nevertheless, they provide a powerful means for thinking through the consequences of moral and epistemological hypotheses.

Combining the use of mathematical models, results from cognitive psychology, and pre-theoretic verdicts on real or imaginary cases constitutes a more robust methodology than reliance on any one or two of those three sources. Each source can alert us to errors made through reliance on the others. A consilience of them gives us more robust grounds for confidence. For instance, mathematical modelling supports the conclusion of Gettier's thought experiments (Williamson 2013c). Moreover, information from those sources must be integrated within the overall setting of informal philosophical theorizing in a broadly abductive spirit, where theories are compared by familiar criteria such as simplicity, strength, unifying power, and fit with the evidence.

[8]   We should also remember that the interpretation of real life experiments can involve cognitive bias of its own, such as concentration on those experiments that give the results one is hoping for.

[9]   Of course, experimental methods may show that many people are willing to assent to "It is and it isn't" when they feel pulled both ways about whether a borderline shade is red. That is roughly as much of a threat to classical logic as experimental evidence that many people are willing to assent to "One plus one equals one" when drops of water coalesce or "One plus one equals ten" when rabbits breed is to standard arithmetic. This is not to deny that there are connections between philosophical logic and the semantics of natural languages (for instance, in the study of conditionals), and that experimental methods are in principle relevant to the latter. Nevertheless, interpreted logical theories are not metalinguistic theories unless they happen to concern metalinguistic logical constants (such as a truth predicate), still less psychological theories. The appropriate methodology for testing them is similar to that for testing interpreted theories in mathematics, for instance set theories.

What happens if we delete the pre-theoretic verdicts on cases from such a methodology? Suppose that we are interested in some philosophically central distinction that neither mathematics nor cognitive psychology themselves supply us with, such as the distinction between right and wrong or between knowledge and ignorance. Mathematics says nothing special about the distinction. Cognitive psychology may tell us how humans apply it, but not whether they apply it correctly or incorrectly. If we want to start talking on our own behalf about the distinction, we must rely initially on our own pre-theoretic applications of it, even though we reserve the right to revise them in the light of subsequent theorizing. If we are not allowed to start from our pre-theoretic judgments about cases, then all we have left are our pre-theoretic *general* judgments about the distinction ("Ought implies can"; "Knowledge implies belief"). But if we do not trust our particular judgments about the distinction, why trust our more general ones? After all, any pressure in the history of our species to apply the distinction correctly is far more likely to have come from the practical need to classify particular cases at hand correctly than from the theoretical desirability of formulating true generalizations about it. "Stick to generalities" and "Avoid examples" are not recipes for good philosophizing, or indeed good theorizing of any kind. Philosophy cannot be reduced to psychology; no clear or plausible picture of an alternative philosophical method has emerged from experimental philosophers' critique of armchair philosophy. There may indeed be a role for experimental philosophy in refining current philosophical method, but only once the method of experimental philosophy has itself been considerably refined.

Acknowledgments

This section first appeared in Justin Sytsma and Wesley Buckwalter (eds.), *A Companion to Experimental Philosophy*, Wiley-Blackwell, as Williamson 2016b. Thanks to an audience in Oxford for discussion and to Joshua Alexander, Wesley Buckwalter, Joshua Knobe, Edouard Machery, Peter Millican, Jennifer Nagel, Justin Sytsma, and Jonathan Weinberg, for detailed written comments on earlier drafts of this section.

10.5   Reply to Dennett, Knobe, and Kuznetsov on "Philosophical Intuitions"

Joshua Knobe (2019)'s title is "Philosophical Intuitions are Surprisingly Robust Across Demographic Differences." He writes that "the aim of experimental philosophy [...] is to find the truth about people's intuitions." He takes for granted that a central issue can be neutrally articulated in the question: how reliable is "a method that relies on intuitions?" According to Anton Kuznetsov (2019), my view in the first edition of this book is ("Roughly speaking") "that there are special philosophical intuitions that support philosophical inquiry" which "are, to some extent, universal and need special philosophical training." In their pieces, neither Knobe nor Kuznetsov makes any attempt to explain what they mean by an "intuition," or by describing one as "philosophical." Daniel Dennett (2019) characterizes "naïve axiomatic auto-anthropology" as "thinking that the royal road to truth is to attempt to axiomatize, with your companions, your shared intuitions," though he is careful not to ascribe that methodology to me. He too does not say what an "intuition" is. Daniel Stoljar (2019) is the only one of the four respondents in the symposium not to use the "i"-word.

In Williamson 2019c, I simply avoided the "i"-word. Given the limitations of space, I preferred not to use any of it explaining my reasons for avoidance. Since "Philosophical 'Intuitions' and Scepticism about Judgment" (Williamson 2004a; the clue is in the scare quotes), I have been arguing that the debate about the reliability of "philosophical intuitions" is ill-posed, because the extension of the quoted phrase is quite unclear. The point is not just that there are borderline cases; we cannot eliminate all vagueness from our vocabulary, and at the margins is usually does little harm. With the term "intuition," it is much worse: most human judgments are in the disputed territory. Let me explain.

Psychologists distinguish between "intuitive" and "reflective" judgments. Roughly, reflective judgments are those based on conscious reasoning; intuitive judgments are those not based on conscious reasoning (for simplicity, I concentrate on judgments, but the distinction can be extended to inhibited inclinations to judgment and the like).

Some philosophers use the word "intuition" with explicit reference to the psychologists' distinction. An example is Jennifer Nagel's excellent paper, Nagel 2012. However, as Nagel emphasizes, one consequence of so defining the term is that normal perceptual judgments (and many others) count as intuitions. Thus relying on normal perceptual judgments would count as relying on intuitions. That is not what the metaphilosophical debate was supposed to be about. Indeed, in that sense of the term, avoiding reliance on intuitions is not an option. For all judgments based on conscious reasoning rely on judgments not based on conscious reasoning. For instance, when you do a complex arithmetical calculation in your head, your final answer is based on conscious reasoning, but you did not go through an infinite regress of conscious reasoning: at some point in the calculation you made a judgment not based on conscious reasoning.

Can one finesse the problem for philosophical purposes by stipulating that "intuitions" are based neither on conscious reasoning nor on perception? That too would wrong-foot the metaphilosophical debate. For our judgments about thought experiments are typically made by using offline, in imagination, the very cognitive capacities we use online, in perception. For example, the proposed stipulation would allow us to sidestep reliance on intuitions in Gettier cases by making judgments based on perception of real-life Gettier cases. We observe someone at 3 o'clock setting his watch by a clock that happened to have stopped at 3 o'clock, and judge that he does not know that it is 3 o'clock. Our judgment that he lacks knowledge is not an "intuition" in the stipulated sense, since it is based on perception, but critics of the case method in epistemology will be just as uneasy about it as they are about the verdict on the corresponding thought experiment – as I have put to the test by tricking audiences at my lectures into real Gettier cases. Thus the proposed restriction misconstrues the metaphilosophical debate.

In Williamson 2013b, I used this easy exchangeability between online and offline judgements to argue that the distinction between the *a priori* and the *a posteriori* is epistemologically superficial. Kuznetsov uses the traditional distinction to characterize my account of armchair philosophy. That is bound to be misleading, given how little I think of the traditional distinction.

As for the problem of defining "intuition," an alternative strategy is to concede that ordinary non-reflective judgments based on perception are intuitions, but deny that they are philosophical intuitions. That too is unpromising. For what is distinctively philosophical about the judgment "He doesn't know that it's 3 o'clock?" "Know" is one of the commonest verbs in the English language. If such an everyday judgment counts as philosophical, it is hard to guess what would count as unphilosophical. Virtually any judgment can be used in a counterexample to some suitably wrong-headed philosophical theory.

To vary the example, for most adults the judgment "2 + 2 = 4" counts as intuitive in the psychologists' sense, since they do not base it on conscious reasoning. They also do not base it on sense perception. Moreover, "2 + 2 = 4" is philosophical in the sense that many philosophers of mathematics rely on the truth of such arithmetical equations in their arguments. I have certainly heard experimental philosophers define "philosophical intuition" in a way that makes "2 + 2 = 4" a philosophical intuition. When the method of relying on "philosophical intuitions" is debated, are elementary arithmetical equations to be included?

The moral is this: do not use the word "intuition" in debates on philosophical methodology unless you have properly clarified what you mean by it. Such clarification requires, at a minimum, answering the questions raised over the past few paragraphs.

Acknowledgment

This section first appeared as part of Williamson 2019d, which was in turn part of a symposium on Williamson 2019c, a short summary of my philosophy of philosophy, in *Epistemology and Philosophy of Science* (Moscow). I thank Daniel Dennett, Joshua Knobe, Anton Kuznetsov, and Daniel Stoljar for their interesting contributions.

11
Naturalism

11.1   Reply to Kornblith

My agreement with Hilary Kornblith (2009) goes deeper than any remaining disagreement. We agree that armchair methods have a legitimate place in philosophy, for instance in logic. We agree that appeals to experimental data also have a legitimate place in philosophy, for instance in the philosophy of mind and the philosophy of time, and that those branches study mind and time themselves, not just our concepts of them. We agree that the proper balance between armchair and other methods cannot be fully determined in advance, but should to some extent emerge from the future development of the discipline. Nevertheless, as Kornblith says, we are not placing quite the same bets on what that balance will be. I expect armchair methods to play legitimately a more dominant role in future philosophy than he expects them to – of course, such differences in emphasis can result in widening divergence in practice.

The first edition welcomes a significant degree of methodological diversity short of "Anything goes," for often the best long-run way to evaluate a philosophical method is for many able philosophers to use it for many years (287, this volume). That includes methods that make heavy use of experimental data. The book is not an attack on experimental philosophy, in which I have even dabbled myself (8, this volume). I could hardly object to Kornblith's suggestion that experimental psychology should contribute to epistemology, since in discussing the epistemology of logic I appeal to experimental data from the psychology of reasoning (105–8, this volume). Indeed, it would be a grave failure of philosophy in its current state of development if it neglected to explore the philosophical applications of experimental data far more extensively than has hitherto been done. It is work that needs doing and surely will be done, although I do not expect to do much of it myself, since my own interests tend to lie elsewhere (as my work makes obvious).

Unfortunately, "experimental philosophy" has acquired a bad name in mainstream philosophy, in view of the crudity with which it is too often carried out: poor experimental design and crass philosophical errors in the interpretation of the data, perhaps as a result of philistine contempt for more traditional philosophical skills and methods (such as long, subtle chains of armchair reasoning). Those defects can charitably be regarded as growing pains, even if holding theoreticians in low esteem is an occupational hazard for experimentalists (and vice versa). Kornblith and I agree that in principle and sometimes in practice the use of experimental data is compatible with the highest degree of philosophical sophistication.

The legitimacy in principle of experimental philosophy does not make armchair philosophy illegitimate in principle. It would be legitimate in principle for mathematicians to conduct large-scale trials concerning the effect of coffee consumption on susceptibility to computational error, and to modify their practice in consequence if sufficiently alarming results were obtained; that does not make it illegitimate in principle for them not to bother. The book defends an armchair methodology as a good way to address many philosophical problems, not as the only good way to address any philosophical problem. It does so without compromising a straightforwardly realist view of what philosophy is about by any restriction to words or concepts.

Kornblith worries that I overplay the scope for armchair methods, especially formal methods. He focuses on a passage in which I advocate the use of mathematical modelling wherever possible in philosophy (293, this volume). He rightly points out that some idealizations yield pointless mathematical models, and that much excellent philosophizing cannot be formalized. It would be a disaster for philosophy to be confined to formal methods, just as it would be a disaster for it to be confined to experimental methods. In the passage I wrote of producing mathematical models of fragments of philosophy: "when we can, we should." The conversational implicature was that sometimes we cannot.

As an example of valuable philosophizing that cannot be formalized, Kornblith cites Laurence BonJour's discussion of coherence. BonJour lists five conditions on coherence (BonJour 1985). They are:

(1) A system of beliefs is coherent only if it is logically consistent.
(2) A system of beliefs is coherent in proportion to its degree of probabilistic consistency.
(3) The coherence of a system of beliefs is increased by the presence of inferential connections between its component beliefs and increased in proportion to the number and strength of such connections.
(4) The coherence of a system of beliefs is diminished to the extent to which it is divided into subsystems of beliefs which are relatively unconnected to each other by inferential connections.
(5) The coherence of a system of beliefs is decreased in proportion to the presence of unexplained anomalies in the believed content of the system.

Although (1)–(5) are of course not fully formal, they are not totally lacking in formal content. Indeed, an attempt at formal modelling is a natural next step in exploring the implications of BonJour's account. His conditions have the sort of complexity that often produces unexpected consequences; working formalizations of them through in toy cases would be an excellent way of gauging their effect. There will certainly be different ways of formalizing them, involving different idealizations. Some of those idealizations will be hopelessly misleading, others will be hard to choose between. Those are just normal hazards of mathematical modelling. They are not fatal in physics, and Kornblith does not really think them fatal in philosophy either.

The use of mathematical models in philosophy is largely neutral over the extent of experimental input. They can figure in an entirely armchair methodology, but they can also play the sort of role they do in physics, economics, and other natural and social sciences. In playing down the role of "highly idealized formal approaches uninformed by such [experimental] input," Kornblith writes "For that very reason, I would see the role of armchair theorizing in philosophy as quite limited, as it is in physics." This underplays the central role of armchair theorizing in physics: many theoretical physicists spend most of their time doing mathematics, string theory being only one of the more extreme examples. Far from being rivals, formal and experimental methods often complement each other. Hypotheses often require some degree of formal modelling before they can deliver predictions that are capable of being experimentally tested as Kornblith recommends; the test results often suggest new models. One might eventually want to test experimentally whether coherence according to BonJour's conditions is increased or decreased in simple real-life cases of learning from perception or testimony. That testing would hardly be possible without some further degree of formalization. My suspicion is that in practice purely armchair methods would provide a far more efficient way of identifying any problems in BonJour's account of coherence, but I will not try to establish that here.

Acknowledgment

This section first appeared as part of my contribution to a symposium on the first edition of the book in *Analysis Reviews* (Williamson 2009a). I thank Hilary Kornblith for his interesting comments, which help bring into relief some main themes of the book.

11.2   Reply to Stalnaker

It is good to find that Robert Stalnaker (2011) and I are in so much agreement about philosophy. I remain reluctant to describe the general picture on which we agree as "philosophical naturalism," because that label inappropriately emphasizes philosophy's affinity to what are usually called "natural sciences" over its affinities to other forms of truth-directed inquiry, such as history, linguistics, economics, and mathematics. Stalnaker says "the general message is that philosophy is continuous with natural science and more generally with empirical inquiry." History, linguistics, and parts of economics presumably count as "empirical inquiry," if not as "natural science," but what sort of inquiry is "empirical" supposed to exclude if not mathematics? Although philosophy *is* continuous with natural science, it is also continuous with mathematics; neglect of that fact has made the near-absence of non-fictional experiments in philosophy look more worrying than it really is. If the term "natural science" is stipulated to cover mathematics, economics, linguistics, and history as well as physics and biology, what sort of inquiry is "natural" supposed to exclude? I suspect, however, that Stalnaker did not intend "natural" and "empirical" in any very exclusive sense, and that the apparent difference of emphasis between us here would largely disappear on clarification.

In the latter half of "The Metaphysical Conception of Analyticity," Stalnaker argues that the first edition's account of most philosophical questions as neither metalinguistic nor meta-conceptual still faces a residual challenge. Most philosophical truths are necessary truths. Consider a philosophical question "P?," where it is non-contingent whether P and we do not know the truth-value of the sentence "P."[1] If "P" is true, it expresses a necessarily true proposition. If "P" is false, it expresses a necessarily false proposition. But any necessarily true proposition is distinct from any necessarily false proposition. Thus, it seems, the proposition "P" expresses if it is true is distinct from the proposition it expresses if it is false. So what proposition "P" expresses depends on the truth-value of "P." Therefore, not knowing its truth-value involves not knowing what proposition it expresses.

---

[1]   Read the quotation marks as Quinean corner quotes.

The philosophical question whether P is inseparable from the metalinguistic question: what proposition does "P" express?

Although Stalnaker does not endorse the reasoning in exactly that form, he takes very similar reasoning quite seriously. But he also takes quite seriously seemingly contrary reasoning. For "P" may be a readily intelligible sentence of English, in which case we surely know what proposition "P" expresses, even before we are in a position to answer the question "P?": "P" expresses the proposition that P. He thinks that "A reconciliation will [...] exploit the obvious context-dependence of the notion of 'knowing what' a sentence means or says." The suggestion may be that the first line of reasoning induces a context in which the sentence "We know what proposition the sentence 'P' expresses" expresses a true proposition, while the second line of reasoning induces a context in which the same "knowledge"-ascribing sentence expresses a different and false proposition.

I agree with Stalnaker that "knowing what" exhibits a sort of context-dependence. In some contexts we count someone familiar with quartz but ignorant of its chemical constitution as "knowing what quartz is"; in other contexts we count the same person at the same time as not "knowing what quartz is."[2] However, it is not clear that the original reasoning to the conclusion "We do not know what proposition 'P' expresses" induces a context in which that conclusion expresses a truth; the reasoning may instead simply be fallacious.

The reasoning as formulated above does not even depend on its being non-contingent whether P. With the modal elements deleted, it runs:

> If "P" is true, it expresses a true proposition. If "P" is false, it expresses a false proposition. But any true proposition is distinct from any false proposition. Thus the proposition "P" expresses if it is true is distinct from the proposition it expresses if it is false. So what proposition "P" expresses depends on the truth-value of "P." Therefore not knowing the truth-value of "P" involves not knowing what proposition it expresses.

---

[2]   Compare Boer and Lycan 1985 on "knowing who." Gareth Evans's neglect of the closely related context-dependence in the phrase "knowing which" is unfortunate for his discussion and use of "Russell's Principle" "that in order to have a thought about a particular object, you must *know which* object it is about which you are thinking" (1982: 74; his italics).

Such an argument would prove far too much: that whenever we do not know the truth-value of a sentence, we do not know what proposition it expresses (by contextually relevant standards). The fallacy is fairly clear. We can grant that *if* "P" is true, the proposition it expresses is true, and that *if* "P" is false, the proposition it expresses is false, where the scope of the definite description "the proposition it expresses" is in each case just the consequent of the relevant conditional. That is just the principle that the truth-value of a sentence reflects the truth-value of the (unique) proposition it expresses, which for present purposes is harmless. But we cannot conclude, concerning "P," that the proposition it expresses if it is true *is* true, or that the proposition it expresses if it is false *is* false. Thus we cannot conclude that the proposition "P" expresses if it is true is distinct from the proposition it expresses if it is false. The displayed argument is really no better than this:

If Oxford has a pre-Roman university, the name "Oxford" denotes a city with a pre-Roman university. If Oxford has no pre-Roman university, "Oxford" denotes a city without a pre-Roman university. But any city with a pre-Roman university is distinct from any city without a pre-Roman university. Thus the city "Oxford" denotes if Oxford has a pre-Roman university is distinct from the city "Oxford" denotes if Oxford has no pre-Roman university. So what city "Oxford" denotes depends on whether Oxford has a pre-Roman university. Therefore not knowing whether Oxford has a pre-Roman university involves not knowing what city "Oxford" denotes.

Such reasoning is spurious. In fact, no city has a pre-Roman university. To either the indicative question "What city does the name 'Oxford' denote if Oxford has a pre-Roman university?" or the subjunctive question "What city would the name 'Oxford' have denoted if Oxford had had a pre-Roman university?," no city (for example, Cambridge) has a better right than Oxford to be the answer. Of course, someone well acquainted with Oxford while uncertain of the denotation of the name "Oxford" might think of a different city, but that is not the case of interest: it fails to show that for ordinary competent speakers the question "Does Oxford have a pre-Roman university?" raises metalinguistic issues in any significant way. Although it is in effect equivalent to the question "Is the sentence 'Oxford has a pre-Roman university' true?," *every* question is in effect equivalent to a metalinguistic one in that uninteresting way, as emphasized in the first edition (28–32, this volume).

Merely switching to non-contingent matters does not improve the displayed form of argument. This instance is equally bad:

> If 8191 is prime, the numeral "8191" denotes a (necessarily) prime number. If 8191 is composite, "8191" denotes a (necessarily) composite number. But any prime number is distinct from any composite number. Thus the number "8191" denotes if 8191 is prime is distinct from the number "8191" denotes if 8191 is composite. So what number "8191" denotes depends on whether 8191 is prime. Therefore not knowing whether 8191 is prime involves not knowing what "8191" denotes.

In fact, 8191 is prime. To either the indicative question "What number does the numeral '8191' denote if 8191 is composite?" or the subjunctive question "What number would the numeral '8191' have denoted if 8191 had been composite?," no number (for example, 8192) has a better right than 8191 to be the answer. Of course, someone well acquainted with advanced arithmetic only through a different notation might think of a different number, but that is not the case of interest: it fails to show that for ordinary competent speakers the question "Is 8191 prime?" raises metalinguistic issues in any significant way. Although it is in effect equivalent to the question "Is the sentence '8191 is prime' true?," *every* question is in effect equivalent to a metalinguistic one in that uninteresting way, as already emphasized.

The antecedent "8191 is composite" is impossible. On many theories of conditionals, including Stalnaker's, a conditional with an impossible antecedent is vacuously true.[3] So interpreted, "If 8191 is composite, '8191' denotes n" is true for any value of "n" (so there is no such thing as *the* number that "8191" denotes if 8191 is composite).[4] We can make the conditional non-vacuous by using the metalinguistic antecedent "The sentence '8191 is composite' is true" instead, if we interpret the inner quotation as referring to an orthographically individuated string that could have had a different meaning.[5] But that

---

[3]   The first edition defends this view of subjunctive conditionals at 173–7, this volume.

[4]   A similar point applies to "If Oxford has no pre-Roman university, 'Oxford' denotes c" on the truth-functional reading of indicative conditionals (which Stalnaker does not accept): it is vacuously true whatever the value of "c" since the antecedent is false.

[5]   This is similar to considering the "diagonal proposition" Stalnaker associates with the sentence "8191 is prime".

hardly helps the argument. To the indicative question "What number does the numeral '8191' denote if '8191 is composite' is true?" still no number has a better right than 8191 to be the answer, for ordinary competent speakers. To the subjunctive question "What number would the numeral '8191' have denoted if '8191 is composite' had been true?" we can imagine that the answer is 8292, because in the closest world in which "8191 is composite" is true the numeral "1" denotes the number 2: but those counterfactual circumstances have no useful bearing on the epistemic predicament of someone who has mastered our actual system of numerals without knowing whether 8191 is prime.

The same lessons apply to Stalnaker's own example, a case of the Kripkean necessary *a posteriori*, taken as a proxy for philosophical claims about non-contingent matters.[6] The crucial reasoning goes thus:

> If the sentence "Hesperus = Phosphorus" is true, it expresses a necessarily true proposition. If "Hesperus = Phosphorus" is false, it expresses a necessarily false proposition. But any necessarily true proposition is distinct from any necessarily false proposition. Thus the proposition "Hesperus = Phosphorus" expresses if it is true is distinct from the proposition it expresses if it is false. So what proposition "Hesperus = Phosphorus" expresses depends on whether it is true. Therefore not knowing whether "Hesperus = Phosphorus" is true involves not knowing what proposition "Hesperus = Phosphorus" expresses.

We should be very suspicious of this argument, given its similarity to the bad arguments displayed earlier. We can grant that *if* "Hesperus = Phosphorus" is true, the proposition it expresses is necessarily true, and that *if* "Hesperus = Phosphorus" is false, the proposition it expresses is necessarily false, where the scope of the definite description "the proposition it expresses" is in each case just the consequent of the relevant conditional. But that does not

---

[6] Stalnaker replies to the first edition's critique of the *a priori/a posteriori* distinction as standardly explained (167–71, this volume) that "if there is to be a notion of a priori knowledge at all, it needs to be explained in a different way," but does not specify any such different way. Note that there is a notion of *a posteriori* knowledge only if there is a notion of *a priori* knowledge.

show, concerning "Hesperus = Phosphorus," that the proposition it expresses if it is true *is* true, or that the proposition it expresses if it is false *is* false. Thus we cannot conclude that the proposition "Hesperus = Phosphorus" expresses if it is true is distinct from the proposition it expresses if it is false.

The potential for Frege puzzles is ubiquitous. For any denoting term *t*, there can be another term *t** that non-obviously has the same denotation as *t*. That "Phosphorus" non-obviously has the same denotation as "Hesperus" does not show that our grasp of the name "Hesperus" is unusually shaky. By normal standards, we all know what proposition ordinary sentences such as "Hesperus is more distant than the moon" and "Phosphorus is more distant than the moon" express. We must therefore know what the names "Hesperus" and "Phosphorus" contribute to such propositions. We also know what the identity sign "=" contributes, and we have mastered the grammar of the sentence "Hesperus = Phosphorus." Thus we know what proposition it expresses, by means of our mastery of the compositional semantics of the language. That we do not know whether the proposition it expresses is necessary just shows that we are not omniscient about it.

Does Stalnaker's puzzle look more compelling if we adopt his own extremely coarse-grained theory of propositions, which identifies a proposition with the set of possible worlds in which it is true? He does not explicitly invoke that theory in "The Metaphysical Conception of Analyticity": dialectically, to do so would be a large concession on his part. Not only is the first edition far from endorsing the theory: conceding that the puzzle arises only on that theory would risk turning the puzzle into an argument against his theory. Nevertheless, let us see whether his theory of propositions strengthens his puzzle.

On Stalnaker's view, exactly one proposition is necessarily true, the set W of all possible worlds, and exactly one proposition is necessarily false, the empty set {}. Thus we know in advance that *if* "Hesperus = Phosphorus" is true it expresses W and *if* "Hesperus = Phosphorus" is false it expresses {}. Since W and {} are evidently distinct, this does create a strong temptation to say that if we do not know whether "Hesperus = Phosphorus" is true, we do not know what proposition it expresses. That temptation must be scrutinized.

The set-theoretic representation of propositions should be bracketed. Although it provides one convenient way of registering Stalnaker's idea that necessarily equivalent propositions are identical, thinking in set-theoretic terms is not supposed to be essential to knowing what proposition a sentence expresses by the relevant standard. For finding out that "Hesperus = Phosphorus" expresses a necessary truth is supposed to be sufficient for knowing what proposition it expresses by the relevant standard, even if the thinker has never been introduced to the theory of propositions as sets of possible worlds. Such a theoretically innocent thinker is also supposed to know what propositions everyday sentences express, despite not knowing that those propositions are sets of possible worlds. For otherwise ordinary people would not know what propositions their sentences expressed, so if philosophers also failed to know what propositions their sentences expressed, that would show nothing peculiar about the situation of philosophy.

We do better to represent the necessary truth and the necessary falsehood by an obvious tautology and an obvious contradiction respectively. For definiteness, we could use "If it's snowing, it's snowing" and "It's both snowing and not snowing." The picture is that once competent English speakers are in a position to know that "Hesperus = Phosphorus" expresses the same proposition as "If it's snowing it's snowing" (rather than the same proposition as "It's both snowing and not snowing"), they know what proposition "Hesperus = Phosphorus" expresses by the relevant standard, but not before.[7] The underlying assumption seems to be this:

COMPARISON If one knows what proposition a sentence s expresses, and one knows what proposition a sentence s^* expresses, then one is in a position to know whether s and s^* express the same proposition.

One knows all along what proposition "If it's snowing it's snowing" expresses. Before one is in a position to know that "Hesperus = Phosphorus" is true, one is not in a position to know that "Hesperus = Phosphorus" and "If it's snowing it's snowing" express the same proposition. By COMPARISON, it follows that one does not then know what proposition "Hesperus = Phosphorus" expresses. When

---

[7] The phrase "in a position to" covers both people who have not considered whether s and s^* express the same proposition and those who have but do not think that for propositions necessary equivalence entails identity, *inter alia*.

one learns that "Hesperus = Phosphorus" is necessarily true, one in effect also learns what proposition it expresses, and is therefore in a position to know whether the two sentences express the same proposition.

However attractive COMPARISON may look, it is too strong for ordinary standards. As already noted, Frege puzzles for a term t are too commonplace to show that competent speakers do not know what propositions ordinary sentences involving t express. Competent speakers who are not in a position to know whether "Hesperus = Phosphorus" is true still count as knowing what propositions the sentences "Hesperus is more distant than the moon" and "Phosphorus is more distant than the moon" express. Therefore, by COMPARISON, those speakers are in a position to know whether "Hesperus is more distant than the moon" and "Phosphorus is more distant than the moon" express the same proposition. But they are not, for if they were they would be in a position to know whether "Hesperus = Phosphorus" was true. Consequently, COMPARISON fails on ordinary standards for knowing what proposition a sentence expresses. If it holds on extraordinary standards, the upshot would merely be an argument that by extraordinary standards we do not know what propositions most of our sentences express, which would again show nothing peculiar about philosophy. Thus, even if we grant Stalnaker's extreme theory of propositions, his puzzle still seems to rest on assumptions too contentious to disturb the conception of much inquiry into non-contingent matters, including much philosophical inquiry, as having no special connection with the metalinguistic or the meta-conceptual.

We can try articulating Stalnaker's concern without using the notion of knowing what proposition a sentence expresses or his theory of propositions. The result that knowing that Hesperus = Hesperus literally just is knowing that Hesperus = Phosphorus is not exclusive to Stalnaker's theory. It can also be defended on the basis of a more moderately coarse-grained Russellian theory of propositions as structured complexes built out of the objects, properties, and relations they are about, on which co-denoting names contribute exactly the same object, their denotation, to the propositions expressed by sentences in which they occur (Salmon 1986).[8] Such a view may tempt one to

---

[8]   There are indications in Stalnaker's comments that he may have taken me to be more sympathetic to Fregean theories of content than I actually am.

describe the ignorance in Frege puzzles as essentially metalinguistic: astronomically ignorant but linguistically competent speakers do in fact know that Hesperus = Phosphorus; what they fail to know is that the sentence "Hesperus = Phosphorus" is true. A similar treatment will then be suggested for many philosophical claims, such as "Pain = π," where "π" is a name whose denotation is fixed by a neuroscientific description (69, this volume): if the identity is true, we knew all along that pain = π, because we knew all along that pain = pain, and knowing that literally just is knowing that pain = π; the ignorance is essentially metalinguistic, as to whether the sentence "Pain = π" is true.

That view of Frege puzzles is inadequate as it stands. Consider this argument:

(P1) If Hesperus = Phosphorus, the sentence "Hesperus = Phosphorus" is true.
(P2) Hesperus = Phosphorus.

(C)   The sentence "Hesperus = Phosphorus" is true.

On the proposed view, astronomically ignorant but logically and linguistically competent speakers know both P1 and P2 but are in no position to know C. Why not? What stops them from applying modus ponens? The answer is that they know P1 only under the guise of a sentence like "If Hesperus = Phosphorus, the sentence 'Hesperus = Phosphorus' is true," whereas they know P2 only under the guise of a sentence like "Hesperus = Hesperus"; since the guises do not match with respect to P2 and the antecedent of P1, the speakers are in no position to apply modus ponens. To understand their epistemic predicament, we must describe not simply what they know but what linguistic guises they know it under. They know that Hesperus = Phosphorus under the guise of the sentence "Hesperus = Hesperus" but not under the guise of the sentence "Hesperus = Phosphorus."[9] Similarly, philosophers may know that pain = π under the guise of the sentence "Pain = pain" but not under the guise of the sentence

[9] Phrases of the form "under the guise of sentence *s*" should be read throughout as outside the sentential complements of "that" and "whether" in the relevant propositional attitude ascriptions.

"Pain = π." As emphasized in the book, "If propositions are individuated in that coarse-grained direct reference way, what matters for progress in philosophy is less which propositions we know than which sentential guises we know them under" (68, this volume).

Once we have this apparatus in place, we can see what a distortion it is to conceive the ignorance in Frege puzzles as metalinguistic. Ancient astronomers wondering "Is Hesperus Phosphorus?" were not wondering about metalinguistic matters; their attention was fixed firmly on the skies. They were not wondering whether a sentence like "Hesperus = Phosphorus" was true; they were wondering under the guise of such a sentence whether Hesperus was Phosphorus. When they looked up in the evening and thought "There's Hesperus" but not "There's Phosphorus," they were not thinking that there was the denotation of the name "Hesperus"; they were just thinking that there was Hesperus, but they were thinking it under the guise of a sentence like "There's Hesperus." Similarly, philosophers wondering "Is pain π?" are not wondering primarily about metalinguistic matters; they are wondering under the guise of the sentence "Pain = π" whether pain is π. The role of the metalinguistic discourse here is not in fully articulating covert contents of philosophical claims: it is in describing how philosophers are related to their overt contents. Metalinguistic discourse plays such a role in the description of any complex inquiry. Perhaps Stalnaker would agree.

Acknowledgment

This section first appeared as part of my contribution to a symposium on the first edition of the book in *Philosophy and Phenomenological Research* (Williamson 2011d).

11.3   Reply to Bianchi

As Andrea Bianchi notes in "What Do Philosophers Do?," many of the main themes of the first edition, such as its anti-exceptionalism about philosophy, can be found in the naturalist tradition, as represented most famously by Quine's "Two Dogmas of Empiricism." He is therefore surprised that the book does not have more to say about naturalism.

In fact, I did take the trouble to situate my critique of analyticity in relation to Quine's (52–4, this volume). I pointed out that although the analytic-synthetic distinction does much less work in contemporary philosophy than it did when Quine wrote, that is not well explained by acceptance of his arguments, since they depend on its interdefinability with other supposedly disreputable semantic distinctions, like that between sameness and difference of meaning, that are now generally considered legitimate. I conjectured that the current marginalization of the analytic-synthetic distinction has more to do with Kripke's redrawing of the interrelations between the necessary, the contingent, the *a priori*, and the *a posteriori* in *Naming and Necessity*, which decisively broke apart the previously dominant stereotypes of the analytic and the synthetic. Nevertheless, I concluded, "There is something robust about 'Two Dogmas of Empiricism': insights remain even when its skepticism towards meaning is stripped away" (54, this volume). I took my critique of analyticity to be a development of those insights.

The reason why I use the term "naturalism" so little in the book is that I regard it as an obstacle to understanding. In my experience, the main function of the words "As a naturalist, I ...," like that of the words "As a Christian, I ...," is to avoid thought. "Naturalism" stands for a loose bundle of logically independent doctrines. If you reject any of them, you count as an anti-naturalist and are expected to reject all of them. If we are to examine each of the constituent doctrines on its merits, we must stop using the word "naturalism" (or "anti-naturalism") as a comfort blanket.

Here is an example. My anti-exceptionalism about philosophy treats it as one more branch of human inquiry, not more different from other branches than they are from each other. I emphasized that this does not imply any special affinity of philosophy with the natural sciences closer than its affinity with, for instance, mathematics (6, this volume). By contrast, Bianchi says "what characterizes naturalism is the idea that philosophy is akin to natural sciences in theorizing starting from empirical data." Indeed, the word "naturalism" almost irresistibly suggests such a special connection with the natural sciences. Central to Quine's naturalism is his privileging of fundamental physics as our best theory of the world, and a reductionist attitude to everything else. Such dogmas tend to be smuggled in under the naturalist label with remarkably little supporting argument, just the implied threat that the only alternative is superstition. How drastically impoverished a view of the philosophical options!

Bianchi seems to assimilate my devaluing of the distinction between the *a priori* and the *a posteriori* to a Quinean rejection of the *a priori*: "If armchair philosophy is philosophy supposedly pursued by traditional *a priori* methods, then certainly philosophical naturalism rules it out, but Williamson does not like it, either." I do indeed regard the traditional stereotype of *a priori* knowledge as almost useless for purposes of serious epistemology, but he neglects to add that I regard the traditional stereotype of *a posteriori* knowledge as equally useless. My attitude to the distinction does not mandate a conception of philosophy modelled exclusively or even primarily on the natural sciences. There is no barrier in principle between philosophy and physics; equally, there is no barrier in principle between philosophy and mathematics. Unless the natural sciences include the social sciences and the humanities (in which case the term "natural science" is uninformatively broad), analogies with disciplines such as economics, linguistics, and history point up other significant and legitimate aspects of philosophy obscured by analogies with the natural sciences.

Bianchi's description of the starting-point of philosophy as "empirical data" also suggests a special connection between philosophy and the natural sciences. The unclear term "empirical" seems to imply "*a posteriori*." Of course, I agree that any data that may be legitimately used in the natural sciences may in principle be legitimately used in philosophy too: the only question is whether they do in fact bear on the question at hand. I also agree that in practice such data sometimes are applied effectively in philosophy. But I also hold that any knowledge that may legitimately be used in mathematics may in principle be legitimately used in philosophy too, and that in practice effective philosophical applications are made of such knowledge. To describe mathematics as theorizing starting from "empirical data" too would be to stretch the description to the point of uninformativeness. Although some parts of philosophy (such as the metaphysics of space, time, and matter) are closer to physics than to mathematics, other parts (such as philosophical logic) are closer to mathematics than to physics. If we cannot understand philosophy by classifying it as *a priori*, no more can we understand it by classifying it as *a posteriori*.[1]

Acknowledgment

This section first appeared as part of my contribution to a symposium on the first edition of this book in Richard Davies (ed.), *Analisi: Annuario e Bollettino della Società Italiana di Filosofia Analytica (SIFA) 2011* (Williamson 2011f). I thank Andrea Bianchi for the care and attention he spent on the book. Like him, I focus on points of divergence. All page references are to the first edition.

---

[1] Sociological note: Despite Bianchi's contrary suggestion, the view of philosophy as linguistic or conceptual analysis is no longer more prominent in Oxford than elsewhere. To judge purely by this symposium, it is considerably more popular in Italy than it is in Oxford or in Britain.

11.4   What is Naturalism?

In the first edition, I defended a view of philosophy as much less different in aims and methods from other forms of intellectual inquiry than its self-images usually suggest. Some commentators treated this anti-exceptionalism about philosophy as a form of *naturalism*, and wondered why I did not characterize it explicitly as such. I will explain why not.

Many contemporary philosophers describe themselves as naturalists. They mean that they believe something like this: there is only the natural world, and the best way to find out about it is by the scientific method. So why do I resist being described as a naturalist? Not for any religious scruple: I am an atheist of the most straightforward kind. But to accept the naturalist slogan without looking beneath the slick packaging is an unscientific way to form one's beliefs about the world, so not something that even naturalists should recommend.

What, for a start, is the natural world? If we define it as the world of matter, or the world of atoms, we are left behind by modern physics, which characterizes the world in far more abstract terms. Anyway, the best current scientific theories will probably be superseded by future scientific developments in various respects. Naturalism is not intended to be hostage to the details of scientific progress. We might therefore define the natural world as whatever the scientific method eventually discovers. Thus naturalism becomes the belief that there is only whatever the scientific method eventually discovers, and (not surprisingly) the best way to find out about it is by the scientific method. That is no tautology. It is not self-evident that there cannot be things only discoverable by non-scientific means, or not discoverable at all.

Still, naturalism is less restrictive than one might think. For example, some of its hard-nosed advocates undertake to postulate a soul or a god, if doing so turns out to be part of the best explanation of our experience, for that would be an application of scientific method. Naturalism is not incompatible in principle with all forms of religion. In practice, however, most naturalists doubt that belief in souls or gods withstands scientific scrutiny.

What is meant by "the scientific method?" Why assume that science only has one method? For naturalists, although natural sciences like physics and biology differ from each other in specific ways, at a sufficiently abstract level they all count as using a single general method. It involves formulating theoretical hypotheses and testing their predictions against systematic observation and controlled experiment. This is the hypothetico-deductive method.

One challenge to naturalism is to find a place for mathematics. Natural sciences rely on it, but should we count it a science in its own right? If we do, then the description of scientific method just given is wrong, for it does not fit the science of mathematics, which proves its results by pure reasoning, rather than the hypothetico-deductive method. Although a few naturalists, such as Quine, argue that the real evidence in favor of mathematics comes from its applications in the natural sciences, so indirectly from observation and experiment, that view does not fit the way the subject actually develops. When mathematicians assess a proposed new axiom, they look at its consequences within mathematics, not outside. On the other hand, if we do not count pure mathematics a science, we thereby exclude mathematical proof by itself from the scientific method, and so discredit naturalism. For naturalism privileges the scientific method over all others, and mathematics is one of the most spectacular success stories in the history of human knowledge.

Which other disciplines count as science? Logic? Linguistics? History? Literary theory? How should we decide? The dilemma for naturalists is this. If they are too inclusive in what they count as science, naturalism loses its bite. Naturalists typically criticize some traditional forms of philosophy as insufficiently scientific, because they ignore experimental tests. How can they maintain such objections unless they restrict scientific method to hypothetico-deductivism? But if they are too exclusive in what they count as science, naturalism loses its credibility, by imposing a method appropriate to natural science on areas where it is inappropriate. Unfortunately, rather than clarify the issue, many naturalists oscillate. When on the attack, they assume an exclusive understanding of science as hypothetico-deductive. When under attack themselves, they fall back on a more inclusive understanding of science that drastically waters down naturalism. Such maneuvering makes naturalism an obscure article of faith. I don't call myself a naturalist because I don't want to be implicated in equivocal dogma. Dismissing an idea as "inconsistent with naturalism" is little better than dismissing it as "inconsistent with Christianity."

Still, I sympathize with one motive behind naturalism, the aspiration to think in a scientific spirit. It's a vague phrase, but one might start to explain it by emphasizing values like curiosity, honesty, accuracy, precision, and rigor. What matters isn't paying lip-service to those qualities – that's easy – but actually exemplifying them in practice – the hard part. To speak of the scientific spirit is not to make the naïve (and unscientific) claim that scientists' motives are always pure. They are human. Science doesn't depend on indifference to fame, professional advancement, money, or comparisons with rivals. Rather, truth is best pursued in social environments, intellectual communities, that minimize conflict between such baser motives and the scientific spirit, by rewarding work that embodies the scientific virtues. Such traditions exist, and not just in natural science.

The scientific spirit is as relevant in mathematics, history, philosophy, and elsewhere as in natural science. Where experimentation is the likeliest way to answer a question correctly, the scientific spirit calls for the experiments to be done; where other methods – mathematical proof, archival research, philosophical reasoning – are more relevant it calls for them instead. Although the methods of natural science could beneficially be applied more widely than they have been so far, the default assumption must be that the practitioners of a well-established discipline know what they are doing, and use the available methods most appropriate for answering its questions. Exceptions may result from a conservative tradition, or one that does not value the scientific spirit. Still, impatience with all methods except those of natural science is a poor basis on which to identify those exceptions.

Naturalism tries to condense the scientific spirit into a philosophical theory. But no theory can replace that spirit, for any theory can be applied in an unscientific spirit, as a polemical device to reinforce prejudice. Naturalism as dogma is one more enemy of the scientific spirit.

Philosophy should be done in a scientific spirit. Therefore we should not do it by invoking slogans about naturalism, or dismissing philosophical theories or methods on the basis of results in natural science whose relevance to them is unclear, or engaging in any of the other forms of lazy-mindedness that the word "naturalism" has so striking a capacity to encourage.

Acknowledgment

This section originally appeared in Matthew Haug (ed.), *Philosophical Methodology: The Armchair or the Laboratory?* (Routledge) as Williamson 2013d.

11.5   The Unclarity of Naturalism

In response to my question "What is Naturalism?," Alex Rosenberg (2013a) defines it as "the philosophical theory that treats science as our most reliable source of knowledge and scientific method as the most effective route to knowledge." In "Why I Am a Naturalist," he nicely exemplifies one of my main complaints, by leaving it unclear what he means by "science" or "scientific method," even though it is crucial for what he is committing himself to as a "naturalist." Still, there are clues. He describes "the test of knowledge that scientific findings attain" as "experimental/observational methods," which suggests that theorems of mathematics would not count as scientific findings. The impression is confirmed by Rosenberg's phrase "mathematicians and scientists," as though he doesn't see mathematicians as scientists. That's bad news for his naturalism, for mathematical proof is just as effective a route to knowledge as experimental/observational methods. Of course, since the natural sciences depend on mathematics, Rosenberg is desperate to find a place for it – but admits that he doesn't know how.

In just the way I noted, Rosenberg's defense of naturalism trades on ambiguities between boring truths and obvious falsehoods. Rightly noting the successes of physics, he says "We should be confident that it will do better than any other approach at getting things right." Which things? If he means questions of physics, what reasonable person denies that physics will do better than any other approach at answering those questions? But if he means all questions, why on earth should we be confident that physics will do better than history at getting right what happened at Gettysburg?

I raised history and literary theory as further test cases. According to Rosenberg, naturalism treats literary criticism as fun, but not as knowledge. Does he really not know whether Mr. Collins is the hero of *Pride and Prejudice*? Every normal reader has that sort of elementary literary critical knowledge. Those who know far more about the historical context in which literary works were produced, read them many times with unusual attention, carefully analyze their structure, and so on, naturally have far more knowledge of those works than casual readers do, whatever the excesses of post-modernism.

As for history, Rosenberg leaves the question of whether it should count as science open. He doubts that it can provide "predictively useful knowledge." Scientific predictions about complex systems with initial conditions of which we have only approximate knowledge are probabilistic. Historical knowledge enables us to make probabilistic predictions too: for example, that if a US president publicly describes his policy on the Middle East as a "crusade," it is more likely to inflame than to calm the situation. Does Rosenberg really think that historical knowledge of the past records of politicians is of zero value in making probabilistic predictions about their future behavior? It isn't even clear how natural science could manage without historical knowledge, as Collingwood long ago pointed out, since knowledge of the results of past experiments and observations is itself historical.

Rosenberg apparently expects it to turn out that "reality contains only the kinds of things that hard science recognizes." By "hard science" he presumably means something like physics. He doesn't explain how that could turn out. How could physics show that reality contains only the kinds of things that physics recognizes? It sounds embarrassingly like physics acting as judge and jury in its own case. That physics does not show that there is such a thing as a debt crisis does not mean that physics shows that there is no such thing as a debt crisis: physics simply does not address the question. That is no criticism of physics; it has other work to do. For it to turn out that reality contains only the kinds of things that hard science recognizes, where they exclude things like debt crises, it would have to turn out that a radically reductionist metaphysical theory is true. That in turn would require industrial-scale argument at a characteristically philosophical level of reasoning. Does Rosenberg count philosophy as hard science?

We can formulate the underlying worry as a sharp argument against the extreme naturalist claim that all truths are discoverable by hard science. If it is true that all truths are discoverable by hard science, then it is discoverable by hard science that all truths are discoverable by hard science. But it is not discoverable by hard science that all truths are discoverable by hard science. Therefore the extreme naturalist claim is not true. "Are all truths discoverable by hard science?" is not itself a question of hard science. Truth is a logical or semantic property, discoverability an epistemic one, and hard science a social process. Although truths discoverable by hard science may be relevant to whether *all* truths are discoverable by hard science, by themselves they do not answer the question, since they are framed in the wrong terms – for example, those of physics.

Such problems pose far less threat to more moderate forms of naturalism, based on a broader conception of science that includes mathematics, history, much of philosophy, and the sensible parts of literary criticism, as well as the natural and social sciences. But we should not take for granted that reality contains only the kinds of things that science even in the broad sense recognizes. My caution comes not from any sympathy for mysterious kinds of cognition alien to science in the broad sense, but simply from the difficulty of establishing in any remotely scientific way that reality contains only the kinds of thing that we are capable of recognizing at all. In any case, Rosenberg does not rest content with some moderate form of naturalism. He goes for something far more extreme, in the process lapsing into hard scientism.

Rosenberg concludes: "What naturalists really fear is not becoming dogmatic or giving up the scientific spirit. It's the threat that the science will end up showing that much of what we cherish as meaningful in human life is illusory." But what people really fear is not always what most endangers them. Those most confident of being undogmatic and possessing the scientific spirit may thereby become all the less able to detect dogmatism and failures of the scientific spirit in themselves. If one tries to assess naturalism in a scientific spirit, one will want to get more precise than most self-labelled naturalists (and anti-naturalists) do about what hypothesis is under test. Nor will one dogmatically assume that, once a clear hypothesis is on the table, testing it will be just a matter for hard science. The evidence so far suggests otherwise.

Acknowledgment

This section originally appeared in Matthew Haug (ed.), *Philosophical Methodology: The Armchair or the Laboratory?* (Routledge) as Williamson 2013e.

11.6   On Penelope Maddy's *What Do Philosophers Do? Skepticism and the Practice of Philosophy*

The hero of this book, whom the author clearly admires, goes by the title of the *Plain Inquirer*. This generic character is the child of the Plain Man. At the beginning of the book she sets off from her birthplace in common sense to explore the world, driven by scientific curiosity. She encounters a variety of philosophers, including Descartes, Locke, Berkeley, Hume, Reid, Moore, Austin, and Wittgenstein, and occasionally glimpses the darker shadow of the contemporary epistemologist. Some of the philosophers try to lure the Plain Inquirer into more radical projects than science requires, but she is never seriously tempted, though she respects their contributions to early vision science and other approved activities. She learns from twentieth-century therapists how weaker spirits fell. The book, based on Maddy's Phi Beta Kappa Romanell Lectures for the public understanding of philosophy, is accessible to non-philosophers, though professionals will find plenty of interest. The text has been left as for lectures, with plural "you" and tasters of what will happen "next time."

The first lecture concerns Descartes' dream argument. When asked "How do you know you're not dreaming?," the Plain Inquirer follows Austin and contemporary science by pointing out various differences between ordinary dreaming and waking experience. In response, the skeptic raises the stakes by asking, as Maddy puts it, "How do you know you're not extraordinary dreaming?" Extraordinary dreams have all the sensory fullness and narrative coherence attributed to waking experience; their content includes all of Plain Inquiry. The Plain Inquirer dismisses that extraordinary question, rightly insisting that the achievements of Plain Inquiry do not depend on being proved "from scratch," a starting-point neutral between scientifically informed common sense on one side and the extraordinary dream hypothesis on the other – though she is disappointingly willing to retreat from proclaiming such achievements as knowledge and describe them only as "probable opinions" instead, in the all-purpose name of fallibilism.

Slightly disingenuously, the Plain Inquirer treats the extraordinary dream question as if it came quite out of the blue, with no affinity to her methods of inquiry. Yet she was reared in the assumptions and methods of the Plain Man, many of which she later had to question and even reject. That must often have involved asking whether she had any independent evidence for the reliability of the assumptions and methods at issue, and at least temporarily distancing herself from them while looking elsewhere for support. Perhaps, for instance, she grew up relying on her father's stories about their ancestors for her view of the distant past, and later wondered whether what he said happened really did happen; she suspended her belief in his stories, and sought different sources of information. In the long run, the result is the serious discipline of history, a Plain Inquiry by any non-philistine standard. We may agree with Maddy that the extraordinary dream question takes that form of testing too far, but insist that even Plain Inquiry involves discovering the limitations of our methods by taking them *beyond* the limits of workability. We have to try meeting the extraordinary dream challenge if we are to understand why it is unreasonable. Similarly, if we want to learn the limitations of mathematical methods, we must be willing to try applying them in areas where they may (or may not) turn out unfruitful. Curiosity killed the cat. The Plain Inquirer should accept that her curiosity will sometimes take her into intellectual danger.

The second lecture concerns the notorious argument from illusion, representative theories of perception, and the corollaries skeptics draw from them. The Plain Inquirer rejects the representative theories as inconsistent with the modern science of perception. Local skeptical questions about perception in specific circumstances are answered by common sense and scientific results about perception in those circumstances. Global skeptical questions about perception as such are rejected as involving an unreasonably radical demand for a basic cognitive faculty to be certified as reliable by other faculties. Maddy rightly emphasizes the weirdness of the idea, still found in some contemporary internalist epistemology, that introspection has epistemic priority over perception, but her central objection is to demands on the Plain Inquirer to justify her methods "from scratch."

The third lecture interprets Moore's much-maligned proof of an external world congenially to the Plain Inquirer, as putting the skeptic on the spot, by meeting the challenge to provide such a proof with a counter-challenge to explain exactly what standard of proof is being demanded and why the demand is legitimate. Wittgenstein is interpreted as a therapist who may cure us of the sick tendency to make such demands, but philosophy escapes being sentenced to be nothing without the sickness, "a sadly crimped view of the philosophical project" (200). It is allowed to survive as a humble part of Plain Inquiry, "employing just common sense and ordinary empirical methods"; the latter can "include some more specialized tools, like ordinary language investigations, appropriate conceptual analyses, and therapeutic cautions" (220).

Although the title asks "What do philosophers do?," much of the book is about what philosophers *should* do. Contemporary philosophers are portrayed as often straying beyond the bounds of Plain Inquiry, and suffering the predictable consequences. Epistemologists are singled out as wrongdoers. Epistemology since Gettier is represented as sterile and inward-looking, having lost touch with natural science, obsessed with increasingly complex counterexamples in the pointless search for an analysis of the concept of knowledge, and neglecting "the central question of how we manage to acquire reliable information about the world" (214). Plain Inquiry is capacious, but not all-inclusive.

Maddy's assessment of current epistemology is neither completely wrong nor completely fair. In one respect it is out of date. Increasingly, epistemologists see themselves as studying knowledge itself, not the concept *knowledge*. They want to understand the nature of epistemological states, not our concepts of those states. Contrary to Maddy's account, they are not doing conceptual analysis. However, if her critique of attempts to analyze the concept *knowledge* were sound, it would also devastate many other current epistemological projects. She endorses Austin's nominalistic deriding of "concept" talk; in her summary: "there are no concepts, the linguistic usage is all there is" (66). If her argument shows that there is no concept *knowledge*, it also shows that there is no relation of knowing (or second-order analogue thereof), and no extension, intension, or Kaplan-style character of the word "know." Attempts to study knowledge itself would be as futile as attempts to study the concept *knowledge*.

Shouldn't the Plain Inquirer's curiosity extend to language? Semantics, as a branch of linguistics, is working towards systematic compositional theories of meaning for natural languages. The best-developed such theories provide a general account of the semantic contribution of factive verbs like "know," which depends in effect on their having something like an intension in a context. The intension of the word "know" in an ordinary context is close enough to a relation of knowing for the analytic epistemologist's project to get started, on terms the Plain Inquirer has no business rejecting.

Of course, "know" may have different intensions in different contexts. But epistemologists are well aware of that possibility, and have been investigating it for decades. Indeed, such inquiries into linguistic usage have 1950s' ordinary language philosophy in their ancestry, but they demonstrate the need to go beyond piecemeal observations by interpreting them within a well-developed theoretical framework. Austin himself was far from anti-theoretical, as his work on speech acts shows.

Maddy cites Weinberg, Nichols, and Stich's famous 2001 paper "Normativity and Epistemic Intuitions" for evidence of cross-cultural variations in the use of "know," for instance on Gettier cases, which might threaten the interest of the analytic project (62n). She does not mention that numerous more recent and methodologically more careful papers have failed to reproduce their results. Instead, they provide evidence of remarkable cross-cultural similarities in judgments about such cases.

To illustrate contemporary epistemology's damaging preoccupation with "ever-more-complex problem cases," Maddy quotes a long description of one from a recent book by Ernest Sosa, and relates it to issues about knowledge (205). But Sosa's case can just as easily be used to explain subtle distinctions concerning "how we manage to acquire reliable information about the world," which Maddy describes as "the central question" of good epistemology. For instance, in the quoted passage, Sosa says:

> my judgments of tomato ripeness are in general apt to be right with no better than even chance. But when it's the particular (and rare) shade of red now displayed, then I am nearly infallible.

Isn't that about acquiring reliable information about the world? Presumably, philosophers are allowed to give complex counterexamples to conjectures; mathematicians do it all the time. Perhaps Maddy thinks that epistemology would be better done in terms of reliable information than of knowledge. But "reliable information" is no more precise or scientific than "knowledge"; both "reliable" and "information" are notoriously slippery words. It is not even clear how reliable information is supposed to differ from knowledge. With the skeptic's arguments defused, realistic standards for knowledge can be applied, as they typically are by contemporary epistemologists. The reader is left with very little idea of how in practice the Plain Inquirer would go about doing epistemology differently.

Maddy is surely right that "no unusual, exclusively philosophical methods appear to be required" for doing philosophy (210). Indeed, no unusual, exclusively philosophical methods *are* required. The methods used elsewhere suffice, though philosophers may sometimes use them more systematically, carefully, and reflectively. Thought experimentation may be an example.

However, the assumption that there are no exclusively philosophical methods leaves philosophy with more flexibility and autonomy than the reader might be led to suppose. For instance, Maddy does not mention the use of formal methods. Such methods are of course not exclusive to philosophy, but they permit far more ambitious and rigorous constructive philosophical theorizing than she hints at. In particular, there are two main traditions of formal epistemology, Bayesian probabilism and epistemic logic, both mathematically highly developed. Philosophers such as Frank Ramsey and Jaakko Hintikka played a key in the growth of both branches. The methods of formal epistemology cannot happily be subsumed under Maddy's concluding description of "common sense and ordinary empirical methods," including "ordinary language investigations, appropriate conceptual analyses, and therapeutic cautions." Although both kinds of formal epistemology have been successfully applied in broadly "empirical" disciplines such as economics, that does not make their methods any more distinctively empirical than those of mathematics.

Some formal epistemology could have been applied with advantage to Maddy's Appendix B, on skepticism and the closure of knowledge under deduction. She formalizes a skeptical argument thus:

(i)   I don't know I'm not extraordinary dreaming.
(ii) If this is a hand, then I'm not extraordinary dreaming.
(iii) Therefore, I don't know this is a hand.

She observes "that (iii) doesn't follow from [TW: (i) and] (ii) alone, that I have to be aware of the logical connection in (ii)" and so makes that assumption (230). But there is no logical connection in (ii). Not only does "if" not specify a *logical* connection, "this is a hand" does not logically entail "I'm not extraordinary dreaming." The connection, such as it is, depends on the meaning of the non-logical constant "dreaming"; moreover, in the possible situation in which I fall asleep and have an extraordinary dream while my hand remains intact, the antecedent of (ii) is true and the consequent false. The connection is at best pragmatic: perhaps I can correctly interpret the perceptual demonstrative "this" only when awake.

Probabilistic distinctions would have clarified the subsequent argument, where Maddy writes "What makes Closure compelling, after all, is the thought that if p implies q, then any evidence I have for p ought to serve just as well as evidence for q" (231). If evidence for a proposition is what raises its probability, that principle is false. For instance, if p is the proposition that the die came up 6, and q is the proposition that the die did not come up 2 or 4, then p implies q, but if our evidence is just that the die came up even, it raises the probability of p from 1/6 to 1/3 while lowering that of q from 2/3 to 1/3. Of course, Maddy's principle holds on another interpretation, where evidence for a proposition is what its probability is high on, but distinguishing such interpretations matters when the transmission of evidence is at issue, as in Maddy's argument.

The Plain Inquirer comes across as ambivalent about philosophy, drawn to the inquiry but scared of losing her reputation for plainness. We wouldn't expect such a half-hearted approach to achieve much in natural science. Why should it do better in philosophy?

Acknowledgment

This section first appeared as a review of Maddy 2017 in *The Journal of Philosophy* (Williamson 2017d).

12

Concepts, Understanding, Analyticity

12.1 Reply to Jackson

Frank Jackson's "Thought Experiments and Possibilities" (Jackson 2009) exhibits a failure to comprehend the extent of the difference between my position and his. In consequence, his arguments are question-begging, because they treat as common ground features of his position that the first edition explicitly calls into question.

A case in point is Jackson's talk of "conceptual possibility" and "conceptual necessity." He writes as if the issue between us is the relative methodological priority for philosophy of conceptual modalities and metaphysical modalities: he ranks the former before the latter; I reverse the order. He says "Williamson isn't telling us that we cannot learn anything about what's conceptually possible," as if I accept such a notion. But the longest chapter in the book (75–135, this volume) is an attack on exactly the sort of epistemological conception of analyticity on which Jackson's appeals to conceptual modalities rely: the idea of matters on which we must agree in order to share a meaning or concept. Although he provides no explanation of the phrases "conceptually possible" and "conceptually necessary," his use of them makes clear that he has something of the sort in mind. In effect, my book argues that there is no such thing as conceptual necessity.

Perhaps Jackson was misled by the passage he quotes from page 208 (this volume), in which for the sake of argument I grant a notion of conceptual possibility in order to argue that thought experiments lose much of their interest if their upshot is characterized in such terms – and that conceptual possibility (unlike metaphysical possibility) does not interact logically in the required way with the counterfactuals that play a central role in thought experiments, although he does not mention the latter point. He also does not mention that the discussion there ends with a reminder that the idea of conceptual modality has already been rejected on the basis of the arguments against epistemological conceptions of analyticity (208–9, this volume).

According to Jackson:

> the most serious problem for Williamson's "metaphysical possibility first" thesis [...] lies in the fact that that our best reasons for concluding that certain claims which aren't conceptually necessary are metaphysically necessary derive from claims that are about what is or is not conceptually necessary conjoined with *a posteriori* claims [...].

In addition to the uncritical reliance on conceptual modality, another fallacy is surfacing here. Jackson's view makes conceptual necessity an epistemological status. But even if the epistemological status of our conclusion that something is metaphysically necessary depended on the epistemological status of some premise as conceptually necessary, it would not follow that the proposition *that* something was conceptually necessary occurred anywhere in the reasoning for the conclusion, as required by his claim that the reasoning is primarily about the conceptual status of the propositions at issue.

A related question-begging feature of Jackson's discussion here is that he freely appeals to a distinction between the "*a priori*" and the "*a posteriori*," without addressing the argument in the book for the untrustworthiness of such a distinction (167–71, this volume).

Although Jackson frequently takes for granted what the book rejects, he does make some comments that bear on the reasons for that rejection. In effect defending an epistemological conception of analyticity, he writes: "communication and knowing what we are disagreeing (or agreeing) about requires substantial agreement about what the words we read and hear signify"; where that is lacking, "we aren't, or need not be, in disagreement." The passage fudges the crucial distinction. If I say "Spurs will win" and you say "Leeds will win" but the word "win" differs in meaning between your mouth and mine, we may not be disagreeing or properly communicating about the match, even if we think we are. If "win" has the same meaning in your mouth and mine, we are (*ceteris paribus*) disagreeing and properly communicating. That is just semantic agreement in the sense of synonymy. It goes no way whatsoever towards establishing what Jackson needs, that synonymy requires agreement *in opinion* on some privileged questions. His wording suggests that he may have in mind agreement in opinion on metalinguistic matters. But that is primarily relevant to whether we *think* we are disagreeing about the initial question, not to whether we actually are. Nor does it address the arguments in the book specifically directed against attempts to save epistemological conceptions of analyticity by appeal to metalinguistic beliefs (111–14, this volume).

In past writings, Jackson defended the idea that shared meanings require shared opinions only by suggesting that there is nothing else for the sharing of meanings to consist in. The first edition responds to that suggestion at length by explaining how the unity of a shared linguistic practice with a word does not require privileged points of agreement and the practice can determine the semantic properties with which all participants use the word (123–31, this volume). Unfortunately, his response does not engage with this alternative.

Jackson conjectures that philosophers with deviant responses to Gettier cases may express a different concept by the word "knowledge," but does not say why it should be classified as a difference of concept rather than of opinion. His introduction of concepts as "our way of categorizing our world" is notably unhelpful in this respect, since there are many different ways of individuating ways. In one way, someone who relies on *The Guardian* in categorizing politicians as "trustworthy" or "untrustworthy" is categorizing in a different way from someone who relies on *The Daily Telegraph*, but it does not follow that they mean different things by the word "trustworthy." In another way, two people who use a word with the same extension use it to categorize in the same way, even if they use it with different intensions. Jackson provides no standard of sameness for concepts or ways of categorizing. If attributing different concepts of "knowledge" to philosophers who respond differently to Gettier cases is just another way of saying that they respond differently, then the terminology is radically misleading. The central question is whether they use the word "knowledge" with the same reference. That is entirely consistent with responding differently to Gettier cases. Consider a class of law students given a statute and a hypothetical case and asked to apply the former to the latter. That they submit different answers is not good evidence of a failure of coreference in their words. They have noticed different features of the statute and the case, assigned different weights to competing considerations. Why should philosophical thought experiments be so different?

Although there is no law against using a common word with an idiosyncratic sense, that is not what philosophers usually do. They want to engage with other philosophers, and in order to do so hold themselves responsible to the public meanings of their words, while using them to deny what others assert. Unorthodox philosophers who think that there is knowledge in Gettier cases are disagreeing with the rest of us, and we should not pretend otherwise. How much progress would one make in philosophy by classifying objectors as expressing different concepts with their words, whether they like it or not?

Jackson's comments fail to answer the arguments of the book against epistemological conceptions of analyticity. Gettier cases tell us something about knowledge and – less directly – something about what we believe about knowledge. Although we can recycle that information as information about words or concepts, we gain little from doing so. If not all justified true belief is knowledge, then not everything in the extension of the words "justified true belief" or of the concept *justified true belief* is in the extension of the word "knowledge" or of the concept *knowledge*, simply because all and only justified true belief is in the extension of "justified true belief" or *justified true belief* and all and only knowledge is in the extension of "knowledge" or *knowledge*. Similarly, if people believe that not all justified true belief is knowledge, then they probably also believe that not everything in the extension of "justified true belief" or *justified true belief* is in the extension of "knowledge" or *knowledge*, if they have the relevant disquotational beliefs. But there is no reason to think of the information we gain from philosophical thought experiments as somehow bearing primarily on words or concepts and only secondarily on what those words or concepts about. The first edition provides a far more straightforward account, which Jackson has failed to undermine.

Jackson briefly suggests that conceptual analysis contributes to other sciences:

Statisticians discuss the best way to analyze the concepts of randomness and probability; physicist discuss the best way to analyze the probabilities that figure in the equations of quantum theory; biologists discuss which concepts of species and genes are best for their purposes.

None of these examples helps his case. He is right, of course, that armchair theorizing of such kinds plays a valuable role in science. But it is not conceptual analysis in a distinctively Jacksonian sense, inquiry into the bounds of conceptual possibility for given concepts. When biologists discuss which concepts of species and genes are best for their purposes, they are discussing which distinctions it would be most useful to draw, which questions it would be most fruitful to ask. That may come down to asking what it would be best to mean by the words "species" and "gene"; it does not come down to asking what we currently mean by them. Nor is Jackson dialectically entitled to assume that word meanings are individuated by conceptual possibility. When physicists discuss the best way to analyze the probabilities that figure in the equations of quantum theory, they are discussing what in physical reality or our knowledge of it corresponds to the probability terms in those equations, on the assumption that our current ways of thinking about them may well be inadequate. When statisticians discuss the best way to analyze the concepts of randomness and probability, they are probably discussing both what there is to mean and what it is best to mean. In no case is the armchair theorizing primarily driven by conceptual competence. In that respect it illustrates a major theme of the book.

Acknowledgments

This section first appeared as part of my contribution to a symposium on the first edition of the book in *Analysis Reviews* (Williamson 2009a). I thank Frank Jackson for his interesting comments, which help bring into relief some main themes of the book.

12.2   Reply to Boghossian

In "Williamson on the *A Priori* and the Analytic" (Boghossian 2011), Paul Boghossian defends a conception of *a priori* knowledge as knowledge in which sense experience plays a purely enabling role: we know *a priori* that all green things are colored even though sense experience was crucial to our acquisition of the concept of green, for that is a purely enabling role. On Boghossian's conception, assent conditions on concept possession are central to at least some *a priori* knowledge, especially of logic. His defense of this view involves him in resisting the arguments of the first edition at several points. In particular, Boghossian maintains that the book's objections to understanding-assent links (assent conditions on concept possession) do not generalize as far as I claim; he rejects my alternative model of understanding, on which understanding-assent links are not required. I will explain why Boghossian's critique leaves me unmoved.

In previous work, Boghossian developed an epistemology of logic based on understanding-assent links corresponding to fundamental rules of logic. His paradigm was modus ponens: a necessary condition for understanding "if" was supposed to be willingness to assent to inferences by modus ponens involving "if." The book presents a series of counterexamples, some actual, some possible, to such putative understanding-assent links, for both modus ponens and other equally fundamental rules (87–123, this volume). The counterexamples concern native speakers of a natural language who come to understand the logical words at issue in the usual way but then go in for deviant logical theorizing without losing their linguistic competence; most philosophers know such people. In response, Boghossian picks what he regards as the clearest understanding-assent link, willingness to assent to "and"-elimination (the inference from "P and Q" to "P" or to "Q") as a condition for understanding "and," and denies that the counterexamples I propose to it (97–8, this volume) make sense.

Strategically, Boghossian's response is not very promising. If he can rely on understanding-assent links only for "and"-elimination and a few other equally banal rules, but not for modus ponens or other fundamental principles, then he is in no position to base either a *general* epistemology of logic or a *general* account of the understanding of logical constants on understanding-assent links. It is a little lame for him to claim in effect that not *every* fundamental rule of logic is a counterexample to his original account. A bolder strategy for him would be to seek a way of defending the claim that *no* fundamental rule of logic is a counterexample to his original account, and in particular of defending his original test case, modus ponens, as a putative understanding-assent link for "if" against my counterexamples. In keeping away from the bolder strategy, Boghossian concedes so much ground that it is quite unclear what his fallback general epistemology of logic or his fallback general account of the understanding of logical constants could be.

In any case, Boghossian's defense of "and"-elimination as a putative understanding-assent link for "and" is unconvincing. Boghossian notes that in some circumstances my proposed counterexample, Simon, will assent to (1) but not to (2):

(1) Booth saw the balding Lincoln and shot him.
(2) Booth shot Lincoln.

Obviously, if we have just met Simon, and know nothing about his background beliefs, we are likely to find his combined reactions to (1) and (2) utterly bewildering. We may reasonably wonder whether he knows what the word "and" means. In practice, independently of his reaction to (1), since it is so well known that Booth shot Lincoln we may also find Simon's rejection of (2) initially puzzling, and wonder whether he is using the name "Booth" to refer to the man we mean. Once we become aware of Simon's conspiracy theory of the assassination, we realize that there was no linguistic misunderstanding over (2); we simply disagree with him about the historical facts. Similarly, once we become aware of Simon's deviant theory of logic, an explanation of his unwillingness to deduce (2) from (1) in terms of linguistic incompetence looks much less attractive. On theoretical grounds, Simon holds that borderline cases for vague terms induce truth-value gaps, and that such gaps should be treated by Kleene's weak three-valued tables, which coincide with the classical two-valued tables when all the constituent sub-sentences are true or false but make the complex sentence gappy when at least one sub-sentence is gappy. Simon also thinks that it is legitimate to assent to gappy sentences as well as to true ones; what matters is to avoid falsity. Since he thinks that Booth saw Lincoln and regards Lincoln as a borderline case for the vague term "bald," he thinks that "Booth saw the balding Lincoln" is gappy, and that (1) inherits its gappiness. He concludes that it is legitimate to assent to (1). The gappiness does not infect (2). Simon rejects (2) as straightforwardly false.

Of course, Simon would be quick to point out that in conversational terms it would be highly misleading to assert (1) on grounds of its gappiness when one's audience had no reason to suspect that one was doing so. In the absence of special background assumptions, asserting "A(P)" leaves it open whether "A(P)" is true or gappy, on Simon's view. If one knows that "A(P)" is gappy because it has the gappy constituent "P," one can therefore make a simpler and more informative assertion by simply asserting that "P" is gappy, omitting the other material in "A(P)" as irrelevant. On Simon's view, one can gain the effect of asserting that "P" is gappy without going meta-linguistic by asserting "P and not P." Thus if Simon asserts (1), his audience is entitled for Gricean reasons to assume that he is not doing so merely on the grounds that "Lincoln was bald" is gappy, since otherwise he is being conversationally uncooperative and should have said something like "Was Lincoln bald? Well, he was and he wasn't" instead. The default conversational assumption is that one is not dealing with borderline cases; under that assumption one can defeasibly move from "P and Q" to "P" and to "Q." Nevertheless, according to Simon, the move is not deductively valid, and the case of (1) and (2) is a counterexample.

Once Simon has explained his view, it is much less plausible that his unwillingness to infer (2) from (1) manifests linguistic incompetence. It looks much more like a case of theoretical disagreement. Imagine a community in which no alternative to geocentrism has ever been contemplated. Now someone develops a heliocentric theory. This first emerges one morning when she dissents from the assertion "The sun has risen." She agrees that before the sun was in that direction (pointing down) and now it is in this direction (pointing up), but refuses to conclude "It has risen." Initially, other speakers are utterly bewildered, and wonder whether she understands the word "risen." However, once she has explained her view, they realize that it is a case of cosmological disagreement. Whether or not her geocentric theory is really correct, and whether or not it really entails the literal falsity of "The sun has risen," her denial of that assertion does not constitute linguistic incompetence. Similarly, an unexplained refusal to conclude "There are more natural numbers than even numbers" from the two premises "Every even number is a natural number" and "Not every natural number is an even number" causes utter bewilderment amongst those unacquainted with Cantorian reasoning, and doubts as to whether the speaker understands the word "more," but filling in that reasoning makes it clear that no linguistic incompetence is involved. Unlike Copernicus and Cantor, Simon chose the wrong direction for theoretical unorthodoxy, but that does not make him linguistically incompetent.

Boghossian objects that Simon's tolerance of assent to gappy statements undermines the presumption that he is assenting to them as true. Quite what Boghossian means by "assenting to something as true" is unclear. If it means assenting to the explicit claim that it is true, then it involves too much theorizing on the speaker's part to be pertinent here. For instance, some bad philosophers assent to "The earth is not flat" but not to "It is true that the earth is not flat," on the grounds that Nietzsche or Derrida has deconstructed the idea of truth. Presumably Boghossian does not want their deviant inferential role for "true" to make their inferential roles for all other words automatically deviant too. Many bad philosophers have quite sensible views about non-philosophical matters. Moreover, unsophisticated thinkers such as children may genuinely assent to various claims about their external environment without having an explicit concept of truth at all.

In any case, Simon applies the same weak Kleene treatment to the sentential operator "it is true that" as he does to other sentential operators. The classical two-valued truth-table for "it is true that" maps true to true and false to false; thus the corresponding weak Kleene three-valued table for "it is true that" maps true to true, gappy to gappy, and false to false. Thus "It is true that A" always has the same status as "A." Consequently, Simon assents to "It is true that A" when and only when he assents to "A." So far, his assenting to something looks like assenting to it as true.

Perhaps it is different when Simon goes meta-linguistic. Let "T" be the predicate in his meta-language corresponding to the top line of his three-valued tables. If quoted occurrences of sentences do not count as constituents, then the object-language sentence "A" is not a constituent of the meta-language sentence T("A"), and we may suppose that T("A") is true when "A" is on the top line but false when "A" is on the second or third line. Thus when Simon regards "A" as gappy, he will assent to "A" but not to T("A"). Does that show that he is not really assenting to "A" as true?

The easiest way to finesse that objection is by refining the example. Let Simon think of the weak Kleene tables as using a three-way classification into the definitely true, the indefinite, and the definitely false, and of being indefinite as a way of being true, indefinitely true. Thus, strictly speaking, "T" does not mean true; it means definitely true. The failures of "and"-elimination on this semantics have the same structure as before: "A" is indefinite, so "A and B" is also indefinite, even though "B" is definitely false. When Simon regards "A" as gappy, he will assent to both "A" and True("A"), which on his view is true when "A" is definitely true or indefinite, although he will not assent to T("A"). Like Graham Priest, Simon is a dialetheist, for when he regards something as gappy he assents to it, to its negation, and their conjunction. Nevertheless, his theoretical aberrations provide no sound basis for denying that his assent is genuine.

Simon's assent to both "Lincoln was bald" and "Lincoln was not bald" may be compared to our assent to both "Every weapon of mass destruction in Iraq belonged to Al Qaeda" and "No weapon of mass destruction in Iraq belonged to Al Qaeda": both are vacuously true, because there never were any weapons of mass destruction in Iraq. In both cases the assent is genuine, even though its unusual grounds defeat various expectations it might arouse in a hearer ignorant of those grounds. Simon regards both "Lincoln was bald" and "Lincoln was not bald" as something like vacuously true. Thus the main counterexample in the book to the understanding-assent link for "and"-elimination goes through, despite Boghossian's protests.

The book briefly mentions two other types of counterexample to the understanding-assent link for "and"-elimination, one concerning actual and robust experimental evidence of a human tendency in some circumstances to treat conjunctions as more probable than their conjuncts, the other concerning possible speakers who dissent from one conjunct in the absence of the others because they mistake a false conversational implicature for a false entailment (96, this volume).

Since Boghossian offers no objection to either of these types of counterexample, they too stand.[1]

In addition to contesting my main counterexample to the understanding-assent link for "and"-elimination, Boghossian asks what competence with a logical word could consist in, if not in assent of the kind understanding-assent links require. The book sketches an alternative answer, one consequence of which is that when the word belongs to a public language, competence with it constitutively involves causal relations with other speakers of the language, which do not supervene on patterns of assent and dissent. As an analogy, consider what competence in the casual game of beach soccer consists in. There is no rule R of beach soccer such that, necessarily, one is competent in beach soccer only if one assents to R. Someone who thinks that the slightly different rule R* is in force, rather than R, can still be competent in beach soccer. Oscar and Twin-Oscar may have the same intrinsic dispositions even though Oscar is competent (although not expert) in beach soccer while Twin-Oscar is not even competent in beach soccer, because the game played in Oscar's world is beach soccer while the game played in Twin-Oscar's world is beach twin-soccer, which differs from beach soccer in subtle respects of which neither Oscar nor Twin-Oscar is aware. Once one has joined a game of beach soccer, it takes rather extreme deviance to get slung out. The same applies to participation in a linguistic practice. The unorthodox theorists who counterexemplify understanding-assent links remain competent with the relevant words because they maintain an adequate level of participation in the social practice of using those words. Of course, such remarks are only a beginning. The discussion in the first edition goes further (123–32, this volume), and far more remains to be done. Nevertheless, the analogy already shows the possibility of

---

[1]   In a footnote, Boghossian suggests that even if all understanding-assent links in the strict sense fail, "A friend of epistemological analyticities might well be satisfied with the existence" of clusters of links of the form "necessarily, anyone who understands **w** accepts S(**w**) or S'(**w**) … or S*(**w**)." To be a genuine alternative, the latter must mean a disjunction of acceptances, not acceptance of a disjunction. Such a disjunctive link will not confer *a priori* status on knowledge of any one of the disjuncts (or on knowledge of their disjunction). Since Boghossian does not explain how it would serve his overall argumentative purposes, I discuss it no further.

an account of linguistic competence that differs structurally from one based on understanding-assent links.

It is not clear that Boghossian has come to grips with the alternative model of linguistic competence. He asks how societies determine the social meanings that on my view a public language makes available to its speakers. He gives as my answer a sentence from the book: "A complex web of interactions and dependences can hold a linguistic or conceptual practice together even in the absence of a common creed that all participants at all times are required to endorse" (127, this volume). Boghossian comments "This repeats the rejection of inferentialism but without providing a substantive alternative." But the quoted sentence was not intended to address the question of how societies determine social meanings. On my view of meaning, that would involve explaining how the referential properties of expressions of the language supervene on lower-level facts, for example about causal connections between uses of those expressions and objects in the environment. That is a huge task for the philosophy of language, whether the language is public or private. It was not the business of the book to attempt to carry out that task, although the comments in the final chapter on knowledge maximization as a principle of charity are at least relevant (264–75, this volume). The quoted sentence addressed a different question: what unifies a linguistic or conceptual practice enough for it to be a locus for the assignment of meanings, by contrast with a mere collection of such loci corresponding to the more or less similar idiolects of different speakers? The partial answer is that the unification consists in causal interrelations of speakers, not merely in their shared monadic properties. Since competence with the public language depends on participation in such a unity, an inferentialist account of competence in terms of understanding-assent links cannot be right, because it has the wrong structure: the understanding-assent links do not capture the causal interrelations. Even someone who rejects that alternative to inferentialism should be able to see that it is substantive on the point at issue.

Boghossian suggests that the inferentialist is better placed than I am to handle empty terms such as "phlogiston." However, purported understanding-assent links for empty terms are subject to counterexamples of just the same sort as purported links for nonempty terms. What is unusual about empty atomic terms such as "phlogiston" is that knowing their referential properties (that they do not refer) is typically of little help in attaining competence with them, whereas knowing the referential properties of nonempty terms (what they refer to) is typically of great help in attaining competence with the latter. That difference is hardly surprising. It does nothing to show that the standard for competence is inferentialist in nature. Even the practice of using "phlogiston" was unified by a complex web of interactions and dependences; it did not require a universally shared creed to hold it together.

Given the failure of Boghossian's attempt to rehabilitate the appeal to understanding-assent links or epistemological analyticity, we may turn to his more general remarks about the *a priori* at the beginning of his piece. In the book, I argue that however the distinction between *a priori* and *a posteriori* knowledge is made precise, it does not cut very deep. Modal claims are used as a test case. The idea is that modal claims are logically equivalent to combinations of counterfactual conditionals, and that our cognitive capacity to handle the latter is what gives us the capacity to handle the former too. Our cognitive capacity to handle counterfactual conditionals involves the offline deployment of cognitive capacities originally developed online to handle the antecedents and consequents of those conditionals separately. Consider the example that Boghossian quotes:

(3) It is necessary that whoever knows something believes it.

I argue that our knowledge of (3) does not involve an understanding-assent link; there is no "epistemologically analytic" connection between "knows" and "believes." Rather, in a nutshell, our knowledge of (3) involves the offline deployment of concepts of knowledge and belief, in a way not radically different from that which occurs in our assessment of a contingent counterfactual such as:

(4) If Mary had known more about John, she would have believed that he was untrustworthy.

Whether we know (3) or (4) depends in part on our skill in applying the concepts of belief and knowledge. That skill was partly developed online, in the classification of cases encountered in sense experience as cases of knowledge or ignorance, belief or unbelief; those encounters are constitutively relevant to the epistemic status of our present applications of our concepts of knowledge and belief. Thus sense experience plays a more than purely enabling role in our knowledge of (3) as well as (4) (170, this volume). Yet our knowledge of (3) would usually be classified as a paradigm of *a priori* knowledge. But it would be no less crude to classify our knowledge of (3) as *a posteriori*, since sense experience does not play a strictly evidential role in that knowledge.

Boghossian complains that the argument ignores the possibility that the difference between those who grasp (3) and assent to it and those who grasp (3) and don't assent may concern "the exercise of a faculty of a priori insight" (although that is not his own view). My argument is openly speculative. It attempts nothing like proof; that would be hopelessly premature for any account of the matter at this stage. Nevertheless, as the book emphasizes (164, this volume), considerations of theoretical economy and psychological plausibility strongly favor explanations of armchair knowledge that invoke more general cognitive capacities for which there is independent evidence (such as our capacity to evaluate counterfactual conditionals) over accounts that postulate specialized faculties to do philosophically exciting things for which there is no independent evidence.

Boghossian briefly expresses skepticism as to whether "knowledge of modal claims can be reduced to knowledge of counterfactuals," on the grounds that "on any plausible account, knowledge of logical, mathematical and constitutive truths will be presupposed in accounting for our knowledge of counterfactuals." Those comments suggest a misunderstanding of what is at issue. *Pace* Boghossian, I did not claim that "knowledge of modal claims is knowledge of counterfactual conditionals." My point was rather that "Despite the non-synonymy of the two sides, our cognitive capacity to evaluate the counterfactual conditionals gives us exactly what we need to evaluate the corresponding modal claims too" (164, this volume). More important, *modal* truths must be distinguished from *necessary* truths. A theorem of first-order non-modal logic expresses a necessary truth; it does not express a modal truth, for it employs no modal terms. "It is necessary that $2 + 2 = 4$ and John knows that $2 + 2 = 4$" does not entail "John knows that it is necessary that $2 + 2 = 4$." Logical, mathematical, and constitutive truths are typically necessary but not modal. Thus even when our prior knowledge of them plays a role in our knowledge of relevant counterfactual conditionals, that role does not imply any circularity in the account of our knowledge of modal truths. In particular, that role does not require us to have prior knowledge that the logical, mathematical, and constitutive truths are necessary; rather, that knowledge of modality is generated by the same means as the knowledge of counterfactuals. The book explains in more detail how the interplay of modal and counterfactual knowledge involves no circularity in its account (171–3, this volume).

The attraction of epistemological analyticity was that it promised to demystify *a priori* knowledge. If there were no promising alternative means to do that, we might have some reason to think that there *must* be understanding-assent link links, despite all the evidence that there are not. Once we see that our ability to handle counterfactual conditionals provides independent evidence of cognitive capacities that are well placed to explain armchair knowledge, we have no need to hanker after epistemological analyticity.

Acknowledgment

This section first appeared as part of my contribution to a symposium on the first edition of the book in *Philosophy and Phenomenological Research* (Williamson 2011c).

12.3 Reply to Peacocke

In "Understanding, Modality, Logical Operators" (Peacocke 2011), Christopher Peacocke contests both the first edition's epistemology of metaphysical modality and its account of linguistic understanding. I discuss each challenge in turn.

1

The book explains our capacity to think about the esoteric topic of metaphysical modality as an accidental byproduct of our capacity to use mundane subjunctive conditionals. The explanation starts from the broadly logical equivalence of a claim of metaphysical necessity with a subjunctive conditional whose consequent is logically false, and the dual equivalence for a claim of metaphysical possibility (159, this volume):

$$\Box A \equiv (\neg A \,\Box\!\!\rightarrow \bot)$$

$$\Diamond A \equiv \neg(A \,\Box\!\!\rightarrow \bot)$$

Here $\bot$ is a logically false sentence. Peacocke concedes these equivalences but denies their epistemological and explanatory significance. In particular, he argues that neither of them constitutes an "explanatory definition" (his phrase).

I explicitly disavowed the claim that the equivalences are strict synonymies (162, this volume). What I suggested they show is that a creature with the cognitive capacity to handle subjunctive conditionals thereby already has the cognitive capacity to handle metaphysical modalities, so that it is explanatorily redundant to postulate an additional cognitive capacity dedicated to the latter. Peacocke argues to the contrary that his account of the concepts of metaphysical possibility and necessity provides a substantive explanation of the metaphysical impossibility of contradictions, while my account provides none. Unfortunately, his argument wavers between at least three different explananda such as these (for concreteness, I have replaced his "q&~q" by a particular contradiction):

(1) It is metaphysically impossible that it is hot and not hot.
(2) The proposition that it is metaphysically impossible that it is hot and not hot is true.
(3) The sentence "It is metaphysically impossible that it is hot and not hot" is true.

When he considers what explanation I can offer, he writes as though only (1) were to be explained: he does not consider how my explanation would treat ascriptions of truth to propositions or sentences. But then he goes on:

> An explanatory definition should contribute to an explanation of why the metaphysical impossibility of q&~q results from the semantic contributions of negation and conjunction, and their mode of combination in q&~q. [...] A simple explanation of the metaphysical impossibility of p&~p draws on the fact that necessity is truth in all possible worlds (taken as sets of propositions), where genuine possibility is constrained, inter alia, by the requirement that in any genuinely possible world, the same rules for evaluating logically complex expressions must hold as actually hold for outright truth.

Such considerations might figure in an explanation of (3). They are quite out of place in an explanation of (1): it could not have been both hot and not hot, whatever the *words* "and" and "not" had meant. The natural form for an explanation of (3) is bipartite: a non-semantic explanation of (1), and a semantic explanation of the Tarskian biconditional of (3) with (1). In effect, Peacocke devotes almost all his explanation to the biconditional. Once it is stripped of that semantic material, virtually nothing is left as an explanation of (1) itself. But of course my explanation of (3) can contain corresponding semantic material pertaining to the biconditional of (3) with (1), just as sensitive as Peacocke's to the semantic roles of conjunction, negation, and the modal operator. What neither of us has, or could reasonably expect, is a story that explains why it could not have been both hot and not hot from a significantly more fundamental starting-point: (1) is close to explanatory bedrock. The best either of us can do is to derive (1) in a very few steps from standard principles of modal logic (in Peacocke's case) or counterfactual logic (in mine), perhaps by deriving the negation of a contradiction in non-modal propositional logic and then applying a rule of necessitation or its analogue in counter-factual logic. Similar points apply to the explanation of (2) (Peacocke sometimes writes of the truth of propositions rather than sentences). In effect, he has produced the illusion of a substantive explanatory task that his account can fulfil and mine cannot by oscillating be-tween use and mention.

2

Peacocke's other challenge is to the book's account of linguistic un-derstanding. In broad terms, he argues that an adequate account of what is to understand expressions of a public language must invoke a level of something like Frege's cognitively individuated senses for those expressions. By contrast, the book dispenses with such a level, dividing the work between meanings individuated at the level of ref-erence (which may include both Carnapian intensional isomorphism and Kaplanian character) and understanding as full engagement with a public practice of using the expressions, on which the shared mean-ings supervene.

For Peacocke, the cognitive psychology that individuates senses is individualistic, not social: "what correct understanding consists in, at the level of sense, has a specification not involving society."[1] An im-mediate problem for such a view is that Oscar and Twin-Oscar may be duplicates at the level of individualistic cognitive psychology even though Oscar correctly understands our word "gold" while Twin-Os-car does not. For Oscar may be a normal English speaker while Twin-Oscar belongs to a speech community whose word "gold" refers to fool's gold. Twin-Oscar does not even *have* our word "gold"; *a for-tiori*, he does not correctly understand it. When he says "That is gold," he speaks truly if and only if the referent of his demonstrative is fool's gold, not if and only if it is gold. He is not using our concept *gold*.

Even if we restrict attention to people who do have our word "gold," it is doubtful that on Peacocke's own conception of understanding the difference between those who understand "gold" and those who do

---

[1] Peacocke's added gloss "(Of course, what makes it the correct specification has something to do with society)" does not help with the problems to be raised here.

not can be specified without involving society. For he claims that "understanding an expression [...] consists in tacit knowledge of the fundamental reference rule for that expression." Presumably Peacocke intends tacit knowledge to be a species of *knowledge*. But then whether a speaker has tacit knowledge of the reference rule or only tacit true belief depends in part on the causal basis of the putative knowledge. Two members of our speech community may be duplicates at the level of individualistic psychology and both have the relevant word with the right reference rule even though one speaker has them in the proper way while the other has them only as a result of a failed attempt to hoax her about the rule by hoaxers who themselves misunderstood the word. The former has tacit knowledge of the reference rule while the latter has mere true belief, yet the difference between them seems constitutively to involve society, since it concerns the difference in their relations to other speakers. If that is not the sort of social difference that Peacocke intends to rule out, it is quite unclear what sort of social difference he does intend to rule out.

Even if understanding is not a matter of tacit knowledge, a sufficiently deviant connection to the public practice of using a word, like the one just sketched, will not constitute understanding.

The preceding examples also reveal a gap in an argument with which Peacocke tries to destabilize my account of meaning and understanding:

> a good formulation of a character-rule, especially at the level of concepts, will plausibly coincide with a fundamental reference-rule. But, provided that we are not concerned with the special subcases in which the fundamental reference or character rule actually mentions other language-users, this implies that character-rules can fix a society-independent understanding-condition at the level of sense.

In specifying the character-rules of many expressions, it is indeed unnecessary to refer to social matters.[2] But that does *not* imply that

---

[2] Peacocke's expression "character-rule" hovers dangerously between the function from contexts to contents (the character in Kaplan's terminology) and the meaning of some descriptive specification of that function. On my account, what constitutes the meaning of the original expression is the function itself, not (regressively) the meaning of a descriptive specification of it. Fregean senses must not be smuggled in under the alternative label of "rules".

"character-rules can fix a society-independent understanding-condition at the level of sense." For one understands a word only if one has that word. Nor will a deviant connection between the word and the right character-rule constitute understanding. Those conditions, as just noted, are not society-independent.

Let us bracket the question of individualism, and consider the example that Peacocke uses to argue that a level of cognitively individuated sense is needed to individuate meanings finely enough:

> It is possible that there is a language with a semantically and syntactically unstructured word W for the shape perceived as a regular-diamond (same length sides, right angles). This shape is, at the level of reference, the same shape as a square. But it can be informative that squares are Ws. The story can be developed in such a way as to make it compelling that the understanding-condition for W mentions shapes perceived as diamonds. Yet W and "square" have the same character.

What Peacocke means by W being "a word for the shape perceived as a regular-diamond" is not entirely clear. He does not mean that a shape ceases to be a W when it ceases to be perceived as a regular-diamond, so what connection does he intend to stipulate between the word W and being perceived as a regular-diamond? It is tempting to distinguish between "square" and "regular-diamond" by contrasting *oriented-shapes* with ordinary shapes: geometrically, oriented-shape is invariant under translations but not under rotations whereas ordinary shape is invariant under both translations and rotations. In a given plane, rotating a token square (two sides horizontal) through 45° gives a regular-diamond (one diagonal horizontal), the same in shape but different in oriented-shape. However, interpreting W and "square" as referring to oriented-shapes rather than ordinary shapes would make them differ in reference, which is not what Peacocke wants. Rather, we should imagine that, when shown a square oriented with two sides horizontal and asked "What shape is that?," if you say "A W" you answer truly, although perhaps infelicitously; likewise if you say "A square" when shown it with one diagonal horizontal. We should also imagine that speakers expect other speakers to prefer to use W when one orientation is salient and "square" when the other orientation is salient.

We might be able to develop the scenario in such a way that W and "square" carry different conventional implicatures about the orientation of the relevant token; the book explicitly allowed conventional implicature as a constituent of meaning (130, this volume). But Frege classifies differences in conventional implicature (such as that between "and" and "but") as differences in coloring, not in sense, because they make no difference to the truth-conditions of the sentences in which they occur. More generally, Peacocke has not explained what difference, if any, the difference between W and "square" makes to the truth-conditions of containing sentences. Without one, Frege would not count it as a difference in sense. As pointed out in the book, synonymous expressions can differ in ways that speakers expect each other to know about. One is expected to know about differences in sociolinguistic register, such as that between "gob" and "mouth," even though such differences hardly qualify as semantic (131, this volume). In the absence of any definite suggestion as to what role the difference between W and "square" might play in a systematic semantic theory for the language, we have no good reason to regard the difference as semantic.

The concern that Peacocke's invocation of senses in semantics is unsystematic is reinforced by his explicit acknowledgement of a category of expressions with reference but no sense. For the sense of a sentence is supposed to be recursively built up out of the senses of its constituent expressions. If some of those constituents lack senses, then the attempt to assign a complete sense to the sentence will fail. In Fregean terms, it will not express a complete Thought, even though it still has a truth-value, since it suffers from no corresponding reference failure. If the compositional semantic theory can smoothly handle those sentences without associating them with Thoughts, the role of Thoughts even for those sentences that do have them is likely to be marginal at best.

Finally, I turn to Peacocke's objection to one of my most extreme examples of someone linguistically competent with a logical constant yet highly deviant in their reasoning with it. Simon, a native speaker of English, regards both truth and indefiniteness as acceptable values for an assertion: what matters is to avoid falsity.[3] Simon also endorses Kleene's weak three-valued tables for evaluating complex sentences

---

[3]   The example is also discussed in Section 12.2. For convenience, relevant points are repeated here.

with indefinite constituents, on which indefiniteness in a part always infects the whole. Thus he rejects the standard rule of conjunction-elimination, since it can lead from an indefinite premise to a false conclusion, when the premise is the conjunction of a false conjunct with an indefinite conjunct (98, this volume). Peacocke objects that Simon lacks general linguistic competence, since he has an inadequate grasp of the practice of assertion, which – Peacocke and I agree – is governed by the rule that one should assert A only if one knows A. Therefore, according to Peacocke, "no one who thinks A is indefinite should be sincerely asserting A."

The matter is not so straightforward. If Simon applies the spirit of Kleene's tables to knowledge ascriptions, he may treat "I know A" as indefinite when A is indefinite, and faithful to his own principles assert "I know A." Thus he may not regard his assertion of A as violating the knowledge rule. Furthermore, conscious acceptance of the knowledge rule is no precondition for linguistic competence. Quite a few philosophers consciously reject the knowledge rule without ceasing to be competent speakers of English, just as someone can play a game while partially misunderstanding its rules. The question is whether Simon's attempts to employ the speech act of assertion will be so deviant as to undermine his engagement in the normal practice of assertion. However, many linguistically competent philosophers have theoretical views that would, unchecked, lead to wildly deviant practice (for example, those who think that no vague sentence is ever strictly speaking true). Typically, they survive by invoking a variety of pragmatic fixes to adjust their practice until it comes within the bounds of the normal. Certainly Simon will not feel obliged to assert *everything* he takes to be indefinite, just as Peacocke and I do not feel obliged to assert everything we take ourselves to know. Perhaps Simon will commit some fallacies or at least make some horribly *ad hoc* moves in adjusting his theory and his practice towards each other. That would not bother me, since my concern is not to defend the truth of Simon's theories. I reject them as false, just as Peacocke does. My concern is just to insist that Simon's deviant theorizing is consistent with his linguistic competence. Peacocke's comments do not show that it is not.

Over recent years, theorists of concepts have tended gradually to water down their once-substantive conditions on concept possession in the face of counter-examples. Despite Peacocke's extended labors, it is doubtful that what remains has enough explanatory power to pay its way.

Acknowledgment

This section first appeared as part of my contribution to a symposium on the first edition of the book in *Philosophy and Phenomenological Research* (Williamson 2011b).

12.4   Reply to Miščević

As Nenad Miščević indicates in "An Uncomfortable Armchair" (Miščević 2013), the main line of argument in the second half of the first edition grew out of a talk I gave to a 2002 workshop on intuition and epistemology at the University of Fribourg, in which we both participated (Miščević 2004, Williamson 2004a). The original talk was far more optimistic about the usefulness of the category of intuition even than my 2004 paper. I set out with the idea of treating "intuit" as a *sui generis* factive mental state operator comparable to "perceive" and "remember," in the sense of *Knowledge and its Limits* (Williamson 2000a: 34–40). Thus "S intuits that P" is semantically unanalyzable but entails "P," and indeed "S knows that P." Formally, such an account is straightforward. What disturbed me somewhat as I prepared the talk, and much more as I started to write it up afterwards, was the difficulty of finding clean examples. Whatever I tried substituting for "P," the knowledge at issue turned out on reflection to involve elements that made the use of the term "intuition" quite misleading. It dawned on me, uncomfortably, that the problem was not my inability to think of good examples but rather the failure of the category of intuition to cut at the epistemological joints. The sneer quotes around the word "intuitions" in the title of the 2004 paper expressed my disillusion.

Miščević defends the category of intuition with what he calls the Moderate Voice-of-Competence view (MoVoC). Although MoVoC contrasts in spirit with my 2002 account, some of the problems it faces are similar; others are different.

MoVoC identifies intuitions in a core sense with the deliverances of various domain-specific, more or less modular "competencies" that normal adult humans are claimed to possess. In Miščević paper, such competencies are postulated for the linguistic, spatial-geometric, mathematical, metaphysical, epistemological, and moral domains. According to MoVoC, their deliverances, intuitions, are judgments or inclinations to judgment about the domains at issue, not about the words or concepts we use in talking or thinking about those domains (compare the face value interpretations that I defend against Trobok's criticisms). In a typical thought experiment, what such an intuition contributes to the verdict is separable from the contribution of background general knowledge. MoVoC's ability to discern such structure is held up as one of its advantages over an undifferentiated holism.

To illustrate how straightforwardly we can separate intuitions from background knowledge, Miščević gives 7** (his label):

> (7**) If John had stolen money from a totally drunk person at a party, that would have been morally unacceptable.

He explains (II.A.3[1]):

> What one needs to judge 7** is some moral competence (practical reason, moral feeling, moral sense, whatever you like); the empirical knowledge about money and about effects of drink is clearly distinguishable from the moral point.

Since the moral point is so easy to distinguish, the reader may assume that Miščević has distinguished it, and captured it in 7**. But 7** depends on background non-moral knowledge. For example, imagine a society in which it is common knowledge that people who get totally drunk at parties usually end the night by paying to sexually abuse and torture children, and that the only effective way to stop them is by stealing their money. In those circumstances, presumably, our moral competence does not tell us that it would be morally unacceptable to steal money from a totally drunk person at a party. Thus 7** does not distinguish a purely moral point from background non-moral knowledge. But 7** was supposed to be a case for which the distinction is easy to make.

We could try refining 7**, to purify it of all such non-moral elements. However, the prospects of success are dim. One strategy is to try to load all the relevant non-moral assumptions into the antecedent of the conditional. But that is a virtually endless process. There is no limit to the complexity of potentially relevant non-moral factors. Moreover, if the deliverances of a moral sense really play a causal role in human life, they must be of humanly tractable complexity, closer to

---

[1]   All such references are to sections in Miščević 2013.

7** than to its imagined refinements. An alternative strategy is to try to abstract some comparatively simple, very general non-moral feature sufficient for moral unacceptability that stealing money from a totally drunk person at a party would have in our circumstances, and put that feature in the antecedent. But that would involve constructive moral theorizing, whereas the intuitional data are supposed to "involve no theory and very little proto-theory" (I). Moreover, many of our particular moral judgments – such as "Hitler was evil" – have much greater epistemic probability for us than any general moral principle from which we could derive them, using relevant non-moral auxiliary premises. To treat knowledge of the particular moral truths as epistemically dependent on knowledge of the more speculative general moral principles is to get the epistemology back to front.[2]

If a moral sense is a cognitive capacity that supplies moral premises independent of non-moral cognition to ordinary moral judgment, then we have no moral sense. Of course, we have the cognitive capacity to make moral judgments, both online and offline. Seeing John stealing money from a totally drunk person at a party, we judge "That is morally unacceptable." Imagining John stealing money from a totally drunk person at a party, we judge "That would be morally unacceptable." But none of that requires a moral module of the sort Miščević postulates.[3]

The preceding considerations also undermine Miščević attempt to use MoVoC to uphold some sort of *prima facie a priori* status for verdicts on thought experiments in ethics, such as 7**. Presumably, what people usually do when they get totally drunk at a party is not an *a priori* matter.

Similar arguments apply to an epistemological module, which Miščević also postulates. He says that Gettier cases "seem to unearth our original and deep seated understanding of what knowledge is" (Miščević 2013, section III), but does not attempt to articulate that understanding. For reasons explained in the first edition, our verdicts

---

[2]   Miščević (II.A.3) suggests that I am inconsistent in criticizing such factorizing (see 194, this volume) while practicing it myself (188, this volume). What I am doing in the relevant passage is arguing that the verdict on a thought experiment is not a conceptual truth, which is not factorizing in the relevant sense.

[3]   See McGrath 2004 for relevant further discussion of moral epistemology.

on specific Gettier cases are not purely epistemological, just as our verdict on 7** is not purely moral. Miščević himself insists that our original untutored responses to Gettier cases are highly specific and precede "more general insights" (end of II.A.1): I agree, but the point makes MoVoC's postulation of purely epistemological premises for those verdicts all the more implausible.[4] Miščević attempt to use Mo-VoC to uphold some sort of limited *prima facie a priori* status for verdicts on thought experiments in epistemology is also undermined.

We have contingently reliable recognitional capacities for both moral and epistemological qualities, but that does not involve having a moral or epistemological competency in Miščević's sense. The cognitive preconditions for making a recognition judgment are not built into the content of the judgment itself, and the subject may be utterly incapable of articulating them. Ethics and epistemology are two of the branches of philosophy in which thought experiments have been most salient. In neither case do our verdicts on them derive from intuitions as characterized by MoVoC. The argument can be generalized to other branches of philosophy.

The case of mathematics is a little different. Many people know many truths of pure mathematics, such as those of arithmetic, whereas pure ethics and pure epistemology are in far less advanced states. But the difference does not help MoVoC. For, blatantly, knowledge of pure mathematics varies massively with cultural circumstances, whereas Miščević seems to regard his modules as innate. If there is an innate mathematical module, why do we have to go to school to learn its deliverances? Of course, children may struggle to learn the grammar

[4] Miščević worries that my formalization of the verdict on a Gettier case with universal quantifiers (188, this volume) over-intellectualizes it by giving it an unrealistically general content. However, as explained on page 186 (this volume), keeping the original fictional names ("Smith," "Jones") in formalizing the thought experiment would be even more problematic, since then the verdict would arguably fail to express a proposition. The natural solution is to replace them by quantified variables. A direct treatment of thought experiments with fictional names would be even more complex, since it would involve discussing both the semantics of fiction and its interaction with the semantics of modality (to explain how fictions can be used to refute a non-fictional theory about knowledge). In doing the semantics of natural languages, it is commonplace to represent the truth-conditions of apparently simple sentences with formulas of a perspicuous formal language that look very different from anything of which native speakers are conscious.

of their native language when it is taught as an explicit theory. But the cases of language and mathematics are quite unlike. For virtually all mature humans have implicit mastery of the highly complex grammar of a natural language, which informs their judgments of well-formedness, whereas nothing comparable holds for mathematics. Without specific mathematical training, our mathematical judgments may not be much better off than our ethical and epistemological judgments.[5]

Miščević has failed to anchor the category of intuition in modularity or domain-specific competence. He may be forced much further towards "undifferentiated holism" than he would like. However, he still has an alternative preliminary characterization of intuitions, on which he lays less weight, in more traditional terms of "their non-inferential, self-evident, clear and distinct character" (III). For that characterization does not rely on modularity.

By "self-evident" Miščević seems not to mean anything technical, such as "knowable merely by being entertained," since he appeals to "our intuition that ordinary material objects exist" (II.A.2). The reading of that phrase relevant to the original context is de dicto rather than de re: the alleged intuition is that there are ordinary material objects; it is not, of some particular ordinary material objects, that there are such things as them. Presumably, one cannot know that there are ordinary material objects merely by entertaining the proposition that there are ordinary material objects. Nor does Miščević seem to mean "clear and distinct" in its technical Cartesian sense. Perhaps his description "self-evident, clear and distinct" can be paraphrased simply and informally as "obvious." But what is the connection between intuition and obviousness? Amongst friends of intuition, it is not uncommon to speak of some intuitions as being firmer or less tentative than others. Obvious and non-obvious judgments can come from the very same source. From that perspective, obviousness looks more like a characteristic of those intuitions on which they would most confidently rely, rather than a precondition for being an intuition in the first place.

Even "non-inferential" is less straightforward than it looks. For in what sense is our intuition that there are ordinary material objects

---

[5] However, Miščević makes an unnecessary concession in suggesting that the conditional "If twelve people had come to the party, more than eleven people would have come to the party" depends on the assumption that partygoers do not fuse (II.A.3); "Twelve Fs G" entails "More than eleven Fs G" whatever weird changes Fs can undergo.

non-inferential? It may not be deduced by existential generalization from any particular premise of the form "o_1, ..., o_n are ordinary material objects," but we reach very few of our beliefs by deduction in the strict sense from prior premises. Even a scientist's educated judgment that one theory is better supported than another by a mixed body of evidence is unlikely to be deductive in that sense. If Miščević means "inferential" in the strict sense, then characterizing intuitions as non-inferential tells us very little. On the other hand, if he means "inferential" in a looser sense that applies to any belief that somehow depends on prior beliefs, then the alleged general intuition that there are ordinary material objects may well *be* inferential, through its dependence on a host of more specific prior beliefs, for example that there are hands and feet, mountains and rivers, sticks and stones.

Thus Miščević auxiliary modularity-independent characterization offers little help in demarcating a useful category of intuition. Since his main modularity-based characterization is also in trouble, he has given us no good reason to indulge in "intuition"-talk. In passages that he quotes, I argue that we have good reason *not* to indulge in it, because its function in much philosophical discourse is to fudge issues about the nature of our evidence in philosophy. When philosophers say "I have the intuition that P," it is typically unclear whether what they are advancing as evidence is the putative non-psychological fact that P or the putative psychological fact that they have the intuition that P.[6] Typically, the former is directly relevant to the philosophical question but easy to contest; the latter is harder to contest but not directly relevant.[7] Miščević gives examples in which "intuition"-talk does not serve that obfuscatory function (II.A.2). He is right that it does not *have* to insinuate any psychologization of our data. But my objection was not that it has to but that it typically *does*, as a contingent tendency of current philosophical discourse. Of course, if it also picked out an important psychological kind, the best policy

---

[6]   The phrase "have the intuition that" is to be read non-factively.

[7]   Miščević suggests that in describing facts as contestable I am treating them as beliefs rather than facts, since they can turn out not to be facts (II.A.2). That is not so. The fact that P is contestable because someone may contest it, in the sense of (falsely) denying that P. No fact ever turns out not be a fact, although someone may falsely believe that it has turned out not to be a fact that P, and indeed it has turned out to be a fact that not P.

might be to continuing use it while remaining on guard against the psychologizing tendency. But since the best efforts of Miščević and many others have failed to pin down any such kind, another good reason not to indulge in "intuition"-talk is to avoid the presupposition that we are dealing with a significant psychological kind.[8]

I turn to Miščević questions at the end of II.A.2 about my positive account of the epistemology of modality and of thought experiments. In the first edition, I argue that our ordinary cognitive capacity to handle counterfactual conditionals carries with it the cognitive capacity to handle ascriptions of metaphysical modalities, at no extra cost.[9] In that case, retorts Miščević, "ordinary capacities have extraordinary powers, and they should be accounted for." But why is any special accounting needed? Consider an analogy with logic. Suppose that our ordinary logical capacities include a capacity to apply the rules of some standard system of natural deduction in arguing from contingent premises to contingent conclusions, all about our local environment. Then by the very same rules we can argue from no premises to a necessary logical truth. For example, we can deduce the conclusion $C \to C$ by conditional proof. No special explanation is needed, beyond the proof itself. Similarly, on my account, the very same procedures that we use to evaluate ordinary counterfactual conditionals can also be used to evaluate the "extraordinary" counterfactual conditionals that are equivalent to ascriptions of metaphysical modalities. No special explanation is needed, beyond the sort of details supplied in the first edition.

It might be objected: the reliability of our ordinary procedures when applied to ordinary cases is no reason to expect them to be reliable when applied to extraordinary cases. Without further support, however, that is just inductive skepticism. Compare the claim that the reliability of our ordinary procedures when applied to past cases is no reason to expect them to be reliable when applied to future cases. To make the doubt serious, the objector must base it on some cognitively pertinent difference between the extraordinary cases and the ordinary

---

[8]   This line of objection to "intuition"-talk is pursued further in Sections 10.3 to 10.5.

[9]   Contrary to Miščević's claim that I need "some very strong assumptions" about the logic of counterfactuals to derive the rules for the necessity operator from it (II.A.3), the counterfactual logic I use to derive the standard modal system KT is in fact quite weak: for instance, it is significantly weaker than David Lewis's preferred counterfactual logic (see 295–303, this volume).

ones. Extraordinariness itself is not enough. After all, in comparison to ordinary proofs with some contingent premises, proofs with no premises are extraordinary, but not in a way that casts serious doubt on the reliability in extraordinary proofs of standard principles of natural deduction already found to be reliable in ordinary proofs. Since Miščević proposes no such difference, I will not pursue the matter here.

Instead, Miščević poses another question for me: are only philosophical intuitions "ordinary?" He draws a potential contrast with moral, mathematical, and linguistic intuitions, for example, and asks whether I want to give a uniform account of both philosophical and non-philosophical intuitions. Although unhappy with the "intuition"-talk, I can say this much. Given the obvious differences between morality, mathematics, and language as subject matters, of course one cannot expect a uniform account to cover all of them in detail, let alone philosophy too. At a more general level of description, however, the same points apply to all of them. Typically, we start with online judgments about perceptually presented cases. We judge actions that we have just witnessed as good or bad; we classify physical objects in front of us by shape, manipulate them to work out which fit inside which, and count collections of them; we hear some people speaking differently from others and comment on the differences. In imagination, we learn to apply the same cognitive skills offline, to hypothetical cases. For example, in deciding what to do, we judge whether an action we could take would be good or bad. By mental manipulation we work out how to make an object of a sort we have never seen, and how to count collections of absent objects. We judge whether a string of words in a foreign language would sound well-formed before uttering it out loud. On the basis of such ordinary cognitive skills, we occasionally go on to think in more general and theoretical terms. Intellectual disciplines emerge: mathematics, philosophy (including moral philosophy), linguistics. In these respects, philosophy is not at all exceptional.

As Miščević notes, he and I agree on many significant points about the nature of philosophy. I hope that they include those made in the preceding paragraph. Indeed, he offers a beautiful illustration of them in the case of mathematics: "understanding the inverse of a function by *imagining* its spatial representation. Our imagination moves from one imagined set to the other, and back, and we can assume that it had been honed through a lifetime of bodily movement in opposite directions" (II.B). Of course, the notion of a (one-one) function and of its inverse are general enough to be used in philosophy as well as in mathematics, for example in discussion of the mind-body problem. Thus the case also shows how a cognitive skill on which philosophy relies may originate in bodily movement. Philosophical methods are rooted in ordinary cognitive skills.[10]

Acknowledgment

This section first appeared as part of my contribution to a symposium on the first edition of the book in the *Croatian Journal of Philosophy* (Williamson 2013g). See also the acknowledgment to Section 12.6.

---

[10]   I confine to this footnote my responses to some specific points Miščević makes about my critique of the *a priori–a posteriori* distinction (II.B). (a) He quotes a passage in which I envisage two people disagreeing as to whether knowledge entails belief as a result of subtle differences between their courses of experience, for instance in the cases to which they hear the words "know" and "believe" applied (170, this volume). He tentatively interprets me as meaning that they use the word "know" with different senses. As he notes, that would sit ill with semantic externalism about meaning that I invoke elsewhere in the book. But in the sentence immediately preceding the one he quotes I say that it would not be plausible to accuse those philosophers who take the minority view that knowledge does not entail belief of failing to understand the words "know" and "believe" (in their public senses, of course). The view I am expressing is exactly the same as in the discussion of epistemological analyticity. Sharp differences in the inferences one treats as valid with words do not entail any difference whatsoever in the senses with which those words are used. (b) Miščević criticizes an example I give in my later, more developed critique of the *a priori–a posteriori* distinction (Williamson 2013b). It involves Norman, who assents to (*) "All crimson things are red" and (**) "All recent volumes of *Who's Who* are red" on the basis of similar imaginative exercises, even though his knowledge of * would normally be classified as *a priori* and his knowledge of ** as *a posteriori*. Miščević objects that if Norman was shown a crimson patch as a sample of "red" then the defender of the distinction can hold that * is built into Norman's concept of "red." However, this neglects the fact that there are many different shades of crimson. Even if Norman learns from the original ostension that all things of the given shade of crimson are red, that does not entail *. On the other horn of his dilemma, Miščević suggests that if Norman was not shown a crimson patch as a sample of "red," his ability to classify crimson shades as red must depend on his having completed something like an inner color solid. But, for the sake of the example, there is no need to suppose that Norman either associates "red" and "crimson" with long exhaustive lists of their maximally specific shades or literally has a quasi-spatial analogue model of color space in his head. He may simply associate the words with relevant focal shades and have a capacity to judge comparative similarity in color, online and offline – which is just what my example requires.

12.5   Reply to Smokrović

In the first edition and some of its predecessor articles (Williamson 2003a, 2006b), I attacked the core tenet of inferentialism: that understanding some words, or grasping the concepts they express, requires a willingness to assent to some key sentences or inferences in which they occur. On the canonical version of inferentialism, assent itself is necessary for understanding when those sentences or inferences come into play. On a weaker, dispositionalist version, only a disposition to assent is necessary. One can have a disposition to do something yet not do it even when the moment comes, because another disposition intervenes to inhibit the first. For example, you may be disposed to assent to a rude comment about someone but not assent because you know that his mother is within earshot. I attacked both the canonical and the dispositionalist versions of inferentialism. In his commentary "Are Dispositions to Believe Constitutive for Understanding?," (Smokrović 2013), Nenad Smokrović accepts my critique of canonical inferentialism but defends dispositional inferentialism. He brings out clearly why the latter doctrine is harder to refute than the former; he may well have identified the best ground for inferentialists to fight on. He is in any case right that unconscious inferential dispositions are cognitively important.

However, dispositional inferentialism may not serve all the purposes for which philosophers have appealed to canonical inferentialism. For instance, Paul Boghossian uses the assumption that we cannot understand some words without assenting to key inferences involving them in his attempt to explain our epistemic right to make those inferences (Boghossian 2003). If we *can* understand those words without assenting to those inferences, because we can overrule our disposition to assent, the prospects for such an explanation are even worse. For a dispositional inferentialist, our understanding still leaves us a choice as to whether, all things considered, we make the inference. If we do make it, we cannot simply plead necessity as our defense. Thus canonical inferentialism was more pertinent to my critique of Boghossian (Williamson 2003a). Similarly, if there were inferences to which our understanding of the relevant words bound us to assent, they could play a far more robust role in the methodology of philosophy than inferences over which we had reflective discretion. However, Smokrović is not concerned to uphold those specific applications of inferentialism. He simply undertakes to defend the truth of dispositional inferentialism itself. That is where I will take issue with him.

My counterexamples to dispositional inferentialism involved characters who originally came to understand words of their native language in the normal way, but then through a process of theoretical reflection reach the conclusion that the sentences or inferences at issue were unsound, and so withdraw their original assent. Smokrović agrees that in so doing they do not cease to understand the words or to grasp the concepts supposedly expressed. So far, nothing excludes the dispositionalist hypothesis that they still retain a sub-personal *disposition* to assent, whose manifestation has been inhibited by higher-level processing. We may assume that as they become used to their new view, they are no longer conscious of any such disposition, but that does not entail its absence from their unconsciowus cognitive structures. Nevertheless, to postulate such an unconscious cognitive disposition is to give a hostage to scientific fortune. In the first edition, I argued that there is scant evidence that such a disposition must survive. Smokrović seems more concerned to argue that a disposition *might* survive than to show that one actually does so.

There is much with which I agree in Smokrović's general account of dispositions as capable of surviving as sub-personal even when overridden, and of beliefs and assent as typically unreflective. My disagreement with him comes at a more specific level.

To clarify the issues, I will consider a different example. In a system of natural deduction for first-order logic, a simple form of the elimination rule ∃-E for the existential quantifier says that if one has derived a conclusion C from a premise A(c) and some or no auxiliary premises, then one can derive C from the premise ∃x A(x) and the auxiliary premises if any, where A(c) results from substituting the constant c for all free occurrences of the variable x in A(x), <u>provided that c does not occur in A(x), the auxiliary premises, or the conclusion C</u>. The constant c is used as though it named an "arbitrary" verifier of the existential premise (which may in fact have many verifiers, or none). Let ∃-E* be the corresponding rule without the underlined restriction. Suppose that when Edward first learns the existential quantifier, he does not realize the need for the underlined restriction on the elimination rule, so he adopts the simple rule ∃-E*, not the correct rule ∃-E. (For present purposes, it does not matter whether at this stage he counts as understanding the quantifier ∃.) At first, everything goes fine; when Edward applies his rule, the restriction happens to be met anyway, so his inferential practice appears normal. However, since A(t) counts as trivially derivable from itself without auxiliary premises, Edward then realizes that he can use his rule to derive A(t) from ∃x A(x). But that is a disaster. For instance, since Edward believes ∃x x = 1, he derives the conclusion 0 = 1. Since he also believes 0 ≠ 1, he has landed in contradiction. Rather than becoming a follower of Parmenides or Graham Priest, he reflects on his predicament and comes to realize that his rule of existential elimination is invalid; he needs to add the underlined restriction. He therefore rejects ∃-E* and accepts the correct rule ∃-E instead.

Does Edward still have a sub-personal disposition to reason by the incorrect rule ∃-E*? He *might*, for all that has been said so far. But he need not. On one legitimate continuation of the example, he loses even the sub-personal disposition to reason by ∃-E*. That is a genuine possibility. Let us take the example that way. After he identifies his mistake, Edward is disposed to reason just by the correct rule ∃-E. He lacks even a sub-personal disposition to assent to an instance of ∃-E* that violates the restriction on ∃-E. Although dispositions are not destroyed simply by being overridden, they can be destroyed.

For clarity, the example concerned a formal language. However, one can easily describe a structurally similar example concerning a natural language. The rule ∃-E corresponds to a natural rule of deduction for a natural language. The general moral is that through reflection and habituation it is possible eventually to lose even the sub-personal disposition to reason by a given rule.

Now compare Edward with Peter and Stephen in the original cases (Chapter 4). Whereas Edward starts with an invalid elimination rule for the existential quantifier and restricts it to form a valid elimination rule, they start with a valid introduction rule for the universal quantifier and restrict it to form introduction rules that are unnecessarily weak, although still valid. Peter's restriction avoids assent to vacuous universal generalizations; Stephen's restriction avoids assent to universal generalizations that involve borderline cases in a specific way. From an internal psychological perspective, however, the cases are very similar. Initially, all three reason by a given rule. Subsequent reflection convinces them that the rule is invalid, and requires a restriction. By the end of the process, all three reason by the restricted rule, and have lost even the disposition to reason by the original unrestricted rule. We have no reason to exclude any of the cases as impossible. Even though some inferential dispositions may be quite robust in human psychology, they are not immutable of necessity.

Once Peter and Stephen have lost the disposition to reason by the original unrestricted rule of universal introduction, do they still understand the universal quantifier? In the first edition, I argued at length that they do, on grounds connected with the nature of understanding and the social determination of meaning. Smokrović's paper provides no criticism of that part of my argument, which I will therefore not repeat.

One further consideration deserves notice. In a very suggestive paper, the late Paolo Casalegno pointed out that inferential dispositions do not exhaust the dispositions relevant to understanding logical constants. We also use such expressions to construct complex descriptions of what we perceive: "Some of the things in front of me are red, and none of them are green." He gives the example of someone who lacks inferential dispositions as a result of some cognitive disability, but still manifests understanding of the logical constants by using them to describe visually presented scenes (Casalegno 2004: 407). Although Boghossian has doubted the possibility of such a case, his criticisms can be met (Boghossian 2012, Williamson 2012). If inferential dispositions are highly modular, as Smokrović conjectures, the inferential disability could be much more localized, and the case correspondingly even easier to envisage. Since specific inferential dispositions ground just one aspect of our use of logical constants, they are all the less essential to our understanding.

In the light of these considerations, I maintain my rejection of dispositional as well as canonical inferentialism.

Acknowledgment

This section first appeared as part of my contribution to a symposium on the first edition of the book in the *Croatian Journal of Philosophy* (Williamson 2013g). See also the acknowledgment to Section 12.6.

12.6   Reply to Trobok

One theme of the first edition is that philosophical questions are normally to be taken at face value. For example, when metaphysicians ask "What is causality?," they are primarily asking about the nature of causality itself, a worldly relation between events, not about the word "cause" or a concept it expresses. Even if a sentence used in philosophical discourse is analytic in some sense, it is still to be given its literal meaning, not reinterpreted as being about words or concepts. For example, "Bachelors are unmarried" is just as much a generalization about bachelors as "Bachelors are untidy is." Like mathematics, philosophy makes generalizations from the armchair about a world of which the armchair is one tiny part. On this theme, I find myself in agreement with Nenad Miščević but in disagreement with Majda Trobok.

In "Defending Analyticity" (Trobok 2013), she starts by arguing that the precedent of mathematics does not help me, because mathematics itself is about concepts. She gives two separable considerations in favor of that claim, with which I will deal in turn.

Trobok's first point is that, on a Fregean analysis, numbers are ascribed to concepts rather than objects. For instance, the purely mathematical statement "There are four prime numbers between 10 and 20" ascribes the number four to the concept *prime number between 10 and 20*. More generally, Frege interprets second-order quantifiers, binding variables in predicate position, as quantifiers over concepts. I accept standard arguments for axiomatizing arithmetic and set theory in a second-order language, in order properly to capture the intended strength of the axioms. Thus, on the Fregean analysis, both arithmetic and set theory routinely involve quantification over concepts. However, none of this poses any threat to what I say about mathematics. For the reading of "concept" ("*Begriff*") relevant to Frege's texts is quite different from those used in the first edition and by most contemporary philosophers. In current philosophical discourse, "concept" means something like "mode of presentation" or "mental representation." Thus, when I deny that metaphysicians are primarily interested in concepts of causation, rather than in the worldly relation itself, I am denying that they are primarily interested in modes of presentation or mental representations of that relation. But "concepts" on the

534 Concepts, Understanding, Analyticity

Fregean reading are *not* modes of presentation, or mental representations, or anything like them. In Frege's terms, modes of presentation are *senses*, whereas concepts belong to the realm of reference, not of sense, and have still less to do with mental representations. For example, although the two predicative expressions "_ is part of Hesperus" and "_ is part of Phosphorus" have different senses, and correspond to different mental representations, they refer to the same concept, the function mapping every part of Hesperus (= Phosphorus) to truth and every other object to falsity. More generally, Frege treats functions, and in particular concepts, extensionally: the analogue of identity for functions is returning the same values for the same arguments, so in particular the analogue of identity for concepts is coextensiveness. By contrast, distinct modes of presentation or mental representations may be coextensive. The Fregean interpretation of mathematics is incompatible with a metaconceptual interpretation in the modern sense of "concept," the only one I will use henceforth.

Trobok's second point is that it is often natural to speak of mathematical axioms as introducing a concept. That holds even on a non-Fregean reading of "concept." But it is not specific to mathematics. For instance, we might describe a physicist as introducing a technical concept of force by laying down some principles about it. Clearly, that does not commit us to the implausible claim that the physicist is primarily interested in the concept of force rather than in the nature of force itself. After all, we might equally well describe her as introducing a technical *term* "force" by laying down some principles about it, but that does not commit us to the claim that she is primarily interested in the term "force" rather than in the nature of force itself. The point is simply that the best way to get people to understand a new scientific term is often by setting forth some axioms involving it. Once they understand the new term, they will be able to take those axioms at face value, as literally about that to which the term refers, which is the reading that fits the role those principles play in ordinary scientific practice. That provides no evidence for the idea that the subject matter of the science itself is metalinguistic or metaconceptual.

Consequently, I am unconvinced by Trobok's case that mathematics is about concepts. I continue to regard mathematics as an impressive paradigm of a non-metaconceptual, non-metalinguistic, armchair discipline. The rest of her paper concentrates mainly on arguing by various means for a metaconceptual reading of analytic sentences, as a precedent for such a reading of philosophical discourse.

Consider these three sentences:

(1) Every vixen is a female fox.
(2) Every female fox is a female fox.
(3) Every vixen is a terrestrial renate.

Here "vixen" is synonymous with "female fox" (and "renate" with "creature with a kidney"). For present purposes we may assume that (1) and (2) are analytic, at least in the sense of being synonymous with the logical truth (2), and that (3) is not analytic in any relevant sense. By the standard compositional semantics for English, (3) has a literal reading as an ordinary first-order universal generalization. In exactly the same way, (1) and (2) have literal readings as first-order universal generalizations with the same overall syntactic and semantic structure as (3). That much is hardly in doubt. Of course, Trobok could still argue that for special reasons in some contexts (1) must be interpreted non-literally, or perhaps that all strings like (1)-(3) are ambiguous in English and have a second literal reading as something other than first-order universal generalizations. However, such an argument would require quite specific semantic or pragmatic considerations of a sort that I do not find in the paper.

In the first edition, I remark as an objection to a metalinguistic reading of (1) that vixens would have been female foxes no matter how words had been used. At the end of section 1 of her paper, Trobok responds to that objection. She correctly points out that the syntactically individuated sentence (1) expresses a falsehood in an alien language in which "vixen" means *female cat* but all other words mean the same as in English. However, she suggests that we disagree with the aliens as to whether vixens are female foxes. We do not. The scenario as she sets it up involves no disagreement between us and the aliens. To be clear, let $(1)_E$ be the English sentence (1) and $(1)_A$ be the Alien sentence (1). The aliens correctly dissent from $(1)_A$. If we interpret them as thereby dissenting from $(1)_E$, we misinterpret them, precisely because the Alien word "vixen" differs in meaning and extension from the English word "vixen." They are not denying that every vixen is a female fox, for every vixen *is* a female fox, so if they were denying it they would be in error while speaking their native language, which they are not in this situation any more than we are. Of course, if at first we and the aliens do not realize that we mean different things by "vixen," we may get into a silly argument with them in which each side makes false statements, literally interpreted, when speaking the language of the other. However, the possibility of such trivial misunderstandings does not help Trobok, because it fails to provide any possibility of not every vixen being a female fox. Although we could have spoken a language like Alien, in those circumstances every vixen would still have been a female fox, although (1)$_A$ would have expressed the false proposition that every female cat is a female fox rather than the true propositions that every female fox is a female fox. Provided that one takes care with the distinction between using an expression and mentioning it, the possibility of alternative stipulations poses no threat to my argument.

In section 2 of her paper, Trobok sketches an epistemic objection to the first-order reading of (1), along the lines that it would make (1) unknowable, or at least not knowable *a priori*. However, it is hard to see how any such objection could succeed. Just focus on the literal reading of (1) as a first-order universal generalization. If you are worried about some hidden complexity of English grammar, focus instead on a standard formalization of (1) in first-order logic. Now ask yourself whether it is true on that reading. Most of us recognize at once that it is, in a way that would be classified as *a priori* by those happy to apply that term. We have no epistemological difficulty with (1) on its first-order reading.

Section 3 of Trobok's paper culminates in the challenge to me to explain how we know (1) if, as I claim in the first edition, (1) is not epistemologically analytic: someone can understand (1) without being disposed to assent to it, because they espouse non-classical principles of logic. Of course, what one regards as an adequate answer to Trobok's challenge will depend on the general shape of one's epistemology, and so on issues beyond the scope of these remarks. I have argued elsewhere for a strongly externalist view of knowledge, with an emphasis on safety from error as a mark of knowledge (Williamson 2000a). Someone who employs standard natural deduction rules for classical logic can easily use them to derive (2), and thence derive (1) by treating "vixen" as interchangeable with "female fox," at least in non-quotational contexts. There is no reason why such a person should not count as safe from error and as satisfying any other reasonable externalist requirement on knowing. No metalinguistic or metaconceptual reflection is needed on their part. In particular, the knower need not wonder why the expressions "vixen" and "female fox" are interchangeable, or even entertain the thought that they are interchangeable; she need only be disposed to interchange them. Most ordinary knowledge involves no such logical or semantic reflection. Contrary to Trobok's claim, the knower does not "*have* to know at least a segment of the metasemantic story." Rather, the role of the metasemantic story is in *making* the knower safe from error, and so on, whether she appreciates that role or not. All of that is perfectly consistent with the literal reading of (1) as a first-order universal generalization. We can take logical truths and their synonyms at face value, just as we can normal stretches of philosophical discourse.

Acknowledgment

This section first appeared as part of my contribution to a symposium on the first edition of the book in the *Croatian Journal of Philosophy* (Williamson 2013g). My exchanges with Majda Trobok, Nenad Smokrović, and Nenad Miščević on themes from the first edition, at the University of Rijeka, the Inter-University Centre in Dubrovnik, and elsewhere, before and after its publication, have been a source of both intellectual pleasure and intellectual profit, at least for me and I hope for them too. In replying here to their thoughtful and sophisticated comments, I follow the usual and fruitful practice of focusing on points of disagreement. Nevertheless, the possibility of such focus on sharp points rather than blurred regions of disagreement indicates how much background agreement there is between us, on matters both philosophical and metaphilosophical.

13

Wittgensteinian Approaches

13.1 Reply to Moore

In his characteristically nuanced "Not to be Taken at Face Value" (Moore 2009), Adrian Moore expresses concern at "Williamson's lack of serious engagement with the history of philosophy." Although that is not the focus of his discussion, I will start with a comment on it. I noted that the book "touches on historical matters only glancingly" (10, this volume). For example, in my critique of the linguistic turn I abjured the attempt to trace all the forms it took in twentieth-century philosophy (13, this volume). Nevertheless, a looming background presence in the book is after all the history of philosophy: most notably, its *recent* history. For the history of philosophy did not stop forty years ago. A central motivation for writing the book was my sense that over the past forty years philosophy has developed in ways to which its inherited twentieth-century self-images cannot do justice (xxx, this volume). They are anachronisms; reliance on them betrays a lack of historical sensitivity, however much one discusses Kant or Wittgenstein. I stressed the need for a new narrative of the history of recent analytic philosophy, uncommitted to obsolescent assumptions about its direction, in order to make sense of its development over our own lifetimes (21, 24, this volume). Much of the evidence for the intellectual bankruptcy of the linguistic turn consists not in one-off arguments against it but in its historical record. That includes both the recent proliferation and flourishing of forms of philosophy that can only be forced into the linguistic turn by crassly Procrustean means and the repeated failure of its ablest proponents to respond fruitfully to objections: for instance, of Wittgenstein's followers to make good on the invocation of grammar in passages such

as the one that Moore displays as his epigraph. Similarly, the basis
for my characterization of anti-realist semantics as a degenerating
research program was largely historical, as befits Lakatos's concept
(286, this volume).

Moore's sympathies are anti-realist. As an example of an anti-
realist account of truth, he gives what he calls "the Wittgensteinian
View" of truth for mathematical discourse (unhistorically, without
attributing it to Wittgenstein). As he presents it, the view is too rudi-
mentary to constitute a serious alternative. It claims that "In asserting
a mathematical truth one is stating a rule, not saying how things are
independently of any such assertion," but it does not specify what the
rule is, or whether in making the assertion one is saying how things
are not independently of any such assertion, or what it is to make
assertive use of a sentence in which a mathematical component is
embedded within the scope of other operators (the standard Frege–
Geach problem), or what it is to ask a mathematical question, ... The
Wittgensteinian View also constrains the epistemology of mathematics: "nothing but a mathematical proof can establish a mathematical
truth." In defending this constraint, Moore claims that "empirical evidence is only ever evidence for an empirical conclusion." Faced with
apparent counterexamples, Moore says "In mathematical terms, the
empirical evidence establishes nothing." But there is a gap between
not *establishing* a mathematical proposition and not being *evidence*
for it. One can accept that in mathematics the agreed standard for assertion (and knowledge) is proof, while not trying to explain away all
the numerous cases in which most mathematicians would agree that
empirical evidence gives some nonconclusive support to mathematical propositions.[1]

In attempting to show how to "sidestep certainly apparently decisive objections" to the Wittgensteinian View, Moore acquiesces in the
charge that it makes the consistency of a mathematical theory a matter of stipulation: we adopt a rule "that guarantees the consistency
of Peano Arithmetic." Here as elsewhere, he leaves the content of the
rules he invokes unspecified. We could indeed add to a given proof
system for the language of Peano Arithmetic the rule that if one of **A**
and **B** is the negation of the other then nothing as long as a proof of **A**

---

[1] If all mathematical truths have probability 1, then the support will need to be understood non-probabilistically.

counts as a proof of **B**, which guarantees that **A** and **B** are never both provable in the *new* proof system. But that does nothing to guarantee that they were not both provable in the *old* proof system, without the extra rule, which was the question at issue. We can no more make the old system consistent by *fiat* than we can the system of the *Grundgesetze*. No doubt anti-realists can always "sidestep" objections in the sense in which defenders of astrology always can (243, this volume), but more than that is needed to maintain a view as a worthwhile protagonist in philosophical discussion.

Moore's main concern is the defensibility of an anti-realist view of philosophical discourse. He discusses my example, the original question "Was Mars always either dry or not dry?" Moore says that he "cannot hear that interrogative sentence, as used in that context [in which TW asks it], except as a question about the workings of the word 'dry' or the concept of dryness." Perhaps he cannot imagine why someone would ask it if they had no interest in words or concepts (I can), but the motivation for asking it should not be confused with the question's content. Moore does not dispute the argument in the book that a strict and literal reading of the original question according to its compositional semantics does not make the answer trivially obvious. So if we believe his profession of inability to hear the question in a non-metalinguistic, non-metaconceptual way, perhaps we should take it as just in his words "an autobiographical observation." However, he does have a more theoretical motivation for denying that the original question has the strict and literal content it appears to have. His theory runs roughly along these lines: when borderline cases come into play, no proposition is expressed. Given that Mars is a borderline case for the vague term "dry" with respect to some past time, the sentence "Mars was always either dry or not dry" fails to express a proposition on its strict and literal reading, and the original question correspondingly lacks strict and literal content (in the relevant context). By contrast, given that Mars clearly falls in the extension of "dry" with respect to the present, the sentence "Mars is dry" expresses a proposition on its strict and literal reading, and the question "Is Mars dry?" correspondingly has strict and literal content (in that context). Needless to say, such a view plays havoc with compositional semantics. Of the property of being dry, we can contentfully ask whether Mars has it but not whether Mars has always either had it or not had it. Standard semantic operations on the proposition strictly and literally expressed by "Mars is dry" in a given context somehow fail to yield a proposition to be strictly and literally expressed by "Mars was always either dry or not dry"; relevant forms of Evans's Generality Constraint will fail. Presumably this does not worry Moore: "I think language is messy." To some extent it is. But that does not justify giving up the attempt to achieve what systematic understanding we can of it at the first sign of difficulty. Moore would probably regard it as scientistic to point out that physicists do not proceed in that way ("I think the world is messy"). Linguists too are reluctant to shrug off systematic constraints as easily as Moore does.

Moore's final comments address my critique of epistemological conceptions of analyticity, in which I argue that even extreme logical unorthodoxy is compatible with using the relevant words with their usual meanings. According to him:

> *Strictly* speaking, when Graham Priest says, "There are true contradictions," he is violating rules that govern the workings of those words in the English language and is not using them with the meanings that these rules help to determine[.]

Moore does not specify exactly which words Priest is using with deviant meanings ("true?" "contradictions?" both? the sentence as a whole?) or what those deviant meanings are. Nor does he specify which rules of English Priest is violating. Is there a rule that simply forbids one to say "There are true contradictions," or is that prohibition derivable from more general rules of English, and if so what is their content? How does he handle the evidence in the book about normal speakers from the psychology of reasoning that looks unfavorable to his rule-based conception of logical understanding (105–9, this volume)? If one had no idea who Graham Priest was and overheard him in a pub saying "There are true contradictions," one might think at first that he was only saying that because he misunderstood the long word "contradiction." Once one starts talking to him, that hypothesis feels rather less attractive. Unconsidered initial judgments are not decisive in determining linguistic rules. Moore allows that Priest may count as using the words with their standard meanings "on a looser way of speaking," but the case is utterly unlike that of a language-learner whom it would be genuinely natural to describe as having only a partial understanding of the words. It is philosophical dogma, not respect for English, that prevents one from seeing that Priest is as linguistically competent with the words as any other normal speaker of the language.

Moore presents himself as representing an alternative way of doing philosophy to the one urged in this book: more humanistic, concerned to preserve unsystematic insights, respectful of the complexities of actual life and language, sensitive to deep differences in conversational and historical context and so responsive to areas of discourse whose underlying purposes need anti-realist treatment, in short *warmer*, by contrast with the cold scientism, the ahistorical, harshly systematic, uniformly realist theory-building that I represent. When one examines his text more closely, however, one finds that its unsystematic, unscientific air depends not on avoiding theoretical commitments but on avoiding making good on them. This is particularly clear in his repeated invocation of unspecified rules. If he were to state the content of the supposed rules, and provide some evidence that they are really in force, his claims would then be open to testing and challenge of kinds that only the evasiveness of his presentation now protects them from. He would become embroiled in just the kind of "scientific" discourse he shuns. The problem is not some individual failing on Moore's part. On the contrary, he is unusually conscientious and fair-minded to his opponents. The problem is with the subtradition he represents, from which he has inherited a style of discourse that effectively discourages the sort of systematic, painfully explicit and articulated questioning (not completely unfamiliar to the victims of Socrates) without which it is just too easy to get away with falsehoods.

Acknowledgment

This section first appeared as part of my contribution to a symposium on the first edition of the book in *Analysis Reviews* (Williamson 2009a). I thank Adrian Moore for his interesting comments, which help bring into relief some main themes of the book.

13.2 Reply to Horwich

In "Williamson's Philosophy of Philosophy" (Horwich 2011), Paul Horwich defends the idea that the proper business of philosophy is clarification rather than systematic theory-building. His target is my methodological sermon "Must Do Better," the afterword to the first edition, which he treats as based on a misconceived assimilation of philosophy to science.

On one point Horwich and I are agreed. Philosophy suffers from a shortage of established constraints of the sort required for a discipline to make scientific progress. For Horwich, this means that scientific progress is an inappropriate model for philosophy. To the contrary, I suggest that the shortage is not a total absence, that skill in science often consists in finding ingenious and surprising ways to extract answers to questions from constraints that seemed too elementary for the task, and that philosophy is no different in that respect.

As an example of philosophy, Horwich contrasts "traditional moral theory" with "the *empirical sciences*": "It isn't founded on *perception*; its central facts are not *contingent*; *causal explanation* seems to be out of place; and so does the very idea of *theoretical depth*" (italics in the original). The oddest claim in that passage is that the very idea of theoretical depth seems to be out of place in traditional moral theory. There is nothing strange in the idea that Kant's moral philosophy has more theoretical depth than Bentham's. Of course, some utilitarians will dissent, but probably by arguing that Bentham's moral philosophy has more theoretical depth than Kant's. Thus Horwich's final contrast between traditional moral theory and the empirical sciences seems to be a figment of his philosophical preconceptions, rather than something independently plausible. At first sight, his other three contrasts seem much less contentious. On further scrutiny, however, they turn out to be less clear-cut.

Horwich presupposes that the "central facts" of the empirical sciences, by contrast with those of traditional moral theory, are contingent. He does not mention Kripke's examples of the necessary *a posteriori*, such as the fact that gold is the element with atomic number 79. Recent philosophy of science has developed Kripke's suggestion that many scientific laws usually classified as physically but not metaphysically necessary may in fact be metaphysically necessary.[1] Even if they are merely physically necessary, Horwich does not say what the methodological significance of the contrast between physical and metaphysical necessity is supposed to be.

Perhaps Horwich has in mind that empirical science starts from observations of contingent facts. In that respect, however, it is not obviously different from moral theory. Perception is arguably a source of moral knowledge. In suitable circumstances one can literally see that someone is being cruel to a child, just as one can literally see that they are acting in anger and causing pain.[2] Such moral knowledge may be the starting point for moral theorizing, and a continuing constraint. Contingent facts about the Nazis are used as a touchstone in moral philosophy: a theory that cannot acknowledge that Hitler acted wrongly must be inadequate. Thus Horwich's claim that traditional moral theory is not founded on perception – in the broad sense in which his empirical sciences are founded on perception – is also dubious. Of course, specific claims to moral knowledge by perception are not beyond question; even if they are granted, they do not take us all the way by themselves to systematic moral theory. But the same goes for Horwich's empirical sciences. Specific claims to physical knowledge by perception are not beyond question; even if they are granted, they do not take us all the way by themselves to systematic physical theory.

Horwich's own description of the starting point of traditional moral theory is "intuitions." Presumably, he has in mind the results of thought experiments, which obviously play a larger role in contemporary moral philosophy than in the empirical sciences he lists (physics, biology, and psychology). He does not address the extended critique of talk of intuitions in the book, nor its positive analysis of thought experiments and their epistemology. On the latter, they typically involve offline applications of the very same skills in applying moral concepts that

---

[1]   Kripke 1980: 164, Bird 2007.

[2]   See McGrath 2004. It is not epistemologically plausible that one merely sees that they acted in non-moral way W and combines that knowledge with the necessary moral principle, known a priori, that whoever acts in way W acts cruelly to reach inferential moral knowledge that they acted cruelly. One may know the conclusion of the supposed inference without knowing the premises. Note also that no faculty dedicated to moral perception is being postulated.

are applied online in judging empirically encountered moral situations. The gulf between "perceptions" and "intuitions" is not as deep as Horwich assumes. After all, the epistemological position of moral philosophy would not be radically transformed if we set up trolley problems and other moral thought experiments in real life rather than the imagination, so that our judgments of them would constitute perceptions rather than intuitions. Of course, supposed moral perceptions are often more controversial than supposed physical perceptions, but Horwich has not begun to show that in this respect they differ in kind rather than in degree.

Thus Horwich's attempts to use perception and contingency to distinguish his empirical sciences from traditional moral theory misfire. His remaining criterion, causal explanation, may look more hopeful for distinguishing traditional moral theory in kind from empirical sciences. Causal explanation is surely not the goal of traditional moral theory. However, it is not obvious that causal explanation is the goal even of all empirical sciences. In fundamental physics, the primary aim may be to discover underlying physical laws. Although hypotheses about those laws figure in causal explanations, from the perspective of fundamental physics the point of those explanations may be to test the hypotheses rather than to explain the phenomena. Indeed, it is doubtful that the notion of cause figures in fundamental physics.[3] Although causal explanation surely plays some role in empirical sciences, it plays some role in traditional moral theory too. In a recent book on ethics, David Wiggins asks: "are we really to believe that the courage of a soldier or the charity (benevolence, kindness, considerateness …) of a Samaritan will not figure in any explanation of anything that exists or comes to pass?"[4] In political philosophy, it would be hard to mount a credible defense of some system of government without considering what effects it causally explains.[5] That an arrangement is unjust may help to explain causally why few of those who live under it thrive. In short, none of Horwich's four criteria establishes a difference in kind between traditional moral theory and the empirical sciences.

Horwich goes further by questioning both whether there are truths in the domain of philosophical theory and, even if there are, whether

[3] Russell 1913, Field 2003.
[4] Wiggins 2008: 380.
[5] A random example: Mill's *On Liberty* is full of causal-explanatory arguments.

we benefit from believing them. The first doubt seems to be correctly answered by Horwich's own minimalist theory of truth. Consider, for instance, a question in the domain of traditional moral theory: is torture always wrong? By the law of excluded middle, either torture is always wrong or torture is not always wrong. By his minimalist condition for propositional truth, if torture is always wrong then the proposition that torture is always wrong is true. Equally, if torture is not always wrong then the proposition that torture is not always wrong is true. Thus, either way, there is a truth of the matter: either the proposition that torture is always wrong is true or the proposition that torture is not always wrong is true. Parallel arguments apply to other questions of philosophical theory.[6]

In the example, Horwich's second question amounts to this: do we benefit from having a true belief as to whether torture is always wrong? Given his minimalism about truth, that is equivalent to asking two conditional questions. If torture is always wrong, do we benefit from believing that torture is always wrong? If torture is not always wrong, do we benefit from believing that torture is not always wrong? The answers seem obvious: the relevant belief will help us act well concerning torture. It would be irresponsible not to care about that.

Most philosophical questions lack direct practical applications. Consider a metaphysician wondering whether people are events. For Horwich's second question, we grant that it is either true or false that people are events. What is wrong with simply wanting to know whether people are events? Horwich speaks of benefits in terms of satisfying one's desires. Presumably, one can desire cognitive goods. One can derive the benefit of satisfying one's desire to know whether people are events. If Horwich has no such desire, he need not pursue the question. But the fact that a philosophical question bores Horwich does not mean that it is not worth asking.

In any discipline, some theoretical questions are not worth asking. However, we have no general method for telling in advance which are worth asking, which are not. We may simply have to trust the instincts of leading practitioners in the field, because we have no basis on which to second-guess them. If the leading practitioners are

---

[6]   Horwich 1998b; he endorses the application of the theory to ethical propositions at 84.

charlatans, the "discipline" is in trouble. Evidence that philosophers are asking worthwhile questions comes from numerous constructive interactions between theoretical philosophy and empirical or partly empirical disciplines such as biology, economics, linguistics, physics, politics, and psychology. That is hardly what one would expect if the philosophers asked bad questions while the others asked good ones.

Horwich has a further line of argument. He suggests that simplicity is a far less appropriate criterion for theory choice in philosophy than in the empirical sciences because our basic conceptual practices, concerning most concepts of philosophical interest, are not simple, being complicated by the variety of ordinary practical purposes for which we deploy those concepts.

One worry here is that Horwich writes as though the main concern of philosophy were with concepts rather than the properties and relations they are concepts of. He does not address the extensive arguments to the contrary in the book. However, he seems to mean that because our conceptual practices are ramshackle, our concepts refer to ramshackle properties and relations – properties and relations with complex boundaries, of which no simple theory is true. He is making the questionable assumption that complexity in the conceptual practice will induce complexity in its referent. If naturalness carries weight in determining the comparative eligibility of candidates for reference, some complexity in the conceptual practice may instead count as error.[7]

As an example of a philosophically interesting ordinary concept whose referent has complex boundaries, Horwich gives the concept of knowledge: "the conditions for mathematical knowledge diverge somewhat from the conditions for empirical knowledge (in not requiring there to be any causal or counterfactual connection between the knowing and what is known)." He describes these conditions for the application of "know" as "*disjunctive*" (his emphasis). The example is misdescribed. Presumably, Horwich's reason for denying that mathematical knowledge requires a causal or counterfactual connection is that the necessity of mathematical truths is incompatible with one. If so, however, the necessity of the truth that gold is the element with atomic number 79 should also rule out a causal or counterfactual connection for knowledge that gold is the element with atomic num-

---

[7] See 258–70 (this volume) and Lewis 1983b.

ber 79. But the latter is empirical knowledge, contrary to Horwich's assumption that empirical knowledge does require such a causal or counterfactual connection. In any case, a unitary epistemological condition may have to be realized in different ways for different subject matters. Thus Horwich has not shown that the conditions for knowledge are disjunctive. Of course, nobody expects them to match those of some fundamental physical relation; such matching is unnecessary for systematic epistemological theorizing. I developed a systematic non-reductive theory of knowledge in Williamson 2000a, partly guided by considerations of theoretical simplicity. Horwich does not attempt a critique of that theory. His use of the example of knowledge fails to help his case.

Horwich mentions the ordinary concept of truth as another example. On his own minimalist conception, the main constraint on it is the simple schema "The proposition that P is true if and only if P." Here too, our conceptual practice does not prevent our concept from referring to something of which a simple theory is true. I applaud the work of Horwich and others in showing how much a minimal characterization of propositional truth can explain, without invoking more elaborate, dubious conceptions of correspondence and the like. Contrary to his impression, I do not regard the semantic paradoxes as the only area in which progress has been made in understanding truth.

Horwich doubts that formal work on the semantic paradoxes has constituted philosophical progress at all. He is right that there has been no convergence on a single solution. However, it is not a zero-sum game between the alternative approaches. They all contribute to our knowledge of how closely a consistent theory can approximate to the original unrestricted and therefore inconsistent disquotational principle for sentential (rather than propositional) truth. They are gradually helping us map out in meticulous detail what truthlike properties there are. It would be philistine to dismiss such new knowledge as "unphilosophical."

As another candidate for philosophical progress, Horwich discusses the development of truth-conditional semantics. He presents the astonishingly *insouciant* view that if truth-conditional semantics were empirically significant, it would not be philosophy, but that deflationism shows it to be an empirically insignificant response to a non-problem about compositionality, whose development has been largely a philosophically insignificant formal exercise.

Horwich does not explain what he means by "empirical significance." A truth-conditional semantic theory for Serbian will tell you,
for example, that the word "krava" applies to all and only cows. In
what sense does that information lack empirical significance? For a
different sort of example, consider the rich tradition of work on generalized quantifiers in natural languages. From it have emerged inductively supported hypotheses about universals in natural language,
specifically, constraints on quantifiers in all human natural languages
that are violated by formally possible languages.[8] If a human natural
language is discovered to violate such a constraint, the hypothesis
will have been refuted. If Horwich's deflationism entails that the hypothesis is nevertheless devoid of empirical significance, so much the
worse for his deflationism.

The case of generalized quantifiers also brings out the hollow-
ness of Horwich's references to "use-theoretic approaches" as though
they constituted a serious alternative to truth-conditional semantics. Standard works on generalized quantifiers in natural languages,
such as the book by Peters and Westerståhl, proceed entirely within
the truth-theoretic approach. What works of comparable detail and
scope do "use-theoretic approaches" have to offer?

As for Horwich's insinuation that truth-conditional semantics has
produced little of philosophical interest, it suggests an extraordinarily
narrow conception of philosophy. For example, Russell's theory of
definite descriptions is an early piece of truth-conditional semantics.
Does Horwich find it of little philosophical interest?

An intriguing issue nevertheless remains as to how we should conceive the relation between philosophy and linguistics in this area.
How can a claim about the meaning of some specific sentences in
a specific natural language be of distinctively philosophical interest? To fix ideas, consider Davidson's treatment of action sentences.
For example, he proposes something like this for the sentence "Shem
kicked Shaun":[9]

(1) "Shem kicked Shaun" is true if and only if there is an event x
    such that x is a kicking of Shaun by Shem.

---

[8]   Peters and Westerståhl 2006: 138–41.
[9]   Davidson 1980: 118.

That is a metalinguistic hypothesis about a particular sentence of English. We may be tempted to regard it as of no distinctively philosophical interest. We may be even more strongly tempted to regard the corresponding homophonic disquotational equivalence as of no distinctively philosophical interest:

(2) "Shem kicked Shaun" is true if and only if Shem kicked Shaun.

We can treat (2), unlike (1), as uncontroversial. But from (1) and (2) we can deduce a consequence that is not metalinguistic:

(3) Shem kicked Shaun if and only if there is an event x such that x is a kicking of Shaun by Shem.

But (3) is obviously of distinctively philosophical interest, since it permits one to move from a premise ("Shem kicked Shaun") that may be common ground between proponents and opponents of an ontology of events to a conclusion ("There is an event x such that x is a kicking of Shaun by Shem") that is explicitly committed to an ontology of events. Those who regard claims of truth-conditional semantics as of merely linguistic and not philosophical interest typically forget how easily disquotational platitudes allow one to move between metalinguistic and non-metalinguistic claims. Since (1) and (2) jointly entail something of philosophical interest, it is unwise to regard them as of no philosophical interest.

Is (3) "empirically significant?" Without clarification of "empirically significant," the question is hardly worth discussing. The critique of the distinction between *a priori* and *a posteriori* knowledge in the book might have warned Horwich that the label "empirically significant" is too vague to do the work he expects of it. Informed assessment of claims such as (3) requires a complicated mix of linguistic, logical and metaphysical considerations, even though (3) is not itself a claim about language. Horwich's dichotomy between empirically significant, philosophically insignificant scientific linguistics and empirically insignificant, philosophically significant reflection on language is hopelessly inadequate to the methodological need for interaction between linguistic and non-linguistic considerations, as continually exemplified by good recent work in many areas of linguistics and philosophy. As so often, Wittgensteinian preconceptions stand in the way of following Wittgenstein's injunction to "look and see."

In Horwich's view, the proper aim of philosophy is to dispel confusions and irrational presuppositions, an activity to be pursued in an unsystematic, untheoretical manner. A familiar feature of Wittgensteinians' attempts at philosophizing in that spirit is that the informality of the presentation conceals rather than avoids theoretical presuppositions of their own. For the presuppositions they expose in others are not blatantly "confused" or "irrational"; they are true or false propositions that cannot be argued against in a theoretically neutral way.

Just about all human discourse involves presuppositions; we must take some things for granted in order to focus on what is relevant. Anyway, the attempt to produce a presupposition-free discourse would lead philosophy in a direction that Horwich could hardly approve, towards the construction of something like Frege's *Begriffsschrift*. Once a presupposition has been identified, the question is whether it is legitimate. That will often be a matter of controversy. Dissatisfaction with dogmatic attempts to end the controversy at a stroke, confused attempts to dispel confusion, is one motive that drives us to systematic theorizing.

For Horwich, the proper task of the philosopher is also to "quell over hasty generalization." But, on his view, can there be generalization in philosophy that is *not* over hasty? He says nothing about how philosophers are to arrive at generalizations without haste, given that they are supposed to avoid systematic theorizing. Are we not supposed to generalize at all? If there are true generalizations in philosophy, it seems a pity that we should not be allowed to look for them. Surely Horwich does not think that there are no true generalizations in philosophy, for that would be an over hasty generalization. If there are no true generalizations in philosophy, then it is a true generalization in philosophy that there are no true generalizations in philosophy, so by *reductio ad absurdum* there are after all true generalizations in philosophy.

We can state the argument in a less paradoxical-sounding way. Either there are true informative first-order generalizations about philosophy or there are not. If there are not, then a true informative second-order generalization about philosophy is that there are no true informative first-order generalizations about it. Therefore, there are true informative first- or second-order generalizations about philosophy. Although they may be difficult to find, we can at least try. In that enterprise, Horwich's lazy philosophy of philosophy is of no help whatsoever. We must do better.

Acknowledgment

This section first appeared as part of my contribution to a symposium on the first edition of the book in *Philosophy and Phenomenological Research* (Williamson 2011e).

13.3   Reply to Frascolla

As a case study of philosophical inquiry and its relation to the linguistic and conceptual turns, I used the original question "Was Mars always either dry or not dry?" I argued that, taken at face value, without reinterpretation as "really" a metalinguistic or metaconceptual question, it already constitutes a challenging starting-point for philosophical inquiry. In "On the face value of the 'original question' and its weight in philosophy," Pasquale Frascolla (2011) disputes my account by distinguishing between philosophical and non-philosophical ways of taking the question. He argues that taking the question philosophically involves not taking it at face value.

The first difficulty with Frascolla's arguments is that he persistently misstates the face value of the original question. Sometimes he does so by gratuitously introducing talk of the truth or falsity of statements. In particular, he characterizes the classical proof of a positive answer to the question as proceeding via the Principle of Bivalence and considerations about truth-tables, rather than simply as a regular proof in the first-order object-language of a universally quantified instance of the law of excluded middle. Adding that extraneous metalinguistic layer misses the point of my insistence in the book on extreme care with the distinction between the logical and the metalogical. Elsewhere, Frascolla misstates the face value of the original question in a quite different way, by treating it as equivalent to the question "Was Mars never a borderline case of dryness?" The difference between the two questions is crucial for both supervaluationists and epistemicists. On such views, the answer to the original question is positive, whether or not Mars was ever a borderline case of dryness. Thus Frascolla never engages with the actual face value of the question.

Nevertheless, Frascolla has an argument that, if sound, would bypass the first difficulty. He correctly notes that the classical proof of the positive answer to the face value original question immediately generalizes to objects other than Mars and to properties other than dryness. He concludes without further ado that in giving the proof we are not really taking the question at face value. He thereby commits a fallacy against which I explicitly warned the reader (28, this volume). It is like claiming that when I ask "Am I mortal?" I am not really asking about myself, because the reason for a positive answer can be generalized to anyone else. Having convinced himself that the question must really be about a generalization, Frascolla compounds the error by assuming that the generalization must be a metalinguistic one – as opposed, for example, to a non-metalinguistic generalization in second-order logic.

Next, Frascolla objects to my discussion of an intuitionist's response to the disputed law of classical logic. He distinguishes between mathematical and philosophical ways of taking the question, confining the intuitionist's distinctively proof-theoretical considerations to the latter. This is a serious misunderstanding of intuitionism. Brouwer and his followers were revisionists about mathematical practice. Their proof-theoretical account was intended to apply to *mathematical* questions, not just to philosophical ones. Frascolla's account of the intuitionist approach is also distorted by a technical error. He discusses what the intuitionist will say on the supposition that a certain formula is neither provable nor refutable. But for intuitionists that supposition is inconsistent: according to them, *A* is unprovable only if it is provably unprovable, in which case ¬*A* is provable on their account of negation, so *A* is refutable.[1]

In summing up, Frascolla diagnoses in me "a meta-philosophical prejudice in favor of the idea that, just like every other discipline that makes truth-claims about how things stand, so too philosophy is concerned with the world (thought and language included)." It is not entirely clear what the content of this prejudice is supposed to be. Is the intended alternative that philosophy makes truth-claims about how things stand, but is not concerned with the world, or simply that it does not make truth-claims about how things stand? I have no restrictive conception of "how things stand" or "the world." If a truth-claim is a claim with a propositional content intended to be true, then it is

---

[1] After reading my reply, Frascolla qualified "provable" by "*de facto*." It is unclear what the distinction between provability and *de facto* provability is supposed to be: perhaps an adaptation of intuitionistic semantics for mathematical language to empirical discourse. Anyway, it makes a difference to my argument only if *de facto* provability satisfies structurally different principles from standard intuitionistic provability. If so, the onus is on Frascolla to explain what alternative structure for intuitionistic semantics he has in mind. Having provided no such alternative, he is in no position to claim, as he does, that "it is clear" what answer the intuitionist will give to a question about *de facto* provability. For some of the difficulties in extending intuitionistic proof-theoretic semantics to empirical discourse see Williamson 1994c.

more or less trivial that such a claim is about how things stand and is concerned with the world. So I take the charge to be that I have a metaphilosophical prejudice in favor of the idea that philosophy makes truth-claims. Certainly I endorse the idea, but is it a prejudice? Is it not rather a piece of commonplace knowledge shared by almost everyone who has read some philosophy, past or present, even if it is denied by some philosophers in the grip of a wildly implausible metaphilosophical theory? Although a few philosophers deny that there are sticks and stones, it is not a *prejudice* that there are such things. Many philosophical texts – Locke's *Essay Concerning Human Understanding*, or Frege's *Die Grundlagen der Arithmetik* – are obviously full of intelligible truth-claims, true or false. What is striking is the ability of some people to persuade themselves of the opposite.

Frascolla goes to a further extreme when he suggests that my claim that "thinking just as much as perceiving is a way of learning how things are" (49, this volume) "stands in urgent need of defense." If I know that the rabbit went this way or that way or the other way, and I check that it did not go this way or that way, by thinking I can learn that it went the other way. By thinking, Andrew Wiles and others learned how things are concerning the truth-value of Fermat's Last Theorem. Those claims stand in far less urgent need of defense than any philosophical view incompatible with them.

Acknowledgment

This section first appeared as part of my contribution to a symposium on the first edition of this book in Richard Davies (ed.), *Analisi: Annuario e Bollettino della Società Italiana di Filosofia Analytica (SIFA) 2011* (Williamson 2011f). I thank Pasquale Frascolla for the care and attention he spent on the book. Like him, I focus on points of divergence. All page references are to the first edition.

13.4 Reply to Marconi

In "Wittgenstein and Williamson on Conceptual Analysis," Diego Marconi (2011) argues that the first edition leaves unscathed a pre-eminent alternative to its account of philosophy: "Wittgenstein's view that philosophical investigations are conceptual investigations." He is right that although the book contains occasional more or less dismissive remarks about Wittgenstein, it has no sustained discussion of his views. He does better than Heidegger, who is passed over in silence. The omissions were, of course, deliberate. I wanted to address the situation of philosophy now, not fifty years ago. To discuss Wittgenstein's conception of philosophy, one must first go through a complex hermeneutic process, not least in order to understand the notorious tensions between his less than transparent philosophical practice and his fragmentary comments on the nature of philosophy – that philosophy makes or should make no controversial theoretical claims is itself a controversial theoretical claim, and so on. One can be quite sure in advance that any account of Wittgenstein's views that forms the basis for a critique of them will be accused of misinterpretation by Wittgenstein scholars. The worse the tensions in his corpus, the easier the charge is to make. That was exactly the sort of stale discussion with which I wanted not to take up my readers' time. For most philosophers today, including me, seeing philosophy Wittgenstein's way is not a live option.

In terms of Marconi's clear version of Wittgenstein's account, it is straightforward to explain why it is no longer a live option for so many philosophers. According to Marconi, "Wittgenstein's view that philosophical investigations are conceptual investigations derives from his conception of necessity"; I will not dispute that interpretative claim. The intended connection is this: If there were philosophical propositions, they would be non-contingent. "However, there are no necessary propositions: if a proposition were necessary, its negation would describe an impossibility. But impossibilities cannot be meaningfully described, hence necessities cannot be meaningfully described either." The false step here is "impossibilities cannot be meaningfully described." For it to serve its function in the argument, the claim must be something like this: whenever a meaningful sentence s expresses the proposition that P, it could be that P. But the claim falls to obvious counter-examples. The sentence "$\sqrt{2}$ is rational" is meaningful; it expresses the proposition that $\sqrt{2}$ is rational, the hypothesis for *reductio ad absurdum* at the start of the standard proof that $\sqrt{2}$ is irrational. But $\sqrt{2}$ could not be rational, for it is irrational and mathematics is not contingent. I have often seen Wittgensteinians confronted with such counter-examples. Their response has always been an appeal to other bits of equally implausible Wittgensteinian dogma. The effect is merely to discredit their own view.

The meaningfulness of the sentence "$\sqrt{2}$ is rational" derives from the meaningfulness of its parts ("$\sqrt{}$," "2," "is," and "rational") and the way in which they are put together to form a well-formed sentence according to the rules of mathematical English. Correspondingly, the compositional structure determines what proposition has been expressed. I briefly went through such an argument in the book, vainly hoping that its application to Wittgenstein's ill-considered claims about modality would be obvious (58–60, this volume). Amusingly, another compositional objection starts from a point that Marconi himself makes in expounding the Wittgensteinian argument: "if p, a proposition that describes a necessity, were meaningful then $\sim p$, the description of an impossibility, would be meaningful as well."[1] By far the best ground for this conditional is the compositional thesis that meaningfulness is preserved under negation: whenever q is meaningful, so is $\sim q$. By the same compositional principle, meaningfulness should also be preserved under conjunction, another truth-function: whenever q and r are meaningful, so is q & r. But together these two principles entail that whenever q is meaningful, so is the contradiction q & $\sim q$, contrary to the Wittgensteinian dogma. One can give a parallel compositional argument at the level of the proposition expressed.

Contemporary theories of propositions have no difficulty with impossible propositions, that is, with propositions that are false with respect to all possible circumstances. I am well aware that such objections provoke no end of special pleading on the part of Wittgensteinians. To the unbiased observer, such independently implausible reactions confirm the bankruptcy of their view.

---

[1] Following an older tradition, Marconi uses "proposition" where I might use "sentence." In contemporary philosophical usage, propositions are things expressed rather than the expressions of them, and so are not candidates for meaningfulness.

Although I am highly sympathetic to Kripke's overall picture of necessity, Marconi overestimates how much of it the book assumes. In particular, my skepticism about the usefulness of the distinction between *a priori* and *a posteriori* knowledge might have indicated that I take Kripke's category of the necessary *a posteriori* with a pinch of salt, while still regarding it as important progress. But no distinctively Kripkean assumptions are needed to reject Wittgenstein's wild claims about necessity. As just seen, far more elementary considerations suffice.

Compositional considerations also tell against Wittgenstein's idea that sentences such as "Knowledge entails truth" express rules for the use of words rather than true propositions about a non-linguistic subject matter. According to Marconi, "Discovering that knowledge entails truth is discovering that within the practices where words such as 'know' and 'true' are used, the concepts of knowledge and truth are so applied that we do not call a propositional content 'knowledge' if we do not take it to be true." The passage seems to involve a use–mention confusion. Ancient philosophers who knew that knowledge entails truth knew nothing about the English words "know" and "true." Even if we restrict attention to competent speakers of English, the two discoveries are entirely distinct. Someone could realize that knowledge entails truth but regard the entailment as a logical subtlety to which few native speakers have access. Conversely, someone could realize that the concepts of knowledge and truth are so applied that we do not call a propositional content "knowledge" if we do not take it to be true, but deny that knowledge entails truth on the grounds that our conceptual practices are incoherent (as witnessed by the Liar paradox) and have no automatic connection to the objective logical relations. Even if such combinations of views are mistaken, they still highlight the cognitive gap between the two discoveries. Even if we were to stipulate the linguistic rule that "knowledge" applies only if "true" applies, for compositional reasons the declarative sentence "Knowledge entails truth" would still express a true or false proposition. The first edition explains the same point in terms of a less philosophical example (73–4, this volume).

One reason for Marconi's failure to notice the anti-Wittgensteinian arguments implicit in the book is its equation of conceptual truth with analyticity and its use of very standard examples of the latter. That may have given the impression that I was relying on a narrow traditional account of analyticity, on which many truths that count as conceptual for Wittgenstein are synthetic. I was not. On the contrary, I was following current usage outside the Wittgensteinian camp, in which there is no clear distinction between "conceptual truth" and "analytic truth" but both terms are regarded as up for grabs, given the manifest inadequacy of the usual explanations as they stand. I used traditional paradigms of analyticity out of charity to my opponents, because their claims were likely to work for those cases if for any. I canvassed a wide variety of alternative explications of "analytic" or "conceptual truth" (50–135, this volume). The reason why I did not directly confront Wittgensteinian formulations about grammatical rules and the like was not definitional sleight of hand, but simply that I find them too unclear and poorly developed to be useful poles of discussion.

Acknowledgments

This section first appeared as part of my contribution to a symposium on the first edition of this book in Richard Davies (ed.), *Analisi: Annuario e Bollettino della Società Italiana di Filosofia Analytica (SIFA) 2011* (Williamson 2011f). I thank Diego Marconi for the care and attention he spent on the book. Like him, I focus on points of divergence. All page references are to the first edition.

13.5 Reply to Tripodi

In the book I give counterexamples to epistemological conceptions of analyticity. They illustrate the point that even a basic disagreement in logic is compatible with shared meanings. In "Peter, Stephen … and Ludwig," Paolo Tripodi (2011) maintains that my argument begs the question. He reasonably takes as one of my primary targets the claim that philosophy is *connective analysis*, which he defines as "the *a priori* description of the conceptual connections (and exclusions) in the web of one or more words" and takes to cover the philosophical practice of the later Wittgenstein, Peter Strawson, and other analytic philosophers of that epoch and general style. He then reasons that if philosophy is indeed connective analysis, two philosophers who give different connective analyses of the same word associate different concepts with it and therefore understand it differently, in which case my counterexamples fail.

One problem for Tripodi is how high he has set the bar for himself. If it is even possible for a few philosophers not to engage in connective analysis but, however mistakenly, to try doing philosophy in a more theoretical or critical spirit, then my counterexamples can involve philosophers of that sort. Thus his argument depends on something more like the premise that necessarily all meaningful philosophical activity is connective analysis. The immense variety in the world history of philosophy suggests that no such flatteningly reductive formula is even approximately correct.

But even if two philosophers do engage in connective analysis, and give different analyses of the same word, why should it follow that they associate different concepts with it or understand it differently in the sense relevant to my counterexamples: that is, why should it follow that they use the word with different meanings? Of course, if their "analyses" were mere proposals to use the word with the stipulated meaning in future, they might bring about a divergence in meaning. But such revisionary meaning stipulations are more in the spirit of Carnap than of Wittgenstein and Strawson. Moreover, the idea that philosophy consists entirely or even mainly of meaning stipulations is hopelessly implausible. In any case, it is not what Tripodi has in mind, since he defines connective analysis as a *description* of conceptual connections. On this picture, the philosopher's task to describe (*a priori*) semantic networks of conceptual connections between words of a public language with which they are competent. That makes the question even more pressing: if two philosophers give inequivalent descriptions of such connections, why should it follow that they are describing different concepts or meanings? Why exclude the possibility that they are describing exactly the same thing, although one or both of them is describing it incorrectly or incompletely?

Tripodi comes closest to facing the objection in this passage: "Of course, the connective analyst intends to describe the conceptual behavior of a *shared* concept. Nonetheless, she ultimately describes the conceptual behavior of *what she takes to be* the standard concept. Her key access to that concept is *her own* individual semantic competence." But such fudging can be used in an attempt to wriggle out of any charge of misdescription of anything whatsoever. Suppose that I describe the wallpaper as having a pattern of pentagons, and you point out that in fact it is a pattern of hexagons. I reply: "Of course, I intended to describe the pattern of the wallpaper itself. Nonetheless, I ultimately described *what I took to be* the pattern of the wallpaper. My key access to that pattern is *my own* individual perception." The analogue of Tripodi's claim is that your description of the pattern on the wallpaper did not conflict with mine, because each of us was correctly describing the pattern of the wallpaper as we perceived it. But that is mere sophistry. In the envisaged case, your description was right and mine was wrong. Each of us intended to describe the pattern on the wallpaper itself, not our perception of it; those intentions set the standard of correctness for our descriptions. Exactly the same applies to the description of a semantic network in a public language.

Tripodi's argument does not even fit the practice or theory of the later Wittgenstein, Strawson, and the other practitioners of connective analysis he lists. Surely they thought that sloppy or prejudiced philosophers can misdescribe conceptual connections: the result is an incorrect description of public concepts, not a correct description of private ones.

Thus, contrary to Tripodi's charge, my counterexamples do not beg the question against the view that philosophy is connective analysis, since they work even on that view. Of course, I deny that philosophy is connective analysis, and part of my reason for doing so is that the critique of epistemological analyticity helps undermine the very idea of a conceptual connection. But that does not make the critique question-begging.[1, 2]

Acknowledgments

This section first appeared as part of my contribution to a symposium on the first edition of this book in Richard Davies (ed.), *Analisi: Annuario e Bollettino della Società Italiana di Filosofia Analytica (SIFA) 2011* (Williamson 2011f). I thank Paolo Tripodi for the care and attention he spent on the book. Like him, I focus on points of divergence. All page references are to the first edition.

[1]   Another tendentious aspect of Tripodi's comments is that he describes my counterexamples to epistemological analyticity as borderline cases of understanding. As I emphasize in the book, they are in fact clear cases of understanding, controversial only for those in the grip of a philosophical theory.

[2]   Contrary to a speculation that Tripodi reports, my imaginary philosopher Stephen was named after Stephen Cole Kleene (for his three-valued tables), not after Stephen Schiffer.

13.6   On Paul Horwich's *Wittgenstein's Metaphilosophy*

"Arguably," says Paul Horwich, "Wittgenstein's singular achievement was to have appreciated the true nature of philosophy" (vii). The book's primary aim is to expound and support a certain conception of philosophy. Arguing that it was Wittgenstein's conception is a secondary aim, although one that Horwich takes to be rather easily achieved on the basis of Part I of *Philosophical Investigations*.

The reader is exposed to just two sorts of philosophy. One of them is traditional theoretical philosophy, which Horwich calls "T-philosophy." The other is Wittgenstein's therapeutic critique of T-philosophy. The latter does not rest on any particular view of meaning, according to Horwich. Rather, it engages in detailed case studies of T-philosophy, showing up its ill-founded scientistic pretensions, its cavalier way with recalcitrant data, its blindness to simple resolutions of supposedly deep problems, and the irrational dogmatism of its practitioners. On the picture that emerges, 90% of philosophy is a waste of space, while the remaining 10% consists of praiseworthy demolitions of the 90%. Horwich does not explain why taxpayers should be expected to fund a branch of the academy with that structure. Would it not be cheaper and more effective simply to abolish philosophy altogether? Proponents of a therapeutic conception of philosophy often argue that it can perform valuable purgative services for the wider culture, so we should not be better off without it. But Horwich does not make that argument. Doing so might generalize the imputation of intellectual bankruptcy to many other domains.

Naturally, Horwich and Wittgenstein's conclusion is not that we should do T-philosophy better, but that we should not do it at all. The upshot of the critique is supposed to be that T-philosophy is a hopeless enterprise, the construction of elaborate theories to solve what are in fact mere pseudo-problems. Of course, that is just the sort of surprising, very general conclusion characteristic of T-philosophy, and so raises the notorious difficulty that Wittgenstein's metaphilosophy seems to be self-refuting. To his credit, Horwich confronts the difficulty head-on. His response is that the critique involves no theory about some hidden reality: it merely draws attention to straightforward matters open to view on the surface, after which the conclusion that T-philosophy is irrational is a statement of the obvious (65–6). Although many philosophers deny that T-philosophy is irrational, Horwich correctly insists that something may be potentially obvious yet highly controversial.

However, some T-philosophers claim that *their* conclusions are potentially obvious, once one has attended to the relevant straight-forward matters. The question is whether Horwich's considerations are really clearer and more decisive than the T-philosophers', whether they really render their conclusions more obvious. They do not. Hor-wich offers arguments of a recognizably philosophical kind; as he says, he writes in the style of contemporary analytic philosophy (xiii). His arguments are better than many in T-philosophy, and worse than many others. Indeed, his arguments tend to suffer from the very faults of which they accuse T-philosophy.

One example is Horwich's discussion of the use of the word "pain," a major part of his attempted dissolution of the "mystery" of con-sciousness. Following Wittgenstein, he claims that "'He thinks he is in pain but perhaps he is mistaken' and 'I am not sure if I am in pain' are considered deviant, anomalous – a sort of violation of linguistic rules" (184). But when my son pinches me, I am sometimes unsure whether the irritating sensation is bad enough to be pain, and people prone to self-pity sometimes mistakenly think that they are in pain when they get a slight bump. In neglecting such common sense cases, Horwich is just as cavalier with the data as he claims T-philosophers to be. On minimal and misdescribed evidence, he postulates an un-specified rule of English unknown to linguists outlawing such ordi-nary utterances: just the sort of reckless theorizing he treats as typical of T-philosophy. Horwich also claims that his account of "pain" talk removes "the worry that other peoples' pain might be different from our own" (194). In dismissing such individual variation, he ignores the everyday differentiations amongst pains in natural language. For instance, a doctor may ask her patient "Is it a throbbing pain?" The phrase "throbbing pain" is not familiarly correlated with specific non-linguistic throbbing-pain behavior in anything like the way in which Horwich, following Wittgenstein, describes "pain" as familiarly cor-related with specific non-linguistic pain behavior. Since Horwich is reaching a general conclusion about different types of pain on the basis of considerations about ordinary talk, while neglecting ordi-nary talk about different types of pain, he is again doing just what he criticizes T-philosophers for doing. Of course, the ordinary possibility that I have a throbbing pain while you have a pain of some other type does not justify regarding consciousness as a mystery. The point is just that Horwich's arguments, far from making his conclusions obvious, clearly belong to T-philosophy as he describes and condemns it.

Similar illustrations can be given from other parts of the book. We are told that "if everything is normal, red things look red, and they look that way to everybody" (204): does "everybody" include the color-blind? On almost no evidence, Horwich proposes a highly speculative use theory of meaning, on which the use of a word is explained by a basic regularity for its use. Although a few examples are given, they are not developed. In each case, the alleged basic regularity for a word w involves using other words too, even though one can understand w perfectly well without having encountered those other words (122–3, 154–5). Nevertheless, we are told, "it is *potentially* obvious" that meaning is use (115). A supposedly non-intentional characterization of use is given in terms of *premises* and *assertions* (113). And so on.

If one could argue by the highest standards of T-philosophy that T-philosophy is irrational (a word Horwich frequently applies to it), that might be taken to show by *reductio ad absurdum* that T-philosophy is indeed irrational, even without making that conclusion *obvious*. But Horwich's arguments fall well short of the highest standards of contemporary T-philosophy. Many past and present T-philosophers do better. Rather, the book resembles a flawed statistical argument for the irrationality of statistical argument. That might constitute a useful warning of the need for high standards in statistical argument; it would not show that statistical argument itself is irrational. Similarly, although Horwich's book may constitute a useful warning of the need for high standards in T-philosophy, it does not show that T-philosophy itself is irrational.

A further reason for skepticism about Horwich's arguments comes from their tendency to generalize from T-philosophy to other branches of inquiry. He considers the objection that arithmetic qualifies as T-philosophy because it too "purports to arrive *a priori* at non-obvious results." But arithmetic is different, says Horwich, "since it arrives at its number-theoretic conclusions by demonstrative proof rather than by the forms of conjectural inference relied upon in T-philosophy" (22). The trouble with that reply is that it does not address the status of the axioms or other first principles of demonstrative proof. If one treats arithmetic as basic, an example is the principle of mathematical induction. If one derives the arithmetical principles from definitions, that merely shifts the problem to the status of the first principles of second-order logic or set theory on which the derivations rely. When one looks at how mathematicians actually justify their first principles of proof, one finds speculative abductive reasoning and stretched appeals to the imagination, both of a kind quite reminiscent of T-philosophy. Considerations of simplicity play a significant role, despite Horwich's talk of "an irrational distortion that tends to occur when the demand for simplicity is carried over from empirical science to *a priori* philosophy" (34). He also asserts that "in the *a priori* domain we cannot reasonably deploy the picture of increasingly profound layers of reality" (39). But mathematicians and logicians often do deploy just that picture, taking new results to give a deeper understanding of old ones. To a much greater extent than Horwich realizes, his critique of T-philosophy relies on features that T-philosophy shares with logic and mathematics.

Horwich's arguments also have an uneasy relationship with the special sciences. He criticizes systematization in philosophy on the grounds that "in all but a few cases the complexity of our data makes it unreasonable to expect interesting results" (49) and that "If a *complex* systematization is all that can be achieved then there are bound to be equally good alternatives; in which case we won't have legitimate epistemic norms that will enable us [to] decide between them" (50). The reader is left wondering why such points, if good, would not also tell against systematization at the level of linguistics, psychology, or biology. In a different connection, Horwich describes the use of ideal laws as "a common and legitimate feature of scientific theorizing," and correctly notes that "the standardly desired blend of empirical adequacy, simplicity, and explanatory power is sometimes best achieved by means of a theory whose two-pronged form is to postulate certain *ideal laws* (or *ceteris paribus* laws) and certain *distorting factors*" (156–7). The natural question is not raised: why shouldn't philosophers achieve systematicity in complex domains by constructing theories with ideal laws? Indeed, in formal epistemology they have already done so, quite successfully. The sense of a double standard at work is confirmed by Horwich's complaint that T-philosophers do not respect their data in the way scientists do, because T-philosophers sometimes reject observations made by normal subjects in normal conditions (37–8, 46). But natural scientists are just as liable as T-philosophers to reject the judgment of a normal observer in normal conditions that the sun is rising or that a fish is breaching. The possible explanations for observational and experimental error are not circumscribed in advance. When done well, both natural science and T-philosophy second-guess their data in flexible but intellectually responsible ways. A more nuanced and accurate description of natural scientific practice in this respect would not support the stark contrast with T-philosophy that Horwich claims.

The book depicts T-philosophy as starting from an unwarranted scientistic presumption that the given abstract domain satisfies simple yet deeply hidden laws. But no such presumption is needed. For example, one can ask what principles of quantified modal logic hold when the modal operators are read as expressing metaphysical modalities and the quantifiers are read as unrestricted. The question is philosophical, not merely technical. It does not presuppose that some principles of quantified modal logic *do* hold on those readings. If none hold, that is itself a simple and deeply hidden answer to the question. As it happens, much progress has already been made towards answering the question. We know many principles to hold universally on the specified readings: for example, all those of the propositional modal logic KT. Other principles remain highly controversial, such as the Barcan formula, and the principle that everything is necessarily something. If some of us are curious whether those further principles hold, why is it irrational for us to try to find out? The book provides no serious evidence that the inquiry must fail.

Of course, a standard Wittgensteinian objection to such an inquiry is that the alleged T-philosophical questions are *meaningless*, because they confuse grammatical matters with factual ones, or spin in the void, or whatever. A refreshing feature of Horwich's book is that he does not rely on that implausible charge, since – whatever its advocates may say – supporting it requires large and distinctively T-philosophical assumptions about the nature of meaning. For Horwich, Wittgenstein's views about meaning and other philosophical topics derive from his metaphilosophy, not the other way round. Whether Horwich is right about that is a question for Wittgenstein scholars to decide.

This review has not addressed the faithfulness of Horwich's interpretation of Wittgenstein to the original, since that is only a secondary aim of the book, albeit one Horwich takes himself to have achieved. However, *if* his interpretation is even roughly faithful, then Wittgenstein is not a philosopher of much depth or consistency. The point emerges the more clearly thanks to Horwich's commendably straightforward and accessible style and his refusal to take refuge in mysticism or dark sayings (but no thanks to the awful proof-reading). One may therefore predict that most Wittgenstein scholars will find Horwich's interpretation unfaithful.

Acknowledgment

This section first appeared as a review of Horwich 2012 in the *European Journal of Philosophy* (Williamson 2013h).

14
Miscellany

14.1 Reply to Ichikawa

The first edition analyses the Gettier thought experiment as an argument whose major premise is a counterfactual conditional. In "Knowing the Intuition and Knowing the Counterfactual" (Ichikawa 2009), Jonathan Ichikawa objects that this misrepresents the thought experiment as more accident-prone than it really is. If the world does not cooperate, the counterfactual will fail: it will be false that if the Gettier text had been realized, there would have been justified true belief without knowledge. Even if the world cooperates enough to make the counterfactual true, it may still not cooperate enough to enable us to know it, if it could too easily have been false. Ichikawa denies that the thought experiment is such a hostage to empirical fortune. The first edition considers such objections, arguing that although the thought experiment is indeed not immune to misfortune, that should not drive us to skepticism. If we identify an unwanted way in which the Gettier text might well have been realized, we can easily fix it by extending the text to rule out that way (202–6, this volume). There is no need to pretend that we had already fixed the problem before we had even thought of it. Rather than repeating those arguments, I will inquire whether Ichikawa's proposed alternative does any better.[1]

The main idea behind his proposal is to replace the Gettier text by the Gettier story. The latter strictly implies far more than the former does, because many things are true in a story without having been explicitly stated in the text of that story. Thus, unlike the Gettier text, the Gettier story is supposed to strictly imply that there is justi-

---

[1] He refers the reader to Ichikawa and Jarvis (2008) for more details.

fied true belief without knowledge, so that the problem of unwanted realizations no longer arises. However, we are not to conceive thinkers performing the thought experiment as conceptualizing the Gettier story to themselves *as* what is true in the fiction presented by the Gettier text. Rather, given their familiarity with the practice of fiction, reading the text puts them in a position to entertain a more specific proposition, which they might articulate to themselves as "Things are like *that*."[2] They can then argue: it is possible for things to be like that; necessarily, if things are like that then there is justified true belief without knowledge; therefore, it is possible for there to be justified true belief without knowledge.

The significance of the proposal does not lie in the use of strict implication rather than the counterfactual conditional to formulate the major premise. For a strict implication entails the corresponding counterfactual, and the latter suffices to validate the passage from the possibility of its antecedent to the possibility of its consequent, while making an epistemically less risky claim. In fact, Ichikawa could take over exactly the formalization of the Gettier argument that the book recommends, counterfactual and all. The only difference would lie in the interpretation of the predicate **GC**. Whereas I explain it in terms of realizing the Gettier text, Ichikawa would explain it in terms of realizing the Gettier story, or verifying the proposition that things are like *that*. What matters for his proposal is that the strict implication be true, not that it be used as the major premise. Its truth is what is supposed to remove the element of epistemic luck.

An obvious danger for Ichikawa's account is that truth in fiction may itself depend on counterfactuals that one can be wrong about if the world does not cooperate, as in David Lewis's classic account (1978). In a world in which it is highly abnormal not to have many alternative sources of knowledge for a given belief, Gettier's text may present a fiction in which it is not true that the protagonist has justified true belief without knowledge. If we are in an abnormal pocket of ignorance within such a world, then the Gettier story does not strictly imply that there is justified true belief without knowledge; perhaps it even strictly implies that there is no justified true belief without knowledge. Thus it is not obvious that Ichikawa's account

---

[2]   Ichikawa and Jarvis (2008).

avoids the epistemic risks to which he objects in mine. That we articulate the proposition as "Things are like *that*" rather than "Whatever is true in the Gettier fiction is true" does not help us avoid the risk of error when we believe that proposition to strictly imply a case of justified true belief without knowledge.

Ichikawa does not address the challenge in exactly that form. He does tell us that when one considers the Gettier text, one "enriches it, considering a more-determinate scenario." He allows that "divergent private fillings-out of the scenario" are possible, but suggests that we normally avoid them because "we have particular conventions, grounded in our practices with fictions, that govern how to move from a weaker description to a stronger scenario in the intended way." This suggests a psychological process, inspired by the Gettier text, of constructing our own fiction, whose additional content can be generated in part by our false beliefs. Thus, even if it is not really true in the Gettier fiction that there is justified true belief without knowledge, the proposition that *we* express by "Things are like *that*" may nevertheless still imply that there is justified true belief without knowledge.

Is such an account psychologically plausible? Often, when we perform a thought experiment, we simply read the text and make a verdict, or hesitate to do so. We need not sit there, daydreaming, adding detail after detail to the story. Visual imagery is absent or, if present, usually irrelevant (one may imagine the protagonist of Gettier's story with black hair). Entertaining the proposition that things are like *that* is not just a matter of demonstrating a possible world that one can already see in one's mind's eye.

In Ichikawa's example, the original Gettier-like text is this:

T1 At 8:28, somebody looked at a clock to see what time it was. The clock was broken; it had stopped exactly twenty-four hours previously. The subject believed, on the basis of the clock's reading, that it was 8:28.

Ichikawa points out that T1 conjoined with the originally unintended T2 no longer works as a Gettier case:

T2 The subject knew in advance that the clock had stopped exactly twenty-four hours previously.

On Ichikawa's view, the normal reader of T1 constructs a more specific proposition than T1 expresses that is incompatible with the proposition that T2 expresses. But how, exactly? Normal readers of T1 are *taken by surprise* when the possibility of elaborating T1 with T2 is pointed out to them. They have not already gone through a psychological process of formulating T2 and elaborating T1 with its negation, still less with the negation of T3 or of T4:[3]

T3 The subject knew in advance that the clock had stopped an exact multiple of twenty-four hours previously.

T4 The subject knew in advance that she suffered from a rare psychological condition that rendered her incapable of reading a clock as saying 8:28 at any time other than 8:28.

If the normal reader of T1 has excluded T2, T3, and T4 before even having formulated them, it is not through a psychological process of explicitly formulating something that, combined with T1, logically implies their negations. The original exclusion, if psychological at all, is dispositional rather than occurrent. The relevant disposition might be to add the negations of T2, T3, and T4 to T1 if the question arises. On this view, what proposition the reader expresses by "Things are like *that*" is determined by the set of sentences she is disposed to add to T1 if the question arises.

Such a view faces many problems.

First, the sentences a given reader is disposed to add to T1 if the question arises are quite likely to form an inconsistent set. This need not mean that she is disposed to continue T1 in an inconsistent way. She may rather be disposed to continue T1 in different individually consistent but jointly inconsistent ways, depending on which question arises first. For example, a mildly suggestible reader may be disposed to add either T5 or T6 to T1, depending on which question arises first:

T5 The subject was not wearing a wristwatch.

T6 The subject was wearing a wristwatch, but it had stopped.

---

[3] Readers of this exchange between Ichikawa and me may be abnormally on the look-out for such loopholes, but even they cannot specifically anticipate each of them.

After all, each of T5 and T6 seems to be a reasonably adequate and natural way of filling out the text of T1. But once such a reader has added T5 to T1, she may lose the disposition to add T6, and *vice versa*. Even the dispositions to add T2, T3, and T4 may be sensitive to what else has already been added. It is by no means obvious how to construct a metaphysically possible proposition out of such a complex web of interrelated dispositions. Yet Ichikawa's rendering of the Gettier argument requires such a proposition, to verify the premise that it is possible for things to be like *that*. Indeed, he requires us to *know* that it is possible, if the argument is to give us knowledge of its conclusion, that it is possible for there to be justified true belief without knowledge. Thus Ichikawa's account makes the epistemology of the first premise of the Gettier argument problematic in ways that mine does not.

Second, an account of the content of "Things are like *that*" in terms of the reader's psychological dispositions to fill out the original text almost guarantees that different readers will express different contents by the sentence. Ichikawa's appeal to our familiarity with the conventions of fiction merely suggests that those contents will tend not to differ too greatly from reader to reader. By hypothesis, the contents do not in general coincide with the shared story itself, on pain of undermining his implied account of the epistemology of the major premise. When two readers apparently disagree in their verdicts on a thought experiment, that already constitutes a difference in their psychological dispositions to fill out the original text, and so provides *prima facie* reason to believe that they associate different contents with "Things are like *that*." If so, they are not really disagreeing on Ichikawa's account. But that is not how philosophical discussion of thought experiments works. We allow the text of the thought experiment to fix a shared content, and then discuss that scenario.

Third, even if one is performing a thought experiment in isolation from other people, one's verdict on it is still in general a judgment that can be true or false independently of one's disposition to make it. Only a very foolish philosopher, on coming to a verdict on a tricky example in ethics, would think "I can't be wrong about this; it's just how I'm envisaging the case." Ichikawa's account has not yet shown enough distance between the specification of the scenario in a thought experiment and our dispositions to make further judgments as to what would be the case in that scenario. Providing that distance will tend to reintroduce the epistemic risks with respect to the major premise of the Gettier argument that he complains about in my account.

Whatever the details of Ichikawa's account, it exemplifies a strategy against which I argued in the first edition: the attempt to combat skepticism about our evidence in philosophy by psychologization. His application of the strategy is quite subtle, since what he psychologizes is not the content of the premises of the Gettier argument but our relation to that content. Rather than grasping it by understanding the public verbal description of the scenario, our filling out of the description is supposed to acquaint us psychologically with the content in a way that not only allows us to articulate it as "Things are like *that*" but somehow enables us to avoid the normal risks of error in judging what would be the case in a scenario. The strategy is no more successful here than elsewhere.

We cannot realistically expect that the method of thought experiments in philosophy will turn out to be much *more* reliable than the methods of the natural sciences. What, then, is so bad about accepting that the former is not immune from a mass of easily corrected small errors like those to which the latter are quite obviously subject?

Acknowledgments

This section originally appeared in *Philosophical Studies* as part of my half of a symposium on the first edition (Williamson 2009b). Thanks to Jonathan Jenkins Ichikawa for his interesting questions and to participants at the Arché workshop in St. Andrews which led to this exchange for discussion.

14.2 Reply to Martin

In "Reupholstering a Discipline" (Martin 2009), Michael Martin contests two themes of the first edition: the idea that philosophy makes progress and knowledge maximization as a principle of charity in interpretation. I will discuss his comments on each theme in turn.

1

Martin suggests that the idea of progress in a discipline, although applicable to mathematics and the natural sciences, fails to fit some of the humanities, such as history, so that we should not be too surprised if it also fails to fit philosophy. In making that suggestion, he does not intend to align himself with post-modern conceptions of inquiry as merely continuing or subverting a conversation.

Does the comparison with history help Martin's case? Of course, historians tend to distance themselves from the idea of progress in history as the succession of human doings and sufferings. But that is not what Martin means. He is questioning whether history as a discipline makes progress. He says very little to support a negative answer. Yet significantly more is known about a vast range of historical matters than was known fifty years ago. That is not just fact-grubbing. Significantly more is understood about those matters too. For instance, the role of religious belief in the English Civil War is better understood than it was. Again, history has vastly extended the range of its inquiries, for instance into the lives of members of marginalized groups. Its methods have developed, not only through the application of advances in science, such as statistics and DNA analysis. More critical and more imaginative ways of learning from documents are available. It seems merely quixotic to deny that if such changes really have taken place, they constitute progress in history as a discipline. Of course, someone may deny that the role of religious belief in the English Civil War is really any better understood now than it was fifty years ago. But, if so, that neither would nor should be a matter of indifference to the historians concerned. It would be a failure on their own terms. Martin does not seem ready to endorse such skepticism about history as a discipline. Although the progress it makes is piecemeal, the sort of progress I suggested philosophy makes is piecemeal too. Thus the comparison with history, to the extent to which it is relevant, undermines Martin's case against progress in philosophy.

Martin is more willing to countenance progress for individual philosophers than for the discipline as a whole. But this individualistic preference is hard to reconcile with the social nature of philosophy. Many of us see ourselves as participating in a collective enterprise, one that goes back to the ancient Greeks if not further and, we hope, will continue for millennia to come. The point of publishing is not only to advance one's career or benefit from feedback. It is to contribute, if only in a very small way, to an inquiry that will continue after one's death. For example, one tries to bring to others' attention a possibility they have missed, so that in the long run philosophers may determine whether it actually obtains. One defines one's individual goals in relation to progress in the discipline.

Even at the level of the individual, Martin is cautious about the idea of philosophical knowledge, and seems happier speaking of understanding. The thought that, individually or collectively, we might progress in understanding without progressing in knowledge is a familiar cop-out in defense of the humanities. Does it withstand scrutiny? If you don't know why Rome fell, you don't understand why Rome fell. If you do know why Rome fell, you have at least made considerable progress towards understanding why it fell. You might know that such-and-such caused Rome to fall without knowing why such-and-such caused Rome to fall, but what you lack there is more knowledge. Nor is knowing why some mysterious sort of nonpropositional knowledge. What constitutes knowing why the barn caught fire is, for instance, knowing that the burning match Innocent dropped in the straw caused the fire. It is not radically different in philosophy. If you don't know why zombies are impossible, you don't understand why zombies are impossible. In such cases, the idea that understanding transcends knowledge depends on too narrow a conception of the facts to be known.[1] In any discipline, practitioners may be reluctant to summarize progress in a one-liner.

---

[1]   In this respect knowing why is worth comparing with knowing how; see Stanley and Williamson 2001.

2

In the latter part of his comments, Martin develops a putative counterexample to knowledge maximization as a principle for determining reference. He assumes that one can simultaneously attend visually
to each of two objects in different parts of one's visual field; I am
quite happy to grant that assumption for the sake of argument. In
the imagined case, one is simultaneously attending visually to each
of two qualitatively identical pink Dolly Mixtures, righty and lefty,
while attending in thought only to lefty. One thinks "That's pink,"
referring only to lefty. Martin suggests that knowledge maximization
cannot determine whether the reference is to righty or to lefty, because the sentence would express knowledge either way. He stipulates that the "salient non-intentional facts" are symmetrical between
righty and lefty.

Presumably, Martin is not suggesting that the symmetry between
righty and lefty at the non-intentional level is perfect. If asked "Which
one?," one will answer "The one on the left," not "The one on the
right." That difference corresponds to some causal asymmetry at the
non-intentional level. The question is whether my account can engage
with that asymmetry. It can if the question is asked; as Martin notes,
only the correct assignment of reference makes the thought "That's
furthest to the left" knowledgeable. But he stipulates, legitimately,
that one has no such actual thought in the given case. The book does
not formulate knowledge maximization in counterfactual terms.

The account of reference determination in the book appeals to naturalness at more than one point. Martin designs the case to pre-empt
a straightforward appeal, but neglects a subtler possibility. Knowledge itself should be a somewhat natural relation (268, this volume).
If one refers to lefty in the counterfactual case in which the question
"Which one?" subsequently occurs, then it is more natural for the
reference to be to lefty in the actual case in which the question does
not occur, for the two cases begin the same. A difference in reference
between them would make knowledge less natural.

Perhaps we can go deeper. For although one is visually attending
to both lefty and righty equally, it does not follow that one's thought
"That's pink" has symmetrical causal relations to righty and lefty.
The simplest suggestion would be that it is causally explained by the
fact that lefty is pink and not by the fact that righty is pink. That is

insufficiently general, for in one version of the example I first think "They are both pink," an event which does have symmetrical causal relations to righty and lefty, and then infer "That's pink" of lefty, with no further causally relevant input from the color of lefty. In such a case, what – if anything – do we imagine the reference of "that" to lefty rather than righty as consisting in?

An appealing picture is that when one starts using "that" with reference to lefty, one opens some sort of mental file, if only a very temporary one, with a predominant causal connection to lefty that enables it to act as a channel for perceptual information about lefty more directly than it can act as a channel for perceptual information about righty: potentially, a channel for *knowledge* of lefty rather than righty. It does not matter whether that knowledge includes the particular item that it is pink, for the thought "That is pink" still has a compositional semantics. Even if no knowledge actually happens to be gained through that channel, the naturalness of the reference relation may still keep the reference constant between the actual case and counterfactual cases in which knowledge of lefty is gained through the channel.

That picture is not the only one consistent with the knowledge maximization principle. However unappealing on other grounds, a descriptivist account on which "that" somehow abbreviates a description such as "The one on the left" or "The one actually on the left" is also consistent with the principle. Other, more complex possibilities are consistent too. But if we suppose that *no* such story is to be told in the example, it ceases to be a clear case of reference to lefty; a verdict of reference failure becomes much more plausible. The case was not intended to be one in which the reference to lefty was puzzling to everyone; it was intended to discredit the knowledge maximization principle by providing a puzzle distinctive to it. But, as just seen, it can be accommodated within the book's framework of knowledge maximization and naturalness.

Acknowledgments

This section originally appeared in *Philosophical Studies* as part of my half of a symposium on the first edition (Williamson 2009b). Thanks to Michael Martin for his interesting questions, and to participants in the Arché workshop in St. Andrews that led to this exchange for discussion.

14.3   On Robert Brandom's *Reason in Philosophy: Animating Ideas*

Humans have a predictable liking for theories of what makes humans special, far above mere beasts and machines. Robert Brandom backs one of the most popular candidates, reason, in a specific form indicated by the word "reasoning": making inferences, reaching conclusions from premises. Are we really the only reasoners? A dog traces its quarry to a place where it could have gone any of three ways, sniffs at two of them and rushes off along the third *without sniffing*. The Stoic Chrysippus interpreted the dog as reasoning "It went this way, that way or the other way; it did not go this way or that way; therefore it went the other way." Far more complex logic is routine for computers. Such examples would not convince Brandom. For him, they lack a normative dimension essential to genuine engagement with reasons. When humans make a judgment, we incur both a responsibility to provide our reasons if challenged and a commitment to endorse consequences of what we claimed or else withdraw the claim. Dogs and computers incur no such responsibilities or commitments. Brandom labels his view "normative rationalism."

Distinguishing humans from others is just one of many achievements attributed to normative rationalism. Brandom is going for broke. In the first half of this short book, "A Semantic Sonata in Kant and Hegel," he depicts normative rationalism as the rightful inheritor of the best and deepest in the German idealist tradition. His argument ranges boldly over norms, selves, concepts, autonomy, community, freedom, history, reason, reality. Selves come in because they incur the responsibilities and commitments. Since contradicting oneself is bad, unlike contradicting someone else, rational norms demarcate the boundaries between selves. Concepts are rules for applying words; they give specific shape to the norms. Those concepts are ours because we make the rules. Our autonomy is that power to bind ourselves with self-given norms. Since it would amount to little if one always acted as judge and jury in one's own case, we must make and maintain the rules as a community, rather than each of us drawing up our own personal rulebook. In particular, concepts are expressed by words in a public language. It is in such a language that we request and supply reasons. The rules develop as a system of case law, not statutory law, for words have meanings in virtue of how we use them, not by a once-for-all act of stipulation. Thus normativity and reason have an essential historical dimension, because applications of rules must be judged by the standard of past applications and in turn modify the standard for judging future applications. Since retrospective criticism is possible too, the process works backwards as well as forwards. We grasp the concept of objective reality by reflecting on that history of self-correction. This does not make reality itself as mind-dependent as the process of self-correction; Brandom's idealism is more semantic than metaphysical. He makes no pretense at detailed exegesis of Kant and Hegel's crucial texts. Rather, he self-consciously engages in a selective rewriting of the history of philosophy as a triumphant progress up to his own views, including the view that so presenting one's views is a central philosophical task.

The second half of the book, less dense with abstractions than the first, is intended to be accessible to non-philosophers, although one wonders how they will get there. It contains five independent essays, two of them previously published, in which Brandom applies his normative rationalism to the nature of philosophy, the value of the philosophical life, the role of truth, problems for an empiricist conception of concepts, and philosophy's lessons for cognitive science. The volume feels slightly miscellaneous and repetitive. There are no big surprises, given his previous four books. However, it offers useful material for assessing his grand program.

Brandom repeatedly argues that reasoning is what matters by contrasts like this: a human assertion "That's red" with a similar-sounding noise made by a parrot or a tape recorder attached to a photocell. Even if the latter two have no concept of red, they may be just as reliable as the human at producing the noise in the presence of red objects. The crucial difference, Brandom argues, is that only the human can do things like reasoning from "That's red" to "That's colored." Although a dog or computer can do things which look like reasoning, he denies them the normative status of reasoning. But if one is going to play the normative card, one could just as easily have played it straight off, contrasting the human judgment "That's red" in normative status with the noise made by the parrot or tape recorder. If it isn't red, the human is getting it *wrong*, unlike the parrot or tape recorder. Although Brandom insists that the normative role of the judgment depends on its inferential connections, his evidence does not support that conclusion. At the critical point, he is using a normative difference between humans and non-humans to justify restricting genuine *reasoning* to humans, but since the normative difference is no worse a justification for restricting genuine *judgment* to humans, it provides no non-circular basis for privileging reasoning over judgment, as his normative rationalism demands.

The norms of judgment are not those of reasoning. To reason is to move from premises to a conclusion. A central norm of reasoning is *validity*: the conclusion should follow from the premises. Thus "Shergar was a racehorse, so he was kidnapped" is invalid, even though Shergar was both, for most racehorses are not kidnapped. The corresponding norm for judgment is *truth*. If you simply judge "Shergar was kidnapped," the question is whether Shergar *was* kidnapped. Since we can use valid reasoning to expand our stock of true beliefs, for instance by applying mathematics in science, it is natural to explain validity in terms of truth: *if* the premises in valid reasoning are true, the conclusion must be true too.

That is not how Brandom sees it. He acknowledges a fundamental norm of validity for reasoning, but no fundamental norm of truth for judgment. He allows truth no important explanatory role in philosophy; in particular, he does not explain validity in terms of truth. On the theory he endorses, "true" is merely a linguistic device similar in function to a pronoun. Just as I sometimes use "he" instead of "Brandom," one can sometimes use "That's true" instead of "Yes, Shergar was kidnapped." Truth is no "metaphysically weighty *property*" (whatever that means). For Brandom, any norm of judgment derives from norms of reasoning.

Brandom's downplaying of truth shapes his theory of meaning. On current orthodoxy, the meaning of "Shergar was kidnapped" demarcates circumstances in which Shergar was kidnapped from all others; the judgment is true if made in the former circumstances, false otherwise. This simple idea has been basic to the massive development of mainstream formal semantics over recent decades, in both linguistics and philosophy of language, for natural and artificial languages. If Brandom is right about truth, that development is profoundly wrongheaded. Semantics will have to be done again from scratch. To illustrate the difficulties: when Brandom applies his approach to the semantics of "if," "necessary," and "possible," all three of his proposals are vitiated by logical errors (46). Although his previous book

Between Saying and Doing (2008) contains a better developed attempt, it remains an isolated fragment by contrast with mainstream semantic theories.

Is Brandom right about truth? He makes little attempt to construct criticisms of orthodoxy sharp enough to worry its defenders. That would not be decisive if his positive account had significant advantages. Its economy is attractive, but cuts can go too far. For example, Brandom's account implies that the probability that the sentence "Snow is white" is true simply equals the probability that snow is white (see 164). That sounds good, until we remember that we can talk about how probable something is for someone else. The probability for us English speakers that "Snow is white" is true equals the probability for us that snow is white, if we are certain that "Snow is white" means that snow is white. But consider a monolingual Inuit who sees the sentence "Snow is white" on a fragment of philosophical text blown by the wind, without knowing what it means. On Brandom's account, the probability for her that the sentence "Snow is white" is true equals the probability for her that snow is white. Since she knows better than we do that snow is white, the probability for her that snow is white is high. But the probability for her that the sentence "Snow is white" is true is not high, since she has no evidence that the sentence means that snow is white rather than that blood is green. Thus Brandom's account is incorrect, and no improvement on orthodoxy.

Even if Brandom is wrong about truth, how much explanatory work can his norms of reasoning do? He does not intend a purely formal or *a priori* standard. Perhaps for that reason, he avoids the word "validity," preferring "good material inference." "Material" signals that the norm can be satisfied by an informal, *a posteriori* connection between premises and conclusion. He emphasizes that "what is *really* a reason for what depends on how things *actually* are." That pushes his norms of reasoning closer to an orthodox norm of truth (what is *really* true depends on how things *actually* are).

Brandom often prefers to work with a relation of material incompatibility in terms of which he can define good material inference. The corresponding norm is to avoid incompatible commitments. As an example of material incompatibility, he gives the triad "*A* is a blackberry," "*A* is red," and "*A* is ripe." The incompatibility depends on the actual nature of blackberries. Avoiding such incompatible commitments is not unlike avoiding false commitments. Presumably the norms are not quite equivalent, since one can avoid incompatible commitments without avoiding false commitments, for example by committing oneself only to "*A* is a blackberry" and "*A* is ripe" when *A* is actually an unripe blackberry. Brandom does not make the standard for material incompatibility explicit, but seems to intend some kind of natural impossibility: it is a natural impossibility for *A* to be a ripe red blackberry (freak cases apart?). This suggests that one has materially incompatible commitments whenever one misidentifies fruit, for if *A* is a raspberry then it is a natural impossibility for *A* to be a blackberry. The reader is left guessing how far "material incompatibility" is supposed to extend.

Some passages give the impression of sneaking a norm of truth back in by using the word "correct" in place of "true." For example, Brandom writes:

> what is represented must provide a standard for normative assessment of [representings'] *correctness*, as representings

and

> In [engaging in discursive practices], we bind ourselves by norms articulated by the contents of the concepts we apply. If I claim that the coin is copper, I have said something that, whether I know it or not, is *correct* only if the coin would melt at 1084°C and would *not* melt at 1083°C.

He does not say how he reconciles such passages with truth's explanatory unimportance.

Brandom contrasts "horizontal" relations between different "representings" with "vertical" relations between those representings and what is represented. Inferential relations are horizontal. Truth, as normally conceived, depends on vertical relations such as that of the word "copper" to the metal copper. Sometimes he seems to hint at explaining the vertical relations in terms of horizontal ones, a highly ambitious form of inferentialism. But then he admits that he is explaining only the horizontal relation of *purporting* to refer to the same thing, which different utterances of "copper" have to each other. However far you extend a horizontal, it will not turn vertical. Brandom's demotion of reference elsewhere is analogous to his demotion of truth and faces analogous problems.

These tensions come from the attempt to have semantic idealism without metaphysical idealism. To put it schematically, Brandom's semantic idealism characterizes meaning in terms of moves in a language game; which is attractive because it ties meaning to speakers' practical abilities. By contrast, metaphysical idealism wildly asserts that there is no world independent of the game. Earlier forms of semantic idealism involved some form of metaphysical idealism too. The most logically sophisticated was the intuitionist school of Brouwer, Heyting, Prawitz, Dummett, and others, which characterized the meaning of mathematical sentences in terms of the structure of their proofs, but in doing so assumed, implausibly, that every mathematical truth is provable by a finite mind. While ignoring such precedents, Brandom tries to avoid their defects. He accepts that a move in the language game can be a true or false statement about something independent of the game. He attempts to explain how the rules provide for such moves by making their legitimacy depend on the independent world. If he goes all the way, however, material incompatibility collapses into falsity, the norms of reasoning collapse into those of judgment, and everything distinctive of inferentialism is lost. The danger is that Brandom has gone far enough to disappoint the original motivation for semantic idealism, but not far enough for a satisfying rejection of metaphysical idealism. Since inferential relations can depend on facts about nature inaccessible to speakers, meaning has not been adequately tied to speakers' practical abilities. Since inferential relations do not fix truth and reference, meaning has not been adequately tied to the language-independent world.

All the erudite sophistication and laborious ingenuity with which Brandom tries explaining meaning in terms of inferential relations may ultimately help convince the reader that it cannot be done. Fifteen years after the publication of his magnum opus, *Making it Explicit*, Brandom's semantic inferentialism remains largely programmatic, unlike more orthodox semantic theories based on truth and reference. If you want an explicit theory of how some particular linguistic construction contributes to the meanings of sentences in which it occurs, the inferentialist is unlikely to have one. Better try the referentialist.

Although Brandom can show awareness that the devil is in the detail, in philosophy as elsewhere, his more grandiose paragraphs discourage any attempt to put his theory into practice by working out and critically testing the details. For philosophical prose style, Kant and Hegel are not the best influences:

It is by placing both within a larger *historical* developmental structure that Hegel fits the model of the synthesis of an original unity of apperception by rational integration together with the model of the synthesis of normative-status-bearing apperceiving selves and their communities by reciprocal recognition so as to make the discursive commitments instituted thereby intelligible as determinately contentful.

(Bold type and italics Brandom's.) Although his writing isn't all as bad as that, its paucity of clear detail has increasingly concentrated his readership amongst those – not few in number – who prefer philosophy to come in vast, vague programs, like the election manifestos of parties that know they will never have to govern. Brandom cannot want such marginalization. This volume will not reverse the trend.

Acknowledgment

This section originally appeared as a review of Brandom 2009a in the *Times Literary Supplement* (Williamson 2010).

14.4 On Peter Unger's *Empty Ideas: A Critique of Analytic Philosophy*

Metaphysics is back in fashion, at least in the analytic tradition that dominates English-speaking philosophy and is growing rapidly across the rest of the world too. It's quite a turnaround. In the mid-twentieth century, the analytic tradition had two main strands: logical positivism and ordinary language philosophy. The logical positivists dismissed metaphysics as cognitively meaningless, unverifiable by observation and logic. Ordinary language philosophers tended to be equally suspicious, diagnosing metaphysical speculation as the pathological result of using words outside the down-to-earth contexts that gave them meaning. But things have changed. These anti-metaphysical arguments rested on assumptions about meaning that have not withstood the test of time. Moreover, the resurgence of metaphysics was led by philosophers such as Saul Kripke and David Lewis, who wrote so clearly and intelligibly about essential properties (think Aristotle), possible worlds (think Leibniz), and the like that the charge of meaninglessness just would not stick.

Contemporary analytic metaphysicians see themselves as theorizing boldly and systematically about the deepest and most general nature of reality. In Peter Unger's view, they are deluded: far from resuming pre-Kantian metaphysics in the grand old style, they do little more than play with words. Their ideas are mostly *empty*. Indeed, he widens the charge to analytic philosophy more generally. Nor does he think better of non-analytic philosophy; he just has no time for it.

One might expect that by "empty" Unger means something like "meaningless." He does not. He allows that some empty ideas are true. For instance, the idea that all red things are colored is true, not meaningless, but is still empty by Unger's standard. What he objects to in empty ideas is their lack of *interest*, rather than of meaning or truth. Thus it's not self-defeating for him to admit, as he does, that some of his own ideas in the book are empty, for analytic philosophers – of whom Unger is one – might have done badly enough to deserve a boring sermon. But Unger does not use "empty" as a synonym for "boring," otherwise the book would be one long yawn. Instead, emptiness is supposed to be a more objective property of some ideas that explains *why* they should not excite our interest.

To assess Unger's critique, one must get clear what he does mean by "empty." He contrasts empty ideas with "substantial" ones. As far as the reader can tell, for an idea to be "substantial" is just for it to be contingent, to concern what could have been otherwise. It's contingent that Napoleon died on Saint Helena, since he could have died elsewhere, but it's not contingent whether all red things are colored. Thus for an idea to be "empty" is just for it to be non-contingent: either necessary or impossible. But, Unger notices, that doesn't give him what he needs, for all purely mathematical truths are necessary too: 5 + 7 could not have been 13. If mathematics yields only empty ideas, to say that analytic philosophy yields only empty ideas is at worst to say that it's as bad as mathematics, which isn't bad at all. To differentiate philosophy from mathematics, Unger distinguishes between concrete reality (including things in space and time) and abstract reality (including numbers). Supposedly, mathematics succeeds by informing us about abstract reality, whereas analytic philosophy tries but fails to inform us about concrete reality. According to Unger, analytic philosophy yields almost no "concretely substantial ideas": that is, contingent information about concrete reality.

Unger's focus on concrete reality doesn't solve the problem. One reason is that logic and mathematics don't only inform us about some realm of abstract objects. They are also useful because they can be applied to concrete reality itself, as in natural science. They give us necessary but far from obvious truths of the form "If concrete reality satisfies these conditions, then it satisfies this other condition." Why assume that analytic philosophy isn't doing the same? Yet such truths are "concretely empty" by Unger's standard. Indeed, many ideas of blatant philosophical interest will be "concretely empty." Abbreviate "being that has, of necessity, all these attributes: omniscience, omnipotence, omnibenevolence, concreteness, and so existence" as "god." Then the idea that there is a god is non-contingent and so concretely empty, because it's not contingent whether something is necessary. But a philosopher who tells us whether there is a god is doing metaphysics in the grand old style. Indeed, a characteristic ambition of such metaphysics past and present is to understand the deepest, most general, *and necessary* nature of reality. Thus Unger's complaint that analytic metaphysicians give us only concretely empty ideas will not threaten them, since it's in line with their hopes.

Unger's use of the term "empty" is just an advertising trick. It's like a competitor who defines "empty" as "containing nothing but brand X fruit juice" and then puts up posters warning that cartons of brand X fruit juice are empty. To read *Empty Ideas*, one must get through the equivalent of numerous elaborate descriptions of cartons of brand X fruit juice of various types, each concluding that the carton was empty, and for contrast some elaborate descriptions of cartons of brand Y fruit juice of various other types, each concluding that the carton was full. The reader's task is made no easier by Unger's loquacious, attention-seeking prose.

The book does have a way of turning up the heat, by adding a second charge against analytic philosophy: its ideas are not just concretely empty, they are "analytically empty." Unger is more evasive about what he means by "analytically empty" than with "concretely empty." His picture seems to be that the truth or falsity of analytically empty ideas depends on semantic interrelations amongst our words or concepts rather than on features of the reality to which those words or concepts refer. For example, the truth of "All red things are colored" is supposed to depend on a semantic relation between the word "red" and the word "colored," or a relation between our concept of red and our concept of color, rather than on a relation between the red things and the colored things. By contrast, the truth of "Napoleon died on St. Helena" is supposed to depend on a relation between the man Napoleon and the island of St. Helena, rather than between the name "Napoleon" and the name "St. Helena," or between our concept of Napoleon and our concept of St. Helena. So if analytic philosophers' ideas are analytically empty, they are asking verbal questions, not engaging with the concrete reality whose deepest and most general nature they were hoping to understand.

Unfortunately for Unger, the picture on which his second charge relies has turned out to be much less useful than it may look at first sight. For a start, whether one speaks truly or falsely in uttering any sentence whatsoever depends on the meanings of the words one utters, or on the concepts one uses them to express. Thus "Napoleon died on St. Helena" expresses a falsehood when uttered by someone who uses "St. Helena" to refer to the town of St. Helens in Lancashire, but the other words normally. Moreover, the truth of "All red things are colored" does turn on a relation between the red things and the colored things: that the latter include the former. Of course, the meaning of "All red things are colored" is such that it expresses a necessary truth, while the meaning of "Napoleon died on St. Helena" is such that it expresses a contingent one, but that just returns to the original contrast between concretely empty and concretely substantial ideas, and so adds nothing to the first charge. Unger shows no awareness of the difficulty, and says nothing that might help to resolve it.

Some philosophers restrict the term "analytic" to cases where the semantic or conceptual relation at issue should be obvious to a competent user of the language or someone who grasps the relevant concepts. On that reading, the second charge would simply be that analytic philosophers deserve no prizes because what they tell us was obvious anyway, like "All red things are colored." But that cannot be what Unger means, for many of the ideas he classifies as analytically empty concern matters that are utterly unobvious even on reflection, hard or even impossible to decide, and he does not pretend otherwise.

Unger's usual procedure is just to report an analytic philosopher's view and then confidently assert without argument that it is concretely empty, often adding with slightly less confidence and still no argument that it is analytically empty. If he had really uncovered some dark secret about what analytic philosophers are up to, one might have expected the case for the prosecution to take a somewhat more elaborate form.

Occasionally, Unger shares with the reader some of his wild fantasies about mind and matter, as a hint of where the sort of concretely substantial philosophy he favors might go. However, he mostly refrains from claiming that those fantasies are true. According to him, serious progress on that front will require a combination of talent and knowledge in both philosophy and physics to a level that only a handful of favored individuals currently attain, not including him. The book ends with the injunction that "we philosophers should assume, or maintain, a deeply held attitude of intellectual modesty." The modesty he has in mind seems to be collective, with respect to practitioners of other disciplines, rather than individual, with respect to other philosophers. For he also tells us:

> what's already presented in this book, much of it first proposed in my earlier *All the Power in the World*, probably comprises more in the way of novel substantial philosophical ideas than everything published by prominent mainstreamers, all taken together, during the last 70 years or so.

To maintain his modesty with respect to non-philosophers, he adds a disclaimer, perhaps in view of the lack of scientific support for his speculations: "precious little of it – maybe none at all – is worth significant or sustained consideration." If one wanted to refute Unger's claim to (probably) outdo the mainstream in novel substantial philosophical ideas, one could start with a mass of recent work in the philosophy of mind about the contingent workings of the human mind, closely engaged with experimental psychology.

Empty Ideas has several virtues, all characteristic of good analytic philosophy. It is often bold, clear, intelligent, ingenious, and independent-minded. In passing, it makes some useful contributions to debates in analytic metaphysics, offering examples that repay further reflection, for instance on the topic of essentialism. But it is vitiated by an overall framework that has not been properly constructed and cannot bear the weight of the argument.

There is a genuine question about how learning necessary truths can bring new knowledge, since they exclude no possibilities. But the first step towards answering it is to realize that it is a special case of a more general question: how can learning necessarily equivalent truths bring different knowledge? For instance, knowing the contingent truth "There are 17^2 tiles on the floor" is somehow different from knowing the necessarily equivalent contingent truth "There are 289 tiles on the floor," just as knowing the trivial necessary truth "$17^2 = 17^2$" is somehow different from knowing the necessarily equivalent but less trivial necessary truth "$17^2 = 289$." It is still unclear what the best framework is for understanding such matters, but it will surely articulate the way in which our thinking about the same state of affairs can be mediated by different sentences. Whatever the details, there is no good reason to expect the explanation to make a big deal of the difference between disciplines that mainly investigate non-contingent matters, such as mathematics, logic, and philosophy, and most other disciplines, which investigate contingent matters. The large differences in methodology between disciplines have more specific sources. A critique based on confusion about such fundamental issues should not move analytic philosophers.

Acknowledgment

This section originally appeared as a review of Unger 2014 in the *Times Literary Supplement* (Williamson 2015b).

14.5   Plato Goes Pop

It was only a matter of time, after the success of Stephen Hawking and the subsequent wave of popular science books, before someone noticed the gap in the market for books of popular philosophy. The gap is now rapidly being filled. A pile of them sits on my desk as I write. But they don't emulate the stereotype of popular science. The authors are not trying to communicate mind-twisting recent developments in philosophy beyond the readership of technical journals. Indeed, several of them seem rather embarrassed about the association with academic philosophy, anxiously emphasizing their credentials as streetsmart, clued-in drinking companions (*Beer and Philosophy, Wine and Philosophy*): despite being philosophers, they are sexy and never in any way in the least boring. The blurb for the Blackwell Philosophy and PopCulture series (*South Park and Philosophy, The Office and Philosophy*) says "Philosophy has had a public relations problem for a few centuries now. This series aims to change that, showing that philosophy is relevant to your life." The titles, not only in that series, tell a slightly different story: "philosophy," "philosopher" (*The Undercover Philosopher*), "philosophical" (*Philosophical Provocations*) are treated as words that sell books, not as put-offs to be concealed until the reader is already hooked. An old-fashioned image is not always bad for business.

Recent changes in philosophy's self-image facilitate popularization. "The linguistic turn" belongs in the last century. Increasingly, philosophers have returned to seeing their subject matter as the world, rather than only our talk or thought about it: not just the word "beer" or the concept of beer, but the stuff you can drink. Philosophers of time study time itself, alert to the possibility that Special Relativity undermines the ordinary language of time. Contemporary moral philosophers do not restrict themselves to describing the rules of moral discourse; they can argue directly about whether torture is absolutely always wrong. In these ways, philosophy no longer defines its questions in ways radically alien to a more innocent understanding.

At the same time, the growing specialization and technicality of academic philosophy has made it ever less accessible to non-specialists, thus ever more in need of popularization. Much work in moral and political philosophy bears on urgent practical issues, public or private, but often in a qualified, indirect way; it may become tractable for decision-makers only after going through several stages of mediation, in what the original author may regard as a process of crass over-simplification. Similarly, philosophers of language are currently debating relativism in terms of subtle issues about the exact structure of a formal theory of meaning. The debate really does implicate popular versions of relativism often invoked when disagreement looks irresolvable ("That's true for us even if it's false for you"). For non-specialists, some mediating process is needed to elucidate what is at stake.

Not much popular philosophy attempts to mediate recent developments in technical or academic philosophy to a wider audience. When philosophers are cited, they tend to be the mighty dead. Philosophy, unlike physics, is apparently best consumed when well pickled. Many of the authors seem too little acquainted with recent developments to be in a position to mediate them. Some seem actively hostile. Academic philosophy is presented as trivial logic-chopping that has lost touch with the deep, simple questions at the heart of real philosophy. Thus popular philosophy steps in to undertake the proper task of philosophy, which the professionals disdain.

The bluff amateur style of philosophy is not without presuppositions. It takes for granted that simple questions ("Why be good?," "What is truth?") have simple answers, and that to find those answers it is unnecessary to take much notice of what other people working on the same questions have recently come up with – popular philosophers tend to ignore each other as well as the professionals. This optimistic procedure is taken to be the way to make philosophy serious again. Naturally, the actual results are riddled with boring old fallacies and confusions, rarely even amusing new ones. For instance, I read "when Jane says she loves Dick, she is actually saying that she is in love with her ideas of Dick," which embodies at least two mistakes as old as the undergraduate essay. Too often, the genre of popular philosophy is abused as an opportunity to pass off one's pet theories dogmatically on a readership unacquainted with the standard objections and alternatives to them, unhampered by the tiresome business of being reviewed by one's peers.

Few professional philosophers that I know have forgotten the fundamental questions from which their inquiry originated, not least because they have to explain the connections every year when teaching undergraduates. The elaborate apparatus of academic writing in philosophy results not from self-indulgent pedantry but from the need to distinguish different interpretations of the question, which may have different answers, to provide non-question-begging evidence in support of one's answers, to assess whether one's answer is any better supported than those carefully developed by others, and so on. Although rigor is sometimes portrayed as the resort of those who lack the courage to speak from the gut, the real risk-taking is in precise statements and explicitly articulated arguments, since the point of such formality is to make errors maximally easy to spot. If you are afraid of being caught out, take refuge behind a smokescreen of vagueness and obscurity.

Of course, similar remarks apply to specialization in any academic discipline. But philosophy seems peculiarly vulnerable to the charge that its nature requires accessibility. It would be more blatantly dumb to tell physicists to drop their equations and start doing real physics, or historians to get out of their archives and start doing real history. According to a venerable tradition, philosophy is an essentially practical activity, whose aim is to improve our lives. If so, it should be accessible, for there is little point in giving people advice they can't understand. This conception is not limited to ethics, the branch of philosophy most obviously relevant to how to live. Descartes, typecast as the founding father of modern epistemology, tried to develop a method of inquiry that would enable one to avoid error and gain genuine knowledge. By contrast, most contemporary epistemologists have lowered their sights. They may tell you what knowledge is, but they won't tell you how to get it. Wouldn't it be nice, though, to have a sort of epistemology that *did* tell you how to get knowledge? Some popular philosophers seem to be moved by the practical calling. For those in a hurry for practical advice, academic philosophy is not the best place to go. That is nothing new. The founder of the Academy gave a lecture *On the Good*. Most of Plato's audience came expecting to be told how to get rich, or stay healthy, or be happy, and were disappointed to hear a lecture full of mathematics, culminating in the statement that the Good is One. Its practical implications were not immediate. As a research instrument, Descartes' method fell short of his advertising.

Not all contemporary academic epistemologists are determined to be practically useless. The Bayesian school applies probability theory in ways that really do help one handle uncertainty better in predicaments that lend themselves to a probabilistic representation. A mass of psychological evidence indicates that, without such training, humans are scarily bad at thinking with probabilities. But Bayesian epistemology is not popular philosophy: it is highly mathematical. There are also theoretical reasons for doubting that any rule of action can be fully practical, although some are less impractical than others. If the rule says "In such-and-such circumstances, do so-and-so," cases can always arise in which it is unclear whether the circumstances are so-and-so, and therefore unclear what you must do to comply with the rule.

Although practical and academic medicine have different and sometimes conflicting imperatives, we don't want practical medicine to ignore academic medicine (as alternative medicine does). It is not wholly different in philosophy. Although there is even more uncertainty in academic philosophy than in academic medicine, in both cases practice should take account of that uncertainty, not hide it from the patients. Philosophical questions are too interesting and important to be left to the professionals. The more people who ask them, the better. It is good that accessible books exist to feed such curiosity. A few do it well. But it is a pity that so much of the genre shows such incuriosity about what is really happening in philosophy now.

Acknowledgment

This section originally appeared in the *Times Literary Supplement* as Williamson 2009c.

14.6 Popular Philosophy and Populist Philosophy

Every intellectual discipline needs to speak to others as well as to itself, both to learn and to teach. If it is getting anywhere, it has something new to say to neighboring disciplines, but also to the general public.

If a discipline has practical applications, it should communicate them where they can help. It should also provide points of entry to the curious. Its survival depends on that: if it can't explain to the uninitiated what it is up to, how will it recruit new members? Politically, it is unwise to tell the taxpayers who fund it "Shut up and give us the money; never you mind how we spend it."

All that applies to philosophy in particular. A civilized society has popular philosophy just as it has popular physics, popular psychology, popular history, … So one might expect the relation between popular and academic philosophy to resemble the corresponding relations for other disciplines. Thus popular philosophy would communicate recent research in academic philosophy to a wider audience.

In my experience, a surprisingly high proportion of popular philosophy is *not* like that. Instead, it sets itself up as a rival to academic philosophy, which it portrays as trivial, sterile, pedantic, irrelevant logic-chopping.

This popular philosophy claims to be the *real* philosophy, the true heir to what was done in ancient times. It asks and answers the questions that really matter, going straight to the point by arguments that can be understood with no previous training. It speaks over the heads of the scholastics to laypeople who approach philosophy fresh and unprejudiced.

The message that with little effort one can do better than the professionals is naturally gratifying to non-professionals; it finds a ready audience. One might call that populist message the Michael Gove view of philosophy, in honor of the British politician who, when asked during the 2016 referendum campaign which economists favored leaving the European Union, replied "people in this country have had enough of experts" – though Covid-19 has changed his public attitude to experts.

Like Gove with economic expertise, populist philosophers are uncomfortable with the idea of genuine expertise in philosophy. They may admit that there are experts on the history of philosophy, who understand numerous difficult texts hardly anyone else has even read. They may also accept that there are experts on formal logic, and expert *teachers* of philosophy. But such concessions are consistent with the populist idea that the apparatus of academic philosophy – all the to-and-fro of point-by-point discussion in conferences and refereed journals – contributes nothing of significance to answering central questions of philosophy, and should be bypassed.

Sometimes I encounter people who take a similar attitude to modern natural science. They say that science went wrong after Aristotle, or send me their theory of "qualitative physics," which bypasses all that boring mathematics to go straight to the secret of the universe. But such ideas are not the stuff of most popular science, which has better things to do.

Philosophy is more vulnerable than natural science to the populist belief that laypeople are just as qualified as professionals. This belief derives from the ideal of the radically autonomous inquirer, who takes nothing for granted and uses nothing second-hand. In other words, such a thinker refuses to learn anything from other people. That's a recipe for the endless repetition of the same elementary mistakes, generation after generation. Anyway, the instructions cannot be carried out; *all* thinking takes much for granted. The ideal of the radically autonomous inquirer is itself stale and nth-hand.

A less arrogant attitude is that we all have much to learn from other people, in philosophy as everywhere else. Philosophy is even harder than it seems; the right response to its difficulty is not to trash all the work already done by thousands of highly gifted and knowledgeable men and women. Compared to the size of the task, their contributions may have been small, and often mistaken, but that does not mean you can do better by ignoring them.

Philosophy is a collective enterprise, which has developed slowly through various traditions over many centuries in many parts of the world. It has never been just the work of a few isolated geniuses. Joining one of those traditions has always involved acquiring the relevant forms of philosophical expertise. We shouldn't be coy about it. We need to explain honestly and openly how philosophy works.

Recent philosophical research has produced lots of fascinating new ideas, which deserve to be better known. Now there's a task for popular philosophy.

Acknowledgment

This section first appeared as a post on the blog *Daily Nous* as part of the series "The Philosophy of Popular Philosophy," edited by Aaron James Wendland.

Bibliography

Adams, E. 1965. "The logic of conditionals," Inquiry 8: 166–97.

Adams, E. 1975. *The Logic of Conditionals*. Dordrecht: Reidel.

Alexander, J. 2012. *Experimental Philosophy: An Introduction*. Cambridge: Polity Press.

Alexander, J. and Weinberg, J. 2007. "Analytic epistemology and experimental philosophy," Philosophy Compass 2: 56–80.

Alexander, J. and Weinberg, J. 2014. "The 'unreliability' of epistemic intuitions," in E. Machery and E. O'Neill, eds., *Current Controversies in Experimental Philosophy*, 128–45. London: Routledge.

Anderson, A. R. 1951. "A note on subjunctive and counterfactual conditionals," Analysis 12: 35–8.

Arntzenius, F. 2008. "Gunk, topology, and measure," Oxford Studies in Metaphysics 4: 225–47.

Austin, J. L. 1956–1957. "A plea for excuses," Proceedings of the Aristotelian Society 57: 1–30.

Ayer, A. J. 1936. *Language, Truth and Logic*. London: Victor Gollancz.

Ayer, A. J. 1956. *The Problem of Knowledge*. London: Macmillan.

Bach, K. 1988. "Burge's new thought experiment: Back to the drawing room," Journal of Philosophy 85: 88–97.

Baker, G. and Hacker, P. 1984. *Frege: Logical Excavations*. Oxford: Blackwell.

Bealer, G. 1998. "Intuition and the autonomy of philosophy," in DePaul and Ramsey 1998, 201–40.

Bealer, G. 2002. "Modal epistemology and the rationalist renaissance," in Gendler and Hawthorne 2002, 71–125.

Bennett, J. 2003. *A Philosophical Guide to Conditionals*. Oxford: Clarendon Press.

Bergmann, G. 1964. *Logic and Reality*. Madison, WI: The University of Wisconsin Press.

Bianchi, A. 2011. "What do philosophers do? A few reflections on Timothy Williamson's *The Philosophy of Philosophy*," in R. Davies, ed., *Analisi: Annuario/Bollettino della Società Italiana di Filosofia Analytica 2011*, 117–25. Milan: Mimesis.

Bird, A. 1998. "Dispositions and antidotes," Philosophical Quarterly 48: 227–34.

Bird, A. 2007. *Nature's Metaphysics: Laws and Properties.* Oxford: Clarendon Press.

Blackburn, S. 1987. "Morals and modals," in G. Macdonald and C. Wright, eds., *Facts, Science and Morality,* 119–41. Oxford: Blackwell.

Boer, S. and Lycan, W. 1985. *Knowing Who.* Cambridge, MA: Bradford Books.

Boghossian, P. 1997. "Analyticity," in B. Hale and C. Wright, eds., *A Companion to the Philosophy of Language,* 331–68. Oxford: Blackwell.

Boghossian, P. 2002. "How are objective epistemic reasons possible?," in J. Bermudez and A. Miller, eds., *Reasons and Nature,* 1–47. Oxford: Oxford University Press.

Boghossian, P. 2003. "Blind reasoning," The Aristotelian Society sup. 77: 225–48.

Boghossian, P. 2011. "Williamson on the a priori and the analytic," Philosophy and Phenomenological Research 82: 488–97.

Boghossian, P. 2012. "Inferentialism and the epistemology of logic: Reflections on Casalegno and Williamson," dialectica 66: 221–36.

Boghossian, P. and Williamson, T. 2020. *Debating the A Priori.* Oxford: Oxford University Press.

Bonini, N., Osherson, D., Viale, R., and Williamson, T. 1999. "On the psychology of vague predicates," Mind and Language 14: 377–93.

BonJour, L. 1985. *The Structure of Empirical Knowledge.* Cambridge, MA: Harvard University Press.

Bradley, F. H. 1893. *Appearance and Reality.* London: Swan Sonnenschein.

Braine, M. and O'Brien, D. 1991. "A theory of *if*: A lexical entry, reasoning program,and pragmatic principles," Psychological Review 98: 182–203.

Brandom, R. 1994. *Making It Explicit: Reasoning, Representing, and Discursive Commitment.* Cambridge, MA: Harvard University Press.

Brandom, R. 2000. *Articulating Reasons: An Introduction to Inferentialism.* Cambridge, MA: Harvard University Press.

Brandom, R. 2009a. *Reason in Philosophy: Animating Ideas.* Cambridge, MA: Harvard University Press.

Brandom, R. 2009b. "Animating ideas of idealism: A semantic sonata in Kant and Hegel," in Brandom 2009a, 27–107.

Burge, T. 1978. "Belief and synonymy," Journal of Philosophy 75: 119–38.

Burge, T. 1979. "Individualism and the mental," Midwest Studies in Philosophy 4: 73–121.

Burge, T. 1986. "Intellectual norms and foundations of mind," Journal of Philosophy 83: 697–720.

Byrne, R. 1989. "Suppressing valid inferences with conditionals," Cognition 31: 1–21.

Byrne, R. 2005. *The Rational Imagination: How People Create Alternatives to Reality.* Cambridge, MA: MIT Press.

Cappelen, H. 2012. *Philosophy without Intuitions.* Oxford: Oxford University Press.

Carnap, R. 1947. *Meaning and Necessity: A Study in Semantics and Modal Logic*. Chicago, IL: University of Chicago Press.

Carnap, R. 1950. *Logical Foundations of Probability*. Chicago, IL: University of Chicago Press.

Casalegno, P. 2004. "Logical concepts and logical inferences," dialectica 58: 395–411.

Casullo, A. 2021. "A defense of the significance of the a priori – a posteriori distinction," forthcoming in D. Dodd and E. Zardini, eds., *The A Priori: Its Significance, Grounds, and Extent*. Oxford University Press.

Chalmers, D. 2002. "Does conceivability entail possibility?" in Gendler and Hawthorne 2002, 145–200.

Chalmers, D. 2006. "The foundations of two-dimensional semantics," in M. García-Carpintero and J. Macià, eds., *Two-Dimensional Semantics*, 55–140. Oxford: Clarendon Press.

Chambers, T. 1998. "On vagueness, *sorites*, and Putnam's 'intuitionistic strategy'," Monist 81: 343–8.

Chisholm, R. 1957. *Perceiving: A Philosophical Study*. Ithaca, NY: Cornell University Press.

Chomsky, N. 1957. *Syntactic Structures*. The Hague: Mouton.

Chomsky, N. 1959. "Review of B. F. Skinner's *Verbal Behavior*," Language 35: 26–58.

Cohen, S. 1988. "How to be a fallibilist," Philosophical Perspectives 2: 91–123.

Collins, J., Hall, N., and Paul, L., eds. 2004. *Causation and Counterfactuals*. Cambridge, MA: MIT Press.

Craig, E. 1985. "Arithmetic and fact," in I. Hacking, ed., *Exercises in Analysis*, 89–112. Cambridge: Cambridge University Press.

Cummins, R. 1998. "Reflections on reflective equilibrium," in DePaul and Ramsey 1998, 113–28.

Currie, G. 1995a. *Image and Mind: Philosophy, Film and Cognitive Science*. New York: Cambridge University Press.

Currie, G. 1995b. "Visual imagery as the simulation of vision," Mind and Language 10: 17–44.

Davidson, D. 1967a. "Truth and meaning," Synthese 17: 304–23.

Davidson, D. 1967b. "The logical form of action sentences," in N. Rescher, ed., *The Logic of Decision and Action*, 81–95. Pittsburgh, PA: University of Pittsburgh Press.

Davidson, D. 1974. "On the very idea of a conceptual scheme," Proceedings and Addresses of the American Philosophical Association 47: 5–20. Reprinted in Davidson 1984, to which page numbers refer.

Davidson, D. 1975. "Thought and talk," in S. Guttenplan, ed., *Mind and Language*, 7–23. Oxford: Clarendon Press. Reprinted in Davidson 1984, to which page numbers refer.

Davidson, D. 1977. "The method of truth in metaphysics," in P. French, T. Uehling, and H. Wettstein, eds., *Midwest Studies in Philosophy, 2: Studies in the Philosophy of Language*, 244–54. Morris, MN: The University of Minnesota. Reprinted in Davidson 1984, to which page numbers refer.

Davidson, D. 1980. *Essays on Actions and Events*. Oxford: Clarendon Press.

Davidson, D. 1983. "A coherence theory of truth and knowledge," in D. Henrich, ed., *Kant Oder Hegel?* 423–38. Stuttgart: Klett-Cotta. Reprinted with "Afterthoughts" in Davidson 2001.

Davidson, D. 1984. *Inquiries into Truth and Interpretation*. Oxford: Clarendon Press.

Davidson, D. 1986. "A nice derangement of epitaphs," in E. LePore, ed., *Truth and Interpretation*, 433–46. Oxford: Blackwell.

Davidson, D. 1991. "Epistemology externalized," Dialectica 45: 191–202. Reprinted in Davidson 2001, to which page numbers refer.

Davidson, D. 2001. *Subjective, Intersubjective, Objective*. Oxford: Clarendon Press.

Davies, M. 1981. *Meaning, Quantification, Necessity*. London: Routledge and Kegan Paul.

Davies, M. and Humberstone, I. L. 1980. "Two notions of necessity," Philosophical Studies 38: 1–30.

Davies, M. and Stone, T., eds. 1995. *Mental Simulation: Evaluation and Applications*. Oxford: Blackwell.

Dennett, D. 1981. *Brainstorms: Philosophical Essays on Mind and Psychology*. Brighton: Harvester.

Dennett, D. 2019. "Philosophy or auto-anthropology," Epistemology and Philosophy of Science 56: 26–8.

DePaul, M. 1998. "Why bother with reflective equilibrium?," in DePaul and Ramsey 1998, 293–310.

DePaul, M. and Ramsey, W., eds. 1998. *Rethinking Intuition: The Psychology of Intuition and Its Role in Philosophical Inquiry*. Lanham, MD: Rowman and Littlefield.

DeRose, K. 1995. "Solving the skeptical problem," Philosophical Review 104: 1–52.

Deutsch, M. 2009. "Experimental philosophy and the theory of reference," Mind and Language 24: 445–66.

Dretske, F. 1970. "Epistemic operators," Journal of Philosophy 67: 1007–23.

Dummett, M. 1959. "Truth," Proceedings of the Aristotelian Society 59: 141–62.

Dummett, M. 1973. *Frege: Philosophy of Language*. London: Duckworth.

Dummett, M. 1975a. "Wang's paradox," Synthese 30: 301–24.

Dummett, M. 1975b. "The philosophical basis of intuitionistic logic," in H. E. Rose and J. Shepherdson, eds., *Logic Colloquium '73*, 5–40. Amsterdam: North-Holland.

Dummett, M. 1977a. *Elements of Intuitionism*. Oxford: Oxford University Press.

Dummett, M. 1977b. "Can analytical philosophy be systematic, and ought it to be?," Hegel Studien 17: 305–26.

Dummett, M. 1978. *Truth and Other Enigmas*. London: Duckworth.

Dummett, M. 1984. "An unsuccessful dig," Philosophical Quarterly 34: 377–401.

Dummett, M. 1991. *The Logical Basis of Metaphysics*. London: Duckworth.

Dummett, M. 1993. *Origins of Analytical Philosophy*. London: Duckworth.

Edgington, D. 2001. "Conditionals," in L. Goble, ed., *The Blackwell Guide to Philosophical Logic*, 385–414. Oxford: Blackwell.

Edgington, D. 2003. "Counterfactuals and the benefit of hindsight," in P. Dowe and P. Noordhof, eds., *Causation and Counterfactuals*, 12–27. London: Routledge.

Eklund, M. 2002. "Inconsistent languages," Philosophy and Phenomenological Research 64: 251–75.

Elbourne, P. 2005. *Situations and Individuals*. Cambridge, MA: MIT Press.

Elugardo, R. 1993. "Burge on content," Philosophy and Phenomenological Research 53: 367–84.

Ericsson, K. A., Charness, N., Feltovich, P., and Hoffmann, R., eds. 2006. *The Cambridge Handbook of Expertise and Expert Performance*. Cambridge: Cambridge University Press.

Etchemendy, J. 1990. *The Concept of Logical Consequence*. Cambridge, MA: Cambridge University Press.

Evans, G. 1979. "Reference and contingency," Monist 62: 161–89.

Evans, G. 1982. *The Varieties of Reference*. Oxford: Clarendon Press.

Evans, G. 1985. *Collected Papers*. Oxford: Clarendon Press.

Evans, J. and Over, D. 2004. *If*. Oxford: Oxford University Press.

Feyerabend, P. 1978. *Science in a Free Society*. London: NLB.

Field, H. 2003. "Causation in a physical world," in M. Loux and D. Zimmerman, eds., *The Oxford Handbook of Metaphysics*, 435–60. Oxford: Oxford University Press.

Fine, K. 1970. "Propositional quantifiers in modal logic," Theoria 36: 336–46.

Fine, K. 1975. "Vagueness, truth and logic," Synthese 30: 265–300.

Fine, K. 1994. "Essence and modality," Philosophical Perspectives 8: 1–16.

Fine, K. 1995. "Senses of essence," in Sinnott-Armstrong et al. 1995, 53–73.

Fintel, K. V. 2001. "Counterfactuals in a dynamic context," in M. Kenstowicz, ed., *Ken Hale: A Life in Language*, 123–52. Cambridge, MA: MIT Press.

Fodor, J. 1975. *The Language of Thought*. New York: Thomas Crowell.

Fodor, J. 1998. *Concepts: Where Cognitive Science Went Wrong*. Oxford: Oxford University Press.

Føllesdal, D. 2004. *Referential Opacity and Modal Logic*. London: Routledge.

Forster, M. and Sober, E. 1994. "How to tell when simpler, more unified, or less *ad hoc* theories will provide more accurate predictions," British Journal for the Philosophy of Science 45: 1–35.

Frascolla, P. 2011. "On the face value of the 'original question' and its weight in philosophy," in R. Davies, ed., *Analisi: Annuario e Bollettino della Società Italiana di Filosofia Analitica (SIFA) 2011*, 81–90. Milan: Mimesis.

Frege, G. 1950. *The Foundations of Arithmetic*, trans. J. L. Austin. Oxford: Blackwell.

French, P., Uehling, T., and Wettstein, H., eds. 1986. *Midwest Studies in Philosophy XI: Studies in Essentialism*. Minneapolis, MN: University of Minnesota Press.

Gallie, W. B. 1964. *Philosophy and the Historical Understanding.* London: Chatto and Windus.

Gauker, C. 2005. *Conditionals in Context.* Cambridge, MA: MIT Press.

Gaut, B. 2006. "Art and cognition," in M. Kieran, ed., *Contemporary Debates in Aesthetics and the Philosophy of Art,* 115–26. Oxford: Blackwell.

Gendler, T. S. 1998. "Galileo and the indispensability of scientific thought experiments," British Journal for the Philosophy of Science 49: 397–424.

Gendler, T. S. 2004. "Thoughts experiments rethought – and reperceived," Philosophy of Science 71: 1152–63.

Gendler, T. S. and Hawthorne, J., eds. 2002. *Conceivability and Possibility.* Oxford: Clarendon Press.

Gettier, E. 1963. "Is justified true belief knowledge?," Analysis 23: 121–3.

Godfrey-Smith, P. 2006a. "The strategy of model-based science," Biology and Philosophy 21: 725–40.

Godfrey-Smith, P. 2006b. "Theories and models in metaphysics," Harvard Review of Philosophy 14: 4–19.

Godfrey-Smith, P. 2012. "Metaphysics and the philosophical imagination," Philosophical Studies 160: 97–113.

Goldberg, S. 2000. "Do anti-individualistic construals of propositional attitudes capture the agent's conceptions?," Noûs 36: 597–621.

Goldman, A. 1992. "Empathy, mind, and morals," Proceedings and Addresses of the American Philosophical Association 66: 17–41.

Goldman, A. 2005. "Kornblith's naturalistic epistemology," Philosophy and Phenomenological Research 71: 403–10.

Goldman, A. and Pust, J. 1998. "Philosophical theory and intuitional evidence," in DePaul and Ramsey 1998, 179–97.

Goodman, N. 1955. *Fact, Fiction and Forecast.* Cambridge, MA: Harvard University Press.

Graff, D. and Williamson, T., eds. 2002. *Vagueness.* Aldershot: Dartmouth.

Grandy, R. 1973. "Reference, meaning, and belief," Journal of Philosophy 70: 439–52.

Greenough, P. and Lynch, M., eds. 2006. *Truth and Realism.* Oxford: Clarendon Press.

Grice, P. 1961. "The causal theory of perception," Aristotelian Society sup. 35: 121–52.

Grice, P. 1975. "Logic and conversation," in D. Davidson and G. Harman, eds., *The Logic of Grammar,* 64–75. Encino, CA: Dickenson.

Grice, P. 1986. "Reply to Richards," in R. Grandy and R. Warner, eds., *Philosophical Grounds of Rationality: Intentions, Categories, Ends,* 45–106. Oxford: Clarendon Press.

Grice, P. 1989. *Studies in the Way of Words.* Cambridge, MA: Harvard University Press.

Grice, P. and Strawson, P. 1956. "In defence of a dogma," Philosophical Review 65: 141–58.

Häggqvist, S. 1996. *Thought Experiments in Philosophy.* Stockholm: Almqvist and Wiksell.

Halbach, V. 2001. "How innocent is deflationism?" Synthese 126: 167–94.

Harman, G. 1965. "The inference to the best explanation," Philosophical Review 74: 88–95.

Harman, G. 1986. *Change in View: Principles of Reasoning.* Cambridge, MA: MIT Press.

Harman, G. 1999. *Reasoning, Meaning, and Mind.* Oxford: Clarendon Press.

Harris, P. 2000. *The Work of the Imagination.* Oxford: Blackwell.

Hawthorne, J. 2004. *Knowledge and Lotteries.* Oxford: Oxford University Press.

Hawthorne, J. 2006. *Metaphysical Essays.* Oxford: Clarendon Press.

Hawthorne, J. and Stanley, J. 2008. "Knowledge and action," Journal of Philosophy 105: 571–90.

Hempel, C. 1965. *Aspects of Scientific Explanation and Other Essays in the Philosophy of Science.* New York: The Free Press.

Hill, C. 2006. "Modality, modal epistemology, and the metaphysics of consciousness," in S. Nichols, ed., *The Architecture of the Imagination: New Essays on Pretense, Possibility and Fiction*, 205–36. Oxford: Oxford University Press.

Hintikka, J. 1962. *Knowledge and Belief.* Ithaca, NY: Cornell University Press.

Hintikka, J. 1999. "The Emperor's new intuitions," Journal of Philosophy 96: 127–47.

Horgan, T. 1995. "Transvaluationism: A Dionysian approach to vagueness," Southern Journal of Philosophy 33 sup.: 97–126.

Horgan, T. 1998. "The transvaluationist conception of vagueness," Monist 81: 313–30.

Horwich, P. 1998a. *Meaning.* Oxford: Clarendon Press.

Horwich, P. 1998b. *Truth*, 2nd edn. Oxford: Clarendon Press.

Horwich, P. 2011. "Williamson's *Philosophy of Philosophy*," Philosophy and Phenomenological Research 82: 524–33.

Horwich, P. 2012. *Wittgenstein's Metaphilosophy.* New York: Oxford University Press.

Howson, C. and Urbach, P. 1993. *Scientific Reasoning: The Bayesian Approach*, 2nd edn. Chicago, IL: Open Court.

Hughes, G. and Cresswell, M. 1996. *A New Introduction to Modal Logic.* London: Routledge.

Ichikawa, J. 2009. "Knowing the intuition and knowing the counterfactual," Philosophical Studies 145: 435–43.

Ichikawa, J. and Jarvis, B. 2008. "Thought experiment intuitions and truth in fiction," Philosophical Studies 142: 221–46.

Inwagen, P. van. 1995. *Material Beings.* Ithaca, NY: Cornell University Press.

Inwagen, P. van. 1997. "Materialism and the psychological-continuity account of personal identity," Philosophical Perspectives 11: 305–19.

Jackson, F. 1977. "A causal theory of counterfactuals," Australasian Journal of Philosophy 55: 3–21.

Jackson, F. 1979. "On assertion and indicative conditionals," Philosophical Review 88: 565–89.

Jackson, F. 1981. "Conditionals and possibilia," Proceedings of the Aristotelian Society 81: 125–37.

Jackson, F. 1987. *Conditionals*. Oxford: Blackwell.

Jackson, F. 1998. *From Metaphysics to Ethics: A Defence of Conceptual Analysis*. Oxford: Clarendon Press.

Jackson, F. 2001. "Responses," Philosophy and Phenomenological Research 62: 653–64.

Jackson, F. 2009. "Thought experiments and possibilities," Analysis 69: 100–9.

Johnson-Laird, P. and Byrne, R. 1993. "Models and deductive rationality," in K. Manktelow and D. Over, eds., *Rationality: Psychological and Philosophical Perspectives*, 177–210. London: Routledge.

Johnston, M. 1993. "Objectivity refigured: Pragmatism without verificationism," in J. Haldane and C. Wright, eds., *Reality, Representation and Projection*, 85–130. Oxford: Oxford University Press.

Jönsson, M. and Hampton, J. 2006. "The inverse conjunction fallacy," Journal of Memory and Language 55: 317–34.

Kahneman, D. and Frederick, S. 2002. "Representativeness revisited: Attribute substitution in intuitive judgment," in T. Gilovich, D. Griffin, and D. Kahneman, eds., *Heuristics and Biases: The Psychology of Intuitive Judgment*, 49–81. Cambridge: Cambridge University Press.

Kahneman, D. and Tversky, A. 1982. "The simulation heuristic," in D. Kahneman, P. Slovic, and A. Tversky, eds., *Judgement under Uncertainty*, 201–8. Cambridge: Cambridge University Press.

Kaplan, D. 1970. "S5 with quantifiable propositional variables," Journal of Symbolic Logic 35: 355.

Kaplan, D. 1989. "Demonstratives: An essay on the semantics, logic metaphysics, and epistemology of demonstratives and other indexicals," in J. Almog, J. Perry, and H. Wettstein, eds., *Themes from Kaplan*, 481–564. Oxford: Oxford University Press.

Kaplan, D. 1990. "Words," Aristotelian Society sup. 64: 93–119.

Keefe, R. 2000. *Theories of Vagueness*. Cambridge: Cambridge University Press.

Keefe, R. and Smith, P., eds. 1997. *Vagueness: A Reader*. Cambridge, MA: MIT Press.

Kleene, S. 1952. *Introduction to Metamathematics*. Amsterdam: North-Holland.

Klein, P. 1986. "Radical interpretation and global skepticism," in LePore 1986, 369–86.

Kment, B. 2006. "Counterfactuals and the analysis of necessity," Philosophical Perspectives 20: 237–302.

Knobe, J. 2019. "Philosophical intuitions are surprisingly robust across demographic differences," Epistemology and Philosophy of Science 56: 29–36.

Kornblith, H. 2002. *Knowledge and Its Place in Nature*. Oxford: Oxford University Press.

Kornblith, H. 2006. "Appeals to intuition and the ambitions of epistemology," in S. Hetherington, ed., *Epistemology Futures*, 10–25. Oxford: Clarendon Press.

Kornblith, H. 2007. "Naturalism and intuitions," Grazer Philosophische Studien 74: 27–49.

Kornblith, H. 2009. "Timothy Williamson's *The Philosophy of Philosophy*," Analysis 69: 109–16.

Kratzer, A. 1977. "What 'must' and 'can' must and can mean," Linguistics and Philosophy 1: 337–55.

Kratzer, A. 1986. "Conditionals," in A. Farley, P. Farley, and K.-E. McCollough, eds., *Papers from the Parasession on Pragmatics and Grammatical Theory*, 10–25. Chicago, IL: Chicago Linguistics Society.

Kripke, S. 1963. "Semantical considerations on modal logic," Acta Philosophica Fennica 16: 83–94.

Kripke, S. 1972. "Naming and necessity," in D. Davidson and G. Harman, eds., *Semantics of Natural Languages*, 253–355 and 763–9. Dordrecht: Reidel. Expanded as Kripke 1980.

Kripke, S. 1976. "Is there a problem about substitutional quantification?," in G. Evans and J. McDowell, eds., *Truth and Meaning*, 325–419. Oxford: Oxford University Press.

Kripke, S. 1979. "A puzzle about belief," in A. Margalit, ed., *Meaning and Use*, 239–83. Dordrecht: Reidel.

Kripke, S. 1980. *Naming and Necessity*. Oxford: Blackwell.

Kripke, S. 1982. *Wittgenstein on Rules and Private Language: An Elementary Exposition*. Oxford: Blackwell.

Kripke, S. 2013. *Reference and Existence: The John Locke Lectures*. Oxford: Oxford University Press.

Kuhn, T. 1970. *The Structure of Scientific Revolutions*, 2nd edn. Chicago, IL: University of Chicago Press.

Kuznetsov, A. 2019. "Armchair science and armchair philosophy," Epistemology and Philosophy of Science 56: 43–5.

Ladusaw, W. 1996. "Negation and polarity items," in S. Lappin, ed., *The Handbook of Contemporary Semantic Theory*, 321–42. Oxford: Blackwell.

Lange, M. 2005. "A counterfactual analysis of logical truth and necessity," Philosophical Studies 125: 277–303.

Langford, C. H. 1942. "The notion of analysis in Moore's philosophy," in P. Schilpp, ed., *The Philosophy of G. E. Moore*, 319–42. Evanston, IL: Northwestern University Press.

LePore, E., ed. 1986. *Truth and Interpretation: Perspectives on the Philosophy of Donald Davidson*. Oxford: Blackwell.

Lewis, D. 1968. "Counterpart theory and quantified modal logic," Journal of Philosophy 65: 113–26.

Lewis, D. 1969. *Convention: A Philosophical Study*. Oxford: Blackwell.

Lewis, D. 1973a. "Counterfactuals and comparative possibility," Journal of Philosophical Logic 2: 418–46. Reprinted in his *Philosophical Papers*, vol. 2. Oxford: Oxford University Press, 1986, to which page numbers refer.

Lewis, D. 1973b. "Causation," Journal of Philosophy 70: 556–67.

Lewis, D. 1974. "Radical interpretation," Synthese 23: 331–44. Reprinted with "Postscripts" in Lewis 1983a, to which page numbers refer.

Lewis, D. 1975a. "Adverbs of quantification," in E. Keenan, ed., *Formal Semantics of Natural Language*, 178–88. Cambridge: Cambridge University Press.

Lewis, D. 1975b. "Languages and language," in K. Gunderson, ed., *Language, Mind, and Knowledge*, 3–35. Minneapolis, MN: University of Minnesota Press.

Lewis, D. 1978. "Truth in fiction," American Philosophical Quarterly 15: 37–46.

Lewis, D. 1979. "Counterfactual dependence and time's arrow," Noûs 13: 455–76.

Lewis, D. 1983a. *Philosophical Papers*, vol. 1. Oxford: Oxford University Press.

Lewis, D. 1983b. "New work for a theory of universals," Australasian Journal of Philosophy 61: 343–77.

Lewis, D. 1986a. *Counterfactuals*, revised edn. Cambridge, MA: Harvard University Press.

Lewis, D. 1986b. *On the Plurality of Worlds*. Oxford: Blackwell.

Lewis, D. 1996. "Elusive knowledge," Australasian Journal of Philosophy 74: 549–67.

Lewis, D. 1997. "Finkish dispositions," Philosophical Quarterly 47: 143–58.

Lipton, P. 2004. *Inference to the Best Explanation*, 2nd edn. London: Routledge, 2004.

Lowe, E. J. 1987. "Not a counterexample to modus ponens," Analysis 47: 44–7.

Lycan, W. 2001. *Real Conditionals*. Oxford: Oxford University Press.

Machery, E. 2011. "Thought experiments and philosophical knowledge," Metaphilosophy 42: 191–214.

Machery, E. 2015. "The illusion of expertise," in E. Fischer and J. Collins, eds., *Experimental Philosophy, Rationalism, and Naturalism: Rethinking Philosophical Method*, 188–203. London: Routledge.

Maddy, P. 2011. *Defending the Axioms: On the Philosophical Foundations of Set Theory*. Oxford: Oxford University Press.

Maddy, P. 2017. *What Do Philosophers Do? Skepticism and the Practice of Philosophy*. New York: Oxford University Press.

Manktelow, K. and Over, D. 1987. "Reasoning and rationality," Mind and Language 2: 199–219.

Marconi, D. 1997. *Lexical Competence*. Cambridge, MA: MIT Press.

Marconi, D. 2011. "Wittgenstein and Williamson on conceptual analysis," in R. Davies, ed., *Analisi: Annuario e Bollettino della Società Italiana di Filosofia Analytica (SIFA) 2011*, 91–102. Milan: Mimesis.

Marion, M. 2000. "Oxford realism: Knowledge and perception," parts I and II, British Journal for the History of Philosophy 8: 299–338, 485–519.

Martin, C. 1994. "Dispositions and conditionals," Philosophical Quarterly 44: 1–8.

Martin, C. and Heil, J. 1998. "Rules and powers," Philosophical Perspectives 12: 283–312.

Martin, M. 2009. "Reupholstering a discipline: Commentary on Williamson," Philosophical Studies 145: 445–53.

Mates, B. 1952. "Synonymity," in L. Linsky, ed., *Semantics and the Philosophy of Language*, 111–38. Urbana, IL: University of Illinois Press.

McCulloch, G. 2003. *The Life of the Mind: An Essay on Phenomenological Externalism*. London: Routledge.

McDowell, J. 1994. *Mind and World*. Cambridge, MA: Harvard University Press.

McGee, V. 1985. "A counterexample to modus ponens," Journal of Philosophy 82: 462–71.

McGee, V. and McLaughlin, B. 2000. "The lessons of the many," Philosophical Topics 28: 129–51.

McGinn, C. 1986. "Radical interpretation and epistemology," in LePore 1986, 356–68.

McGrath, S. 2004. "Moral knowledge by perception," Philosophical Perspectives 18: 209–28.

McKinsey, M. 1991. "Anti-individualism and privileged access," Analysis 51: 9–16.

Melis, G. and Wright, C. 2021. "Williamsonian scepticism about the a priori," forthcoming in D. Dodd and E. Zardini, eds., *The A Priori: Its Significance, Grounds, and Extent*. Oxford: Oxford University Press.

Mercier, H. and Sperber, D. 2009. "Intuitive and reflective inferences," in J. Evans and K. Frankish, eds., *In Two Minds: Dual Processes and Beyond*, 149–70. Oxford: Oxford University Press.

Mill, J. S. 1859. *On Liberty*. London: J. W. Parker and Son.

Miščević, N. 2004. "The explainability of intuitions," dialectica 58: 43–70.

Miščević, N. 2013. "An uncomfortable armchair: Tim Williamson against a priorism," Croatian Journal of Philosophy 13: 5–28.

Montague, R. 1970. "English as a formal language," in B. Visentini and C. Olivetti, eds., *Linguaggi nella Società e nella Tecnica*, 189–224. Milan: Edizioni di Comunità.

Montague, R. 1973. "The proper treatment of quantification in ordinary English," in J. Hintikka, J. Moravcsik, and P. Suppes, eds., *Approaches to Natural Language: Proceedings of the 1970 Stanford Workshop on Grammar and Semantics*, 221–42. Dordrecht: Reidel.

Moore, A. 2009. "Not to be taken at face value," Analysis 69: 116–25.

Moore, G. E. 1925. "A defence of common sense," in J. Muirhead, ed., *Contemporary British Philosophy* (2nd series), 192–233. London: George Allen & Unwin.

Moss, S. 2018. "Moral encroachment," Proceedings of the Aristotelian Society 118: 177–205.

Mumford, S. 1998. *Dispositions*. Oxford: Oxford University Press.

Nagel, J. 2008. "Knowledge ascriptions and the psychological consequences of changing stakes," Australasian Journal of Philosophy 86: 279–94.

Nagel, J. 2010. "Knowledge ascriptions and the psychological consequences of thinking about error," Philosophical Quarterly 60: 286–306.

Nagel, J. 2012. "Intuitions and experiments: A defense of the case method in epistemology," Philosophy and Phenomenological Research 85: 495–527.

Nagel, T. 1974. "What is it like to be a bat?," Philosophical Review 83: 435–50.

Nagel, T. 1986. *The View from Nowhere*. Oxford: Oxford University Press.

Neale, S. 1990. *Descriptions*. Cambridge, MA: MIT Press.

Newstead, S., Handley, S., Harley, C., et al., 2004. "Individual differences in deductive reasoning," Quarterly Journal of Experimental Psychology 57A: 33–60.

Nichols, S. and Stich, S. 2003. *Mindreading: An Integrated Account of Pretence, Self-Awareness, and Understanding of Other Minds*. Oxford: Clarendon Press.

Nichols, S., Stich, S., Leslie, A., and Klein, D. 1996. "Varieties of off-line simulation," in P. Carruthers and P. Smith, eds., *Theories of Theories of Mind*, 39–74. Cambridge: Cambridge University Press.

Nolan, D. 1997. "Impossible worlds: A modest approach," Notre Dame Journal for Formal Logic 38: 535–72.

Nolan, D. 2003. "Defending a possible-worlds account of indicative conditionals," Philosophical Studies 116: 215–69.

Norton, J. 1991. "Thought experiments in Einstein's work," in T. Horowtz and G. Massey, eds., *Thought Experiments in Science and Philosophy*, 129–48. Savage, MD: Rowman and Littlefield.

Norton, J. 2004. "Why thought experiments do not transcend empiricism," in C. Hitchcock, ed., *Contemporary Debates in the Philosophy of Science*, 44–66. Oxford: Blackwell.

Nozick, R. 1981. *Philosophical Explanations*. Oxford: Oxford University Press.

Nozick, R. 2001. *Invariances: The Structure of the Objective World*. Cambridge, MA: Harvard University Press.

Oaksford, M. 2005. "Reasoning," in N. Braisby and A. Gellatly, eds., *Cognitive Psychology*, 366–92. Oxford: Oxford University Press.

Over, D. 1987. "Assumptions and the supposed counterexamples to modus ponens," Analysis 47: 142–6.

Paul, L. 2012. "Metaphysics as modelling: The handmaiden's tale," Philosophical Studies 160: 1–29.

Peacocke, C. 1985. "Imagination, experience and possibility," in J. Foster and H. Robinson, eds., *Essays on Berkeley: A Tercentennial Celebration*, 19–35. Oxford: Clarendon Press.

Peacocke, C. 1992. *A Study of Concepts*. Cambridge, MA: MIT Press.

Peacocke, C. 1999. *Being Known*. Oxford: Clarendon Press.

Peacocke, C. 2004. *The Realm of Reason*. Oxford: Oxford University Press.

Peacocke, C. 2011. "Understanding, modality, logical operators," Philosophy and Phenomenological Research 82: 472–80.

Peters, S. and Westerståhl, D. 2006. *Quantifiers in Language and Logic*. Oxford: Clarendon Press.

Planck, M. 1949. *Scientific Autobiography and Other Papers*, trans. F. Gaynor. New York: Philosophical Library.

Priest, G. 1995. *Beyond the Limits of Thought*. Cambridge: Cambridge University Press.

Priest, G., Beall, J. C., and Armour-Garb, B., eds. 2004. *The Law of Non-Contradiction: New Philosophical Essays*. Oxford: Clarendon Press.

Prior, A. 1957. *Time and Modality*. Oxford: Clarendon Press.

Prior, A. 1960. "The runabout inference-ticket," Analysis 21: 38–9.

Pust, J. 2001. "Against explanationist skepticism regarding philosophical intuitions," Philosophical Studies 106: 227–58.

Putnam, H. 1975. *Mind, Language and Reality: Philosophical Papers, Volume 2*. Cambridge: Cambridge University Press.

Putnam, H. 1978. *Meaning and the Moral Sciences*. London: Routledge and Kegan Paul.

Putnam, H. 1994. "Sense, nonsense, and the senses: An inquiry into the powers of the human mind," Journal of Philosophy 91: 445–517.

Quine, W. V. O. 1936. "Truth by convention," in O. H. Lee, ed., *Philosophical Essays for A. N. Whitehead*, 90–124. New York: Longmans.

Quine, W. V. O. 1951. "Two dogmas of empiricism," Philosophical Review 60: 20–43.

Quine, W. V. O. 1953. *From a Logical Point of View*. Cambridge, MA: Harvard University Press.

Quine, W. V. O. 1960. *Word and Object*. Cambridge, MA: MIT Press.

Quine, W. V. O. 1966. *The Ways of Paradox and Other Essays*. New York: Random House.

Quine, W. V. O. 1969. "Foreword," in Lewis 1969, xi–xii.

Quine, W. V. O. 1970. *Philosophy of Logic*. Englewood Cliffs, NJ: Prentice-Hall.

Ramsey, F. 1978. *Foundations: Essays in Philosophy, Logic, Mathematics and Economics*, ed. H. Mellor. London: Routledge and Kegan Paul.

Rawls, J. 1951. "Outline of a decision procedure for ethics," Philosophical Review 60: 167–97.

Rawls, J. 1971. *A Theory of Justice*. Cambridge, MA: Harvard University Press.

Roberts, C. 1996. "Anaphora in intensional contexts," in S. Lappin, ed., *The Handbook of Contemporary Semantic Theory*, 215–46. Oxford: Blackwell.

Roese, N. and Olson, J. 1993. "The structure of counterfactual thought," Personality and Social Psychology Bulletin 19: 312–19.

Roese, N. and Olson, J. 1995. "Functions of counterfactual thinking," in N. Roese and J. Olson, eds., *What Might Have Been: The Social Psychology of Counterfactual Thinking*, 169–98. Mahwah, NJ: Erlbaum.

Rooij, R. van. 2006. "Free choice counterfactual donkeys," Journal of Semantics 23: 383–402.

Rorty, R., ed. 1967. *The Linguistic Turn: Recent Essays in Philosophical Method*. Chicago, IL: University of Chicago Press.

Rorty, R. 1979. *Philosophy and the Mirror of Nature*. Princeton, NJ: Princeton University Press.

Rorty, R. 1989. *Contingency, Irony and Solidarity*. Cambridge: Cambridge University Press.

Rose, D. and Danks, D. 2013. "In defense of a broad conception of experimental philosophy," Metaphilosophy 44: 512–32.

Rosen, G. 1990. "Modal fictionalism," Mind 99: 327–54.

Rosenberg, A. 2013a. "Why I am a naturalist," in M. Haug, ed., *Philosophical Methodology: The Armchair or the Laboratory?*, 32–5. London: Routledge.

Rosenberg, A. 2013b. "Can naturalism save the humanities?," in M. Haug, ed., *Philosophical Methodology: The Armchair or the Laboratory?'*, 39–42. London: Routledge.

Russell, B. 1912. *The Problems of Philosophy*. London: Williams and Norgate.

Russell, B. 1913. "On the notion of cause," Proceedings of the Aristotelian Society 13: 1–26.

Russell, B. 1919. *Introduction to Mathematical Philosophy*. London: George Allen and Unwin.

Russell, B. 1973. "The regressive method of discovering the premises of mathematics," in D. Lackey, ed., *Essays in Analysis*, 272–83. London: George Allen and Unwin. Written 1907.

Russell, J. S. 2008. "The structure of gunk: Adventures in the ontology of space," Oxford Studies in Metaphysics 4: 248–74.

Sainsbury, R. M. 1997. "Easy possibilities," Philosophy and Phenomenological Research 57: 907–19.

Salmon, N. 1982. *Reference and Essence*. Oxford: Blackwell.

Salmon, N. 1986. *Frege's Puzzle*. Cambridge, MA: MIT Press.

Salmon, N. 1989. "The logic of what might have been," Philosophical Review 98: 3–34.

Salmon, N. 1993. "This side of paradox," Philosophical Topics 21: 187–97.

Schechter, J. 2006. "Can evolution explain the reliability of our logical beliefs?," typescript. Ancestor of Schechter 2013.

Schechter, J. 2013. "Could evolution explain our reliability about logic?" Oxford Studies in Epistemology 4: 214–39.

Schroeter, L. and Schroeter, F. 2006. "Rational improvisation," typescript.

Schroyens, W. and Schaeken, W. 2003. "A critique of Oaksford, Chater, and Larkin's (2000) conditional probability model of conditional reasoning," Journal of Experimental Psychology: Learning, Memory and Cognition 29: 140–9.

Searle, J. 1969. *Speech Acts: An Essay in the Philosophy of Language*. Cambridge: Cambridge University Press.

Shanteau, J. 1992. "Competence in experts: The role of task characteristics," Organizational Behavior and Human Decision Processes 53: 252–66.

Shin, H. S. and Williamson, T. 1994. "Representing the knowledge of Turing machines," Theory and Decision 37: 125–46.

Shin, H. S. and Williamson, T. 1996. "How much common belief is necessary for a convention?," Games and Economic Behavior 13: 252–68.

Shope, R. 1983. *The Analysis of Knowing: A Decade of Research*. Princeton, NJ: Princeton University Press.

Sides, A., Osherson, D., Bonini, N., and Viale, R. 2002. "On the reality of the conjunction fallacy," Memory and Cognition 30: 191–8.

Siegel, S. 2017. *The Rationality of Perception*. Oxford: Oxford University Press.

Sinnott-Armstrong, W. 1999. "Begging the question," Australasian Journal of Philosophy 77: 174–91.

Sinnott-Armstrong, W., Moor, J., and Fogelin, R. 1986. "A defense of modus ponens," Journal of Philosophy 83: 296–300.

Sinnott-Armstrong, W., Raffman, D., and Asher, N., eds. 1995. *Modality, Morality, and Belief: Essays in Honor of Ruth Barcan Marcus*. Cambridge: Cambridge University Press.

Smart, J. 1984. *Ethics, Persuasion and Truth*. London: Routledge, Kegan and Paul.

Smart, J. 1987. *Essays Metaphysical and Moral: Selected Philosophical Papers*. Oxford: Blackwell.

Smokrović, N. 2013. "Are dispositions to believe constitutive for understanding?," Croatian Journal of Philosophy 13: 37–47.

Soames, S. 1995. "T-sentences," in Sinnott-Armstrong et al. 1995, 250–70.

Soames, S. 1999. *Understanding Truth*. Oxford: Oxford University Press.

Sober, E. 2000. "Quine," Aristotelian Society sup. 74: 237–80.

Sorensen, R. 1992. *Thought Experiments*. Oxford: Oxford University Press.

Sorensen, R. 2001. *Vagueness and Contradiction*. Oxford: Clarendon Press.

Sosa, E. 2005. "A defense of the use of intuitions in philosophy," in D. Murphy and M. Bishop, eds., *Stich and His Critics*, 101–12. Oxford: Blackwell.

Sosa, E. 2006. "Intuitions and truth," in Greenough and Lynch 2006, 208–26.

Sosa, E. 2007. "Experimental philosophy and philosophical intuitions," Philosophical Studies 132: 99–107.

Srinivasan, A. 2020. "Radical externalism," Philosophical Review, forthcoming.

Stalnaker, R. 1968. "A theory of conditionals," American Philosophical Quarterly Monographs 2(*Studies in Logical Theory*): 98–112.

Stalnaker, R. 1984. *Inquiry*. Cambridge, MA: MIT Press.

Stalnaker, R. 1999. *Context and Content*. Oxford: Oxford University Press.

Stalnaker, R. 2003. *Ways a World Might Be*. Oxford: Clarendon Press.

Stalnaker, R. 2011. "The metaphysical conception of analyticity," Philosophy and Phenomenological Research 82: 507–14.

Stanley, J. 2005. *Knowledge and Practical Interests*. Oxford: Oxford University Press.

Stanley, J. and Williamson, T. 2001. "Knowing how," Journal of Philosophy 98: 411–44.

Stanovich, K. and West, R. 2000. "Individual differences in reasoning: Implications for the rationality debate?," Behavioral and Brain Sciences 23: 645–65.

Stich, S. 1998. "Reflective equilibrium, analytic epistemology and the problem of cognitive diversity," in DePaul and Ramsey 1998, 95–112.

Stine, G. 1976. "Skepticism, relevant alternatives, and deductive closure," Philosophical Studies 29: 249–61.

Stoljar, D. 2019. "Williamson on laws and progress in philosophy," Epistemology and Philosophy of Science 56: 37–42.

Strawson, P. 1950. "On referring," Mind 59: 320–44.

Strawson, P. 1952. *Introduction to Logical Theory*. London: Methuen.

Strawson, P. 1959. *Individuals: An Essay in Descriptive Metaphysics*. London: Methuen.

Strawson, P. 1971. "Meaning and truth," in his Logico-Linguistic Papers, 131–46. London: Methuen.

Strawson, P. 1977. "Analitička filozofija," Theoria (Belgrade) 12: 61–71.

Strawson, P. 1992. *Analysis and Metaphysics: An Introduction to Philosophy.* Oxford: Oxford University Press.

Strawson, P. 1998. "Intellectual autobiography," in L. Hahn, ed., *The Philosophy of P. F. Strawson*, 3–21. La Salle, IL: Open Court.

Sutton, J. 2007. *Without Justification.* Cambridge, MA: MIT Press.

Tappenden, J. 1993. "Analytic truth – It's worse (or perhaps better) than you thought," Philosophical Topics 21: 233–61.

Tappolet, C. 1997. "Mixed inferences: A problem for pluralism about truth predicates," Analysis 57: 209–10.

Tarski, A. 1983a. "The concept of truth in formalized languages," trans. J. H. Woodger, in J. Corcoran, ed., *Logic, Semantics, Metamathematics*, 2nd edn, 152–278. Indianapolis, IN: Hackett.

Tarski, A. 1983b. "On the concept of logical consequence," trans. J. H. Woodger, in J. Corcoran, ed., *Logic, Semantics, Metamathematics*, 2nd edn, 409–20. Indianapolis, IN: Hackett.

Tripodi, P. 2011. "Peter, Stephen … and Ludwig," in R. Davies, ed., *Analisi: Annuario e Bollettino della Società Italiana di Filosofia Analytica (SIFA) 2011*, 103–15. Milan: Mimesis.

Trobok, M. 2013. "Defending analyticity: Remarks on Williamson's *The Philosophy of Philosophy*," Croatian Journal of Philosophy 13: 29–35.

Tversky, A. and Kahneman, D. 1983. "Extensional versus intuitive reasoning: The conjunction fallacy in probability judgment," Psychological Review 90: 293–315.

Unger, P. 2014. *Empty Ideas: A Critique of Analytic Philosophy.* New York: Oxford University Press.

Vahid, H. 2004. "Varieties of epistemic conservativism," Synthese 141: 97–122.

van Ditmarsch, H., Halpern, J., van der Hoek, W., and Kooi, B. 2015. *Handbook of Epistemic Logic.* London: College Publications.

Wason, P. and Shapiro, D. 1971. "Natural and contrived experience in a reasoning problem," Quarterly Journal of Experimental Psychology 23: 63–71.

Weatherson, B. 2003. "What good are counterexamples?," Philosophical Studies 115: 1–31.

Weinberg, J. 2009. "On doing better, experimental-style," Philosophical Studies 145: 455–64.

Weinberg, J., Gonnerman, C., Buckner, C., and Alexander, J. 2010. "Are philosophers expert intuiters?," Philosophical Psychology 23: 331–55.

Weinberg, J., Stich, S., and Nichols, S. 2001. "Normativity and epistemic intuitions," Philosophical Topics 29: 429–60.

Weisberg, M. 2007. "Who is a modeller?," British Journal for the Philosophy of Science 58: 207–33.

Weisberg, M. 2013. *Simulation and Similarity: Using Models to Understand the World.* Oxford: Oxford University Press.

Wiggins, D. 1976. "Truth, invention, and the meaning of life," Proceedings of the British Academy 62: 331–78.

Wiggins, D. 2001. *Sameness and Substance Renewed.* Cambridge: Cambridge University Press.

Wiggins, D. 2008. *Ethics: Twelve Lectures on the Philosophy of Morality*. London: Penguin.

Williams, B. 1966. "Imagination and the self," Proceedings of the British Academy 52: 105–24.

Williams, B. 1970. "The self and the future," Philosophical Review 79: 161–80.

Williamson, T. 1984. "The infinite commitment of finite minds," Canadian Journal of Philosophy 14: 235–55.

Williamson, T. 1988. "First-order logics for comparative similarity," Notre Dame Journal of Formal Logic 29: 457–81.

Williamson, T. 1990. *Identity and Discrimination*. Oxford: Blackwell.

Williamson, T. 1994a. *Vagueness*. London: Routledge.

Williamson, T. 1994b. "Crispin Wright, *Truth and Objectivity*," International Journal of Philosophical Studies 2: 130–44.

Williamson, T. 1994c. "Never say never," Topoi 13: 135–45.

Williamson, T. 1999a. "Truthmakers and the converse Barcan formula," dialectica 53: 253–70.

Williamson, T. 1999b. "Schiffer on the epistemic theory of vagueness," Philosophical Perspectives 13: 505–17.

Williamson, T. 2000a. *Knowledge and Its Limits*. Oxford: Oxford University Press.

Williamson, T. 2000b. "Existence and contingency," Proceedings of the Aristotelian Society 100: 117–39.

Williamson, T. 2001. "Ethics, supervenience and Ramsey sentences," Philosophy and Phenomenological Research 62: 625–30.

Williamson, T. 2003a. "Understanding and inference," Aristotelian Society sup. 77: 249–93.

Williamson, T. 2003b. "Vagueness in reality," in M. Loux and D. Zimmerman, eds., *The Oxford Handbook of Metaphysics*, 690–715. Oxford: Oxford University Press.

Williamson, T. 2004a. "Philosophical 'intuitions' and scepticism about judgement," dialectica 58: 109–53.

Williamson, T. 2004b. "Past the linguistic turn?," in B. Leiter, ed., *The Future for Philosophy*, 106–28. Oxford: Oxford University Press.

Williamson, T. 2005a. "Armchair philosophy, metaphysical modality and counterfactual thinking," Proceedings of the Aristotelian Society 105: 1–23.

Williamson, T. 2005b. "Contextualism, subject-sensitive invariantism, and knowledge of knowledge," Philosophical Quarterly 55: 213–35.

Williamson, T. 2005c. "Knowledge and scepticism," in F. Jackson and M. Smith, eds., *The Oxford Handbook of Contemporary Philosophy*, 681–700. Oxford: Oxford University Press.

Williamson, T. 2006a. "Indicative versus subjunctive conditionals, congruential versus non-hyperintensional contexts," Philosophical Issues 16: 310–33.

Williamson, T. 2006b. "Conceptual truth," Aristotelian Society sup. 80: 1–41.

Williamson, T. 2006c. "Must do better," in Greenough and Lynch 2006, 177–87.

Williamson, T. 2007. "Philosophical knowledge and knowledge of counterfactuals," Grazer Philosophische Studien 74: 89–123.

Williamson, T. 2008a. "Why epistemology can't be operationalized," in Q. Smith, ed., *Epistemology: New Philosophical Essays*, 277–300. Oxford: Oxford University Press.

Williamson, T. 2008b. "Reference, inference and the semantics of pejoratives," in J. Almog and P. Leonardi, eds., *Essays for David Kaplan*, 137–58. Oxford: Oxford University Press.

Williamson, T. 2009a. "Replies to Kornblith, Jackson and Moore," Analysis 69: 125–35. Reprinted in this volume as Sections 11.1, 12.1, and 13.1.

Williamson, T. 2009b. "Replies to Ichikawa, Martin and Weinberg," Philosophical Studies 145: 465–76. Reprinted in this volume as Sections 14.1, 14.2, and 10.1 in this volume.

Williamson, T. 2009c. "Plato goes pop," Times Literary Supplement 5529: 15. Reprinted as Section 14.5 in this volume.

Williamson, T. 2010. "Review of Robert Brandom, *Reason in Philosophy*," Times Literary Supplement 5579: 22–3. Reprinted as Section 14.3 in this volume.

Williamson, T. 2011a. "Philosophical expertise and the burden of proof," Metaphilosophy 42: 215–29. Reprinted as Section 10.2 in this volume.

Williamson, T. 2011b. "Reply to Peacocke," Philosophy and Phenomenological Research 82: 481–7. Reprinted as Section 12.3 in this volume.

Williamson, T. 2011c. "Reply to Boghossian," Philosophy and Phenomenological Research 82: 498–506. Reprinted as Section 12.2 in this volume.

Williamson, T. 2011d. "Reply to Stalnaker," Philosophy and Phenomenological Research 82: 515–23. Reprinted as Section 11.2 in this volume.

Williamson, T. 2011e. "Reply to Horwich," Philosophy and Phenomenological Research 82: 481–7. Reprinted as Section 13.2 in this volume.

Williamson, T. 2011f. "Three Wittgensteinians and a naturalist on *The Philosophy of Philosophy*," in R. Davies, ed., *Analisi: Annuario e Bollettino della Società Italiana di Filosofia Analitica (SIFA) 2011*, 127–37. Milan: Mimesis. Reprinted as Sections 11.3, 13.3, 13.4, and 13.5 in this volume.

Williamson, T. 2012. "Boghossian and Casalegno on understanding and inference," dialectica 66: 237–47. Reprinted in Boghossian and Williamson 2020: 108–16.

Williamson, T. 2013a. *Modal Logic as Metaphysics*. Oxford: Oxford University Press.

Williamson, T. 2013b. "How deep is the distinction between a priori and a posteriori knowledge?," in A. Casullo and J. Thurow, eds., *The A Priori in Philosophy*, 291–312. Oxford: Oxford University Press. Reprinted in Boghossian and Williamson 2020: 117–36.

Williamson, T. 2013c. "Gettier cases in epistemic logic," Inquiry 56: 1–14.

Williamson, T. 2013d. "What is naturalism?," in M. Haug, ed., *Philosophical Methodology: The Armchair or the Laboratory?*', 29–31. London: Routledge. Reprinted as Section 11.4 in this volume.

Williamson, T. 2013e. "The unclarity of naturalism," in M. Haug, ed., *Philosophical Methodology: The Armchair or the Laboratory?*', 36–8. London: Routledge. Reprinted as Section 11.5 in this volume.

Williamson, T. 2013f. "Review of Joshua Alexander, *Experimental Philosophy: An Introduction*," Philosophy 88: 467–74. Reprinted as Section 10.3 in this volume.

Williamson, T. 2013g. "Replies to Trobok, Smokrović, and Miščević on *The Philosophy of Philosophy*," Croatian Journal of Philosophy 13: 49–64. Reprinted as Sections 12.4, 12.5, and 12.6 in this volume.

Williamson, T. 2013h. "Review of Paul Horwich, *Wittgenstein's Metaphilosophy*," European Journal of Philosophy 21: e7–e10. Reprinted as Section 13.6 in this volume.

Williamson, T. 2014a. "How did we get here from there? The transformation of analytic philosophy," Belgrade Philosophical Annual 27: 7–37. Reprinted as Section 9.1 in this volume.

Williamson, T. 2014b. "Very improbable knowing," Erkenntnis 79: 971–99.

Williamson, T. 2014c. "Replies to Bricker, Divers, and Sullivan on *Modal Logic as Metaphysics*," Philosophy and Phenomenological Research 88: 744–64.

Williamson, T. 2015a. "A note on Gettier cases in epistemic logic," Philosophical Studies 172: 129–40.

Williamson, T. 2015b. "Review of Peter Unger, *Empty Ideas: A Critique of Analytic Philosophy*," Times Literary Supplement 5833: 22–3. Reprinted as Section 14.4 in this volume.

Williamson, T. 2016a. "Abductive philosophy," Philosophical Forum 47: 263–80. Reprinted as Section 9.2 in this volume.

Williamson, T. 2016b. "Philosophical criticisms of experimental philosophy," in J. Sytsma and W. Buckwalter, eds., *A Companion to Experimental Philosophy*, 22–36. Oxford: Wiley Blackwell. Reprinted as Section 10.4 in this volume.

Williamson, T. 2016c. "Knowing by imagining," in A. Kind and P. King, eds., *Knowledge through Imagination*, 113–23. Oxford: Oxford University Press. Reprinted in Boghossian and Williamson 2020: 175–85.

Williamson, T. 2017a. "Model-building in philosophy," in R. Blackford and D. Broderick, eds., *Philosophy's Future: The Problem of Philosophical Progress*, 159–73. Oxford: Wiley-Blackwell. Reprinted as Section 9.3 in this volume.

Williamson, T. 2017b. "Semantic paradoxes and abductive methodology," in B. Armour-Garb, ed., *The Relevance of the Liar*, 325–46. Oxford: Oxford University Press.

Williamson, T. 2017c. "Acting on knowledge," in J. Adam Carter, E. Gordon, and B. Jarvis, eds., *Knowledge-First*, 163–81. Oxford: Oxford University Press.

Williamson, T. 2017d. "Review of Penelope Maddy, *What Do Philosophers Do? Skepticism and the Practice of Philosophy*," Journal of Philosophy 114: 492–7. Reprinted as Section 11.6 in this volume.

Williamson, T. 2017e. "Counterpossibles in semantics and metaphysics," Argumenta 2: 195–226.

Williamson, T. 2018a. *Doing Philosophy: From Common Curiosity to Logical Reasoning*. Oxford: Oxford University Press.

Williamson, T. 2018b. "Alternative logics and applied mathematics," Philosophical Issues 28: 399–424.

Williamson, T. 2018c. "Counterpossibles," Topoi 37: 357–68.

Williamson, T. 2018d. "Doing philosophy', 'Reply to Nigel Collins', 'Reply to Amanda McBride', 'Reply to Edward Gibney', 'Reply to Hisham El Edrissi," The Philosopher 106: 4–6, 9–10, 12–13, 16–17, 19–20.

Williamson, T. 2019a. "Morally loaded cases in philosophy," Proceedings and Addresses of the American Philosophical Association 93: 159–72. Reprinted as Section 9.4 in this volume.

Williamson, T. 2019b. "Evidence of evidence in epistemic logic," in M. Skipper and A. Steglich-Petersen, eds., Higher-Order Evidence: New Essays, 265–97. Oxford: Oxford University Press.

Williamson, T. 2019c. "Armchair philosophy," Epistemology and Philosophy of Science 56: 19–25.

Williamson, T. 2019d. "Reply to Dennett, Knobe, Kuznetsov, and Stoljar on philosophical methodology," Epistemology and Philosophy of Science 56: 46–52. Reprinted as Sections 9.5, 9.6, and 10.5 in this volume.

Williamson, T. 2020a. Suppose and Tell: The Semantics and Heuristics of Conditionals. Oxford: Oxford University Press.

Williamson, T. 2020b. "The KK principle and rotational symmetry," Analytic Philosophy 61: 000–000.

Williamson, T. 2020c. "Review of Arnon Levy and Peter Godfrey-Smith (eds.), The Scientific Imagination: Philosophical and Psychological Perspectives," Notre Dame Philosophical Reviews, 2020.04.03, https://ndpr.nd.edu/news/the-scientific-imagination-philosophical-and-psychological-perspectives

Williamson, T. 2020d. "Popular philosophy and populist philosophy," Daily Nous, http://dailynous.com/2020/06/08/popular-philosophy-populist-philosophy-guest-post-timothy-williamson. Reprinted as Section 14.6 in this volume.

Williamson, T. 2021a. "Justifications, excuses, and sceptical scenarios," forthcoming in F. Dorsch and J. Dutant, eds., The New Evil Demon: New Essays on Knowledge, Justification, and Rationality. Oxford: Oxford University Press.

Williamson, T. 2021b. "More Oxonian scepticism about the a priori," forthcoming in D. Dodd and E. Zardini, eds., The A Priori: Its Significance, Grounds, and Extent. Oxford University Press.

Williamson, T. 2021c. "Reply to Casullo's defence of the significance of the a priori – A posteriori distinction," forthcoming in D. Dodd and E. Zardini, eds., The A Priori: Its Significance, Grounds, and Extent. Oxford University Press.

Williamson, T. 2021d. "The counterfactual-based approach to modal epistemology," forthcoming in O. Bueno and S. Shalkowski, eds., Routledge Handbook of Modality. London: Routledge.

Williamson, T. 2021e. "E = K, but what about R?," forthcoming in M. Lasonen-Aarnio and C. Littlejohn, eds., The Routledge Handbook of Evidence. London: Routledge.

Wilson, J. C. 1926. *Statement and Inference*, 2 vols. Oxford: Clarendon Press.
Wilson, M. 2008. "Beware of the blob: Cautions for would-be metaphysicians," Oxford Studies in Metaphysics 4: 275–320.
Wright, C. 1975. "On the coherence of vague predicates," Synthese 30: 325–65.
Wright, C. 1989. "Necessity, caution and scepticism," Aristotelian Society sup. 63: 203–38.
Wright, C. 1993. *Realism, Meaning and Truth*, 2nd edn. Oxford: Blackwell.
Yablo, S. 2002. "Coulda, woulda, shoulda," in Gendler and Hawthorne 2002, 441–92.
Zimmerman, D. 2004. "Prologue: Metaphysics after the twentieth century," Oxford Studies in Metaphysics 1: ix–xxii.

Index

CPSIA information can be obtained
at www.ICGtesting.com
Printed in the USA
BVHW050533070323
659799BV00002B/115

9 781119 616672